FINANCIAL ECONOMETRIC MODELING

FINANCIAL ECONOMETRIC MODELING

STAN HURN, VANCE L. MARTIN,
PETER C. B. PHILLIPS, AND JUN YU

OXFORD
UNIVERSITY PRESS

Oxford University Press is a department of the University of Oxford.
It furthers the University's objective of excellence in research, scholarship,
and education by publishing worldwide. Oxford is a registered trade mark of
Oxford University Press in the UK and certain other countries.

Published in the United States of America by Oxford University Press
198 Madison Avenue, New York, NY 10016, United States of America.

© 2021 by Oxford University Press

For titles covered by Section 112 of the US Higher Education
Opportunity Act, please visit www.oup.com/us/he for the latest
information about pricing and alternate formats.

CIP data is on file at the Library of Congress
978–0–19–085706–6

Printing number: 1 3 5 7 9 8 6 4 2
Printed by LSC Communications, Inc., United States of America

PREFACE

Financial econometrics is an exciting young discipline that began to take on its present form around the turn of the millennium. The subject brings financial theory and econometric methods together with the power of data to advance our understanding of the global financial universe on which all modern economies depend. Two major developments underscored its rapid growth and expanding capabilities. First, the massive importance of well-functioning financial markets to the global economy and to global financial stability was universally acknowledged following the dot-com bubble of the late 1990s in the United States and the global financial crisis of 2008 coupled with its prolonged aftermath. Second, modern methods of econometrics emerged that proved equal to some of the special challenges presented by financial data and the ideas of financial theory.

Among the most significant of these challenges are the complex interdependencies of financial, commodity, and real estate markets, the dynamic and spatial linkages within financial data, the random wandering behavior of asset prices, anomalies such as financial bubbles and market crashes in the data, the difficulties in modeling rapidly changing volatility in financial returns, the growth in high-dimensional ultra-high frequency data, and the attention to market microstructure effects that all such data require. While not entirely unique to financial data, these challenges presented the econometrics profession with the need to re-fashion methods, develop new tools of inference, and tackle a wide selection of new empirical goals associated with a growing number of financial instruments and vast data sets being generated in the financial world.

This book, like the subject itself, is motivated by all of these challenges. We seek to provide a broad and gentle introduction to this rapidly developing subject of financial econometrics where theory, measurement, and data play equal roles in our development and where empirical applications occupy a central position. Our target audiences are intermediate and advanced undergraduate students who wish to learn about financial econometrics, and postgraduate students with limited backgrounds in econometrics who are doing masters courses designed to offer an introduction to finance and its applications. We hope the book will also prove useful to practitioners in the industry as an introductory reference source for relevant tools and approaches to modern empirical work in finance.

Throughout the book, special emphasis is placed on the exposition of core concepts, their illustration using relevant financial data sets, and a hands-on approach to learning by doing that involves practical implementation. The guiding principle we have adopted is that only by working through plenty of applications and exercises can a coherent understanding of the properties of financial econometric models, interrelationships with the underlying finance theory, and the role of econometric tools of inference be achieved.

Our philosophy has been to write a book on financial econometrics, not an econometrics text that illustrates techniques with data sets drawn from finance. Our goal is centered on the subject of financial econometrics explaining how evidence-based research in applied finance is conducted. Econometrics is viewed as the vehicle that makes the ideas and theories about financial markets face the reality of observations.

To ensure the book is self-contained for a first course in financial econometrics, some foundational theory and methods of relevant econometric technique are provided. But the methods covered in this book travel along a customized path designed to ease the reader's transition from concepts and methods to empirical work. The book tracks its way forward from data to modeling through to estimation, inference, and prediction.

A consistent thematic throughout the book is to motivate each topic with the presentation of relevant data. The journey begins with data and a simple grounding in regression and inference. From this foundation, it moves on to more advanced financial econometric methods that open up empirical applications with many different types of data from various financial markets. The path promises to keep readers motivated throughout their journey by means of many examples and to reinforce their learning by extensive data-based exercises. Several introductory appendices are included to assist students with limited mathematics and no econometric background in understanding more technical aspects of the discussion, particularly in the second half of the book.

ORGANIZATION OF THE BOOK

Part I—Fundamentals—is designed to form the basis of a semester-long first course in financial econometrics directed at an introductory level. Technical difficulty is kept to an absolute minimum, with an emphasis on the data, financial concepts, appropriate econometric methodology, and the intuition that draws these essential components of modeling together. Methodology is largely confined to descriptive methods and ordinary least squares regression, a choice that limits the extent of the analysis and promotes heuristic discussion on some topics that are revisited later in the book for a more complete and rigorous development.

In Part II—Methods—the level of difficulty steps up slightly in treating the relevant econometric estimation methods of instrumental variables, generalized method of moments, and maximum likelihood. These core estimators are used extensively throughout the second half of the book and knowledge of them is a key asset in working through the later material. Also included in Part II are methods that deal with panel data and models with latent factors. A second course in financial econometrics might usefully begin with Chapters 8–12, taking Part I as a given foundation.

Part III—Topics—introduces a number of special topics in financial econometrics, covering models of volatility, financial market microstructure, the econometrics of options, and methods relating to extreme values and copulas. One of the dominant features of financial time series is their volatility. Financial theory and empirical experience both demonstrate that there is often much less to explain in the levels of financial returns than there is to explain in their variation. Accordingly, Chapters 13–15 of the book are devoted to modeling volatility. These chapters treat parametric univariate and multivariate models of volatility and introduce the more recent nonparametric modeling approach that is based on market realized volatility measured using high-frequency data.

As in any project of this nature, sacrifices were made to keep the length of the book manageable. Some topics, for instance, are treated by example and illustration within a chapter rather than by devoting an entire chapter to their development. As a result, the book is rich in real-world examples drawn from financial markets for stocks, fixed income securities, exchange rates, and derivatives. As such, the coverage is intended to be extensive while not treating every topic in the same depth.

COMPUTATION

A fundamental principle guiding the inclusion of material in this book is whether the methods are available for easy implementation. In consequence, all results reported in the book may be reproduced using existing software packages like Stata and EViews.[1] This choice is intended to enhance the usefulness of the material for beginning students. In some cases, the programming languages in these packages need to be used to achieve full implementation of the illustrations. Of course, for those who actively choose to learn by programming themselves, the results are also reproducible in any of the common matrix programming languages, such as R.[2] The numerical computations reported in the book are primarily rounded versions of the results generated using Stata.

The data files are all available for download from the book's companion website (https://global.oup.com/academic/instructors/finects) in Stata format (.dta), EViews format (.wf1), comma delimited files (.csv), and as Excel spreadsheets (.xlsx).

ACKNOWLEDGMENTS

Many colleagues, students, and research assistants have read and commented on parts of the book and in some cases even taught from early versions of the book. We are particularly grateful to Ahmad Bahir, Kit Baum, Jimmy Chan, Han Chen, Ye Chen, Xiaohong Chen, Jieyang Chong, Adam Clements, Fulvio Corsi, Mark Doolan, Renée Fry-McKibbin, Zhuo Huang, Marko Krause, Bei Luo, Cheng Liu, Andrew Patton, Shuping Shi, Daniel Smith, Chrismin Tang, Timo Teräsvirta, Stephen Thiele, Tomasz Woźniak, and Lina Xu. A special thank you goes to Annastiina Silvennoinen and Glen Wade who were relentless in picking up typographical errors and factual inconsistencies, as well as suggesting alternative ways of presenting material. All remaining errors are the responsibility of the authors.

Stan Hurn, Vance L. Martin, Peter C. B. Phillips, and Jun Yu
June 2019

---

[1] Stata is the copyright of StataCorp LP, www.stata.com, and EViews is the copyright of IHS-Inc., www.eviews.com.

[2] R is a free software environment for statistical computation and graphics that is part of the GNU Project, see www.r-project.org.

CONTENTS

LIST OF FIGURES

Fundamentals

CHAPTER 1

Financial Asset Prices and Returns

1.1 WHAT IS FINANCIAL ECONOMETRICS?

There is no simple definition of financial econometrics. The subject is best described through its many different activities. These include the formulation of financial models intended for empirical implementation, methods of estimation and inference with these models, and their use for forecasting, for policy analysis, and for understanding financial phenomena.

As a subject, financial econometrics is interdisciplinary. It draws on ideas and methods from finance, economics, probability, statistics, and applied mathematics, while at the same time providing a rich source bed of new ideas for modeling, estimation, and inference. Partly because of this diversity, financial econometrics is a vast and growing discipline with applications that stretch across the social and business sciences. Its primary tasks stem from the particular nature of financial data and the body of financial theory that has been developed to explain the complex world of finance and financial instruments that surrounds us.

While the origins of financial econometrics may be traced back to early empirical studies of stock prices, bond yields, and interest rates, the subject began to take aspects of its modern form during the 1980s. At this time, the methods of time series econometrics evolved in ways that were especially beneficial to studying financial data, taking account of features such as the wandering nature of financial asset prices, the volatility of financial returns, and the availability of ultra-high-frequency observations. These new modeling and inferential tools drawn from time series econometrics and other constituent disciplines joined with a growing specialization among econometricians working with financial data to promote the development of a new discipline with the common goal of searching for a deeper understanding of the way in which financial markets work and financial asset prices are determined. Out of this understanding and sustained research, it is to be hoped, regulators and policymaker will be better equipped to assist in monitoring markets toward the lofty goal of financial stability and to guide the smooth functioning of financial markets in the face of crisis.

Central to the success of this scientific process is the initial step of establishing a reliable data set that is well-suited to the various tasks of econometric investigation. The financial data of primary interest in applications are the prices of financial assets and the yields or returns to investments from those assets. The first logical step in the study of financial econometrics, therefore, is to become familiar with the many different types of financial assets, how prices for these assets are quoted and reported, and how yields or returns to investment in such assets are constructed.

A distinguishing feature of financial econometrics that sets the subject apart from many other applications of econometrics, particularly macroeconomics, is the abundance of financial data. Table 1.1 gives a selective listing of commonly used data sources, some of which are free while others require institutional subscription. The vast global financial industry now creates terabytes of data daily covering a huge array of financial assets, producing high dimensional data sets that carry fine-grained transaction level details recording the continuous pulse of financial markets. These data are used in the

TABLE 1.1   Common sources for finding data on financial variables.

Bloomberg
bloomberg.com
Current and historical data on stocks, preferred stock, indices, bonds, commodities, futures, options, exchange rates, mortgages, and money market instruments.

Datastream International
solutions.refinitiv.com/datastream-macroeconomic-analysis
Comprehensive historical data on stocks, indices, bonds, commodities, futures, options, earning forecasts, economic conditions, interest rates, exchange rates, and economic forecasts.

Federal Reserve Economic Data (FRED)
fred.stlouisfed.org
FRED collects over 200,000 US and international economic time series. Data coverage includes growth, inflation, employment, interest rates, exchange rates, production and consumption, income and expenditure, savings and investment, and more.

Kenneth French Data Library
mba.tuck.dartmouth.edu/pages/faculty/ken.french/data_library.html
US equity returns and data on the Fama–French factors together with returns to sorted portfolios.

Global Financial Data
globalfinancialdata.com
Data on bonds, commodities, interest rates, stock markets and indices, futures, macroeconomic variables, stock market capitalization, dividend yields, price/earnings ratios, total return performance indices, and Global Financial Data's World Stock Market Indices. Historical data on selected macroeconomic variables dates to the 1700s and even earlier.

Robert Shiller Data Library
econ.yale.edu/ shiller/data.htm
An eclectic collection of historical data including stock, bond, interest rate, and consumption data together with stock market confidence and real estate indices.

Thompson Reuters Tick History
financial-risk-solutions.thomsonreuters.info/TickHistory
Based on the DataScope Select platform, TRTH provides access to historical high-frequency data across global asset classes dating to 1996.

Wharton Research Data Service (WRDS)
wrds-web.wharton.upenn.edu
Interface to many important financial and economic databases.

Yahoo Finance
finance.yahoo.com
Comprehensive data on stocks and currencies (including cryptocurrencies).

industry by financial firms searching for investment opportunities and they provide an extraordinary digitized resource for financial econometricians. Unlike macroeconomics, in finance there is no paucity of data for testing hypotheses of interest. But superabundance of observations is no testament to quality or the absence of measurement error, missing observations, data revisions, or subtleties associated with transaction-level data.

Much work is frequently needed to get financial data into the clean form that is necessary for meaningful empirical analysis. These problems go well beyond the superficial and they can involve deep questions associated with the very structure of trading in financial markets. Addressing the plethora of financial data, the risks associated with data mining, the subtleties involved in transaction-level observations, and the probabilistic foundations of modeling and inference with such data have galvanized the energies of the large and growing community of scholars in financial econometrics. This chapter does not attempt to cover all the interesting twists and turns of data creation in the financial world that applied researchers in financial econometrics have to face in their empirical work. But it will highlight some of these issues and stimulate a renewed awareness of the famous adage that empirical results are only as good as the data on which they are based.

1.2 FINANCIAL ASSETS

Although they may have no intrinsic physical worth, financial assets derive value from the contractual claims they place on a stream of services or cash flows. The major categories of financial assets that will be used in this book are cash, fixed-income securities, equity securities, and derivative securities.

Cash

Cash represents a claim on the stream of services that it can secure by virtue of its role as a medium of exchange. One particularly important financial transaction that may be regarded as a cash investment is dealing in foreign exchange. The exchange rate is simply the price of one currency in terms of another. So trading in currencies may be regarded as investments in cash.

Fixed-Income Securities

Fixed-income securities provide two sources of return. The first corresponds to a stream of interest payments (or coupons) that are made at fixed, regular intervals, and the second is to the eventual return of principal at maturity. Although the original distinguishing feature of this class of financial asset was that the periodic payment was known in advance, recent developments in financial markets link many of these payments to a particular short-term interest rate and some are even linked to the prevailing inflation rate.

Money market fixed-income securities are short-term assets whose markets are particularly active (or liquid). There is now a bewildering array of money market instruments available to study. But only two will feature in this book.

- *Treasury Bills* are the simplest form of government debt. The government sells Treasury Bills in the money market and redeems them at the maturity of the bill.

No interest is payable during the life of the bill and so they trade at discount to the face value of the bill that will be paid at maturity. The most common maturities are 3, 6, and 9 months.

- *Eurodollar Deposits* are the deposits of US banks that are denominated in US$ but held with banks outside the United States. Most of these deposits have a relatively short maturity (less than 6 months) and the Eurodollar deposit rate is commonly used as a representative short-term interest rate.

The *bond market* is the place where longer term borrowing of governments or corporations is conducted. A bond is a security which promises to pay the owner of the bond its face value at the time of the maturity of the bond and usually an ongoing coupon payment prior to maturity. There are also zero-coupon bonds that pay no regular interest and are therefore traded at prices that are below their face value. In recent times, this distinction has become less important because zero-coupon bonds may be created from coupon paying bonds by separating the coupons from the principal and trading each of these components independently. This process is known as stripping.

Another common way in which the fixed-income securities market is classified is by the issuer of the securities. For instance, a distinction is sometimes made between bonds issued by financial intermediates (FI bonds) and non-financial intermediaries (NFI bonds). Financial intermediaries are entities that facilitate financial transactions between two or more parties and include commercial banks, investment banks, and insurance companies.

Equity Securities

Equities or common stocks give the owner an equity stake in a company and a corresponding claim on company assets and earnings. Equities can be bought and sold on stock markets. Stocks give the owner the right to a payment that represents the distribution of some of the company's earnings, which is known as a dividend. The dividend is usually expressed as the amount each share receives or as a percentage of the current market price, which is referred to as the dividend yield.

Derivative Securities

Derivative securities provide a payoff based on the value(s) of other assets such as commodities, bonds, or stocks. Such securities therefore *derive* their own value from the market performance of the other underlying assets to which they are attached. Derivatives started out as over-the-counter (OTC) trades where interested parties made mutually beneficial trades. In recent years, as more standardized contracts have emerged, derivatives have been very actively traded on exchanges such as the Chicago Board of Exchange.

Two classes of derivative securities are emphasized in this book.

- *Options* contracts offer the buyer the right, but not the obligation, to buy (call option) or sell (put option) some designated financial asset (the underlying asset from which the option derives its value) at a particular price during a certain period of time or on a specific date.
- *Futures* contracts specify the delivery of either an asset or a cash value at a time known as the maturity for an agreed price, which is payable at maturity. The entity

who commits to purchase the asset on delivery takes a *long* position. The entity who commits to delivering the asset takes a *short* position.

One of the most significant developments in financial markets in recent years has been the growth of derivatives markets as illustrated in Figure 1.1. The problem with measuring the size of the derivatives market stems from the fact that there is a large volume of OTC trades which make it difficult to quantify the exact volume of derivative trading. What is clear from Figure 1.1, however, is that the combined outstanding value of derivatives is several orders larger than world gross domestic product, particularly in the latter part of the period.

1.3 EQUITY PRICES AND RETURNS

In this section, the prices of financial assets and the returns to holding these assets will be couched in terms of common stocks. Stocks represent an equity claim on the company and typically, although not always, receive a regular stream of dividend payments. Prices and returns associated with other financial assets are determined in a similar way.

1.3.1 Prices

The most basic data in financial econometrics are the prices of financial assets. The price of an equity security is defined in terms of the dollar (or other currency denomination) amount at which a transaction can occur (a quoted price) or has occurred (an historical transaction price). When dealing with high-frequency data the appropriate prices are usually quoted prices. An illustration is provided in Table 1.2 that gives quoted

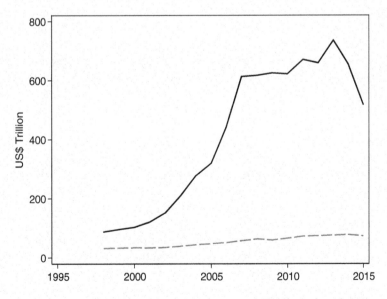

FIGURE 1.1 Total outstanding value of derivatives contracts (solid line) plotted against gross world product (dashed line) from 1998 to 2015.

TABLE 1.2   Quoted prices on Yahoo! Finance for The Boeing Company (BA) for 12 September 2014.

The Boeing Company (BA) – NYSE			
127.64 ↓ 0.58(0.45%)			
Prev Close:	128.22	Day's Range:	127.20 – 127.99
Open	127.82	52wk Range:	109.14 – 144.57
Bid:	127.50	Volume:	1,988,616
Ask:	127.84	Market Cap:	91,98 bn.

Source: https://finance.yahoo.com.

prices obtained from Yahoo Finance for common stock in the US company Boeing on September 2014.

Recording a price for the purpose of econometric analysis is not as straightforward as it might seem. A number of alternatives are available. In addition to the previous day closing price and the current day opening price, there are also prevailing bid and ask prices. The bid price is the maximum price that buyers are willing to pay for the stock, and the ask price is the minimum price that sellers are willing to accept for the stock. The differential between the bid and ask price is called the spread. Many studies that use intra-day data (popularly known as high-frequency data) compromise this complexity by using the midpoint of the bid and ask prices as the best summary estimate of the prevailing current price. This convention simplifies data analysis but circumvents important details of the transaction price determination process. In doing so it produces intriguing econometric problems arising from the impact of the neglected market microstructure in modeling prices, as we now explain.

The practice of using summary estimates of prices, like the midpoint of the bid-ask spread, points to an unusual feature of high-frequency data that affects econometric work: increasing the number of observations by using intra-day data need not always increase efficiency or improve understanding. More data often means that there is more to explain. Indeed, in the present case, adding more data by using more frequent observations changes the focus of attention toward a microscopic focus on the transaction process itself. This new focus in turn raises the dimensionality of the econometric problem by virtue of the complexity of the transaction process, which brings buyers and sellers together through a market determination process that involves multiple bid-ask order layers in which random elements may enter the price determination process in the microcosm of market forces.

When dealing with historical prices recorded at lower frequencies the situation is less complex. Table 1.3 reports the historical daily prices for the US stock Microsoft for the month of August 2014. The choice for the researcher is now simpler. We have the recorded opening price, closing price, daily highs and lows, and the adjusted closing price. In most cases it is convenient to choose the adjusted closing price (denoted by Close*), which is adjusted for stock splits and dividends.

The effect of a dividend payment is to lower the price by the amount of the dividend so that the closing price on 18 August is greater than the opening price on 19 August. In order to ensure that the effect of the dividend is smoothed out in historical prices, the correction is to subtract the dividend from the closing price on the previous day, compute the quotient $(P_{t-1} - D_t)/P_{t-1}$, and then multiply all previous prices by this factor. On 18 August the closing price and the adjustment factor are given by

TABLE 1.3 Daily prices for the United States stock Microsoft (MSFT) for the month of August 2014. All prices are quoted in US$. The column Close* gives the closing price adjusted for dividends and stock splits. A dividend of US$ 0.28 per share was paid on 19 August 2014.

Date	Open	High	Low	Close	Volume	Close*
29 Aug 2014	45.09	45.44	44.86	45.43	21607600	45.43
28 Aug 2014	44.75	44.98	44.61	44.88	17657600	44.88
27 Aug 2014	44.90	45.00	44.76	44.87	20823000	44.87
26 Aug 2014	45.31	45.40	44.94	45.01	14873100	45.01
25 Aug 2014	45.40	45.44	45.04	45.17	16898100	45.17
22 Aug 2014	45.35	45.47	45.07	45.15	18294500	45.15
21 Aug 2014	44.84	45.25	44.83	45.22	22272000	45.22
20 Aug 2014	45.34	45.40	44.90	44.95	24750700	44.95
19 Aug 2014	44.97	45.34	44.83	45.33	28115600	45.33
Dividend US$ 0.28						
18 Aug 2014	44.94	45.11	44.68	45.11	26891100	44.83
15 Aug 2014	44.58	44.90	44.40	44.79	41611300	44.51
14 Aug 2014	44.08	44.42	44.01	44.27	19313200	44.00
13 Aug 2014	43.68	44.18	43.52	44.08	22889500	43.81
12 Aug 2014	43.04	43.59	43.00	43.52	21431100	43.25
11 Aug 2014	43.26	43.45	43.02	43.20	20351600	42.93
8 Aug 2014	43.23	43.32	42.91	43.20	28942700	42.93
7 Aug 2014	42.84	43.45	42.65	43.23	30314900	42.96
6 Aug 2014	42.74	43.17	42.21	42.74	24634000	42.47
5 Aug 2014	43.31	43.46	42.83	43.08	26266400	42.81
4 Aug 2014	42.97	43.47	42.81	43.37	34277400	43.10
1 Aug 2014	43.21	43.25	42.60	42.86	31170300	42.59

Source: https://finance.yahoo.com.

$$\$44.83 = 45.11 - 0.28 \quad \text{and} \quad \frac{45.11 - 0.28}{45.11} = 0.9938,$$

respectively. In consequence, the adjusted closing price on 15 August is

$$\$44.51 = 44.79 \times 0.9938.$$

Note that this process of adjustment means that the historical prices do not necessarily reflect the actual prices at which trades took place.

The adjustment process for a stock split is similar. Suppose, for instance, that a 2-for-1 stock split occurs in which a company replaces each existing share by two shares (or some other multiple). Then the price of an individual share is immediately halved (or scaled by the otherwise appropriate fraction). Such splits make shares appear more affordable even though the underlying market capitalization of the company has not changed. To avoid the artificially induced discontinuity in the share price at the time of the split, all historical prices need to be divided by 2 and the historical volume series correspondingly multiplied by 2 so that the price after the split and the price before the split are comparable.

A further issue of data comparability is the presence of non-trading days in the raw data. For instance, a close look at the calendar days in the first column of Table 1.3 reveals a number of missing days, each of which corresponds (in this instance) to weekends and public holidays. But there may be days other than public holidays and weekends when a stock does not trade. In addition, when comparing time series of stock prices from different countries, public holidays do not always fall on the same days. In preparing data for empirical work, all these details need attention.

1.3.2 Returns

The return to a financial asset probably receives more attention in financial econometrics than does the price of an asset, although the movement of stock prices over long historical periods is also of substantial interest to investors and is relevant in practical econometric work dealing with longer term trends. Broadly speaking, a financial return provides a measure of outcome of the decision to invest in a financial asset. This measure accounts not only for the capital gain or loss due to the price change over the holding period of the asset but also for the cumulative impact of the contractual stream of cash flows that take place over the course of the holding period.

In principle, a financial asset might be held for an indeterminate period. Historically, stock prices were usually measured at daily, weekly, and monthly frequencies. In that case, the holding period of the investment is limited to a multiple of this frequency. But with the advent of readily available high-frequency data, returns can be computed for most holding periods, even extremely short ones. The latter have become much more important with computerized trading practice.

Dollar Returns

The simplest measure of return on holding an asset for k periods between time $t - k$ and t is the dollar return, denoted $\$R_{kt}$, given by the price differential over this period,

$$\$R_{kt} = P_t - P_{t-k}.$$

Although this measure is a simple intuitive response to the problem of computing the return to an investment, its major drawback is that it is not scale-free and does not measure the return relative to the initial investment. Moreover, this measure depends on the unit in which prices (and dividends) are quoted. To make returns comparable across assets and across international financial markets, scale-free measures of returns are required.

Simple Returns

The simple return on an asset between time $t - 1$ and t is given by

$$R_t = \frac{P_t - P_{t-1}}{P_{t-1}} = \frac{P_t}{P_{t-1}} - 1. \qquad (1.1)$$

The relative price ratio P_t/P_{t-1}, also known as the price relative (or prel for short), is a useful quantity to compute. If the ratio is greater than 1 then returns are positive; and if it is less than 1 returns are negative. Equation (1.1) may be rearranged as

$$1 + R_t = \frac{P_t}{P_{t-1}},$$

in which $1 + R_t$ is known as the simple gross return. The usefulness of the simple gross return is that it represents the value at time t of investing $\$1$ at time $t - 1$.

The return to holding an asset for k periods, $R_t(k)$, is given by

$$
\begin{aligned}
R_t(k) &= \frac{P_t}{P_{t-k}} - 1 \\
&= \frac{P_t}{P_{t-1}} \times \frac{P_{t-1}}{P_{t-2}} \times \cdots \times \frac{P_{t-k+2}}{P_{t-k+1}} \times \frac{P_{t-k+1}}{P_{t-k}} - 1 \\
&= (1 + R_t) \times (1 + R_{t-1}) \times \cdots \times (1 + R_{t-k+2}) \times (1 + R_{t-k+1}) - 1 \\
&= \prod_{j=0}^{k-1} (1 + R_{t-j}) - 1.
\end{aligned}
\tag{1.2}
$$

The point to be emphasized in this calculation is that simple returns are not additive when computing multi-period returns because of the multiplicative effect of period-by-period returns.

If the data frequency is monthly, then the simple return for a holding period of 1 year is given by

$$
R_t(12) = \left[\prod_{j=0}^{11} (1 + R_{t-j}) \right] - 1.
\tag{1.3}
$$

The most common period over which a return is quoted is 1 year, and returns data are commonly presented in per annum terms. This means that the current monthly return needs to be appropriately scaled so that it is interpretable as an annual return and expressed on a per annum basis. In the case of monthly returns, the associated annualized simple return is computed as

$$
\text{Annualized } R_t(12) = (1 + R_t)^{12} - 1.
\tag{1.4}
$$

Expression (1.4) is obtained from equation (1.3) by making the assumption that the best guess of the per annum return is that the current monthly return will persist for the next 12 months. In this case, all the terms in the product expansion (in square brackets) of equation (1.3) will be identical.

Log Returns

The log return of an asset is defined as

$$
r_t = \log(1 + R_t) = \log P_t - \log P_{t-1}.
\tag{1.5}
$$

Log returns are also referred to as continuously compounded returns. To understand why this is so, it is convenient to use the exponential constant e. The Swiss mathematician Leonhard Euler (1707–1783) named this constant, introduced the letter e to represent it, showed its now well-known exponential series representation, and proved its form in terms of the limiting operation

$$
e \equiv \lim_{s \to \infty} \left(1 + \frac{1}{s} \right)^s \approx 2.71828.
$$

Somewhat earlier in 1683, another Swiss mathematician Jacob Bernoulli (1655–1705) attempted to find this limit in studying the effect of continuously compounded interest. Its discovery is often attributed to him and links the mathematics of compound interest with the subjects of accounting, finance, and economics. The limit formula above represents the value of an account at the end of the year that started with $1.00 and paid 100% interest per year but with the interest compounded continuously over time rather than at discrete intervals during the year.

If m is the compounding period and r_t the return, then it follows from above that

$$P_t = P_{t-1}\left(1 + \frac{r_t}{m}\right)^m.$$

Continuous compounding is produced when $m \to \infty$ leading to

$$P_t = P_{t-1} \lim_{m \to \infty} \left(1 + \frac{r_t}{m}\right)^m. \tag{1.6}$$

Let $s = m/r_t$ in this formula. Then the expression in (1.6) may be rewritten as

$$P_t = P_{t-1} \lim_{s \to \infty} \left[\left(1 + \frac{1}{s}\right)^{s r_t}\right]$$

$$= P_{t-1} \left[\lim_{s \to \infty} \left(1 + \frac{1}{s}\right)^s\right]^{r_t}$$

$$= P_{t-1} e^{r_t}. \tag{1.7}$$

Taking logarithms of expression (1.7) yields the definition of the log returns given in equation (1.5).

Log returns are particularly useful because of the simplification they allow in dealing with multiperiod returns. For example, the 2-period return is given by

$$r_t(2) = \log P_t - \log P_{t-2}$$

$$= (\log P_t - \log P_{t-1}) + (\log P_{t-1} - \log P_{t-2})$$

$$= r_t + r_{t-1}. \tag{1.8}$$

By extension, the k-period return is

$$r_t(k) = \log P_t - \log P_{t-k}$$

$$= (\log P_t - \log P_{t-1}) + (\log P_{t-1} - \log P_{t-2}) + \cdots + (\log P_{t-k+1} - \log P_{t-k})$$

$$= r_t + r_{t-1} + \cdots + r_{t-(k-1)}$$

$$= \sum_{j=0}^{k-1} r_{t-j}. \tag{1.9}$$

In other words, the k-period log return is simply the sum of the single period log returns over the pertinent period.

For the case of data observed monthly, the annual log return is

$$r_t(12) = \log P_t - \log P_{t-12} = \sum_{j=0}^{11} r_{t-j}. \tag{1.10}$$

Once again, expression (1.9) may be used to obtain the returns expressed on a per annum basis by simply multiplying all monthly returns by 12, making the implicit assumption that the best guess of the per annum return is that the current monthly return will persist for the next 12 months.

By analogy, if prices are observed quarterly, then the individual quarterly returns can be annualized by multiplying the quarterly returns by 4. Similarly, if prices are observed daily, then the daily returns are annualized by multiplying the daily returns by the number of trading days 252. The choice of 252 for the number of trading days in a calendar year is an approximation because of the effect of public holidays, leap years, and additional days of trading interruption. Other choices are 250; and, very rarely, the number of calendar days, 365.

Table 1.4 provides calculations based on historical monthly prices for the US stock Microsoft showing the mechanics of return computations from the price of a stock. Note that no return figures are reported for January 2012. Their absence emphasizes that an observation is lost at the beginning of the sample when computing returns because the price of the stock before the start of the sample period is not available. The monthly dollar, simple, and log returns to Microsoft for February 2012 are, respectively,

$$\$R_t = 31.74 - 29.53 = \$2.210,$$

$$R_t = \frac{31.74 - 29.53}{29.53} = 0.075 = 7.5\%,$$

$$r_t = \log(1 + 0.075) = 0.072 = 7.2\%.$$

TABLE 1.4 Monthly prices for the US stock Microsoft for the years 2012 and 2013. Also shown are alternative measures of the one-month return to holding Microsoft. Prices are month-end closing prices adjusted for splits and dividends quoted in US$.

Date	Price	Prel	Monthly Dollar Return	Monthly Simple Return	Monthly Log Return	Annual Simple Return	Annual Log Return
Jan 2012	29.530	...	...	...	...	...	...
Feb 2012	31.740	1.075	2.210	0.075	0.072	1.378	0.866
Mar 2012	32.250	1.016	0.510	0.016	0.016	0.211	0.191
Apr 2012	32.020	0.993	−0.230	−0.007	−0.007	−0.082	−0.086
May 2012	29.190	0.912	−2.830	−0.088	−0.093	−0.671	−1.110
Jun 2012	30.590	1.048	1.400	0.048	0.047	0.754	0.562
Jul 2012	29.470	0.963	−1.120	−0.037	−0.037	−0.361	−0.448
Aug 2012	30.820	1.046	1.350	0.046	0.045	0.712	0.537
Sep 2012	29.780	0.966	−1.040	−0.034	−0.034	−0.338	−0.412
Oct 2012	28.530	0.958	−1.245	−0.042	−0.043	−0.401	−0.512
Nov 2012	26.620	0.933	−1.915	−0.067	−0.069	−0.566	−0.834
Dec 2012	26.730	1.004	0.110	0.004	0.004	0.051	0.049
Jan 2013	27.470	1.028	0.740	0.028	0.027	0.388	0.328
Feb 2013	27.800	1.012	0.330	0.012	0.012	0.154	0.143
Mar 2013	28.610	1.029	0.810	0.029	0.029	0.411	0.345
Apr 2013	33.100	1.157	4.490	0.157	0.146	4.751	1.749
May 2013	34.880	1.054	1.780	0.054	0.052	0.875	0.629
Jun 2013	34.530	0.990	−0.350	−0.010	−0.010	−0.114	−0.121
Jul 2013	31.830	0.922	−2.700	−0.078	−0.081	−0.624	−0.977
Aug 2013	33.400	1.049	1.570	0.049	0.048	0.782	0.578
Sep 2013	33.310	1.097	−0.090	−0.003	−0.003	−0.032	−0.032
Oct 2013	35.350	1.061	2.040	0.061	0.059	1.041	0.713
Nov 2013	38.130	1.079	2.780	0.079	0.076	1.480	0.908
Dec 2013	37.430	0.982	−0.700	−0.018	−0.019	−0.199	−0.222

Source: Bloomberg.

These calculations demonstrate that continuously compounded returns are very similar to simple returns as long as the return is relatively small, which it generally will be for monthly or daily returns. Indeed, it is only really at the third decimal place that the differences between the two definitions of returns become readily apparent.

Despite the similarities in the two measures of returns, appreciable differences emerge when the returns are annualized. For the simple return in February 2012 the calculation is

$$R_t(12) = (1 + 0.075)^{12} - 1 = 1.378 = 137.8\%.$$

By contrast, the annualized log return is

$$r_t(12) = 12 \times 0.072 = 0.866 = 86.6\%.$$

Note that the practice of quoting figures as annual rates is usually related to scaling the data. Returns, when computed over the time interval of a day or even shorter intervals, can be relatively small in value and this may lead to arithmetic errors when doing complex computations involving the returns. Annualizing the return scales can help to alleviate this problem.

Dealing with Dividends
Adjusting the computation of returns for the payment of a dividend, D_t, between time $t-1$ and t, is relatively straightforward. The dollar return becomes

$$\$R_t = P_t + D_t - P_{t-1},$$

in which P_t and P_{t-1} are the unadjusted prices. The simple and gross returns are then given by

$$R_t = \frac{P_t + D_t - P_{t-1}}{P_{t-1}} = \frac{P_t}{P_{t-1}} + \frac{D_t}{P_{t-1}} - 1, \tag{1.11}$$

$$(1 + R_t) = \frac{P_t + D_t - P_{t-1}}{P_{t-1}} = \frac{P_t}{P_{t-1}} + \frac{D_t}{P_{t-1}}, \tag{1.12}$$

respectively. It is apparent from equations (1.11) and (1.12) that the simple and gross returns to a stock in the presence of a dividend payment are easily computed in terms of the price relative, P_t/P_{t-1} and the dividend yield, D_t/P_{t-1}.

Adjusting log returns for a dividend payment simply requires using the correct definition of gross simple returns when taking logarithms

$$r_t = \log(1 + R_t) = \log\left(1 + \frac{P_t + D_t - P_{t-1}}{P_{t-1}}\right) = \log\left(\frac{P_t}{P_{t-1}} + \frac{D_t}{P_{t-1}}\right).$$

Much of the earlier discussion concerning the computation of returns has reflected common practice and ignored the issue of dividends. This practice stems from the reality that dividends are paid relatively infrequently and constitute a minor proportion of the overall return compared with price movements.

Excess Returns
The difference between the return on a risky financial asset and a risk-free interest rate, denoted r_{ft}, is known as the excess return. The risk-free rate is often taken to be the interest rate on a government bond. The simple and log excess returns on an asset are therefore

defined as $R_t - r_{ft}$ and $r_t - r_{ft}$, respectively. In computing the excess returns it is important to ensure that the risk-free interest rate is expressed in the same unit of time as the return on the risky financial asset. For example, interest rates are normally quoted as annual rates, so in the case of monthly log returns the quoted annual risk-free interest rate would need to be divided by 12.

1.3.3 Portfolio Returns

Financial econometric work is often concerned not with the return to a single asset as the prime object of the investigation but rather the return to a portfolio of financial assets. Attention to a portfolio of assets accords more closely with individual and firm investment decisions. In order to deal with this revised focus, it is necessary to address the aggregation of the returns of the assets in the portfolio.

Consider a portfolio with only two assets whose portfolio shares are w_1 and w_2, respectively. The portfolio shares represent the fraction of the total portfolio value allocated to each of the assets with the normalization condition

$$w_1 + w_2 = 1.$$

Using the definition of simple gross returns for each asset, the value of the portfolio between $t - 1$ and t may be calculated as

$$P_t = P_{t-1} w_1 (1 + R_{1t}) + P_{t-1} w_2 (1 + R_{2t}) = P_{t-1} \big(w_1 (1 + R_{1t}) + w_2 (1 + R_{2t}) \big).$$

Rearranging slightly, this expression becomes

$$(1 + R_{Pt}) \equiv \frac{P_t}{P_{t-1}} = w_1 (1 + R_{1t}) + w_2 (1 + R_{2t}). \tag{1.13}$$

In words, the one-period gross return to a portfolio, $1 + R_{Pt}$, is given by the weighted sum of the gross returns to each of the assets using portfolio shares as weights. Expanding the right-hand side of equation (1.13) gives

$$1 + R_{Pt} = w_1 + w_1 R_{1t} + w_2 + w_2 R_{2t},$$

which yields the important result that for simple returns, the portfolio rate of return is equal to the weighted average of the returns to the assets

$$R_{Pt} = w_1 R_{1t} + w_2 R_{2t},$$

since $w_1 + w_2 = 1$. For N assets, the simple portfolio return is given by

$$R_{Pt} = \sum_{i=1}^{N} w_i R_{it}, \qquad \sum_{i=1}^{N} w_i = 1. \tag{1.14}$$

This result does not extend to the case of log returns. From equation (1.5) and using the result in (1.14) it follows that the log return on a portfolio, r_{Pt}, is

$$r_{Pt} = \log(1 + R_{Pt}) = \log \left(1 + \sum_{i=1}^{N} w_i R_{it} \right) \neq \sum_{i=1}^{N} w_i r_{it}. \tag{1.15}$$

In most practical situations, the fact that the log return to the portfolio is not the weighted sum of the log returns to the constituent assets is simply ignored. This is acceptable when the log returns are small, as is likely for short holding periods, in which case the log return on the portfolio is negligibly different to the weighted sum of the logarithm of the constituent asset returns because the approximation $r_{Pt} = \log(1 + R_{Pt}) \approx R_{Pt}$ is reasonably accurate when R_{Pt} is small.

The result in equation (1.15) begs the question of how to combine log returns into the portfolio return. Consider again the case of two assets. Using the definition of log returns for each asset and expression (1.7), the value of the portfolio between $t-1$ and t may be calculated as

$$P_t = P_{t-1} w_1 e^{r_{1t}} + P_{t-1} w_2 e^{r_{2t}},$$

so that

$$\log\left(\frac{P_t}{P_{t-1}}\right) \equiv r_{Pt} = \log\left(w_1 e^{r_{1t}} + w_2 e^{r_{2t}}\right).$$

For N assets, the log portfolio return is then

$$r_{Pt} = \log\left(\sum_{i=1}^{N} w_i e^{r_{it}}\right). \tag{1.16}$$

More often than not, financial econometric work uses log returns and simply takes a weighted aggregate of these returns to find portfolio returns. Although not strictly correct, this approach will also be used in Chapter 3 where simple portfolios are constructed using linear regression.

Once returns, either simple returns or log returns, are available, then equations (1.2) and (1.9) may be used for temporal aggregation of the portfolio returns. The situation is summarized in Table 1.5.

1.4 STOCK MARKET INDICES

A problem of particular importance is the return to a portfolio that comprises all or at least a selection of prominent stocks on a stock exchange. An aggregate summary measure of the performance of the stock market as a whole is known as a stock market index. Indices combine a selection of (a large number of) stocks in a particular way to create a portfolio. The index then represents the value of the portfolio and is expressed in terms of an average price that has been normalized in some way. Because stock market indices are price indices, the computation of returns to the index can be performed in exactly the same way as if it were a single stock.

The major stock market indices are constructed in one of two ways. *Price-weighted indices* construct a portfolio of all the stocks in the index in which one share of each of

TABLE 1.5 Summary of expressions for computing portfolio returns using simple and log returns and how to aggregate portfolio returns to obtain the k-period portfolio return.

Aggregation	Simple Returns	Log Returns
Portfolio Return	$R_{Pt} = \sum_{i=1}^{N} w_i R_{it}$	$r_{Pt} = \log\left(\sum_{i=1}^{N} w_i e^{r_{it}}\right)$
k-period Return	$R_{Pt}(k) = \prod_{i=0}^{k-1}(1 + R_{Pt-i}) - 1$	$r_{Pt}(k) = \sum_{i=0}^{k-1} r_{Pt-i}$

the stocks appears and the weight given to the share is therefore simply the price of the share. In other words, the total monetary value invested in each share is only proportional to the price of that share. *Value-weighted indices* construct a portfolio of all the stocks in the index in which the weight given to each stock is proportional to the total market value of its outstanding equity.

The six indices commonly used in financial econometric work are plotted in Figure 1.2.

(i) *Deutscher Aktien Index* (DAX) comprises the 30 largest German companies that trade on the Frankfurt Stock Exchange. It is a value-weighted index although the weights are computed in a slightly more complex way than in a simple value weighting scheme.

(ii) *Dow Jones Industrial Average Index* (Dow Jones or DJIA) is computed using 30 prominent United States corporations. The DJIA is a price-weighted index.

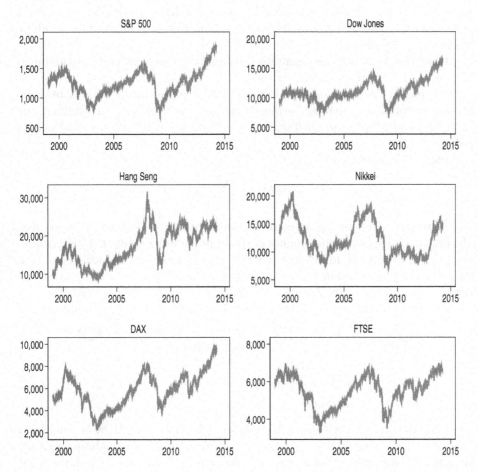

FIGURE 1.2 Daily observations on six international stock market indices for the period 4 January 1999 to 2 April 2014.

(iii) *Financial Times Stock Exchange 100 Index* (FTSE) is a value-weighted index computed using the 100 largest companies listed on the London Stock Exchange.

(iv) *Hang Seng Index* (Hang Seng or HSX) comprises 40 of the largest companies that trade on the Hong Kong Exchange. It is a value-weighted index.

(v) *Nikkei 225 Index* (Nikkei or NKX) is a price-weighted index made up of 225 prominent companies listed on the Tokyo Stock Exchange.

(vi) *Standard and Poor's Composite 500* (S&P 500) is a value-weighted index. The index is computed by summing the market value of the outstanding equity in each firm in the index.

The falls in these market indices that occurred around the collapse of the dot-com bubble in the early 2000s and the global financial crisis of 2008–2009 are evident in each of the graphs plotted in Figure 1.2.

In addition to these six indices, another commonly encountered index is the NASDAQ Composite Index, which is a value-weighted index of all the stocks listed on the NASDAQ stock exchange. It is usually regarded as an index of the performance of technology companies and is particularly associated with the dot-com bubble of the late 1990s, which created and destroyed some $8 trillion dollars of shareholder wealth over a period of 5–6 years.

Table 1.6 lists the 30 component stocks of the Dow Jones obtained from Bloomberg in September 2014. The monthly closing price for December 2013 is also listed together with the market capitalization (US$ billion) of the component stocks (price of share × number of outstanding shares). Despite the fact that the DJIA is a price-weighted index, Table 1.6 also shows the notional share that each stock would have in a value-weighted index.

The DJIA is computed as

$$DJIA_t = \frac{1}{D} \sum_{j=1}^{30} P_{jt},$$

where the quantity D that appears in the denominator is known as the Dow Jones divisor. The divisor started out as the number of stocks in the index so the DJIA was a simple average, but subsequent adjustment due to stock splits and structural changes required the divisor to be adjusted in order to preserve the continuity of the index. For example, the appropriate value of the divisor in December 2013 was 0.15571590501117.

Using the closing prices in Table 1.6, the DJIA for December 2013 is computed as

$$DJIA_{Dec13} = \frac{140.25 + 90.73 + 35.15 + \cdots + 222.68 + 78.69 + 76.40}{0.15571590501117}$$

$$= \frac{2581.25}{0.15571590501117}$$

$$= 16576.662,$$

which is identical to the value of the index, 16576.66, quoted by Bloomberg for December 2013. The DJIA is a price-weighted average. The main advantage of price weighting is its simplicity but its primary disadvantage is that stocks with the highest prices, like Visa ($222.68), IBM ($187.57), and Goldman Sachs ($177.26), have a greater relative impact on the index than perhaps they should have.

TABLE 1.6 The 30 US stocks used in the construction of the Dow Jones. Month-end closing prices adjusted for splits and dividends and quoted in US$ are shown for the month of December 2013 together with total outstanding value of the company's shares ($ billion).

Company	Ticker	Closing Price (Dec. 2013)	Market Cap. (Dec. 2013)	Market Share
3M Co.	MMM	140.250	93.300	0.020
American Express Co.	AXP	90.730	97.196	0.021
AT&T Inc.	T	35.150	97.196	0.021
The Boeing Co.	BA	136.490	102.566	0.022
Caterpillar Inc.	CAT	90.810	57.787	0.012
Chevron Corp.	CVX	124.910	240.224	0.051
Cisco Systems Inc.	CSCO	22.450	120.032	0.025
The Coca-Cola Co.	KO	41.310	182.422	0.039
El du Pont de Nemours & Co.	DD	64.970	60.169	0.013
Exxon Mobil Corp.	XOM	101.200	442.094	0.094
General Electric Co.	GE	28.030	283.590	0.060
The Goldman Sachs Group Inc.	GS	177.260	83.353	0.018
The Home Depot Inc.	HD	82.340	115.953	0.025
Intel Corp.	INTC	25.960	129.047	0.027
International Business Machine	IBM	187.570	203.674	0.043
Johnson & Johnson	JNJ	91.590	258.415	0.055
JPMorgan Chase & Co.	JPM	58.480	219.837	0.047
McDonald's Corp.	MCD	97.030	96.548	0.020
Merck & Co. Inc.	MRK	50.050	146.242	0.031
Microsoft Corp.	MSFT	37.430	312.464	0.066
NIKE Inc.	NKE	78.640	69.955	0.015
Pfizer Inc.	PFE	30.630	198.515	0.042
The Procter & Gamble Co.	PG	81.410	221.291	0.047
The Travelers Companies Inc.	TRV	90.540	32.963	0.007
United Technologies Corp.	UTX	113.800	104.421	0.022
United Health Group Inc.	UNH	75.300	75.809	0.016
Verizon Communications Inc.	VZ	49.140	140.626	0.030
Visa Inc.	V	222.680	141.756	0.030
Wal-Mart Stores Inc.	WMT	78.690	254.623	0.054
The Walt Disney Co.	DIS	76.400	134.256	0.028

Source: Bloomberg.

The other major type of weighting scheme is to weight stocks by market capitalization, giving a value-weighted average. In consequence, stocks like Exxon (0.094), Microsoft (0.066), and General Electric (0.060), would have the largest weights in the index if they were value weighted. The primary disadvantage of value weighting is that constituent securities whose prices have risen the most (or fallen the most) have a greater (or lower) weight in the index. This weighting method can potentially lead to overweighting stocks that have risen in price (and may be overvalued) and underweighting stocks that have declined in price (and may be undervalued).

The differences between price weighting and value weighting are illustrated in Figure 1.3 in which the 30 constituent stocks of the Dow Jones are combined to form two hypothetical indices, one based on simple price weighting and the other using shares

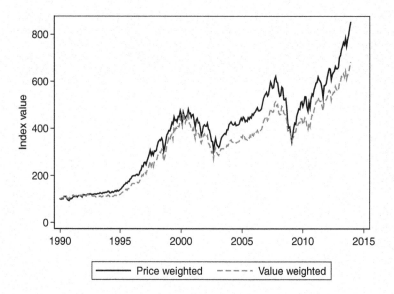

FIGURE 1.3   The effect of price weighting and value weighting on an index comprising 30 stocks that make up the Dow Jones. The indices are computed using monthly data on prices and market capitalization for the period January 1990 to December 2013 with each index scaled to start from 100.

constructed from market capitalization as shown in Table 1.6. Both indices in Figure 1.3 are normalized to take the value 100 in January 1990. While the price-weighted and value-weighted indices track each other fairly closely over the period, the price-weighted index seems to overemphasize market movements during the period of the dot-com bubble during the latter half of the 1990s as well as the speed of the recovery from the 2008 global financial crisis.

1.5 BOND YIELDS

As noted in Section 1.2, zero-coupon bonds may be created from coupon paying bonds by separating the coupons from the principal and trading each of these components independently. Consequently, much of the econometric analysis of the bond market uses data based on zero-coupon bonds. The critical concept when dealing with bonds, which relates to the return on a stock, is the yield to maturity. If a zero-coupon bond has a face value of $1 paid at maturity, n, the price of the bond purchased at time t equals the discounted present value of the principal, which is given by

$$P_{nt} = 1 \times \exp\left(-n y_{nt}\right), \tag{1.17}$$

where y_{nt} is the discount rate or yield and is commonly expressed in per annum terms. The yield on a bond is therefore the discount rate that equates the present value of the bond's face value to its price.

Taking natural logarithms and rearranging equation (1.17) gives

$$y_{nt} = -\frac{1}{n} \log P_{nt} = -\frac{1}{n} p_{nt}, $$

where $P_{nt} = \text{lop } P_{nt}$. $\tag{1.18}$

This expression shows that the yield is inversely proportional to the natural logarithm of the price of the bond, where the proportionality constant is $-1/n$. Moreover, as the price of the bond P_{nt} is always less than \$1 then from the properties of logarithms, p_{nt} is a negative number, and the yield in equation (1.18) will always be positive.

Governments issue bonds of differing lengths to maturity. Bonds at the shorter end of the maturity spectrum (maturity less than 12 months) are generally zero-coupon bonds (bonds that pay no coupon or interest), while the coupon bonds (for which the holder receives regular interest payments) can have a maturity as long as 30 years. The *term structure* of interest rates is the relationship between time to maturity and yield to maturity, and the *yield curve* is a plot of the term structure of yield to maturity against time to maturity at a specific time. Figure 1.4 presents scatter plots of observed US zero-coupon bond yield curves for the months of March, May, July, and August 1989, for yields ranging from 1 to 120 months. The yields are computed from the end-of-month price quotes taken from the CRSP government bonds files, the same data as that used in Diebold and Li (2006).

The plots of the yield curves in Figure 1.4 reveal a few well-known features.

(i) At any point in time when the yield curve is observed, all the maturities may not be represented. This is particularly true at longer maturities where the number of observed yields is much sparser than at the short end of the maturity spectrum.

(ii) The yields at longer maturities tend to be less volatile than the yields at the shorter end of the maturity spectrum.

(iii) On the assumption that longer term financing should carry a risk premium, a natural expectation would be for the yield curve to slope upward. However, the empirical plots in Figure 1.4 show that the yield curve can in practice assume a variety of shapes, including upward sloping, downward sloping, humped, and even inverted humped. These shapes are ultimately determined by the demand and supply of bonds of various maturities, market expectations, and risk assessments.

Modeling bond yields and the term structure are important and often challenging tasks in financial econometric work. Various aspects of these tasks in modeling bond yields and the tools designed to address them are examined in Chapters 6, 9, and 12.

1.6 EXERCISES

The data required for the exercises are available for download as EViews workfiles (*.wf1), Stata datafiles (*.dta), comma delimited text files (*.csv), and as Excel spreadsheets (*.xlsx).

1. Equity Prices, Dividends, and Returns

(a) Access the Yahoo Finance website (https://finance.yahoo.com) and load the current quoted prices for The Boeing Company (BA). Compare the current situation with that reported in Table 1.2.

(b) Observe the historical daily prices for Boeing. What do you notice about the order in which they are presented?

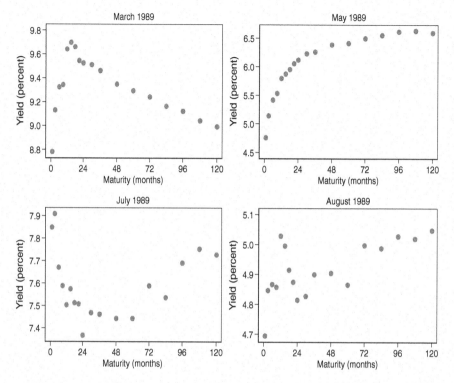

FIGURE 1.4 Scatter plots of observed yields for the months of March, May, July, and August 1989 for US zero-coupon bonds.

(c) Examine the daily prices and scrutinize the days on which dividend payments are made. Verify that the dividend adjustments made to the historical price series are correct.

(d) Obtain monthly price data on Boeing. Are the quoted monthly prices beginning or end-of-month quotes?

2. US Stocks

capm.*

The data are monthly observations for the period April 1990 to July 2004 on the equity prices of Exxon, General Electric, IBM, and Microsoft and Walmart, together with the price of gold.

(a) Plot the price indices and comment on the results.

(b) Compute simple and logarithmic returns to each of the assets. For each asset plot the two returns series and comment on any differences.

(c) Assume that you hold each of the stocks in a portfolio. Compute the portfolio returns in both simple and logarithmic form for the first 7 months of 2004.

3. Dow Jones Index

DJindexstocks.*

The data are monthly observations for the period January 1990 to 31 December 2013 on the Dow Jones, the prices and market capitalization of the 30 constituent stocks of the index, and the risk-free interest rate.

(a) Consider the historical prices for Microsoft for the years 2012 and 2013. For these two years, compute the price relative, simple, and logarithmic monthly returns, and simple and logarithmic annualized returns. Compare your results with Table 1.4.

(b) Compute the logarithmic and simple returns to holding each of the 30 stocks in the Dow Jones for the month of December 2012.

(c) Assuming equal shares, compute the simple and logarithmic returns to holding a portfolio comprising each of the 30 Dow Jones stocks for the month of December 2012.

(d) Verify that your result is identical to THE quoted value of the Dow for that month

$$DJIA_t = \frac{1}{D} \sum_{j=1}^{30} P_{jt},$$

where the Dow Jones divisor, D, is taken to be 0.15571590501117. Verify that your result is identical to quoted value of the Dow for that month.

(e) Construct portfolio shares for each of the Dow Jones stocks based on market capitalization for the month of December 2013. Comment on which stocks that receive the most weight in the Dow under the price and market capitalization weighting schemes, respectively.

(f) Combine the 30 constituent stocks of the Dow Jones to form two indices, one based on simple price weighting and the other using shares constructed from market capitalization. Plot the indices over the sample period and comment on the differences.

4. International Stock Indices

stockindices.*

The data are daily observations on the Dow Jones, S&P 500, Hang Seng, Nikkei, Dax, and FTSE stock indices for the period 4 January 1999 to 2 April 2014.

(a) Plot the indices. Compare your results with Figure 1.2.

(b) Compute the daily logarithmic and simple returns of each of the indices and plot them. Comment on any differences.

(c) Express the daily logarithmic and simple returns in annualized form and plot the resultant series. Comment on your results.

(d) Compute the returns to holding each of the indices over the entire sample period in both logarithmic and simple form. Comment on the results.

5. Australian Stocks

> AusFirms.*

The data are monthly observations on the prices of the largest 136 stocks in Australia from December 1999 to June 2014. Consider a portfolio constructed by holding one share in every stock in the data set that records a price, P_{it}, at every time t in the sample period. In other words, drop those stocks that have any missing observations.

(a) Compute the simple and log returns to the portfolio over the full sample period using

$$R = \frac{P_T}{P_1} - 1, \qquad r = \log\left(\frac{P_T}{P_1}\right),$$

respectively, where P_1 is the first observation and

$$P_t = \sum_{i=1}^{N} P_{it}.$$

Note that P″ is the price of the portfolio in December 1999 and P′ is the price of the portfolio in June 2014. Comment on the results.

(b) Compute the portfolio weights of each stock in the portfolio for every time t using the formula

$$w_{it} = \frac{P_{it}}{\sum_{i=1}^{N} P_{it}},$$

in which N is the number of stocks in the portfolio.

(c) Compute simple and log returns to the portfolio in each time period, respectively,

$$R_{Pt} = \sum_{i=1}^{N} w_{it-1} R_{it}, \qquad r_{Pt} = \log\left(\sum_{i=1}^{N} w_{it-1} e^{r_{it}}\right),$$

remembering to use the weight at the beginning of the holding period.

(d) Compare the results obtained in (a) and (c).

CHAPTER 2

Statistical Properties
of Financial Data

The financial pages of newspapers and magazines, online financial sites, and academic journals all routinely report a plethora of financial statistics. Even within a specific financial market, the data may be recorded at multiple observation frequencies and the same data may be presented in various ways. As will be seen, the time series based on these representations have very different statistical properties and reveal distinct features of the underlying phenomena relating to both long-run and short-run behavior.

The characteristics of financial data may also differ across markets. For example, there is no reason to expect that equity markets behave the same way as currency markets, or for commodity markets to behave the same way as bond markets. In some cases, like currency markets, trading is a nearly continuous activity, while other markets open and close in a regulated manner according to specific times and days. Real estate markets differ further in terms of their intermittent transactions, limited liquidity, and supply side constraints. Yet their importance to other financial markets such as the mortgage market and wider linkages to the macroeconomy are now especially evident in the aftermath of the 2008 financial crisis. Options markets also have their own special characteristics and offer a wide and growing range of financial instruments that relate to other financial assets and markets.

One important preliminary role of statistical analysis is to find stylized facts that characterize different types of financial data and particular markets. Such analysis is primarily descriptive and helps us to understand the prominent features of the data and the differences that can arise from basic elements like varying the sampling frequency and implementing various transformations. Accordingly, the primary aim of this chapter is to highlight the main characteristics of financial data and establish a set of stylized facts for financial time series. These characteristics will be used throughout the book as important inputs in the building and testing of financial models.

2.1 A FIRST LOOK AT THE DATA

This section gives special attention to the key characteristics of some commonly used financial time series data, starting with stock prices, returns, dividends and bond yields.

2.1.1 Prices

Figure 2.1 gives a plot of the monthly US equity price index (S&P 500) for the period January 1950 to September 2016. The time path of equity prices shows long-run growth over this period whose general shape is captured by the exponential trend graphed against the data in the figure. While the exponential trend prescribes a general pattern of movement in prices over this historical period, it is also clear that there are major swings in which prices wander above and below this exponential trend for sustained periods. This observed exponential pattern in the equity price index may be expressed formally as

$$P_t = P_{t-1} \exp(r_t), \tag{2.1}$$

where P_t is the current equity price, P_{t-1} is the previous month's price, and r_t is the rate of the increase between month $t-1$ and month t.

If r_t is restricted to take the same constant value, r, in all time periods, then equation (2.1) becomes

$$P_t = P_{t-1} \exp(r). \tag{2.2}$$

The relationship between the current price, P_t, and the price two months earlier, P_{t-2}, is

$$P_t = P_{t-1} \exp(r) = P_{t-2} \exp(r) \exp(r) = P_{t-2} \exp(2r).$$

By continuing this recursion, the relationship between the current price, P_t, and the price t months earlier, P_0, is given by

$$P_t = P_0 \exp(rt). \tag{2.3}$$

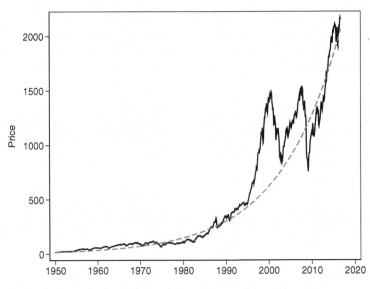

FIGURE 2.1 Monthly S&P 500 equity price index from January 1950 to September 2016. Fitted values (dashed line) are obtained using the exponential model in equation (2.3) with $r = 0.006$.

It is this exponential function that is plotted in Figure 2.1 in which $P_0 = 16.88$ is the equity price in January 1950 and the constant growth rate in monthly prices is set at $r = 0.006$.

The exponential function in equation (2.3) provides a within-sample predictive relationship based on the observed long-run growth behavior over 1950–2016. If an investor in January 1950 assumed that the long-run exponential growth rate was 0.006, then this investor could predict the price of equities in September 2016. As there are 800 months between these dates, the forecast price for September 2016 is

$$P(Sep.\ 2016) = 16.88 \times \exp(0.006 \times 800) = 2051.10.$$

The actual equity price in September 2016 for the data plotted in Figure 2.1 is 2157.69, showing that the predicted price is fairly accurate with a percentage forecast error of

$$100 \times \frac{2157.69 - 2051.10}{2157.69} = 4.94\%.$$

Forecasting methods for financial variables are discussed in Chapter 7.

An alternative way of analyzing the long-run time series behavior of asset prices is to plot the logarithm of prices over time. An example is given in Figure 2.2 where the natural logarithm of the equity price given in Figure 2.1 is presented. Comparing the two series shows that while prices grow exponentially (Figure 2.1), the logarithm of price increases at a constant rate (Figure 2.2). To see why this is the case, take natural logarithms of equation (2.3) to give

$$p_t = p_0 + rt, \tag{2.4}$$

where lower case letters now denote the natural logarithms of the variables, namely, $p_t = \log P_t$ and $p_0 = \log P_0$. This is now a linear equation between p_t and t in which the slope is

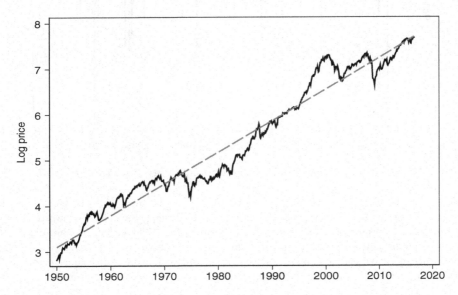

FIGURE 2.2 The natural logarithm of the monthly S&P 500 equity price index from January 1950 to September 2016. The dashed line is a linear function with slope 0.006.

equal to the constant r. This equation also forms the basis of the definition of log returns, a point that is now developed in more detail.

2.1.2 Returns

Figure 2.3 plots monthly log equity returns for the United States defined as

$$r_t = \log(P_t) - \log(P_{t-1}) = p_t - p_{t-1},$$

over the period January 1950 to September 2016. The log returns are seen to hover around a return value that is near zero over the sample period.[1] This value is in fact $r = 0.006$, which is the estimate used in the earlier computations in Section 2.1.1. This feature of equity returns contrasts dramatically with the trending character of the corresponding equity prices presented in Figure 2.1.

The marked empirical difference in the two series for prices and returns reveals an interesting aspect of stock market behavior. It is often emphasized in the financial literature that investment in equities should be based on long-run considerations rather than the prospect of short-run gains. The reason is that stock prices can be very volatile in the short-run. This short-run behavior is reflected in the high variability of the stock returns shown in Figure 2.3. Yet, although stock returns hover around a value

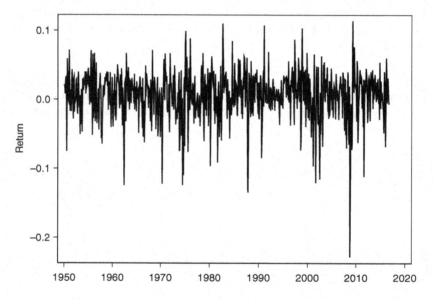

FIGURE 2.3   Monthly US log equity returns for the period January 1950 to September 2016.

---

[1] In computing returns, one observation is lost from the original sample period (unless the period under consideration happens to be a subsample of a longer time series). An immediate question arises as to how to quote the sample period. The convention used throughout this book will be to quote the original sample period without shortening it to account for missing observations due to the returns computation. A similar issue arises in Chapter 4 where observations are lost due to the nature of the model.

of approximately zero, stock prices (which accumulate these returns) tend to trend noticeably upward over time, as is apparent in Figure 2.1. This tendency of stock prices to drift upward over time is taken up again in Chapter 5. For present purposes, it is sufficient to remark that when returns are measured over very short periods of time, any tendency of prices to drift upward is virtually imperceptible because that effect is so small and is swamped by the apparent volatility of the returns. This interpretation puts emphasis on the fact that returns generally focus on short-run effects whereas price movements can trend noticeably upward (or downward) over extended periods of time.

2.1.3 Dividends

In many applications in finance, as in economics, the focus is on understanding the relationships among two or more series. For instance, in present value models of equities, the price of an equity is equal to the discounted future stream of dividend payments

$$P_t = \mathrm{E}_t\left[\frac{D_{t+1}}{(1+\delta_t)} + \frac{D_{t+2}}{(1+\delta_t)^2} + \frac{D_{t+3}}{(1+\delta_t)^3} + \cdots\right], \tag{2.5}$$

where $\mathrm{E}_t(D_{t+n})$ represents the expectation of dividends in the future at time $t+n$ given information available at time t and δ_t is the discount rate at time t.

The relationship between equity prices and dividends is highlighted in Figure 2.4, which plots US equity prices and dividend payments from January 1950 to September 2016. There appears to be a relationship between the two series as both series exhibit positive exponential-like trends with intermittent downturns that are more striking for equity prices.

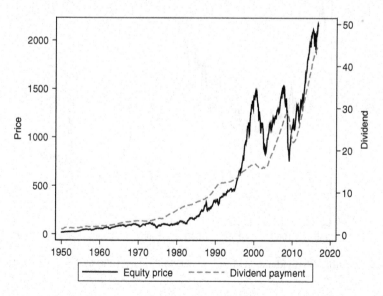

FIGURE 2.4 Monthly US equity prices and dividend payments for the period January 1950 to September 2016.

To analyze the relationship between equity prices and dividends more closely, assume that current expectations of future dividends are given by present dividends, $E_t(D_{t+n}) = D_t$. The present value relationship in equation (2.5) can now be written as

$$P_t = D_t \left(\frac{1}{(1+\delta_t)} + \frac{1}{(1+\delta_t)^2} + ... \right)$$

$$= \frac{D_t}{1+\delta_t} \left(1 + \frac{1}{(1+\delta_t)} + \frac{1}{(1+\delta_t)^2} + ... \right)$$

$$= \frac{D_t}{1+\delta_t} \left(\frac{1}{1 - 1/(1+\delta_t)} \right)$$

$$= \frac{D_t}{\delta_t}, \qquad (2.6)$$

where the penultimate step uses the sum of a geometric progression.[2] Rearranging this expression gives

$$\delta_t = \frac{D_t}{P_t}, \qquad (2.7)$$

which defines the dividend yield plotted in Figure 2.5 based on the data in Figure 2.4. The dividend yield exhibits no upward trend and instead wanders randomly around the level of 0.03. This behavior is in stark contrast to the equity price and dividend series, which both exhibit a strong tendency to trend upward.

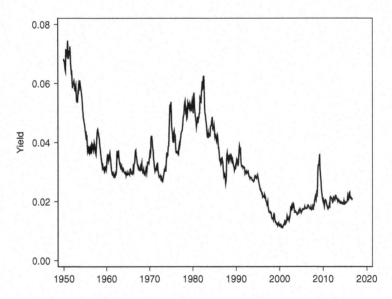

FIGURE 2.5   Monthly US dividend yield for the period January 1950 to September 2016.

[2] Recall that an infinite geometric progression is summed as

$$1 + \lambda + \lambda^2 + \lambda^3 + ... = \frac{1}{1-\lambda}, \qquad |\lambda| < 1,$$

where in the example $\lambda = 1/(1+\delta_t)$.

The example of the dividend yield illustrates how combining two or more series in an appropriate way can change the time series properties of the data in the present case by apparently eliminating the strong upward trending behavior in two series by standardizing one series in terms of the other. The process of combining trending financial variables into new variables that do not exhibit trends is a form of trend reduction by means of variable combination. This idea is explored in more detail in Chapter 6.

An alternative representation of the present value model suggested by equation (2.6) is to take natural logarithms and rearrange for $\log P_t$ to give

$$\log P_t = -\log \delta_t + \log D_t.$$

Assuming equities are priced according to the present value model, this equation reveals a linear relationship between $\log P_t$ and $\log D_t$.

2.1.4 Bond Yields

Figure 2.6 gives plots of yields on US zero-coupon bonds for maturities of 3 and 9 months. The yields to the different maturities are not distinguished from one another as the primary purpose is to discover some of the time series properties of bond yields.

The bond yield plots shown in Figure 2.6 reveal three important properties.

1. The yields are increasing over time, so they exhibit some form of trending behavior. This feature of financial time series is the subject matter of Chapter 5.
2. The variance of the yields tends to grow as the levels of the yields increase. This is called the *levels effect* and is investigated in more detail in Chapter 9.

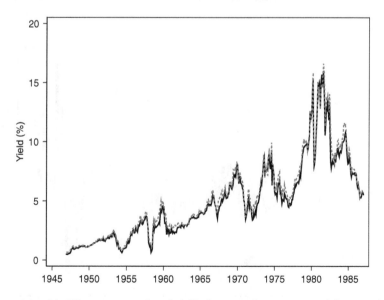

FIGURE 2.6 Monthly US zero-coupon bond yields (expressed as percentages) for maturities of 3 months (black line) and 9 months (gray line) over the period December 1946 to February 1987. The different maturities are hardly distinguishable, emphasizing the fact that yields of different maturities track each other closely.

3. The yields of different maturities follow one another closely, indeed so closely that they are hardly distinguishable in the scale of Figure 2.6. This is yet another example of variables that exhibit trending behavior and move commonly over time.

Property 3 of bond yields may be highlighted by computing the spread between the yields on a long maturity bond and a short maturity bond. Figure 2.7 gives the spread between the long maturity bond (9 months) and the short maturity bond (3 months). Comparison of Figures 2.6 and 2.7 reveals that yields exhibit vastly different time series patterns to spreads, with the latter showing no evidence of trends. However, there is still evidence that the variability of the spread is not constant over the sample, a feature that may be interpreted as a form of trend behavior in the variance.

2.1.5 Financial Distributions

An important but limiting assumption underlying many theoretical models and empirical methods in finance is that returns are normally distributed. This assumption has been widely used in portfolio allocation models, in pricing options, and in many other applications. An example of an empirical returns distribution is given in Figure 2.8, which gives the histogram of hourly US exchange rate returns computed relative to the British pound. Even though this distribution exhibits some characteristics that are consistent with a normal distribution such as symmetry, the distribution differs from normality in two important ways, namely, the presence of a sharp peak in the center of the distribution and evidence of slightly heavier tails. This feature suggests that there are many more observations where the exchange rate hardly moves and for which there are a greater

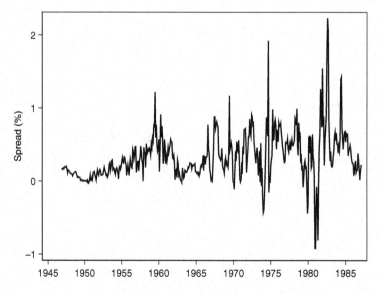

FIGURE 2.7   Spread between the US 9-month and 3-month bond yields for the period December 1946 to February 1987.

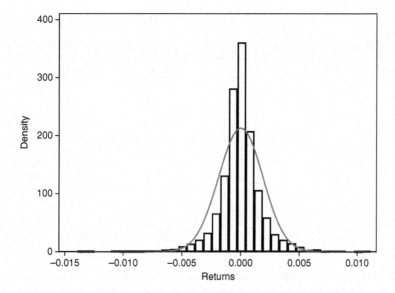

FIGURE 2.8 Empirical distribution of hourly \$/£ exchange rate returns for the period 1 January 1986 00:00 to 15 July 1986 11:00 with a normal distribution overlaid.

number of smaller returns than there would be if returns were drawn randomly from a normal population. Distributions exhibiting these properties are called leptokurtic.

The example given in Figure 2.8 is for exchange rate returns. But the property of heavy tails and peakedness of the distribution of returns is common for other asset markets including equity and commodity markets. All of these empirical distributions are therefore inconsistent with the assumption of normality in terms of these empirical characteristics. Financial models that are derived from normal distributions may therefore result in financial instruments such as options being incorrectly priced or measures of risk being underestimated due to their failure to incorporate these features of asset returns.

2.1.6 Transactions

A property of all of the financial data analyzed so far is that observations on a particular variable are recorded at discrete and regularly spaced points in time. The data on equity prices and dividend payments in Figure 2.4 and the data on zero-coupon bond yields in Figure 2.6 are all recorded every month. In fact, higher frequency data are also available at daily and hourly frequencies.

More recently, high-frequency transactions data that records the price of every trade conducted during the trading day has become available. An example is given in Table 2.1, which gives a snapshot of the trades recorded for American Airlines (AMR) on 1 August 2006 at 09:42. The variable Trade, x_t, is a binary variable signifying whether a trade has taken place at time t so that

$$x_t = \begin{cases} 1 : \text{Trade occurs} \\ 0 : \text{No trade occurs.} \end{cases}$$

TABLE 2.1   A snapshot of American Airlines (AMR) transactions data on 1 August 2006, at 09:42.

Second	Trade	Duration	Price
	x_t	u_t	P_t
5	1	1	$21.58
6	0	.	$21.58
7	0	.	$21.58
8	0	.	$21.58
9	0	.	$21.58
10	0	.	$21.58
11	1	6	$21.59
12	1	1	$21.59
13	0	.	$21.59
14	1	2	$21.59

The duration between trades is measured in seconds, and the corresponding price of the asset at the time of the trade is also recorded. Table 2.1 shows that there is a trade at the 5-second mark where the price is $21.58. The next trade occurs at the 11-second mark at a price of $21.59, so the duration between trades is 6 seconds. There is another trade straight away at the 12-second mark at the same price of $21.59, in which case the duration is just 1 second. There is no trade in the following second, but there is another 2 seconds later at the 14-second mark, again at the same price of $21.59, so the duration is 2 seconds.

The time differences between trades of AMR shares is further highlighted by the histogram of the duration times given in Figure 2.9. This distribution has an exponential shape with the duration time of 1 second being the most common. However, there are a number of durations in excess of 25 seconds and there are some times even in excess of 50 seconds.

The important feature of transactions data that distinguishes it from the time series data discussed earlier is that the time interval between trades is not regular or equally spaced. In fact, if high-frequency data are used, such as 1-minute data, there will be periods where no trades occur in the window of time and the price will not change. This is especially so in thinly traded markets. The implication of using such transactions data is that the models specified in econometric work need to incorporate those features, including the apparent randomness in the observation interval between trades. Such features end up being important in applied work because they connect most closely with the institutional structure of the market and the manner in which trades are conducted. Correspondingly, the appropriate statistical techniques for analyzing such data are expected to be different from the techniques used to analyze regularly spaced financial time series data. These issues apply for very high frequency, irregularly spaced data and are investigated further in Chapter 16 on financial microstructure effects.

2.2 SUMMARY STATISTICS

Thus far the time series properties of financial data are explored using graphical tools such as line charts and histograms in conjunction with tabulation. In assessing investment

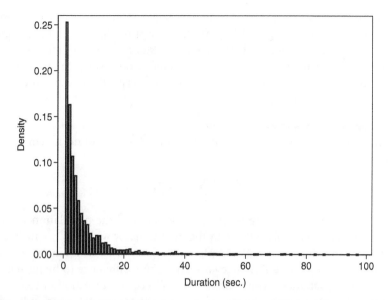

FIGURE 2.9 Empirical distribution of durations (in seconds) between trades of American Airlines (AMR) on 1 August 2006 from 09:30 to 16:00.

opportunities, it is natural for investors to seek summary information about the financial assets of interest to them. This section introduces some simple descriptive statistical methods to summarize the main characteristics of the data. While these summary measures are useful in general, there are situations where they are inappropriate, and a few examples are given to highlight such cases where these simple measures may break down or fail to reveal important characteristics of the data.

2.2.1 Univariate

In particular, investors would like to know about the return that is to be expected from investing in the asset, as well as the risk of the investment where risk refers to the uncertainty surrounding the value or payoff from investing. In addition, the information about the relative likelihood of extreme returns is also of interest. This information is provided in terms of the following summary statistics.

Sample Mean

A simple measure of the expected return is given by the sample mean

$$\bar{r} = \frac{1}{T} \sum_{t=1}^{T} r_t.$$

The returns to monthly S&P 500 data, r_t, are plotted for the period January 1950 to September 2016 in Figure 2.3. The sample mean of these data is $\bar{r} = 0.006$ per month. Expressed in annual terms, the mean return is $0.006 \times 12 = 0.072$, so that the average return over the period 1950 to 2016 is 7.2% per annum. The sample mean represents the level around which r_t fluctuates and therefore represents a summary measure of the location of the data.

An example where the sample mean is an inappropriate summary measure occurs when the data are trending. Figure 2.10 plots the equity price index with the sample mean of prices, $\overline{P} = 501.5$, superimposed. The sample mean, $\overline{P}$, no longer represents a useful long-run level about which P_t is located and is therefore not a suitable summary measure of the location of the data. In fact, the price data spend very little time around this sample mean level, as is evident in Figure 2.10.

Sample Variance and Standard Deviation

A measure of the deviation of the actual return on an asset around its sample mean is given by the sample variance,

$$s^2 = \frac{1}{T} \sum_{t=1}^{T} (r_t - \overline{r})^2.$$

This form of the sample variance is a biased estimator of the population variance. An unbiased estimator is to replace the T in the denominator with $T - 1$, which is known as a degrees of freedom or small sample correction. In most financial econometric applications, the sample size T is large enough for this difference to be negligible. This form of the sample variance involves no degrees of freedom correction to account for the estimation of the mean return. Degrees of freedom corrections are commonly employed in small samples to improve estimation and here would involve replacing the T in the denominator with $T - 1$. In most financial econometric applications, this correction is ignored because the sample size T is large enough for the difference to be negligible. In the case of the S&P 500 returns data, the sample variance is $s^2 = 0.0348^2 = 0.0012$.

In finance, the sample standard deviation[3], which is the square root of the sample variance,

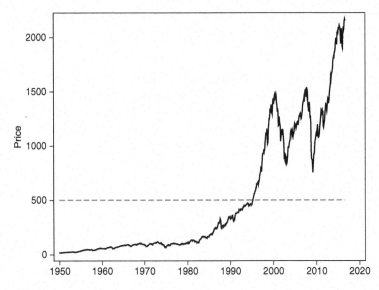

FIGURE 2.10 Monthly US equity price index for the period January 1950 to September 2016 with the sample mean (dashed line) superimposed.

[3] The terminology standard deviation was introduced by a famous English scientist and polymath, Sir Francis Galton (1822–1911), who conceived this measure as a quantity to represent dispersion in the same measurement scale as the data.

$$s = \sqrt{\frac{1}{T}\sum_{t=1}^{T}(r_t - \bar{r})^2},$$

is often used as a measure of the riskiness of an investment and is called the volatility of a financial return. For the S&P 500 data, the standard deviation or volatility of returns is $s = 0.0348$. In the present context, the standard deviation of returns is therefore easily interpretable in terms of the returns data, whereas the sample variance has the scale of returns squared.

Sample Skewness

If the extreme returns in any sample are mainly positive (negative), the distribution of r_t is positively (negatively) skewed. A measure of skewness in the sample is

$$SK = \frac{1}{T}\sum_{t=1}^{T}\left(\frac{r_t - \bar{r}}{s}\right)^3.$$

If the sample skewness is zero, then the distribution is said to be symmetric.

Figure 2.11 gives a histogram of the US log equity returns previously plotted in Figure 2.3. The sample skewness is computed to be $SK = -1.005$, where the sign of the statistic emphasizes negative skewness. The result is supported by the evidence of a heavier left tail in the distribution of returns in comparison with a normal distribution, as shown in Figure 2.11.

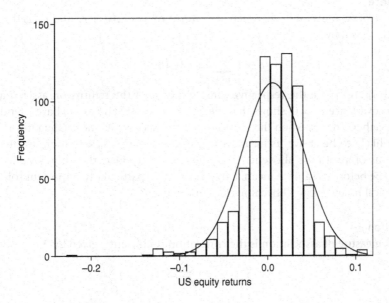

FIGURE 2.11 Empirical distribution of monthly US log equity returns for the period January 1950 to September 2016. Superimposed on the returns distribution is the best fitting normal distribution.

Sample Kurtosis

If there are extreme returns relative to a benchmark distribution (usually the normal distribution), the distribution of r_t is said to exhibit excess kurtosis.[4] A measure of kurtosis in the sample is

$$KT = \frac{1}{T} \sum_{t=1}^{T} \left(\frac{r_t - \bar{r}}{s} \right)^4.$$

Comparing this value to $KT = 3$, which is the kurtosis value of a normal distribution, gives a measure of excess kurtosis

$$EXCESS\ KT = \frac{1}{T} \sum_{t=1}^{T} \left(\frac{r_t - \bar{r}}{s} \right)^4 - 3.$$

In the case of the US log equity returns, the sample kurtosis is $KT = 6.938$. This value is much greater than 3, revealing that there are more extreme returns in the data (or heavier tails) than would be predicted by the normal distribution.

2.2.2 Bivariate

The statistical measures discussed so far summarize the characteristics of the returns to a single asset. Perhaps even more important in finance is understanding the interrelationships between two or more financial assets. For example, in constructing a diversified portfolio, the aim is to include assets whose fluctuations in returns do not match each other perfectly. In this way, the value of the portfolio is partially protected even though there will be certain assets in the portfolio that are performing poorly.

Covariance

A measure of co-movements between the returns on two assets, r_{it} and r_{jt}, is the sample covariance given by

$$s_{ij} = \frac{1}{T} \sum_{t=1}^{T} (r_{it} - \bar{r}_i)(r_{jt} - \bar{r}_j),$$

in which $\bar{r}_i$ and $\bar{r}_j$ are the respective sample means of the returns on assets i and j. A positive covariance, $s_{ij} > 0$, shows that the returns of asset i and asset j have a tendency to move together. That is, when the return on asset i is above its mean, the return on asset j is also likely to be above its mean. A negative covariance, $s_{ij} < 0$, indicates that when the returns of asset i are above its sample mean, on average, the returns on asset j are likely to be below its sample mean. Covariance has a particularly important role to play in empirical finance, as will become clear in Chapter 3.

Correlation

Another measure of association is the correlation coefficient [5] given by

$$c_{ij} = \frac{s_{ij}}{\sqrt{s_{ii}s_{jj}}},$$

---

[4] Kurtosis comes from a Greek word *kurtos* meaning "arching or bulging".

[5] This concept and terminology were also introduced by Sir Francis Galton, in this case independently of ideas developed by a French scientist, Auguste Bravais.

in which

$$s_{ii} = \frac{1}{T}\sum_{t=1}^{T}(r_{it} - \bar{r}_i)^2, \qquad s_{jj} = \frac{1}{T}\sum_{t=1}^{T}(r_{jt} - \bar{r}_j)^2,$$

represent the respective variances of the returns of assets i and j. The correlation coefficient is the covariance scaled by the standard deviations of the two returns. The correlation has the properties that it has the same sign as the covariance, as well as the additional property that it lies in the range $-1 \leq c_{ij} \leq 1$ and is not unit dependent because the measurement units are scaled out in the construction of the ratio.

2.3 PERCENTILES AND VALUE AT RISK

The percentiles of a distribution are a set of statistics that summarize both the location and the spread of a distribution. Formally, a percentile is a measure that indicates the value below which a given percentage of observations in the sample fall. So the important measure of the location of a distribution, the median, below which 50% of the observations of the random variable fall, is also the 50th percentile. The median[6] is an alternative to the sample mean as a measure of location and can be very important in financial distributions in which large outliers are encountered. The difference between the 25th percentile (or first quartile) and the 75th percentile (or third quartile) is known as the interquartile range, which provides an alternative to the standard deviation or variance as a measure of the dispersion of the distribution. It transpires that the percentiles of the distribution, particularly the 1st and 5th percentiles, are important statistics in the computation of a risk measure in finance known as value at risk (VaR).

Losses faced by financial institutions have the potential to be propagated through the financial system and undermine its stability. The onset of heightened fears for the riskiness of the banking system can be rapid and have widespread ramifications. The potential loss faced by banks is therefore a crucial measure of the stability of the financial sector. Pérignon and Smith (2010) examine the daily trading revenues, a measure of a bank's fundamental soundness, for Bank of America. Summary measures and percentiles of the daily trading revenues from 2001 to 2004 are presented in Table 2.2.

TABLE 2.2 Descriptive statistics and percentiles for daily trading revenue (in $ millions) of Bank of America for the period 2 January 2001 to 31 December 2004.

Statistics		Percentiles	
Observations	1008	1%	−24.82
Mean	13.8699	5%	−9.45
Standard Deviation	14.9089	10%	−2.72
Skewness	0.1205	25%	4.84
Kurtosis	4.9260	50%	13.15
Maximum	84.3271	75%	22.96
Minimum	−57.3886	90%	30.86
		95%	36.44
		99%	57.10

---

[6] Yet another example of terminology introduced by Sir Francis Galton.

A wave of banking collapses in the 1990s encouraged financial regulators to require banks to hold capital buffers against possible losses, following recommendations from the Basel Committee on Banking Supervision (1996) within the Bank of International Settlements (BIS). The mechanism for measuring bank exposure to possible losses based on value at risk (VaR) quantifies the loss that a bank can face on its trading portfolio within a given period and for a given confidence interval. In the context of a bank, value at risk is defined in terms of the lower tail of the distribution of trading revenues. Specifically, the 1% value at risk for the next h periods conditional on information at time T is the 1st percentile of expected trading revenue at the end of the next h periods. For example, if the daily 1% h-period value at risk is $30 million, then there is a 1% chance the bank will lose $30 million or more. Although $30 million is a loss, by convention the value at risk is quoted as a positive amount.

There are three common ways to compute value at risk.

1. **Historical Simulation**

   The historical method simply computes the percentiles of the empirical distribution from historical data. Based on the sample percentiles in Table 2.2, the 1% daily value at risk for Bank of America using all available historical data (2001–2004) is

   $$VaR\left(1\%, daily\right) = \$24.82 \text{ million.}$$

2. **The Variance Method**

   This method assumes that the trading revenues are normally distributed. Since 1% of the normal distribution lies in the tail delimited by -2.33, then, using the summary statistics reported in Table 2.2,

   $$VaR\left(1\%, daily\right) = 13.8699 - 2.33 \times 14.9089 = \$20.87 \ m.$$

   This value is slightly lower than that provided by historical simulation because the assumption of normality ignores the slightly fatter tails exhibited by the empirical distribution of daily trading revenues.

3. **Monte Carlo Simulation**

   The third method involves simulating a model for daily trading revenues several times and constructing simulated percentiles. This approach is revisited in Chapter 7.

Figure 2.12 plots the daily trading revenue of the Bank of America together with the 1% daily value at risk reported by the bank on each day. For comparative purposes, the 1% historical value at risk is also shown. By construction, daily trading revenue will fall below the historical value at risk 1% of the time. During this period, however, the Bank of America had only four violations of the 1% daily reported value at risk. Since $4/1008 = 0.4\%$, it follows that during this period the Bank of America was over-conservative in its estimation of daily value at risk.

2.4 THE EFFICIENT MARKET HYPOTHESIS

An important and controversial theory in finance is the efficient market hypothesis, which states in its most general form that all available information concerning the value of a risky asset is factored into the current price of the asset (Fama, 1965; Samuelson, 1965).

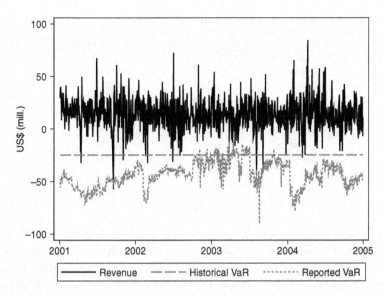

FIGURE 2.12 Time series plot of the daily trading revenue of Bank of America from 2 January 2001 to 31 December 2004. Also shown is the 1% historical value at risk of $24.82 million (dashed line) and the 1% value at risk actually reported by Bank of America on each day.

There are many ways to test this theory and the literature on the subject is vast. Two simple ways to use sample statistics to examine this proposition are first to test asset returns for predictability and second to compare the variance of asset returns over different time horizons.

2.4.1 Return Predictability

An implication of the efficient market hypothesis is that there is no predictable pattern in financial returns, that is, they behave randomly over time. One way to test the predictability of returns is based on the autocorrelation statistic

$$acf(k) = \frac{T^{-1} \sum_{t=k+1}^{T} (r_t - \bar{r})(r_{t-k} - \bar{r})}{T^{-1} \sum_{t=1}^{T} (r_t - \bar{r})^2}. \tag{2.8}$$

This statistic measures the strength of association between the current return, r_t, and the return on the same asset k periods earlier, r_{t-k}. In equation (2.8), the numerator represents the autocovariance of returns k periods apart and the denominator represents the variance of returns. If returns exhibit no autocorrelation then future movements in returns are unpredictable in terms of their own past history. But if returns exhibit positive or negative autocorrelation, then this pattern can be exploited in predicting the future behavior of returns.

Column 2 of Table 2.3 gives the first 10 autocorrelations of hourly returns on the Deutsche Mark-US dollar (DM/$) exchange rate.[7] All the autocorrelations appear close to zero, suggesting that these exchange rate returns are not predictable using their own

---

[7] The Deutsche Mark was the currency used in West Germany prior to the adoption of the Euro.

TABLE 2.3 Autocorrelation properties of returns and functions of returns for the hourly DM/$ exchange rate for the period January 1986 00:00 to 15 July 1986 11:00.

Lag	r_t	r_t^2	$|r_t|$	$|r_t|^{0.5}$
1	−0.0610	0.1340	0.2036	0.2003
2	−0.0013	0.0845	0.1241	0.1296
3	0.0202	0.0164	0.0678	0.0710
4	−0.0318	0.0512	0.0778	0.0650
5	0.0318	0.0327	0.0316	0.0224
6	−0.0584	0.0093	0.0237	0.0310
7	0.0152	−0.0258	−0.0333	−0.0238
8	−0.0182	−0.0257	−0.0127	0.0064
9	−0.0013	−0.0297	−0.0385	−0.0375
10	0.0190	−0.0205	−0.0377	−0.0338

past history. The foreign exchange market is therefore considered to be efficient. For an interesting counter argument in favor of return predictability, see Cochrane (2008).

Autocorrelations of returns reveal information about the temporal dependence properties of the levels of returns. Applying the same approach to squared returns gives

$$acf^2(k) = \frac{T^{-1}\sum_{t=k+1}^{T}\left(r_t^2 - \overline{r^2}\right)\left(r_{t-k}^2 - \overline{r^2}\right)}{T^{-1}\sum_{t=1}^{T}\left(r_t^2 - \overline{r^2}\right)^2},$$ (2.9)

where

$$\overline{r^2} = \frac{1}{T}\sum_{t=1}^{T}r_t^2.$$

This statistic reveals information about the autocorrelation properties of the squared levels of returns. Column 3 of Table 2.3 suggests that while the level of returns are not predictable, the same cannot be said of their squared level or variation. Note that this conclusion does not violate the efficient markets hypothesis, which is solely concerned with the expected value of the level of returns. The application of autocorrelations to squared returns represents an important diagnostic tool in models of time-varying volatility which is dealt with in Chapters 13, 14 and 15.

Autocorrelations can also be computed for various power transformations of returns, such as

$$r_t^3, \quad r_t^4, \quad |r_t|, \quad |r_t|^\alpha.$$

The first two transformations provide evidence of autocorrelations in skewness and kurtosis, respectively. The third transformation, which employs the modulus (or absolute magnitude) of returns, leads to an alternative measure of the presence of autocorrelation in the variance. The last case simply represents a general power transformation. For example, setting $\alpha = 0.5$ computes the autocorrelation of the standard deviation (the square root of the variance). The presence of stronger autocorrelation in squared returns than returns themselves, suggests that other transformations of returns may reveal even stronger autocorrelation patterns and this conjecture is borne out by the results reported in Table 2.3.

2.4.2 The Variance Ratio

An alternative way to examine the efficient market hypothesis is to compare the variance on returns over different time horizons. Consider the variances of the 1-period returns and the n-period returns,

$$s_1^2 = \frac{1}{T} \sum_{t=1}^{T} (r_t - \bar{r})^2, \qquad s_n^2 = \frac{1}{T} \sum_{t=1}^{T} (r_{nt} - n\bar{r})^2,$$

in which

$$r_t = \log P_t - \log P_{t-1}$$
$$r_{nt} = \log P_t - \log P_{t-n} = r_t + r_{t-1} + \cdots + r_{t-(n-1)},$$

and $n\bar{r}$ represents the sample mean of the n-period returns r_{nt}.

If there is no autocorrelation the variance of n-period returns should equal n times the variance of the 1-period returns. The ratio

$$VR_n = \frac{s_n^2}{n s_1^2}$$

is known as the variance ratio and has the following implications for the properties of excess returns:

$$VR_n = \begin{cases} = 1 & \text{[No autocorrelation]} \\ > 1 & \text{[Positive autocorrelation]} \\ < 1 & \text{[Negative autocorrelation]}. \end{cases}$$

The first of these results is easily demonstrated. Consider an $n = 3$ period return

$$r_{3t} = r_t + r_{t-1} + r_{t-2},$$

which is the sum of the three 1-period returns. Let the sample mean for the 1-period returns be $\bar{r}$. Subtracting $\bar{r}$ from both sides three times gives

$$(r_{3t} - 3\bar{r}) = (r_t - \bar{r}) + (r_{t-1} - \bar{r}) + (r_{t-2} - \bar{r}).$$

Squaring both sides and averaging over a sample of size T gives

$$
\begin{aligned}
s_3^2 &= \frac{1}{T} \sum_{t=1}^{T} (r_{3t} - 3\bar{r})^2 \\
&= \frac{1}{T} \sum_{t=1}^{T} (r_t - \bar{r})^2 && \text{[Variance of } r_t\text{]} \\
&+ \frac{1}{T} \sum_{t=1}^{T} (r_{t-1} - \bar{r})^2 && \text{[Variance of } r_{t-1}\text{]} \\
&+ \frac{1}{T} \sum_{t=1}^{T} (r_{t-2} - \bar{r})^2 && \text{[Variance of } r_{t-2}\text{]} \\
&+ \frac{2}{T} \sum_{t=1}^{T} (r_t - \bar{r})(r_{t-1} - \bar{r}) && \text{[Autocovariance of } r_t, r_{t-1}\text{]} \\
&+ \frac{2}{T} \sum_{t=1}^{T} (r_t - \bar{r})(r_{t-2} - \bar{r}) && \text{[Autocovariance of } r_t, r_{t-2}\text{]} \\
&+ \frac{2}{T} \sum_{t=1}^{T} (r_{t-1} - \bar{r})(r_{t-2} - \bar{r}) && \text{[Autocovariance of } r_{t-1}, r_{t-2}\text{]}.
\end{aligned}
$$

This expansion requires values for r_0 and r_{-1}. To implement this formulation in practice, the summation ranges are suitably adjusted to the available data. In the case of zero sample autocovariances (or no sample autocorrelation) the relationship simplifies to

$$s_3^2 = \frac{1}{T}\sum_{t=1}^{T}(r_t - \bar{r})^2 + \frac{1}{T}\sum_{t=1}^{T}(r_{t-1} - \bar{r})^2 + \frac{1}{T}\sum_{t=1}^{T}(r_{t-2} - \bar{r})^2.$$

Assuming that the sample variance for r_t is the same as the sample variance for r_{t-1} and r_{t-2} then gives

$$s_3^2 = 3s_1^2,$$

when there is no sample autocorrelation in the $n = 3$ period returns. A more detailed discussion of the autocorrelation function is provided in Chapter 4. The assumption of equal variances for r_{t-1} and r_{t-2} falls under a general assumption known as (covariance) stationarity and is addressed in detail in Chapters 4 and 5. Modeling with variables that do not satisfy this assumption is dealt with in Chapter 6.

2.5 EXERCISES

The data required for the exercises are available for download as EViews workfiles (*.wf1), Stata datafiles (*.dta), comma delimited text files (*.csv), and as Excel spreadsheets (*.xlsx).

1. Equity Prices, Dividends, and Returns

> pv.*

The data are monthly observations on US equity prices and dividends for the period January 1871 to September 2016. For the sub-sample January 1950 to September 2016 do the following.

(a) Plot the equity price over time and interpret its time series properties.
(b) Plot the natural logarithm of the equity price over time and interpret its time series properties.
(c) Plot the return on equities over time and interpret its time series properties.
(d) Plot the price and dividend series and comment on the results.
(e) Compute the dividend yield and plot this series and comment on the results.
(f) Compare the graphs in parts (a) and (e) and discuss the time series properties of equity prices, dividend payments, and dividend yields.
(g) The present value model predicts a linear relationship between the logarithm of equity prices and the logarithm of dividends. Use a scatter diagram to verify this property and comment on your results.
(h) For the returns on US equities calculate the sample mean, variance, skewness, and kurtosis. Interpret the statistics.

2. **Yields**

zero.*

The data are monthly observations from December 1946 to February 1987 on US zero-coupon bond yields for maturities ranging from 2 months to 9 months.

(a) Plot the 2, 3, 4, 5, 6, and 9 months US zero-coupon yields using a line chart and comment on the results.
(b) Compute the spreads on the 3-month, 5-month, and 9-month zero-coupon yields relative to the 2-month yield. Plot these spreads using a line chart and comment on their properties.
(c) Compare the graphs in parts (a) and (b) and discuss the time series properties of yields and spreads.

3. **Duration Times Between American Airlines (AMR) Trades**

amr.*

The file contains high-frequency data (1-second intervals) giving a snapshot of the trades recorded by AMR from 09:30 to 16:00 on 1 August 2006.

(a) Use a histogram to graph the empirical distribution of the duration times between AMR trades. Compare the graph with Figure 2.9.
(b) Interpret the shape of the distribution of duration times.

4. **Exchange Rates**

hour.*

The data are hourly observations for the period 00:00 1 January 1986 to 11:00 15 July 1986 on the $/£ and $/DM exchange rates.

(a) Draw a line chart of the $/£ exchange rate and discuss its time series characteristics.
(b) Compute the log returns on the $/£ exchange rate. Draw a line chart of this series and discuss its time series characteristics.
(c) Compare the graphs in parts (a) and (b) and discuss the time series properties of exchange rates and exchange rate log returns.
(d) Use a histogram to graph the empirical distribution of the log returns on the $/£ exchange rate. Compare the graph with Figure 2.11.
(e) Compute the first 10 autocorrelations of the log returns, squared log returns, absolute log returns, and the square root of the absolute value of log returns. Comment on the results.
(f) Repeat parts (a) to (e) using the $/DM exchange rate and comment on the time series characteristics, empirical distributions, and patterns of autocorrelation for the two series. Discuss the implications of these results for the efficient market hypothesis.

5. Value-at-Risk (VaR)

bankamerica.*

The data are daily observations for the period 2 January 2001 to 31 December 2004 on the trading revenue and reported VaR values for Bank of America.

(a) Compute summary statistics and percentiles for the daily trading revenues of Bank of America. Compare the results with Table 2.2.

(b) Draw a histogram of the daily trading revenue and superimpose a normal distribution on top of the plot. What do you deduce about the distribution of the daily trading revenues?

(c) Plot the trading revenue together with the historical 1% VaR and the reported 1% VaR. Compare the results with Figure 2.12.

(d) Now assume that a weekly VaR is required. Repeat parts (a) to (c) for weekly trading revenues.

6. Solnik-Roulet Measure of Financial Integration

integration.*

The data consist of daily stock prices in US$ on 10 Asian stocks (China, Hong Kong, Indonesia, Japan, Malaysia, Philippines, Singapore, South Korea, Taiwan, Thailand), as well as the US stock price, from 1 January 1997 to 27 May 2016.

(a) Compute the percentage log returns of all 11 stocks

$$r_{it} = 100 \times (\log P_{it} - \log P_{it-1}),$$

where P_{it} is the stock price index. Plot the log returns and discuss the change in volatility over the sample period.

(b) Solnik and Roulet (2000) measure the change in financial integration over time using the standard deviation of cross-market returns based on

$$\sigma_t = \sqrt{\frac{1}{N} \sum_{i=1}^{N} (r_{it} - \bar{r}_i)^2},$$

where a decrease in σ_t represents an improvement in financial market integration. Compute σ_t^2 for the $N = 10$ Asian stocks and discuss the change in regional financial integration in Asia over the sample period.

(c) Use the Hodrick-Prescott filter to smooth the integration measure computed in part (b) for the $N = 10$ Asian stocks and discuss the change in financial integration in the region.

(d) Repeat parts (b) and (c) by extending the number of stocks to $N = 11$ by including US log returns.

(e) An alternative measure of financial integration to σ_t is to compute the range at each point in time,

$$RANGE_t = \max_i r_{it} - \min_i r_{it}.$$

Using all Asian and US stock returns ($N = 11$) compute $RANGE_t$ at each point in time and compare this measure of integration and the measure based on σ_t.

CHAPTER 3

Linear Regression Models

One of the most important tools in empirical finance is linear regression.[1] Its use is ubiquitous in financial econometrics and much more widely throughout the social and business sciences. The linear regression model provides a framework by which the movements of one financial variable are explained and predicted in terms of other variables called explanatory variables or covariates. One of the most important applications of linear regression in financial econometrics is to the capital asset pricing model (CAPM), which provides a powerful way in which to model the risk of an asset from its exposure to the market. Multi-factor extensions of CAPM are also conveniently captured by extending the set of explanatory variables to contain size and growth factors as well as momentum.

The linear model can be developed and applied in a myriad of ways, including ranking the performance of portfolios and the construction of minimum variance portfolios. One important application is known as event analysis, which provides a framework to capture qualitative effects of financial events by using explanatory variables known as dummy variables. Even in the case of simple linear regression, financial data produce fascinating complications that take us beyond standard textbook theory.

The treatment of linear regression presented here focusses more on its financial applications, with many of the theoretical results stated without detailed derivations. These derivations are widely available in standard introductory econometrics textbooks with some of the key results summarized for convenience in Appendix C.

3.1 THE CAPITAL ASSET PRICING MODEL

The capital asset pricing model (CAPM) encapsulates the risk characteristics of an asset in terms of its so-called β-risk, which is given by the ratio

$$\beta = \frac{\text{cov}(r_{it} - r_{ft}, r_{mt} - r_{ft})}{\text{var}(r_{mt} - r_{ft})}. \tag{3.1}$$

---

[1] The concept of a regression line was invented by Sir Francis Galton (mentioned earlier in Chapter 2 in the context of the median, standard deviation, and correlation coefficient) in the course of his studies of sibling and parental heights. Among his many other accomplishments, Galton coined the terms regression and correlation and introduced the use of the letter r to represent the correlation coefficient, which was studied in Chapter 2. Versions of Galton's correlation diagram for bivariate distributions still appear in introductory statistics texts.

This quantity is a measure of the exposure of the returns r_{it} on the asset to movements in the market r_{mt}, relative to a risk-free rate of interest r_{ft}. Individual stocks, or even the portfolios of stocks, are classified as follows in terms of their degree of β-risk:

Aggressive:	$\beta > 1$
Benchmark:	$\beta = 1$
Conservative:	$0 < \beta < 1$
Uncorrelated:	$\beta = 0$
Imperfect Hedge:	$-1 < \beta < 0$
Perfect Hedge:	$\beta = -1$.

The returns on the market index such as the S&P 500 for the United States is the usual standard that stocks are benchmarked against to measure their performance. Aggressive stocks on average move in excess to movements in the market. This is a particularly common characteristic of technology stocks. On the upside these stocks are expected to earn higher returns than the market in bull markets but in bear markets their returns are expected to be lower than the market. Benchmark stocks mimic the market so their movements tend to track the market one for one. Conservative stocks such as blue chip stocks also move in the same direction as the market, although their movements are attenuated. Unlike aggressive stocks, the returns on conservative stocks are lower than the market on average during periods of market growth, whereas during periods of market decline the falls in returns of conservative stocks tend to be smaller than the falls experienced by the market.

Stocks that bear no market risk as they move independently of the market represent zero-beta stocks such as Treasury bonds and so by definition earn the risk-free rate of return. Hedge stocks such as gold tend to move in the opposite direction to the market thereby counterbalancing market movements. For an imperfectly hedged stock the absolute movements in the stock are less than the market movements whereas for perfectly hedged stocks, these movements match the movements in the market one for one on average, but in the opposite direction. Thus, a portfolio containing the market index and a perfectly hedged stock would bear no risk. Assuming an absence of arbitrage this portfolio would earn the risk-free rate.

The CAPM is formulated in terms of a linear regression model by expressing the relationship between the excess return on the asset $r_{it} - r_{ft}$ and the market $r_{mt} - r_{ft}$ as

$$r_{it} - r_{ft} = \alpha + \beta(r_{mt} - r_{ft}) + u_t, \tag{3.2}$$

where the excess return on the asset represents the dependent variable and the excess return on the market represents the explanatory variable. The disturbance term u_t captures additional movements in the dependent variable not predicted by CAPM. Assuming that these additional movements are also independent of $r_{mt} - r_{ft}$, then $E[(r_{mt} - r_{ft})u_t] = 0$. The regression model in equation (3.2) contains two unknown parameters. The first is the intercept parameter α, which captures the abnormal return to the asset over and above the asset's exposure to the excess return on the market. The second is the slope parameter β, which corresponds to the asset's β-risk as defined in (3.1).

An important advantage of expressing the CAPM as a linear regression model is that it provides a convenient method of decomposing the total risk of an asset into systematic risk (or risk that is inherent to the entire market) from exposure to movements in the market, and idiosyncratic risk caused by other factors. Formally, this decomposition is achieved by squaring both sides of equation (3.2) and then taking expectations

$$\underbrace{E[(r_{it} - r_{ft})^2]}_{\text{Total risk}} = \underbrace{E[(\alpha + \beta(r_{mt} - r_{ft}))^2]}_{\text{Systematic risk}} + \underbrace{E(u_t^2),}_{\text{Idiosyncratic risk}} \qquad (3.3)$$

which uses the zero correlation property $E[(r_{mt} - r_{ft})u_t] = 0$. The systematic risk is also known as nondiversifiable risk while the idiosyncratic risk represents the diversifiable risk.

It is convenient to re-express the linear regression form of the CAPM in equation (3.2) by defining the dependent variable as $y_t = r_{it} - r_{ft}$ and the explanatory variable as $x_t = r_{mt} - r_{ft}$, so the CAPM is rewritten as

$$y_t = \alpha + \beta x_t + u_t, \qquad (3.4)$$

in which α and β are the α-risk and β-risk of the asset y_t, respectively. The disturbance term, u_t, represents movements in y_t that are not explained by the model and it has the properties

$$E(u_t) = 0, \quad E(u_t^2) = \sigma_u^2, \quad E(u_t u_{t-j}) = 0, j \neq 0, \quad E(x_t u_t) = 0. \qquad (3.5)$$

The first property $E(u_t) = 0$ implies that the additional movements in y_t that are in excess of the movements predicted by CAPM balance out to be zero on average. The second property implies that the (squared) idiosyncratic risk as given by the variance of u_t is taken to be constant over time, a property that is known by the technical term of homoskedasticity. This assumption tends to hold for lower frequency data of a month or a quarter, but not for higher frequency data that is observed weekly, daily or intradaily. For such data, it is common for variation to be time dependent in the sense that variation may be higher (or lower), especially according to the magnitude of recent shocks, a property known as conditional heteroskedasticity. Techniques for relaxing the assumption of a constant σ_u^2 are discussed in Chapters 13 to 15 when the class of autoregressive conditional heteroskedasticity models (ARCH) is introduced. A test for time-varying variance is introduced later in this chapter.

The third property is that the movements in u_t are uncorrelated with previous (or future) movements. If this is not the case the idiosyncratic component u_t exhibits autocorrelation, a property that raises potential profit making (called arbitrage) opportunities because this information may be utilized to improve the predictions of future movements in y_t. The fourth and final property ensures that movements in the market (x_t) are not connected in any way with other factors (manifesting via u_t) caused by non-market movements. This assumption is also used in the decomposition of the total risk of an asset into its systematic and idiosyncratic risk components in equation (3.3).

To estimate the population risk parameters α and β in the CAPM in equation (3.4) using data on y_t and x_t for $t = 1, 2, \cdots, T$, the linear regression approach chooses estimates that minimize the sum of squares function

$$S = \sum_{t=1}^{T}(y_t - \alpha - \beta x_t)^2. \qquad (3.6)$$

The solution of this minimization problem is demonstrated graphically in Figure 3.1 for the β-risk parameter. The estimate of β-risk, $\widehat{\beta}$, is chosen here to minimize the function S in equation (3.6) for some given α.

Formally, the full solution for both parameters α and β is obtained by differentiating the sum of squares function S with respect to α and β. Setting the derivatives to zero and rearranging these expressions yields the ordinary least squares estimators

$$\beta\text{-risk:}\qquad \widehat{\beta} = \frac{T^{-1}\sum_{t=1}^{T}(y_t - \overline{y})(x_t - \overline{x})}{T^{-1}\sum_{t=1}^{T}(x_t - \overline{x})^2} \tag{3.7}$$

$$\alpha\text{-risk:}\qquad \widehat{\alpha} = \overline{y} - \widehat{\beta}\overline{x},$$

where $\overline{y} = T^{-1}\sum_{t=1}^{T} y_t$ and $\overline{x} = T^{-1}\sum_{t=1}^{T} x_t$ are the sample means. The standard errors of these estimators are, respectively,

$$se(\widehat{\alpha}) = \sqrt{\frac{\widehat{\sigma}_u^2 \sum_{t=1}^{T} x_t^2}{T\sum_{t=1}^{T}(x_t - \overline{x})^2}}, \quad se(\widehat{\beta}) = \sqrt{\frac{\widehat{\sigma}_u^2}{\sum_{t=1}^{T}(x_t - \overline{x})^2}}, \tag{3.8}$$

in which

$$\widehat{\sigma}_u^2 = \frac{1}{T}\sum_{t=1}^{T}(y_t - \widehat{\alpha} - \widehat{\beta}x_t)^2,$$

is the estimate of the residual variance corresponding to a measure of the idiosyncratic risk of the asset. In computing the residual variance the degrees of freedom correction $T - 2$ is often used in the denominator of the expression. The standard errors measure the precision of the estimators – the smaller the standard error, the more precise the least

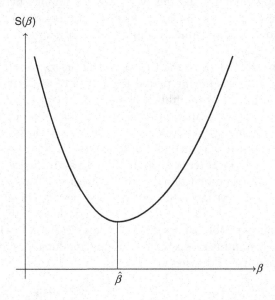

FIGURE 3.1 Illustrating the ordinary least squares estimator of the parameter β in the simple regression model for the case of given α. The estimator $\widehat{\beta}$ is the argument that minimizes the function $S(\beta)$.

squares estimator of the population parameter. The properties of ordinary least squares estimators will be discussed more formally in Section 3.3.

The sample counterpart of the CAPM regression model in equation (3.4) is obtained by replacing the population parameters by their respective estimators as

$$y_t = \widehat{\alpha} + \widehat{\beta} x_t + \widehat{u}_t. \tag{3.9}$$

The term $\widehat{\alpha} + \widehat{\beta} x_t$ represents the regression line, while $\widehat{u}_t$ is known as the regression residual which provides an estimator of the idiosyncratic risk of the asset at time t. An important property of the least squares estimators that immediately follows from solving (3.6) is that the residual sum of squares,

$$RSS = \sum_{t=1}^{T} \widehat{u}_t^2, \tag{3.10}$$

is a minimum. It is for this reason that the least squares regression line is commonly referred to as the line of best fit.

The connection between the usual definition of β-risk given in equation (3.1) and the least squares estimator given in equation (3.7) is made transparent by noting that the numerator of $\widehat{\beta}$ in equation (3.7) is the sample covariance between the excess returns on the asset and the market, while the denominator is the sample variance of the market. This is exactly the same estimator that would follow by directly replacing the population quantities in equation (3.1) with their sample counterparts, a result that establishes the link between β-risk and the linear regression model in this context. Finally, the estimator of α-risk, $\widehat{\alpha}$, is obtained by computing the difference between the average return on the asset over the sample period $\bar{y}$ and the average return implied by the CAPM model, namely, $\widehat{\beta}\bar{x}$. If the estimate $\widehat{\alpha} > 0$ the asset earns higher (abnormal) returns in excess of the return predicted by CAPM, while the opposite occurs if abnormal returns are lower and $\widehat{\alpha} < 0$.

To illustrate the estimation of the CAPM, a data set comprising monthly returns to 10 US industry portfolios for the period January 1927 to December 2013 is used, together with a benchmark of monthly returns to the market and a risk-free rate of interest. The industry portfolios are Consumer Nondurables, Consumer Durables, Manufacturing, Energy, Technology, Telecommunications, Wholesale and Retail, Healthcare, Utilities, and Other, which is a catch-all portfolio that includes mining, construction, entertainment, and finance. The return on the market is constructed as the value-weighted return of all CRSP firms incorporated in the United States and listed on the NYSE, AMEX, or NASDAQ; and the risk-free rate is the 1-month US Treasury Bill rate.

The computation of the ordinary least squares estimates of the α-risk and β-risk parameters is illustrated in Table 3.1 using the Nondurables portfolio. The first 2 columns give, respectively, the monthly excess returns for the Nondurables portfolio, y_t, and the market, x_t. The least squares estimates are

$$\widehat{\beta} = \frac{T^{-1} \sum_{t=1}^{T} (x_t - \bar{x})(y_t - \bar{y})}{T^{-1} \sum_{t=1}^{T} (x_t - \bar{x})^2} = \frac{23273.5059/1044}{30712.9719/1044} = 0.7578,$$

$$\widehat{\alpha} = \bar{y} - \widehat{\beta}\bar{x} = 0.6942 - 0.757 \times 0.6449 = 0.2055,$$

TABLE 3.1 Calculations to estimate the CAPM for the Nondurables portfolio by ordinary least squares. The data are monthly from January 1927 to December 2013, where y_t is the excess return on the Nondurables portfolio, x_t is the excess return on the market, and $\hat{u}_t$ is the least squares residual.

Data	y_t	x_t	$y_t - \bar{y}$	$x_t - \bar{x}$	$(y_t - \bar{y})(x_t - \bar{x})$	$(x_t - \bar{x})^2$	$\hat{u}_t$
1927 Jan.	−0.92	−0.11	−1.6142	−0.7549	1.2186	0.5699	−1.0421
1927 Feb.	3.16	4.11	2.4658	3.4651	8.5442	12.0067	−0.1599
1927 Mar.	2.46	−0.15	1.7658	−0.7949	−1.4037	0.6319	2.3682
1927 Apr.	3.12	0.52	2.4258	−0.1249	−0.3031	0.0156	2.5205
1927 May.	7.88	5.4	7.1858	4.7551	34.1690	22.6107	3.5825
1927 Jun.	−2.03	−2.04	−2.7242	−2.6849	7.3143	7.2089	−0.6896
⋯	⋯	⋯	⋯	⋯	⋯	⋯	⋯
2013 July	2.95	5.65	2.2558	5.0051	11.2905	25.0507	−1.5369
2013 Aug.	−4.00	−2.69	−4.6942	−3.3349	15.6548	11.1218	−2.1671
2013 Sep.	1.94	3.76	1.2458	3.1151	3.8808	9.7036	−1.1147
2013 Oct.	4.75	4.17	4.0558	3.5251	14.2970	12.4261	1.3846
2013 Nov.	1.29	3.12	0.5958	2.4751	1.4747	6.1260	−1.2797
2013 Dec.	2.65	2.81	1.9558	2.1651	4.2345	4.6875	0.3152
	$\bar{y} = 0.6942$	$\bar{x} = 0.6449$			$\sum_{t=1}^{T} = 23273.5059$	$\sum_{t=1}^{T} = 30712.9719$	

and the estimate of the residual variance is

$$\hat{\sigma}_u^2 = \frac{1}{T-2}\sum_{t=1}^{T}(y_t - \hat{\alpha} - \hat{\beta}x_t)^2 = \frac{1}{T-2}\sum_{t=1}^{T}\hat{u}_t^2 = \frac{5026.2404}{1044-2} = 4.8236,$$

where the degrees of freedom adjustment is used in the computation. The standard errors of $\hat{\alpha}$ and $\hat{\beta}$ are, respectively,

$$\text{se}(\hat{\alpha}) = \sqrt{\frac{\hat{\sigma}_u^2 \sum_{t=1}^{T} x_t^2}{T\sum_{t=1}^{T}(x_t - \bar{x})^2}} = \sqrt{\frac{4.8236 \times 31147.2117}{1044 \times 30712.9719}} = \sqrt{0.0047} = 0.0684,$$

$$\text{se}(\hat{\beta}) = \sqrt{\frac{\hat{\sigma}^2}{\sum_{t=1}^{T}(x_t - \bar{x})^2}} = \sqrt{\frac{4.8236}{30712.9719}} = \sqrt{0.0002} = 0.0125.$$

The computations are repeated in Appendix C using the matrix formulation of the linear regression model.

The results obtained by estimating the CAPM for all 10 of the industry portfolios are given in Table 3.2. The aggressive portfolios ($\hat{\beta} > 1$) are Durables, Manufacturing, Technology, and Other. The remaining six portfolios are conservative portfolios ($0 < \hat{\beta} < 1$). As expected, none of the industry portfolios provide a perfect hedge against systematic

TABLE 3.2 Ordinary least squares estimates of the CAPM in equation (3.2) for 10 industry portfolios using monthly data for the United States beginning January 1927 and ending December 2013. Standard errors are given in parentheses. The diagnostic statistics given in the last three columns are the coefficient of determination, equation (3.17), the adjusted coefficient of determination, equation (3.18), and the residual sum of squares, equation (3.10), respectively.

Industry	$\hat{\alpha}$	$\hat{\beta}$	R^2	$\bar{R}^2$	RSS
Nondurables	0.205 (0.068)	0.758 (0.013)	0.778	0.778	5026.2
Durables	0.003 (0.123)	1.244 (0.022)	0.747	0.747	16110.2
Manufacturing	0.008 (0.055)	1.128 (0.010)	0.924	0.923	3234.9
Energy	0.231 (0.119)	0.856 (0.022)	0.595	0.595	15289.8
Tech	0.009 (0.096)	1.236 (0.018)	0.825	0.825	9939.8
Telecom	0.152 (0.092)	0.657 (0.017)	0.591	0.591	9176.5
Retail	0.107 (0.085)	0.969 (0.016)	0.789	0.788	7734.7
Health	0.255 (0.104)	0.841 (0.019)	0.650	0.650	11696.9
Utilities	0.089 (0.113)	0.782 (0.021)	0.576	0.576	13805.6
Other	−0.103 (0.072)	1.126 (0.013)	0.876	0.876	5524.7

risk. All the portfolios indicate positive abnormal profits ($\widehat{\alpha} > 0$) with the exception of the Other portfolio where the estimate of α-risk is -0.103.

3.2 A MULTIFACTOR CAPM

The CAPM has been extended in a number of ways to allow for additional determinants of excess returns. In a seminal paper, Fama and French (1993) augment the CAPM by including two additional risk factors to explain the return on a risky investment. These factors are the performance of small stocks relative to big stocks (SMB), known as a *Size* factor; and the performance of value stocks relative to growth stocks (HML), known as a *Value* factor. In addition, Carhart (1997) suggests a further extension based on momentum (MOM), which captures the returns to a portfolio constructed by buying stocks with high returns over the past 3 to 12 months and selling stocks with low returns over the same period. This factor captures the presence of herd behavior among investors who are following market movements. The market factor of the CAPM and these three additional factors are plotted in Figure 3.2 for the United States from January 1927 to December 2013.

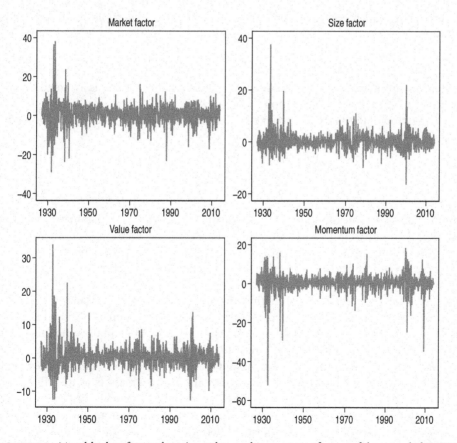

FIGURE 3.2 Monthly data for market, size, value, and momentum factors of the extended CAPM model for the period January 1927 to December 2013.

The CAPM in equation (3.2) is extended to allow for the additional size, value, and momentum factors by expressing the multifactor CAPM as a multiple regression model (that is, a regression model with multiple regressors). Letting EMKT_t be the excess return on the market factor, which is $(r_{mt} - r_{ft})$ in equation (3.2); SMB_t and HML_t represent the Fama–French size and growth factors; and MOM_t be the momentum factor; the multifactor CAPM is specified as

$$r_{it} - r_{ft} = \alpha + \beta_1 \mathrm{EMKT}_t + \beta_2 \mathrm{SMB}_t + \beta_3 \mathrm{HML}_t + \beta_4 \mathrm{MOM}_t + u_t, \tag{3.11}$$

where u_t, as before, is a disturbance term. The term $\alpha + \beta_1 \mathrm{EMKT}_t$ on the right hand side is the CAPM component of the model, with α representing α-risk and with β_1 representing the β-risk of the asset. The contributions of the size, value, and momentum factors are controlled, respectively, by the parameters β_2, β_3, and β_4. The special case where these additional factors do not explain movements in the excess return, $r_{it} - r_{ft}$, on the asset implies the restrictions $\beta_2 = \beta_3 = \beta_4 = 0$, which, if supported by the data, reduce the model to the standard CAPM regression equation.

The multiple regression representation of the multifactor CAPM in equation (3.11) is generalized by redefining y_t as the dependent variable and $x_{1t}, x_{2t}, \cdots, x_{Kt}$ as a set of K explanatory variables representing all of the factors. The multiple linear regression model is

$$y_t = \alpha + \beta_1 x_{1t} + \beta_2 x_{2t} + \cdots + \beta_K x_{Kt} + u_t, \tag{3.12}$$

which contains $K + 1$ unknown parameters. The disturbance term u_t is assumed to have the same properties given in equation (3.5).

Estimation of the $K + 1$ unknown parameters in equation (3.12) proceeds as before by redefining the sum of squares function in equation (3.6) as

$$S = \sum_{t=1}^{T} (y_t - \alpha - \beta_1 x_{1t} - \beta_2 x_{2t} - \cdots - \beta_K x_{Kt})^2. \tag{3.13}$$

Minimizing this expression with respect to the unknown $K + 1$ parameters yields a solution that is the multivariate analogue of the bivariate solution given in equation (3.7). In dealing with the multiple regression model it is convenient to use matrix notation. An introduction to the general linear regression model in matrix notation is given in Appendix C.

The results obtained by estimating the multifactor CAPM for the 10 industry portfolios are given in Table 3.3. A comparison of the α-risk estimates $(\widehat{\alpha})$ and the beta risk estimates $(\widehat{\beta}_1)$ obtained from the multifactor CAPM model and the estimates based on the CAPM presented in Table 3.2 show that the two sets of parameter estimates are qualitatively very similar in terms of signs and magnitudes. This result also suggests that the role of the market factor is still very important in pricing assets as its influence is undiminished through the addition of other factors into the model. Inspection of the signs on the parameter estimates of the size, $\widehat{\beta}_2$, value, $\widehat{\beta}_3$, and momentum, $\widehat{\beta}_4$, factors reveals that different industries have vastly differing exposures to these factors.

A primary shortcoming of the multifactor CAPM model is the absence of a theory that explains how the additional risk factors are priced by the market. Without such

TABLE 3.3   Ordinary least squares estimates of the multifactor CAPM for 10 industry portfolios using monthly data for the United States from January 1927 and December 2013. Standard errors are given in parentheses.

Industry	α	β_1	β_2	β_3	β_4	R^2	$\overline{R}^2$	RSS
Nondurables	0.179	0.767	−0.032	0.028	0.025	0.779	0.778	5001.6
	(0.071)	(0.014)	(0.022)	(0.021)	(0.016)			
Durables	0.089	1.172	0.034	0.145	−0.152	0.763	0.762	15098.7
	(0.123)	(0.024)	(0.039)	(0.037)	(0.028)			
Manuf	−0.012	1.104	−0.001	0.128	−0.021	0.929	0.929	2994.7
	(0.055)	(0.011)	(0.017)	(0.016)	(0.013)			
Energy	0.072	0.895	−0.210	0.265	0.116	0.627	0.626	14083.4
	(0.119)	(0.023)	(0.037)	(0.035)	(0.027)			
Tech	0.190	1.242	0.098	−0.372	−0.089	0.853	0.852	8380.0
	(0.091)	(0.018)	(0.029)	(0.027)	(0.021)			
Telecom	0.258	0.678	−0.140	−0.095	−0.070	0.606	0.604	8846.6
	(0.094)	(0.019)	(0.030)	(0.028)	(0.022)			
Retail	0.170	0.960	0.075	−0.121	−0.039	0.794	0.794	7527.0
	(0.087)	(0.017)	(0.027)	(0.026)	(0.020)			
Health	0.297	0.893	−0.105	−0.166	0.023	0.666	0.665	11172.6
	(0.106)	(0.021)	(0.033)	(0.032)	(0.024)			
Utilities	0.007	0.777	−0.180	0.311	0.008	0.620	0.618	12386.6
	(0.111)	(0.022)	(0.035)	(0.033)	(0.025)			
Other	−0.141	1.043	0.064	0.335	−0.081	0.918	0.918	3635.7
	(0.060)	(0.012)	(0.019)	(0.018)	(0.014)			

a theory additional factors are constantly being suggested to augment the model. See for example, Bekaert et al. (2017) for a recent example in an international setting. These factors may serve as proxies for more fundamental risk factors for which investors demand additional compensation. Explanations for mispricing are, however, increasingly being sought in the field of behavioral finance, where the performance of stocks is related to the psychological mindset of investors. This branch of research dates back to Shiller (1981, 1984) who makes the point that irrational investors can overreact to convincing storytelling and can cause prices to diverge from fundamentals. For more recent work in this area, see Malmendier and Nagel (2011) and Bekaert and Hoerova (2016).

3.3 PROPERTIES OF ORDINARY LEAST SQUARES

The ordinary least squares estimators of the parameters of the CAPM in equation (3.4) and more generally the multiple linear regression model in equation (3.12), have a number of useful properties in both small and large samples. As large samples are of particular interest in financial econometrics given the availability of high-frequency, large data sets, only these properties of the ordinary least squares estimators are discussed here. In particular, the properties considered are called asymptotic properties and these correspond to the (theoretical) situation where sample sizes progressively increase to become infinitely large so that $T \to \infty$. Asymptotic analysis of this type is particularly valuable because it enables us to understand the properties of fitting regression equations in the ideal situation of having an infinite amount of data. In these situations, good performance in regression estimation is to be expected.

Three important asymptotic properties are presented below, which describe such performance of the estimators in relation to the respective population parameters. The first property focuses on the probability of an estimator being arbitrarily close to the true parameter value (consistency), which describes the capacity to locate the true parameter when there is an infinite amount of data. The second concerns the variance of its distribution (asymptotic efficiency) in infinitely large samples, which measures how good the estimator is in relation to other procedures. The third property relates to the shape of the distribution (asymptotic normality), which provides valuable information for constructing confidence intervals and testing.

Consistency

The least squares estimators of α-risk, $\widehat{\alpha}$, and β-risk, $\widehat{\beta}$, are based on extracting information from the data over the period $t = 1, 2, \cdots, T$. If the assumptions on the disturbance term of the multiple linear regression model in equation (3.5) remain satisfied as more and more information is employed by increasing T, these estimators approach the population α- and β-risk parameters, α and β, in the limit as $T \to \infty$. This property is known as *consistency* and shows that closer estimates of the population parameters are typically obtained by having more information.

A more formal statement of consistency of the two risk estimators is

$$\text{plim}(\widehat{\alpha}) = \alpha, \qquad \text{plim}(\widehat{\beta}) = \beta, \tag{3.14}$$

where the use of the term plim denotes a limit that is taken in probability. The use of a probability limit rather than a deterministic limit (denoted as lim) is in recognition that $\widehat{\beta}$ is a random quantity, being a function of data that is itself random. Even though $\widehat{\beta}$ approaches β as T increases, the inherent randomness of $\widehat{\beta}$ ensures that the path to β remains random as T increases, unlike that of a convergent deterministic sequence. In recognition of this characteristic, convergence is said to occur *in probability* as $T \to \infty$.

Figure 3.3 illustrates the consistency of $\widehat{\alpha}$ and $\widehat{\beta}$ in the CAPM regression. The CAPM is simulated with population parameters of $\alpha = 1$ and $\beta = 1$, and sample sizes ranging from $T = 10$ to $T = 10000$. The excess returns on the market, x_t, are simulated from the standard normal distribution $x_t \sim N(0, 1)$, while the disturbance term u_t is simulated from the normal distribution $u_t \sim N(0, 0.25)$. For each sample, the estimates of α and β are plotted in the figure. The property of consistency is clearly demonstrated with both $\widehat{\alpha}$ and $\widehat{\beta}$ approaching their true values of 1, as the sample size progressively increases. This figure also demonstrates the random character of the estimators and the random nature of the convergence toward the population values. Even for very large samples of $T = 10000$, random fluctuations in the path occur, but these continue to contract as T increases, revealing the nature of the probabilistic convergence.

Asymptotic Efficiency

In discussing the property of consistency with the aid of Figure 3.3, it was observed that the parameter estimates from the simulation experiment did not monotonically converge toward the population parameters as $T \to \infty$. Instead, each estimate continued to exhibit random fluctuations about the true population parameter but with its randomness

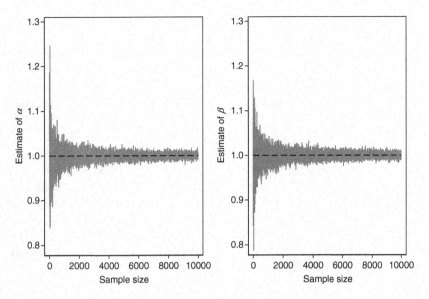

FIGURE 3.3 Illustrating the convergence of the least squares estimates of α and β in the CAPM regression equation (3.4). Estimates of α (left panel) and β (right panel) are shown for sample sizes from 10 to 10000 in increments of 1 observation.

diminishing as T increased. A measure of the spread of this randomness in estimation is captured by estimating the asymptotic variance.

The asymptotic variances of the ordinary least squares estimators with respect to their population parameters in equation (3.4) are given by the following expressions

$$\text{var}(\widehat{\alpha}) = \text{E}[(\widehat{\alpha} - \alpha)^2] = \frac{\sigma_u^2}{\sigma_x^2} \frac{\sigma_x^2 + \mu_x^2}{T}$$

$$\text{var}(\widehat{\beta}) = \text{E}[(\widehat{\beta} - \beta)^2] = \frac{\sigma_u^2}{\sigma_x^2} \frac{1}{T}, \tag{3.15}$$

where σ_u^2 is the variance of the disturbance term u_t, and $\mu_x = \text{E}(x)$ and $\sigma_x^2 = \text{E}[(x - \mu_x)^2]$ are, respectively, the mean and variance of the explanatory variable x. An important feature of these expressions is that the asymptotic variances are inversely related to the sample size T. Since σ_u^2, σ_x^2, and μ_x^2 are all constants by definition, increasing the sample size progressively diminishes the spread of the estimators around their population parameters. In fact, doubling the sample size decreases the asymptotic variances by 50%. This property of the asymptotic variances is demonstrated by the simulation experiment presented in Figure 3.3. In the simulation experiments $\mu_x = 0$, $\sigma_x^2 = 1$, and $\sigma_u^2 = 0.25$, so the asymptotic variances in equation (3.15) are calculated to be

$$\text{var}(\widehat{\alpha}) = \frac{\sigma_u^2}{\sigma_x^2} \frac{\sigma_x^2 + \mu_x^2}{T} = \frac{0.25}{1} \frac{1 + 0^2}{T} = \frac{0.25}{T}$$

$$\text{var}(\widehat{\beta}) = \frac{\sigma_u^2}{\sigma_x^2} \frac{1}{T} = \frac{0.25}{1} \frac{1}{T} = \frac{0.25}{T},$$

with the spread of the parameter estimates progressively falling as the sample size progressively increases.

An important property of the ordinary least squares estimator is that under the assumptions described above and certain mild technical conditions, the asymptotic variances given in equation (3.15) are the smallest possible variances attainable by any consistent estimator. The ordinary least squares estimator is therefore said to be asymptotically efficient.

Asymptotic Normality

The first and second properties of the least squares estimators $\widehat{\alpha}$ and $\widehat{\beta}$ are concerned with the mean and the variance of the asymptotic distributions of these estimators. The third and final property is concerned with the shape of the asymptotic distribution. Under the same conditions described above, the asymptotic distributions of $\widehat{\alpha}$ and $\widehat{\beta}$, are normal with means given by equation (3.14) and variances given by equation (3.15). Upon appropriate scaling of the estimation errors by $\sqrt{T}$, the asymptotic normality property of the least squares estimators is formalized by writing

$$\sqrt{T}(\widehat{\alpha} - \alpha) \overset{d}{\to} N\left(0, \frac{\sigma_u^2(\sigma_x^2 + \mu_x^2)}{\sigma_x^2}\right), \qquad \sqrt{T}(\widehat{\beta} - \beta) \overset{d}{\to} N\left(0, \frac{\sigma_u^2}{\sigma_x^2}\right), \qquad (3.16)$$

where the symbol $\overset{d}{\to}$ represents convergence in distribution as $T \to \infty$, signifying that the sequence of distributions converges to a well-defined asymptotic distribution, which in this case is a normal distribution.

Figure 3.4 illustrates the asymptotic normality property of the least squares β-risk estimator $\widehat{\beta}$. Using the same simulation setup as before for a fixed x_t series, the asymptotic

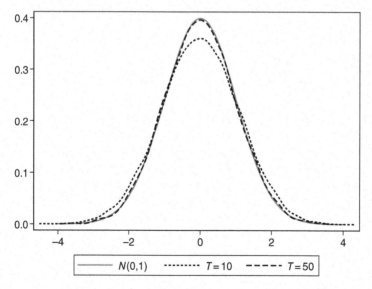

FIGURE 3.4 Illustrating asymptotic normality of the least squares estimator, $\widehat{\beta}$, in the regression model equation (3.4). Estimates of the densities of the distribution of $\sqrt{T}(\widehat{\beta} - 1)/0.5$ for sample sizes 10 and 50 are computed using 10000 replications in each case. Also shown is the standard normal distribution, $N(0,1)$.

distributions are presented by using equation (3.16) to construct the standardized statistic

$$\sqrt{T}\frac{\widehat{\beta}-\beta}{\sqrt{\sigma_u^2/\sigma_x^2}} = \sqrt{T}\frac{\widehat{\beta}-1}{0.5},$$

which has a standard normal asymptotic distribution, $N(0,1)$. In Figure 3.4 two sampling distributions are presented for samples of size $T=10$ and $T=50$, and are shown against the asymptotic $N(0,1)$ distribution. These distributions are all centered on zero as predicted by the consistency property of equation (3.14). Even the sampling distribution based on samples of size $T=10$ is reasonably close to the asymptotic $N(0,1)$ distribution. Increasing the sample size to $T=50$ delivers an extremely close correspondence with the asymptotic distribution.

3.4 DIAGNOSTICS

The estimated CAPM and its linear regression model representation in equation (3.9) are based on the assumption that this model is correctly specified and corresponds to the process that generated the data used to fit the regression. But if asset returns are determined by several factors, as in the multifactor CAPM equation (3.11), then the 1-factor CAPM misspecifies the true generating mechanism of the data. To test this fundamental assumption a number of diagnostic procedures are available. These may be classified into three categories involving diagnostics on the dependent variable y_t, the explanatory variables $\{x_{1t}, x_{2t}, \cdots, x_{Kt}\}$, and the disturbance term u_t.

3.4.1 Diagnostics on the Dependent Variable

A natural measure of the success of an estimated model is given by the proportion of the variation in the dependent variable explained by the model. This measure is called the coefficient of determination and is defined by the ratio

$$R^2 = \frac{\text{Explained sum of squares}}{\text{Total sum of squares}} = \frac{\sum\limits_{t=1}^{T}(y_t-\overline{y})^2 - \sum\limits_{t=1}^{T}\widehat{u}_t^2}{\sum\limits_{t=1}^{T}(y_t-\overline{y})^2}. \tag{3.17}$$

The coefficient of determination satisfies the inequality $0 \le R^2 \le 1$, with values close to unity suggesting a good model fit and values close to zero representing a poor fit. Given the decomposition of the total risk of an asset into systematic and idiosyncratic components in equation (3.3), this expression suggests that R^2 provides an estimate of the proportion of the total risk that is due to systematic risk, with the proportion attributable to idiosyncratic risk estimated by $1-R^2$.

The R^2 statistics for the estimated CAPM applied to the 10 portfolios are given in Table 3.2. The Manufacturing portfolio is estimated to have the highest proportion of systematic risk with an R^2 of 0.924, with the Other portfolio having the second highest with an R^2 of 0.876. The Utilities portfolio has the lowest estimated proportion of systematic risk, with the split between systematic and idiosyncratic being roughly 50-50.

A related measure to the R^2 statistic is the adjusted coefficient of determination

$$\overline{R}^2 = 1 - (1 - R^2)\frac{T-1}{T-K-1}, \tag{3.18}$$

which penalizes the R^2 statistic for specifying a model with additional parameters arising from the inclusion of more explanatory variables. For the multifactor CAPM in equation (3.11) the additional factors are the size, growth, and momentum factors. If these additional factors contribute further (that is, beyond the effect of the penalty) to explaining movements in the excess returns on an asset then $\overline{R}^2$ increases, whereas if they do not then $\overline{R}^2$ falls. However, in both scenarios R^2 increases, a fact which implies that the R^2 of the multifactor CAPM is always greater than the R^2 computed for the CAPM. This result is confirmed by comparing the R^2 statistics in Table 3.2 for the CAPM, which are all lower than the corresponding statistics in Table 3.3 for the multifactor CAPM. A comparison of the $\overline{R}^2$ across the two tables identifies the relative importance of the additional factors included in the multifactor CAPM. Inspection of these statistics shows evidence in favor of the 4-factor CAPM with $\overline{R}^2$ increasing for all portfolios with the exception of the Nondurables portfolio, where it does not change.

3.4.2 Diagnostics on the Explanatory Variables

The CAPM in equation (3.2) explains the price of a risky asset in terms of its exposure to systematic risk. To establish the significance of these risk factors, statistical tests are now performed on the estimated parameters of the CAPM.

Single Parameter Tests

To test the importance of the market factor in the CAPM regression equation in (3.2), the β-risk parameter estimate is tested to assess whether the true parameter is zero using a t test. The null and alternative hypotheses are

$$H_0 : \beta = 0 \quad \text{[market factor not priced]}$$
$$H_1 : \beta \neq 0 \quad \text{[market factor priced]}.$$

The t statistic to perform this test is given by the ratio

$$t = \frac{\widehat{\beta}}{\mathrm{se}(\widehat{\beta})}, \tag{3.19}$$

where $\widehat{\beta}$ is the estimated coefficient of β and $\mathrm{se}(\widehat{\beta})$ is the corresponding standard error. Note that in computing the standard errors, the estimate of the residual variance $\widehat{\sigma}_u^2$ is computed using the degrees of freedom correction $T - K - 1$ to take account of the $K + 1$ unknown parameters in the regression model. The test statistic in equation (3.19) has an asymptotic normal distribution under the null hypothesis. In small samples and under certain conditions (including normally distributed errors u_t), this statistic has a Student t distribution with $T - K - 1$ degrees of freedom.[2]

---

[2] The Student t distribution was developed by the English statistician William Gosset in 1908 who wrote under the pen name Student. He worked in the Guinness brewery and on farms in Ireland, where only

For a 5% significance level the decision rule is

$$p \text{ value} < 0.05 : \text{Reject } H_0 \text{ at the 5\% level of significance}$$
$$p \text{ value} > 0.05 : \text{Fail to reject } H_0 \text{ at the 5\% level of significance,} \qquad (3.20)$$

where the p value is the probability calculated under the null hypothesis of finding a more extreme value of the test statistic than the computed one. From Table 3.2, the t statistic on the coefficient representing β-risk in the Nondurables portfolio is

$$t = \frac{\widehat{\beta}}{se(\widehat{\beta})} = \frac{0.7578}{0.0125} = 60.62.$$

This t statistic yields a p value of $0.000 < 0.05$ showing that the excess return on the market is significant at the 5% level in determining movements in the excess return on the Nondurables portfolio. Inspection of the t statistics for the remaining portfolios reveals qualitatively similar results with the excess market return being significant in all cases. This result provides strong support for the applicability of the CAPM in all sectors of the US economy.

The application of a t test to determine the strength of the β-risk of an asset can also be applied to test for the asset's α-risk by testing the hypothesis $\alpha = 0$. More generally, t tests can be constructed for other types of hypotheses such as testing whether an asset benchmarks the market by testing the hypothesis $\beta = 1$. In this case the t statistic in equation (3.19) becomes

$$t = \frac{\widehat{\beta} - 1}{se(\widehat{\beta})}. \qquad (3.21)$$

Applications of these types of t tests are developed in the exercises.

Joint Parameter Tests

In many financial applications, it is of interest to perform tests of hypotheses on several parameters jointly. In the case of the multifactor CAPM in equation (3.11), a joint test of the significance of all of the additional factors is based on the null and alternative hypotheses

$$H_0 : \beta_2 = \beta_3 = \beta_4 = 0 \qquad \text{[CAPM preferred]}$$
$$H_1 : \text{at least one restriction fails} \qquad \text{[Multifactor CAPM preferred],}$$

which corresponds to $R = 3$ restrictions to be tested. Under the null hypothesis the restrictions imply that CAPM is the preferred model; whereas under the alternative hypothesis the more general multifactor CAPM is preferred.

The general form of the joint test statistic involves estimating the model twice: first, under the null hypothesis in which the restrictions are imposed; and second, under the alternative hypothesis in which the restrictions are relaxed. Letting RSS_0 represent the residual sum of squares from the restricted model as given by CAPM, and RSS_1 the residual sum of squares from the unrestricted model as given by the multifactor CAPM, the test statistic takes the form

---

small samples of data were available on different varieties of barley that he was testing for effectiveness in production. In his honor, the process of taking the ratio in equation (3.19) of an estimate to its standard error is now universally known as studentization.

$$J = \frac{(RSS_0 - RSS_1)}{RSS_1/(T - K - 1)}, \tag{3.22}$$

where T is the sample size and K is the number of factors in the unrestricted model, which for the multifactor CAPM is $K = 4$. If the restrictions are consistent with the true model there will be little difference in the two sums of squares resulting in a small value of the test statistic in equation (3.22). However, if the restrictions are not valid then imposing the restrictions typically leads to a large increase in RSS_0 relative to RSS_1, resulting in a large value of the test statistic. Distinguishing between the null and alternative hypothesis is achieved formally by assessing the *significance* of the statistic. Significance is established by using the property that the test statistic in equation (3.22) has a chi-square distribution with R degrees of freedom (written χ_R^2) in large samples, a property that holds under conditions covered by the assumptions already made. This distribution is used to generate critical values and p values of the test statistic.[3]

In small samples the statistic $F = J/R$ has an F distribution with R and $T - K - 1$ degrees of freedom (written $F_{R,T-K-1}$). Like the t distribution, the F distribution is the exact small sample distribution of the ratio under the assumption that the data are normally distributed.[4]

To implement the test of the multifactor CAPM for the Nondurables portfolio, the restricted residual sum of squares is $RSS_0 = 5026.2$ from the column of Table 3.2 and the unrestricted sum of squares is $RSS_1 = 5001.6$ from the last column of Table 3.3. Substituting these values into equation (3.22) together with $T = 1044$ and $K = 4$ yields a statistic of

$$J = \frac{(RSS_0 - RSS_1)}{RSS_1/(T - K - 1)} = \frac{(5026.2 - 5001.6)}{5001.6/(1044 - 4 - 1)} = 5.11.$$

Under the null hypothesis J is distributed asymptotically as χ_3^2 with a p value of 0.1640. This result provides statistical support for the one-factor CAPM suggesting that the additional risk factors given by the growth, value, and momentum factors are not priced for this portfolio. The opposite result occurs however, for all of the remaining industry portfolios, with the joint test providing strong support for the multifactor CAPM at the 5% level.

3.4.3 Diagnostics on the Disturbance Term

The third set of diagnostic tests concerns the properties of the disturbance term u_t. For the CAPM regression model to be specified correctly there should be no systematic and useful information about excess returns remaining in the disturbance term. Otherwise there will be arbitrage opportunities that can be used to improve predictions of the dependent

---

[3] A critical value is a cut-off point in the distribution that determines whether the observed value of the statistic is significant—or extreme enough—to reject the null hypothesis.

[4] This distribution is named after the English statistician Sir Ronald Fisher (1890–1962), one of the founders of modern experimental agricultural research who developed many new statistical methods to analyze experimental data at the Rothamsted Experimental Station located in the country town of Harpenden near London.

variable (excess returns) and thereby enhance profits. This property suggests that model specification tests can be based on the following set of hypotheses,

$$H_0 : u_t \text{ is random} \qquad \text{[model is specified correctly]}$$
$$H_1 : u_t \text{ is non-random} \qquad \text{[model is misspecified]}.$$

The adoption of tests concerning u_t is especially important for those situations where the coefficient of determination is found to be extremely small. Even though a low R^2 suggests that the estimated model provides a poor fit of the dependent variable, this does not necessarily mean that the model is misspecified. As is often the case with high-frequency financial returns data, the data may be extremely noisy. An R^2 lower than 5% is not at all uncommon in these regressions because financial returns are notoriously difficult to predict. Indeed, from an efficient markets point of view, there may be no effective predictor of future returns. In this scenario, the estimated model can nonetheless still be viewed as well specified provided that the null hypothesis that u_t is random is not rejected.

Testing for Autocorrelation

The aim of a test for residual autocorrelation is to detect the presence of temporal dependence in the disturbance terms. The null and alternative hypotheses are, respectively,

$$H_0 : \text{No autocorrelation in the disturbances}$$
$$H_1 : \text{Autocorrelation in the disturbances}.$$

Failing to reject the null hypothesis of no autocorrelation provides support for the model, whereas rejection of the null hypothesis suggests that the model excludes important information that may aid prediction. In the presence of autocorrelation the ordinary least squares estimator is no longer efficient.

The autocorrelation test is based on the correlation between the least squares residuals $\widehat{u}_t$ and past residuals obtained by specifying the following multiple regression equation

$$\widehat{u}_t = \gamma_0 + \gamma_1 x_{1t} + \gamma_2 x_{2t} + \cdots + \gamma_K x_{K,t} + \rho_1 \widehat{u}_{t-1} + \rho_2 \widehat{u}_{t-2} + \cdots + \rho_p \widehat{u}_{t-p} + v_t, \qquad (3.23)$$

where v_t is a disturbance term. The autocorrelation in the residuals is captured by the regressors $\{\widehat{u}_{t-1}, \widehat{u}_{t-2}, \cdots, \widehat{u}_{t-p}\}$, which allow for autocorrelation for up to p lags in this specification. The choice of p may be informed by theory or guided by the frequency of the data. For example, in monthly data p might be set to 12. A test of the null hypothesis of no autocorrelation is performed by testing the joint restrictions $\rho_1 = \rho_2 = \cdots = \rho_p = 0$. The test statistic of autocorrelation of order p is given by

$$AR(p) = TR^2, \qquad (3.24)$$

where T is the sample size and R^2 is the coefficient of determination from estimating equation (3.23) by ordinary least squares. Under the null hypothesis $AR(p)$ has a χ_p^2 distribution, which is used in determining significance and the outcome of the test.

A test for first order autocorrelation of the residuals of the estimated CAPM for the Nondurables portfolio yields a statistic of 22.646. Using the χ_1^2 distribution the p value is 0.000, showing a strong rejection of the null hypothesis in favor of autocorrelation. The presence of autocorrelation in the residuals may be the result of the exclusion of factors that are also important in pricing the portfolio such as the additional factors included in the multifactor CAPM. Alternatively, the problem may arise because important dynamics such as lagged dependent and explanatory variables have been incorrectly excluded. Extensions of the linear regression model to allow for dynamic relationships are discussed in Chapter 4.

Testing for Heteroskedasticity

An important assumption of the linear regression model given in equation (3.5) is that the variance of the disturbance term σ_u^2 is assumed to be constant over the sample. In the context of the CAPM this assumption implies that the (squared) idiosyncratic risk does not vary over time. As discussed earlier, constant variance is known as homoskedasticity, whereas non-constant variance is known as heteroskedasticity. To test this assumption the null and alternative hypotheses are, respectively,

$$H_0 : \text{Homoskedasticity} \quad [\sigma_u^2 \text{ is constant}]$$
$$H_1 : \text{Heteroskedasticity} \quad [\sigma_u^2 \text{ is time-varying}].$$

Just as in the case of autocorrelation, the presence of heteroskedasticity in the residuals will mean that the ordinary least squares estimator is no longer efficient.

A test for heteroskedasticity is based on determining whether the squared residuals $\widehat{u}_t^2$ are influenced by the explanatory variables in the regression model. For the CAPM the test is constructed by first specifying the following regression equation

$$\widehat{u}_t^2 = \gamma_0 + \gamma_1 x_{1t} + \gamma_2 x_{1t}^2 + v_t, \tag{3.25}$$

where v_t is a disturbance term, and then testing the joint restrictions $\gamma_1 = \gamma_2 = 0$. The test statistic for heteroskedasticity is

$$\text{HETERO} = TR^2, \tag{3.26}$$

where T is the sample size and R^2 is the coefficient of determination from estimating equation (3.25) by ordinary least squares. This test is also known as White's test of heteroskedasticity (White, 1980). Under the null hypothesis $HETERO$ has a χ_2^2 distribution. Although the discussion here focuses on the case of only a single regressor, the test is easily generalized to accommodate multiple regressors. Figure 3.5 provides a plot of the squared residuals from estimating the CAPM for the Nondurables portfolio. Performing the White test yields a test statistic of 34.990. The associated p value is 0.000, providing strong evidence against the null hypothesis of a constant disturbance variance.

Testing for ARCH

One possible reason for this rejection is the presence of volatility clustering whereby large (small) movements are associated with further large (small) movements. This phenomenon, known as autoregressive conditional heteroskedasticity (ARCH), was originally introduced by Engle (1982), and is dealt with in detail in Chapter 13.

To perform a test for ARCH in the disturbance variance, the null and alternative hypotheses are, respectively,

$$H_0 : \text{No ARCH}$$
$$H_1 : \text{ARCH}.$$

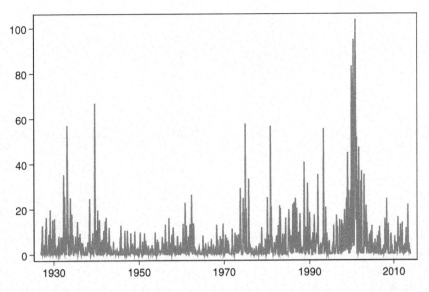

FIGURE 3.5 A plot of the squared residuals, $\widehat{u}_t^2$, from the CAPM regression for Nondurables.

A test for ARCH of arbitrary order p is performed by estimating the following regression equation

$$\widehat{u}_t^2 = \gamma_0 + \gamma_1 \widehat{u}_{t-1}^2 + \gamma_2 \widehat{u}_{t-2}^2 + \cdots \gamma_p \widehat{u}_{t-p}^2 + v_t, \tag{3.27}$$

where v_t is a disturbance term. To establish the presence of ARCH it is usually only necessary to run the test for small values of p. The test statistic is

$$\text{ARCH}(p) = TR^2, \tag{3.28}$$

where T is the sample size and R^2 comes from the estimating equation (3.27) by ordinary least squares. Under the null hypothesis $\text{ARCH}(p)$ has a χ_p^2 distribution.

A test of first order ARCH by setting $p = 1$ in equation (3.27) for the Nondurables portfolio generates a test statistic of 51.911 with a p value of 0.000. This strong rejection of the No ARCH null hypothesis is not surprising given the strong visual evidence of volatility clustering already identified in Figure 3.5. This empirical result also suggests that the CAPM linear regression specification needs to be extended to allow for a time-varying disturbance variance.

Testing for Normality

The diagnostic tests discussed so far are concerned with either the mean of the linear regression model (autocorrelation) or its variance (White and ARCH). The Jarque-Bera statistic (Jarque and Bera, 1987) provides a test of normality of the disturbance distribution. Even though the assumptions given in (3.5) to establish the properties of the least squares estimator do not require the assumption of normality, the properties of the diagnostic tests presented are nonetheless affected by the underlying disturbance distribution.

The null and alternative hypotheses of the test of normality are, respectively,

$$H_0 : u_t \text{ is normally distributed}$$
$$H_1 : u_t \text{ is nonnormally distributed.}$$

The test statistic is

$$JB = T \left(\frac{SK^2}{6} + \frac{(KT - 3)^2}{24} \right), \tag{3.29}$$

where T is the sample size, and SK and KT are skewness and kurtosis measures, respectively, of the least squares residuals

$$SK = \frac{1}{T} \sum_{t=1}^{T} \left(\frac{\widehat{u}_t}{\widehat{\sigma}_u} \right)^3, \qquad KT = \frac{1}{T} \sum_{t=1}^{T} \left(\frac{\widehat{u}_t}{\widehat{\sigma}_u} \right)^4.$$

The JB statistic is a joint test for the presence of skewness and excess kurtosis relative to the normal distribution. Under the null hypothesis the JB statistic is asymptotically distributed as χ_2^2.

The value of the JB statistic of the residuals from the CAPM using the Nondurables portfolio is 192.8. Using the χ_2^2 distribution, the p value is 0.000, resulting in strong rejection of the null hypothesis at the 5% level. An implication of nonnormality is that it affects the standard errors of the parameter estimates resulting in incorrect inferences.

In cases where the null hypothesis is rejected in favor of nonnormal disturbances three potential solutions are available. The first solution is to try to address the problem at its source. One possible option is to use indicator variables to capture extreme observations, which are creating the nonnormality problem (see Exercise 7), thereby effectively removing those observations from being covered in the regression model. The second is to model the nonnormality directly by replacing the normal distribution with a more appropriate alternative, a solution that is explored in Chapter 10 when using maximum likelihood estimation. The third approach, also discussed in Chapter 10, is to do nothing in terms of estimation but to adjust the estimates of the standard errors that are used in statistical testing to take account of the presence of nonnormality in the data, a solution that is based on quasi maximum likelihood estimation.

3.5 MEASURING PORTFOLIO PERFORMANCE

The performance of a portfolio is commonly measured in terms of its expected return in excess of the return from a risk-free asset relative to the risk of the portfolio. Three well-known measures of a portfolio's performance are

$$\text{Sharpe ratio:} \qquad S = \frac{\mu_p - r_f}{\sigma_p}$$

$$\text{Treynor index:} \qquad T = \frac{\mu_p - r_f}{\beta} \tag{3.30}$$

$$\text{Jensen's alpha:} \qquad \alpha = \mu_p - r_f - \beta(\mu_m - r_f),$$

where μ_p and μ_m are, respectively, the expected returns on the portfolio and the market, r_f is the risk-free rate, and the risk measures are portfolio risk σ_p and β-risk from the CAPM. The Sharpe ratio, S, demonstrates how well the return of an asset compensates the investor for the risk taken, which is measured as the average excess return to the

TABLE 3.4 Performance measures and rankings for 10 US industry portfolios computed using monthly returns data for the period January 1927 to December 2013.

Industry	Mean $\widehat{\mu}_p$	Std. Dev. $\widehat{\sigma}_p$	Sharpe Ratio	Treynor Index	Jensen's Alpha	Rank Sharpe	Rank Treynor	Rank Jensen
Nondur	0.98	4.66	0.15	0.92	0.21	1	2	3
Durables	1.09	7.79	0.10	0.65	0.00	9	9	9
Manuf	1.02	6.36	0.12	0.65	0.01	6	8	7
Energy	1.07	6.01	0.13	0.92	0.23	3	3	2
Tech	1.09	7.37	0.11	0.65	0.01	7	7	7
Telecom	0.86	4.64	0.12	0.88	0.15	4	4	4
Retail	1.02	5.91	0.12	0.76	0.11	5	6	5
Health	1.09	5.66	0.14	0.95	0.26	2	1	1
Utilities	0.88	5.59	0.11	0.76	0.09	8	5	6
Other	0.91	6.52	0.10	0.55	−0.10	10	10	10

portfolio per unit of total portfolio risk (Sharpe, 1966). The Treynor index, $\mathcal{T}$, is similar to the Sharpe ratio except that the risk of the portfolio is defined in terms of systematic risk using the β-risk from the CAPM (Treynor, 1966). Jensen's alpha, α, is the abnormal return on a portfolio relative to its systematic risk, which is obtained from the CAPM regression (Jensen, 1968). Of the three measures Jensen's alpha is possibly the most widely used as a positive α is a necessary condition for good performance.

The relative performance rankings of the 10 portfolios used in the CAPM application are presented in Table 3.4, which are computed by replacing the population parameters in equation (3.30) with their corresponding sample quantities. The estimates of the expected portfolio returns and risk are given in columns 2 and 3 of the table as $\widehat{\mu}_p$ and $\widehat{\sigma}_p$. To complete the calculations the expected excess return on the market is estimated as $\widehat{\mu}_m - r_f = 0.6449$, where the risk-free rate is taken as the sample average $r_f = 0.2873$. In the case of the Nondurables portfolio the three performance measures are computed as

Sharpe: $$\widehat{S} = \frac{\widehat{\mu}_p - r_f}{\widehat{\sigma}_p} = \frac{0.9814 - 0.2873}{4.6608} = 0.1489$$

Treynor: $$\widehat{\mathcal{T}} = \frac{\widehat{\mu}_p - r_f}{\widehat{\beta}} = \frac{0.9814 - 0.2873}{0.7577} = 0.9161$$

Jensen: $$\widehat{\alpha} = \widehat{\mu}_p - r_f - \widehat{\beta}(\widehat{\mu}_m - r_f)$$
$$= 0.9814 - 0.2873 - 0.7577 \times (0.6449) = 0.2054,$$

with $\widehat{\beta}$ taken from the CAPM regressions in Table 3.2. The Health portfolio has the highest rankings being ranked number one by the Treynor index and Jensen's alpha, and second by the Sharpe ratio. The Nondurables portfolio is also highly ranked by all three measures with a top ranking using the Sharpe ratio, second using the Treynor index and third by Jensen's alpha. The worst performing portfolio is Others, which is ranked last by all three measures. Despite some broad consistency in the rankings of many of the portfolios, the rankings are clearly not perfectly consistent, a phenomenon that is commonly encountered in practical performance evaluation.

Indeed, different rankings among these measures are to be expected as the Sharpe ratio, for instance, accounts for total portfolio risk, whereas the Treynor measure adjusts excess portfolio returns for systematic risk only. However, some similarity between the rankings provided by Treynor's index and Jensen's alpha is also unsurprising given that the alpha measure is derived from a CAPM regression that explicitly accounts for systematic risk via the inclusion of the market factor.

3.6 MINIMUM VARIANCE PORTFOLIOS

A common goal in choosing a portfolio of assets is to minimize the overall risk of the portfolio, as measured by its variance, or squared volatility. The minimum variance portfolio problem can be formulated neatly in terms of linear regression where many of the key statistics have precise interpretations. To illustrate the problem of constructing a minimum variance portfolio in a two-asset case, monthly equity prices for the US stocks Microsoft and Walmart are used.

To derive the minimum variance portfolio, consider a portfolio consisting of two assets with returns r_{1t} and r_{2t} that satisfy

Mean: $\quad\quad\quad \mu_1 = E[r_{1t}], \quad\quad\quad\quad\quad\quad \mu_2 = E[r_{2t}],$

Variance: $\quad\quad \sigma_1^2 = E[(r_{1t} - \mu_1)^2], \quad\quad\quad \sigma_2^2 = E[(r_{2t} - \mu_2)^2],$

Covariance: $\quad \sigma_{12} = E[(r_{1t} - \mu_1)(r_{2t} - \mu_2)].$

The return on the portfolio is

$$r_{pt} = w_1 r_{1t} + w_2 r_{2t}, \quad\quad w_1 + w_2 = 1, \quad\quad\quad\quad (3.31)$$

in which w_1 and w_2 are the weights that define the relative contributions of each asset in the portfolio.

The expected return on this portfolio is

$$\mu_p = E(w_1 r_{1t} + w_2 r_{2t}) = w_1 E(r_{1t}) + w_2 E(r_{2t}) = w_1 \mu_1 + w_2 \mu_2, \quad\quad (3.32)$$

which is a weighted sum of the expected returns on the two assets. A measure of the portfolio risk is given by the variance

$$\sigma_p^2 = E[(r_{pt} - \mu_p)^2] = w_1^2 \sigma_1^2 + w_2^2 \sigma_2^2 + 2 w_1 w_2 \sigma_{12}. \quad\quad\quad (3.33)$$

Using the adding-up restriction in equation (3.31), the risk of the portfolio is re-expressed in terms of the portfolio weight on the first asset as

$$\sigma_p^2 = w_1^2 \sigma_1^2 + (1 - w_1)^2 \sigma_2^2 + 2 w_1 (1 - w_1) \sigma_{12}. \quad\quad\quad (3.34)$$

To find the optimal portfolio that minimizes risk, the following optimization problem is solved

$$\min_{w_1} \sigma_p^2.$$

Differentiating equation (3.34) with respect to w_1, setting the derivative to zero and solving for w_1 gives the minimum variance weights

$$w_1 = \frac{\sigma_2^2 - \sigma_{12}}{\sigma_1^2 + \sigma_2^2 - 2\sigma_{12}}, \quad w_2 = \frac{\sigma_1^2 - \sigma_{12}}{\sigma_1^2 + \sigma_2^2 - 2\sigma_{12}}, \quad\quad\quad (3.35)$$

where the solution for w_2 uses the adding-up condition $w_2 = 1 - w_1$. The minimum variance weights are a function of the returns variances σ_1^2 and σ_2^2 and the covariance σ_{12}.

Figure 3.6 contains the log returns on Microsoft and Walmart for the period April 1990 to July 2004. The sample averages and covariance matrix of the returns are, respectively,

$$\widehat{\mu}_1 = 0.020877, \quad \widehat{\mu}_2 = 0.013496, \quad \begin{bmatrix} \widehat{\sigma}_1^2 & \widehat{\sigma}_{12} \\ \widehat{\sigma}_{12} & \widehat{\sigma}_2^2 \end{bmatrix} = \begin{bmatrix} 0.011333 & 0.002380 \\ 0.002380 & 0.005759 \end{bmatrix}.$$

In computing the elements of the covariance matrix the biased form, presented in Chapter 2, is used in which T appears in the denominator instead of $T - 1$ in the sample variance matrix. To compute the minimum variance portfolio using the data on Microsoft and Walmart, the weights in equation (3.35) are estimated by replacing the population parameters by their sample quantities. The minimum variance weights are

$$\begin{aligned} \widehat{w}_1 &= \frac{\widehat{\sigma}_2^2 - \widehat{\sigma}_{12}}{\widehat{\sigma}_1^2 + \widehat{\sigma}_2^2 - 2\widehat{\sigma}_{12}} \\ &= \frac{0.005759 - 0.002380}{0.011333 + 0.005759 - 2 \times 0.002380} = 0.274, \\ \widehat{w}_2 &= 1 - \widehat{w}_1 = 1 - 0.274 = 0.726. \end{aligned} \qquad (3.36)$$

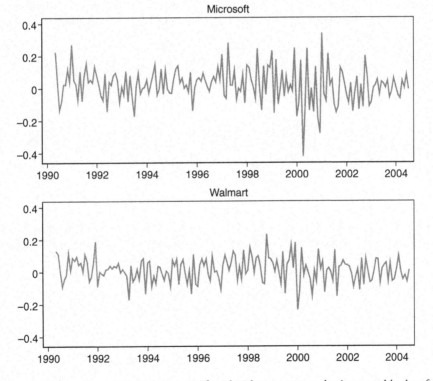

FIGURE 3.6 The returns to US stocks Microsoft and Walmart computed using monthly data for the period April 1990 to July 2004.

Thus, the optimal portfolio to minimize risk is to allocate 0.274 of the investor's wealth to Microsoft and 0.726 to Walmart.

The average return on the minimum variance portfolio is estimated as

$$\widehat{\mu}_p = \widehat{w}_1 \widehat{\mu}_1 + \widehat{w}_2 \widehat{\mu}_2 = 0.274 \times 0.020877 + 0.726 \times 0.013496 = 0.015519. \qquad (3.37)$$

An estimate of the risk of the minimum variance portfolio is

$$\begin{aligned}
\widehat{\sigma}_p^2 &= \widehat{w}_1^2 \widehat{\sigma}_1^2 + (1 - \widehat{w}_1)^2 \widehat{\sigma}_2^2 + 2\widehat{w}_1(1 - \widehat{w}_1)\widehat{\sigma}_{12} \\
&= 0.274^2 \times 0.011333 + (1 - 0.274)^2 \times 0.005759 \\
&\quad + 2 \times 0.274 \times (1 - 0.274) \times 0.002380 \\
&= 0.004833. \qquad\qquad\qquad\qquad\qquad\qquad\qquad\qquad\qquad (3.38)
\end{aligned}$$

Comparing this estimate to the individual risks on Microsoft and Walmart shows that the risk on the portfolio is indeed reduced.

To explore the relationship between the linear regression model in equation (3.2) and the minimum variance portfolio, consider the following regression equation

$$r_{2t} = \alpha + \beta(r_{2t} - r_{1t}) + u_t,$$

where $y_t = r_{2t}$ is the dependent variable corresponding to the return on Walmart, and the explanatory variable is defined as $x_t = r_{2t} - r_{1t}$, the excess return between Microsoft and Walmart. Using the log returns data on Microsoft and Walmart in Figure 3.6, the sample statistics of y_t and x_t are

$$\bar{y} = 0.013496, \quad \bar{x} = -0.007380, \quad \widehat{\sigma}_x^2 = 0.012331, \quad \widehat{\sigma}_{yx} = 0.003379.$$

The least squares parameter estimates are

$$\widehat{\beta} = \frac{\widehat{\sigma}_{yx}}{\widehat{\sigma}_{x^2}} = \frac{0.003379}{0.012331} = 0.274,$$

$$\widehat{\alpha} = \bar{y} - \widehat{\beta}\bar{x} = 0.013496 - 0.274 \times (-0.007380) = 0.015519.$$

A comparison of the slope parameter estimate of $\widehat{\beta} = 0.274$ and the estimate of the minimum variance weight on Microsoft based on the finance calculations in equation (3.36) shows that they are equal. In addition, the estimate of the intercept $\widehat{\alpha} = 0.015519$ also equals the estimate of the average return on the portfolio given in equation (3.37).

The standard error of the estimated regression equation is $\widehat{\sigma}_u = 0.069931$, while the variance is $\widehat{\sigma}_u^2 = 0.069931^2 = 4.8903 \times 10^{-3}$. This value is similar to the estimate of the risk of the minimum variance portfolio given in equation (3.38), but it is not the same. The difference between the two risk estimates is simply due to the degrees of freedom correction used to compute $\widehat{\sigma}_u^2$. Readjusting this estimate as

$$\frac{T-2}{T}\widehat{\sigma}_u^2 = \frac{171-2}{171} \times 0.069931^2 = 0.004833,$$

now yields exactly the same value reported using the minimum variance calculations.

3.7 EVENT ANALYSIS

Event analysis is widely used in empirical finance to model the effects of qualitative changes on financial variables arising from a discrete event. Typical events that are relevant in finance arise from announcements such as the change in a company's CEO, an antitrust decision, a monetary policy announcement, or dramatic news events. In undertaking an event study the overall event is decomposed into three sub-events: the part that is anticipated by the market, the part that occurs at the time of the event, and the part that happens after the event has occurred.

To model qualitative effects in an event analysis an indicator variable, I_t, is defined, which takes the value 1 if the event occurs at a point in time t and 0 for a non-occurrence of the event. This indicator variable is also commonly referred to as a dummy variable. A typical event study involves specifying a regression equation based on some given model that represents *normal* market returns, and then modifying this equation to account for designated events through the inclusion of indicator variables. The modifications involve the inclusion of separate dummy variables at each point in time over the event window to capture the abnormal returns, whether these may be positive or negative. The parameter on a particular dummy measures the *abnormal* return associated with that event, representing the return over and above the normal return.

In December of 2005, Lee Raymond retired as the CEO of Exxon receiving, at the time, the largest retirement package ever recorded of around \$400 million. To determine how the market viewed this event, an event study is performed on the returns on Exxon around the time the announcement is made. A multiple regression model with a 5-month event window is specified as

$$r_t = \underbrace{\beta_0 + \beta_1 r_{mt}}_{\text{Normal return}}$$

$$\underbrace{+ \delta_{-2} I_{Oct,t} + \delta_{-1} I_{Nov,t} + \delta_0 I_{Dec,t} + \delta_1 I_{Jan,t} + \delta_2 I_{Feb,t}}_{\text{Abnormal return}} + u_t. \tag{3.39}$$

The first term in this equation is known as the market model. The indicator variables are defined around the event in December of 2005 as

$$\text{Pre-event:} \quad I_{Oct,t} = \begin{cases} 1 : \text{Oct. 2005} \\ 0 : \text{Otherwise} \end{cases} \quad I_{Nov,t} = \begin{cases} 1 : \text{Nov. 2005} \\ 0 : \text{Otherwise} \end{cases},$$

$$\text{Actual event:} \quad I_{Dec,t} = \begin{cases} 1 : \text{Dec. 2005} \\ 0 : \text{Otherwise} \end{cases},$$

$$\text{Post-event:} \quad I_{Jan,t} = \begin{cases} 1 : \text{Jan. 2006} \\ 0 : \text{Otherwise} \end{cases}, \quad I_{Feb,t} = \begin{cases} 1 : \text{Feb. 2006} \\ 0 : \text{Otherwise} \end{cases}.$$

The abnormal return in the month of the announcement is δ_0; in the months prior to the announcement, the abnormal returns are given by δ_{-2} and δ_{-1}; and for the months after the announcement they are given by δ_1 and δ_2.

Using returns on Exxon (r_t) and the market (r_{mt}), the multiple regression model in equation (3.39) is estimated from January 1970 to February 2006. As the sample period stops in February 2006 the event window corresponds to the last 5 sample observations. The estimated model with standard errors in parentheses is

$$r_t = \underset{(0.002)}{0.009} + \underset{(0.044)}{0.651}\, r_{mt} - \underset{(0.041)}{0.121}\, I_{Oct,t} + \underset{(0.041)}{0.007}\, I_{Nov,t}$$
$$- \underset{(0.041)}{0.041}\, I_{Dec,t} + \underset{(0.041)}{0.086}\, I_{Jan,t} - \underset{(0.041)}{0.059}\, I_{Feb,t} + \widehat{u}_t.$$

Inspection of the parameter estimates and standard errors suggests that the market not only anticipated the event in December 2005 two months earlier where the parameter estimate on the October indicator variable is statistically significant, but that it viewed the retirement package unfavorably with the return on Exxon falling by 0.121 in October. This result is also supported by the fact that on the day that the announcement is made in December of 2005, the estimated return of −0.041 is also negative, although not statistically significant. However, there appears to be a market correction in the month following the announcement with a statistically significant increase in the return on Exxon of 0.086 in January of 2006.

The net effect of the retirement package on the market is negative with the total abnormal return equaling

$$\text{Total} = -0.121 + 0.007 - 0.041 + 0.086 - 0.059 = -0.128.$$

The significance of this value is determined by performing a joint test of the hypothesis that the parameters on the 5 event indicator variables in equation (3.39) are zero. The null and alternative hypotheses are

$$H_0 : \delta_{-2} = \delta_{-1} = \delta_0 = \delta_1 = \delta_2 = 0 \qquad \text{[Normal returns]}$$
$$H_1 : \text{at least one restriction is not valid} \quad \text{[Abnormal returns]}.$$

Under the null hypothesis that $\delta_{-2} = \delta_{-1} = \delta_0 = \delta_1 = \delta_2 = 0$, the regression model in equation (3.39) reduces to the market model. Using a chi square test the statistic is 16.399. As there are 5 restrictions being tested this statistic has a p value of 0.0058. These findings suggest that the net effect of the retirement package was to dampen the returns on Exxon and that the dampening effect was statistically significant.

3.8 EXERCISES

The data required for the exercises are available for download as `EViews` workfiles (*.wf1), `Stata` datafiles (*.dta), comma delimited text files (*.csv), and as `Excel` spreadsheets (*.xlsx).

1. The CAPM

capm.*

The data are monthly observations for the period April 1990 to July 2004 on the equity prices of Exxon, General Electric, IBM, Microsoft, and Walmart, together with the price of Gold, the S&P 500 index, and a short-term interest rate.

(a) Compute the monthly excess returns on Exxon, General Electric, Gold, IBM, Microsoft, and Walmart. Be particularly careful when computing the correct risk-free rate to use. [*Hint: the variable* TBILL *is quoted as an annual rate.*]

(b) Letting $r_{it} - r_{ft}$ represent the excess return on asset i and $r_{mt} - r_{ft}$ represent the excess return on the market, estimate the CAPM

$$r_{it} - r_{ft} = \alpha + \beta(r_{mt} - r_{ft}) + u_t,$$

for each asset where u_t is a disturbance term. Interpret the estimated β- and α-risks.

(c) For each asset, test the restrictions $\alpha = 0$ and $\beta = 1$ individually and jointly. Interpret the results of these tests.

2. Fama–French Three Factor Model

> fama_french.*

The data set contains the monthly Fama–French data for market, risk-free, size, book-to-market, and momentum factors for the period January 1927 to December 2013. The return on the market is constructed as the value-weighted return of all CRSP firms incorporated in the United States and listed on the NYSE, AMEX, or NASDAQ; and the risk-free rate is the 1-month US Treasury Bill rate. The file also contains the monthly returns to 25 US portfolios formed by sorting on size and book-to-market. The data are from Ken French's webpage, http://mba.tuck .dartmouth.edu/pages/faculty/ken.french/.

(a) Estimate the Fama–French three factor model

$$r_{it} - r_{ft} = \alpha + \beta_1 \text{EMKT}_t + \beta_2 \text{SMB}_t + \beta_3 \text{HML}_t + u_t,$$

for each of the 25 portfolios where EMKT_t is the excess return on the market, SMB_t is the size factor, HML_t is the value factor, and u_t is a disturbance term. Interpret the parameter estimates on all three risk factors.

(b) Repeat part (a) for the 1-factor CAPM by imposing the restrictions $\beta_2 = \beta_3 = 0$. Interpret the estimated β-risk and compare with the estimates obtained in part (a).

(c) Perform a joint test of the size (SMB) and value (HML) risk factors in explaining excess returns in each portfolio.

3. Present Value Model

> pv.*

The data file contains monthly US data on equity prices, P_t, and dividend payments, D_t, for the period January 1871 to September 2016.

(a) Estimate the present value model

$$p_t = \alpha + \beta d_t + u_t,$$

where $p_t = \log P_t$, $d_t = \log D_t$, and u_t is a disturbance term.

(b) Examine the properties of the estimated model by performing the following diagnostic tests.

(i) Plot the ordinary least squares residuals and interpret their time series patterns.

(ii) Test for autocorrelation of orders 1 to 6.

(iii) Test for ARCH of orders 1 to 2.

(iv) Test for normality.

(c) Estimate the implied discount factor used to compute the present value of the dividend stream.

(d) Test the restriction $\beta = 1$ and interpret the result. If the restriction is satisfied re-estimate the present value model subject to this restriction and redo part (c).

4. Fisher Hypothesis

> fisher.*

The data file contains US quarterly data for the period September 1954 to December 2007 on the annualized nominal interest rate expressed as a percentage, r_t, and the price level, P_t. The Fisher hypothesis states that r_t fully reflects long-run movements in expected inflation, $E(\pi_t)$.

(a) To examine the Fisher hypothesis estimate the following linear regression

$$r_t = \alpha + \beta \pi_t + u_t,$$

where actual inflation is used as a proxy for expected inflation, and u_t is a disturbance term. Compute inflation as an annual percentage measure.

(b) Examine the properties of the estimated model by performing the following diagnostic tests.

(i) Plot the ordinary least squares residuals and interpret their time series patterns.

(ii) Test for autocorrelation of orders 1 to 4.

(iii) Test for ARCH of orders 1 to 2.

(iv) Test for normality.

(c) If the Fisher hypothesis holds, $\beta = 1$. Test this restriction and interpret the result. If the restriction is satisfied, re-estimate the model subject to this restriction and use the estimated model to generate an estimate of the real (ex post) interest rate $i_t = r_t - \pi_t$.

5. Measuring Portfolio Performance

> fama_french.*

The data set contains the monthly Fama–French data for market, risk-free, size, book-to-market, and momentum factors for the period January 1927 to December 2013. The file also contains the monthly returns to 10 US industry portfolios,

namely, Nondurables, Durables, Manufacturing, Energy, Technology, Telecommunications, Retail/Wholesale, Health, Utilities, and Other. The data are from Ken
French's webpage, http://mba.tuck.dartmouth.edu/pages/faculty/ken.french/.

(a) For each of the 10 industry portfolios, estimate the Fama–French four-factor
model

$$r_{it} - r_{ft} = \alpha + \beta_1 \text{EMKT}_t + \beta_2 \text{SMB}_t + \beta_3 \text{HML}_t + \beta_4 \text{MOM}_t + u_t,$$

where EMKT_t is the excess return on the market, SMB_t is the size risk factor,
HML_t is the value factor, MOM_t is the momentum factor, and u_t is a disturbance
term. Interpret the parameter estimates on all four risk factors.

(b) If μ_p is the expected return on the portfolio, μ_m is the expected return on
the market, r_f is the risk-free rate, σ_p is the risk of a portfolio, and β is the
β-risk obtained from the single-factor CAPM, estimate the following portfolio
performance measures for each of the 10 industry portfolios

$$\text{Sharpe ratio:} \quad \mathcal{S} = \frac{\mu_p - r_f}{\sigma_p}$$

$$\text{Treynor index:} \quad \mathcal{T} = \frac{\mu_p - r_f}{\beta}$$

$$\text{Jensen's alpha:} \quad \alpha = \mu_p - r_f - \beta(\mu_m - r_f).$$

Discuss the rankings of the portfolios based on each measure.

6. **Minimum Variance Portfolios**

> capm.*

The data are monthly observations for the period April 1990 to July 2004 on the
equity prices of Exxon, General Electric, IBM, Microsoft, and Walmart, together
with the price of Gold, the S&P 500 index, and a short-term interest rate.

(a) Consider the minimum variance portfolio regression model consisting of
equity stocks in GE and Walmart

$$r_{2t} = \alpha + \beta(r_{2t} - r_{1t}) + u_t,$$

where r_{1t} is the log return on GE, r_{2t} is the log return on Walmart, and u_t is a
disturbance term. Assume the mean and variance on the ith asset are μ_i and σ_i^2
with covariance σ_{12}.

(i) Show that the slope parameter satisfies

$$\beta = \frac{\text{cov}(y_t, x_t)}{\text{var}(x_t)} = \frac{\sigma_2^2 - \sigma_{12}}{\sigma_1^2 + \sigma_2^2 - 2\sigma_{12}},$$

which is the weight on GE in a minimum variance portfolio given by w_1.

(ii) Letting w_1 and w_2 represent the weights attached to the two stocks in the portfolio, show that the intercept parameter satisfies

$$\alpha = w_1\mu_1 + (1 - w_1)\mu_2 = \mu_p,$$

which is the expected return on the minimum variance portfolio.

(b) Estimate the minimum variance portfolio regression model in part (a). Interpret the parameter estimates and the variance of the least squares residuals, without any degrees of freedom adjustment.

(c) Using the results in part (b), do the following tasks.

   (i) Construct a test of an equal weighted portfolio, $w_1 = w_2 = 0.5$.
   (ii) Construct a test of portfolio diversification.

(d) Repeat parts (b) and (c) for the technology stocks, IBM and Microsoft.
(e) Repeat parts (b) and (c) for Exxon and Gold.

7. **Microsoft and the Dot-Com Crisis**

> capm.*

The data are monthly observations for the period April 1990 to July 2004 on the equity prices of Exxon, General Electric, IBM, Microsoft, and Walmart, together with the price of Gold, the S&P 500 index, and a short-term interest rate. The dot-com crash began on 10 March 2000 which led to very large falls in the equity value of Microsoft and technology stocks in general.

(a) Plot the price and log returns of Microsoft and identify the large movements in its share value during the period of the dot-com crisis.
(b) Estimate the CAPM model for Microsoft

$$r_{it} - r_{ft} = \alpha + \beta(r_{mt} - r_{ft}) + u_t,$$

in which r_{ft} and r_{mt} are the risk free and market returns, respectively. Plot the residuals and perform the Jarque-Bera test of normality.

(c) To capture the effects of the dot-com crisis, construct 11 indicator variables for each month of the crisis beginning with March 2000 and ending in January 2001

$$I_{1t} = \begin{cases} 1 : \text{Mar. 2000} \\ 0 : \text{Otherwise} \end{cases}, \quad I_{2t} = \begin{cases} 1 : \text{Apr. 2000} \\ 0 : \text{Otherwise} \end{cases}, \cdots, \quad I_{11t} = \begin{cases} 1 : \text{Jan. 2001} \\ 0 : \text{Otherwise} \end{cases}.$$

The last date is chosen as this corresponds to the time of the positive correction in Microsoft shares. Now estimate the augmented CAPM regression

$$r_{it} - r_{ft} = \alpha + \beta_1(r_{mt} - r_{ft}) + \sum_{j=1}^{11} \beta_{j+1} I_{jt} + u_t.$$

(i) Plot the residuals and redo the Jarque-Bera test of normality. Compare the result of this test with results of the test in part (b) based on the CAPM residuals.

(ii) Interpret the parameter estimates of the dummy variables.

(iii) Perform a joint test of the effects of the dot-com crisis on Microsoft by testing the restrictions $\beta_2 = \beta_3 = \cdots = \beta_{12}$.

8. **The Retirement of Lee Raymond as the CEO of Exxon**

---
raymond.*

The data are monthly observations on the equity price of EXXON together with the S&P 500 index and a short-term interest rate for the period January 1970 to March 2010. In December of 2005, Lee Raymond retired as the CEO of Exxon receiving the largest retirement package ever recorded of around $400 million. How did the markets view this event?

(a) Estimate the market model for Exxon for the sub-period from January 1970 to September 2005

$$r_t = \alpha + \beta r_{mt} + u_t,$$

where r_t is the log return on Exxon and r_{mt} is the market log return computed from the S&P 500 and u_t is a disturbance term. Compute the abnormal returns over the 5-month event window from October 2005 to February 2006 by substituting in the actual values of r_{mt} over this period into the estimated model.

(b) Estimate the augmented market model

$$r_t = \alpha + \beta_1 r_{mt} + \sum_{j=1}^{5} \beta_{j+1} I_{jt} + u_t,$$

over the extended sample period from January 1970 to February 2006, where the 5 indicator variables are defined as

$$I_{1t} = \begin{cases} 1: \text{Oct. 2005} \\ 0: \text{Otherwise} \end{cases}, \quad I_{2t} = \begin{cases} 1: \text{Nov. 2005} \\ 0: \text{Otherwise} \end{cases}, \cdots, \quad I_{5t} = \begin{cases} 1: \text{Feb. 2006} \\ 0: \text{Otherwise} \end{cases}.$$

Compare the abnormal returns over the event window with the estimates in part (a).

9. **Properties of Ordinary Least Squares for Dependent Data**

The minimum variance portfolio regression in Section 3.6 does not satisfy the assumption $E(x_t u_t) = 0$ given in equation (3.5) as the dependent variable y_t is also present in the definition of the explanatory variable x_t. To investigate the sampling properties of the least squares estimator in this situation, assume that the returns on two assets, r_{1t} and r_{2t}, are summarized in terms of the following bivariate normal distribution

$$\begin{bmatrix} r_{1t} \\ r_{2t} \end{bmatrix} \sim N\left(\begin{bmatrix} 0.020877 \\ 0.013496 \end{bmatrix}, \begin{bmatrix} 0.011333 & 0.002380 \\ 0.002380 & 0.005759 \end{bmatrix}\right).$$

The minimum variance portfolio regression is defined as

$$y_t = \alpha + \beta x_t + u_t,$$

where $y_t = r_{2t}$, and $x_t = r_{2t} - r_{1t}$. From the properties of the minimum variance portfolio the true population parameter values are

$$\beta = \frac{\sigma_2^2 - \sigma_{12}}{\sigma_1^2 + \sigma_2^2 - 2\sigma_{12}} = \frac{0.005759 - 0.002380}{0.011333 + 0.005759 - 2 \times 0.002380} = 0.274$$

$$\alpha = w_1\mu_1 + (1 - w_1)\mu_2 = 0.274 \times 0.020877 + 0.726 \times 0.013496 = 0.0155$$

$$\sigma_u^2 = 0.004833$$

$$\sigma_x^2 = 0.012331.$$

(a) Using simulated data, estimate the slope coefficient β in the minimum variance portfolio regression model for a sample of size $T = 20$. Repeat this estimation 1000 times, plot the histogram of the resultant estimates, and show that even in small samples the estimator $\widehat{\beta}$ is well-centered on the population parameter.

(b) Demonstrate the efficiency of the least squares estimators of the parameters α and β by allowing the sample to grow from $T = 10$ to $T = 10000$ in increments of 1 observation. For each sample size compute $\widehat{\alpha}$ and $\widehat{\beta}$, plot the resultant sequences of estimates, and comment on the results.

(c) Compute and plot the asymptotic distribution of $(\widehat{\beta} - \beta)/\text{se}(\widehat{\beta})$ where the standard error is $\text{se}(\widehat{\beta}) = \sigma_u^2/T\sigma_x^2$. Compare the asymptotic distribution with the simulated distribution of $\widehat{\beta}$ constructed from samples of size $T = \{20, 50, 500, 1000\}$.

CHAPTER 4

Stationary Dynamics for Financial Time Series

A feature of the linear regression model discussed in Chapter 3 is that all the variables that appear in the model are designated as being measured at the same point in time. To allow financial variables to adjust to shocks over time this model is now extended to incorporate dynamic effects. These effects enable the impact of shocks and transitions in a model to take place over a period of time rather than instantaneously. A primary class of dynamic models involves only a single variable and is called univariate or scalar. In a scalar dynamic model, a single dependent financial variable is explained using its own past history as well as lags of other relevant financial variables.

In financial applications, single dependent variable models are often extended to multivariate specifications in which several financial variables are jointly determined and modeled together. Such models are heavily used in central banks, treasuries, international agencies, and the financial industry. An important characteristic of the multivariate class of models investigated in this chapter is that each variable in the system is expressed as a linear function of its own lags as well as the lags of all of the other variables in the system. This type of model is known as a vector autoregression (VAR) and was first explored systematically in a pioneering article by Mann and Wald (1943). The model has the distinguishing feature that each equation has the same set of explanatory variables, a feature that brings several advantages in practical implementation. Structural VAR models were also considered in the original article of Mann and Wald. These models allow for contemporaneous interactive effects among the variables and have received much subsequent attention in recent years from researchers investigating the impact of policy changes on economic activity.

4.1 STATIONARITY

The models in this chapter, which use standard linear regression techniques, require that the variables involved satisfy a simplifying condition known as stationarity. Stationarity requires that all joint distributions of the time series remain unchanged when shifted over time. When this property is specialized to the first two moments of the distribution, a time series is said to be covariance stationary so that the mean, variance, and autocovariances all remain invariant to the time periods in which they are calculated. These conditions fail when the mean, variance, or autocovariances become time dependent. In particular, when the mean has a time trend or when the variance is time varying, then the time series has a nonstationary character. Such series are especially important in financial econometrics because many financial variables such as asset prices and interest rates have means and variances that exhibit changes over time. For now, a simple illustration will indicate the central idea. Consider Figures 4.1 and 4.2, respectively, which show the daily S&P 500 index and associated log returns for the period January 1871 to September 2016.

Assume that an observer takes a snapshot of the two series over two different decades during this historical period (shown as lightly shaded regions in the Figures 4.1 and 4.2): The first snapshot shows the trajectory of the series for the decade of the 1960s and the second shows the trajectory over 2000–2010. It is clear in Figure 4.1 that the pattern of behavior of the series is completely different in these two decades. What the observer sees in 1960–1970 looks quite unlike what happens over 2000–2010. The situation is different for the log returns plotted in Figure 4.2. Casual inspection suggests that the behavior in the two shaded areas is remarkably similar given the long intervening time span of 30 years. Over both decades 1960–1970 and 2000–2010 the data fluctuate about the same level (which is approximately zero). The main difference is that during 2000–2010 the returns show evidence of greater variation largely because of the financial

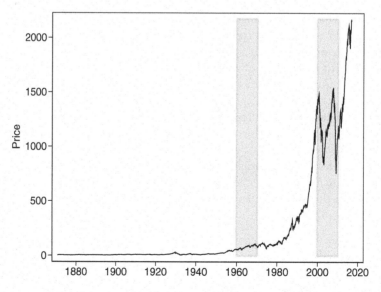

FIGURE 4.1 Snapshots of the time series of the S&P 500 index comprising monthly observations for the period January 1871 to September 2016.

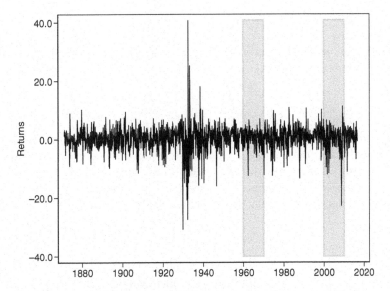

FIGURE 4.2 Snapshots of the time series of log returns to the S&P 500 index computed from monthly observations for the period January 1871 to September 2016.

crisis of 2008–2009, with evidence of more extreme outliers than during 1960–1970. So there are differences between the periods even for returns. But the dominating difference occurs in prices, where the random wandering and fluctuating behavior of the S&P 500 distinguishes the 2000–2010 period from 1960–1970.

For present purposes, it will be assumed that the series we deal with exhibit stationary behavior over time, closer in form to that of the returns data shown in Figure 4.2 than the levels data shown in Figure 4.1. This assumption enhances the usefulness of historical data in estimating relationships, interpreting findings, and forecasting future behavior by extrapolating from the past. Statistical corroboration of supporting assumptions like stationarity or specific forms of nonstationarity is important in empirical work because the validity of the methods used to make inferences often depends on these assumptions. In practical work, evidence for stationarity can be assessed using some of the techniques described in Chapter 5.

4.2 UNIVARIATE TIME SERIES MODELS

This section considers dynamic models for a single stationary dependent variable. The dynamics enter the model either through the lags of the dependent variable, or through the lags of the disturbances, or both. This type of model has been extensively studied and the discussion here will be brief and selective. Thorough theoretical treatments may be found in Brockwell and Davis (1991) or Hamilton (1994). A less theoretical treatment with more emphasis on implementation is in Martin, Hurn, and Harris (2013).

4.2.1 Autoregressive Models

Specification

A linear dynamic model for the dependent variable, y_t, in which movements in y_t are explained in terms of its own lags y_{t-j} with the longest lag included being the pth lag, is given by

$$y_t = \phi_0 + \phi_1 y_{t-1} + \phi_2 y_{t-2} + \cdots + \phi_p y_{t-p} + u_t, \qquad u_t \sim iid\,(0, \sigma_u^2), \qquad (4.1)$$

in which $\phi_0, \phi_1, \cdots, \phi_p$ are unknown parameters. Instead of assuming that the disturbance term is normally distributed, drawing on the discussion of the previous section concerning the importance of stationarity, the assumption is instead that u_t is independently and identically distributed, abbreviated as iid. Equation (4.1) is referred to as an autoregressive model with p lags, or simply an AR(p). An AR(1) model is then given by

$$y_t = \phi_0 + \phi_1 y_{t-1} + u_t, \qquad u_t \sim iid\,(0, \sigma_u^2). \qquad (4.2)$$

If the stability condition, $|\phi_1| < 1$, is satisfied and the initial (start-up) condition of y_t is set to ensure a common mean and variance (which will be so if the initial condition is in the infinite past) then y_t is stationary. This condition is discussed in more detail in Chapter 5.

The unconditional mean and variance of an AR(1) model are easily derived. Applying the unconditional expectations operator to both sides of equation (4.2) gives

$$E(y_t) = E(\phi_0 + \phi_1 y_{t-1} + u_t) = \phi_0 + \phi_1 E(y_{t-1}).$$

One of the important implications of stationarity is that the unconditional expectations are the same at each point in time, so that $E(y_t) = E(y_{t-1})$. Applying this condition and rearranging gives

$$E(y_t) = \frac{\phi_0}{1 - \phi_1}.$$

The unconditional variance is defined as

$$\mathrm{var}(y_t) = \gamma_0 = E\{[y_t - E(y_t)]^2\}.$$

Recognizing that

$$y_t - E(y_t) = \phi_0 + \phi_1 y_{t-1} + u_t - \phi_0 - \phi_1 E(y_{t-1}) = \phi_1 [y_t - E(y_{t-1})] + u_t,$$

and then squaring both sides and taking unconditional expectations gives

$$E\{[y_t - E(y_t)]^2\} = \phi_1^2 E\{[y_{t-1} - E(y_{t-1})]^2\} + E(u_t^2) + 2 E\{[y_{t-1} - E(y_{t-1})]u_t\}$$
$$= \phi_1^2 E\{[y_{t-1} - E(y_{t-1})]^2\} + E(u_t^2),$$

using the property that $E\{[y_{t-1} - E(y_{t-1})]u_t\} = 0$. Moreover, because

$$\gamma_0 = E\{[y_t - E(y_t)]^2\} = E\{[y_{t-1} - E(y_{t-1})]^2\}$$

represents the variance of y_t, it follows that

$$\gamma_0 = \phi_1^2 \gamma_0 + \sigma_u^2,$$

and upon rearrangement,

$$\gamma_0 = \frac{\sigma_u^2}{1 - \phi_1^2}.$$

Estimation

The unknown parameters $\theta = \{\phi_0, \phi_1, \cdots, \phi_p, \sigma_u^2\}$ of the AR(p) model in equation (4.1) are estimated by least squares. The residual sum of squares function for the AR(p) model is

$$S = \sum_{t=p+1}^{T} u_t^2 = \sum_{t=p+1}^{T} (y_t - \phi_0 - \phi_1 y_{t-1} - \phi_2 y_{t-2} - \cdots - \phi_p y_{t-p})^2, \qquad (4.3)$$

where the sample sum of squares begins at $t = p + 1$, as p observations are lost because of the inclusion of p lags in the model. The effective sample size in estimation is therefore $T - p$ rather than T. This criterion function equation (4.3) is differentiated with respect to the parameters $\{\phi_0, \phi_1, \cdots, \phi_p\}$ yielding $p + 1$ first-order conditions. Setting these derivatives to zero and rearranging gives the least squares estimators of the parameters. That is, estimation of the AR(p) model simply involves treating the lagged variables of y_t as regressors, so estimation amounts to regressing y_t on a constant and its p lags.

After estimating the parameters the least squares residuals are computed as

$$\widehat{u}_t = y_t - \widehat{\phi}_0 - \widehat{\phi}_1 y_{t-1} - \widehat{\phi}_2 y_{t-2} - \cdots - \widehat{\phi}_p y_{t-p}, \qquad (4.4)$$

which are used to compute the residual variance

$$\widehat{\sigma}_u^2 = \frac{1}{T - p - 1} \sum_{t=p+1}^{T} \widehat{u}_t^2. \qquad (4.5)$$

4.2.2 Moving Average Models

Specification

An alternative way to introduce dynamics into univariate models is to allow for time dependence in the dependent variable y_t to be determined via the disturbance term u_t. The specification of the model then has the form

$$y_t = \psi_0 + u_t + \psi_1 u_{t-1} + \psi_2 u_{t-2} + \cdots + \psi_q u_{t-q}, \qquad u_t \sim iid\,(0, \sigma_u^2), \qquad (4.6)$$

where $\psi_0, \psi_1, \cdots, \psi_q$ are unknown parameters. Since the disturbance term is formulated as a moving weighted sum of current and past disturbances with ψ_i representing the weights, this model is referred to as a moving average model with q lags, or more simply as MA(q). An MA(1) model is then given by

$$y_t = \psi_0 + u_t + \psi_1 u_{t-1}, \quad u_t \sim iid\,(0, \sigma_u^2), \qquad (4.7)$$

where the stability condition $|\psi_1| \leq 1$ is often imposed.

Applying the unconditional expectations operator to both sides of equation (4.7) gives the unconditional mean of the MA(1) process

$$E(y_t) = E(\psi_0 + u_t + \psi_1 u_{t-1}) = \psi_0 + E(u_t) + \psi_1 E(u_{t-1}) = \psi_0,$$

where the property $E(u_t) = E(u_{t-1}) = 0$ has been used. Using the result that $E(u_t u_{t-1}) = 0$ by virtue of the *iid* assumption on u_t, the unconditional variance is

$$\gamma_0 = E\{[y_t - E(y_t)]^2\} = E[(u_t + \psi_1 u_{t-1})^2] = \sigma_u^2(1 + \psi_1^2).$$

Estimation

Unlike the AR(p) model where estimation of the parameters is based on ordinary least squares, the unknown parameters $\theta = \{\psi_0, \psi_1, \cdots, \psi_q, \sigma_u^2\}$ of the MA(q) model in equation (4.6) are estimated by nonlinear methods. The residual sum of squares function for the MA(q) model is

$$S = \sum_{t=q+1}^{T} u_t^2 = \sum_{t=q+1}^{T} (y_t - \psi_0 - \psi_1 u_{t-1} - \psi_2 u_{t-2} - \cdots - \psi_q u_{t-q})^2, \qquad (4.8)$$

where the sample sum of squares begins at $t = q + 1$, as q observations are lost because the disturbances $u_q, u_{q-1}, \cdots, u_1$ are (unobserved) initializations. The effective sample size for estimating the parameters is therefore $T - q$.

The residual sum of squares function is differentiated with respect to the parameters $\{\psi_0, \psi_1, \cdots, \psi_p\}$ yielding $q + 1$ first-order conditions. Numerical complications in estimating the MA(q) model's parameters arise in this step, as the unknown parameters appear directly in equation (4.8) as well as indirectly through the lagged disturbance terms u_{t-1} to u_{t-q}. For example, the derivative with respect to the parameter ψ_i is

$$\frac{\partial S}{\partial \psi_i} = 2 \sum_{t=q+1}^{T} u_t \left(-u_{t-i} - \psi_1 \frac{\partial u_{t-1}}{\partial \psi_i} - \psi_2 \frac{\partial u_{t-2}}{\partial \psi_i} - \cdots - \psi_q \frac{\partial u_{t-q}}{\partial \psi_i} \right).$$

The existence of this indirect channel means that it is now no longer possible to rearrange the first-order conditions to derive direct analytical solutions of the unknown parameters as was the case with the AR model. Even though no analytical solution is available to compute the parameter estimates, a numerical solution is nonetheless available by using an iterative algorithm. A general introduction to these algorithms is given in Appendix D. An alternative estimation strategy is developed in the exercises that uses a two-step procedure that does not require an iterative solution.

Having estimated the parameters by numerical methods, the nonlinear least squares residuals are computed recursively as follows

$$\widehat{u}_t = y_t - \widehat{\psi}_0 - \widehat{\psi}_1 \widehat{u}_{t-1} - \widehat{\psi}_2 \widehat{u}_{t-2} - \cdots - \widehat{\psi}_p \widehat{u}_{t-q}, \qquad (4.9)$$

and these residuals may be used to compute the residual variance, $\widehat{\sigma}_u^2$, as in equation (4.5), with p replaced by q and with initial conditions $u_q = \cdots = u_1 = 0$ set to the mean value $E(u_t) = 0$.

4.2.3 Autoregressive Moving-Average Models

Specification

Autoregressive and moving average forms may be combined to yield a model containing both components called an autoregressive moving-average (ARMA) model

$$y_t = \phi_0 + \phi_1 y_{t-1} + \cdots + \phi_p y_{t-p} + u_t + \psi_1 u_{t-1} + \cdots + \psi_q u_{t-q}, \qquad u_t \sim iid\,(0, \sigma_u^2).$$

This model has p autoregressive lags and q moving average lags and is therefore denoted as ARMA(p,q). In the case of an ARMA(1,1) model

$$y_t = \phi_0 + \phi_1 y_{t-1} + u_t + \psi_1 u_{t-1}, \qquad u_t \sim iid\,(0, \sigma_u^2), \qquad (4.10)$$

the unconditional mean and variance are, respectively,

$$\mathrm{E}(y_t) = \frac{\phi_0}{1 - \phi_1}, \qquad \gamma_0 = \frac{1 + \psi_1^2 + 2\phi_1\psi_1}{1 - \phi_1^2}\sigma_u^2.$$

As with the AR and MA models, the first two moments of the ARMA model are not functions of time.

Estimation

In view of its MA component, ARMA models also require numerical methods such as nonlinear or iterative least squares procedures to estimate the unknown parameters. In the case of the ARMA(1,1) model the residual sum of squares function is

$$S = \sum_{t=2}^{T} u_t^2 = \sum_{t=2}^{T} (y_t - \phi_0 - \phi_1 y_{t-1} - \psi_1 u_{t-1})^2, \qquad (4.11)$$

where the sample begins at $t = 2$ as a result of the presence of the lagged dependent variable y_{t-1} and the lagged disturbance u_{t-1}. Differentiating with respect to the unknown parameters gives

$$\frac{\partial S}{\partial \phi_0} = 2 \sum_{t=2}^{T} u_t \left(-1 - \psi_1 \frac{\partial u_{t-1}}{\partial \phi_0} \right)$$

$$\frac{\partial S}{\partial \phi_1} = 2 \sum_{t=2}^{T} u_t \left(-y_{t-1} - \psi_1 \frac{\partial u_{t-1}}{\partial \phi_1} \right)$$

$$\frac{\partial S}{\partial \psi_1} = 2 \sum_{t=2}^{T} u_t \left(-u_{t-1} - \psi_1 \frac{\partial u_{t-1}}{\partial \psi_1} \right).$$

This is a nonlinear set of equations in the unknown parameters that requires an iterative solution. As with the AR(p) and MA(q) models, once the parameter estimates are obtained the least squares residuals $\widehat{u}_t$ are computed as well as the residual variance, $\widehat{\sigma}_u^2$, based on equation (4.5) with the appropriate correction for lost observations.

4.2.4 Regression Models with Dynamics

As already noted, the regression models discussed in Chapter 3 have the property that dependent and explanatory variables are all measured concurrently at the same time t.

To allow for dynamic effects, regression models may be combined with the ARMA class of models. Some examples are as follows

$$
\begin{array}{lll}
y_t = \alpha + \beta x_t + u_t, & u_t = \phi_1 u_{t-1} + v_t & \text{[AR disturbance]} \\
y_t = \alpha + \beta x_t + u_t, & u_t = v_t + \psi_1 v_{t-1} & \text{[MA disturbance]} \\
y_t = \alpha + \beta x_t + \lambda y_{t-1} + u_t & & \text{[Lagged dependent]} \\
y_t = \alpha + \beta x_t + \gamma x_{t-1} + u_t & & \text{[Lagged explanatory]} \\
y_t = \alpha + \beta x_t + \lambda y_{t-1} + \gamma x_{t-1} + u_t & & \text{[Joint specification]} \\
\quad u_t = \phi_1 u_{t-1} + v_t + \psi_1 v_{t-1}. & &
\end{array}
$$

A natural mechanism for the introduction of dynamics in linear regression occurs in the case of models of forward market efficiency. Lags arise in these models for two reasons. First, the forward rate acts as a natural predictor of future spot rates. Second, if the data are overlapping so that the maturity of the forward rate is longer than the frequency of observations, the disturbance term has an induced moving average structure.

One reason for including dynamics in a regression model is to correct for potential misspecification problems that arise from incorrectly excluding explanatory variables. In Chapter 3, it was shown how misspecification of this type may be detected using an autocorrelation test applied to the residuals of the estimated regression model.

4.3 AUTOCORRELATION AND PARTIAL AUTOCORRELATIONS

In addition to the unconditional mean and variance not being functions of time, the discussion on stationarity in Section 4.1 emphasizes that the autocovariance of a stationary process is also invariant with respect to the time period in which they are computed.

The autocovariance at order k gives the covariance between y_t and y_{t-k}. The first k autocovariances of y_t are therefore defined as

$$
\gamma_1 = E\{[y_t - E(y_t)][y_{t-1} - E(y_{t-1})]\}
$$
$$
\gamma_2 = E\{[y_t - E(y_t)][y_{t-2} - E(y_{t-2})]\}
$$
$$
\vdots \qquad \vdots \qquad \vdots \qquad \vdots
$$
$$
\gamma_k = E\{[y_t - E(y_t)][y_{t-k} - E(y_{t-k})]\}.
$$

The autocorrelation function is obtained by standardizing the autocovariances by the variance, γ_0, and is given by

$$
\rho_k = \gamma_k / \gamma_0. \tag{4.12}
$$

Consider again the AR(1) model in equation (4.2). The first-order autocovariance is

$$
\gamma_1 = E\{[\phi_1 y_{t-1} - \phi_1 E(y_{t-1}) + u_t][y_{t-1} - E(y_{t-1})]\}
$$
$$
= \phi_1 E\{[y_{t-1} - E(y_{t-1})]^2\}
$$
$$
= \phi_1 \gamma_0,
$$

where the second step is based on the result, stated previously, that $E\{[y_{t-1} - E(y_{t-1})]u_t\} = 0$. It follows that the *kth* autocovariance for $k > 0$ is

$$\gamma_k = \phi_1^k \gamma_0. \tag{4.13}$$

By virtue of the definition $\gamma_k = \gamma_{-k}$, for general integer k, we have $\gamma_k = \phi_1^{|k|}\gamma_0$. From this result it can be seen that the autocovariances of a stationary AR model are not functions of time but do depend on the lag parameter k in the autocovariance.

The autocorrelation function (ACF) of the AR(1) model is

$$\rho_k = \frac{\gamma_k}{\gamma_0} = \phi_1^{|k|}. \tag{4.14}$$

For $0 < \phi_1 < 1$, the AFC of y_t declines exponentially for increasing k so that the effects of previous values on y_t gradually diminish. For $-1 < \phi_1 < 0$, the AFC of y_t alternates in sign, as k is even or odd and its modulus declines exponentially. For higher order AR models the properties of the ACF are more complicated in analytic form but nonetheless follow similar patterns with their moduli having exponential decay with increasing k whenever the AR model is stable.

The pattern of autocovariances and associated autocorrelations for the MA(1) model in equation (4.7) is quite different from the AR(1) case. The first-order auto covariance is

$$\begin{aligned}
\gamma_1 &= E\{[y_t - E(y_t)][y_{t-1} - E(y_{t-1})]\} \\
&= E[(u_t + \psi_1 u_{t-1})(u_{t-1} + \psi_1 u_{t-2})] \\
&= \psi_1 \sigma_u^2,
\end{aligned}$$

which uses the properties

$$E(u_t u_{t-1}) = E(u_{t-1}u_{t-2}) = E(u_t u_{t-2}) = 0, \qquad E(u_t^2) = E(u_{t-1}^2) = \sigma_u^2.$$

For autocovariances of y_t for $k > 1$, $\gamma_k = 0$. The ACF of an MA(1) model is summarized as

$$\rho_k = \frac{\gamma_k}{\gamma_0} = \begin{cases} \dfrac{\psi_1}{1 + \psi_1^2} & : k = 1 \\ 0 & : \text{otherwise.} \end{cases} \tag{4.15}$$

This result contrasts with the ACF of the AR(1) model as there is now a single spike in the ACF at lag 1 that corresponds to the lag length of the model. In a similar way, the ACF of an MA(q) model has non-zero values for the first q lags and zero thereafter.

The first-order autocorrelation of the ARMA(1,1) model in equation (4.10) is

$$\rho_1 = \frac{(1 + \phi_1\psi_1)(\phi_1 + \psi_1)}{1 + \psi_1^2 + 2\phi_1\psi_1},$$

while higher-order autocorrelations are given by

$$\rho_k = \phi_1 \rho_{k-1}, \qquad k \geq 2.$$

Setting $\psi_1 = 0$ produces the autocorrelation function of the AR(1) model given in equation (4.2). Similarly, setting $\phi_1 = 0$ results in the autocorrelation function of the

MA(1) model given in equation (4.15). For the special case where $\psi_1 = -\phi_1$, the AR and MA components cancel and the model contains no dynamics since it reduces to

$$y_t = \frac{\phi_0}{1 - \phi_1} + u_t, \quad \Rightarrow y_t \sim iid\left(\frac{\phi_0}{1 - \phi_1}, \sigma_u^2\right),$$

with $\rho_k = 0$ for all $k \geq 1$.

To compute the sample ACF, the following sequence of AR models may be estimated equation by equation by ordinary least squares

$$y_t = \phi_{10} + \rho_1 y_{t-1} + u_{1t},$$
$$y_t = \phi_{20} + \rho_2 y_{t-2} + u_{2t},$$

$$\vdots \qquad \vdots \qquad \vdots$$

$$y_t = \phi_{k0} + \rho_k y_{t-k} + u_{kt},$$

giving the estimated ACF $\{\widehat{\rho}_1, \widehat{\rho}_2, \cdots, \widehat{\rho}_k\}$. The notation adopted for the constant term in the above regressions emphasizes that this term differs for each equation.

To illustrate, consider US monthly data from January 1871 to September 2016 on equity returns[1] expressed as a percentage, given by

$$re_t = 100 \times (\log P_t - \log P_{t-1}), \tag{4.16}$$

where P_t is the equity price index. The ACF of the equity returns is computed by means of a sequence of regressions. Specifically, the ACF for lags 1 to 3 is computed using the following three regressions (standard errors in parentheses):

$$re_t = \underset{(0.094)}{0.253} + \underset{(0.023)}{0.284}\, re_{t-1} + \widehat{u}_{1t},$$

$$re_t = \underset{(0.098)}{0.350} + \underset{(0.024)}{0.005}\, re_{t-2} + \widehat{u}_{2t},$$

$$re_t = \underset{(0.098)}{0.365} - \underset{(0.024)}{0.041}\, re_{t-3} + \widehat{u}_{3t}.$$

The estimated ACF is $\widehat{\rho}_1 = 0.284$, $\widehat{\rho}_2 = 0.005$, and $\widehat{\rho}_3 = -0.041$. Notice that the standard errors on each of the $\widehat{\rho}_k$ are approximately the same. In fact a useful result is that the standard errors of the autocorrelations are approximately $1/\sqrt{T}$, where T is the sample size. These standard errors are commonly referred to as Bartlett standard errors (see, for example, Brockwell and Davis, 1991).

Another measure of the dynamic properties of AR models is the partial autocorrelation function (PACF) at lag k, which measures the relationship between y_t and y_{t-k} but now with the intermediate lags included in the regression model, so that their effects are controlled for. The PACF at lag k is denoted by ϕ_{kk}. By implication the PACF for an AR(p) model is zero for lags greater than p. For example, in the AR(1) model the PACF has a spike at lag 1 and thereafter is $\phi_{kk} = 0$, $\forall\, k > 1$. This is in contrast to the ACF, which in general has non-zero values for higher lags. Note that by construction the ACF and PACF at lag 1 are equal to each other.

---

[1] Strictly speaking, these are log equity returns expressed as percentages, but the "log" will be dropped for expositional ease when referring to re_t as defined in equation (4.16). The same applies to the log dividend returns, rd_t, which are formally defined in equation (4.17).

To compute the sample PACF, the following AR models are estimated equation by equation by ordinary least squares

$$y_t = \phi_{10} + \phi_{11} y_{t-1} + u_{1t}$$

$$y_t = \phi_{20} + \phi_{21} y_{t-1} + \phi_{22} y_{t-2} + u_{2t}$$

$$y_t = \phi_{30} + \phi_{31} y_{t-1} + \phi_{32} y_{t-2} + \phi_{33} y_{t-3} + u_{3t}$$

$$\vdots \qquad \vdots \qquad \vdots \qquad \vdots$$

$$y_t = \phi_{k0} + \phi_{k1} y_{t-1} + \phi_{k2} y_{t-2} + \cdots + \phi_{kk} y_{t-k} + u_{kt},$$

where the estimated PACF is therefore given by $\{\widehat{\phi}_{11}, \widehat{\phi}_{22}, \cdots, \widehat{\phi}_{kk}\}$.

The PACF for lags 1 to 3 for the equity returns data is then obtained from

$$re_t = \underset{(0.094)}{0.253} + \underset{(0.023)}{0.284} \, re_{t-1} + \widehat{u}_{1t},$$

$$re_t = \underset{(0.094)}{0.272} + \underset{(0.024)}{0.307} \, re_{t-1} - \underset{(0.024)}{0.082} \, re_{t-2} + \widehat{u}_{2t},$$

$$re_t = \underset{(0.094)}{0.277} + \underset{(0.025)}{0.305} \, re_{t-1} - \underset{(0.025)}{0.075} \, re_{t-2} - \underset{(0.024)}{0.021} \, re_{t-3} + \widehat{u}_{3t}.$$

The estimated sample PACF is $\{\widehat{\phi}_{11} = 0.284, \widehat{\phi}_{22} = -0.082, \widehat{\phi}_{33} = -0.021\}$.

Plots of the sample autocorrelation and partial autocorrelation functions can yield valuable insights into the appropriate dynamic model for a process. Consider US monthly data from January 1871 to September 2016 on dividend returns expressed as a percentage,

$$rd_t = 100 \times (\log D_t - \log D_{t-1}), \tag{4.17}$$

where D_t is the dividend payment. Figure 4.3 shows both the autocorrelation and partial autocorrelation functions for this series, with associated 95% confidence intervals, out to $k = 15$. The autocorrelation function demonstrates exponential decay while the partial autocorrelation function has a large spike at $k = 1$. This pattern is very suggestive that an AR(1) model is a suitable one to model dividend returns. There are other significant partial autocorrelations at $k = 4$ and $k = 13$ indicating that there may be some additional structure in the series that needs to be modeled.

4.4 MEAN AVERSION AND REVERSION IN RETURNS

A well-known empirical result in finance is that asset returns exhibit mean aversion (positive autocorrelation) for relatively short time horizons and mean reversion (negative autocorrelation) for longer time horizons (Fama and French, 1988; Kim, Nelson, and Startz, 1991). This property is illustrated by computing the autocorrelations of log returns on the NASDAQ share index for alternative frequencies. Using monthly, quarterly, and annual frequencies for the period 1989 to 2009, the following results are obtained from estimating a simple AR(1) model in each case:

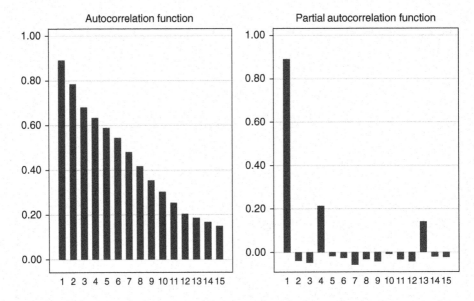

FIGURE 4.3 Autocorrelation and partial autocorrelation functions of dividend returns to the S&P 500 computed from monthly observations for the period January 1871 to September 2016.

$$
\begin{aligned}
\text{Monthly:} \quad & re_t = 0.599 + 0.131\, re_{t-1} + \widehat{u}_{1t}, \\
\text{Quarterly:} \quad & re_t = 1.950 + 0.058\, re_{t-1} + \widehat{u}_{2t}, \\
\text{Annual:} \quad & re_t = 8.974 - 0.131\, re_{t-1} + \widehat{u}_{3t},
\end{aligned}
$$

where the $\widehat{u}_{it}$ are the ordinary least squares residuals. There appears to be mean aversion in returns for time horizons less than a year as the first-order autocorrelation is positive for monthly and quarterly returns. By contrast, there is mean reversion for horizons of at least a year as the first-order autocorrelation is now negative with a value of -0.131 for annual returns.

To understand the change in the autocorrelation properties of returns over different maturities, consider the following model proposed by Poterba and Summers (1988),

$$
\begin{aligned}
p_t &= f_t + u_t, \\
f_t &= f_{t-1} + v_t, & v_t &\sim iid\, N(0, \sigma_v^2), \\
u_t &= \phi_1 u_{t-1} + w_t, & w_t &\sim iid\, N(0, \sigma_w^2),
\end{aligned}
$$

where p_t is the log of prices, f_t is the log of market fundamentals, and v_t and u_t are disturbance terms assumed to be independent of each other. The disturbance term u_t represents transient deviations of p_t from f_t, while v_t captures shocks to the market fundamentals.

The 1-period log return on the asset is

$$
re_t = p_t - p_{t-1} = v_t + u_t - u_{t-1},
$$

and the k-period return is

$$
\begin{aligned}
re_t(k) = p_t - p_{t-k} &= re_t + re_{t-1} + \cdots + re_{t-k+1} \\
&= (v_t + u_t - u_{t-1}) + (v_{t-1} + u_{t-1} - u_{t-2}) + \cdots \\
&\quad + (v_{t-k+1} + u_{t-k+1} - u_{t-k}) \\
&= v_t + v_{t-1} + \cdots v_{t-k+1} + u_t - u_{t-k}.
\end{aligned}
$$

Using the property that $E(re_t) = 0$, the autocovariance is

$$
\begin{aligned}
\gamma_k &= E[(p_t - p_{t-k})(p_{t-k} - p_{t-2k})] \\
&= E[(v_t + v_{t-1} \cdots v_{t-k+1} + u_t - u_{t-k}) \\
&\quad \times (v_{t-k} + v_{t-k-1} + \cdots v_{t-2k+1} + u_{t-k} - u_{t-2k})] \\
&= E(u_t u_{t-k}) - E(u_t u_{t-2k}) - E(u_{t-k}^2) + E(u_{t-k} u_{t-2k}) \\
&= 2\,E(u_t u_{t-k}) - E(u_t u_{t-2k}) - E(u_{t-k}^2).
\end{aligned}
$$

Since u_t is an AR(1) process, it follows that

$$
\gamma_k = \frac{\sigma_w^2}{1 - \phi_1^2}(2\phi_1^k - \phi_1^{2k} - 1).
$$

For small values of k, γ_k can be positive, but in the limit as $k \to \infty$, γ_k eventually becomes negative because

$$
\lim_{k \to \infty} \gamma_k = -\frac{\sigma_w^2}{1 - \phi_1^2} = -\sigma_u^2.
$$

4.5 VECTOR AUTOREGRESSIVE MODELS

Once a decision is made to move into a multivariate setting, it becomes difficult to delimit a single variable as the dependent variable to be explained in terms of all the other variables. Given the interdependence of economic systems and the joint decision-making involved in portfolio choice, it is reasonable to suppose that variables are jointly determined within a system of equations. This way of thinking about economic data has a long history that goes back to the earliest empirical work on price determination by demand and supply. The approach became firmly established during the 1940s with the work of the Cowles Commission researchers at the University of Chicago. From a time series perspective, Mann and Wald (1943) made the fundamental contribution of developing a complete theory of estimation and inference for systems of equations in vector autoregressive (VAR) form under stationarity conditions. Their work also allowed for contemporaneous simultaneous equations effects within the VAR framework, corresponding to what is now known as a structural vector autoregression (SVAR). From an empirical perspective, the major contribution, complete with new methodology for studying a system's impulse responses to shocks, was provided by Sims (1980) using US data on nominal interest rates, money, prices, and output.

The adoption of a VAR modeling framework in empirical finance has many advantages.

(i) Estimation is straightforward, involving the application of ordinary least squares to each equation in the VAR. Multivariate analogues of MA models and ARMA models, known respectively as VMA and VARMA models, are alternative multivariate model specifications. Estimation of these models, however, is less straightforward than for VARs and for this reason are less widely used in empirical work.

(ii) The VAR system provides a convenient framework to forecast financial variables.

(iii) The model provides a basis for performing causality tests between financial variables.

(iv) The dynamics of the VAR can be modeled using impulse response analysis, which reveals the effects of shocks on the system variables.

(v) The volatility of financial variables can be decomposed in terms of their risk components.

(vi) Theoretical models in finance can be tested through the imposition of restrictions on the VAR parameters.

(vii) There is a convenient direct link between a VAR and an important type of model, which will be introduced in Chapter 6, known as an error correction model.

As a consequence of these advantages, VARs enjoy great popularity in applied research.

4.5.1 Specification

All the variables are treated as endogenous by specifying a model in which each of the variables has an equation that explains its movements using past information on all the variables in the system. A distinguishing feature of this approach is that each equation has precisely the same set of explanatory variables. An example of a trivariate VAR(p) is

$$y_{1t} = \phi_{10} + \sum_{i=1}^{p} \phi_{11,i} y_{1t-i} + \sum_{i=1}^{p} \phi_{12,i} y_{2t-i} + \sum_{i=1}^{p} \phi_{13,i} y_{3t-i} + u_{1t},$$

$$y_{2t} = \phi_{20} + \sum_{i=1}^{p} \phi_{21,i} y_{1t-i} + \sum_{i=1}^{p} \phi_{22,i} y_{2t-i} + \sum_{i=1}^{p} \phi_{23,i} y_{3t-i} + u_{2t}, \qquad (4.18)$$

$$y_{3t} = \phi_{30} + \sum_{i=1}^{p} \phi_{31,i} y_{1t-i} + \sum_{i=1}^{p} \phi_{32,i} y_{2t-i} + \sum_{i=1}^{p} \phi_{33,i} y_{3t-i} + u_{3t},$$

where y_{1t}, y_{2t}, and y_{3t} are the jointly dependent variables, p is a prescribed lag length, which is the same for all equations, and u_{1t}, u_{2t}, and u_{3t} are disturbance terms. Even though this model contains just three variables, the total number of parameters can become quite large especially if long lag structures are entertained. In the case of the trivariate VAR the number of unknown parameters in each equation is $1 + 3p$, making the total number of parameters for the whole model $3(1 + 3p)$. If $p = 6$, for instance, then the total number of unknown parameters is $3(1 + 3 \times 6) = 57$.

Higher dimensional VARs containing N variables $\{y_{1t}, y_{2t}, \cdots, y_{Nt}\}$ are specified in the same way as they are for the trivariate VAR in equation (4.18). In matrix notation, the VAR is conveniently represented as

$$y_t = \Phi_0 + \Phi_1 y_{t-1} + \Phi_2 y_{t-2} + \cdots + \Phi_p y_{t-p} + u_t, \qquad (4.19)$$

where the parameter matrices are given by

$$
\Phi_0 = \begin{bmatrix} \phi_{10} \\ \phi_{20} \\ \vdots \\ \phi_{N0} \end{bmatrix}, \qquad \Phi_i = \begin{bmatrix} \phi_{11,i} & \phi_{12,i} & \cdots & \phi_{1N,i} \\ \phi_{21,i} & \phi_{22,i} & & \phi_{2N,i} \\ \vdots & \vdots & \ddots & \vdots \\ \phi_{N1,i} & \phi_{N2,i} & \cdots & \phi_{NN,i} \end{bmatrix}.
$$

The disturbances $u_t = \{u_{1t}, u_{2t}, ..., u_{Nt}\}' \sim iid\,(0, \Omega)$ are independent over t with zero mean and covariance matrix

$$
\Omega = E(u_t u_t') = \begin{bmatrix} \sigma_1^2 & \sigma_{12} & \cdots & \sigma_{1N} \\ \sigma_{21} & \sigma_2^2 & \cdots & \sigma_{2N} \\ \vdots & \vdots & \ddots & \vdots \\ \sigma_{N1} & \sigma_{N2} & \cdots & \sigma_N^2 \end{bmatrix}. \tag{4.20}
$$

This matrix has two properties. First, it is a symmetric matrix so that the upper triangular part of the matrix mirrors the lower triangular part

$$
\sigma_{ij} = \sigma_{ji}, \qquad i \neq j.
$$

Second, the disturbance terms in each equation are generally correlated with the disturbances of other equations, so that

$$
\sigma_{ij} \neq 0, \qquad i \neq j.
$$

This last property allows for interdependence among the shocks that drive the VAR system. It is particularly relevant when undertaking impulse response analysis and in computing variance decompositions.

4.5.2 Estimation

Despite the VAR in equation (4.19) being a multivariate system of equations with lagged values of each variable potentially influencing all the others, estimation of the parameters $\{\Phi_0, \Phi_1, \Phi_2, \cdots, \Phi_p\}$ is performed by simply applying ordinary least squares to each equation one at a time. This strategy is appropriate because the set of explanatory variables is the same in each equation and there are no restrictions on the coefficients of the system.

To estimate the covariance matrix Ω in equation (4.20), let $\widehat{u}_t = \{\widehat{u}_{1t}, \widehat{u}_{2t}, \cdots, \widehat{u}_{Nt}\}$ represent the least squares residuals for each equation in the VAR. An estimate of the covariance matrix is computed using the sample residual moment matrix defined by

$$
\widehat{\Omega} = \begin{bmatrix} \widehat{\sigma}_1^2 & \widehat{\sigma}_{12} & \cdots & \widehat{\sigma}_{1N} \\ \widehat{\sigma}_{21} & \widehat{\sigma}_2^2 & & \widehat{\sigma}_{2N} \\ \vdots & & \ddots & \vdots \\ \widehat{\sigma}_{N1} & \widehat{\sigma}_{N2} & \cdots & \widehat{\sigma}_N^2 \end{bmatrix} \tag{4.21}
$$

or more explicitly,

$$
\widehat{\Omega} = \frac{1}{T} \begin{bmatrix} \sum_{t=p+1}^{T} \widehat{u}_{1t}^2 & \sum_{t=p+1}^{T} \widehat{u}_{1t}\widehat{u}_{2t} & \cdots & \sum_{t=p+1}^{T} \widehat{u}_{1t}\widehat{u}_{Nt} \\ \sum_{t=p+1}^{T} \widehat{u}_{2t}\widehat{u}_{1t} & \sum_{t=p+1}^{T} \widehat{u}_{2t}^2 & & \sum_{t=p+1}^{T} \widehat{u}_{2t}\widehat{u}_{Nt} \\ \vdots & & \ddots & \vdots \\ \sum_{t=p+1}^{T} \widehat{u}_{Nt}\widehat{u}_{1t} & \sum_{t=p+1}^{T} \widehat{u}_{Nt}\widehat{u}_{2t} & \cdots & \sum_{t=p+1}^{T} \widehat{u}_{Nt}^2 \end{bmatrix}.
$$

As an example, consider a bivariate model for equity returns as defined in equation (4.16), re_t, by adding as an explanatory variable lagged dividend returns as defined in equation (4.17), rd_t. Such an extension is justified on theory grounds given the link between equity prices and dividends that is established in the present value model and discussed in Chapter 2. Equally important is the need for a model to explain dividend returns. A natural specification is to include as explanatory variables both its own lags and lags of equity returns in this model. Then, equity returns, re_t, and dividend returns, rd_t, may be treated as potentially endogenous and jointly determined. Consequently, a VAR(6) model is estimated with monthly US data from 1871 to 2016. The parameter estimates, with standard errors in parentheses, are given in Table 4.1.

Notice that the parameter estimates of the effects of dividend returns on equity returns are borderline significant for lags 2 and 6 at the 5% level. The parameter estimates of the effects of equity returns on dividend returns at lags 2, 3, 5, and 6 are also statistically significant at this level, so that lagged values of re_t are important in explaining the behavior of rd_t.

The estimated covariance matrix of the residuals in equation (4.20) is constructed using the parameter estimates reported in Table 4.1, giving

$$\widehat{\Omega} = \begin{bmatrix} 14.8943 & -0.0916 \\ -0.0916 & 0.2411 \end{bmatrix}. \tag{4.22}$$

This estimate shows that there is a large difference in the residual variance in the two equations and that there is a negative covariance between the residuals of the equity and dividend return equations. As discussed next, the matrix $\widehat{\Omega}$ provides an important input concerning model fit, one that is particularly useful in methods designed to select lag length specification in the VAR.

4.5.3 Lag Length Selection

An important part of the specification of a VAR model is the choice of the lag structure whose key parameter is the lag length order p. If the lag length is too short, there is a risk

TABLE 4.1   Parameter estimates of a bivariate VAR(6) model for US monthly equity and dividend returns for the period January 1871 to September 2016.

Lag	Equity Returns		Dividend Returns	
	re	rd	re	rd
1	0.297	−0.049	0.001	0.910
	(0.024)	−(0.187)	(0.003)	(0.024)
2	−0.070	0.519	0.007	0.016
	−(0.025)	(0.254)	(0.003)	(0.032)
3	−0.029	−0.248	0.008	−0.252
	−(0.025)	−(0.250)	(0.003)	−(0.032)
4	0.030	0.318	0.002	0.224
	(0.025)	(0.251)	(0.003)	(0.032)
5	0.052	−0.231	0.012	0.016
	(0.025)	−(0.254)	(0.003)	(0.032)
6	−0.005	−0.341	0.014	−0.023
	−(0.024)	−(0.186)	(0.003)	−(0.024)
Constant	0.264		0.017	
	(0.097)		(0.012)	

that aspects of the dynamic mechanism are excluded from the model. If the lag structure is too long, then there are redundant lags that can reduce the precision of the parameter estimates, thereby raising the standard errors and yielding t statistics that may be biased downward.

In choosing the lag structure of a VAR, care must be exercised in relation to the sample size as degrees of freedom quickly diminish for even moderate lag lengths. For each integer increase in the lag length, an additional matrix of coefficients must be estimated. In a K dimensional system, this means an additional K^2 coefficients are needed for each extra lag. For these reasons, an important practical consideration in constructing and estimating a VAR(p) model is the choice of the lag order p. A common data-driven approach to selecting lag order is to use information criteria. These criteria are scalar statistics that provide a simple but effective way of balancing improvements in sample period fit of the equations against the loss of degrees of freedom in estimation that results from increasing the lag order. Many such criteria are now available for use in econometric work.

The three most commonly used information criteria (IC) for selecting a parsimonious time series model are the Akaike information criterion (AIC; Akaike, 1974, 1976), the Hannan information criterion (HIC; Hannan and Quinn, 1979; Hannan, 1980) and the Schwarz information criterion (SIC; Schwarz, 1978). The versions reported here follow Lütkepohl (2005). If K is the number of variables in the VAR(p) system, then these information criteria are as follows:

$$\text{AIC} = \log|\widehat{\Omega}| + \frac{2pK^2}{T}, \tag{4.23}$$

$$\text{HIC} = \log|\widehat{\Omega}| + \frac{2\log(\log(T))}{T}pK^2, \tag{4.24}$$

$$\text{SIC} = \log|\widehat{\Omega}| + \frac{\log(T)}{T}pK^2. \tag{4.25}$$

In these expressions, $\widehat{\Omega}$ is an estimate of the covariance matrix given in equation (4.21) with the numerical estimate reported in equation (4.22). In the scalar case, the determinant of the estimated covariance matrix, $|\widehat{\Omega}|$, is replaced by the estimated residual variance, $\widehat{\sigma}_u^2$.

Choosing an IC optimal lag order using any of the above criteria requires the following steps.

Step 1: Choose a maximum number of lags, $p_{\max}$, for the VAR model. This choice may be informed by the ACFs and PACFs of the data, the frequency with which the data are observed, and the sample size.

Step 2: Estimate the model sequentially for all lags up to and including $p_{\max}$. For each regression, compute the relevant information criterion, holding the sample size fixed.

Step 3: Choose the specification corresponding to the minimum values of the information criterion. In some cases, there will be disagreement between different information criteria on the choice of lag length. The final decision is then a matter of individual judgement.

The bivariate VAR(6) for equity and dividend returns in Table 4.1 used an arbitrarily chosen maximum lag length $p_{max} = 12$. In order to provide a data-determined choice, the information criteria can be used. For example, calculations of the AIC, HIC, and SIC values for this VAR for lags from 1 to 8 are as follows:

Lag:	1	2	3	4	5	6	7	8
AIC:	7.073	7.062	7.055	7.011	6.992	6.983	6.982	6.973
HIC:	7.080	7.073	7.071	7.032	7.018	7.013	7.017	7.012*
SIC:	7.092	7.093	7.099	7.068	7.062*	7.065	7.077	7.080

These results are typical of many applications. AIC has not yet reached a minimum value after the inclusion of 8 lags, HIC suggests the choice of 8 lags is optimal (indicated by an asterisk), whereas the minimum value of the SIC statistic (also indicated by an asterisk) is SIC $= 7.062$, corresponding to a lag structure with $p = 5$. The AIC criterion is well known to favor longer lag lengths, whereas SIC imposes a higher penalty on additional lags and therefore usually chooses shorter optimal lag lengths. The present results provide empirical evidence that suggest the choice of a lag length $p = 6$ in this example is reasonable.

4.6 ANALYZING VARs

4.6.1 Granger Causality Testing

In a VAR model, all lagged variables are assumed to contribute information in determining the behavior of each dependent variable. But in most empirical applications of VARs there are often large numbers of estimated coefficients that are statistically insignificant. A question of considerable importance in empirical work is whether the coefficients of all the lagged values of a particular explanatory variable in a given equation are zero or not. This question bears on whether the information content of the past values of one variable influences the behavior of another variable in the system. This notion has a close connection with that of causal influence in the sense that predictions might be improved by measuring and including such influences.

In the VAR given in equation (4.18), for example, the information content of variable y_2 on variable y_1 might be tested by considering the joint restrictions

$$\phi_{12,1} = \phi_{12,2} = \phi_{12,3} = \cdots = \phi_{12,p} = 0.$$

These restrictions on the coefficients of the lagged variables $y_{2t-1}, ...y_{2t-p}$ can be tested jointly using a χ^2 test with p degrees of freedom.

If y_{2t} plays a role in predicting future values of y_{1t}, then y_{2t} is said to cause y_{1t} in Granger's sense (Granger, 1969). It is important to remember that Granger causality is based on the presence (or absence) of predictability and does not of itself signify causal influence. On the other hand, if a causal influence from a certain variable is present, then it is to be expected that such a variable will play a role in prediction. Evidence of Granger causality and the lack of Granger causality from y_{2t} to y_{1t} are denoted, respectively, as

$$y_{2t} \to y_{1t}, \qquad y_{2t} \nrightarrow y_{1t}.$$

It is also possible to test for Granger causality in the reverse direction by performing a joint test of the lags of y_{1t} in the y_{2t} equation. Combining both sets of causality results can yield a range of statistical causal patterns:

Unidirectional:	$y_{1t} \rightarrow y_{2t}$
(from y_{1t} to y_{2t})	$y_{2t} \nrightarrow y_{1t}$
Unidirectional:	$y_{2t} \rightarrow y_{1t}$
(from y_{2t} to y_{1t})	$y_{1t} \nrightarrow y_{2t}$
Bidirectional:	$y_{2t} \rightarrow y_{1t}$
(feedback)	$y_{1t} \rightarrow y_{2t}$
Independence:	$y_{2t} \nrightarrow y_{1t}$
	$y_{1t} \nrightarrow y_{2t}$

Table 4.2 gives results of the Granger causality tests based on the χ^2 statistic in a fitted bivariate VAR(6) model for equity and dividend returns, re_t and rd_t, respectively. Both p values are less than 0.05, showing that there is bidirectional Granger causality between equity and dividend returns (re_t and rd_t). The results of the Granger causality tests reported in Table 4.2 may be corroborated using estimates from the univariate model in which equity returns are formulated to depend on lags 1 to 6 of both re_t and rd_t. In this formulation, a test of the information value of dividend returns in explaining equity returns is given by the statistic $\chi^2 = 20.075$. Since there are 6 degrees of freedom, the p value is 0.003, which confirms that dividend returns are statistically relevant in explaining equity returns at the 5% level. This is consistent with many models in finance that emphasize the information content of dividends in determining equity returns.

4.6.2 Impulse Response Analysis

Granger causality testing is one method of identifying the system dynamics of a VAR that enhances understanding of variable interactions over time. An alternative but related approach focuses on impulse responses by tracking the transmission effects of shocks to the system on the dependent variables. This approach to examining system dynamics is called impulse response analysis.

A potential candidate for the shocks in a VAR system is the vector of disturbances $u_t = \{u_{1t}, u_{2t}, ..., u_{Nt}\}$, which represents contributions to the dependent variable that are not predicted from past information. The primary problem in the direct use of the fitted disturbances in studying impulse responses is that these terms are correlated, which complicates the interpretation of the shocks u_t with respect to the underlying economic and financial forces. In the foregoing example, for instance, the estimated covariance matrix

TABLE 4.2 Results of Granger causality tests based on estimates of a bivariate VAR(6) model for US monthly equity returns, re_t, and dividend returns, rd_t, for the period January 1871 to September 2016.

Null Hypothesis:	Chi-square	Degrees of Freedom	p value
$rd \nrightarrow re$	20.075	6	0.003
$re \nrightarrow rd$	68.279	6	0.000

Ω in equation (4.22) contains non-zero off-diagonal elements, showing correlations between the equation shocks. One solution that aids interpretation is to transform the VAR into a new system in which the disturbances in the equations are uncorrelated so that the effects of these uncorrelated shocks on the system variables can be traced over time, thereby enabling determination of the responses to impulses associated with the individual shocks.

To illustrate, consider the bivariate VAR model of equity returns and dividend returns estimated in Table 4.1 based on $p = 6$ lags

$$re_t = \phi_{10} + \sum_{i=1}^{6} \phi_{11,i} re_{t-i} + \sum_{i=1}^{6} \phi_{12,i} rd_{t-i} + u_{1t}, \tag{4.26}$$

$$rd_t = \phi_{20} + \sum_{i=1}^{6} \phi_{21,i} re_{t-i} + \sum_{i=1}^{6} \phi_{22,i} rd_{t-i} + u_{2t}.$$

Let the relationship between the two VAR disturbances u_{1t} and u_{2t} be represented by the linear regression equation

$$u_{2t} = \rho u_{1t} + v_{2t}, \tag{4.27}$$

where ρ is a parameter capturing the correlation between u_{1t} and u_{2t}, and v_{2t} is a new disturbance term, which, from the properties of the linear regression model, is uncorrelated with u_{1t}. The equation (4.27) may be interpreted as a structural relationship between the two shocks u_{1t} and u_{2t} in which the residual v_{2t} is that part of the impulse u_{2t} that is uncorrelated with u_{1t}. Using equation (4.26) to substitute for u_{1t} and u_{2t} in equation (4.27) and rearranging yields an alternative equation for rd_t given by

$$rd_t = (\phi_{20} - \rho\phi_{10}) + \rho\, re_t + \sum_{i=1}^{6} (\phi_{21,i} - \rho\phi_{11,i}) re_{t-i} + \sum_{i=1}^{6} (\phi_{22,i} - \rho\phi_{12,i}) rd_{t-i} + v_{2t},$$

or

$$rd_t = \beta_{20} + \rho\, re_t + \sum_{i=1}^{6} \beta_{21,i} re_{t-i} + \sum_{i=1}^{6} \beta_{22,i} rd_{t-i} + v_{2t}, \tag{4.28}$$

in which $\beta_{20} = \phi_{20} - \rho\phi_{10}$, $\beta_{21,i} = \phi_{21,i} - \rho\phi_{11,i}$, and $\beta_{22,i} = \phi_{22,i} - \rho\phi_{12,i}$.

The difference between equation (4.28) and the VAR equation for rd_t in equation (4.26) is the inclusion of equity returns at time t, re_t, as an explanatory variable. Moreover, since v_{2t} is uncorrelated with u_{1t} because of equation (4.27), the VAR equation for re_t in equation (4.26) and the equation for rd_t in equation (4.28) contain disturbances that are now uncorrelated with each other. To highlight this property, the two equations are written as

$$re_t = \beta_{10} + \sum_{i=1}^{6} \beta_{11,i} re_{t-i} + \sum_{i=1}^{6} \beta_{12,i} rd_{t-i} + v_{1t},$$

$$\tag{4.29}$$

$$rd_t = \beta_{20} + \rho\, re_t + \sum_{i=1}^{6} \beta_{21,i} re_{t-i} + \sum_{i=1}^{6} \beta_{22,i} rd_{t-i} + v_{2t},$$

where $\beta_{10} = \phi_{10}$, $\beta_{11,i} = \phi_{11,i}$, $\beta_{12,i} = \phi_{12,i}$, and $v_{1t} = u_{1t}$. This system of equations represents a structural VAR (SVAR) where the disturbances v_{1t} and v_{2t} represent structural disturbances or primitive shocks that are uncorrelated, $E(v_{1t}v_{2t}) = 0$. It is this system that can now be used to construct impulse responses for re_t and rd_t with respect to the structural shocks v_{1t} and v_{2t}.

The structural system of equations in equation (4.29) is estimated equation by equation by ordinary least squares and the resultant parameter estimates are given in Table 4.3, together with the size of the estimation sample, T, and the residual sum of squares for the two equations, RSS. The estimates of the first equation of the SVAR for equity returns, re_t, are taken directly from Table 4.1. The equation for dividend returns, rd_t, is estimated by regressing rd_t on a constant, re_t and 6 lags of re_t and rd_t.

Impulse responses are constructed by allowing for a shock in the SVAR disturbances v_{1t} and v_{2t} in equation (4.29). As the SVAR model is dynamic the shocks have a contemporaneous effect as well as a dynamic effect. As the model is bivariate, in total there are 4 sets of impulse responses with the two dependent variables re_t and rd_t each being affected by equity shocks, v_{1t}, and dividend shocks, v_{2t}.

Equity Shock

To estimate the contemporaneous effect of a shock in re_t on itself, let the size of the shock be equal to the estimate of the standard deviation of v_{1t}, which from Table 4.3 is

$$\Delta re_t = \sqrt{\frac{25945.84}{1742}} = 3.8593. \tag{4.30}$$

TABLE 4.3 Parameter estimates of a bivariate SVAR(6) model for the US monthly equity and dividend returns for the period January 1871 to September 2016.

Lag	Equity Returns		Dividend Returns	
	re	rd	re	rd
0			−0.006 (0.003)	
1	0.297 (0.024)	−0.049 (0.188)	0.003 (0.003)	0.910 (0.024)
2	−0.070 (0.025)	0.520 (0.255)	0.007 (0.003)	0.019 (0.032)
3	−0.029 (0.025)	−0.248 (0.251)	0.008 (0.003)	−0.254 (0.032)
4	0.030 (0.025)	0.318 (0.251)	0.002 (0.003)	0.226 (0.032)
5	0.052 (0.025)	−0.231 (0.255)	0.012 (0.003)	0.014 (0.032)
6	−0.005 (0.024)	−0.341 (0.186)	0.014 (0.003)	−0.025 (0.024)
Constant	0.264 (0.100)		0.019 (0.012)	
T	1742		1742	
RSS	25945.84		419.0077	

Here the estimate of the standard deviation is chosen not to be adjusted for degrees of freedom.[2] As the change in re_t is 3.8593, this implies from the SVAR equation for rd_t in equation (4.29) that dividend returns change by

$$\Delta rd_t = \widehat{\rho} \times 3.8593 = -0.0061 \times 3.8593 = -0.0237. \tag{4.31}$$

To compute the effect of the equity shock on equities and dividends in the next month, rewrite the SVAR in equation (4.29) as

$$
\begin{aligned}
re_{t+1} &= \beta_{10} + \sum_{i=1}^{6} \beta_{11,i} re_{t+1-i} + \sum_{i=1}^{6} \beta_{12,i} rd_{t+1-i} + v_{1t+1}, \\
rd_{t+1} &= \beta_{20} + \rho \, re_{t+1} + \sum_{i=1}^{6} \beta_{21,i} re_{t+1-i} + \sum_{i=1}^{6} \beta_{22,i} rd_{t+1-i} + v_{2t+1}.
\end{aligned}
\tag{4.32}
$$

This suggests that the expected change in equities next month is the result of two sources: the change in equities and the change in dividends at time t

$$E_t(\Delta re_{t+1}) = \beta_{11,1} \Delta re_t + \beta_{12,1} \Delta rd_t.$$

Thus, the impulse response of equities at time $t+1$ to an equity shock is estimated as

$$E_t(\Delta re_{t+1}) = 0.2974 \times 3.8593 - 0.0489 \times (-0.0237) = 1.1491.$$

In the case of dividends at $t+1$ the effect of the equity shock at t has three sources given by

$$E_t(\Delta rd_{t+1}) = \rho \Delta re_{t+1} + \beta_{21,1} \Delta re_t + \beta_{22,1} \Delta rd_t,$$

which is estimated as

$$
\begin{aligned}
E_t(\Delta rd_{t+1}) &= -0.0061 \times 1.1491 + 0.0028 \times 3.8593 + 0.9096 \times (-0.0237) \\
&= -0.0179.
\end{aligned}
$$

This process of tracing the effect of a shock over time is formally known as the recursive substitution method, which is also used in Chapter 7 to generate forecasts of time series models.

Dividend Shock

The size of the dividend shock is estimated as the standard deviation of v_{2t}, which from Table 4.3 is

$$\Delta rd_t = \sqrt{\frac{419.0077}{1742}} = 0.4904. \tag{4.33}$$

As rd_t does not enter the structural equation for re_t in equation (4.32), the effect of a dividend shock on equities at time t is simply

$$\Delta re_t = 0.0000.$$

---

[2] Other definitions of the size of the shock can be adopted, including adjusting the standard deviation by the degrees of freedom, or defining the shock to be a 1% shock, for example. These alternative shocks would change the magnitude of the shock, but not the dynamic shape of the impulse response patterns.

The effects of the dividend shock at time t are

$$E_t(\Delta re_{t+1}) = \beta_{11,1}\Delta re_t + \beta_{12,1}\Delta rd_t,$$

which is estimated as

$$E_t(\Delta re_{t+1}) = 0.2974 \times 0.00 + (-0.0489) \times 0.4904 = -0.0240.$$

The effect of the dividend shock on dividends the next month is

$$E_t(\Delta rd_{t+1}) = \rho\,\Delta re_{t+1} + \beta_{21,1}\Delta re_t + \beta_{22,1}\Delta rd_t,$$

which is estimated as

$$E_t(\Delta rd_{t+1}) = -0.0061 \times (-0.0241) + 0.0028 \times 0.00 + 0.9097 \times 0.4904 = 0.4463.$$

To compute impulse responses for longer time horizons the sequence of steps based on recursive substitution proceeds as above. Figure 4.4 shows the effects of shocks to the bivariate VAR(6) equity-dividend model for a 30-month horizon. Four graphics are shown in Figure 4.4 to capture four different sets of impulses. The first column of the figure shows responses to a shock in equity returns, and the second column shows responses to a shock in dividends. A positive shock to equity returns has a damped oscillatory effect on itself that quickly dissipates. The effect on dividend returns is initially negative but quickly turns positive and reaches a peak after 8 months, before decaying monotonically. The effect of a positive shock to dividend returns on later dividend returns slowly dissipates, approaching zero after nearly 30 periods. The immediate effect of this

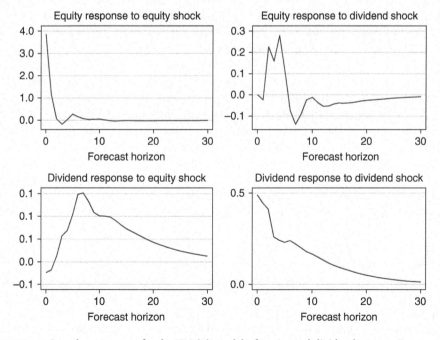

FIGURE 4.4 Impulse responses for the VAR(6) model of equity and dividend returns. Data are monthly for the period February 1871 to September 2016.

shock on equity returns is zero by construction in the first period. Subsequently, the effects exhibit a damped oscillatory pattern before decaying rapidly.

Cholesky Decomposition

The calculation of impulse responses is presented within a regression framework that involves estimating the SVAR by least squares and then using recursive substitution methods to compute the effects of the structural shocks on the variables in the model. Although the discussion is presented for a bivariate model, the approach can be extended to N-dimensional systems. However, a more convenient approach in the multivariate case is to perform the calculations using matrices. Formally this is achieved by defining a lower triangular matrix L with the property that the estimated VAR covariance matrix $\widehat{\Omega}$ in equation (4.22) is decomposed as

$$\widehat{\Omega} = LL'. \tag{4.34}$$

This decomposition of a matrix is commonly referred to as the Cholesky decomposition. As the matrix being decomposed in this case is the covariance matrix, L can be referred to as the standard deviation matrix, or even square-root matrix, as multiplying L by the transposition of itself recovers the covariance matrix.

The Cholesky decomposition of $\widehat{\Omega}$ in equation (4.22) is

$$\widehat{\Omega} = \begin{bmatrix} 3.8593 & 0.0000 \\ -0.0237 & 0.4904 \end{bmatrix} \begin{bmatrix} 3.8593 & -0.0237 \\ 0.0000 & 0.4904 \end{bmatrix} = \begin{bmatrix} 14.8943 & -0.0916 \\ -0.0916 & 0.2411 \end{bmatrix}. \tag{4.35}$$

The main diagonal of L gives the size of the equity and dividend shocks, which are, respectively, 3.8593 and 0.4904. The first column of L gives the effects of an equity shock on re_t and rd_t, with the contemporaneous effect of an equity shock on dividends given by -0.0237. The second column gives the effects of a dividend shock on re_t and rd_t, which are, respectively, 0.0 and 0.4904. These impulse responses at time t are also the same estimates obtained using the recursive substitution method applied earlier to the estimated SVAR model in Table 4.3.

In specifying the bivariate SVAR model in equation (4.32) and hence in calculating the impulse responses, a particular ordering is imposed in which re_t affects rd_t contemporaneously, but rd_t only affects re_t with a lag. An alternative ordering is where rd_t can affect re_t contemporaneously, but re_t now only affects rd_t with a lag. For this SVAR specification, the VAR equation for rd_t in equation (4.26) is retained, whereas the equation for re_t will be a function of a constant, rd_t and the 6 lags on re_t and rd_t. For more details of the construction of impulse responses, see Lütkepohl (2005).

4.6.3 Variance Decomposition

Impulse response graphics of the type just displayed show the trajectories of system variable responses to incoming structural shocks. These graphics impart interpretable information about the internal dynamics within a VAR system that govern the transmission effects of shocks. To gain explicit quantitative insight on the relative importance of various structural shocks on the variables in the system, a variance decomposition can also be performed. The discussion of the variance decomposition will use some notation relating to forecasting, a topic that is formally dealt with in Chapter 7.

In this additional analysis, the forecast variances for each variable over alternative forecast horizons are decomposed into the separate relative effects of each structural shock, with the results expressed as a percentage of the overall movement. In the case of the SVAR model of equities and dividends given in equation (4.29), the approach is to express the forecast error variances of equities and dividends in terms of the structural shocks v_{1t} and v_{2t}. For additional details on the computation of the variance decomposition, see Martin, Hurn, and Harris (2013, pp. 498–500).

Forecast Error Variance at $T + 1$ for Equity

The one-step-ahead forecast error for equities at time $T + 1$ conditional on information at time T is defined as

$$e_{1T+1} = re_{T+1} - E_T(re_{T+1}). \tag{4.36}$$

Writing the expression for re_t in equation (4.29) at $T + 1$ and taking conditional expectations based on information at T gives

$$E_T(re_{T+1}) = E(\beta_{10} + \sum_{i=1}^{6} \beta_{11,i} re_{T+1-i} + \sum_{i=1}^{6} \beta_{12,i} rd_{T+1-i} + v_{1T+1})$$

$$= \beta_{10} + \sum_{i=1}^{6} \beta_{11,i} re_{T+1-i} + \sum_{i=1}^{6} \beta_{12,i} rd_{T+1-i},$$

since $E_T(v_{1T+1}) = 0$. The one-step-ahead forecast error for equities in equation (4.36) simply equals the equity structural shock

$$e_{1T+1} = v_{1T+1}. \tag{4.37}$$

The forecast error variance of equities at $T + 1$ is defined as

$$\text{var}(e_{1T+1}) = E_T[(e_{1T+1} - E_T(e_{1T+1}))^2] = E_T(e_{1T+1}^2) = E_T(v_{1T+1}^2), \tag{4.38}$$

which uses the property that $E_T(e_{1T+1}) = 0$ and uses the result in equation (4.37). This result shows that the equities forecast error variance at $T + 1$ is totally determined by its own shocks. This result immediately follows from the triangular ordering of the SVAR model specified in equation (4.29). Using the results in Table 4.3 the forecast error variance of equities at $T + 1$ is estimated as

$$\widehat{\text{var}}(e_{1T+1}) = 3.8593^2 = 14.8940.$$

This expression shows that 100% of the equities forecast error variance 14.8940 at $T + 1$ is the result of its own shocks to equities and nothing from dividend shocks. This decomposition is reported in the column headed "Decomposition of re" in Table 4.4 for Period 1.

Forecast Error Variance at $T + 1$ for Dividends

The one-step-ahead forecast error of dividends at $T + 1$ conditional on information at T is defined as

$$e_{2T+1} = rd_{T+1} - E_T(rd_{T+1}). \tag{4.39}$$

TABLE 4.4 Variance decomposition expressed in percentages computed from a VAR(6) model estimated using monthly data on US equity returns, re_t, and dividend returns, rd_t, over the period January 1871 to September 2016.

Period	Decomposition of *re*		Decomposition of *rd*	
	re	rd	re	rd
1	100.000	0.000	0.234	99.766
2	99.996	0.004	0.201	99.799
3	99.684	0.316	0.172	99.828
4	99.531	0.469	0.631	99.369
5	99.057	0.943	1.217	98.783
10	98.785	1.215	8.822	91.178
15	98.732	1.267	11.522	88.478
20	98.694	1.306	12.571	87.429
25	98.680	1.320	12.911	87.089
30	98.675	1.325	13.012	86.988

To derive an expression for the dividend forecast error in terms of the structural shocks, the expression for rd_t in equation (4.29) is rewritten at $T + 1$ as

$$rd_{T+1} = \beta_{20} + \rho\, re_{T+1} + \sum_{i=1}^{6} \beta_{21,i} re_{T+1-i} + \sum_{i=1}^{6} \beta_{22,i} rd_{T+1-i} + v_{2T+1}. \tag{4.40}$$

Taking expectations conditional on information at T gives

$$\mathrm{E}_T(rd_{T+1}) = \mathrm{E}_T\Big(\beta_{20} + \rho\, re_{T+1} + \sum_{i=1}^{6} \beta_{21,i} re_{T+1-i} + \sum_{i=1}^{6} \beta_{22,i} rd_{T+1-i} + v_{2T+1}\Big)$$

$$= \beta_{20} + \rho \mathrm{E}_T(re_{T+1}) + \sum_{i=1}^{6} \beta_{21,i} re_{T+1-i} + \sum_{i=1}^{6} \beta_{22,i} rd_{T+1-i}. \tag{4.41}$$

The forecast error for dividends in equation (4.39) is obtained by subtracting equation (4.41) from equation (4.40), resulting in

$$e_{2T+1} = \rho(re_{T+1} - \mathrm{E}_T(re_{T+1})) + v_{2T+1} = \rho v_{1T+1} + v_{2T+1}. \tag{4.42}$$

The forecast error at $T + 1$ for dividends is now a function of both structural shocks unlike the corresponding expression for equities in equation (4.37), which is simply a function of its own shock v_{1T+1}.

The forecast error variance of dividends at $T + 1$ is defined as

$$\mathrm{var}(e_{2T+1}) = \mathrm{E}_T[(e_{2T+1} - \mathrm{E}_T(e_{2T+1}))^2] = \mathrm{E}_T(e_{2T+1}^2), \tag{4.43}$$

which uses the property that $\mathrm{E}_T(e_{2T+1}) = 0$. From equation (4.42)

$$\mathrm{var}(e_{2T+1}) = \mathrm{E}_T[(\rho v_{1T+1} + v_{2T+1})^2]$$
$$= \mathrm{E}_T(\rho^2 v_{1T+1}^2 + v_{2T+1}^2 + 2\rho v_{1T+1} v_{2T+1})$$
$$= \rho^2 \mathrm{E}_T(v_{1T+1}^2) + \mathrm{E}_T(v_{2T+1}^2).$$

The last step uses the property that the structural shocks are independent of each other, $\mathrm{E}_T(v_{1T+1} v_{2T+1}) = 0$. From the results given in Table 4.3 and equations (4.30),

(4.31), and (4.33), the dividend forecast error variance at $T+1$ in equation (4.43) is estimated as

$$\widehat{\text{var}}(e_{2T+1}) = (-0.0061)^2 \times 3.8593^2 + 0.49044^2 = 0.0010 + 0.24053 = 0.2411.$$

This expression shows that for the dividends forecast error variance of 0.2411, $0.24053/0.2411 = 0.99766$, or 99.766%, is due to its own shocks and the remaining is due to equity shocks. This decomposition is reported in the column headed "Decomposition of rd" in Table 4.4 for Period 1.

Forecast Error Variances at Longer Horizons

Forecast error variances for equities and dividends for longer horizons are derived and decomposed in terms of the structural shocks using the same substitution techniques as adopted to derive the one-period forecast error variances. In the case of equities the forecast error variance at $T+2$ conditional on information at T is defined as

$$e_{1T+2} = re_{T+2} - \text{E}_T(re_{T+2}). \tag{4.44}$$

Now use equation (4.29) to rewrite the expression for equities at $T+2$ as

$$re_{T+2} = \beta_{10} + \sum_{i=1}^{6} \beta_{11,i} re_{T+2-i} + \sum_{i=1}^{6} \beta_{12,i} rd_{T+2-i} + v_{1T+2}.$$

Taking conditional expectations based on information at T gives

$$\text{E}_T(re_{T+2}) = \beta_{10} + \sum_{i=1}^{6} \beta_{11,i} \text{E}_T(re_{T+2-i}) + \sum_{i=1}^{6} \beta_{12,i} \text{E}_T(rd_{T+2-i}),$$

and the resulting equities forecast error variance at $T+2$ as

$$\begin{aligned}
e_{1T+2} &= re_{T+2} - \text{E}_T(re_{T+2}) \\
&= \beta_{11,1}(re_{T+1} - \text{E}_T(re_{T+1})) + \beta_{12,1}(rd_{T+1} - \text{E}_T(rd_{T+1})) + v_{1T+2} \\
&= \beta_{11,1} v_{1T+1} + \beta_{12,1} v_{2T+1} + v_{1T+2}. \tag{4.45}
\end{aligned}$$

This equities forecast error variance at $T+2$ is a function of three components: its own equity shock at $T+2$ as well as both equity and dividend shocks at $T+1$.

The equity forecast error variance at $T+2$ is defined as

$$\begin{aligned}
\text{var}(e_{1T+2}) &= \text{E}_T(e_{1T+2}^2) \\
&= \text{E}_T[(\beta_{11,1} v_{1T+1} + \beta_{12,1} v_{2T+1} + v_{1T+2})^2] \\
&= \beta_{11,1}^2 \text{E}_T(v_{1T+1}^2) + \beta_{12,1}^2 \text{E}_T(v_{2T+1}^2) + \text{E}_T(v_{1T+2}^2), \tag{4.46}
\end{aligned}$$

which uses equation (4.45). As the structural variances are time invariant, $\text{E}_T(v_{1T+2}^2) = \text{E}_T(v_{1T+1}^2)$, a comparison of equation (4.38) and (4.46) shows that the forecast error variance increases from $T+1$ to $T+2$, with the difference given by

$$\beta_{11,1}^2 \text{E}_T(v_{1T+1}^2) + \beta_{12,1}^2 \text{E}_T(v_{2T+1}^2) > 0.$$

From the results given in Table 4.3 the equity forecast error variance at $T+2$ in equation (4.46) is estimated as

$$\widehat{\text{var}}(e_{1T+2}) = 0.297^2 \times 3.8593^2 + (-0.049)^2 \times 0.49044^2 + 3.8593^2$$
$$= 1.3138 + 5.7752 \times 10^{-4} + 14.8940$$
$$= 16.209,$$

by using the assumption $E_T(v_{1T+2}^2) = E_T(v_{1T+1}^2)$. The total contribution of equity shocks to the equity forecast error variance is $(1.3138 + 14.8940)/16.209 = 0.9999$ or 99.99% with the remaining component due to dividend shocks. This decomposition is reported in the column headed "Decomposition of re" in Table 4.4 corresponding to Period 2.

Table 4.4 provides the variance decomposition expressed in percentages for equities and dividends up to a 30-period horizon. Evidently, dividend shocks contribute very little to equity returns with the maximum contribution being less than 2%. In contrast, equity return shocks after 15 periods contribute more than 10% of the variance in dividend returns. These results suggest that the effects of shocks to equity on dividends are relatively more important than in the reverse direction.

4.7 DIEBOLD–YILMAZ SPILLOVER INDEX

An important application of the variance decomposition in a VAR model is the spillover index proposed by Diebold and Yilmaz (2009). The objective in constructing this index is to calculate the total contribution of shocks on an asset market arising from the other variables in the VAR. Table 4.5 gives the volatility decomposition for a 10-week horizon of the weekly asset log returns of 19 countries based on a VAR with 2 lags and a constant. The sample period is from 4 December 1996 to 23 November 2007.

The first row of the table gives the contributions to the 10-week forecast variance of shocks in all 19 asset markets on US weekly returns. By excluding own market shocks, which equal 93.6%, the total contribution of the other 18 asset markets is given in the first cell of the last column (headed Others in the table) and equals

$$1.6 + 1.5 + \cdots + 0.3 = 6.4\%.$$

Similarly, for the United Kingdom in the second row of the table, the total contribution of the other 18 asset markets to its forecast variance is

$$40.3 + 0.7 + \cdots + 0.5 = 44.3\%.$$

Of the 19 asset markets, the US appears to be the most independent of all international asset markets as it has the lowest contributions from all other markets, equal to just 6.4%. The next lowest is Turkey with a contribution of 14.2%. Germany's asset market

TABLE 4.5 Diebold-Yilmaz spillover index of global stock market log returns. Based on a variance decomposition (expressed as a percentage) from estimating a 19 variable VAR with 2 lags and a constant.

To	US	UK	FRA	GER	HKG	JPN	AUS	IDN	KOR	MYS	PHL	SGP	TAI	THA	ARG	BRA	CHL	MEX	TUR	Others
US	93.6	1.6	1.5	0	0.3	0.2	0.1	0.1	0.2	0.3	0.2	0.2	0.3	0.2	0.1	0.1	0.0	0.5	0.3	6.4
UK	40.3	55.7	0.7	0.4	0.1	0.5	0.1	0.2	0.2	0.3	0.2	0.0	0.1	0.1	0.1	0.1	0.0	0.4	0.5	44.3
FRA	38.3	21.7	37.2	0.1	0.0	0.2	0.3	0.3	0.3	0.2	0.2	0.1	0.1	0.3	0.1	0.1	0.1	0.1	0.3	62.8
GER	40.8	15.9	13.0	27.6	0.1	0.1	0.3	0.4	0.6	0.1	0.3	0.3	0	0.2	0.0	0.1	0.0	0.1	0.1	72.4
HKG	15.3	8.7	1.7	1.4	69.9	0.3	0.0	0.1	0.0	0.3	0.1	0	0.2	0.9	0.3	0.0	0.1	0.3	0.4	30.1
JPN	12.1	3.1	1.8	0.9	2.3	77.7	0.2	0.3	0.3	0.1	0.2	0.3	0.3	0.1	0.1	0.0	0.0	0.1	0.1	22.3
AUS	23.2	6.0	1.3	0.2	6.4	2.3	56.8	0.1	0.4	0.2	0.2	0.2	0.4	0.5	0.1	0.3	0.1	0.6	0.7	43.2
IDN	6.0	1.6	1.2	0.7	6.4	1.6	0.4	77.0	0.7	0.4	0.1	0.9	0.2	1.0	0.7	0.1	0.3	0.1	0.4	23.0
KOR	8.3	2.6	1.3	0.7	5.6	3.7	1.0	1.2	72.8	0.0	0.0	0.1	0.1	1.3	0.2	0.2	0.1	0.1	0.7	27.2
MYS	4.1	2.2	0.6	1.3	10.5	1.5	0.4	6.6	0.5	69.2	0.1	0.1	0.2	1.1	0.1	0.6	0.4	0.2	0.3	30.8
PHL	11.1	1.6	0.3	0.2	8.1	0.4	0.9	7.2	0.1	2.9	62.9	0.3	0.4	1.5	1.6	0.1	0	0.1	0.2	37.1
SGP	16.8	4.8	0.6	0.9	18.5	1.3	0.4	3.2	1.6	3.6	1.7	43.1	0.3	1.1	0.8	0.5	0.1	0.3	0.4	56.9
TAI	6.4	1.3	1.2	1.8	5.3	2.8	0.4	0.4	2.0	1.0	1.0	0.9	73.6	0.4	0.8	0.3	0.1	0.3	0.0	26.4
THA	6.3	2.4	1.0	0.7	7.8	0.2	0.8	7.6	4.6	4.0	2.3	2.2	0.3	58.2	0.5	0.2	0.1	0.4	0.3	41.8
ARG	11.9	2.1	1.6	0.1	1.3	0.8	1.3	0.4	0.4	0.6	0.4	0.6	1.1	0.2	75.3	0.1	0.1	1.4	0.3	24.7
BRA	14.1	1.3	1.0	0.7	1.3	1.4	1.6	0.5	0.5	0.7	1.0	0.8	0.1	0.7	7.1	65.8	0.1	0.6	0.7	34.2
CHL	11.8	1.1	1	0.0	3.2	0.6	1.4	2.3	0.3	0.3	0.1	0.9	0.3	0.8	2.9	4.0	65.8	2.7	0.4	34.2
MEX	22.2	3.5	1.2	0.4	3.0	0.3	1.2	0.2	0.3	0.9	1.0	0.1	0.3	0.5	5.4	1.6	0.3	56.9	0.6	43.1
TUR	3.0	2.5	0.2	0.7	0.6	0.9	0.6	0.1	0.6	0.3	0.6	0.1	0.9	0.8	0.5	1.1	0.6	0.2	85.8	14.2
Others	291.9	84.1	31	11.2	80.8	19.2	11.5	31.4	13.6	16.2	9.9	8.2	5.9	11.8	21.4	9.4	2.6	8.4	6.7	675.1
Own	385.5	139.8	68.2	38.8	150.6	96.9	68.3	108.3	86.4	85.4	72.8	51.2	79.5	70.0	96.7	75.2	68.4	65.4	92.4	Index = 35.5%

appears to be the most affected by international shocks with shocks from external markets contributing 72.4% to its forecast variance.

Adding the separate contributions to each asset market in the last column gives the total contributions of external (to own market) shocks on all 19 asset markets

$$6.4 + 44.3 + \cdots + 14.2 = 675.1\%.$$

As the contributions to the total forecast variance by construction are normalized to sum to 100% for each of the 19 asset markets, the percentage contribution of external shocks to these 19 asset markets is given by the spillover index

$$SPILLOVER = \frac{675.1}{19} = 35.5\%.$$

This value shows that on average approximately one-third of the forecast variance of asset returns in these countries is the result of foreign shocks, with the remaining two-thirds arising from local shocks.

4.8 EXERCISES

The data required for the exercises are available for download as EViews workfiles (*.wf1), Stata datafiles (*.dta), comma delimited text files (*.csv), and as Excel spreadsheets (*.xlsx).

1. Equity and Dividend Returns

pv.*

The data are monthly observations on US equity prices and dividends for the period January 1871 to September 2016.

(a) Compute the percentage monthly log returns on equities and dividends expressed as percentages, defined as

$$re_t = 100 \times (\log P_t - \log P_{t-1})$$
$$rd_t = 100 \times (\log D_t - \log D_{t-1}).$$

Plot the two series and interpret their time series patterns.

(b) Compute the ACF of equity returns for up to 6 lags. Compare a manual procedure with an automated version provided by econometric software.

(c) Compute the PACF of equity returns for up to 6 lags. Compare a manual procedure with an automated version provided by econometric software.

(d) Repeat parts (b) and (c) for dividend returns.

(e) Estimate an AR(6) model of equity returns. Interpret the parameter estimates.

(f) Estimate an MA(3) model of equity returns using the following two-step method (Durbin, 1959) to circumvent the necessity of using a nonlinear estimation procedure. The steps are as follows.

(i) Estimate an autoregressive model for y_t with a constant term and $p > 3$ autoregressive terms,

$$re_t = \phi_0 + \phi_1 y_{t-1} + \cdots + \phi_p y_{t-p} + u_t$$

and save the residuals $\widehat{u}_t$.

(ii) Estimate the MA(3) parameters by estimating the model

$$re_t = \psi_0 + \psi_1 \widehat{u}_{t-1} + \psi_2 \widehat{u}_{t-2} + \psi_3 \widehat{u}_{t-3} + v_t,$$

by ordinary least squares. Comment on the results.

(g) Using the same two-step procedure, estimate an ARMA(1,1) model of equity returns. The procedure is now as follows.

(i) Estimate an AR(p) model with P and save the residuals, $\widehat{u}_t$.
(ii) Estimate an ARMA(p, q) model using 1 lag of the dependent variable and 1 lag of the fitted residuals, $\widehat{u}_{t-1}$. Interpret your results.

2. Forward Market Efficiency

> spot.*

The data are weekly observations (all recorded on a Wednesday) for the period 4 January 1984 to 31 December 1990 on the spot US/Australian exchange rate and the 1-month, 3-month, and 6-month forward US/Australian exchange rates.

(a) The forward market is efficient if the lagged forward rate is an unbiased predictor of the current spot rate. Estimate the following model of the spot and the lagged 1-month forward rate

$$s_t = \beta_0 + \beta_1 f_{t-4} + u_t,$$

where the forward rate is lagged four periods (the data are weekly). Test the restriction $\beta_1 = 1$ and interpret the result.

(b) Compute the ACF and PACF of the least squares residuals, $\widehat{u}_t$, for the first 8 lags. Interpret the results.

(c) Repeat parts (a) and (b) for the 3-month (12 lags) and the 6-month (24 lags) forward rates.

3. Mean Aversion and Reversion in Stock Returns

> international_annual.*, international_quarterly.*, international_monthly.*

The data files contain, respectively, annual, monthly, and weekly log returns data (expressed as percentages) for the years 1989 to 2009 on the Australian share index, the NASDAQ index, and the Singapore Straits Times index.

(a) Estimate the following regression equation using returns on the NASDAQ, re_t, for each frequency (monthly, quarterly, annual)

$$re_t = \phi_0 + \phi_1 re_{t-1} + u_t,$$

where u_t is a disturbance term. Interpret the results.
(b) Repeat part (a) for the Australian share price index.
(c) Repeat part (a) for the Singapore Straits Times stock index.

4. An Equity–Dividend VAR

pv.*

Use the same data set as in Exercise 1 and also the same definitions of equity, re_t, and dividend, rd_t, returns.

(a) Compute the percentage monthly returns on equities and dividends and estimate a bivariate VAR(6) for these variables.
(b) Test for the optimum choice of lag length using information criteria and specifying a maximum lag length of 12.
(c) Test for Granger causality between equities and dividends and interpret the results.
(d) Compute the impulse responses for 30 periods and interpret the results.
(e) Compute the variance decomposition for 30 periods and interpret the results.

5. Campbell–Shiller Present Value Model

cam_shiller.*

The data are monthly data for the period January 1933 to December 1990 comprising observations on US equity prices and dividend payments. Let y_t be dividend yields (expressed in percentage terms), and let v_t be deviations from the present value model

$$p_t = \beta + \alpha d_t + v_t,$$

where p_t is the log of equity prices and d_t log dividend payments. Campbell and Shiller (1987) develop a VAR(1) model for y_t and v_t given by

$$\begin{bmatrix} y_t \\ v_t \end{bmatrix} = \begin{bmatrix} \phi_{10} \\ \phi_{20} \end{bmatrix} + \begin{bmatrix} \phi_{11} & \phi_{12} \\ \phi_{21} & \phi_{22} \end{bmatrix} \begin{bmatrix} y_{t-1} \\ v_{t-1} \end{bmatrix} + \begin{bmatrix} u_{1t} \\ u_{2t} \end{bmatrix}.$$

(a) Estimate the parameter α and compute the least squares residuals $\widehat{v}_t$.
(b) Estimate the VAR(1) containing the dividend yields, y_t, and $\widehat{v}_t$.
(c) Campbell and Shiller show that

$$\phi_{22} = \delta^{-1} - \alpha \phi_{12},$$

where δ represents the discount factor. Use the parameter estimate of α obtained in part (a) and the parameter estimates of ϕ_{12} and ϕ_{22} obtained in part (b) to estimate δ. Interpret the result.

6. Campbell–Shiller Model of Interest Rates

> yields_us.*

The data are monthly observations on US zero-coupon bonds with maturities of $\{1, 3, 6, 12, 24, 36, 60, 84, 120\}$ months. The sample period is from July 2001 to September 2010. Campbell and Shiller (1991) proposed testing the relationship between short-term rates of maturity m and longer-term rates of maturity $n > m$ using the regression.

$$r_{n-m,t} - r_{n,t-m} = \alpha + \beta(r_{n,t-m} - r_{m,t-m}) + u_t,$$

where u_t is a disturbance term. Of particular interest is whether or not the slope coefficient β satisfies the relationship $\beta = m/(n-m)$.

(a) Test this relationship for maturities of $m = 3$ months and $n = 6$ months.
(b) Test this relationship for maturities of $m = 1$ year and $n = 2$ years.
(c) Test this relationship for maturities of $m = 1$ year and $n = 3$ years.

7. Diebold–Yilmaz Spillover Index

> diebold.*

Diebold and Yilmaz (2009) construct spillover indices of international real asset returns and volatility based on the variance decomposition of a VAR. The data file contains weekly data on real asset returns, *rets*, and volatility, *vol*, of 7 developed countries and 12 emerging countries from the first week of January 1992 to the fourth week of November 2007.

(a) Compute descriptive statistics of the 19 real asset market returns given in *rets*. Compare the estimates with the results reported in Table 1 of Diebold and Yilmaz.
(b) Estimate a VAR(2) containing a constant and the 19 real asset market returns.
(c) Estimate VD_{10}, the variance decomposition for horizon $h = 10$. Using the results, compute the "Contribution from Others" by summing each row of VD_{10} excluding the diagonal elements, and the "Contribution to Others" by summing each column of VD_{10} excluding the diagonal elements. Compare these estimates with the results reported in Table 3 of Diebold and Yilmaz.
(d) Repeat parts (a) to (c) with the 19 series in *rets* replaced by the series in *vol*, and the comparisons now based on Tables 2 and 4 in Diebold and Yilmaz.

CHAPTER 5

Nonstationarity in Financial Time Series

An important property of asset prices identified in Chapter 2 is that they exhibit strong evidence of trends over long periods of time. Trend behavior often manifests in a tendency for a time series to drift over time in such a way that no fixed mean value is revealed. This property is highlighted in Figure 2.1, which shows that the S&P 500 stock price index displays a general pattern of exponential growth over a long historical period from 1950 to 2016. But this long term growth is coupled with extended sub-periods in which prices wander above and below the growth line. Such time series are said to be nonstationary and may embody both a deterministic drift, which manifests in the exponential growth path shown in Figure 2.1, and a stochastic process trend, which arises from the accumulation of random forces that drive prices to wander above and below the path of deterministic drift.

Nonstationarity in this complex form that combines deterministic and random forces is one of the primary characteristics of financial time series. Nonstationary behavior needs to be respected in empirical work because of the importance of linkages between trending financial time series that are often the subject of investigation, because of the serious impact that trends can have on forecasting performance, and because of major changes in the econometric apparatus of inference when trends are present in the data.

Financial series that exhibit no such trending behavior and whose mean, variance, and autocovariances are time invariant are said to be stationary and are the subject matter of Chapter 4. This chapter provides an introduction to some of the main properties of nonstationary time series and the models that generate such series. Its primary focus is on identifying and testing for nonstationarity in financial time series.

Identification of stochastic, as distinct from deterministic, nonstationarity typically hinges on testing evidence in support of a unit root restriction, $\rho = 1$, in an autoregressive model of the form

$$y_t = \rho y_{t-1} + v_t, \tag{5.1}$$

in which v_t is a stationary disturbance term. If the restriction $\rho = 1$ is satisfied and $v_t \sim iid(0, \sigma_v^2)$, where, from Chapter 4, iid stands for independently and identically distributed, this model is commonly known as a random walk without drift. Tests of the restriction $\rho = 1$ are referred to as unit root tests and have very different characteristics from traditional regression tests in stationary time series models where $|\rho| < 1$. The trajectories of unit root processes may be regarded as random draws of a function that is observed at discrete points in time over the interval of observation. In consequence, under a unit root null hypothesis, estimates of the parameter ρ and test statistics of the hypothesis that $\rho = 1$ have asymptotic distributions that rely on the distribution of these entire trajectories. These distributions differ considerably from a normal distribution and lead to new procedures for testing.

The classification of variables as either stationary or nonstationary has implications in both finance and econometrics. From a finance perspective, stochastic nonstationarity is important because the ubiquity of the random forces driving financial asset prices leads to the wandering price trajectories that are typically observed in practice. Within this class of models, unit root processes like equation (5.1) with $\rho = 1$ have special significance because they are compatible with common formulations of the efficient markets hypothesis. According to this hypothesis in its general form, all the information about the future price of an asset is embodied in the most recently observed price. So the conditional expectation of tomorrow's price, given the price history to today, is simply today's price.

Small departures from the unit root class both above and below unity are also important. If nonstationarity takes the form of an explosive process with $\rho > 1$, then this may be taken as evidence of the emergence of financial exuberance associated with the expansionary phase of a bubble in the price of the asset. For values of ρ less than unity, as already noted, y_t in equation (5.1) is a stationary process with statistical properties that are very different from the unit root ($\rho = 1$) and explosive ($\rho > 1$) processes.

5.1 THE RANDOM WALK WITH DRIFT

Specification

The return to a risky asset in an efficient market may be written as

$$r_t = p_t - p_{t-1} = \alpha + v_t, \qquad v_t \sim iid(0, \sigma_v^2), \tag{5.2}$$

where p_t is the logarithm of the asset price. The parameter α represents the average return on the asset. From an efficient markets point of view, v_t is not autocorrelated, r_{t+1} cannot be predicted using information at time t.

Another way of expressing equation (5.2) is to write the equation in terms of p_t as

$$p_t = \alpha + p_{t-1} + v_t. \tag{5.3}$$

The parameter α is the drift parameter with y_t now representing a random walk with drift, so that the dependence of p_t on the past history of shocks v_j and the origination of the process is apparent. Start by lagging the random walk with drift model in equation (5.3) by one period, giving

$$p_{t-1} = \alpha + p_{t-2} + v_{t-1},$$

and substituting this expression for p_{t-1} in equation (5.3) gives

$$p_t = \alpha + \alpha + p_{t-2} + v_t + v_{t-1}.$$

Repeating this recursive substitution process for t-steps gives

$$p_t = p_0 + \alpha t + v_t + v_{t-1} + v_{t-2} + \cdots + v_1 = \alpha t + \sum_{j=1}^{t} v_j + p_0, \qquad (5.4)$$

in which p_t is fully determined by its initial value, p_0, a deterministic trend component, and the accumulation of the complete history of shocks since initialization of the process at $t = 0$.

The unit root mechanism is evident in the equation both in the unit coefficient of the lagged price variable p_{t-1} and in the accumulation process $\sum_{j=1}^{t} v_j$ whose weights are unity in all time periods. The drift parameter α now determines the extent of the deterministic drift measured by the linear time trend αt. From an efficient market perspective, this equation shows that in predicting the price of an asset in the next period, all of the relevant information is contained in the current price when $\alpha = 0$.

Properties

Taking expectations of expression (5.4) and using the property that $E(v_t) = E(v_{t-1}) = \cdots = 0$, gives the mean of p_t

$$E(p_t) = p_0 + \alpha t.$$

Evidently when $\alpha > 0$, the mean price drifts upward and increases over time at the same constant rate α. Even when the drift parameter α is small, over long periods of time the upward drift in the mean price becomes a prominent characteristic of the time series. The variance of p_t is given at each point in time by

$$\text{var}(p_t) = E\{[p_t - E(p_t)]^2\} = t\sigma_v^2,$$

which uses the *iid* property that the component shocks v_j are uncorrelated. Just as for the mean, the variance is also a linear increasing function over time. So the asset price p_t exhibits greater overall variation, or fluctuations with increasing amplitude, as time passes. These properties reveal some of the implications of the efficient market hypothesis on the time series behavior of financial asset prices. Specifically, in an efficient market, asset prices may be expected to exhibit trending behavior in levels and in long-term fluctuations.

To appreciate the capabilities of a simple time series model such as equation (5.4) in capturing the main time series features of financial asset prices, it is useful to view a simulation of this time series. Figure 5.1 plots a simulated random walk with drift based on equation (5.4). The parameters of the random walk with drift are taken to be[1] $p_0 = 1.491$, $\alpha = 0.0035$, and $\sigma_v^2 = 0.002$.

Observe that the simulated price exhibits two major characteristics: an increasing mean, associated with the positive drift upward in the series; and an increasing variance over time, associated with the accumulation of shocks, $\sum_{j=1}^{t} v_j$, that appears in the model solution in equation (5.4). The simulated price series has similar characteristics to the observed logarithm of the price index given in Figure 2.2 in Chapter 2.

---

[1] These values are based on the S&P 500 index from January 1871 to September 2016, where p_0 is the log price in January 1871, and α and σ_v^2 are, respectively, the mean and the variance of log returns over the sample period.

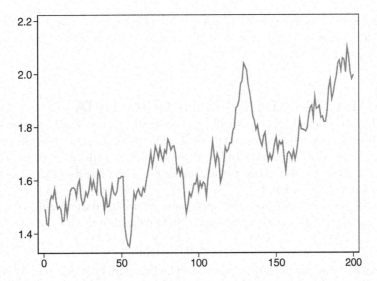

FIGURE 5.1 Simulated trajectory of a random walk with drift based on equation (5.4) with parameter values $p_0 = 1.491$, $\alpha = 0.0035$, and $\sigma_v^2 = 0.002$. The distribution of the disturbance term, v_t in equation (5.3), is taken to be normal.

Order of Integration

The partial summation component of p_t, namely, $\sum_{j=1}^{t} v_j$ in equation (5.4), is known as a stochastic trend component, which aggregates (or integrates) up the component shocks v_j. Simply removing the deterministic trend, αt, from the process y_t will not be sufficient to obtain a stationary series because the stochastic trend component is still retained. This partial summation component is the origin of an important concept concerning nonstationarity, namely, *the order of integration* of a time series. A process is integrated of order d, denoted by $I(d)$, if it can be rendered stationary by differencing d times. Setting $d = 1$ to ensure differencing once, we have

$$\Delta p_t = \alpha + v_t,$$

where the symbol Δ is known as the difference operator, leading to $\Delta p_t = p_t - p_{t-1}$. The series Δp_t is stationary with mean α, variance σ_v^2, and disturbance v_t, which in the case of model equation (5.3) is serially uncorrelated.

A general time series y_t is said to be integrated of order one, denoted $I(1)$, if it is rendered stationary by differencing once that is, y_t is nonstationary, but $\Delta y_t = y_t - y_{t-1}$ is stationary[2]. If $d = 2$, then y_t is $I(2)$ and needs to be differenced twice to achieve stationarity as follows

$$\Delta(y_t - y_{t-1}) = (y_t - y_{t-1}) - (y_{t-1} - y_{t-2}) = y_t - 2y_{t-1} + y_{t-2}.$$

---

[2] Strictly speaking, the $I(1)$ property also requires that Δy_t not be representable as a difference of some stationary time series w_t, in which case $\Delta y_t = y_t - y_{t-1} = w_t - w_{t-1}$; and then $y_t = w_t$ would itself be stationary.

It is rare for financial series to exhibit orders of integration greater than $d = 2$. By analogy, a stationary process is integrated of order zero, $I(0)$, because it does not require any differencing to achieve stationarity.[3]

5.2 CHARACTERISTICS OF FINANCIAL DATA

Most financial econometricians agree that the dominant characteristics of many financial time series arise from the random forces involved in stochastic process trends rather than deterministic trends. It is particularly hard to reconcile the strong predictability that is implied by a deterministic trend with the complications and surprises that are continually faced by financial forecasters.[4]

To illustrate the point about the importance of the stochastic trend component in bond market data, consider fitting a simple AR(1) regression model

$$y_t = \alpha + \rho y_{t-1} + v_t, \tag{5.5}$$

to bond yields. The empirical results obtained by fitting this regression to monthly data on US zero-coupon bonds with maturities ranging from 2 months to 9 months for the period January 1947 to February 1987 are given in Table 5.1.

The primary result of interest in the estimated regressions reported in Table 5.1 is that the fitted slope coefficient, $\widehat{\rho}$, is universally close to unity and strongly indicative of the presence of a stochastic trend in the data. A secondary result of importance is that the fitted intercept $\widehat{\alpha}$ is small and positive, indicative of a very small (and possibly insignificant) drift in the time series over time, an outcome that is consistent across all maturities and, accordingly, the more persuasive. This general pattern in the estimated

TABLE 5.1   Ordinary least squares estimates of an AR(1) model estimated using monthly data on US zero-coupon bonds with maturities ranging from 2 months to 9 months for the period January 1947 to February 1987.

Maturity	Intercept		Slope	
(months)	$(\widehat{\alpha})$	$se(\widehat{\alpha})$	$(\widehat{\rho})$	$se(\widehat{\rho})$
2	0.090	0.046	0.983	0.008
3	0.087	0.045	0.984	0.008
4	0.085	0.044	0.985	0.007
5	0.085	0.045	0.985	0.007
6	0.087	0.045	0.985	0.007
9	0.088	0.046	0.985	0.007

[3] Fractional values of d are also possible and these correspond to more general forms of nonstationarity (sometimes referred to as long-memory) in the data. While these long-memory processes are appropriate in some instances in financial econometric work, attention here is confined to $I(d)$ processes with integer values of d.

[4] Indeed, it was the astonishing failure of stock market forecasters, including some leading economists such as Irving Fisher, during the period leading up to the great stock market crash of October 1929 that led Alfred Cowles in 1932 to establish the Cowles Commission for Research in Economics whose immediate goal was to advance a scientific understanding of stock market forecasting.

coefficients observed in Table 5.1 is indicative of a much more general finding that is almost ubiquitous in other financial markets, such as currency markets (spot and forward exchange rates), equity markets (share prices and dividends), and commodity markets (such as oil, gas, gold, and copper).

As an example of financial data drawn from equity rather than bond markets, consider Figure 5.2 that shows time series of US equity prices and various transformations of this series over the period from January 1871 to June 2004. Even casual inspection of these plots reveals prominent characteristics of equity prices that relate to the discussion concerning the random walk with drift model and the importance of the stochastic trend component. It is clear from Figure 5.2 that equity prices and the logarithm of equity prices are nonstationary. Both these series exhibit a general upward drift in mean, signalling $\alpha > 0$ and confirming a positive trend over this long historical period.

Simple first differencing of equity prices, on the other hand, renders the series constant in mean over time but with an apparent nonstationarity in the variance, as the variability of the first differences increases dramatically over time. The implication is that first differencing equity prices does not on its own produce a stationary series. Finally, equity returns defined as the first differences of the logarithms of prices evidently manifest greater stability over time, both in mean and in variance. But considerable fluctuations in the variance are still apparent in the equity returns series, indicating some instability or potential nonstationarity in variance.

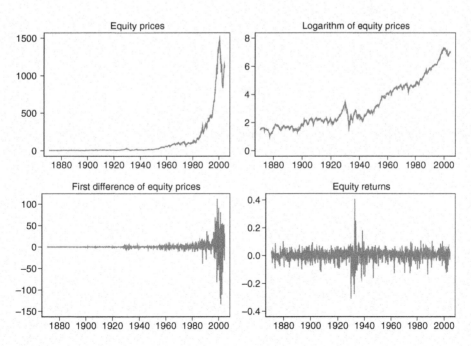

FIGURE 5.2 Monthly US equity prices and various transformations of the equity price process for the period January 1871 to June 2004.

The plots shown in Figure 5.2 reveal that certain transformations of time series, such as taking logarithms and first differencing, can be useful in revealing underlying characteristics of the series.[5] The preceding discussion points to some of their advantages and limitations. In particular, first differencing prices may help to remove nonstationarity in the mean, and first differencing logarithms of prices may help to stabilize the variance as well. While such transformations are helpful in interpreting properties of financial time series and are heavily used in practical work, there are limitations to what they can accomplish. As the plot of equity returns in Figure 5.2 shows, however, there is still much to explain in the apparent time-varying volatility of this series.

5.3 DICKEY–FULLER METHODS AND UNIT ROOT TESTING

The methods considered in Dickey and Fuller (1979, 1981) were developed as tests of the hypothesis $\rho = 1$ in equation (5.5) with the additional assumption that the disturbance term, v_t, is normally distributed.[6] With some modifications to the form of these tests and under more general assumptions and asymptotic theory, these procedures provide a framework for assessing evidence for the presence of a unit root in fairly general time series settings. This framework is now extensively used in applied econometric work and it remains one of the most popular methods of testing for nonstationarity in financial time series. The approach is called unit root testing.

5.3.1 The Dickey–Fuller (DF) Unit Root Tests

Consider again the AR(1) regression equation

$$y_t = \alpha + \rho y_{t-1} + v_t, \tag{5.6}$$

in which $v_t \sim N(0, \sigma_v^2)$. The relevant null and alternative hypotheses are stated as follows

$$\begin{aligned} &H_0 : \ \rho = 1 \ [\text{Variable } y_t \text{ is nonstationary}] \\ &H_1 : |\rho| < 1 \ [\text{Variable } y_t \text{ is stationary}]. \end{aligned} \tag{5.7}$$

Importantly, H_1 is a left-sided alternative to the unit root null H_0. To perform the test, equation (5.6) is estimated by ordinary least squares regression and a t statistic is constructed in the usual manner to test whether $\rho = 1$. This statistic has the conventional ratio form

$$t_\rho = \frac{\widehat{\rho} - 1}{\text{se}(\widehat{\rho})}, \tag{5.8}$$

---

[5] These transformations are examples of filters. Filters are particularly useful in detrending data and removing recurrent effects such as seasonality. They are therefore heavily used in empirical work.

[6] Extension to more general conditions where the data are not normally distributed and the innovations are serially dependent and possibly heterogeneous involves what is known as an *invariance principle* because the final asymptotic result is invariant to the assumption of normality. Phillips (1987) verified the existence of such an invariance principle in this setting, showing that the results obtained by Dickey and Fuller (1979, 1981) have more general representations and with certain adjustments to the statistics, the asymptotic theory remains valid under much more general conditions.

where $se(\hat{\rho})$ is the standard error of $\hat{\rho}$. There is no deviation from normal practice up to this point in testing the hypothesis: Estimation of equation (5.6) by ordinary least squares, construction of the standard error of $\hat{\rho}$, and the use of the t statistic in equation (5.8) to test the hypothesis H_0 are all sound procedures. The difficulty in executing the test arises from the fact that under the null hypothesis, the time series y_t is nonstationary and nonstationarity affects both the finite sample and asymptotic distribution of the statistic t_ρ. Even under the normality assumption used by Dickey and Fuller (1979, 1981) the statistic t_ρ does not have a t distribution.

In practice, it is convenient to transform equation (5.6) in a way that converts the t statistic in equation (5.8) to a test of a zero slope coefficient in the transformed equation. This transformation has the great advantage that the t statistic commonly reported in standard regression packages directly yields the unit root test statistic. To achieve this transformation, simply subtract y_{t-1} from both sides of equation (5.6) and collect terms to give

$$y_t - y_{t-1} = \alpha + (\rho - 1)y_{t-1} + v_t. \tag{5.9}$$

Defining $\beta = \rho - 1$ gives the regression equation

$$y_t - y_{t-1} = \alpha + \beta y_{t-1} + v_t. \tag{5.10}$$

Equations (5.6) and (5.10) are precisely the same equations with the connection between them being the simple reparameterization $\beta = \rho - 1$ in equation (5.10).

To illustrate this equivalence in a practical application, consider the monthly data on US zero-coupon bonds with maturities ranging from 2 months to 9 months for the period January 1947 to February 1987. This data is used in the estimation of the AR(1) regressions reported in Table 5.1. Estimation of equation (5.6) yields the following results (with standard errors given in parentheses)

$$y_t = \underset{(0.046)}{0.090} + \underset{(0.008)}{0.983}\, y_{t-1} + \hat{v}_t. \tag{5.11}$$

On the other hand, estimating the transformed equation (5.10) yields

$$y_t - y_{t-1} = \underset{(0.046)}{0.090} - \underset{(0.008)}{0.017}\, y_{t-1} + \hat{v}_t. \tag{5.12}$$

Comparison of the estimated equations in (5.11) and (5.12) shows that they differ only in terms of the slope estimate on y_{t-1}. The difference in the two slope estimates is easily reconciled as the slope estimate of (5.11) is $\hat{\rho} = 0.983$, whereas an estimate of β may be recovered as

$$\hat{\beta} = \hat{\rho} - 1 = 0.983 - 1 = -0.017.$$

This is also the slope estimate obtained in equation (5.12). To perform a statistical test of the null hypothesis $H_0 : \rho = 1$, the two relevant t statistics in these two regressions are

$$t_\rho = \frac{\hat{\rho} - 1}{se(\hat{\rho})} = \frac{0.983 - 1}{0.008} = -2.120,$$

$$t_\beta = \frac{\hat{\beta} - 0}{se(\hat{\beta})} = \frac{-0.017 - 0}{0.008} = -2.120,$$

demonstrating that the two methods are indeed equivalent.

These tests can be extended to deal with the possibility that under the alternative hypothesis the time series may be stationary around a deterministic trend. As discussed in Sections 5.1 and 5.2, financial data typically exhibit trends and empirical researchers therefore face the difficulty of distinguishing between stochastic and deterministic trends. If the data do trend over time and if the null hypothesis of nonstationarity is rejected, it is important that the maintained model under the alternative hypothesis is able to account for the major characteristics displayed by the series being tested.

If the regression equation (5.10) is used for testing and the null hypothesis of a unit root is rejected, the alternative hypothesis is that of a process which is stationary around a constant. In other words, the model under the alternative hypothesis contains no deterministic trend. The maintained hypothesis is therefore not general enough to accommodate a trend stationary time series as an alternative. Consequently, an important extension of the unit root testing framework is to include a linear time trend in the test regression to account for any deterministic drift that may be present in the time series.

The form of the equation to be estimated is

$$y_t - y_{t-1} = \alpha + \delta t + \beta y_{t-1} + v_t. \tag{5.13}$$

The Dickey–Fuller test still consists of testing $\beta = 0$. But under the alternative hypothesis, y_t is now a stationary process with a deterministic trend.

Once again using the monthly data on US zero-coupon bonds, the estimated regression including the time trend gives the following results (with standard errors in parentheses)

$$\Delta y_t = \underset{(0.052)}{0.030} + \underset{(0.001)}{0.001}\, t - \underset{(0.014)}{0.046}\, y_{t-1} + \widehat{v}_t.$$

The value of the Dickey–Fuller test statistic is

$$t_\beta = \frac{\widehat{\beta} - 0}{\mathrm{se}(\widehat{\beta})} = \frac{-0.046 - 0}{0.014} = -3.172.$$

In general, three basic forms of the Dickey–Fuller unit root test are available, based on the following simple regression equations

$$
\begin{aligned}
\textbf{Model 1:} \quad & \Delta y_t = \beta y_{t-1} + v_t, \\
\textbf{Model 2:} \quad & \Delta y_t = \alpha + \beta y_{t-1} + v_t, \\
\textbf{Model 3:} \quad & \Delta y_t = \alpha + \delta t + \beta y_{t-1} + v_t,
\end{aligned}
\tag{5.14}
$$

where Model 3 corresponds to equation (5.13). For each of these three models, the null hypothesis of the unit root test remains the same, namely, $H_0: \beta = 0$. Unlike conventional statistical testing, however, the pertinent critical value for determining statistical significance in each case is different. The differences arise because the distribution of the unit root test statistic changes substantially depending on which model is used as the test regression. Thus, changing the regression equation by adding an intercept and/or a linear time trend not only affects the fitted regression coefficients and t statistics, it also changes their asymptotic distributions.

To illustrate these differences, the distributions of the scaled coefficient statistic $T\widehat{\beta}$ for the different versions of the Dickey–Fuller test regression are shown in Figure 5.3. In addition, Figure 5.4 shows the distributions of the Dickey–Fuller t statistics for each of the models. The key point to note in these distributions is that all three distributions

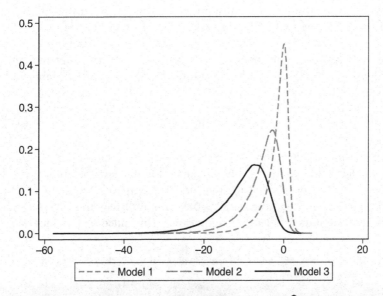

FIGURE 5.3 Comparisons of the simulated scaled distributions of $T\widehat{\beta}$ for the Dickey–Fuller regressions in Model 1 (dashed line), Model 2 (long-dashed line), and Model 3 (solid line).

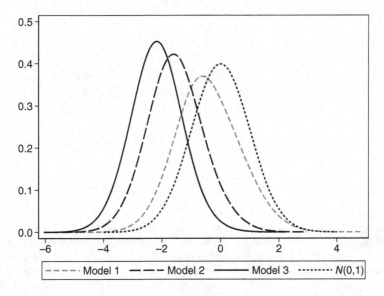

FIGURE 5.4 Comparisons of the simulated distributions of the t statistic from the three Dickey–Fuller regressions in Model 1 (dashed line), Model 2 (long-dashed line), and Model 3 (solid line). The standard normal curve (dotted line) is provided as a reference point.

are heavily skewed to the left and are also located to the left of a standard normal distribution.[7] In addition, these distributions become more dispersed, more located to the left of the origin, and less negatively skewed as more deterministic components (constants and time trends) are included.[8] This skewness has a major impact on statistical inference because the critical values of the test statistic are very different from those of conventional statistical tests with an asymptotic normal distribution. Table 5.2 provides critical values of the tests for the 1%, 2.5%, 5%, and 10% levels of significance. Note, however, that most econometric packages will report critical values and p values for the Dickey–Fuller test regressions based on the response surface regressions calculated by MacKinnon (1994).

As an empirical illustration, the monthly US zero-coupon bond data are used to estimate Model 2 and Model 3, and p values for the tests are those derived from MacKinnon (1994). The p value for the Model 2 unit root test statistic (-2.120) is found to be 0.237; and because $0.237 > 0.05$, the null hypothesis of nonstationarity cannot be rejected at the 5% level of significance. This outcome provides evidence that

TABLE 5.2 The 1%, 2.5%, 5%, and 10% critical values of the Dickey–Fuller test for Models 1, 2, and 3 for various sample sizes.

	T	1%	2.5%	5%	10%
Model 1	25	−2.66	−2.26	−1.95	−1.60
	50	−2.62	−2.25	−1.95	−1.61
	100	−2.60	−2.24	−1.95	−1.61
	250	−2.58	−2.23	−1.95	−1.61
	500	−2.58	−2.23	−1.95	−1.61
	∞	−2.58	−2.23	−1.95	−1.61
Model 2	25	−3.75	−3.33	−3.00	−2.62
	50	−3.58	−3.22	−2.93	−2.60
	100	−3.51	−3.17	−2.89	−2.58
	250	−3.46	−3.14	−2.88	−2.57
	500	−3.44	−3.13	−2.87	−2.57
	∞	−3.43	−3.12	−2.86	−2.57
Model 3	25	−4.38	−3.95	−3.60	−3.24
	50	−4.15	−3.80	−3.50	−3.18
	100	−4.04	−3.73	−3.45	−3.15
	250	−3.99	−3.69	−3.43	−3.13
	500	−3.98	−3.68	−3.42	−3.13
	∞	−3.96	−3.66	−3.41	−3.12

---

[7] These asymptotic distributions are derived using a body of probability theory known as functional central limit theory. Functional central limit theory is concerned with establishing that certain function-valued random elements have limits as Gaussian stochastic processes, the most famous of which is Brownian motion. Brownian motion was discovered by the British botanist Robert Brown in 1827, after whom the process is named. Its properties were explored and explained for the first time by Albert Einstein in 1905. Somewhat later, the mathematician Norbert Wiener provided its probabilistic foundations in the function space of continuous functions, and for his fundamental contribution Brownian motion is often called the Wiener process.

[8] This phenomenon was explained analytically in Phillips (2002).

the interest rate is stochastically nonstationary and its generating mechanism has a unit root. For Model 3, the p value of the test statistic (-3.172) is found to be 0.091; because $0.091 > 0.05$, the null hypothesis of a unit root is still not rejected at the 5% level of significance. This result is qualitatively the same as the unit root test based on Model 2, although there is a large reduction in the p value from 0.237 in the case of Model 2 to 0.091 in Model 3.

5.3.2 The Augmented Dickey–Fuller (ADF) Test

In estimating any of the regression specifications given in equation (5.14), there is a real possibility that the disturbance term will exhibit autocorrelation. One reason for the presence of autocorrelation in the residuals is that many financial series interact with each other over time, which can induce joint dependence and serial dependence. Because the test regression specifications in equation (5.14), are univariate equations, the effects of these interactions are ignored. Adjustments to the specifications to account for these interactions are therefore desirable in practical work.

One common solution to correct for induced autocorrelation is to proceed as suggested in Chapter 4 and include lags of the dependent variable Δy_t in the test regressions in equation (5.14). Additional lagged variables help to remove this autocorrelation. With adjustments for the extra lagged variables, the equations take the augmented form

$$\text{Model 1:} \quad \Delta y_t = \beta y_{t-1} + \sum_{i=1}^{p} \phi_i \Delta y_{t-i} + v_t,$$

$$\text{Model 2:} \quad \Delta y_t = \alpha + \beta y_{t-1} + \sum_{i=1}^{p} \phi_i \Delta y_{t-i} + v_t, \qquad (5.15)$$

$$\text{Model 3:} \quad \Delta y_t = \alpha + \delta t + \beta y_{t-1} + \sum_{i=1}^{p} \phi_i \Delta y_{t-i} + v_t.$$

In practice, the lag length p in these specifications is an unknown parameter and may be chosen by model selection methods, such as those outlined in Chapter 4, to ensure that the disturbances u_t do not exhibit autocorrelation. The unit root test procedures remain the same and involve the use of the same t statistic for testing $\beta = 0$ after taking into account the new specification of the various models given in equation (5.15).

The inclusion of lagged values of (differences in) the dependent variable represents an augmentation of the regression equation. Accordingly, the test is commonly referred to as the Augmented Dickey–Fuller (ADF) test, which was explored in Said and Dickey (1984). Setting $p = 0$ in any version of the test regressions in equation (5.15) gives the simple Dickey–Fuller test discussed earlier. Importantly, the asymptotic distributions of the ADF statistics in these augmented regressions are identical to the corresponding unit root asymptotic distributions in the original specifications in equation (5.14). Hence, the same critical values as given in Table 5.2 may be used in conducting tests of the unit root hypothesis $\beta = 0$.

For example, using Model 2 in equation (5.15) to construct the ADF test with $p = 2$ lags for the US zero-coupon, 2-month bond yield, the estimated regression equation is

$$\Delta y_t = \underset{(0.046)}{0.092} - \underset{(0.008)}{0.017} \, y_{t-1} + \underset{(0.045)}{0.117} \, \Delta y_{t-1} - \underset{(0.046)}{0.080} \, \Delta y_{t-2} + \widehat{v}_t.$$

The value of the ADF test statistic is

$$t_\beta = \frac{\widehat{\beta} - 0}{se(\widehat{\beta})} = \frac{-0.017 - 0}{0.008} = -2.157.$$

Using the Dickey–Fuller distribution the p value is 0.223. Since $0.223 > 0.05$ the null hypothesis is not rejected at the 5% level of significance. This result is qualitatively the same as the earlier Dickey–Fuller test with $p = 0$ lags.

If p is chosen to be too small, then substantial autocorrelation may remain in the disturbance term in equation (5.15) and this will result in distorted statistical inference because the asymptotic distribution under the null hypothesis no longer applies in the presence of autocorrelation. However, including an excessive number of lags has an adverse effect on the ability of the test to reject the null hypothesis if it is false, referred to as a loss of power, because the extra lags serve to absorb variation in the data and tend to reduce its ability to discriminate.

To select the lag length p used in the ADF test, a common approach is to base the choice on information criteria such as those considered in Chapter 4. Two commonly used criteria are the Akaike Information criterion (AIC) and the Schwarz information criteria (SIC), otherwise known as the Bayesian information criterion (BIC). A lag-length selection procedure that is known to have good properties in unit root testing is the modified Akaike information criterion (MAIC) method proposed by Ng and Perron (2001). The lag length is chosen to satisfy

$$\widehat{p} = \arg\min_p \text{MAIC}(p) = \log(\widehat{\sigma}_v^2) + \frac{2(\tau_p + p)}{T - p_{\max}}, \tag{5.16}$$

in which

$$\tau_p = \frac{\widehat{\beta}^2}{\widehat{\sigma}_v^2} \sum_{t=p_{\max}+1}^{T} \widehat{v}_{t-1}^2,$$

and the maximum lag length is chosen as $p_{\max} = \text{int}[12(T/100)^{1/4}]$ where int[.] signifies the integer part of the argument. In computing $\widehat{p}$, it is important that the sample over which the computations are performed is held constant.

5.4 BEYOND THE SIMPLE UNIT ROOT FRAMEWORK

There is now a vast literature on unit root testing, much of which dealing with extensions of the framework just described to admit a far wider class of nonstationary time series. These extensions are particularly important in financial applications because they allow for typical characteristics of financial data. A number of these developments are now standard in econometric software packages and are considered briefly below. Further extensions are considered in Chapter 11 where unit roots are applied to nonstationary panel data models.

5.4.1 Structural Breaks

The major form of nonstationarity considered so far is that of a stochastic trend that is generated by the presence of a unit root. There are other forms that nonstationarity in a time series may take and one of these occurs when the data are known to be disrupted by a permanent structural change. Such a break might arise from institutional changes, new policy implementations, or external shocks that have a permanent effect. The simplest structural break of this type involves a shift in the intercept of a time series, which delivers a level break or "crash" in the event that the break is negative. Another type of structural break occurs when there is a shift in the slope as well as the intercept of a linear time trend. Breaks of this kind were discussed in the context of the use of dummy variables in Chapter 3.

When the timing of such structural breaks is known, it is straightforward to accommodate such shifts in the regression model. For instance, a simple mechanism for dealing with a level shift is to include a dummy variable in equation (5.15) to capture the structural break through the specification

$$\Delta y_t = \beta y_{t-1} + \alpha + \delta t + \sum_{i=1}^{p} \phi_i \Delta y_{t-i} + \gamma \, \text{LBREAK}_t + v_t, \tag{5.17}$$

where the structural break dummy variable is defined as

$$\text{LBREAK}_t = \begin{cases} 0 : t \leq \tau \\ 1 : t > \tau, \end{cases} \tag{5.18}$$

and τ is the observation (assumed to be known) where the break occurs.

Unit root tests are now constructed and performed just as before by testing the hypothesis $\beta = 0$ in equation (5.17). However, because the regression equation (5.17) has changed through the inclusion of the covariate LBREAK_t, the distribution of the ADF statistic under the null also changes to accommodate the presence of this covariate. Accordingly, the p values change from those of a statistic computed without these covariates and they now become a function of the timing of the structural break τ. These changes in the distribution theory mean that different tables of critical values must be employed when conducting a unit root test in the presence of breaks.

In a similar way, a companion variable can be introduced to capture a possible additional shift in the time trend slope, as in the following specification

$$\Delta y_t = \beta y_{t-1} + \alpha + \delta t + \sum_{i=1}^{p} \phi_i \Delta y_{t-i} + (\gamma_\alpha + \gamma_\delta t)\text{LBREAK}_t + v_t. \tag{5.19}$$

The structural break dummy variable LBREAK_t in equation (5.19) is the same as in equation (5.18) but now affects both the level and the time trend. Again, unit root tests are conducted in precisely the same manner as earlier. All that changes is the critical value used in the test. Tabulations of critical values for unit root tests of the above type against alternative hypotheses that involve a structural break that occurs at some exogenously given date are calculated by simulation.

5.4.2 Generalized Least Squares Detrending
Consider the following model

$$y_t = \alpha + \delta t + u_t, \tag{5.20}$$

$$u_t = \phi u_{t-1} + v_t, \tag{5.21}$$

in which u_t is a disturbance term with zero mean and constant variance σ_u^2. This is the fundamental equation from which Model 3 of the Dickey–Fuller test is derived. If the aim is still to test for a unit root in y_t, the null and alternative hypotheses are

$$H_0 : \phi = 1 \qquad \text{[Nonstationary]}$$
$$H_1 : \phi < 1. \qquad \text{[Stationary]} \tag{5.22}$$

Instead of proceeding in the manner described previously and using Model 3 in either equation (5.14) or equation (5.15), an alternative approach is to use a two-step procedure.

Step 1: Detrending

Estimate the parameters of equation (5.20) by ordinary least squares and then construct a detrended version of y_t given by

$$y_t^* = y_t - \widehat{\alpha} - \widehat{\delta} t.$$

Step 2: Testing

Test for a unit root using the deterministically detrended data, y_t^*, from the first step using the Dickey–Fuller or augmented Dickey–Fuller test. Model 1 in equation (5.14) will be the appropriate model to use because, by construction, y_t^* will have zero mean and no deterministic trend.

This procedure is equivalent to the single-step approach based on Model 3 in equation (5.14).

Elliott, Rothenberg, and Stock (1996) suggested an alternative approach to detrending the data prior to testing for a unit root. Their approach aims to address an important shortcoming of the Dickey–Fuller approach that the tests may have low power. The modified detrending approach is based on the premise that the test is more likely to reject the null hypothesis of a unit root if under the alternative hypothesis the detrending process takes into account that the process may have a root that is in the region of unity (more specifically, local to unity in a manner dependent on the sample size). The modified detrending step proceeds as follows. Define the constant ϕ^* in specific local to unity form as

$$\phi^* = 1 + \bar{c}/T \qquad \text{where } \bar{c} = \begin{cases} -7 & \text{[Constant } (\alpha \neq 0, \delta = 0)] \\ -13.5. & \text{[Trend } (\alpha \neq 0, \delta \neq 0)], \end{cases}$$

and use it to construct the following variables

$$y_t^* = y_t - \phi^* y_{t-1},$$
$$\alpha^* = 1 - \phi^*, \tag{5.23}$$
$$t^* = t - \phi^*(t - 1).$$

The starting values for each of these variables at $t = 1$ are $y_1^* = y_1$, and $\alpha_1^* = 1$ and $t_1^* = 1$, respectively. The starting values are important because if $\bar{c} = -T$ then this differencing procedure has no effect. If, on the other hand, $\bar{c} = 0$, then the procedure reverts to a simple first difference. This kind of detrending is commonly referred to as generalized least squares detrending, but is also known as quasi-differencing and partial generalized least squares (Phillips and Lee, 1995).

The choice of the value of the constant $\bar{c}$ in this detrending process is determined so that the test reaches the envelope of maximum power under certain conditions when optimal power is around 50%. In this sense, the test is considered to be *point optimal* for local departures from unity with autoregressive coefficient $\phi = 1 + c/T$ and localizing coefficient $c = \bar{c}$. For example, based on a sample size of $T = 200$, $\phi^* = 1 + \bar{c}/T = 1 - 7/200 = 0.9650$ for a regression with only a constant and 0.9325 for a regression with a constant and a time trend.

Using the newly defined variables in equation (5.23), run the regression

$$y_t^* = \pi_0 \alpha^* + \pi_1 t^* + u_t^*, \tag{5.24}$$

in which u_t^* is a composite disturbance term. Once the ordinary least squares estimates $\widehat{\pi}_0$ and $\widehat{\pi}_1$ are available, detrended data

$$\widehat{u}_t^* = y_t^* - \widehat{\pi}_0 \alpha^* - \widehat{\pi}_1 t^* \tag{5.25}$$

can be constructed. The detrended data from equation (5.25) can now be tested for a unit root. If Model 1 of the Dickey–Fuller framework is used then the test is referred to as the generalized least squares Dickey–Fuller (GLS-DF) test. Note, however, that because the detrended data depend on the value of $\bar{c}$, the critical values are different to the Dickey–Fuller critical values that rely on simple detrending.

This modified approach to unit root testing relies on the assumption that departures from unit roots are uniformly of the local to unity form $\phi = 1 + c/T$. Many realistic departures (including structural breaks) are not of this simple form; and, in such cases, GLS tests suffer power losses, are no longer point optimal tests, and do not necessarily dominate standard unit root tests (Bykhovskaya and Phillips, 2020).

5.4.3 Nonparametric Adjustment for Autocorrelation

Phillips and Perron (1988) proposed an alternative method for adjusting the Dickey–Fuller test for autocorrelation of general form and some forms of heterogeneity. The adjustment is nonparametric rather than parametric and therefore produces a unit root test of wide applicability. The test is based on estimating the Dickey–Fuller regression equation, either equation (5.10) or equation (5.13), by ordinary least squares, but the test statistic uses a nonparametric approach to correct for the autocorrelation. The Phillips–Perron statistic is

$$\widetilde{t}_\beta = t_\beta \left(\frac{\widehat{\gamma}_0}{\widehat{f}_0} \right)^{1/2} - \frac{T(\widehat{f}_0 - \widehat{\gamma}_0)\text{se}(\widehat{\beta})}{2\widehat{f}_0^{1/2} s}, \tag{5.26}$$

where t_β is the ADF statistic, s is the standard deviation of the residuals from the Dickey–Fuller test regression, and $\widehat{f}_0$ is known as the long-run variance. The long-run variance is computed as

$$\widehat{f}_0 = \widehat{\gamma}_0 + 2 \sum_{j=1}^{p} \left(1 - \frac{j}{p} \right) \widehat{\gamma}_j, \tag{5.27}$$

where p is the length of the lag, and $\widehat{\gamma}_j$ is the jth estimated autocovariance function of the ordinary least squares residuals obtained from estimating either equation (5.10) or equation (5.13)

$$\widehat{\gamma_j} = \frac{1}{T-j} \sum_{t=j+1}^{T} \widehat{v_t}\widehat{v}_{t-j}. \tag{5.28}$$

The critical values are the same as the Dickey–Fuller critical values when the sample size is large, which makes this general test very easy to apply in practical work.

5.4.4 Unit Root Testing with a Null of Stationarity
The Dickey–Fuller testing framework, including the GLS detrending and Phillips–Perron variants, are designed for testing the null hypothesis that a time series y_t is nonstationary or $I(1)$. There is also a popular test commonly known as the KPSS test, after Kwiatkowski, Phillips, Schmidt, and Shin (1992) that is often reported in the empirical literature, which has a null hypothesis of stationarity or $I(0)$. Consider the regression model

$$y_t = \alpha + \delta t + w_t + u_t,$$

where u_t is a disturbance term and w_t is given by

$$w_t = w_{t-1} + v_t, \qquad v_t \sim iid N(0, \sigma_v^2).$$

The null hypothesis that y_t is a stationary $I(0)$ process is tested in terms of the null hypothesis $H_0 : \sigma_v^2 = 0$, in which case w_t is simply a constant equal to zero. Define $\{\widehat{u}_1, \cdots, \widehat{u}_T\}$ as the ordinary least squares residuals from a regression of y_t on a constant and a deterministic trend. The standardized test statistic is now given by

$$S = \frac{1}{T^2 \widehat{f_0}} \sum_{t=1}^{T} \left(\sum_{j=1}^{t} \widehat{u}_j \right)^2,$$

in which $\widehat{f_0}$ is a consistent estimator of the long-run variance of u_t, as defined in equation (5.27).

5.5 ASSET PRICE BUBBLES
During the 1990s, led by dot-com stocks and the internet sector, the US stock market experienced a spectacular rise in all major indices, especially the NASDAQ index. Figure 5.5 plots the monthly NASDAQ index, expressed in real terms, for the period February 1973 to January 2009. The series grows fairly steadily until the early 1990s and then begins to surge. The steep upward movement in the series continues until the late 1990s as investment in dot-com stocks grows in popularity. Early in the year 2000 the Index drops abruptly and then continues to fall to the mid-1990s level. In summary, over the decade of the 1990s, the NASDAQ index rose to its historical high on 10 March 2000 and then collapsed, in the process creating and destroying some US$8 trillion dollars of shareholder wealth.

Concomitant with the striking rise in stock market indices during this period there was much popular talk among economists about the effects of the internet and computing technology on productivity and the emergence of a new economy associated with these changes. The information revolution, it was argued, may have provided a new fundamental driver that explained the surge in stock prices. What actually caused this and other unusual surges and subsequent falls in prices, whether there were bubbles and, if

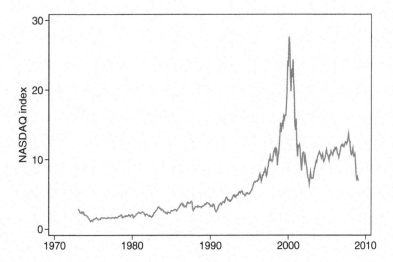

FIGURE 5.5 The monthly NASDAQ index expressed in real terms for the period February 1973 to January 2009.

so, whether they were rational or behavioral, are among the most actively debated issues in macroeconomics and finance.

A recent line of research has developed empirical tests for bubbles and rational exuberance in financial asset markets, with applications to phenomena such as the dot-com bubble, the US property market bubble, and the 2008 global financial crisis (Phillips and Yu, 2011; Phillips, Wu, and Yu, 2011). This development provides an interesting new variant in the field of unit root testing. Instead of concentrating on performing a test of a unit root against the alternative of stationarity (which employs a one-sided test where the critical region is defined in the left-hand tail of the distribution of the test statistic), financial time series may be tested for explosive behavior by testing against the alternative of an explosive root, leading to a right-sided unit root test where the critical value of the test lies in the right tail of the distribution. Such tests are appropriate for asset prices exhibiting exuberance or bubble-like behavior. The null hypothesis of interest is still $\rho = 1$ but the alternative hypothesis is now $\rho > 1$ in equation (5.6), or

$$
\begin{aligned}
&H_0 : \rho = 1 \quad \text{[Variable is nonstationary, no price bubble]} \\
&H_1 : \rho > 1. \quad \text{[Variable is explosive, price bubble]}
\end{aligned}
\tag{5.29}
$$

To motivate the presence of a price bubble, consider the following model

$$
P_t(1 + R) = E_t [P_{t+1} + D_{t+1}],
\tag{5.30}
$$

where P_t is the price of an asset, R is the risk-free rate of interest assumed to be constant for simplicity, D_t is the dividend payment and $E_t [\cdot]$ is the conditional expectations operator that conditions on information up to time t. This equation highlights two types of investment strategies. The first is given by the left hand-side, which involves investing in a risk-free asset at time t yielding a payoff of $P_t(1 + R)$ in the next period. Alternatively, the right-hand side shows that by holding the asset the investor earns the capital gain from owning an asset with a potentially higher price the next period plus a dividend payment.

In equilibrium, there are no arbitrage opportunities so the two types of investment are equal to each other.

Now divide both sides of equation (5.30) by $(1 + R)$ to yield

$$P_t = \beta\, E_t\,[P_{t+1} + D_{t+1}], \tag{5.31}$$

where $\beta = (1 + R)^{-1}$ is the discount factor. Writing this expression at $t + 1$

$$P_{t+1} = \beta\, E_t\,[P_{t+2} + D_{t+2}], \tag{5.32}$$

means that it can be used to substitute out P_{t+1} in equation (5.31)

$$P_t = \beta\, E_t\,[\beta\, E_t\,[P_{t+2} + D_{t+2}] + D_{t+1}] = \beta\, E_t\,[D_{t+1}] + \beta^2\, E_t\,[D_{t+2}] + \beta^2\, E_t\,[P_{t+2}].$$

Repeating this approach $N - 1$ times gives the price of the asset in terms of two components

$$P_t = \sum_{j=1}^{N} \beta^j E_t\,[D_{t+j}] + \beta^N E_t\,[P_{t+N}]$$

$$= \sum_{j=1}^{N} \beta^j E_t\,[D_{t+j}] + B_t, \tag{5.33}$$

where

$$B_t = \beta^N E_t\,[P_{t+N}].$$

The first term on the right-hand side of equation (5.33) is the standard present value of an asset whereby the price of an asset equals the discounted present value stream of expected dividends. The second term is a bubble component. Diba and Grossman (1988) argue that this bubble component has an explosive property given by

$$E_t\,[B_{t+1}] = (1 + R)B_t.$$

In the absence of bubbles ($B_t = 0$), the degree of nonstationarity of the asset price is controlled by the character of the dividend series, but asset prices will be explosive in the presence of bubbles because $1 + R > 1$. The implied conditional expectation at time t of the value of the process h periods ahead is

$$E_t\,[B_{t+h}] = (1 + R)^h B_t.$$

It follows that $E_t\,[B_{t+h}]$ grows exponentially with the horizon h. The process B_t is known as the rational bubble component of the solution equation (5.33) and will always be present in the solution unless the initial value $B_0 = 0$.

As indicated earlier, one way of testing for the presence of a bubble process like B_t in asset prices is to apply a right-sided unit root test to the price process itself. Interestingly enough, if that convention were followed and the ADF test were applied to the full sample (February 1973 to January 2009), the unit root test would not reject the null hypothesis $H_0 : \rho = 1$ in favor of the right-tailed alternative $H_1 : \rho > 1$ at the 5% level of significance. This outcome would lead to the conclusion that there is no significant evidence of exuberance in the behavior of the NASDAQ index over the sample period.

This conclusion would sit comfortably with a consensus view that was held before the NASDAQ experience that there is little empirical evidence to support the hypothesis of explosive behavior in stock prices (see, for example, Campbell, Lo, and MacKinlay, 1997, p. 260).

On the other hand, Evans (1991) argued that explosive behavior in prices is only temporary in the sense that bubbles eventually collapse. Consequently, observed trajectories of asset prices may appear more like an I(1) or even a stationary series rather than an explosive one even when bubbles occur in the trajectory, thereby confounding empirical evidence about the existence of bubbles in financial data. Using simulations, Evans demonstrated that standard unit root tests have difficulties in detecting such periodically collapsing bubbles.

To address the lack of power of the full sample-based unit root test in detecting periodically collapsing bubbles, Phillips et al. (2011) suggest implementing recursively a unit root test based on expanding windows of observations, starting with $T_0 = [Tr_0]$ observations in the first regression and ending with T observations in the final regression, where T is the full sample size and $r_0 \in (0, 1)$ is the sample fraction of T used for initializing the test recursion. The test statistic is the maximum of the t statistics obtained in this way over the expanding windows of data. The asymptotic distribution of the test statistic is then the supremum of the unit root distributions taken over this range of values. Critical values for the recursive test are obtained by simulation. The test then provides a test of explosive behavior over the sample period $[T_0, T]$.

An important outcome of this testing framework is that it also delivers a date-stamping procedure for the origination and termination of bubbles. By matching the recursive t statistics with the path of the right-tailed critical values an estimate of the origination of bubble behavior in the data is obtained by determining the first observation for which the test statistic crosses the critical value path. This is known as the first crossing time principle. Similarly, an estimate of the termination of the bubble is obtained by noting the observation for which the recursive test statistic crosses back over and falls below the critical value path. This use of recursive unit root testing provides a valuable approach to the detection and dating of bubbles in financial data.

Figure 5.6 is a plot of the forward recursive ADF statistic with 1 lag computed from forward recursive regressions by fixing the start of the sample period and progressively increasing the sample size observation by observation until the entire sample is used. The startup sample is 39 observations. The NASDAQ shows no evidence of rational exuberance prior to June 1995 as the ADF statistics lie below the dashed line. In July 1995, the test detects the presence of explosive behavior (which can be interpreted as exuberance) in stock prices ($\rho > 1$), which is indicated by a significant test statistic. The supporting evidence for the presence of a bubble tends to become progressively stronger in terms of the test statistic's deviation from the critical value path and it reaches a peak in February 2000. The bubble continues until February 2001 and by March 2001 the bubble appears to have dissipated. Interestingly, the first occurrence of the bubble is July 1995, which is more than a year before the remark by Alan Greenspan, the then Chairman of the Federal Reserve Board, on 5 December 1996, who coined the phrase irrational exuberance to characterize irrationally optimistic herding behavior in stock markets.

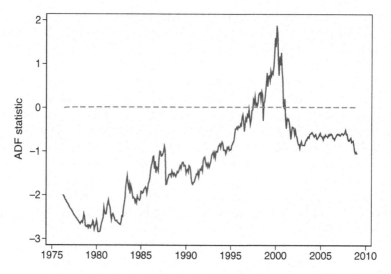

FIGURE 5.6 The Phillips, Wu, and Yu (2011) procedure to test for price bubbles in the log of the monthly NASDAQ index expressed in real terms for the period February 1973 to January 2009 by means of a recursive expanding window ADF test with 1 lag. The startup sample is 39 observations from February 1973 to April 1976. The approximate 5% critical value is shown by the dashed line.

To check the robustness of these findings, Figure 5.7 plots the ADF statistic with 1 lag for a series of rolling window regressions. Each regression is based on a subsample of size $T = 77$, with the first sample period from February 1973 to June 1979. The fixed window is then rolled forward one observation at a time. The general pattern to emerge is completely consistent with the results reported in Figure 5.6. Tests for exuberance based on these rolling window regressions and recursively evolving versions of such regressions are developed in Phillips, Shi, and Yu (2015a, 2015b).

Given that the model used to produce these results has a reduced form structure, the findings do not deliver a causal explanation for the exuberance of the 1990s in dot-com stocks. Several possibilities exist, including the presence of a rational bubble, herding behavior, or explosive effects on economic fundamentals arising from time variation in discount rates. Identification of explicit economic source(s) of this observed price behavior will involve more explicit formulation of structural models of behavior that enables identification of the driving force(s).

What the recursive testing methodology does provide is clear support for the presence of a mildly explosive propagating mechanism in the NASDAQ index and estimates of the origination and termination of this phenomena in the data. A further advantage of the recursive methodology is that it can be used in real time to make ongoing assessments of the state of the stock market. The methods can be applied in this way to study recent phenomena in many different markets such as real estate, commodity, foreign exchange, and equity markets, all of which have attracted considerable attention. They are now being used by regulators and central banks to assist in monitoring the state of financial markets.

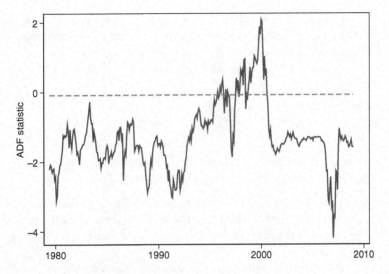

FIGURE 5.7 The Phillips, Shi, and Yu (2015a, 2015b) procedure to test for price bubbles in the log of the monthly NASDAQ index expressed in real terms for the period February 1973 to January 2009 by means of a rolling window ADF test with 1 lag. The size of the window is set to 77 observations so that the starting sample is February 1973 to June 1979. The approximate 5% critical value is shown by the dashed line in the figure.

5.6 EXERCISES

The data required for the exercises are available for download as EViews workfiles (*.wf1), Stata datafiles (*.dta), comma delimited text files (*.csv), and as Excel spreadsheets (*.xlsx).

1. Commodity Price Data

> commodity.*

The data comprise monthly observations on a number of US traded commodity price indices for the period January 1957 to November 2003.

(a) Use the commodity prices to construct the following transformed series: the natural logarithm of commodity prices, the first difference of commodity prices, and log returns of commodity prices. Plot the series and discuss the stationarity properties of each series.

(b) Use the following unit root tests to test for stationarity of the natural logarithm of commodity prices.

(i) Dickey–Fuller test with a constant and no time trend.

(ii) Augmented Dickey–Fuller test with a constant and no time trend and $p = 2$ lags.

(iii) Phillips–Perron test with a constant and no time trend and $p = 2$ lags.

(c) Repeat part (b) for the first differences and log returns of commodity prices.

(d) Now construct the *first difference of log returns* of commodity prices. Repeat part (b). Are you able to reach a conclusion about the appropriate level of differencing, *d*, required to achieve stationarity for the logarithm of commodity prices, assuming the *d* takes an integer value?

2. Equity Market Data

pv.*

The data are monthly observations on US equity prices, dividends and earnings for the period January 1871 to September 2016.

(a) Use the equity price series to construct the following transformed series: the natural logarithm of equity prices, the first difference of equity prices, and log returns of equity prices. Plot the series and discuss the stationarity properties of each series.

(b) Construct similarly transformed series for dividend payments and discuss the stationarity properties of each series.

(c) Construct similarly transformed series for earnings and discuss the stationarity properties of each series.

(d) Use the following unit root tests to test for stationarity of the natural logarithms of prices, dividends, and earnings.

  (i) Dickey–Fuller test with a constant and no time trend.
  (ii) Augmented Dickey–Fuller test with a constant and no time trend and $p = 1$ lag.
  (iii) Phillips–Perron test with a constant and no time trend and $p = 1$ lag.
  (iv) Repeat parts (ii) and (iii) where the lag length for the ADF and PP tests is based on a data driven selection of the optimal lag length.

(e) Repeat part (d) for the first differences and log returns of equity prices, dividends, and earnings.

3. Bond Market Data

zero.*

The data are monthly observations from December 1946 to February 1987 on US zero-coupon bond yields for maturities ranging from 2 months to 9 months.

(a) Use the following unit root tests to determine the stationarity properties of each yield.

  (i) Dickey–Fuller test with a constant and no time trend.
  (ii) Augmented Dickey–Fuller test with a constant and no time trend and $p = 2$ lags.
  (iii) Phillips–Perron test with a constant and no time trend and $p = 2$ lags.

(b) Now construct the spreads between the longer-term maturities and the 2-month yield. Repeat (a) and hence test the stationarity properties of the spreads.

4. Fisher Hypothesis

fisher.*

The data file contains US quarterly data for the period September 1954 to December 2007 on the annualized nominal interest rate expressed as a percentage, r_t, and the price level, P_t. The Fisher hypothesis states that the nominal interest rate fully reflects the long-run movements in the inflation rate.

(a) Construct the percentage annualized inflation rate, π_t.
(b) Plot the nominal interest rate and inflation rate.
(c) Perform unit root tests to determine the level of integration of the nominal interest rate and inflation. In performing the unit root tests, test the sensitivity of the results by using a model with a constant and no time trend, and a model with a constant and a time trend. Let the lags be determined by the automatic lag length selection procedure. Discuss the results in terms of the level of integration of each series.
(d) Compute the real interest rate as

$$r_t = i_t - \pi_t.$$

Test the real interest rate r_t for stationarity using a model with a constant but no time trend based on a data driven selection of optimal lag length. Does the Fisher hypothesis hold? Discuss.

5. Testing for Price Bubbles in the Share Market

bubbles.*

The data are monthly observations of the NASDAQ price index and the dividends for the period January 1960 to December 1989. The present value model implies that the fundamental driver of the share price P_t is the dividend payment D_t. A bubble occurs when the actual share price persistently deviates from fundamentals.

(a) Create the log price-dividend ratio, $p_t - d_t$, whereas customary lower case variables refer to logarithms. Use right-tailed unit root tests applied to the entire sample to determine whether or not a bubble exists. Take the minimum window size to be 39 observations.
(b) Use the forward recursive, right-tailed, Dickey–Fuller test procedure to test for a bubble in the log price-dividend ratio.
(c) Use a rolling window, right-tailed, Dickey–Fuller test procedure to test for a bubble in the log-price dividend ratio. Discuss your results.

CHAPTER 6

Cointegration

As discussed in Chapter 5, a single nonstationary time series can often be rendered stationary by differencing. In a multivariate context, the same differencing technique may be applied to each component to achieve stationarity. But an alternative method may also be available to remove nonstationarity. When there is more than one nonstationary time series and the series tend to move together over time, it is often possible to form linear combinations of the nonstationary series that produce a stationary series. This ability to generate stationary time series through carefully chosen linear combinations of nonstationary time series is known as cointegration. The weights that together constitute this special linear combination of the original series are known as cointegrating coefficients.

The idea that nonstationary time series may be reduced to stationary time series by means of well-defined regression specifications has long been implicit in much of the empirical research in economics as well as the adjustment mechanisms that underpinned the form of many models formulated in economic theory for aggregate economic data, such as trade cycle and cyclical growth models in macroeconomics. Bergstrom (1967) provides an extensive discussion of such models and many references. In econometrics, the central contribution to this subject was made by Engle and Granger (1987) and acknowledged in the award of the 2003 Nobel Prize in Economic Science.

The concept of cointegration provides a useful basis for interpreting many financial models in terms of meaningful long-run relationships. Such relationships are often obtained as equilibrium path solutions of intertemporal decision-making problems that face economic agents or in linkages that explain asset prices in terms of expected returns. The empirical relevance of such theories can then be investigated in applied work by examining evidence in support of cointegration. Having uncovered long-run relationships between financial variables by establishing evidence of cointegration, the transient or short-run properties of the variables may be separately modeled or even modeled simultaneously by building transient responses directly into the specification of the equations that define the long-run relationships. The latter type of model is useful because it can sometimes be interpreted in terms of the adjustment mechanisms present in some underlying financial theory. The approach has a practical advantage because the econometric specification, which is known as a vector error-correction model

(VECM), is simply a restricted form of the commonly used VAR model considered in Chapter 4.

The existence of cointegration between nonstationary time series has important theoretical, statistical, and dynamic implications.

(i) A number of theoretical models in finance can be couched within a cointegrating framework.

(ii) Estimates of the parameters in the cointegrating equations, including ordinary least squares estimates, converge to their population values at a rate faster than is the case for stationary variables, a property known as super-consistency.

(iii) Special methods of estimation have been developed to provide asymptotically efficient estimates, to address bias and serial dependence, and to facilitate inference. These methods are easy to use, some involve simple modifications of least squares procedures, and many are now available in standard software packages.

(iv) Modeling a system of cointegrated variables allows for the joint specification of long-run and short-run dynamics of financial variables in terms of the VECM.

6.1 THE PRESENT VALUE MODEL AND COINTEGRATION

An important property of asset prices identified in both Chapters 2 and 5 is that they exhibit stochastic trends. This is indeed the case for the United States as seen in Figure 6.1, which shows that the logarithms of monthly equity prices, $p_t = \log P_t$, dividend payments, $d_t = \log D_t$, and earnings $e_t = \log E_t$ all exhibit strong (largely positive) trends over the period January 1871 to September 2016. These series are indicative of many financial time series that exhibit trending, nonstationary characteristics that are well-represented as integrated $I(1)$ processes, as discussed in Chapter 5.

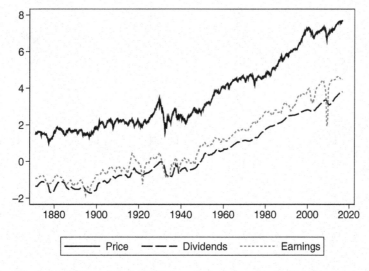

FIGURE 6.1   Time series plots of monthly US log equity prices, log dividend payments, and log earnings per share for the period January 1871 to September 2016.

6.1.1 Equilibrium Relationships

Even though the pattern of behavior of the series in Figure 6.1 indicates that equity prices and dividends are trending $I(1)$ series, the present value model of equity prices provides a theoretical link between equity prices and dividends that is strongly suggestive of co-movement in the two series over time. From Chapter 2, this relationship is expressed as

$$p_t = \beta_0 + \beta_d d_t + u_t, \tag{6.1}$$

where p_t is the log equity price, d_t is the log dividend, u_t is a disturbance term, and β_0 and β_d are unknown parameters. Both p_t and d_t are well-modeled as $I(1)$ processes. Yet the present value model indicates that the differences $p_t - \beta_0 - \beta_d d_t = u_t$ are simply transient shocks that do not disturb the nature of the relationship in equation (6.1) over time. The linkage between p_t and d_t in equation (6.1) is therefore regarded as a long-run (or permanent) relationship between trending $I(1)$ series and the disturbances u_t are viewed as transient shocks or $I(0)$. The linear combination of the $I(1)$ variables p_t and d_t that results in the $I(0)$ variable given by u_t is known as a cointegrating relationship or simply as cointegration. The reduction of the trending $I(1)$ character of p_t and d_t to the transient $I(0)$ character of u_t is the essential condition of cointegration. When these conditions hold, then equation (6.1) is known as a cointegrating equation and the parameters β_0 and β_d are the cointegrating coefficients.

An alternative way of viewing the present value model in equation (6.1) as a cointegrating system is through the scatter diagram in Figure 6.2 for p_t and d_t using the same data presented in Figure 6.1. Superimposed on the scatter plot is an estimate of the present value model equation

$$p_t = 3.1375 + 1.1957\, d_t + \widehat{u}_t, \tag{6.2}$$

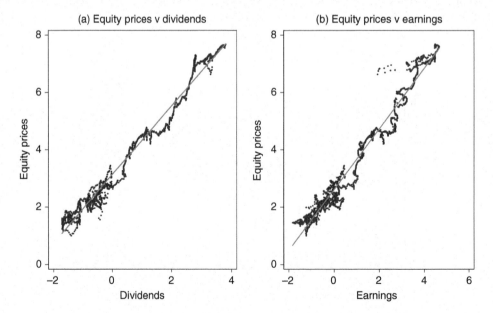

FIGURE 6.2 Scatter plots of monthly US log equity prices and log dividends, in panel (a), and log equity prices and log earnings per share, in panel (b), for the period January 1871 to September 2016.

obtained by regressing p_t on a constant and d_t. Even though p_t and d_t are both nonstationary, prices and dividends never deviate too far away from the line given by $3.1375 + 1.1957\, d_t$, suggesting that this relationship captures an equilibrium path between these variables. If there were no cointegration between the variables, the scatter diagram would have points much more evenly scattered about the two dimensional plane. In other words, cointegration has the effect of an attractor among nonstationary series, in the present case compressing equity prices and dividends close to a one-dimensional relationship.

This interpretation of the scatter diagram also suggests that actual movements in p_t can be decomposed into a long-run component representing the (dynamic) equilibrium price as determined by dividends and a short-run, transient component that represents temporary deviations of p_t from its long-run path. This decomposition is expressed as

$$\underbrace{p_t}_{\text{Actual path}} = \underbrace{\beta_0 + \beta_d d_t}_{\text{Long-run path}} + \underbrace{u_t}_{\text{Short-run deviations}}$$

6.1.2 Equilibrium Dynamics

The scatter plot between equity prices and dividends in Figure 6.2 suggests that not only are the shocks arising from u_t transitory but that there are forces continually pushing the system back toward the equilibrium path whenever there is a shock. These adjustment dynamics are highlighted in Figure 6.3 where the line containing the points ADC represents the equilibrium line of the present value model in equation (6.2) and pressure from points B and E above and below the line drive the system toward the equilibrium path.

To understand the equilibrium forces within the present value model, consider the effects of a shock u_t at time t, assuming initially that dividends d_t are unaffected by this shock. For a positive shock with $u_t > 0$, equities appear overvalued relative to the long-run level since the stock price p_t lies above its long-run equilibrium price as determined by dividend flows (Point B in Figure 6.3). Similarly, with a negative shock $u_t < 0$, equities

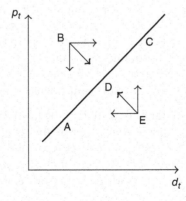

FIGURE 6.3 Phase diagram to demonstrate the equilibrium adjustment if two variables are cointegrated.

appear undervalued because p_t lies below its long-run equilibrium price (Point E in Figure 6.3).

Consider the effect of a positive shock that takes the share price above its equilibrium price at Point A in Figure 6.3. The disequilibrium induced by this price shock in the system leads to forces of adjustment that operate to drive prices back toward the equilibrium path somewhere along the ADC line in Figure 6.3. There are three potential scenarios to consider.

(i) Equity prices adjust

For equilibrium to be re-established in this scenario, equity prices need to decrease back to point A from point B without any change in dividends. Assuming that the fall in equity prices is proportional to the size of the shock $u_t = p_t - \beta_0 - \beta_d d_t$, the change in the equity price in the next period $p_{t+1} - p_t$ is represented by the adjustment equation

$$p_{t+1} - p_t = \delta_1 + \alpha_1 (p_t - \beta_0 - \beta_d d_t) + v_{1t+1}, \tag{6.3}$$

where v_{1t+1} is a disturbance term capturing additional future movements in p_t not arising from the shock u_t. Given that equity prices need to adjust downward in this scenario to restore equilibrium, the adjustment parameter α_1 satisfies the restriction $\alpha_1 < 0$.

(ii) Dividends adjust

For equilibrium to be re-established in this scenario, dividends need to increase from point B to point C while equity prices remain fixed. Adopting the assumption that the adjustment in dividends is also proportional to the size of the shock $u_t = p_t - \beta_0 - \beta_d d_t$, the change in future dividends is represented by the adjustment equation

$$\Delta d_{t+1} = \delta_2 + \alpha_2 (p_t - \beta_0 - \beta_d d_t) + v_{2t+1}, \tag{6.4}$$

where v_{2t+1} is a disturbance term capturing additional future movements in d_t not arising from the initial shock u_t. Given that dividends need to increase to restore equilibrium in this scenario, the adjustment parameter α_2 satisfies the restriction $\alpha_2 > 0$.

(iii) Equity prices and dividends adjust

In this scenario, both the equity price and dividend adjustment equations (6.3) and (6.4) operate with p_t decreasing and d_t increasing. The relative strength of the movements in equity prices and dividends is determined by the relative magnitudes of the adjustment parameters α_1 and α_2. If, for example, the movement is from point B to point D as shown in Figure 6.3, then both equity prices and dividends bear an equal share of the adjustment toward equilibrium.

As it is equity prices that adjust over time in the first scenario toward equilibrium, this variable is classified as endogenous, whereas the dividend variable is treated as exogenous[1] given that it does not adjust to restore equilibrium in response to the disequilibrium $p_t - \beta_0 - \beta_d d_t$ and $\alpha_2 = 0$ accordingly. The opposite is the case for the second scenario where the dividend variable is the endogenous variable and the equity

---

[1] The concept of exogeneity is dealt with in more detail in Section 6.5.

price is treated as exogenous, by setting $\alpha_1 = 0$. For the third scenario, equity prices and dividends are jointly determined and endogenous as both variables adjust the system toward equilibrium, and in this event, $\alpha_1, \alpha_2 \neq 0$.

To gauge the relative strength of the adjustment parameters, α_1 and α_2, in restoring equilibrium in the present value model for the United States, equations (6.3) and (6.4) are estimated by ordinary least squares using the equity price and dividends data presented in Figure 6.1. Letting $\widehat{u}_t$ represent the ordinary least squares residuals from equation (6.2), the parameter estimates of the price adjustment equation are computed by regressing Δp_{t+1} on a constant and $\widehat{u}_t$, with the estimated model given by

$$\Delta p_{t+1} = 0.0035 - 0.0011\,\widehat{u}_t + \widehat{v}_{1t+1}. \tag{6.5}$$

Similarly, the parameter estimates of the dividend adjustment equation are computed by regressing Δd_{t+1} on a constant and $\widehat{u}_t$, resulting in the estimated model

$$\Delta d_{t+1} = 0.0029 + 0.0078\,\widehat{u}_t + \widehat{v}_{2t+1}. \tag{6.6}$$

An alternative representation of the estimated adjustment equations in equations (6.5) and (6.6) is to use the estimated long-run equilibrium relationship in equation (6.2) to substitute out $\widehat{u}_t$ so that

$$\begin{aligned}
\Delta p_{t+1} &= 0.0035 - 0.0011\,(p_t - 3.1375 - 1.1957\,d_t) + \widehat{v}_{1t+1} \\
\Delta d_{t+1} &= 0.0029 + 0.0078\,(p_t - 3.1375 - 1.1957\,d_t) + \widehat{v}_{2t+1}.
\end{aligned} \tag{6.7}$$

The signs of the adjustment parameter estimates are consistent with the dynamics presented in Figure 6.3, with equity prices decreasing ($\widehat{\alpha}_1 < 0$) and dividends increasing ($\widehat{\alpha}_2 > 0$) to restore equilibrium after a positive shock to equity prices. Moreover, since

$$|\widehat{\alpha}_2| = 0.0078 > |\widehat{\alpha}_1| = 0.0011,$$

dividends appear to be the stronger driving force in restoring equilibrium in the system after a shock to the equity price.

6.2 VECTOR ERROR CORRECTION MODELS

The bivariate set of equations containing equity prices and dividends in equations (6.3) and (6.4) is known as a VECM. To generalize this model, it is convenient to re-express the present value cointegrating model as

$$\begin{aligned}
\Delta y_{1t} &= \delta_1 + \alpha_1 (y_{1t-1} - \beta_0 - \beta_2 y_{2t-1}) + v_{1t} \\
\Delta y_{2t} &= \delta_2 + \alpha_2 (y_{1t-1} - \beta_0 - \beta_2 y_{2t-1}) + v_{2t},
\end{aligned} \tag{6.8}$$

where y_{1t} and y_{2t} are two $I(1)$ variables, and for convenience the time subscript t is redefined by replacing $t+1$ by t. The parameters β_0 and β_2 represent the cointegrating or long-run parameters with the long-run parameter on y_{1t}, namely, β_1 normalized to unity. The adjustment parameters α_1 and α_2 are known as the error correction parameters, as they control the relative strengths of the adjustments in the dependent variables with respect to the (lagged) equilibrium error. These terms control the error-correction mechanism. Finally, the parameters δ_1 and δ_2 allow the time series y_{1t} and y_{2t} to have some deterministic drift. However, a model that is often used in empirical work imposes the restriction $\delta_1 = \delta_2 = 0$, which is appropriate if the two time series y_{1t} and y_{2t} exhibit random walk behavior without evidence of any deterministic trends.

6.2.1 Extensions

VECM specifications such as equation (6.8) often include additional endogenous variables and more complex short-run dynamics that are captured using extra lags of the endogenous variables, or equivalently, changes in those variables. An important extension of the VECM in empirical work is to allow for multiple cointegrating equations. This extension is appropriate where it is known or hypothesized that there are several equilibrium relationships operating simultaneously among the $I(1)$ variables. Deterministic variables such as time trends can also be included in the same way that these variables appear in unit root models and tests. In multivariate settings, deterministic variables may also appear in the long-run cointegrating equation, in which case the variables are considered to be deterministically as well as stochastically cointegrated.

Additional $I(1)$ Variables

The present value model is a bivariate model containing two $I(1)$ variables with y_{1t} representing log equity prices and y_{2t} representing log dividend payments. This model is extended in Section 6.6 to a trivariate model that allows for earnings. In the models of the term structure of interest rates discussed in Section 6.7, the dimension of the system is governed by the number of yields with different maturities that are included in the model. Extending the framework from a bivariate model as in equation (6.8) to N variables that are all $I(1)$ with a common scalar long-run relationship simply involves augmenting the two VECM equations in equation (6.8) to N equations according to the following scheme

$$\Delta y_{1t} = \delta_1 + \alpha_1 u_{t-1} + v_{1t}$$
$$\Delta y_{2t} = \delta_2 + \alpha_2 u_{t-1} + v_{2t}$$
$$\vdots \qquad \vdots \qquad\qquad (6.9)$$
$$\Delta y_{Nt} = \delta_N + \alpha_N u_{t-1} + v_{Nt},$$

where the error correction term from the scalar cointegrating equation is now defined in terms of the equilibrium error

$$u_t = y_{1t} - \beta_0 - \beta_2 y_{2t} - \beta_3 y_{3t} - \cdots - \beta_N y_{Nt}. \qquad (6.10)$$

A property of equation (6.10) is that the long-run parameter on y_{1t} is set at $\beta_1 = 1$, which is a normalization that specifies y_{1t} as the dependent variable in this cointegrating equation. Such a normalization is usually specified because it has an explicit economic or financial interpretation. However, as all variables in a VECM are endogenous and jointly determined, any normalization that makes one of the N variables the dependent variable in the cointegrating equation is permissible, provided that variable does enter the cointegrating relation. So, for example, if $\beta_2 \neq 0$, setting $\beta_2 = 1$ by rescaling the equation would make y_{2t} the dependent variable of the cointegrating equation. The scalar used in this rescaling is simply $1/\beta_1$ and it is absorbed in each of the loading factors α_i in the N equations.[2]

---

[2] This invariance of the cointegrating equation specification has implications for the finite sample properties of maximum likelihood estimators of the cointegrating parameters that are analogous to those in simultaneous equations models. In particular, these estimates typically have heavy tailed behavior in finite samples that increases the probability of outliers, as shown in Phillips (1994).

Additional *I*(0) Variables

Thus far the VECM has been specified in terms of $I(1)$ variables only. Stationary variables can also be included to contribute to the transient dynamics of the system. In the case of the present value model, these additional determinants could be business cycle factors or external influences from world equity markets. As these additional variables are $I(0)$ by definition, the natural place for them to enter the model is in the error correction equations, as these equations govern the short-term movements in the nonstationary variables. To include a stationary variable x_t with an additional lag x_{t-1} into the bivariate VECM in equation (6.8), the model may be rewritten as

$$\Delta y_{1t} = \delta_1 + \alpha_1(y_{1t-1} - \beta_0 - \beta_2 y_{2t-1}) + \psi_{10}x_t + \psi_{11}x_{t-1} + v_{1t}$$
$$\Delta y_{2t} = \delta_2 + \alpha_2(y_{1t-1} - \beta_0 - \beta_2 y_{2t-1}) + \psi_{20}x_t + \psi_{21}x_{t-1} + v_{2t},$$

(6.11)

where ψ_{ij} is the parameter on x_{t-j} in the *ith* equation of the VECM. In this instance, the x_t variable is specified to enter all equations. A more restrictive choice is to allow x_t to enter only some of the VECM equations by setting the appropriate ψ_{ij} parameters to zero.

Short-run Dynamics

To allow the bivariate VECM in equation (6.8) to have additional short-run dynamics the model may be respecified as

$$\Delta y_{1t} = \delta_1 + \alpha_1(y_{1t-1} - \beta_0 - \beta_2 y_{2t-1})$$
$$+ \sum_{i=1}^{k-1} \gamma_{11,i}\Delta y_{1t-i} + \sum_{i=1}^{k-1} \gamma_{12,i}\Delta y_{2t-i} + v_{1t}$$
$$\Delta y_{2t} = \delta_2 + \alpha_2(y_{1t-1} - \beta_0 - \beta_2 y_{2t-1})$$
$$+ \sum_{i=1}^{k-1} \gamma_{21,i}\Delta y_{1t-i} + \sum_{i=1}^{k-1} \gamma_{22,i}\Delta y_{2t-i} + v_{2t},$$

(6.12)

where k controls the length of the lag structure in the transient dynamics. The multivariate nature of a VECM means that all lagged dependent variables appear in all equations. Moreover, as these lags correspond to the changes in the endogenous variables Δy_{it}, they affect the short-run dynamic path as the system adjusts toward its long-run equilibrium path. The short-run movements could be monotonic, as is the case with the adjustment path from point B to point D in Figure 6.3, or they could now be more involved paths that embody cycles or even overshooting behavior.

Time Trends

A further generalization of the VECM in equation (6.12) is to include a time trend in the cointegrating equation as in the following specification

$$\Delta y_{1t} = \delta_1 + \alpha_1 (y_{1t-1} - \beta_0 - \beta_2 y_{2t-1} - \phi t)$$

$$+ \sum_{i=1}^{k-1} \gamma_{11,i} \Delta y_{1t-i} + \sum_{i=1}^{k-1} \gamma_{12,i} \Delta y_{2t-i} + v_{1t}$$

$$\Delta y_{2t} = \delta_2 + \alpha_2 (y_{1t-1} - \beta_0 - \beta_2 y_{2t-1} - \phi t)$$

$$+ \sum_{i=1}^{k-1} \gamma_{21,i} \Delta y_{1t-i} + \sum_{i=1}^{k-1} \gamma_{22,i} \Delta y_{2t-i} + v_{2t}, \tag{6.13}$$

with the strength of the trend in the cointegrating equation controlled by the parameter ϕ. Imposing the restriction $\phi = 0$ eliminates the trend and reduces the VECM in equation (6.13) to equation (6.8). As a further extension, a time trend could also be included in the error correction equations, which, because the equation is formulated in differences, would result in the level variables y_{1t} and y_{2t} having quadratic deterministic time trends.

General Specification
The extensions discussed above are conveniently combined by expressing the VECM in matrix notation. Define the following $(N \times 1)$ vectors

$$y_t = \begin{bmatrix} y_{1t} \\ y_{2t} \\ \vdots \\ y_{Nt} \end{bmatrix} \quad \delta = \begin{bmatrix} \delta_1 \\ \delta_2 \\ \vdots \\ \delta_N \end{bmatrix} \quad \alpha = \begin{bmatrix} \alpha_1 \\ \alpha_2 \\ \vdots \\ \alpha_N \end{bmatrix} \quad \beta = \begin{bmatrix} 1 \\ -\beta_2 \\ \vdots \\ -\beta_N \end{bmatrix} \quad v_t = \begin{bmatrix} v_{1t} \\ v_{2t} \\ \vdots \\ v_{Nt} \end{bmatrix},$$

so that the VECM in equations (6.9) and (6.10) can be written as

$$\Delta y_t = \delta + \alpha (\beta' y_{t-1} - \beta_0) + v_t, \tag{6.14}$$

where β_0 is a scalar. To capture the proposed extensions to the VECM, a general specification is given by

$$\Delta y_t = \delta + \alpha (\beta' y_{t-1} - \beta_0 - \phi t) + \sum_{i=1}^{k-1} \Gamma_i \Delta y_{t-i} + \Psi x_t + v_t, \tag{6.15}$$

where ϕ is a scalar, Γ_i is an $(N \times N)$ matrix of parameters at lag i, and Ψ is a $(N \times K)$ matrix of parameters associated with the K stationary variables contained in x_t.

6.2.2 Relationship with VARs
An important property of a VECM is that it represents a restricted form of a VAR system. The restrictions arise from the property that the variables within the system are connected by the same long-run cointegrating equation. To highlight the nature of these restrictions consider the following bivariate VECM

$$y_{1t} - y_{1t-1} = \alpha_1 (y_{1t-1} - \beta_2 y_{2t-1}) + v_{1t}$$

$$y_{2t} - y_{2t-1} = \alpha_2 (y_{1t-1} - \beta_2 y_{2t-1}) + v_{2t}, \tag{6.16}$$

in which there is one cointegrating equation and no lagged difference terms on the right-hand side. There are three parameters to be estimated, namely, the cointegrating parameter β_2 and the two error correction parameters α_1 and α_2. Now re-express each equation in terms of the levels of the variables as

$$y_{1t} = (1+\alpha_1)y_{1t-1} - \alpha_1\beta_2 y_{2t-1} + v_{1t}$$
$$y_{2t} = \alpha_2 y_{1t-1} + (1-\alpha_2\beta_2)y_{2t-1} + v_{2t}, \tag{6.17}$$

or

$$y_{1t} = \phi_{11}y_{1t-1} + \phi_{12}y_{2t-1} + v_{1t}$$
$$y_{2t} = \phi_{21}y_{1t-1} + \phi_{22}y_{2t-1} + v_{2t}. \tag{6.18}$$

The parameters in equation (6.18) are related to those in equation (6.17) by the restrictions

$$\phi_{11} = 1+\alpha_1, \quad \phi_{12} = -\alpha_1\beta_2, \quad \phi_{21} = \alpha_2, \quad \phi_{22} = 1-\alpha_2\beta_2. \tag{6.19}$$

Equation (6.18) represents a VAR in the levels of the variables as discussed in Chapter 4. Although equations (6.17) and (6.18) look very similar (they both represent models containing the levels of the variables and the same number of lags), careful comparison of the VECM in equation (6.17) and the VAR in equation (6.18) reveals three details worth emphasizing.

(i) The model in equation (6.17) is a restricted VAR containing 3 parameters, whereas equation (6.18) is an unrestricted VAR containing 4 parameters. This difference in the number of unknown parameters is encapsulated by the set of restrictions in equation (6.19) that arise from the y_{it} variables jointly having the same long-run equation.

(ii) If y_{1t} and y_{2t} are cointegrated, then the VECM system specified in levels in equation (6.17) is embedded within the VAR model in equation (6.18), suggesting that a VAR in levels is an appropriate general specification because it allows for both the VECM system by way of specialization of the system as well as cases where there is no cointegration. When there is cointegration, the long-run and short-run relationships manifest through the parameters on the lagged variables of the VAR in equation (6.18) that satisfy the restrictions in equation (6.19). But when there is no cointegration between y_{1t} and y_{2t}, the adjustment parameters $\alpha_1 = \alpha_2 = 0$ and there are no equilibrating forces present to return the system toward a long-run equilibrium. Imposing the restrictions $\alpha_1 = \alpha_2 = 0$ on equations (6.16) or (6.17) reduces the model to a simple VAR in first differences, that is, a VAR model in which each equation has a unit root and there are no cointegrating links between the $I(1)$ variables. In such cases, there are a full set of unit roots in the system, and short-run dynamics can be modeled by examining the corresponding equation specified in differences.

(iii) The VAR in equation (6.18) contains one lag, whereas the VECM specification in equation (6.16) contains no additional lags of the dependent variable other than those embodied in the error correction component. This difference in specification of the lag structure extends to VARs with k lagged dependent variables, with the corresponding VECM containing only $k-1$ additional lagged dependent variables, all of which are specified in terms of differences. Thus, the number of additional lags in the VECM specification in equation (6.15) is $k-1$. Since those additional lags involve differences Δy_{t-i}, the corresponding unrestricted levels VAR specification has k lags. This connection between the lag structures of the VAR and the VECM specifications is important in practical work. It means that the information criteria used in Chapter 4 to determine the optimal lag structure of a VAR are also valid for determining the optimal lag length of a VECM: If k is the optimal lag structure in the levels VAR determined by information criteria, then the corresponding number of additional lags in differences in the VECM model is $k-1$.

The possible relationships between VECM and VAR models may be summarized using a bivariate VAR(1) model expressed as

$$\Delta y_t = \Phi y_{t-1} + v_t, \tag{6.20}$$

or in the equivalent form

$$y_t = (I_2 + \Phi)y_{t-1} + v_t, \tag{6.21}$$

in which I_2 is a 2×2 identity matrix.[3] Three versions of this model are possible, each of which involves a different rank of the matrix Φ, which is denoted by r.

Full rank case ($r = 2$)

$$\begin{bmatrix} \Delta y_{1t} \\ \Delta y_{2t} \end{bmatrix} = \begin{bmatrix} \phi_{11} & \phi_{12} \\ \phi_{21} & \phi_{22} \end{bmatrix} \begin{bmatrix} y_{1t-1} \\ y_{2t-1} \end{bmatrix} + \begin{bmatrix} v_{1t} \\ v_{2t} \end{bmatrix}.$$

If Φ is of full rank, $r = 2$, then all the elements of Φ may be freely estimated without restriction. In this instance, the correct specification of the model is an unrestricted VAR in levels. The system is stationary and all variables are $I(0)$ when the matrix $(I_2 + \Phi)$ is stable.

Reduced rank case ($r = 1$)

$$\begin{bmatrix} \Delta y_{1t} \\ \Delta y_{2t} \end{bmatrix} = \begin{bmatrix} \alpha_1 \\ \alpha_2 \end{bmatrix} [1, -\beta_2] \begin{bmatrix} y_{1t-1} \\ y_{2t-1} \end{bmatrix} + \begin{bmatrix} v_{1t} \\ v_{2t} \end{bmatrix}.$$

In this case, there is a cointegrating linear combination $y_{1t-1} - \beta_2 y_{2t-1} = \beta' y_{t-1}$ between the two variables in levels and the matrix Φ has the outer product form $\Phi = \alpha\beta'$ where the vector $\alpha' = (\alpha_1, \alpha_2)$, and the vector $\beta' = (\beta_1, \beta_2)$. Examination of the matrix Φ reveals that the first row is simply a multiple of the second row, so that its rank $r = 1$. Looked at another way, constraining Φ to be the outer product of two vectors implies that the matrix has at most the rank of its constituent parts, which both have rank $r = 1$. The model may be specified as a restricted VAR expressed in levels or as a VECM expressed in differences and levels. The concept of reduced rank is extensively used in the estimation and testing of cointegrated systems of equations.

---

[3] Appendix A provides a short introduction to matrices including discussion of the identity matrix and the rank of a matrix.

Zero rank case (r = 0)

$$\begin{bmatrix} \Delta y_{1t} \\ \Delta y_{2t} \end{bmatrix} = \begin{bmatrix} 0 & 0 \\ 0 & 0 \end{bmatrix} \begin{bmatrix} y_{1t-1} \\ y_{2t-1} \end{bmatrix} + \begin{bmatrix} v_{1t} \\ v_{2t} \end{bmatrix}.$$

The most restricted model is the VAR in first differences given by the third model. This model has zero rank as the coefficient matrix Φ is merely a matrix of zeros, the outcome of four coefficient restrictions. In this case, the model is a VAR in first differences, each variable is $I(1)$, and the system is sometimes called a full rank $I(1)$ VAR model.

6.3 ESTIMATION

Two methods for estimating the unknown parameters of the VECM introduced in Section 6.2 are now discussed.[4] These are the fully modified ordinary least squares (FM-OLS) regression-based estimator proposed by Phillips and Hansen (Phillips and Hansen, 1990) and the Johansen reduced rank regression estimator (Johansen, 1988, 1991, 1995).

These estimators both possess two important properties.

(i) They are consistent for the true population parameters at the rate T, which is considerably faster than the $\sqrt{T}$ rate at which coefficients are estimated in stationary time series models (see, for example, Appendix B). This faster rate of convergence is sometimes referred to as super-consistency. It arises because the variables $\{y_{1t}, y_{2t}, \cdots, y_{Nt}\}$ are nonstationary $I(1)$ series, whose stochastically trending nature facilitates estimation of the cointegrating relationships.

(ii) The asymptotic distributions of these two estimators of the cointegrating parameters can be used to conduct hypothesis tests in much the same way as for models based on stationary variables. This important feature is not true for all cointegrating regression estimators.[5]

6.3.1 The Fully Modified Estimator

The FM-OLS estimator of Phillips and Hansen (Phillips and Hansen, 1990) is a regression-based estimator that circumvents the problems associated with the simple least squares regression estimation (Engle and Granger, 1987) by appropriately modifying the ordinary least squares estimator of the cointegrating equation.[6]

---

[4] Other methods for obtaining estimates of long-run cointegrating parameters have been proposed by Engle and Yoo (1987), Phillips and Loretan (1991), Saikkonen (1991), and Stock and Watson (1993). Most recently, methods that rely on deterministic trend instrumental variable regressions have been introduced by Phillips (2014b) and Hwang and Sun (2018). These latter methods have the advantage of simplicity and have good performance in both estimation and inference.

[5] The least squares estimator of the cointegrating parameters that were used in the original study by Engle and Granger (1987) and for estimating the parameters of the present value model in equation (6.7) has the super-consistency property, but the standard errors of the estimator do not allow conventional inference.

[6] FM-OLS may also be used in a system of equations and in a VAR context, where it is called FM-VAR (Phillips, 1995).

To highlight the features of the FM estimator, the present value model is specified more completely in terms of the following system

$$p_t = \beta_0 + \beta_d d_t + u_t$$
$$\Delta d_t = v_t. \tag{6.22}$$

The first equation is the cointegrating equation, while the second equation makes explicit the unit root stochastic trend property of dividends. The disturbances u_t and v_t are $I(0)$: the former because of cointegration and the latter because dividends are assumed to be difference stationary.

Although ordinary least squares estimation of the cointegrating regression in equation (6.22) delivers super-consistent estimation, inferences based on these estimates are generally invalid for several reasons

(i) d_t is an endogenous regressor;
(ii) u_t and v_t are correlated; and
(iii) u_t and v_t are autocorrelated.

The FM estimator takes into account these general features of the generating mechanism of the data and modifies least squares by correcting for endogeneity and autocorrelation. In both cases, long-run covariances are used to implement the corrections and these involve multivariate extensions of the long-run variance estimator introduced in Chapter 5. Long-run covariances are required in these corrections because equation (6.22) is a long-run relationship.

The long-run matrices that are needed are defined in terms of the following two-sided and one-sided sums of autocovariances

$$\Omega = \begin{bmatrix} \omega_{11} & \omega_{12} \\ \omega_{21} & \omega_{22} \end{bmatrix} = \sum_{j=-\infty}^{\infty} \Gamma_j \qquad \text{[2-sided]}$$
$$\Lambda = \begin{bmatrix} \lambda_{11} & \lambda_{12} \\ \lambda_{21} & \lambda_{22} \end{bmatrix} = \sum_{j=0}^{\infty} \Gamma_j, \qquad \text{[1-sided]} \tag{6.23}$$

where $\Gamma_j = E(w_t w'_{t-j})$ with $w_t = (u_t, v_t)'$.

The required estimates of the long-run quantities are obtained by first estimating equation (6.22) by least squares. Letting $\widehat{u}_t$ and $\widehat{v}_t = \Delta d_t = v_t$ be the least squares residuals from estimating equation (6.1), the two-sided and one-sided long-run covariance matrices can be estimated by the following weighted sums of sample autocovariances

$$\widehat{\Omega} = \begin{bmatrix} \widehat{\omega}_{11} & \widehat{\omega}_{12} \\ \widehat{\omega}_{21} & \widehat{\omega}_{22} \end{bmatrix} = \sum_{j=-m}^{m} \left(1 - \frac{j}{m+1}\right) \widehat{\Gamma}_j \qquad \text{[2-sided]}$$
$$\widehat{\Lambda} = \begin{bmatrix} \widehat{\lambda}_{11} & \widehat{\lambda}_{12} \\ \widehat{\lambda}_{21} & \widehat{\lambda}_{22} \end{bmatrix} = \sum_{j=0}^{m} \left(1 - \frac{j}{m+1}\right) \widehat{\Gamma}_j, \qquad \text{[1-sided]} \tag{6.24}$$

where m is the lag length, and $\widehat{\Gamma}_j$ is the autocovariance matrix at lag j given by

$$\widehat{\Gamma}_j = \frac{1}{T} \sum_{t=1+j}^{T} \begin{bmatrix} \widehat{u}_t \widehat{u}_{t-j} & \widehat{u}_t \widehat{v}_{t-j} \\ \widehat{v}_t \widehat{u}_{t-j} & \widehat{v}_t \widehat{v}_{t-j} \end{bmatrix}. \tag{6.25}$$

The diagonal elements of $\widehat{\Gamma}_j$ are the sample autocovariances of $\widehat{u}_t$ and $\widehat{v}_t$, and the off-diagonal elements contain their sample cross-covariances. The weighting scheme used in equation (6.22) employs the triangular weights $(1 - j/(m+1))$ and was introduced by Bartlett (1950) and used by Newey and West (1987) in the development of robust methods for constructing standard errors in econometrics.

The FM estimator of the cointegrating regression in equation (6.22) corrects for endogeneity and serial dependence and has the following explicit form

$$
\widehat{\beta}_{FM} = \left[\begin{array}{c} \widehat{\beta}_0 \\ \widehat{\beta}_d \end{array} \right] = \left[\begin{array}{cc} T & \sum\limits_{t=1}^{T} d_t \\ \sum\limits_{t=1}^{T} d_t & \sum\limits_{t=1}^{T} d_t^2 \end{array} \right]^{-1} \left[\begin{array}{c} \sum\limits_{t=1}^{T} p_t^+ \\ \sum\limits_{t=1}^{T} (d_t p_t^+ - \widehat{c}) \end{array} \right], \tag{6.26}
$$

where $p_t^+ = p_t - \widehat{\rho} \Delta d_t$ and $\widehat{\rho} = \widehat{\omega}_{12} \widehat{\omega}_{22}^{-1}$. There are two correction terms in equation (6.26) that modify the usual ordinary least squares formulae.

(i) The estimator $\widehat{\rho} = \widehat{\omega}_{12} \widehat{\omega}_{22}^{-1}$ is an estimator of the long-run regression coefficient $\omega_{12} \omega_{22}^{-1}$ of u_t on v_t. The correction term $p_t^+ = p_t - \widehat{\rho} \Delta d_t$ then adjusts the dependent variable p_t for its long-run joint dependence on d_t. This is the endogeneity correction.

(ii) The quantity $\widehat{c} = \widehat{\lambda}_{12} - \widehat{\rho} \, \widehat{\lambda}_{22}$ provides an adjustment that compensates for the contemporaneous and serial dependence of the price equation errors u_t with the errors $\Delta d_t = v_t$ in the dividend equation. This adjustment leads to the modification of sample moment $\sum_{1=1}^{T} (d_t p_t^+ - \widehat{c})$ that appears in the final member of the right side of equation (6.26).

Combining the adjustments (i) and (ii) leads to the fully modified version of least squares regression. To help understand the properties of the FM estimator, consider the special case where the equation errors u_t and v_t are not cross-correlated at leads and lags. The estimator of the covariance matrix in equation (6.25) is computed just using the sample contemporaneous covariance matrix between the $\widehat{u}_t$ and $\widehat{v}_t$ since $\Gamma_j = 0$ for all $j \neq 0$. For this special case, the estimators of the long-run covariance matrices in equation (6.24) are equal to each other

$$
\left[\begin{array}{cc} \widehat{\omega}_{11} & \widehat{\omega}_{12} \\ \widehat{\omega}_{21} & \widehat{\omega}_{22} \end{array} \right] = \left[\begin{array}{cc} \widehat{\lambda}_{11} & \widehat{\lambda}_{12} \\ \widehat{\lambda}_{21} & \widehat{\lambda}_{22} \end{array} \right] = \frac{1}{T} \sum_{t=1}^{T} \left[\begin{array}{cc} \widehat{u}_t^2 & \widehat{u}_t \widehat{v}_t \\ \widehat{v}_t \widehat{u}_t & \widehat{v}_t^2 \end{array} \right],
$$

which results in the correction term $\widehat{c}$ in equation (6.26) disappearing since

$$
\widehat{c} = \widehat{\lambda}_{12} - \widehat{\rho} \widehat{\lambda}_{22} = \widehat{\omega}_{12} - \widehat{\rho} \widehat{\omega}_{22} = \widehat{\omega}_{12} - \widehat{\omega}_{12} \widehat{\omega}_{22}^{-1} \widehat{\omega}_{22} = 0.
$$

The FM estimator is now simply obtained by regressing the modified dependent variable $p_t^+ = p_t - \widehat{\rho} \Delta d_t$ on a constant and d_t, with the remaining correction term $\widehat{\rho}$ computed from a simple least squares regression of $\widehat{u}_t$ on $\widehat{v}_t$.

A further special case is where there is no contemporaneous or serial correlation between u_t and v_t at all in equation (6.22) so the appropriate estimator for the remaining correction term is just $\widehat{\rho} = 0$. In this case, where there is no endogeneity and no serial correlation and this information is used, there is equivalence of the FM-OLS and ordinary least squares estimates. In general, of course, endogeneity and serial correlation are to be expected in the data and in the absence of any explicit information to the contrary, FM-OLS is constructed using both corrections.

The FM-OLS estimator is implemented by the following steps.

Step 1: Estimate equation (6.22) by ordinary least squares to obtain $\widehat{\beta}_0$ and $\widehat{\beta}_d$ and the residuals $\widehat{u}_t$, as well as $\widehat{v}_t = v_t = \Delta d_t$.

Step 2: Compute the long-run covariance matrices in equation (6.24) using the matrices in equation (6.25) with the lag length m selected according to some fixed value or data determined according to some optimal selection criterion.

Step 3: Use equation (6.26) to compute the FM parameter estimates.

Applying these steps to the US data on equity prices and dividends presented in Figure 6.1 gives the FM estimates of the present value cointegrating equation with standard errors in parentheses

$$p_t = \underset{(0.038)}{3.127} + \underset{(0.023)}{1.195}\, d_t + \widehat{u}_t. \tag{6.27}$$

The long-run covariance matrices in equation (6.24) are computed using a lag length of $m=8$. The FM-OLS parameter estimates are qualitatively very similar to the OLS parameter estimates presented in equation (6.2), which reflects the fact that both estimators generate super-consistent parameter estimates. However, the standard errors associated with the FM-OLS estimates given in equation (6.27) are robust to endogeneity and serial dependence by virtue of their construction.

6.3.2 The Johansen Reduced Rank Regression Estimator

The reduced rank regression estimator (Johansen, 1988, 1991, 1995) yields estimates for all of the parameters in an explicit parametric form of the VECM in equation (6.15), including both the long-run cointegrating parameters and the short-run error-correction parameters. This is in contrast to the semi-parametric regression-based FM estimator that yields estimates of only the long-run parameters because the transient dynamics are treated nonparametrically by FM-OLS.

To demonstrate the operation of the Johansen estimator, consider the following VECM of equity prices and dividends with the short-run dynamics captured by an additional lagged difference in the two variables

$$
\begin{aligned}
p_t &= \beta_0 + \beta_d d_t + u_t \\
\Delta p_t &= \delta_1 + \alpha_1 (p_{t-1} - \beta_0 - \beta_d d_{t-1}) + \gamma_{11}\Delta p_{t-1} + \gamma_{12}\Delta d_{t-1} + v_{1t} \\
\Delta d_t &= \delta_2 + \alpha_2 (p_{t-1} - \beta_0 - \beta_d d_{t-1}) + \gamma_{21}\Delta p_{t-1} + \gamma_{22}\Delta d_{t-1} + v_{2t},
\end{aligned}
\tag{6.28}
$$

where $v_t = (v_{1t}, v_{2t})'$ is a (2×1) vector of the VECM disturbances. As pointed out in Section 6.2, a VECM is a restricted VAR model in which the restrictions arise from a common long-run equation relation that leads to a reduced rank VAR structure. From inspection of the VECM in equation (6.28), the cointegrating link between prices and dividends yields a set of nonlinear, cross-equation restrictions in which the cointegrating parameters β_0 and β_d appear in both equations.

Johansen develops a computationally efficient algorithm to estimate the parameters of the VECM using reduced rank regression under the assumption of Gaussian innovations.[7] The Johansen estimator is implemented using the following steps.

Step 1: Construct the conditional residuals from 4 auxiliary regressions by regressing $\{\Delta p_t, \Delta d_t, p_{t-1}, d_{t-1}\}$ on $\{1, \Delta p_{t-1}, \Delta d_{t-1}\}$.

Step 2: Use the conditional residuals in the previous step to perform an eigen decomposition and compute $\widehat{\beta}_0$ and $\widehat{\beta}_d$ using the eigenvector corresponding to the largest eigenvalue.[8]

Step 3: Construct the cointegrating residuals $\widehat{u}_t = p_t - \widehat{\beta}_0 - \widehat{\beta}_d d_t$ and estimate the VECM in equation (6.28) by regressing $\{\Delta p_t, \Delta d_t\}$ in turn, on the regressors $\{1, \widehat{u}_{t-1}, \Delta p_{t-1}, \Delta d_{t-1}\}$.

The Johansen parameter estimates are presented in Table 6.1 using the US data on equity prices and dividends presented in Figure 6.1. The cointegrating parameter estimate of β_d is 1.1773, which is marginally smaller that the FM estimate of 1.195 given in equation (6.27). The signs of the error-correction parameters are $\widehat{\alpha}_1 = -0.0068 < 0$ and $\widehat{\alpha}_2 = 0.0024 > 0$. These signs are consistent with the system adjusting toward its long-run equilibrium by means of the price and dividend changes discussed earlier. The results are similar qualitatively to those obtained in equation (6.7) where the cointegrating residual $\widehat{u}_t$ is based on the OLS estimator.

The estimate of the intercept parameter β_0 does not have an associated standard error, whereas the estimates of the intercepts in the 2 error correction equations do have standard errors. The reason for this difference is that the dimension of the system is $N = 2$ and there are therefore only 2 unique intercepts corresponding to the levels of the 2

TABLE 6.1 The parameter estimates of the price-dividend VECM in equation (6.28) with standard errors in parentheses. The sample period is January 1871 to September 2016. The estimated cointegrating equation is

$$p_t = 3.4034 + \underset{(0.0303)}{1.1773}\, d_t + \widehat{u}_t.$$

Variable	Δp_t	Δd_t
Constant	0.000	0.001
	(0.0013)	(0.0002)
$\widehat{u}_{t-1}$	−0.007	0.002
	(0.0032)	(0.0004)
Δp_{t-1}	0.290	0.001
	(0.0231)	(0.0030)
Δd_{t-1}	0.137	0.879
	(0.0841)	(0.0110)

[7] The Johansen estimator is based on the maximum likelihood principle, which is introduced in Chapter 10. The treatment here does not emphasize this aspect of the estimator.

[8] The eigenvalue decomposition is also used to estimate factor models based on principal components in Chapter 12.

variables p_t and d_t. The reduced rank regression estimator apportions these values among the 3 intercepts that appear in the model (β_0, δ_1 and δ_2) thereby delivering estimates of the 3 intercepts. Only 2 standard errors are computed and provided because there are only two random intercepts from which the 3 intercepts in the VECM system are obtained.

From the theory underlying the present value model, equation (2.7) in Chapter 2 shows that the intercept β_0 in the cointegration equation of the present value model can be used to generate an estimate of the implied discount factor. This estimate is

$$\exp(-\widehat{\beta_0}) = \exp(-3.4034) = 0.0333,$$

resulting in a discount factor of 3.33%, which is just slightly below the estimate of 5% obtained from Figure 2.5 in Chapter 2.

The parameter estimates of the present value model presented in Table 6.1 are based on specifying the VECM in equation (6.15) with a single lag. This choice is arbitrary and is made here to simplify the implementation and the presentation of the results for the present value model. Formal data-based approaches to select the lag structure may be used instead. A simple method is to estimate the unrestricted VAR form of a VECM that is discussed in Section 6.2 and use information criteria to determine an appropriate lag length k of the VAR. The corresponding lag length for the VECM, where the lags are formulated in differences, is $k-1$. A preferred approach is to use information criteria to select both the lag length in the reduced rank regression and the cointegrating rank simultaneously by information criteria. This approach was suggested by Phillips (1996) and yields consistent estimates of both lag length and cointegrating rank (Chao and Phillips, 1999). More recent work (Cheng and Phillips, 2009, 2012) has shown that information criteria may be used to consistently estimate cointegrating rank without requiring explicit specification of the transient dynamics in the fitted model.

Determination of an appropriate lag structure is very important in implementing reduced rank regression in practice. The parameter estimates of the cointegrating equation and the choice of cointegrating rank (or the number of cointegrating relations) can both be extremely sensitive to the choice of k. This fragility is particularly the case in large dimensional systems where a large loss in degrees of freedom occurs as k increases, which in turn leads to imprecise parameter estimates. In such cases, it is desirable to employ data-determined methods for joint determination of lag length and cointegrating rank. Another strategy is to employ semi-parametric methods such as FM-OLS regression, which has been found to be more robust in estimating the cointegrating equation than reduced rank regression estimation in which the lag structure is determined parametrically. The sensitivities of reduced rank regression to choice of lag length in the present value VECM are explored in the exercises.

6.4 COINTEGRATION TESTING

Both the FM-OLS and Johansen estimators discussed in Section 6.3 proceed under the assumption that a cointegrating long-run relationship between the $I(1)$ variables exists. For the bivariate model relating equity prices and dividends, the long-run relationship originates in the present value finance model of equity prices and the presumption made in estimation is that this relationship is satisfied empirically.[9]

In this section, two methods are proposed to test for the presence of cointegration. The first method is easy to conduct and applies the univariate unit root tests of Chapter 5 to the residuals obtained from estimating the cointegrating equation. The second method relies on reduced-rank regression and may be interpreted as a multivariate extension of the univariate unit root test.

6.4.1 Residual-based Tests

To illustrate the residual-based test of cointegration, consider the present value model

$$p_t = \beta_0 + \beta_d d_t + u_t, \tag{6.29}$$

where the log equity price p_t and log dividend d_t are $I(1)$, and u_t is the disturbance term that will be $I(0)$ when p_t and d_t are cointegrated. A natural way to test for cointegration is a two-step procedure consisting of estimating the cointegrating regression in equation (6.29) by ordinary least squares in the first step and testing the residuals for stationarity in the second step. As the unit root test treats the null hypothesis as nonstationary, the null hypothesis corresponds to no cointegration, whereas the alternative hypothesis of stationarity corresponds to cointegration

$$\begin{aligned} H_0 &: \text{No Cointegration} \quad [u_t \text{ is nonstationary}] \\ H_1 &: \text{Cointegration.} \quad\;\; [u_t \text{ is stationary}] \end{aligned} \tag{6.30}$$

The distribution of the residual-based cointegration test is non-standard, as might be expected because the procedure tests for a unit root null hypothesis (Phillips and Ouliaris, 1990). In a similar way to unit root tests, residual-based cointegration tests have critical values that depend on the sample size and the number of deterministic terms in the regression. But unlike standard unit root tests, residual-based tests have asymptotic distributions and critical values that also depend on the number of $I(1)$ regressors in the cointegrating equation.[10] Tables are provided by MacKinnon (1991), which gives response surface estimates of the critical values that are now used in many computer packages.

Using the monthly data on equity prices and dividends for the United States from January 1871 to September 2016, the residuals from estimating the cointegrating

---

[9] If no such long-run relationship exists, then empirical regressions of $I(1)$ variables that are not cointegrated produce spurious results in the sense that the variables may appear to be related because of the existence of their individual underlying trends even though these trends are not common to both variables. This problem is known as the spurious regression problem. In cases where there is no underlying long-run relationship, an unrestricted VAR in first differences (instead of a VECM formulation) may still be employed and can deliver valid inference about the short-run dynamics. Valid inference may also be made in VAR regressions formulated in levels, provided appropriate methods are used, such as FM-OLS regression (Phillips, 1995) or lag augmented VAR regression (Toda and Yamamoto, 1995).

[10] No degrees of freedom adjustment is necessary if the cointegrating parameters are known, as is the case for the present value model if the long-run restriction of $\beta_d = 1$ is imposed on equation (6.29). In this case, the critical values used to test for a unit root in a variable are still appropriate.

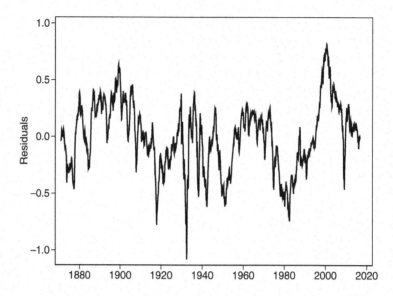

FIGURE 6.4   Plot of the residuals from the first stage of the Engle–Granger two-stage procedure applied to the present value model. Data are monthly observations from January 1871 to September 2016 on US equity prices and dividends.

equation in (6.29) by ordinary least squares are plotted in Figure 6.4. The series has mean zero and there is no trend apparent, giving the appearance of stationarity.

Formal tests of the stationarity of the residuals in Figure 6.4 are presented in Table 6.2. Two cointegration tests are provided based on the Augmented Dickey–Fuller (ADF) and Phillips–Perron (PP) unit root tests with lag lengths running from 0 to 4 lags. The ADF tests based on lags 1 to 4 all yield statistics which are greater than the 5% critical values, thereby providing strong evidence for rejecting the null of no cointegration in favor of the alternative hypothesis of cointegration. Similar qualitative results are obtained for the PP test for all lags. These results in general confirm the intuition provided by Figure 6.4, thereby providing strong support for the present value model as a valid long-run relationship between equity prices and dividends.

TABLE 6.2   **Residual-based tests of cointegration between US equity prices and dividends using equation (6.29). The test regression has no constant term, with lags running from 0 to 4.**

Lags	Augmented Dickey–Fuller	Phillips–Perron
0	−3.028	−3.028
1	−4.287	−3.493
2	−4.029	−3.680
3	−4.037	−3.770
4	−4.317	−3.849

Note: Critical values are, respectively, 1%, −2.580; 5%, −1.950; and 10%, −1.620.
* In the ADF test, "Lags" represents the number of lagged differences of the dependent variable included in the regression. In the Phillips–Perron test, "Lags" represents the number of Newey–West lags employed in the estimates of the nonparametric components of the test statistic.

6.4.2 Johansen Reduced Rank Regression Tests

The Johansen reduced rank regression test of cointegration is based on the VECM, which for the present value model is given by the two error correction equations for p_t and d_t as

$$\Delta p_t = \delta_1 + \alpha_1 (p_{t-1} - \beta_0 - \beta_d d_{t-1}) + \gamma_{11} \Delta p_{t-1} + \gamma_{12} \Delta d_{t-1} + v_{1t}$$
$$\Delta d_t = \delta_2 + \alpha_2 (p_{t-1} - \beta_0 - \beta_d d_{t-1}) + \gamma_{21} \Delta p_{t-1} + \gamma_{22} \Delta d_{t-1} + v_{2t}. \tag{6.31}$$

Unlike the residual-based tests of cointegration, which involve testing a single set of hypotheses as in equation (6.30), the Johansen test is based on testing a sequence of different hypotheses. In the case of the present value model where there are $N = 2$ equations, there are two stages to the testing procedure with different null and alternative hypotheses in each case

$$\begin{aligned}
&\text{Stage 1} && H_0 : \text{No cointegration, all variables are } I(1) \\
& && H_1 : \text{1 or more cointegrating equations}
\end{aligned}$$

$$\tag{6.32}$$

$$\begin{aligned}
&\text{Stage 2} && H_0 : \text{1 cointegrating equation} \\
& && H_1 : \text{All variables are stationary } I(0)
\end{aligned}$$

The first stage is effectively equivalent to the null and alternative hypotheses used in expression (6.30). The null hypothesis is no cointegration, which occurs when p_t and d_t are $I(1)$, and the error correction term $u_t = p_t - \beta_0 - \beta_d d_t$ is also $I(1)$. The alternative hypothesis at the first stage is that cointegration exists and u_t is $I(0)$. If the null hypothesis in the first stage is not rejected testing is complete with the conclusion that there is no cointegration.

If the first stage null hypothesis is rejected in favor of the alternative hypothesis in expression (6.32), the second stage hypotheses are tested. Here the null hypothesis is that there is one cointegrating equation and so u_t is $I(0)$. Interestingly, the alternative hypothesis for this second stage is not that there are two cointegrating equations, but that p_t and d_t are actually stationary or $I(0)$.

A simple way of interpreting this sequence of tests is to view them as a test for determining the number of unit roots in the system or the number of unit roots in the VAR model expressed in levels. The null hypothesis in Stage 1 is that there is a full set of unit roots. The alternative hypothesis in Stage 1 is that there are at most $N - 1$ unit roots (or at least one cointegrating relation). The null hypothesis in Stage 2 is that there are $N - 1$ unit roots and one cointegrating relation. The alternative hypothesis in Stage 2 is that there are $N - 2$ unit roots and, since $N = 2$ in this example, the system is stationary. Thus, the reduced rank regression test sequence is really just a sequence of tests concerning the number of unit roots in the system, thereby making these tests just a multivariate form of unit root test.

To test the sequence of hypotheses in expression (6.32), the first, most restrictive case involves estimating the VECM in equation (6.31) under the null hypothesis of no cointegration ($r = 0$) by restricting the error correction parameters to be zero $\alpha_1 = \alpha_2 = 0$. The VECM in equation (6.31) then reduces to a VAR with $k - 1$ lags, with all of the variables in this case expressed in first differences. This is a VAR with a full set of unit roots. The second set of restrictions corresponds to the alternative hypothesis in the first stage in expression (6.32), equivalent to the null hypothesis in the second stage, by estimating the VECM subject to the cross-equation restrictions arising from cointegration ($r = 1$). The third set corresponds to the alternative hypothesis in the second stage where all variables are stationary ($r = 2$). In this scenario, the VECM becomes a VAR with k lags with all of the variables in levels. Since this approach to testing for cointegration is based on the rank of the system, it is referred to as a reduced rank regression test or a Johansen test.

A computationally efficient way of performing the sequence of tests is to express the statistic in terms of the estimated eigenvalues obtained from applying the reduced rank regression estimator to the VECM in (6.15) (Johansen, 1988, 1991, 1995). For an N-dimensional system, the form of the statistic is

$$TRACE = -(T - k) \sum_{i=r+1}^{N} \log(1 - \widehat{\lambda}_i), \tag{6.33}$$

where $\widehat{\lambda}_i$, $i = 1, 2, \cdots, N$ are the eigenvalues obtained from estimating the VECM using the reduced rank regression estimator, ordered from highest to lowest.[11] The subscript r represents the rank of the system. Under the null hypothesis in Stage 1 of expression (6.32), the rank of the system is $r = 0$, with the statistic in equation (6.33) representing a joint test that all N eigenvalues are zero. The null hypothesis in Stage 2 is that $r = 1$. The statistic in this case is a test that the smallest eigenvalue is zero. The test statistic is called the trace test because the trace of a matrix is determined by the number of non-zero eigenvalues. Large values of the trace statistic relative to the critical value result in rejection of the null hypothesis.

In the present value model $N = 2$ and therefore a sequence of two stages is sufficient. For higher dimensional VECMs with $N > 2$, there may be more than a single cointegrating long-run equation connecting the nonstationary variables up to a possible maximum of $N - 1$ cointegrating equations. Examples of VECMs with multiple cointegrating equations are discussed in Sections 6.6 ($r = 3$) and 6.7 ($r = 5$).

The results of the Johansen test applied to the US equity prices and dividends from January 1871 to September 2016 ($T - k = 1747$) are given in Table 6.3. The estimates of the eigenvalues are $\widehat{\lambda}_1 = 0.0207$ and $\widehat{\lambda}_2 = 0.0008$. The value of the test statistic for the first null hypothesis of no cointegration ($r = 0$) is computed as

$$TRACE(r = 0) = -1747 \left(\log(1 - 0.0207) + \log(1 - 0.0008) \right) = 37.9330.$$

TABLE 6.3 Johansen test of cointegration between US equity prices and dividends. Testing is based on the VECM in equation (6.31). Both the 5% critical value (CV) and the p value of the test are reported.

Null Hypothesis	Eigenvalue	Statistic	5% CV	p value
$r = 0$: No cointegration	0.0207	37.9330	15.41	0.000
$r = 1$: 1 cointegrating equation	0.0008	1.3910	3.76	0.238

---

[11] This test is, in fact, a likelihood ratio (LR) test since the reduced rank estimator is a maximum likelihood estimator under Gaussian assumptions. This type of test is dealt with in Chapter 10. However, unlike the standard chi-square distribution of the usual LR statistic, the trace test has a nonstandard distribution due to the nonstationarity of the variables being tested.

The null is easily rejected at the 5% level with a p value of 0.0000, providing evidence of at least one cointegrating equation between equity prices and dividends. The value of the test statistic for the next null hypothesis corresponding to one cointegrating equation $(r = 1)$ is

$$TRACE(r = 1) = -1747 \left(\log(1 - 0.0008)\right) = 1.3910.$$

As the p value is 0.2382, which is greater than 0.05, this null is not rejected at the 5% level. This sequence of tests provides strong support for the present value model because cointegration between equity prices and dividends is confirmed, thereby complementing the results obtained using the residual-based tests for cointegration.

6.4.3 Relationship with Unit Root Testing

As indicated in the previous discussion, the reduced-rank regression test for cointegration is a form of multivariate unit root test in which the variables are tested jointly for nonstationarity. If the null hypothesis in Stage 1 of expression (6.32) is not rejected, then testing concludes with the result that all variables in the system are $I(1)$. This test may be compared with the approach in Chapter 5 where unit root tests are performed on each series at a time. In fact, the asymptotic distribution of the reduced-rank test is the analogue for a multivariate time series of the scalar unit root limit distribution for a single time series.

In the extreme case where all null hypotheses in expression (6.32) are rejected, the final alternative hypothesis that all variables are $I(0)$ is accepted. If $N = 1$, this set of hypotheses reduces to the set of hypotheses underlying unit root tests discussed in Chapter 5, with the intermediate hypotheses of cointegration no longer relevant. A system that involves $N > 1$ variables allows for intermediate cases of cointegration where linear subsets of $I(1)$ variables can be constructed that are $I(0)$. If there are r linearly independent subsets of this type, then there are still $N - r$ unit roots in the system and the reduced-rank regression test is a test for the presence of such unit roots.

The Johansen test provides a computationally efficient mechanism for computing unit root tests on several variables jointly with a single statistic. It also circumvents situations where individual unit root tests may not provide a consensus view of the nonstationarity properties of the variables in the system. Cointegration testing may be interpreted as a step toward formulating a multivariate dynamic model of the VECM form. In doing so, the approach works to preserve the potential multivariate linkages between variables and thereby helps to avoid possible misspecification that can arise in making inference based on univariate specifications alone.

6.5 PARAMETER TESTING

When there is cointegration in the system, the FM-OLS and reduced-rank regression estimators deliver super-consistent parameter estimates of the cointegrating parameters associated with the $I(1)$ variables together with standard errors that can be used to construct asymptotically valid t tests concerning these parameters. In contrast to the unit root tests discussed in Chapter 5 and the reduced rank regression tests for cointegration discussed above, both of which have non-standard asymptotic distributions, the distributions of these t tests are, in fact, asymptotically normally distributed as $N(0, 1)$

despite the component variables being nonstationary. This property arises because when it is correctly specified, the VECM system is expressed in stationary variable form involving either first differences of $I(1)$ variables or long-run equilibrium errors such as u_{t-1}.

In testing the parameters of a VECM three broad sets of hypotheses can be explored. These hypotheses relate to the cointegrating parameters, the equilibrium adjustment parameters, and the transient dynamic parameters. The tests are illustrated for the present value cointegrating model using the reduced-rank regression parameter estimates in Table 6.1.

Cointegrating Parameters

The long-run parameter estimate on dividends in the cointegrating equation in (6.28) is $\widehat{\beta}_d = 1.1773$, which is numerically close to the theoretical value predicted by the present value model of $\beta_d = 1$. Testing this restriction that $\beta_d = 1$ proceeds under the null hypothesis as usual and is based on the t statistic

$$t(\beta_d = 1) = \frac{1.1773 - 1}{0.0303} = 5.8515.$$

Despite the point estimate being numerically close to the theoretical value of $\beta_d = 1$, the large value of the t statistic provides strong evidence that the null hypothesis is rejected at the 5% level.

Error Correction Parameters and Weak Exogeneity

The relative strengths of the equilibrating mechanisms are controlled by the adjustment or error correction parameters α_1 and α_2 in equation (6.28). A test that p_t does not adjust to restore equilibrium is based on the null hypothesis that $\alpha_1 = 0$. This test is sometimes referred to as a test of weak exogeneity because under the null hypothesis, movements in p_t are independent of the error correction term $u_{t-1} = p_{t-1} - \beta_0 - \beta_d d_{t-1}$ and hence the long-run parameters β_0 and β_d. The t statistic to test for weak exogeneity of p_t is

$$t(\alpha_1 = 0) = \frac{-0.0068 - 0}{0.0032} = -2.1015.$$

The p value is 0.0356, resulting in a rejection of the null hypothesis at the 5% level of significance, but not at the 1% level. A similar test of weak exogeneity is performed for dividends where the null hypothesis is $\alpha_2 = 0$. The t statistic is

$$t(\alpha_2 = 0) = \frac{0.0024 - 0}{0.0004} = 5.7796,$$

resulting in a p value of 0.000 and strong rejection of the null hypothesis. The outcome of these tests is that at the 5% level, both p_t and d_t are important in adjusting to restore long-run equilibrium, whereas at the 1% level, the primary role in the adjustment mechanism is taken by d_t.

Dynamic Parameters and Strong Exogeneity

The short-run parameters γ_{ij} in equation (6.28) combined with the error correction parameters, α_1 and α_2, control the short-run dynamic paths toward long-run equilibrium.

To test the role of the γ_{ij} parameters in the present value model, four t tests are conducted. The first two tests are for the Δp_t error correction equation given by

$$t(\gamma_{11} = 0) = \frac{0.2901 - 0}{0.0231} = 12.54, \quad t(\gamma_{12} = 0) = \frac{0.1366 - 0}{0.0841} = 1.626.$$

The first is statistically significant, whereas the second is not. Repeating these tests for the Δd_t error correction equation yields

$$t(\gamma_{21} = 0) = \frac{0.0006 - 0}{0.0030} = 0.21, \quad t(\gamma_{22} = 0) = \frac{0.8792 - 0}{0.0110} = 80.17.$$

Here the second test is statistically significant, whereas the first is not. This group of tests shows that own lags are statistically important in contributing to the short-run dynamic adjustment paths, but other lagged variables are not.

The results of the weak exogeneity tests show that at the 1% significance level, it is d_t that primarily adjusts to the error correction term u_{t-1}, while p_t is weakly exogenous. Combining this result with the transient dynamic tests in the Δp_t error correction equation, Δp_t appears to depend primarily on its own past history and to be independent of past movements of d_t. Following the discussion of causality in Chapter 4, these empirical results suggest that d_t fails to Granger cause p_t in which case p_t may be interpreted as being exogenous. The findings also indicate that d_t is the primary endogenous variable in the system and it is this variable that plays the primary role in making adjustments toward the long-run equilibrium path.

6.6 COINTEGRATION AND THE GORDON MODEL

The present value model of equity price determination is based on a bivariate relationship between log equity prices and log dividends. An early influential paper on equity prices by Gordon (1959) actually proposes two competing models of asset prices. The first is the present value model already discussed. The second is based on earnings. For this second model, it is assumed the investor buys equity in order to obtain income per share and is indifferent as to whether returns to investment are packaged in terms of the fraction of earnings distributed as a dividend or in terms of a rise in the share's value.

Defining p_t as log equity prices, d_t as log dividends, and e_t as log earnings, these two competing models of equity prices are summarized as

$$\begin{aligned} p_t &= \beta_{10} + \beta_{1d}d_t + u_{1t}, \quad \text{[Price-Dividend long-run equation]} \\ p_t &= \beta_{20} + \beta_{2e}e_t + u_{2t}, \quad \text{[Price-Earnings long-run equation]} \end{aligned} \qquad (6.34)$$

where u_{1t} and u_{2t} are disturbance terms representing the pricing errors for the two models. This set of equations is often referred to as the Gordon model. Provided that p_t, d_t, and e_t are $I(1)$ and the two disturbances are $I(0)$, the system of equations in equation (6.34) represents two cointegrating equations within a trivariate $(N = 3)$ model. The corresponding VECM now contains two error correction terms that capture the equilibrating mechanisms that push to restore the long-run equilibrium path after transient shocks to the variables may drive the system away from the equilibrium path.

Figure 6.5 gives a 3-dimensional scatter plot of monthly observations of the variables p_t, d_t, and e_t from January 1871 to September 2016 for the US. All three variables tend to move closely around a single 1-dimensional path running through the 3-dimensional space. This near-linear path is strong visual evidence supporting the presence of two cointegrating equations that together work to reduce the 3-dimensional variation. By contrast, there would be no visual evidence of cointegration if the observations were scattered evenly throughout the 3-dimensional cube, a point already made regarding the 2-dimensional scatter plot in Figure 6.2. The effect of a single cointegrating equation would be to reduce the number of dimensions by 1, in which case the observations would be attracted toward a 2-dimensional surface within the cube. The presence of a second cointegrating equation compresses the dimension of the scatter plot further from a 2-dimensional surface toward a 1-dimensional path within the 3-dimensional cube.

The results of performing the Johansen cointegration test to identify the number of cointegrating equations among the $N = 3$ variables are presented in Table 6.4. In implementing this test, the VECM in equation (6.15) is specified as

$$\Delta y_t = \delta + \alpha(\beta' y_{t-1} - \beta_0) + \Gamma_1 \Delta y_{t-1} + v_t, \tag{6.35}$$

with the $N = 3$ variables ordered as $y_t = (p_t, d_t, e_t)$. The dimensions of the parameters are as follows: δ is a (3×1) vector of constants in the VECM, α and β are $(3 \times r)$ matrices of error-correction and cointegrating parameters, respectively; where r is the number of cointegrating equations, β_0 is an $(r \times 1)$ vector of constants corresponding to the r cointegrating equations, and Γ_1 is a (3×3) matrix of transient dynamic parameters serving as coefficients on Δy_{t-1}. The choice of a single additional lag in this VECM is adopted for convenience to simplify the presentation of the model. In the exercises, the analysis is repeated for a lag length of $k - 1$ in the VECM chosen using information criteria applied to the corresponding VAR model.

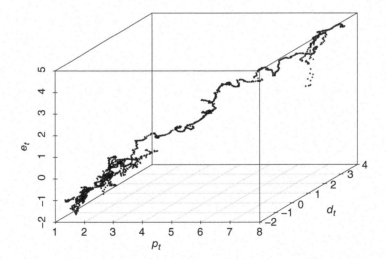

FIGURE 6.5 Three dimensional scatter plot of the equity price index, dividends, and earnings (all expressed in logs). The Gordon model implies the existence of two cointegrating vectors, which is illustrated by the scatter being attracted to a line in three dimensional space. The data are monthly observations from January 1871 to September 2016.

TABLE 6.4 Johansen cointegration test of the Gordon model of equity prices in equation (6.35) between US log equity prices, log dividends, and log earnings. The sample period is January 1871 to September 2016.

Null Hypothesis	Eigenvalue	Statistic	5% CV	p value
$r = 0$: No cointegration	0.0647	145.6367	29.68	0.0001
$r = 1$: 1 cointegrating equation	0.0157	28.7756	15.41	0.0003
$r = 2$: 2 cointegrating equations	0.0007	1.1765	3.76	0.2781

As the dimension of the system is $N = 3$ variables, there are 3 sets of hypotheses to consider. The first null hypothesis is of no cointegration ($r = 0$), with the alternative being there is at least 1 cointegrating equation. The test statistic is 145.6367. The 5% critical value is 29.68, resulting in a p value that is less than 0.05, thereby providing strong evidence against the null of no cointegration and in favor of the alternative hypothesis of cointegration. To identify the actual number of cointegrating equations, testing proceeds to the next set of hypotheses where the null is now 1 cointegrating equation and the alternative is that there are at least 2 cointegrating equations. The test statistic for this hypothesis is 28.7756. The 5% critical value is 15.41, resulting in a rejection at the 5% level of the null hypothesis that there is just 1 cointegrating equation. To determine if there is an additional cointegrating equation, testing proceeds to the third set of hypotheses where the null is that there are 2 cointegrating equations. The corresponding test statistic is 1.1765, which now provides strong evidence in favor of the null hypothesis at the 5% level since the critical value of the test is 3.76. These results support the graphical analysis in Figure 6.5, which shows visual evidence of 2 cointegrating equations.

The specification of the dividends and earnings cointegrating equations in equation (6.34) is based on the theoretical models proposed by Gordon (1959). However, these two equations can be rearranged to generate an alternative long-run cointegrating equation that is still perfectly consistent with the cointegrating system associated with the Gordon model. For example, setting the two equations in equation (6.34) equal to each other eliminates p_t as follows,

$$\beta_{10} + \beta_{1d}d_t + u_{1t} = \beta_{20} + \beta_{2e}e_t + u_{2t}.$$

Rearranging this equation for d_t as a function of e_t gives

$$d_t = \beta_{30} + \beta_{3e}e_t + u_{3t}, \qquad \text{[Dividend-Earnings long-run equation]} \qquad (6.36)$$

with $\beta_{30} = (\beta_{20} - \beta_{10})/\beta_{1d}$, $\beta_{3e} = \beta_{2e}/\beta_{1d}$ and $u_{3t} = (u_{2t} - u_{1t})/\beta_{1d}$. Equation (6.36) also represents a cointegrating equation as d_t and e_t are $I(1)$, while the disturbance term u_{3t} is a linear function of $I(0)$ disturbances, which must also be $I(0)$. Any two of the three cointegrating equations in (6.34) and (6.36) provide a valid and observationally equivalent representation of the long-run properties underlying equity prices, dividends, and earnings. Obtaining a unique representation of the cointegrated system requires a specific normalization process, such as that given in equation (6.34) where each equation is normalized so that the coefficient of the price variable p_t is unity.

The Gordon model can be formulated by using the price-earnings equation (6.34) and the dividends-earnings equation (6.36) as the two normalized cointegrating equations to be estimated by reduced rank regression. The specification of the VECM for this version of the Gordon trivariate model containing two cointegrating equations and one lag has the explicit form

$$\Delta p_t = \delta_1 + \alpha_{11}u_{2t-1} + \alpha_{12}u_{3t-1} + \gamma_{11}\Delta p_{t-1} + \gamma_{12}\Delta d_{t-1} + \gamma_{13}\Delta e_{t-1} + v_{1t}$$
$$\Delta d_t = \delta_2 + \alpha_{21}u_{2t-1} + \alpha_{22}u_{3t-1} + \gamma_{21}\Delta p_{t-1} + \gamma_{22}\Delta d_{t-1} + \gamma_{23}\Delta e_{t-1} + v_{2t}$$
$$\Delta e_t = \delta_3 + \alpha_{31}u_{2t-1} + \alpha_{32}u_{3t-1} + \gamma_{31}\Delta p_{t-1} + \gamma_{32}\Delta d_{t-1} + \gamma_{33}\Delta e_{t-1} + v_{3t}.$$

The parameter estimates of this system are presented in Table 6.5. The long-run parameter estimates on the earnings variable in the two cointegrating equations are both numerically very close to unity. Testing the restriction $\beta_{2e} = 1$ from the price-earnings cointegrating regression in equation (6.34) yields a t statistic of

$$t(\beta_{2e} = 1) = \frac{1.0900 - 1}{0.0349} = 2.5788,$$

which is nonetheless still statistically significant at the 5% level with a p value of 0.0099. Applying the same test to the parameter β_{3e} in the dividend-earnings cointegrating regression in equation (6.36) yields a t statistic of

$$t(\beta_{3e} = 1) = \frac{0.9170 - 1}{0.0110} = -7.5170,$$

which also leads to a rejection of the null hypothesis at the 5% level with a p value of 0.0000.

Inspection of the error correction parameter estimates in Table 6.5 shows that equity prices adjust to the equity-earnings error correction term $\hat{u}_{2t-1}$, but not the dividend-earnings error correction term $\hat{u}_{3t-1}$. In fact, all three variables respond when the price-earnings relationship is not in long-run equilibrium. The negative sign on $\hat{u}_{2t-1}$ in the Δp_t equation of the VECM shows that when equity prices operate above (below) the

TABLE 6.5   Reduced-rank regression parameter estimates of the Gordon model, with standard errors in parentheses. The sample period is January 1871 to September 2016. The estimated cointegrating equations are

$$p_t = 2.7677 + 1.0900e_t + \hat{u}_{2t}$$
$$\text{\footnotesize(0.0349)}$$

$$d_t = -0.5052 + 0.9170e_t + \hat{u}_{3t}.$$
$$\text{\footnotesize(0.0110)}$$

Variable	Δp_t	Δd_t	Δe_t
Constant	0.0004	0.0011	0.0003
	(0.0013)	(0.0002)	(0.0007)
$\hat{u}_{2t-1}$	−0.0082	0.0018	0.0048
	(0.0033)	(0.0004)	(0.0019)
$\hat{u}_{3t-1}$	0.0061	−0.0064	0.0135
	(0.0056)	(0.0007)	(0.0033)
Δp_{t-1}	0.2845	−0.0012	0.0459
	(0.0232)	(0.0030)	(0.0137)
Δd_{t-1}	0.0768	0.8328	0.1786
	(0.0957)	(0.0123)	(0.0562)
Δe_{t-1}	0.0488	0.0082	0.7889
	(0.0261)	(0.0033)	(0.0153)

price-earnings long-run relationship, this results in short-run decreases (increases) in equity prices.

By contrast, the positive signs on $\widehat{u}_{2t-1}$ in the dividend and earnings error correction equations show that these variables restore equilibrium by increasing (decreasing) when equity prices are above (below) the price-earnings long-run equilibrium. Dividends and earnings also adjust toward the equilibrium path when the dividend-earnings relationship is not in equilibrium, with dividends falling and earnings increasing when dividends are above their long-run value (when $\widehat{u}_{3t-1} > 0$). These error-correction mechanisms show that equity prices, dividends, and earnings are all endogenous within the trivariate system and all operate to restore long-run equilibrium in the equity market arising from temporary shocks pushing the system into disequilibrium.

The estimated model presented in Table 6.5 is based on the price-earnings and dividend-earnings cointegrating relationships in equations (6.34) and (6.36). To recover the estimates of the present value cointegrating relationship between p_t and d_t note that

$$\beta_{10} = \beta_{20} - \beta_{3e}\beta_{30}/\beta_{2e}, \qquad \beta_{1d} = \beta_{2e}/\beta_{3e},$$

which are obtained by using the expressions for β_{30} and β_{3e} given immediately below equation (6.36). Using the parameter estimates reported in Table 6.5, the price-dividend cointegrating parameter estimates are

$$\widehat{\beta}_{10} = 2.7677 + 0.9170 \times 0.5052/1.0900 = 3.1927, \quad \widehat{\beta}_{1d} = \frac{1.0900}{0.9170} = 1.1887.$$

These estimates would also have been achieved if the cointegrating system was expressed as in equation (6.34).

6.7 COINTEGRATION AND THE YIELD CURVE

The expectations hypothesis of the term structure of interest rates posits that the yield on a long-maturity bond is the average of the current and expected future yields on a short maturity bond (see Chapter 2). If the long-term bond has maturity of $m = 3$ months with yield r_{3t} and the short-term bond is an $m = 1$ month bond with yield r_{1t}, the investor at time $t = 0$ can either invest \$1 for 3 months at the 3-month yield or invest the \$1 in a 1-month bond at the current yield, r_{1t}, and reinvest at the (expected) prevailing 1-month yield in months 2 and 3. To ensure that there are no arbitrage opportunities, the expectations hypothesis requires that these two strategies result in the same return, so that

$$r_{3t} = \frac{1}{3}E_t(r_{1t} + r_{1t+1} + r_{1t+2}). \tag{6.37}$$

Equation (6.37) is rearranged to generate an expression for the spread between the long and short interest rates by subtracting r_{1t} from both sides, and adding and subtracting $r_{1t+1}/3$ from the right-hand side as follows

$$r_{3t} - r_{1t} = E_t\left(-\frac{2}{3}r_{1t} + \frac{1}{3}r_{1t+1} + \frac{1}{3}r_{1t+1} - \frac{1}{3}r_{1t+1} + \frac{1}{3}r_{1t+2}\right)$$
$$= E_t\left(-\frac{2}{3}r_{1t} + \frac{2}{3}r_{1t+1} - \frac{1}{3}r_{1t+1} + \frac{1}{3}r_{1t+2}\right)$$
$$= E_t\left(\frac{2}{3}\Delta r_{1t+1} + \frac{1}{3}\Delta r_{1t+2}\right). \tag{6.38}$$

The spread between the long and the short yields is expressed as a weighted sum of future changes in the 1-month short yield. This equation can be generalized to arbitrary maturities of m months according to

$$r_{mt} - r_{1t} = E_t \sum_{j=1}^{m-1}\left(1 - \frac{j}{m}\right)\Delta r_{1t+j}. \tag{6.39}$$

Equation (6.39) represents a system of cointegrating equations. As bond yields are found to be $I(1)$ from the direct application of unit root tests in Chapter 5, the right-hand side of this expression must be stationary, as it is a function of future changes in the short-term yield, which by definition are $I(0)$. This, in turn, implies that the spread $r_{mt} - r_{1t}$ is stationary, making r_{mt} and r_{1t} cointegrated as the spread is a linear function of two $I(1)$ variables that becomes an $I(0)$ variable. An important property of equation (6.39) is that because it holds for all m, the expectations theory of the term structure predicts that there are $m - 1$ cointegrating long-term relationships with the short-term rate r_{1t}.

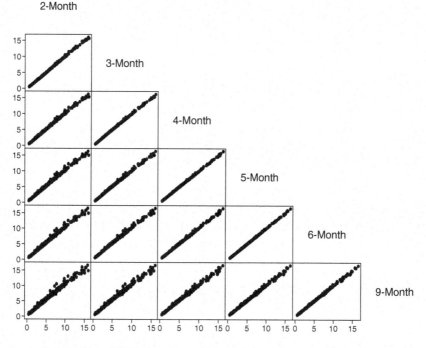

FIGURE 6.6 Scatter plots of the US zero-coupon bond yields of various maturities. The data are monthly for the period December 1946 to February 1987.

Figure 6.6 contains scatter plots of US zero-coupon bond yields from December 1946 to February 1987 for maturities of $m = \{2, 3, 4, 5, 6, 9\}$ months. Inspection of the 5 scatter plots in the first column between the short-term yield and the 5 longer-term yields shows strong evidence of long-run equilibria between each of these pairs of yields. This figure also shows similar long-run relationships between other combinations of yields in the other columns. This result is a reflection of the property already established for the Gordon model in Section 6.6, namely, that when there are multiple cointegrating equations in a system, the cointegrating equations may be expressed in a variety of forms, whereas the space defined by the cointegrating relations is well defined and unique. For the term structure data with 6 maturities, the scatter plots in Figure 6.6 show 15 paired linkages among the various maturities. However, the overall dimension of the linkages or cointegrated system is only 5 (such as those shown in the first column) because the remaining 10 paired linkages can be recovered by taking combinations of these chosen 5 cointegrating equations. In the empirical analysis that follows, the cointegrating equations are based on the pairs of yields presented in the first column, although undertaking the analysis on other combinations of yields would also be appropriate.

A formal test of the number of cointegrating equations between the 6 yields is conducted using the Johansen cointegration test. To perform this test, it is necessary to specify the VECM in equation (6.15). To identify the lag structure of the VECM, Table 6.6 contains the results of using information criteria to determine the lag length of a VAR containing all 6 yields, expressed in levels. Information criteria are presented for lags running from $k = 0$ to $k = 8$. Using the information criteria defined in Chapter 4, the HIC and SIC both choose 2 lags, whereas the AIC chooses 6 lags. Adopting the HIC and SIC chosen lag structure of $k = 2$, the appropriate lag length for the VECM model, where the lagged variables are expressed as lagged differences, is $k - 1 = 1$.

Given the results of the lag structure tests on the VAR, the VECM in equation (6.15) is specified for the $N = 6$ bond yields as

$$\Delta y_t = \alpha(\beta' y_{t-1} - \beta_0) + \Gamma_1 \Delta y_{t-1} + v_t, \qquad (6.40)$$

with the yields ordered as $y_t = (r_{9t}, r_{6t}, r_{5t}, r_{4t}, r_{3t}, r_{2t})$, where the subscript gives the maturity of the bond. The respective error-correction and cointegrating parameter matrices α and β are $(6 \times r)$, where r is the number of cointegrating equations, which, from the theory of the term structure of interest rates, is $r = N - 1 = 5$. The $(r \times 1)$ vector of

TABLE 6.6 **Lag structure test of the 6-variate VAR of bond yields. The maximum lag length is set at 8 lags. The sample period is December 1946 to February 1987.**

Lag	AIC	SC	HQ
0	−11.3622	−11.3096	−11.3415
1	−16.5112	−16.1431	−16.3665
2	−16.8283	−16.1447	−16.5595
3	−16.8407	−15.8415	−16.4478
4	−16.8513	−15.5366	−16.3343
5	−16.9090	−15.2787	−16.2679
6	−16.9097	−14.9639	−16.1445
7	−16.8908	−14.6295	−16.0015
8	−16.8898	−14.3129	−15.8764

constants β_0 allows for the possibility of non-zero risk premia in the longer-term bond yields, while Γ_1 is a (6×6) matrix of short-run dynamic parameters. This choice of specification is based also on two additional restrictions regarding deterministic time trends. The first is that there are no time trends in the cointegrating equations, $\phi = 0$ in equation (6.15), as the risk premia on bond yields are assumed constant given that spreads are not observed to widen persistently over time. The second is that there are no intercepts in the error correction equations, $\delta = 0$ in equation (6.15). This set of restrictions is different to the VECM specified for the Gordon model and is motivated by the property that as bonds have a finite maturity, bond yields cannot increase or decrease without bound over time, as would be the case with series exhibiting deterministic trends.

The results of the Johansen cointegration test are given in Table 6.7 based on the VECM in equation (6.40). There are $N = 6$ sets of hypotheses, where the first null is of no cointegration among the $I(1)$ yields, and the last null corresponds to $N - 1 = 5$ cointegrating equations. The first 5 null hypotheses are all soundly rejected at the 5% level with p values of 0.0001 or smaller. The last null hypothesis of 5 cointegrating equations is not rejected at the 5% level given the p value is $0.3335 > 0.05$. This sequence of tests supports the visual analysis of the scatter plots presented in Figure 6.6 showing strong evidence of 5 cointegrating equations among the 6 bond yields in y_t.

The estimates of the long-run equations based on the VECM in equation (6.40) with $r = 5$ cointegrating equations are

$$r_{9t} = \underset{(0.0809)}{0.2450} + \underset{(0.0134)}{1.0424} r_{2t} + \widehat{u}_{1t}$$

$$r_{6t} = \underset{(0.0568)}{0.1662} + \underset{(0.0097)}{1.0364} r_{2t} + \widehat{u}_{2t}$$

$$r_{5t} = \underset{(0.0469)}{0.1379} + \underset{(0.0080)}{1.0301} r_{2t} + \widehat{u}_{3t} \tag{6.41}$$

$$r_{4t} = \underset{(0.0335)}{0.0984} + \underset{(0.0057)}{1.0225} r_{2t} + \widehat{u}_{4t}$$

$$r_{3t} = \underset{(0.0168)}{0.0518} + \underset{(0.0029)}{1.0133} r_{2t} + \widehat{u}_{5t}.$$

All of the long-run slope parameter estimates are numerically close to the theoretical value of unity, although the differences are statistically significant based on t tests. For example, in the case of the cointegrating equation between r_{9t} and r_{2t}, the t statistic is

$$t(\beta_{12} = 1) = \frac{1.0424 - 1.0}{0.0134} = 3.1642,$$

TABLE 6.7 Johansen cointegration test of the 6-variate model of the term structure of interest rates based on the VECM in equation (6.40). The sample period is December 1946 to February 1987.

Null Hypothesis	Eigenvalue	Statistic	5% CV	p value
$r = 0$: No cointegration	0.3023	557.1008	103.8473	0.0000
$r = 1$: 1 cointegrating equation	0.2421	383.9215	76.9728	0.0001
$r = 2$: 2 cointegrating equations	0.2228	250.5879	54.0790	0.0000
$r = 3$: 3 cointegrating equations	0.1448	129.3162	35.1927	0.0000
$r = 4$: 4 cointegrating equations	0.0978	54.0827	20.2618	0.0000
$r = 5$: 5 cointegrating equations	0.0095	4.5730	9.1645	0.3335

which has a p value of 0.0000, providing strong rejection of the null hypothesis that $\beta_{12} = 1$.

Inspection of the parameter estimates on the intercepts in equation (6.41) reveals positive risk premia that increase with maturity starting from $\widehat{\beta}_{50} = 0.0518$ for the 3-month yield and growing to $\widehat{\beta}_{10} = 0.2450$ for the 9-month yield. The risk premia are also found to be statistically significant for all spreads. In the case of the spread between r_{9t} and r_{2t}, the t statistic associated with the null hypothesis that $\beta_{10} = 0$ is

$$t(\beta_{10} = 0) = \frac{0.2450 - 0.0}{0.0809} = 3.03.$$

The p value is 0.0000, which provides strong evidence against the null hypothesis of no risk premia. All of the statistical tests show that while there is strong evidence in favor of the term structure of interest rates model in equation (6.39), the statistical evidence does reject the pure form of this model with $(1, -1)$ spreads and no risk premia.

To investigate the stability properties of the estimated model of the term structure, Figure 6.7 shows the impulse responses of all 6 bond yields to a shock in the 2-month yield as given by the last element in v_t, namely, v_{6t}, in equation (6.40).[12] The impulse responses are shown for a 24-month or 2-year horizon. The system is stable with all impulse responses nearly converging to a steady state level within a year, thereby providing strong support for cointegration and the presence of long-run equilibria among the 6 yields. The impulse responses after 2 years reported in Figure 6.7 are

$$\frac{\partial y_{1t+24}}{\partial v_{6t}} = 0.5065, \quad \frac{\partial y_{2t+24}}{\partial v_{6t}} = 0.5038, \quad \frac{\partial y_{3t+24}}{\partial v_{6t}} = 0.5007,$$

$$\frac{\partial y_{4t+24}}{\partial v_{6t}} = 0.4971, \quad \frac{\partial y_{5t+24}}{\partial v_{6t}} = 0.4928, \quad \frac{\partial y_{6t+24}}{\partial v_{6t}} = 0.4864.$$

These estimates can also be used to generate the long-run relationships between the yields, which provides an internal consistency check on the cointegrating parameter estimates in equation (6.41). In the case of the long yield, y_{1t}, and the short yield, y_{6t}, this relationship is

$$\frac{\partial r_{91t+24}}{\partial r_{2t+24}} = \frac{\partial y_{1t+24}}{\partial y_{6t+24}} = \frac{\partial y_{1t+24}}{\partial v_{6t}} \frac{\partial v_{6t}}{\partial y_{6t+24}} = \frac{0.5065}{0.4864} = 1.0413,$$

which is in agreement with the long-run estimate of 1.0424 reported for the first long-run equation in equation (6.41). Extending the impulse horizon to 3 years improves the accuracy of this calculation to 4 decimal places and, in the limit, the estimate obtained from the impulse responses would perfectly match the estimate obtained from the cointegrating parameter estimate.

---

[12] Technically, the size of the shock to the 2-month yield is not determined by the standard deviation of v_{6t} in the VECM in equation (6.40), as the impulse responses are expressed in terms of structural shocks using the Cholesky triangular decomposition, discussed in Chapter 4.

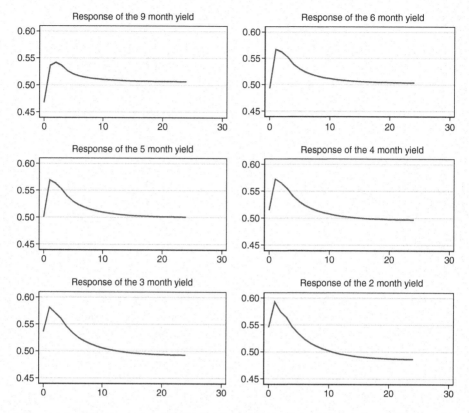

FIGURE 6.7 Impulse responses of the VECM showing how the zero-coupon bond yields respond to a shock in the 2-month yield. The VECM uses the restricted constant specification with one lag.

6.8 EXERCISES

The data required for the exercises are available for download as EViews workfiles (*.wf1), Stata datafiles (*.dta), comma delimited text files (*.csv), and as Excel spreadsheets (*.xlsx).

1. **The Present Value Model**

pv.*

The data are monthly observations on US equity prices and dividends for the period January 1871 to September 2016. The present value model predicts the following relationship between price and dividends

$$p_t = \beta_0 + \beta_d d_t + u_t,$$

where p_t is the log equity price, d_t is the log of dividend payments, u_t is a disturbance term, $\exp(-\beta_0)$ is the discount rate, and $\beta_d = 1$ if the present value model holds.

(a) Estimate a bivariate VAR with an intercept for the variables p_t and d_t, choosing an appropriate lag structure k.

(b) Test for cointegration between $y_t = (p_t, d_t)$ by specifying the VECM

$$\Delta y_t = \delta + \alpha(\beta' y_{t-1} - \beta_0) + \sum_{j=1}^{k-1} \Gamma_j \Delta y_{t-i} + v_t,$$

where the number of lags in the VECM is determined by the choice of the lag structure of the VAR in part (a).

(c) Given the results in part (b), estimate a bivariate VECM for p_t and d_t. Interpret the results paying particular attention to the long-run parameter estimates, $\widehat{\beta}_0$ and $\widehat{\beta}_d$, and the error correction parameter estimates, $\widehat{\alpha}_1$ and $\widehat{\alpha}_2$.

(d) Derive an estimate of the long-run real discount rate from $\exp(-\beta_0)$ and interpret the result.

(e) Test the restriction $H_0 : \beta_d = 1$. Discuss whether the empirical results support the present value model.

2. Forward Market Efficiency

spot.*

The data files contain weekly data (all recorded on a Wednesday) for the period 4 January 1984 to 31 December 1990 on the spot \$/AUD exchange rate together with forward rates for 1, 3, and 6 months. The data are from Corbae, Lim, and Ouliaris (1992) who test for speculative efficiency by considering the equation

$$s_t = \beta_0 + \beta_f f_{t-n} + u_t,$$

where s_t is the log spot rate, f_{t-n} is the log forward rate lagged n periods, and u_t is a disturbance term. In the case of weekly data and when the forward rate is the 1-month rate, f_{t-4} is an unbiased estimator of s_t if $\beta_f = 1$ and $\beta_0 = 0$.

(a) Use unit root tests to determine the level of integration of s_t and f_t.

(b) Test for cointegration between $y_t = (s_t, f_{t-4})$ by specifying the VECM

$$\Delta y_t = \alpha(\beta' y_{t-1} - \beta_0) + v_t.$$

(c) Given the results in part (b), estimate a bivariate VECM.

(d) Interpret the parameter estimates $\widehat{\beta}_0$ and $\widehat{\beta}_f$, and test the restriction $\beta_f = 1$.

(e) Repeat parts (a) to (d) for the 3-month and 6-month forward rates. *Hint: remember that the frequency of the data is weekly.*

3. Fisher Hypothesis

fisher.*

The data file contains US quarterly data for the period September 1954 to December 2007 on the annualized nominal interest rate expressed as a percentage,

r_t, and the price level, P_t. Under the Fisher hypothesis, the nominal interest rate i_t fully reflects the long-run movements in the inflation rate π_t. The Fisher hypothesis is represented by

$$i_t = \beta_0 + \beta_\pi \pi_t + u_t,$$

where u_t is a disturbance term, and the slope parameter is $\beta_\pi = 1$ if the Fisher hypothesis holds.

(a) Construct the percentage annualized inflation rate, π_t.
(b) Use a bivariate VAR (with an intercept) for i_t and π_t to choose an appropriate lag structure k.
(c) Test for cointegration between i_t and π_t based on the VECM

$$\Delta y_t = \alpha(\beta' y_{t-1} - \beta_0) + \sum_{j=1}^{k-1} \Gamma_j \Delta y_{t-i} + v_t,$$

where the number of lags in the VECM is determined by the optimal lag structure of the VAR chosen in part (b).
(d) Test for cointegration subject to the restriction that $\beta_\pi = 1$. Does the Fisher hypothesis hold in the long run? Discuss.

4. Purchasing Power Parity

PPP.*

The data are monthly observations for the period January 1979 to December 2008 for the consumer price index in Australia and the US, respectively, together with the $/AUD exchange rate. Under the assumption of purchasing power parity (PPP), the nominal exchange rate, S, adjusts in the long run to the price differential between foreign (F) and domestic (P) countries according to

$$S = \frac{P}{F}.$$

This expression suggests that the relationship between the nominal exchange rate and the prices in the two countries is given by

$$s_t = \beta_0 + \beta_p p_t + \beta_f f_t + u_t,$$

where lower case letters denote variables expressed in logarithms, and u_t is a disturbance term representing short-run departures from PPP.

(a) Construct the relevant variables, s_t, f_t, p_t, and the foreign price differential $p_t - f_t$.
(b) Use unit root tests to determine the level of integration of all of these series based on 12 lags. Discuss the results in terms of the level of integration of each series.

(c) Test for cointegration between $y_t = (s_t, p_t, f_t)$ using the VECM

$$\Delta y_t = \delta + \alpha(\beta' y_{t-1} - \beta_0) + \sum_{j=1}^{k-1} \Gamma_j \Delta y_{t-i} + v_t,$$

with $k = 12$ lags.

(d) Given the results in part (c) estimate a trivariate VECM for s_t, p_t, and f_t.

(e) Interpret the long-run parameter, error correction, and short-run parameter estimates.

(f) Test the restriction $H_0 : \beta_p = -\beta_f$. Is PPP satisfied?

5. The Gordon Equity Model

pv.*

The data are monthly observations on US equity prices, dividends, and earnings for the period January 1871 to September 2016. The Gordon equity model, is represented by two long-run equations involving the variables log equity prices p_t, log dividends d_t, and log earnings e_t, according to the specification

$$p_t = \beta_{10} + \beta_{1d} d_t + u_{1t}$$
$$p_t = \beta_{20} + \beta_{2e} e_t + u_{2t},$$

where u_{1t} and u_{2t} are disturbance terms representing the pricing errors for the two models.

(a) Estimate a VAR (with an intercept) containing p_t, d_t, and e_t based on an optimal choice of the lag structure k.

(b) Test for cointegration between $y_t = (p_t, d_t, e_t)$ by specifying the VECM

$$\Delta y_t = \delta + \alpha(\beta' y_{t-1} - \beta_0) + \sum_{j=1}^{k-1} \Gamma_j \Delta y_{t-i} + v_t,$$

where the number of lags in the VECM is determined by the optimal lag structure of the VAR obtained in part (a).

(c) Given the results in part (b), estimate the VECM and write out the estimated long-run cointegrating equation(s) in terms of earnings, e_t. Interpret the long-run parameter estimates.

(d) Derive estimates of the long-run relationship between p_t and d_t for the following cases.

   (i) Using the parameter estimates reported in part (c).
   (ii) After re-estimating the VECM with the ordering of the variables chosen as $y_t = (p_t, e_t, d_t)$.

6. The Term Structure of Interest Rates

zero.*

The data are monthly observations from December 1946 to February 1987 on US zero-coupon bond yields for maturities ranging from 2 months to 9 months.

The expectations hypothesis of the term structure of interest rates predicts the following relationship between a long-term interest rate of maturity n and a short-term rate of maturity $m < n$

$$r_{nt} = \beta_0 + \beta_m r_{mt} + u_t,$$

where u_t is a disturbance term and β_0 represents the term premium. The pure expectations hypothesis requires that $\beta_0 = 0$ and $\beta_m = 1$.

(a) Estimate a VAR with a fitted intercept and $N = 6$ variables containing the yields $y_t = (r_{9t}, r_{6t}, r_{5t}, r_{4t}, r_{3t}, r_{2t})$ using a data-determined lag structure k.

(b) Test for cointegration among the $N = 6$ yields by specifying the VECM

$$\Delta y_t = \alpha(\beta' y_{t-1} - \beta_0) + \sum_{j=1}^{k-1} \Gamma_j \Delta y_{t-i} + v_t,$$

where the number of lags in the VECM is based on the optimal lag structure of the VAR from part (a).

(c) Given the results in part (b), estimate the VECM and write out the estimated long-run equations in terms of the short-term yield r_{2t}.

(d) Perform a joint test that all of the cointegrating parameters are of the form $(1, -1)$.

(e) Test each of the $N = 6$ yields individually for weak exogeneity.

(f) Given the results in part (e), test each of the $N = 6$ yields for strong exogeneity.

7. Spurious Regression Problem

If there is no long-run relationship binding $I(1)$ variables over time, a regression involving such unrelated or independent nonstationary variables should not be expected to find any statistical relationship connecting them, as is the case when the variables are independent and stationary. Spurious regressions among $I(1)$ variables were investigated in a simulation study by Granger and Newbold (1974), showing that major inferential distortions can arise in such cases. Phillips (1986, 1998) demonstrates that in regressions of this type, the t statistics will always diverge to $\pm\infty$ because the trends within each series inevitably correlate with each other and suggest statistical significance. Against this background, the present exercise is based on a Monte Carlo study conducted by Banerjee, Dolado, Galbraith, and Hendry (1993) that investigates the spurious regression problem.

(a) Consider the following bivariate models

(i) $y_{1t} = v_{1t}$	$y_{2t} = v_{2t}.$
(ii) $y_{1t} = y_{1t-1} + v_{1t}$	$y_{2t} = y_{2t-1} + v_{2t}.$
(iii) $y_{1t} = y_{1t-1} + v_{1,t}$	$y_{2t} = 2y_{2t-1} - y_{2t-2} + v_{2t}.$
(iv) $y_{1t} = 2y_{1t-1} - y_{1t-2} + v_{1t}$	$y_{2t} = 2y_{2t-1} - y_{2t-2} + v_{2t}.$

Assume v_{1t} and v_{2t} are both $N(0, 1)$. Simulate each bivariate model 10000 times for a sample of size $T = 100$ and compute the correlation coefficient, $\widehat{\rho}$, of each draw. Compute the sampling distributions of $\widehat{\rho}$ for the four sets of bivariate models and discuss the properties of these distributions in the context of the spurious regression problem.

(b) Repeat part (a) but with $T = 500$. What do you conclude?

(c) Repeat part (a), but for each draw estimate the following regression equation by least squares

$$y_{2t} = \beta_0 + \beta_1 y_{1t} + u_t.$$

Compute the sampling distributions of the least squares estimator $\widehat{\beta}_1$ and its t statistic for the four sets of bivariate models. Discuss the properties of these distributions in the context of the spurious regression problem.

CHAPTER 7

Forecasting

Considerations of the future values of financial and economic variables play an important role in decision-making by agents in financial markets. Forecasting the future course of financial markets and economic activity is therefore of intense interest to investors, banking institutions, policymakers, and regulatory authorities.

A forecast is a quantitative estimate about the most likely future value of a particular variable. Forecasts are typically based on past and current information about the variable itself and other observable variables that are thought to be related to it. In econometric forecasting, this information is typically embodied in an empirical model whose solution shows the dependence of the variable of interest on other observable variables and unobserved random variables representing errors and disturbances. The mechanism of econometric forecasting then relies on the estimation of the equations of these models with observed data and the use of the fitted equations to create projections of future values.

Previous chapters have studied a wide variety of econometric models suited to financial time series data, covering both univariate and multivariate models. The empirical specification and estimation of these models provides a groundwork for producing forecasts that are objective in the sense that they can be replicated exactly with knowledge of the structure of the model, the estimation procedure, and the data used in estimation. Replicability is important because it provides a mechanism for evaluating the performance characteristics of a particular model or method in relation to other models and methods. This approach contrasts with methods that involve purely subjective assessments that are not reproducible or testable in simulation exercises.

Forecasting also serves a useful purpose as a means to compare and rank alternative models and to assess different methods of estimation. In carrying out such exercises, forecast errors are useful in directing attention toward the potential weaknesses in model specification that lead to systematic errors in forecast performance. Forecast evaluation based on past successes and failures also provides a useful way of choosing between alternative models and a way to combine models using the information that is contained in past performance.

7.1 TYPES OF FORECASTS

Illustrative examples of forecasting in financial markets are as follows.

(i) The determination of the price of an asset based on present value methods requires discounting the present and forecasted future dividend stream at a discount rate that may be allowed to change over time.

(ii) Firms are interested in forecasting the future health of the economy when making decisions about current capital outlays. Investments in capital equipment earn streams of returns over time that depend on the future state of the economy and that need to be discounted to assess the viability of the investments.

(iii) In currency markets, forward exchange rates may be used to provide an estimate, or forecast, of the future spot exchange rate.

(iv) In options markets, the Black–Scholes method and other methods for pricing options rely on present information such as the price of the underlying asset, the strike price, and expiration date together with forecasts (or assumptions) about the asset's volatility over the life of the option.

(v) In futures markets, buyers and sellers enter a contract to buy and sell commodities at a future date based on forecasts of future prices of those commodities.

(vi) Model-based computation of value at risk requires repeated forecasting of the value of a portfolio over a given time horizon.

Although these illustrations differ considerably, the principles and issues involved in forecasting are typically similar, involving the form of the model being used, the nature of the data, and the methods of projection employed. Before developing the mechanisms for forecast generation some terminology is useful.

Consider an observed sample of data $\{y_1, y_2, \cdots, y_T\}$ and an econometric model that is to be used to generate forecasts of y_t over a horizon of H periods. The forecasts of y_t are denoted by $\widehat{y}_t$ and are of two main types.

Ex Ante Forecasts: The entire sample $\{y_1, y_2, \cdots, y_T\}$ is used to estimate the model and the task is to forecast the variable y over the future horizon $T+1$ to $T+H$.

Ex Post Forecasts: The model is estimated over a restricted sample period that excludes the last H observations, $\{y_1, y_2, \cdots, y_{T-H}\}$. The model is then forecasted out-of-sample from y_{T-H+1} through to y_T. Since the actual values of these later observations are known, it is possible to compare the accuracy of the forecasts with the actual values.

Ex post and ex ante forecasts may be illustrated as follows

Sample	$y_1, y_2, \cdots, y_{T-H}, y_{T-H+1}, y_{T-H+2}, \cdots, y_T$
Ex Post	$y_1, y_2, \cdots, y_{T-H}, \widehat{y}_{T-H+1}, \widehat{y}_{T-H+2}, \cdots, \widehat{y}_T$
Ex Ante	$y_1, y_2, \cdots, y_{T-H}, y_{T-H+1}, y_{T-H+2}, \cdots, y_T, \quad \widehat{y}_{T+1}, \cdots, \widehat{y}_{T+H}$

It is clear therefore that forecasting ex ante for H periods ahead requires the successive generation of $\widehat{y}_{T+1}, \widehat{y}_{T+2}$ up to and including $\widehat{y}_{T+H}$. This is referred to as a *multi-step* dynamic forecast. On the other hand, ex post forecasting allows some latitude for choice. The forecast $\widehat{y}_{T-H+1}$ is based on data up to and including y_{T-H}. In generating the forecast $\widehat{y}_{T-H+2}$, the observation y_{T-H+1} is available for use. Forecasts that use this observation are referred to as *one-step-ahead* or *static* forecasts. Ex post forecasting also allows for multi-step forecasting using data up to and including y_{T-H}, known as *dynamic* forecasting.

There is a distinction between forecasting based on dynamic time series models and forecasts based on broader linear or nonlinear regression models. Forecasts based on dynamic univariate or multivariate time series models such as those developed in Chapter 4 are sometimes referred to as *recursive* forecasts. Forecasts that are based on structural econometric models are sometimes known as *structural* forecasts. However, the distinction between these two types of forecasts is often unclear because econometric models often involve both structural and dynamic time series features.

Finally, forecasts in which only a single quantity $\widehat{y}_{T+H}$ is reported for period $T+H$ are known as *point* forecasts. A point forecast of y_{T+H} represents an estimate of this future value of y. Even if it is known from past performance that this estimate is a particularly good one, there is inevitably uncertainty associated with every such forecast. *Interval* forecasts represent this uncertainty by providing a range of forecast values about the estimate $\widehat{y}_{T+H}$, called a prediction interval, within which the actual value y_{T+H} is expected to lie with some given level of confidence. Density forecasting goes beyond interval forecasting by building an estimate of the probability distribution of a future value of y conditional on past information. These density forecasts can be particularly useful in financial risk management where value at risk calculations are needed which, in turn, depend on the probability density forecasts of portfolio values.

7.2 FORECASTING UNIVARIATE TIME SERIES MODELS

To understand the most basic principles of forecasting from financial econometric models a univariate AR(1) model is sufficient to demonstrate the key elements. Extending the model to more general univariate and multivariate models only increases the complexity to the computation but not the underlying techniques of how the forecasts are generated.

AR(1) Model
Consider the AR(1) model

$$y_t = \phi_0 + \phi_1 y_{t-1} + v_t, \qquad v_t \sim iid\, N(0, \sigma_v^2). \tag{7.1}$$

Suppose that the data consist of T sample observations $y_1, y_2, \cdots, y_T$. Now consider using the model to forecast the variable one period into the future, at $T+1$. If there is no change in the generating mechanism, the model at time $T+1$ is

$$y_{T+1} = \phi_0 + \phi_1 y_T + v_{T+1}. \tag{7.2}$$

To be able to compute a perfect forecast of y_{T+1} it is necessary to know everything on the right-hand side of equation (7.2). Inspection of this equation reveals that some of these terms are known and some are unknown at time T

$$
\begin{array}{lll}
\text{Observations:} & y_T & \text{Known} \\
\text{Parameters:} & \phi_0, \phi_1 & \text{Unknown} \\
\text{Disturbance:} & v_{T+1} & \text{Unknown.}
\end{array}
$$

The aim of forecasting is to produce the best possible estimate of y_{T+1}. A natural approach is then to replace the unknowns with their best estimates. In the case of the parameters, the obvious procedure is to replace them with point estimates, $\widehat{\phi}_0$ and $\widehat{\phi}_1$, that are known to have good properties such as consistency and where the full sample is used to obtain the estimates. Formally this involves replacing the conditional mean $\phi_0 + \phi_1 y_T$ of the distribution of y_{T+1} by the sample estimate $\widehat{\phi}_0 + \widehat{\phi}_1 y_T$. If the estimates $(\widehat{\phi}_0, \widehat{\phi}_1)$ are consistent, then the conditional mean estimate $\widehat{\phi}_0 + \widehat{\phi}_1 y_T$ will be consistent for $\phi_0 + \phi_1 y_T$. In the same way, the unknown disturbance term v_{T+1} in equation (7.2) is replaced by using the mean of its distribution, which will be simply $E(v_{T+1}) = 0$ if the model is correctly specified and there is no structural change in the forecast period. The resulting forecast of y_{T+1} based on equation (7.2) is given by

$$
\widehat{y}_{T+1} = \widehat{\phi}_0 + \widehat{\phi}_1 y_T + 0 = \widehat{\phi}_0 + \widehat{\phi}_1 y_T, \tag{7.3}
$$

where $\widehat{y}_{T+1}$ signifies that it is a forecast quantity.

Now consider extending the forecast horizon to $T + 2$, the second period after the end of the sample period. The strategy is the same as before in which the first step is to express the model at time $T + 2$ as

$$
y_{T+2} = \phi_0 + \phi_1 y_{T+1} + v_{T+2}, \tag{7.4}
$$

in which all terms are now unknown at the end of the observation period at time T, that is

$$
\begin{array}{lll}
\text{Observations:} & y_{T+1} & \text{Unknown} \\
\text{Parameters:} & \phi_0, \phi_1 & \text{Unknown} \\
\text{Disturbance:} & v_{T+2} & \text{Unknown.}
\end{array}
$$

As before, the parameters ϕ_0 and ϕ_1 are replaced by the estimates $\widehat{\phi}_0$ and $\widehat{\phi}_1$, respectively, and the disturbance v_{T+2} by its mean $E[v_{T+2}] = 0$. What is new in equation (7.4) is the presence of the unknown quantity y_{T+1} on the right-hand side of the equation. Again, the strategy of replacing unknowns by a best estimate suggests that the forecast of this variable obtained in the previous step, $\widehat{y}_{T+1}$, be used in place of y_{T+1}. Accordingly, the forecast for the second period is obtained

$$
\widehat{y}_{T+2} = \widehat{\phi}_0 + \widehat{\phi}_1 \widehat{y}_{T+1} + 0 = \widehat{\phi}_0 + \widehat{\phi}_1 \widehat{y}_{T+1}.
$$

Clearly extending this analysis to H periods ahead implies a forecasting equation of the form

$$
\widehat{y}_{T+H} = \widehat{\phi}_0 + \widehat{\phi}_1 \widehat{y}_{T+H-1} + 0 = \widehat{\phi}_0 + \widehat{\phi}_1 \widehat{y}_{T+H-1}.
$$

The need to use the result from the previous step to generate a forecast in the subsequent step is commonly referred to as recursive forecasting. The process is dynamic because earlier forecasts are needed in order to produce forecasts at longer horizons. Moreover, as all of the information embedded in the forecasts $\widehat{y}_{T+1}, \widehat{y}_{T+2}, \cdots, \widehat{y}_{T+H}$ is based on information up to and including the last observation in the sample at time T, the forecasts are commonly referred to as conditional mean forecasts where conditioning is based on information available at the end of the observation period, which is time T.

Forecasting Equity Returns with an AR(1) Model

This univariate recursive forecasting procedure is easily demonstrated in an empirical example. Consider the log returns to the monthly US equity index for the period February 1871 to September 2016 expressed in percentage terms as

$$re_t = 100 \times (\log P_t - \log P_{t-1}),$$

where P_t is the equity price index. To generate ex ante forecasts of returns using a simple AR(1) model, the parameters are estimated using the entire available sample period and these estimates, together with the actual return for September 2016, are used to generate the recursive forecasts. Consider the case where ex ante forecasts are required for October and November 2016. The estimated model is

$$re_t = 0.2527 + 0.2839 \, re_{t-1} + \widehat{v}_t,$$

where $\widehat{v}_t$ is the least squares fitted residual. Given that the actual return for September 2016 is -0.6127%, the forecasts for October and November are, respectively,

$$
\begin{aligned}
\text{October:} \quad \widehat{re}_{T+1} &= 0.2527 + 0.2839 \, re_T \\
&= 0.2527 + 0.2839 \times (-0.6127) = 0.0788\% \\
\text{November:} \quad \widehat{re}_{T+2} &= 0.2527 + 0.2839 \, \widehat{re}_{T+1} \\
&= 0.2527 + 0.2839 \times 0.0788 \quad = 0.2751\%.
\end{aligned}
$$

AR(2) Model

Extending the AR(1) model to an AR(2) model gives

$$y_t = \phi_0 + \phi_1 y_{t-1} + \phi_2 y_{t-2} + v_t,$$

and the same simple strategy may be used to forecast y_t in this model. First, the model at time $T+1$ is written as

$$y_{T+1} = \phi_0 + \phi_1 y_T + \phi_2 y_{T-1} + v_{T+1}.$$

Replacing the parameters $\{\phi_0, \phi_1, \phi_2\}$ by their sample estimates $\{\widehat{\phi}_0, \widehat{\phi}_1, \widehat{\phi}_2\}$ and the disturbance v_{T+1} by its mean $E[v_{T+1}] = 0$, the forecast for the first period into the future is

$$\widehat{y}_{T+1} = \widehat{\phi}_0 + \widehat{\phi}_1 y_T + \widehat{\phi}_2 y_{T-1}.$$

To generate the forecasts for the second period, the AR(2) model is written at time $T+2$ as

$$y_{T+2} = \phi_0 + \phi_1 y_{T+1} + \phi_2 y_T + v_{T+2}.$$

Replacing all of the unknowns on the right-hand side by their corresponding estimates, including the forecast $\widehat{y}_{T+1}$ of y_{T+1}, gives

$$\widehat{y}_{T+2} = \widehat{\phi}_0 + \widehat{\phi}_1 \widehat{y}_{T+1} + \widehat{\phi}_2 y_T.$$

Similarly, to derive the forecast of y_t at time $T+3$, the AR(2) model is written at $T+3$ as

$$y_{T+3} = \phi_0 + \phi_1 y_{T+2} + \phi_2 y_{T+1} + v_{T+3}.$$

All terms on the right-hand side are unknown and need to be estimated, so the forecasting equation becomes

$$\widehat{y}_{T+3} = \widehat{\phi}_0 + \widehat{\phi}_1 \widehat{y}_{T+2} + \widehat{\phi}_2 \widehat{y}_{T+1}.$$

The same procedure applies in higher order autoregressive models where unknown future values of the time series are replaced by forecasts in making forecasts at horizons beyond a single period.

Forecast Properties

Looking at recursive forecasts as successive estimates of corresponding conditional means is useful conceptually and in developing statistical properties of these forecasts. In the context of an AR(1) model, consider the expected value of the next period observation given information to time T, which is

$$E_T(y_{T+1}) = \phi_0 + \phi_1 y_T.$$

Under quite general conditions, least squares estimates $(\widehat{\phi}_0, \widehat{\phi}_1)$ are consistent estimates of (ϕ_0, ϕ_1), and so the conditional expectation is consistently estimated by the forecast $\widehat{y}_{T+1}$ in equation (7.3). In the same way, the conditional expectation of y_{T+2} given information to time T is

$$E_T(y_{T+2}) = E_T(\phi_0 + \phi_1 y_{T+1} + v_{t+2}) = \phi_0 + \phi_1(\phi_0 + \phi_1 y_T) = \phi_0 + \phi_0\phi_1 + \phi_1^2 y_T.$$

By analogy, it follows that

$$E_T(y_{T+3}) = \phi_0 + \phi_0\phi_1 + \phi_0\phi_1^2 + \phi_1^3 y_T,$$

and more generally at horizon H

$$\begin{aligned}
E_T(y_{T+h}) &= \phi_0 + \phi_0\phi_1 + \phi_0\phi_1^2 + \cdots + \phi_0\phi_1^{H-1} + \phi_1^H y_T \\
&= \phi_0(1 + \phi_1 + \phi_1^2 + \cdots \phi_1^{H-1}) + \phi_1^H y_T.
\end{aligned} \tag{7.5}$$

This conditional expectation is consistently estimated by the forecast

$$\widehat{y}_{T+H} = \widehat{\phi}_0(1 + \widehat{\phi}_1 + \widehat{\phi}_1^2 + \cdots \widehat{\phi}_1^{H-1}) + \widehat{\phi}_1^H y_T. \tag{7.6}$$

Using equations (7.5) and (7.6), a number of key properties of these recursive forecasts of conditional expectations may be obtained.

(i) When the model is stationary with $|\phi_1| < 1$, then it follows from equation (7.5) that as $H \to \infty$

$$E_T(y_{T+H}) \to \frac{\phi_0}{1 - \phi_1}.$$

In other words, the conditional mean converges to the unconditional mean of y_t. This result relies on $(1 + \phi_1 + \phi_1^2 + \cdots + \phi_1^{H-1})$ being a convergent series and also on the elimination of the second term on the right-hand side of equation (7.5). Both these conditions follow from $|\phi_1| < 1$ by virtue of the stationarity assumption. Further, when $(\widehat{\phi}_0, \widehat{\phi}_1)$ is consistent for (ϕ_0, ϕ_1), the forecast $\widehat{y}_{T+H}$

in equation (7.6) converges to the unconditional mean, $\phi_0/(1-\phi_1)$, as the sample size $T \to \infty$ and the horizon $H \to \infty$.

(ii) The forecasts at all horizons are also consistent estimates of the corresponding conditional means. The conditional mean may be regarded as an optimal forecast because it does not involve any variability due to the estimation of unknown parameters. The optimal forecast errors at differing horizons may be obtained from equation (7.5) as follows

$$y_{T+1} - E_T(y_{T+1}) = \phi_0 + \phi_1 y_T + v_{t+1} - (\phi_0 + \phi_1 y_T) = v_{t+1}$$

$$y_{T+2} - E_T(y_{T+2}) = \phi_0 + \phi_0\phi_1 + \phi_1^2 y_T + v_{t+2} + \phi_1 v_{t+1} - (\phi_0 + \phi_0\phi_1 + \phi_1^2 y_T)$$

$$= v_{t+2} + \phi_1 v_{t+1}.$$

It follows that the optimal forecast error at $T+H$ can be written as

$$y_{T+H} - E_T(y_{T+H}) = v_{t+H} + \phi_1 v_{t+H-1} + \cdots + \phi^{H-1} v_{t+1}. \qquad (7.7)$$

Since $E(v_{t+H}) = 0$ for all H, the expected value of the optimal forecast error is 0, and hence the optimal forecast is unbiased.

(iii) The results established so far imply that the variance of the forecasts at different horizons are as follows

$$\text{var}[y_{T+1} - E_T(y_{T+1})] = \sigma_v^2$$

$$\text{var}[y_{T+2} - E_T y_{T+2})] = \sigma_v^2(1 + \phi_1^2)$$

$$\vdots \qquad = \qquad \vdots$$

$$\text{var}[y_{T+H} - E_T(y_{T+H})] = \sigma_v^2(1 + \phi_1^2 + \phi_1^4 + \phi_1^6 + \cdots + \phi_1^{2(H-1)}),$$

where $\sigma_v^2 = E(v_t^2)$ is the variance of the one-step-ahead optimal forecast error. Importantly, the variance of the optimal forecast is an increasing function of the forecast horizon H. Thus, even in the optimal situation where no parameters need to be estimated, raising the forecast horizon inevitably raises the forecast error variance.

7.3 FORECASTING MULTIVARIATE TIME SERIES MODELS

The recursive method used to generate the forecasts of a univariate time series model is easily generalized to multivariate models, including VARs and VECMs.

7.3.1 Vector Autoregressions

Consider a bivariate vector autoregression with one lag, VAR(1), given by

$$y_{1t} = \phi_{10} + \phi_{11} y_{1t-1} + \phi_{12} y_{2t-1} + v_{1t}$$

$$y_{2t} = \phi_{20} + \phi_{21} y_{1t-1} + \phi_{22} y_{2t-1} + v_{2t}, \qquad (7.8)$$

where v_{1t} and v_{2t} are disturbance terms. Given data up to time T, a forecast one period ahead is obtained by writing the model at time $T+1$

$$y_{1T+1} = \phi_{10} + \phi_{11}y_{1T} + \phi_{12}y_{2T} + v_{1T+1}$$
$$y_{2T+1} = \phi_{20} + \phi_{21}y_{1T} + \phi_{22}y_{2T} + v_{2T+1}.$$

The knowns on the right-hand side are the last observations of the two variables, y_{1T} and y_{2T}, and the unknowns are the disturbance terms v_{1T+1} and v_{2T+1} and the parameters $\{\phi_{10}, \phi_{11}, \phi_{12}, \phi_{20}, \phi_{21}, \phi_{22}\}$. Replacing the unknowns with estimates, just as in the univariate AR model, the forecasts for the two variables at time $T+1$ are

$$\widehat{y}_{1T+1} = \widehat{\phi}_{10} + \widehat{\phi}_{11}y_{1T} + \widehat{\phi}_{12}y_{2T}$$
$$\widehat{y}_{2T+1} = \widehat{\phi}_{20} + \widehat{\phi}_{21}y_{1T} + \widehat{\phi}_{22}y_{2T}.$$

To generate forecasts of the VAR(1) model in equation (7.8) for two periods ahead, the model is written at time $T+2$

$$y_{1T+2} = \phi_{10} + \phi_{11}y_{1T+1} + \phi_{12}y_{2T+1} + v_{1T+2}$$
$$y_{2T+2} = \phi_{20} + \phi_{21}y_{1T+1} + \phi_{22}y_{2T+1} + v_{2T+2}.$$

All terms on the right-hand side are now unknown. As before, the parameters are replaced by estimates and the disturbances are replaced by their means, while y_{1T+1} and y_{2T+1} are replaced by their forecasts from the previous step, resulting in the two-period ahead forecasts

$$\widehat{y}_{1T+2} = \widehat{\phi}_{10} + \widehat{\phi}_{11}\widehat{y}_{1T+1} + \widehat{\phi}_{12}\widehat{y}_{2T+1}$$
$$\widehat{y}_{2T+2} = \widehat{\phi}_{20} + \widehat{\phi}_{21}\widehat{y}_{1T+1} + \widehat{\phi}_{22}\widehat{y}_{2T+1}.$$

In general, the forecasts of the VAR(1) model for H periods ahead are

$$\widehat{y}_{1T+H} = \widehat{\phi}_{10} + \widehat{\phi}_{11}\widehat{y}_{1T+H-1} + \widehat{\phi}_{12}\widehat{y}_{2T+H-1}$$
$$\widehat{y}_{2T+H} = \widehat{\phi}_{20} + \widehat{\phi}_{21}\widehat{y}_{1T+H-1} + \widehat{\phi}_{22}\widehat{y}_{2T+H-1}.$$

An important new feature of this result is that even if forecasts are required for just one of the variables, say y_{1t}, it is necessary to generate forecasts of the other variables in the model as well.

To illustrate forecasting using a VAR, consider log returns to equity, re_t, and log returns to dividends, rd_t, defined in percentage terms as follows

$$p_t = 100 \times \log P_t, \qquad re_t = p_t - p_{t-1}$$
$$d_t = 100 \times \log D_t, \qquad rd_t = d_t - d_{t-1},$$

where P_t is the equity price index, and D_t is the dividend payment. As before, data are available for the period February 1871 to September 2016, and suppose ex ante forecasts are required for October and November 2016. The estimated bivariate VAR (1) model is

$$re_t = 0.2216 + 0.2836\, re_{t-1} + 0.1058\, rd_{t-1} + \widehat{v}_{1t}$$
$$rd_t = 0.0316 + 0.0029\, re_{t-1} + 0.8902\, rd_{t-1} + \widehat{v}_{2t},$$

where $\widehat{v}_{1t}$ and $\widehat{v}_{2t}$ are the residuals from the two equations. The forecasts for equity and dividend log returns in October are

$$\widehat{re}_{T+1} = 0.2216 + 0.2836 \, re_T + 0.1058 \, rd_T$$
$$= 0.2216 + 0.2836 \times (-0.6127) + 0.1058 \times 0.4228$$
$$= 0.0926\%$$
$$\widehat{rd}_{T+1} = 0.0316 + 0.0029 \, re_T + 0.8902 \, rd_T$$
$$= 0.0316 + 0.0029 \times (-0.6127) + 0.8902 \times 0.4228$$
$$= 0.4062\%.$$

The corresponding forecasts for November are

$$\widehat{re}_{T+2} = 0.2216 + 0.2836 \, \widehat{re}_{T+1} + 0.1058 \, \widehat{rd}_{T+1}$$
$$= 0.2216 + 0.2836 \times 0.0926 + 0.1058 \times 0.4062$$
$$= 0.2908\%$$
$$\widehat{rd}_{T+2} = 0.0316 + 0.0029 \, \widehat{re}_{T+1} + 0.8902 \, \widehat{rd}_{T+1}$$
$$= 0.0316 + 0.0029 \times 0.0926 + 0.8902 \times 0.4062$$
$$= 0.3934\%.$$

7.3.2 Vector Error Correction Models

An important relationship between systems of VARs and VECMs that was discussed in Chapter 6 is that a VECM may be considered as a restricted VAR model where the restrictions are embodied in a reduced rank coefficient matrix in the VAR. This correspondence means that a VECM can be re-expressed in VAR form, which, in turn, can be used to forecast the variables of the model.

To illustrate, consider the following bivariate VECM that is a restricted version of equation (6.12) in which $k = 2$ and $\delta_1 = \delta_2 = 0$,

$$\Delta y_{1t} = \alpha_1 (y_{1t-1} - \beta_0 - \beta_2 y_{2t-1}) + \gamma_{11} \Delta y_{1t-1} + \gamma_{12} \Delta y_{2t-1} + v_{1t}$$
$$\Delta y_{2t} = \alpha_2 (y_{1t-1} - \beta_0 - \beta_2 y_{2t-1}) + \gamma_{21} \Delta y_{1t-1} + \gamma_{22} \Delta y_{2t-1} + v_{2t}.$$

Rearranging the VECM as a (restricted) VAR(2) in the levels of the variables gives

$$y_{1t} = -\alpha_1 \beta_0 + (1 + \gamma_{11} + \alpha_1) y_{1t-1} - \gamma_{11} y_{1t-2} + (\gamma_{12} - \alpha_1 \beta_2) y_{2t-1} - \gamma_{12} y_{2t-2} + v_{1t}$$
$$y_{2t} = -\alpha_2 \beta_0 + (\gamma_{21} + \alpha_2) y_{1t-1} - \gamma_{21} y_{1t-2} + (1 + \gamma_{22} - \alpha_2 \beta_2) y_{2t-1} - \gamma_{22} y_{2t-2} + v_{2t}.$$

Alternatively, it is possible to write this system in VAR form as

$$y_{1t} = \phi_{10} + \phi_{11} y_{1t-1} + \phi_{12} y_{1t-2} + \phi_{13} y_{2t-1} + \phi_{14} y_{2t-2} + v_{1t}$$
$$y_{2t} = \phi_{20} + \phi_{21} y_{1t-1} + \phi_{22} y_{1t-2} + \phi_{23} y_{2t-1} + \phi_{24} y_{2t-2} + v_{2t}, \tag{7.9}$$

in which the VAR and VECM parameters are related as follows,

$$
\begin{aligned}
\phi_{10} &= -\alpha_1 \beta_0 & \phi_{20} &= -\alpha_2 \beta_0 \\
\phi_{11} &= 1 + \alpha_1 + \gamma_{11} & \phi_{21} &= -\alpha_2 + \gamma_{21} \\
\phi_{12} &= -\gamma_{11} & \phi_{22} &= -\gamma_{21} \\
\phi_{13} &= -\alpha_1 \beta_2 + \gamma_{12} & \phi_{23} &= 1 - \alpha_2 \beta_2 + \gamma_{22} \\
\phi_{14} &= -\gamma_{12} & \phi_{24} &= -\gamma_{22}.
\end{aligned}
\tag{7.10}
$$

These equations give the explicit form of the reduced rank restrictions implicit in the VECM system. Once the VECM is expressed as a VAR in the levels of the variables as in equation (7.9), forecasts are generated for the VAR as in Section 7.3.1, with the VAR parameter estimates computed from the VECM parameter estimates based on the explicit relationships given in (7.10).

Using the same data set as that used in producing the ex ante VAR forecasts, the procedure is easily repeated for the VECM. The estimated VECM with one lag[1] and also relaxing the restriction $\delta_1 = \delta_2 = 0$ is

$$re_t = 0.0353 - 0.0068(p_{t-1} - 1.1773\,d_{t-1} - 340.3414)$$
$$+ 0.2901\,re_{t-1} + 0.1366\,rd_{t-1} + \widehat{v}_{1t}$$
$$rd_t = 0.0984 + 0.0024(p_{t-1} - 1.1773\,d_{t-1} - 340.3414)$$
$$+ 0.0006\,re_{t-1} + 0.8792\,rd_{t-1} + \widehat{v}_{2t},$$

where $\widehat{v}_{1t}$ and $\widehat{v}_{2t}$ are the residuals from the two equations. Since $re_t = p_t - p_{t-1}$ and $rd_t = d_t - d_{t-1}$, the VECM(1) is rewritten as a VAR(2) in levels as follows,

$$p_t = (0.0353 + 0.0068 \times 340.3414)$$
$$+ (1 - 0.0068 + 0.2901)p_{t-1} - 0.2901\,p_{t-2}$$
$$+ (0.0068 \times 1.1773 + 0.1366)d_{t-1} - 0.1366\,d_{t-2} + \widehat{v}_{1t}$$
$$d_t = (0.0984 + 0.0024 \times 340.3414)$$
$$+ (0.0024 + 0.0006)p_{t-1} - 0.0006\,p_{t-2}$$
$$+ (1 - 0.0024 \times 1.1773 + 0.8792)d_{t-1} - 0.8792\,d_{t-2} + \widehat{v}_{2t},$$

or

$$p_t = 2.3350 + 1.2980\,p_{t-1} - 0.2901\,p_{t-2} + 0.1433\,d_{t-1} - 0.1366\,d_{t-2} + \widehat{v}_{1t}$$
$$d_t = 0.9232 + 0.0035\,p_{t-1} - 0.0006\,p_{t-2} + 1.8816\,d_{t-1} - 0.8792\,d_{t-2} + \widehat{v}_{2t}.$$

The forecast for the October 2016 log equity price and log dividend payment given their values in August, p_{T-1} and d_{T-1}, and September, p_T and d_T, are obtained using these equations as

$$\widehat{p}_{T+1} = 2.3350 + 1.2980\,p_T - 0.2901\,p_{T-1} + 0.1433\,d_T - 0.1366\,d_{T-1}$$
$$= 767.7360,$$

and

$$\widehat{d}_{T+1} = 0.9232 + 0.0035\,p_T - 0.0006\,p_{T-1} + 1.8816\,d_T - 0.8792\,d_{T-1}$$
$$= 381.1519.$$

Similar calculations reveal that the respective forecasts for the November 2016 log equity price and log dividend payment (both scaled by 100) are

$$\widehat{p}_{T+2} = 767.9893$$
$$\widehat{d}_{T+2} = 381.5670.$$

---

[1] These estimates are the same as the estimates reported in Chapter 6 with the exception that the intercepts now reflect the fact that the variables are scaled by 100.

Based on these forecasts, percentage equity returns in October and November are, respectively,

$$\widehat{re}_{T+1} = 767.7360 - 767.6793 = 0.0567\%$$
$$\widehat{re}_{T+2} = 767.9893 - 767.7360 = 0.2533\%,$$

and the corresponding forecasts for dividend returns are, respectively,

$$\widehat{rd}_{T+1} = 381.1519 - 380.7329 = 0.4190\%$$
$$\widehat{rd}_{T+2} = 381.5670 - 381.1519 = 0.4151\%.$$

7.4 COMBINING FORECASTS

Models are stylized representations of real world phenomena that, at best, capture only approximately the complexities of the underlying processes. Even though models can never be expected to represent the true generating process exactly, some models can be very useful in modeling and forecasting economic and financial variables. In approximating the true process and in forecasting future realizations, certain models may prove to be better than others. To take advantage of the good properties of certain models and the robustness of others, it is sometimes helpful to combine models and the forecasts from these models in a manner that exploits their individual properties.

Such combinations have often been found in practical work to reduce forecast error variance. It is not surprising, therefore, that the concept and methodology of forecast combination has attracted much academic interest. Timmerman (2006) and Elliott and Timmerman (2008, 2016) provide extensive references to the vast literature on this subject. In practical forecasting work, the media often report consensus forecasts of key economic and financial variables such as GDP and inflation that are important in financial decision-making. Such forecasts are obtained by taking simple averages of forecasts of the same quantity that are provided by different forecasting units or different forecasting techniques. The availability of multiple forecasts raises an important question in forecasting: Is it better to rely on an individual forecast with known good properties or are there potential gains to averaging several competing forecasts?

Suppose that two unbiased forecasts of a variable y_t are available, given by $\widehat{y}_t^1$ and $\widehat{y}_t^2$, with respective forecast variances σ_1^2 and σ_2^2 and covariance σ_{12}. A weighted average of these two forecasts is

$$\widehat{y}_t = \omega\widehat{y}_t^1 + (1 - \omega)\widehat{y}_t^2,$$

which depends on a weight parameter $\omega \in [0, 1]$. The combined forecast $\widehat{y}_t$ is also unbiased and its variance is

$$\sigma^2 = \omega^2\sigma_1^2 + (1 - \omega)^2\sigma_2^2 + 2\omega(1 - \omega)\sigma_{12}.$$

A natural approach to selecting the combined forecast is to choose the weight ω in order to minimize its forecast variance. The first-order condition for a minimum is given by

$$\frac{d\sigma^2}{d\omega} = 2\omega\sigma_1^2 - 2(1 - \omega)\sigma_2^2 + 2\sigma_{12} - 4\omega\sigma_{12},$$

and setting this expression to zero and solving gives the optimal weight parameter

$$\omega = \frac{\sigma_2^2 - \sigma_{12}}{\sigma_1^2 + \sigma_2^2 - 2\sigma_{12}}.$$

It is clear, therefore, that the weight attached to $\widehat{\gamma}_t^1$ varies inversely with its variance. In passing, it is worth noting that these weights are identical to the optimal weights for the minimum variance portfolio derived in Chapter 3.

This point can be illustrated more clearly if the forecasts are assumed to be uncorrelated so that $\sigma_{12} = 0$. In this case,

$$\omega = \frac{\sigma_2^2}{\sigma_1^2 + \sigma_2^2}, \qquad 1 - \omega = \frac{\sigma_1^2}{\sigma_1^2 + \sigma_2^2},$$

and it is clear that both forecasts have weights varying inversely with their individual variances. By rearranging the expression for ω as follows

$$\omega = \left(\frac{\sigma_2^2}{\sigma_1^2 + \sigma_2^2}\right)\left(\frac{\sigma_2^{-2}\sigma_1^{-2}}{\sigma_2^{-2}\sigma_1^{-2}}\right) = \frac{\sigma_1^{-2}}{\sigma_1^{-2} + \sigma_2^{-2}}, \qquad (7.11)$$

the inverse proportionality is now manifest in the numerator of expression (7.11). The inverse of the forecast variance, σ_1^{-2}, may be interpreted as a measure of the imprecision of the forecast $\widehat{\gamma}_t^1$ (that is, the larger the variance, the lower the precision of the forecast). The implication of equation (7.11) is that the lower the precision of the forecast $\widehat{\gamma}_t^1$ (relative to the overall precision), the less weight (ω) is placed on that forecast in the combination.

This simple intuition in the two forecast case translates into a situation in which there are N forecasts $\{\widehat{\gamma}_t^1, \widehat{\gamma}_t^2, \cdots, \widehat{\gamma}_t^N\}$ of the same variable γ_t. If these forecasts are all unbiased and uncorrelated and if the weights satisfy

$$\sum_{i=1}^{N} \omega_i = 1 \qquad \omega_i \geq 0 \qquad i = 1, 2, \cdots, N,$$

then from equation (7.11), the optimal weights are

$$\omega_i = \frac{\sigma_i^{-2}}{\sum_{j=1}^{N} \sigma_j^{-2}},$$

and the weight on forecast i is inversely proportional to its variance.

The weights in expression (7.11) are intuitively appealing as they are based on the principle of producing a minimum variance portfolio of the forecasts. Important questions remain, however, about how best to implement the combination of forecasts approach in practice. Bates and Granger (1969) suggested using equation (7.11) to construct the weights, with the required estimates of the forecast variances, $\widehat{\sigma}_i^2$, given by the forecast mean square error based, for instance, on within-sample performance. All this approach requires then is an estimate of the mean square error of all the competing forecasts in order to compute estimates of the optimal weights, $\widehat{\omega}_i$. Granger and Ramanathan (1984) later show that this method is numerically equivalent to weights constructed from running the restricted regression

$$y_t = \omega_1 \widehat{y}_t^1 + \omega_2 \widehat{y}_t^2 + \cdots + \omega_N \widehat{y}_t^N + v_t,$$

in which the constant term is zero and the coefficients are constrained to be non-negative and to sum to one. Enforcing these restrictions involves constrained optimization that can be difficult in practice and sometimes ad hoc methods are adopted instead. One method is the sequential elimination of forecasts with weights estimated to be negative until all the remaining forecasts in the proposed combination forecast have positive weights.

Yet another approach to averaging forecasts is based on the use of information criteria (Buckland, Burnham, and Augustin, 1997; Burnham and Anderson, 2002), which may be interpreted as an estimate of the relative quality of an econometric model. Suppose there are N different models, each with an estimated Akaike information criterion $AIC_1, AIC_2, \cdots, AIC_N$, then the model that returns the minimum value of the information criterion is usually the model of choice. Denote the minimum value of the information criterion for this set of models as AIC_{min}. Then the expression[2]

$$\exp[\Delta I_i/2] = \exp[(AIC_i - AIC_{min})/2]$$

may be interpreted as a relative measure of the loss of information from using model i instead of the model that produces AIC_{min}. It is therefore natural to allow the forecast combination to reflect this relative information by computing the weights in terms of the ratios

$$\widehat{\omega}_i = \frac{\exp[\Delta I_i/2]}{\sum\limits_{j=i}^{N} \exp[\Delta I_i/2]}.$$

The Schwarz (Bayesian) Information Criterion (SIC) has also been suggested as an alternative information criterion to use in the application of this method (Garratt, Koop, and Vahey, 2008; Kapetanios, Labhard, and Price, 2008).

The simplest approach of all is to assign equal weights to these forecasts and construct the simple average

$$\widehat{y}_t = \frac{1}{N} \sum_{i=1}^{N} \widehat{y}_t^i.$$

Interestingly, simulation studies and practical work indicate that this simplistic strategy of averaging forecasts often works better than other more sophisticated methods, especially

---

[2] The exact form of this expression derives from the likelihood principle, which is discussed in Chapter 10. The AIC is an asymptotically unbiased estimator of -2 times the log-likelihood function of model i, so that after dividing by -2 and exponentiating, the result is a measure of the likelihood that model i actually generated the observed data.

when there are large numbers of forecasts to be combined, notwithstanding all the subsequent work on the optimal estimation of weights (Stock and Watson, 2001). Two possible explanations for why simple averaging might work better in practice than constructing an optimal combination with estimated weights are as follows.

(i) There may be significant errors in the estimation of the weights, due to either parameter instability (Clemen, 1989; Winkler and Clemen, 1992; Smith and Wallis, 2009) or structural breaks (Hendry and Clements, 2004).

(ii) If the forecast variances of the competing forecasts are similar and their covariances are positive, then large gains obtained by constructing optimal weights are unlikely (Elliott, 2011). Note, for example, in the two-forecast combination case, if the forecast variances are the same, the weight formula is

$$\omega = \frac{\sigma^2 - \sigma_{12}}{2\sigma^2 - 2\sigma_{12}} = \frac{1}{2},$$

delivering equal weights.

7.5 FORECAST EVALUATION STATISTICS

The discussion so far has concentrated on ex ante forecasting of a variable or variables over a forecast horizon, H, beginning after the last observation in the data set. However, it is also of interest to be able to compare the forecasts with the actual values that are observed in order to assess accuracy. One approach is simply to wait until the future values are observed, but this is not convenient if information about the forecasting capability of a model is required before ex ante forecasting is conducted.

A common solution that is adopted to determine the forecast accuracy of a model is to estimate the model over a restricted sample period that excludes the last H observations. The model is then forecasted out-of-sample over these observations. Since the actual values of the variables over these H time periods have already been observed, it is now possible to compare forecasts with historical values to assess accuracy. Forecasts computed in this way are known as ex post forecasts according to the definition given earlier.

Suppose now that ex post forecasts are required for the period January 2016 to September 2016 for US equity returns, re_t, using the same data set used to generate the ex ante forecasts of the previous section based on the AR(1) model. The model is estimated over the restricted period February 1871 to December 2015 to yield

$$re_t = 0.2518 + 0.2840\, re_{t-1} + \widehat{v}_t,$$

where $\widehat{v}_t$ is the least squares residual. The forecasts are now generated recursively using the estimated model and also the fact that the equity return in December 2015 is $re_{T-H} = -1.2838\%$

Jan: $\widehat{re}_{T-H+1} = 0.2518 + 0.2840\, re_{T-H}$

$\qquad = 0.2518 + 0.2840 \times (-1.2838) = -0.1127\%$

Feb: $\widehat{re}_{T-H+2} = 0.2518 + 0.2840\, \widehat{re}_{T-H+1}$

$\qquad = 0.2518 + 0.2840 \times (-0.1127) = \ \ 0.2198\%,$

Mar: $\widehat{re}_{T-H+3} = 0.2518 + 0.2840\, \widehat{re}_{T-H+2}$

$\qquad = 0.2518 + 0.2840 \times \ \ 0.2198 = \ \ 0.3143\%$

Apr: $\widehat{re}_{T-H+4} = 0.2518 + 0.2840\, \widehat{re}_{T-H+3}$

$\qquad = 0.2518 + 0.2840 \times \ \ 0.3143 = \ \ 0.3411\%$

May: $\widehat{re}_{T-H+5} = 0.2518 + 0.2840\, \widehat{re}_{T-H+4}$

$\qquad = 0.2518 + 0.2840 \times \ \ 0.3411 = \ \ 0.3487\%$

Jun: $\widehat{re}_{T-H+6} = 0.2518 + 0.2840\, \widehat{re}_{T-H+5}$

$\qquad = 0.2518 + 0.2840 \times \ \ 0.3487 = \ \ 0.3509\%$

Jul: $\widehat{re}_{T-H+7} = 0.2518 + 0.2840\, \widehat{re}_{T-H+6}$

$\qquad = 0.2518 + 0.2840 \times \ \ 0.3509 = \ \ 0.3515\%$

Aug: $\widehat{re}_{T-H+8} = 0.2518 + 0.2840\, \widehat{re}_{T-H+7}$

$\qquad = 0.2518 + 0.2840 \times \ \ 0.3515 = \ \ 0.3517\%$

Sep: $\widehat{re}_{T-H+9} = 0.2518 + 0.2840\, \widehat{re}_{T-H+8}$

$\qquad = 0.2518 + 0.2840 \times \ \ 0.3517 = \ \ 0.3517\%.$

The ex post forecasts of US equity returns are illustrated in Figure 7.1. It is readily apparent how quickly the forecasts are driven toward the unconditional mean of returns

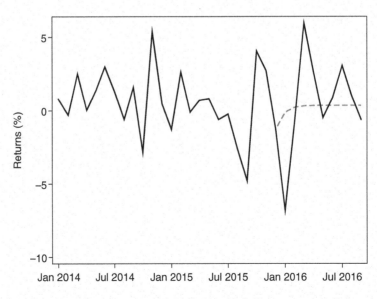

FIGURE 7.1   Ex post forecasts (shown by the dashed line) of US equity returns (%) generated by an AR(1) model. The sample period of the data is January 1871 to December 2015 and the forecast period is from January 2016 to September 2016.

0.3539%. As pointed out previously, this pattern is typical of time series forecasts based on stationary data.

There are a number of simple summary statistics that are used to determine the accuracy of ex post forecasts. Define the forecast errors as the differences between the actual values and the forecasted values over the forecast horizon, namely,

$$y_{T+1} - \widehat{y}_{T+1}, y_{T+2} - \widehat{y}_{T+2}, \cdots, y_{T+H} - \widehat{y}_{T+H}.$$

The smaller these forecast errors are, the better the forecasts. So the differences may be used to compute a summary statistic. The most commonly used summary measures of overall closeness of the forecasts to the actual values are the mean absolute error (MAE), mean absolute percentage error (MAPE), the mean squared error (MSE), and the root mean squared error (RMSE). These metrics are defined as follows

$$\text{MAE} = \frac{1}{H} \sum_{h=1}^{H} |y_{T+h} - \widehat{y}_{T+h}|$$

$$\text{MAPE} = \frac{1}{H} \sum_{h=1}^{H} \left| \frac{y_{T+h} - \widehat{y}_{T+h}}{y_{T+h}} \right|$$

$$\text{MSE} = \frac{1}{H} \sum_{h=1}^{H} (y_{T+h} - \widehat{y}_{T+h})^2$$

$$\text{RMSE} = \sqrt{\frac{1}{H} \sum_{h=1}^{H} (y_{T+h} - \widehat{y}_{T+h})^2}.$$

To compute the MSE for the forecast period, the actual sample observations of equity returns from January 2016 to September 2016 are required. These percentage returns are

$$1.8746, 1.0696, 2.8859, 4.6891, 0.9526, -1.7095, 0.8311, -2.7352, \text{ and } 2.6822.$$

The MSE is

$$
\begin{aligned}
\text{MSE} &= \frac{1}{9} \sum_{h=1}^{9} \left(re_{T+h} - \widehat{re}_{T+h} \right)^2 \\
&= \frac{1}{9} \big((1.8746 - (-0.1127))^2 + (1.0696 - 0.2198)^2 + (2.8859 - 0.3143)^2 \\
&\quad + (4.6891 - 0.3411)^2 + (0.9526 - 0.3487)^2 + (-1.7095 - 0.3509)^2 \\
&\quad + (0.8311 - 0.3515)^2 + (-2.7352 - 0.3517)^2 + (2.6822 - 0.3517)^2 \big) \\
&= 10.3423.
\end{aligned}
$$

The RMSE is

$$\text{RMSE} = \sqrt{\frac{1}{9} \sum_{h=1}^{9} \left(re_{T+h} - \widehat{re}_{T+h} \right)^2} = \sqrt{10.3423} = 3.2159.$$

Taken on its own, the RMSE of the forecast, 3.2159, does not provide a good descriptive measure of the relative accuracy of this model because its value can be changed by simply changing the units of measurement of the data. For example, expressing the data as returns and not as percentage returns results in the RMSE falling by a factor of 100. Clearly this smaller RMSE does not mean that the forecasting performance of the AR(1) model has improved. The way that the RMSE and the MSE are typically used to evaluate the forecasting performance of a model is to compute the same statistics for an alternative model. The model with the smaller RMSE or MSE is judged to be the better forecasting model.

The forecasting performance characteristics of several models are now compared in a practical exercise. The models employed are an AR(1) model of equity returns, a VAR(1) model containing both equity and dividend returns, and a VECM(2) with an unrestricted constant, containing log equity prices and log dividend payments. Each model is estimated using a reduced sample on US monthly percentage equity returns from February 1871 to December 2015 and used to generate forecasts from January to September 2016. The resulting forecasts are then compared using the MSE and RMSE statistics.

The results in Table 7.1 show that the VECM(2) is the best forecasting model as it yields the smallest MSE and RMSE. This result is not surprising given the earlier discussion in Chapter 6 that revealed the usefulness of a cointegrating link in capturing the interdependence between dividends and equity prices. The VECM is designed to capture this long-term linkage and use the link in forecasting. The fact that the VAR(1), which is formulated with both equity returns and dividend returns data, provides the second best forecasting performance suggests that transient linkages between these variables is also important. In particular, the findings indicate that accounting for short-run dynamic feedback effects between equity returns and dividend returns is worth doing even when long-term linkages are ignored, giving forecast performance that is superior to a univariate specification for equity returns.

A widely used formal test for comparing two different forecasts is due to Diebold and Mariano (1995). Suppose we have two competing forecasts and we are able to compute the forecast error, $\widehat{u}_{T+H}(M_j) = y_{T+H} - \widehat{y}_{T+H}$, for the jth model, M_j. Now define the difference

$$w_t = \widehat{u}_{T+H}(M_1) - \widehat{u}_{T+H}(M_2).$$

TABLE 7.1   Forecasting performance of models of US monthly percentage equity returns. The sample period of the data is January 1871 to December 2015 and forecasts are from January to September 2016.

2016	AR(1)	VAR(1)	VECM(2)
Jan	−0.1127%	−0.0713%	−0.1013%
Feb	0.2198%	0.2678%	0.2426%
Mar	0.3143%	0.3599%	0.3410%
Apr	0.3411%	0.3825%	0.3677%
May	0.3487%	0.3859%	0.3737%
Jun	0.3509%	0.3841%	0.3738%
Jul	0.3515%	0.3811%	0.3723%
Aug	0.3517%	0.3781%	0.3705%
Sep	0.3517%	0.3753%	0.3687%
MSE	10.3423	10.3234	10.3076
RMSE	3.2159	3.2130	3.2106

The Diebold–Mariano test of equal predictive accuracy is based on a simple t test that $E(w_t) = 0$. Proper construction of this t test relies on the use of an appropriate standard error for the difference w_t.

There is an active research area in financial econometrics in which these statistical (or *direct*) measures of forecast performance are replaced by problem-specific (or *indirect*) measures of forecast performance in which the evaluation relates specifically to some relevant economic decision (Elliott and Timmerman, 2008; Patton and Sheppard, 2009). Examples of the indirect approach to forecast evaluation appear in Engle and Colacito (2006), who evaluate forecast performance in terms of portfolio return variance; and Fleming, Kirby, and Ostdiek (2001, 2003), who apply a quadratic utility function that values one forecast relative to another. Becker, Clements, Doolan, and Hurn (2015) survey and compare these different approaches to forecast evaluation.

7.6 EVALUATING THE DENSITY OF FORECAST ERRORS

The above discussion of forecast generation for financial variables has focused on first and second moment properties: the conditional mean point forecast and the conditional variance of the forecast distribution, which can both be used to help construct an interval forecast. A natural extension is to include forecasts of higher order moments such as skewness and kurtosis or even the entire probability distribution. The latter is of particular interest in the area of risk management where assessments of such quantities as future value at risk are relevant.

As is the case with point forecasts, where statistics are computed to determine the relative accuracy of the forecasts, density forecasts may also be evaluated to determine their relative accuracy. The approach that is typically used is to consider the entire distribution by using a quantity known as the probability integral transform (PIT), which is now discussed.

7.6.1 Probability Integral Transform

To fix ideas in a simple case, consider the constant mean model of returns given by

$$y_t = \mu + v_t, \qquad v_t \sim N(0, \sigma_v^2), \tag{7.12}$$

in which $\mu = 0$. Denote the cumulative distribution function (cdf) of the standard normal distribution evaluated at any point z as $\Phi(z)$. If the observed values y_t are indeed generated correctly according to this simple model, then the transformed quantity

$$u_t = \Phi\left(\frac{y_t - \mu}{\sigma_v}\right), \qquad t = 1, 2, \cdots, T, \tag{7.13}$$

takes values in the unit interval $[0, 1]$ because of the fundamental property of the cdf, Φ. Furthermore, and again assuming that y_t is generated by equation (7.12), the transformed time series u_t has a standard uniform distribution on this interval because

$$P(u_t \le u) = P\left(\Phi\left(\frac{y_t - \mu}{\sigma_v}\right) \le u\right)$$

$$= P\left(\frac{y_t - \mu}{\sigma_v} \le \Phi^{-1}(u)\right) \qquad \textbf{(7.14)}$$

$$= \Phi(\Phi^{-1}(u)) = u.$$

The transformation of equation (7.13) is known as the probability integral transform because use of the cdf, Φ, involves a transform of probability as shown in equation (7.14).

Figure 7.2 illustrates how the transformed times series u_t is obtained from the actual time series y_t where the specified model is $N(0, 1)$. This result reflects the property that if the cumulative distribution is indeed the correct distribution, transforming y_t to u_t means that each transformed quantity u_t has the same probability of being realized as any other value of u_t, as corroborated directly by equation (7.14).

The probability integral transform in the case where the specified model is chosen correctly is highlighted in panel (a) of Figure 7.3. A time series plot of 1000 simulated observations, y_t, drawn from a $N(0, 1)$ distribution is transformed into u_t using the cumulative normal distribution in equation (7.13). In the third column of panel (a) the histogram of the transformed time series u_t is shown. Inspection of the histogram corroborates empirically that the distribution used in transforming y_t is indeed the correct one because distribution of u_t is close to uniform over the whole interval $[0, 1]$.

Next consider the case where the true data generating process for y_t is a $N(0.5, 1)$ distribution, but the incorrect distribution based on equation (7.12) is used as the forecast distribution to perform the probability integral transform. The effect of misspecifying the mean of the forecast distribution is illustrated in panel (b) of Figure 7.3. A time series

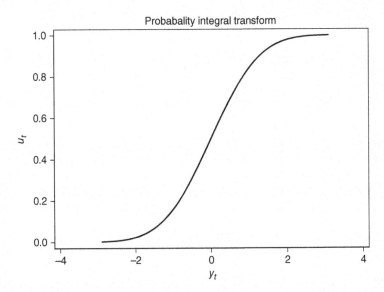

FIGURE 7.2 The probability integral transform showing how the time series y_t is transformed into u_t based on the distribution $N(0, 1)$.

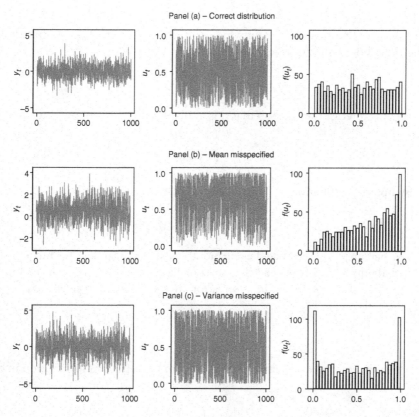

FIGURE 7.3 Simulated time series to show the effects of misspecification using the probability integral transform. In panel (a) there is no misspecification; while panels (b) and (c) demonstrate the effect of misspecification in the mean and variance of the distribution, respectively.

of 1000 simulated observations from a $N(0.5, 1.0)$ distribution, y_t, is transformed using the incorrect distribution, $N(0, 1)$, and the histogram of the transformed time series, u_t, is plotted in the third column. The histogram of u_t appears to rise systematically over the interval $[0, 1]$ and clearly departs from a uniform distribution. The departure from uniformity in this case is a reflection of the misspecified mean model in the forecasting model. The histogram exhibits a positive slope reflecting the fact that larger values of u_t, and hence y_t, have relatively higher probability of occurrence than smaller values of u_t and y_t.

Finally, consider the case where the variance of the model is misspecified. If the data generating process is a $N(0, 2)$ distribution, but the forecast distribution used in the probability integral transform is again $N(0, 1)$, then it is to be expected that the forecast distribution will understate the true spread of the data. This is visible in panel (c) of Figure 7.3. The histogram of u_t is now U-shaped implying that large negative and large positive values have a higher probability of occurring than are predicted by the $N(0, 1)$ distribution.

7.6.2 Equity Returns

The models used to forecast US equity log returns r_t in Section 7.2 are all based on the assumption of normality. Consider the AR(1) model

$$r_t = \phi_0 + \phi_1 r_{t-1} + v_t, \qquad v_t \sim N(0, \sigma_v^2).$$

Assuming the forecast is ex post so that r_t is available, the one-step-ahead forecast error is given by

$$\widehat{v}_t = r_t - \widehat{\phi}_0 - \widehat{\phi}_1 r_{t-1},$$

with asymptotic distribution

$$\widehat{v}_t \sim N(r_t - \phi_0 - \phi_1 r_{t-1}, \sigma_v^2), \qquad (7.15)$$

where the parameters are estimated using monthly data from January 1871 to September 2016. For the purpose of this exercise, the calculations do not take into account the distributional effects of the estimation error in the fitted coefficients $(\widehat{\phi}_0, \widehat{\phi}_1)$. The distribution in equation (7.15) is

$$\widehat{v}_t \sim N(r_t - 0.2527 - 0.2839\, r_{t-1}, 3.9036^2).$$

The probability integral transform corresponding to the estimated distribution in equation (7.15) is then

$$u_t = \Phi\left(\frac{\widehat{v}_t}{\widehat{\sigma}_v}\right),$$

in which $\widehat{\sigma}_v = 3.9036$ is the standard error of the regression. A histogram of the transformed time series, u_t, is given in Figure 7.4. It appears that the AR(1) forecasting model of equity returns is misspecified because the distribution of u_t is non-uniform. The interior peak of the distribution of u_t suggests that the distribution of y_t is more peaked than that predicted by the normal distribution. Also, the peak in the distribution of u_t at zero suggests that there are some observed large negative values of y_t that are not consistent with the specification of a normal distribution. These two properties together indicate that the specified model fails to take into account the presence of kurtosis and skewness in the actual data.

The analysis of the one-step-ahead AR(1) forecasting model can easily be extended to the other estimated models of equity returns including the VAR model and the VECM investigated in Section 7.3 to forecast equity returns. As applied here, the probability integral transform is performed ex post because it uses within sample, one-step-ahead prediction errors to conduct the analysis. The application is also a graphical implementation in which misspecification is detected by simple visual inspection of the histogram of the transformed time series u_t. It is possible to relax both these limitations in practice. In particular, Diebold, Gunther, and Tsay (1998) discuss an alternative approach suited to ex ante applications, and Ghosh and Bera (2005) propose a class of formal statistical tests of the null hypothesis that u_t is uniformly distributed.

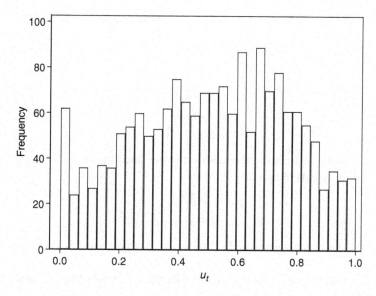

FIGURE 7.4 Probability integral transform applied to the estimated one-step-ahead forecast errors of the AR(1) model of US equity returns, January 1871 to September 2016.

7.7 REGRESSION MODEL FORECASTS

The forecasting techniques for univariate and multivariate models that have been discussed so far are all based on time series models in which each dependent variable is expressed as a function of its own lags and lags of other variables. Additional explanatory variables may be used in forecasting exercises.

A simple framework for using explanatory variables in forecasting exercises is the linear regression model

$$y_t = \beta_0 + \beta_1 x_t + u_t,$$

where y_t is the dependent variable, x_t is the explanatory variable, u_t is a disturbance term, and the sample period is $t = 1, 2, \cdots, T$. To generate a forecast of y_t at time $T + 1$, as before, the model is written at $T + 1$ as

$$y_{T+1} = \beta_0 + \beta_1 x_{T+1} + u_{T+1}.$$

The unknown values on the right hand-side are x_{T+1} and u_{T+1}, as well as the parameters $\{\beta_0, \beta_1\}$. As before, the equation error in the forecast period u_{T+1} is replaced by its expected value of $E[u_{T+1}] = 0$, and the parameters are replaced by their sample estimates, $(\widehat{\beta}_0, \widehat{\beta}_1)$. However, unlike autoregressive formulations in which lagged values of the dependent variable are observed in a one-period ahead forecast, the future value of the explanatory variable x_{T+1} is unobserved.

One strategy is to specify hypothetical future values of the explanatory variable that represent potential outcomes of interest. A less subjective approach is to specify a time series model for x_t and use this model to generate forecasts of future values x_{T+H} by means of the methods discussed previously. For example, if an AR(2) model is proposed for x_t, the overall model becomes a bivariate system of equations of the form

$$y_t = \beta_0 + \beta_1 x_t + u_t \tag{7.16}$$
$$x_t = \phi_0 + \phi_1 x_{t-1} + \phi_2 x_{t-2} + v_t. \tag{7.17}$$

To generate the first forecast at time $T+1$, the system of equations is written as

$$y_{T+1} = \beta_0 + \beta_1 x_{T+1} + u_{T+1}$$
$$x_{T+1} = \phi_0 + \phi_1 x_T + \phi_2 x_{T-1} + v_{T+1}.$$

Replacing the unknown parameters with estimates and the unknown equation errors with expectations yields the predictive system

$$\widehat{y}_{T+1} = \widehat{\beta}_0 + \widehat{\beta}_1 \widehat{x}_{T+1} \tag{7.18}$$
$$\widehat{x}_{T+1} = \widehat{\phi}_0 + \widehat{\phi}_1 x_T + \widehat{\phi}_2 x_{T-1}. \tag{7.19}$$

Equation (7.19) is used to generate the forecast $\widehat{x}_{T+1}$, which is utilized in equation (7.18) to generate $\widehat{y}_{T+1}$.

These calculations can be performed in a single step by substituting equation (7.19) for $\widehat{x}_{T+1}$ into equation (7.18) to give

$$\widehat{y}_{T+1} = \widehat{\beta}_0 + \widehat{\beta}_1 (\widehat{\phi}_0 + \widehat{\phi}_1 x_T + \widehat{\phi}_2 x_{T-1})$$
$$= \widehat{\beta}_0 + \widehat{\beta}_1 \widehat{\phi}_0 + \widehat{\beta}_1 \widehat{\phi}_1 x_T + \widehat{\beta}_1 \widehat{\phi}_2 x_{T-1}.$$

Using the same approach, multiple explanatory variables are easily handled by specifying a VAR to generate the required multivariate forecasts of these variables.

As an illustration, a regression model may be used to forecast US equity returns, re_t, using dividend returns, rd_t. As in earlier examples, the data employed are from February 1871 to September 2016. Estimation of equations (7.16) and (7.17) is conducted by ordinary least squares. For simplicity, the model for the explanatory variable is restricted to an AR(1). The fitted system is

$$re_t = 0.3433 + 0.0360 rd_t + \widehat{u}_t$$
$$rd_t = 0.0326 + 0.8903 rd_{t-1} + \widehat{v}_t.$$

The forecasts for dividend returns in October and November are then

$$\widehat{rd}_{T+1} = 0.0326 + 0.8903\, rd_T = 0.0326 + 0.8903 \times 0.4228 = 0.4090\%$$
$$\widehat{rd}_{T+2} = 0.0326 + 0.8903\, \widehat{rd}_{T+1} = 0.0326 + 0.8903 \times 0.4090 = 0.3967\%,$$

and the corresponding equity return forecasts are

$$\widehat{re}_{T+1} = 0.3433 + 0.0360\, \widehat{rd}_{T+1} = 0.3433 + 0.0360 \times 0.3982 = 0.3580\%$$
$$\widehat{re}_{T+2} = 0.3433 + 0.0360\, \widehat{rd}_{T+2} = 0.3433 + 0.0360 \times 0.3871 = 0.3576\%.$$

7.8 PREDICTING THE EQUITY PREMIUM

Forecasting in finance using time series regression models is a highly active field of research in applied finance. One area where the methods have been extensively used is in predicting the equity premium. Two influential papers on this topic are by Goyal and Welch (2003, 2008). They address the problem of predicting the equity premium, which is defined as the excess return from investment in equities over the return from a risk-free investment. The relevant equations are

$$EQP_t = rm_t - rf_t$$
$$rm_t = \log(P_t + D_t) - \log(P_{t-1})$$
$$rf_t = \log(1 + Rf_t),$$

where P_t is an equity price index, D_t is the dividend payment stream associated with the index, and Rf_t is a representative risk-free interest rate. Two explanatory predictors are used in the regressions, namely, the dividend-price ratio and the dividend-yield ratio, which are defined as

$$DP_t = \log(D_t) - \log(P_t)$$
$$DY_t = \log(D_t) - \log(P_{t-1}).$$

Table 7.2 provides summary statistics of the annual data used by Goyal and Welch (2003). For these calculations, P_t is the value-weighted CRSP index, D_t is the dividend paid on the index, DP_t is the corresponding dividend price ratio, and the equity premium EQP_t is obtained using the 3-month Treasury Bill rate as the risk-free rate Rf_t and the annual market return on the S&P 500 index rm_t. Figure 7.5 provides plots of the time series of the logarithms of the equity premium, dividend yield, and dividend-price ratio.

Two predictive regressions for EQP_t are considered, namely,

$$EQP_t = \alpha_p + \beta_p DP_{t-1} + v_{pt} \qquad (7.20)$$
$$EQP_t = \alpha_y + \beta_y DY_{t-1} + v_{yt}. \qquad (7.21)$$

The parameter estimates obtained from estimating these equations for two different sample periods (1926 to 1990 and 1926 to 2002) are reported in Table 7.3.

These results suggest that the lagged dividend price ratio, DP_{t-1}, and the lagged dividend yield, DY_{t-1}, have some forecasting power for the equity premium over the period 1926–1990, at least when EQP_t is defined using the S&P 500 index. It is notable,

TABLE 7.2 Descriptive statistics for the annual total market return to the S&P 500 Index, rm_t, the equity premium, EQP_t, the dividend price ratio, DP_t, and the dividend yield ratio, DY_t. All variables are in percentages and the data are for the period 1926 to 2002.

	Mean	Std. Dev.	Min.	Max.	Skew.	Kurt.
			1926–2002			
rm_t	9.29	19.80	−58.74	45.71	−0.89	3.95
EQP_t	5.57	20.00	−59.82	45.41	−0.75	3.66
DP_t	−3.30	0.42	−4.48	−2.36	−0.68	3.76
DY_t	−3.252	0.40	−4.53	−2.56	−1.17	4.50
			1946–2002			
rm_t	10.34	16.00	−32.72	40.72	−0.52	2.75
EQP_t	5.69	16.37	−40.46	39.86	−0.53	2.98
DP_t	−3.41	0.41	−4.48	−2.73	−0.80	3.43
DY_t	−3.34	0.42	−4.53	−2.56	−0.87	3.76

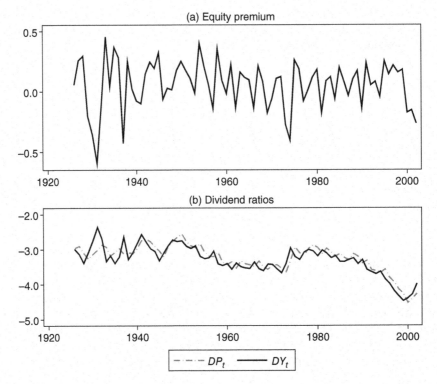

FIGURE 7.5   Plots of the time series of the logarithms of the equity premium, the dividend-price ratio and dividend yield. Data are for the period 1926 to 2002.

TABLE 7.3   Predictive regressions for the equity premium using the dividend price ratio, $d_t - p_t$, and the dividend yield, $d_t - p_{t-1}$, as explanatory variable predictors. Figures in parentheses are t statistics.

Predictor	α	β	R^2	$\overline{R}^2$	$\hat{\sigma}_v$	T
Sample 1926–1990						
DP_{t-1}	0.612 (2.146)	0.176 (1.959)	0.058	0.043	0.203	64
DY_{t-1}	0.898 (2.851)	0.270 (2.683)	0.104	0.090	0.1983	64
Sample 1926–2002						
DP_{t-1}	0.390 (2.128)	0.102 (1.839)	0.044	0.031	0.198	76
DY_{t-1}	0.504 (2.639)	0.138 (2.364)	0.070	0.058	0.195	76

however, that the size of both slope coefficients are substantially reduced when the sample size is increased.

The subsample instability of the estimated regression coefficients in Table 7.3 is further illustrated by considering the recursive plots of the slope coefficients from equations (7.20) and (7.21). Figure 7.6 reveals that the coefficient on DP_{t-1} increases over time, while the coefficient on DY_{t-1} steadily decreases. In other words, as time progresses forecasts appear to rely less on DY_{t-1} and more on DP_{t-1} despite the fact that the coefficient on DY_{t-1} appears more reliable in terms of statistical significance measured by the size of its t ratio.

The main tool for interpreting the performance of the predictive regressions used by Goyal and Welch is a plot of the cumulative sum of squared one-step-ahead forecast errors of the predictive regressions expressed relative to the forecast error of the best current estimate of the mean of the equity premium. Let the one-step-ahead forecast errors of the dividend yield and dividend price ratio models be $\widehat{v}_{yt}$ and $\widehat{v}_{pt}$, respectively, and let the

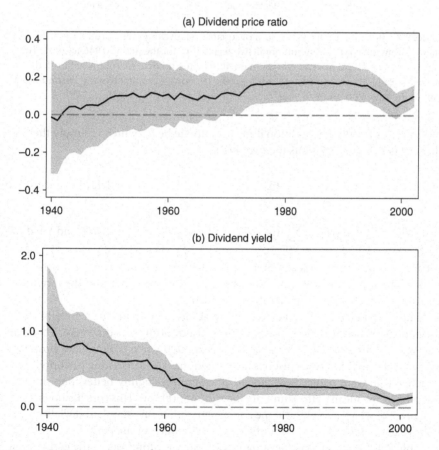

FIGURE 7.6 Recursive estimates of the slope coefficients on the dividend-price ratio and the dividend yield from equations (7.20) and (7.21), respectively, computed for the period 1940 to 2002. The grey area denotes a one standard deviation band around the estimate.

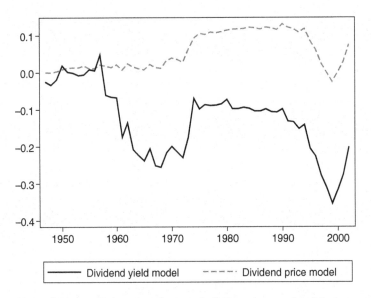

FIGURE 7.7 Plots of the cumulative sum of squared relative one-step-ahead forecast errors obtained from the equity premium predictive regressions for the period 1946 to 2002. The squared one-step-ahead forecast errors obtained from the models are subtracted from the squared one-step-ahead forecast errors based solely on the best current estimate of the unconditional mean of the equity premium.

forecast errors for the unconditional mean estimate be $\hat{u}_t$, which is simply the centered value of EQP_t. Figure 7.7 plots the two series

$$SSE(p) = \sum_{t=1946}^{2002} (\hat{u}_t^2 - \hat{v}_{pt}^2) \qquad \text{[Dividend-Price Ratio Model]}$$

$$SSE(y) = \sum_{t=1946}^{2002} (\hat{u}_t^2 - \hat{v}_{yt}^2). \qquad \text{[Dividend Yield Model]}$$

A positive value for SSE means that the model forecasts are superior to the forecasts based solely on the mean thus far. A positive slope implies that over the recent year the forecasting model performs better than the mean.

Figure 7.7 indicates that the forecasting ability of a predictive regression using the dividend yield is poor because $SSE(y)$ is almost uniformly less than zero. There are two main years in the mid-1970s and again around 2000 when $SSE(y)$ has a positive slope (yet still negative) but these episodes are exceptions. The forecasting performance of the predictive regression using the dividend price ratio is slightly better than the forecasts generated by the mean as the summary measure $SSE(p) > 0$. This conclusion is supported by Figure 7.6, which shows the slope coefficient and its one standard deviation bands to be above the origin, albeit close to the origin over much of the period.

Table 7.4 provides forecast evaluation statistics for forecasts of the equity premium that are based on an estimation sample of 1926–1992 and a forecast period of 1993–2002. The forecasts are obtained from the dividend-price ratio model, the dividend yield

TABLE 7.4 Performance of forecasts of the equity premium obtained from the dividend-price ratio model, the dividend yield model, a simple combination forecast, and a combination forecast that uses optimal weights. The estimation period is 1926–1992 and the forecast period is 1993–2002.

Forecast Statistic	Dividend Price	Dividend Yield	Simple Combination	Optimal Combination
MAE	0.1614	0.1875	0.1701	0.1676
MAPE	0.9531	1.1621	1.0067	0.9840
MSE	0.0392	0.0525	0.0444	0.0434
RMSE	0.1980	0.2292	0.2107	0.2085

model, a simple combination of the two forecasts, and a combination that uses optimal weights. The optimal weights are constructed according to the suggestion of Bates and Granger (1969) outlined in Section 7.4. The RMSE values for the dividend-price ratio model and the dividend yield model reported are used to compute the optimal weight on the dividend-price ratio model. The weight is computed to be 0.5726 so that the weight on the dividend yield model is 0.4274. These values reflect the fact that the RSME for the dividend-price ratio model is smaller than that of the dividend yield model. So the former is accorded a larger weight in forming the optimal combination.

The results in Table 7.4 indicate that the dividend-price ratio predictor of the equity premium unambiguously provides the better forecast. The two combination forecasts provide only slender support for using forecast combinations in this illustration, these forecasts being dominated by the dividend price predictor. The simplicity of this forecasting problem, the small number of competing models, the fact that the dividend price ratio predictor dominates the dividend yield predictor, and the relative short horizon all make conditions less favorable for a successful combination forecast. In situations that involve many competing forecast models, each with its own potential advantages, and in forecast exercises over longer horizons where successful forecasting is inevitably more challenging, there is much greater potential for successful implementation of forecast combination.

There are some important practical lessons to learn from predictive regressions. The first is that good in-sample performance does not necessarily imply that a fitted regression equation will provide good forecasts. Parameter instability and structural change are inevitable realities that challenge good predictive performance. Second, there are major conceptual and technical difficulties that arise from differences in the time series properties of explanatory predictors and dependent variables. The dependent variable of interest in forecasting exercises is often a stationary variable such as the equity premium, which is difficult to predict well, as witnessed by the low R^2 statistics and poor predictive capability of the regressors demonstrated by the findings in Table 7.4. Furthermore, the explanatory predictors that are chosen for such regressions as being the most relevant variables are often time series whose autoregressive roots are typically near unity, signifying near nonstationarity.

Regression equations that relate such variables potentially suffer from an imbalance in the time series properties of the explanatory predictors and the dependent variable. For instance, Stambaugh (1999) found that dividend ratios have time series behavior similar to random walks, whereas equity premia are typically stationary. Dividend ratios may then be good predictors of their own future behavior but may be viewed as only marginally relevant predictors of the future path of the equity premium. Therefore, the coefficients in such imbalanced regressions must naturally be expected to be small, and the explanatory power, as well as predictive power, of the regressions is similarly expected to be slight. Since much of the data that are employed in financial predictive regression exercises have nonstationary characteristics, these complications present major challenges for forecasters, and active research on this topic is ongoing (Campbell and Yogo, 2006; Phillips and Lee, 2013; Phillips, 2014a; Kostakis, Magdalinos, and Stamatogiannis, 2014; Kasparis, Andreou, and Phillips, 2015). For an interesting argument in favor of the predictability of equity returns that challenges the conventional view, see Cochrane (2008).

7.9 STOCHASTIC SIMULATION OF VALUE AT RISK

Forecasting need not necessarily be about point forecasts or best guesses. Sometimes important information is conveyed by the degree of uncertainty inherent in the best guess. One important application of this uncertainty is the concept of value at risk, which was introduced in Chapter 2. Stated formally, value at risk represents the losses that are expected to occur with probability α on an asset or portfolio of assets, P, after N days.

Recall from Chapter 2 that value at risk may be computed by historical simulation, the variance-covariance method, or Monte Carlo simulation. Using a model to make forecasts of future values of the asset or portfolio and then assessing the uncertainty in the forecast is the method of Monte Carlo simulation. In general, simulation refers to any method that randomly generates repeated trials of a model and seeks to summarize uncertainty in the model forecast in terms of the distribution of these random trials. The steps to perform a simulation for a simple AR(1) model are as follows

Step 1: **Estimate the model**

Given observations $y_t = \{y_1, \cdots, y_T\}$, estimate the proposed model

$$y_t = \phi_0 + \phi_1 y_{t-1} + v_t,$$

and compute and store the residuals, $\widehat{v}_t$.

Step 2: **Simulate the model**

Now use the model to make a forecast; but instead of making a single forecast based on a best guess for the unknowns, make explicit allowance for uncertainty by including a disturbance term. This disturbance term may be obtained either by drawing from some assumed distribution (such as the normal distribution) or by taking a random draw from the residuals, $\widehat{v}_t$, computed in Step 1. The forecasts are constructed as follows

$$\widehat{y}^1_{T+1} = \phi_0 + \phi_1 y_T + \tilde{v}_{T+1},$$
$$\widehat{y}^1_{T+2} = \phi_0 + \phi_1 \widehat{y}_{T+1} + \tilde{v}_{T+2},$$

$$\vdots$$

$$\widehat{y}^1_{T+H} = \phi_0 + \phi_1 \widehat{y}_{T+H-1} + \tilde{v}_{T+H},$$

where $\tilde{v}_{T+H}$ represents a random draw from $\widehat{v}_t$.

Step 3: **Repeat**

Step 2 is now repeated S times to obtain

$$\begin{array}{cccccc}
\hat{y}^1_{T+1} & \hat{y}^2_{T+1} & \hat{y}^3_{T+1} & \cdots & \hat{y}^{S-1}_{T+1} & \hat{y}^S_{T+1} \\
\hat{y}^1_{T+2} & \hat{y}^2_{T+2} & \hat{y}^3_{T+1} & \cdots & \hat{y}^{S-1}_{T+2} & \hat{y}^S_{T+2} \\
\vdots & \vdots & \hat{y}^3_{T+1} & \vdots & \vdots & \vdots \\
\hat{y}^1_{T+H} & \hat{y}^2_{T+H} & \hat{y}^3_{T+1} & \cdots & \hat{y}^{S-1}_{T+H} & \hat{y}^S_{T+H}.
\end{array}$$

Step 4: **Summarize the uncertainty**

Each column of this ensemble of forecasts is a possible outcome of the model and therefore collectively the forecasts capture the uncertainty of the future value of y_t. In particular, the percentiles of these simulated forecasts for each time period $T + i$ provide an estimate of the distribution of the forecast at that time. The disturbances used to generate the forecasts are drawn from the actual one-step-ahead prediction errors and not from a normal distribution and the forecast uncertainty will then reflect any non-symmetry or fat tails present in the estimated prediction errors.

Consider the case of US monthly data on equity prices. Suppose that the asset in question is one that pays the value of the index. An investor who holds this asset in September 2016, the last date in the sample, would observe that the value of the portfolio is $2157.69. Suppose the investor wishes to know what the value of the asset will be in 6 months time in March 2017. It is not so much the best guess of the future value that is important, but rather it is the spread of the distribution of the forecast. The situation is illustrated in Figure 7.8 where the shaded region captures the 90% confidence interval

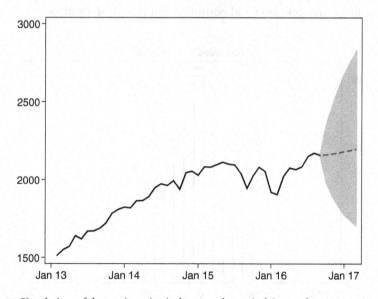

FIGURE 7.8 Simulation of the equity price index over the period September 2016 to March 2017. The ex ante forecasts are shown by the dashed line, while the confidence interval encapsulates the uncertainty inherent in the forecast.

of the forecast. Clearly, the investor needs to take this spread of likely outcomes into account when thinking of the future value of the investment.

Consider now the problem of computing the 99% value at risk for the asset that pays the value of the US equity index over a time horizon of 6 months. On the assumption that equity returns are generated by an AR(1) model, the estimated equation is

$$r_t = 0.2527 + 0.2839 \, r_{t-1} + \widehat{v}_t,$$

which may be used to forecast returns for period $T + 1$, but ensuring that uncertainty is explicitly introduced. The forecasting equation is therefore

$$\widehat{r}_{T+1} = 0.2527 + 0.2839 \, r_T + \tilde{v}_{T+1},$$

where $\tilde{v}_{T+1}$ is a random draw from the computed one-step-ahead forecast errors computed by means of an in-sample static forecast. The value of the asset at $T + 1$ in repetition s is computed as

$$\widehat{P}^s_{T+1} = P_T \exp\left[\widehat{r}_{T+1}/100\right],$$

where the forecast returns are adjusted so that they are no longer expressed as percentages. A recursive procedure is now used to forecast the value of the asset out to $T + 6$ and the whole process is repeated S times. The distribution of the value of the asset at $T + 6$ after S replications is shown in Figure 7.9 based on the initial value at time T of $P_T =$ \$2157.69. The distribution of simulated losses obtained by subtracting the initial value of the asset from the terminal value is shown in Figure 7.9. The first percentile value of this distribution is −\$675.97 so that the 6-month 99% value at risk is \$675.97, where by convention the minus sign is dropped when reporting value at risk. Of course this approach is equally applicable to simulating value at risk for more complex portfolios comprising more than one asset and portfolios that include derivatives.

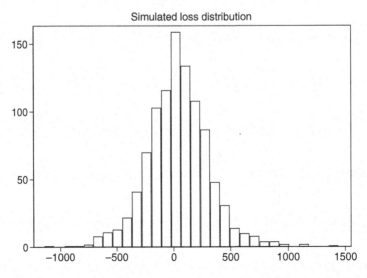

FIGURE 7.9 Simulated distribution of the equity index and the profit/loss on the equity index over a 6-month horizon from July 2004.

7.10 EXERCISES

The data required for the exercises are available for download as EViews workfiles (*.wf1), Stata datafiles (*.dta), comma delimited text files (*.csv), and as Excel spreadsheets (*.xlsx).

1. **Ex Ante Forecasts of Equity Returns**

pv.*

   The data are monthly observations on US equity prices and dividends for the period January 1871 to September 2016. Compute equity returns and dividend returns as

   $$re_t = 100 \times (\log P_t - \log P_{t-1})$$
   $$rd_t = 100 \times (\log D_t - \log D_{t-1}),$$

   where P_t is the equity price index and D_t are dividend payments. Compare the ex ante forecasts of equity returns obtained from the following alternative models

   (a) Estimate an AR(1) model of equity returns, re_t, with the sample period ending in September 2016. Generate forecasts of re_t from October to December 2016.
   (b) Estimate an AR(2) model of equity returns, re_t, with the sample period ending in September 2016. Generate forecasts of re_t from October to December 2016.
   (c) Repeat parts (a) and (b) for dividend returns, rd_t.
   (d) Estimate a VAR(1) for re_t and rd_t with the sample period ending in September 2016. Generate forecasts of equity returns from October to December 2016.
   (e) Estimate a VAR(2) for re_t and rd_t with the sample period ending in September 2016. Generate forecasts of equity returns from October to December 2016.
   (f) Estimate a VECM(1) for the equity price, p_t, dividend payments, d_t, (where the lower cases denote logarithms) with the sample period ending in September 2016 and where the VECM specification contains a constant in both the VAR and the cointegrating equation. Generate forecasts of equity returns from October to December 2016.
   (g) Repeat part (f) with the lag length in the VECM increasing from 1 to 2.
   (h) Repeat part (g) with the VECM specification containing a constant in the cointegrating equation but not the VAR.
   (i) Now estimate a VECM(1) containing the equity price, p_t, dividend payments, d_t, and earnings, e_t, with the sample period ending in September 2016 and the specification as in part (f). Assume a cointegrating rank of 1. Generate forecasts of equity returns from October to December 2016.
   (j) Repeat part (i) with the lag length in the VECM increasing from 1 to 2.

2. **Ex Post Forecasts of Equity Returns**

pv.*

   The data are monthly observations on US equity prices and dividends for the period January 1871 to September 2016. Compute equity returns and dividend returns as

$$re_t = 100 \times (\log P_t - \log P_{t-1})$$
$$rd_t = 100 \times (\log D_t - \log D_{t-1}),$$

where P_t is the equity price index and D_t are dividend payments.

(a) Estimate an AR(1) model of equity returns, re_t, with the sample period ending December 2015, and generate ex post forecasts from January to September 2016.

(b) Estimate a VAR(1) model of equity returns, re_t, and dividend returns, rd_t, with the sample period ending December 2015, and generate ex post forecasts from January to September 2016.

(c) Estimate a VECM(1) model of the equity price, p_t, and dividend payments, d_t, using a constant in both the cointegrating equation and the VAR, with the sample period ending December 2015. Generate ex post forecasts for equity prices and returns from January to September 2016.

(d) For each set of forecasts generated in parts (a) to (c), compute the MSE and the RMSE. Which is the better forecasting model? Discuss.

3. Regression Based Forecasts of Equity Returns

pv.*

The data are monthly observations on US equity prices and dividends for the period January 1871 to September 2016. Compute equity returns and dividend returns as

$$re_t = 100 \times (\log P_t - \log P_{t-1})$$
$$rd_t = 100 \times (\log D_t - \log D_{t-1}),$$

where P_t is the equity price index and D_t are dividend payments.

(a) Estimate the following regression for a sample period ending in September 2016,

$$re_t = \beta_1 + \beta_2 rd_t + u_t.$$

Estimate an AR(1) model of dividend returns

$$rd_t = \rho_0 + \rho_1 rd_{t-1} + v_t,$$

and combine this model with the estimated model in the first equation to generate forecasts of equity returns from October to December 2016.

(b) Estimate an AR(2) model of dividend returns

$$rd_t = \rho_0 + \rho_1 rd_{t-1} + \rho_2 rd_{t-2} + v_t,$$

and combine this model in place of the AR(1) model in part (a) to generate forecasts of equity returns from October to December 2016.

(c) Use the estimated model in part (a) to generate forecasts of equity returns from October to December 2016 assuming that dividend returns are the following.

(i) 3% per annum.

(ii) 10% per annum.

(iii) 3% per annum in October and 10% in November and December.

4. Pooling Forecasts

> hedgefunds.*

The data are daily percentage log returns to seven hedge fund indices, from 1 April 2003 to 28 May 2010.

(a) Estimate an AR(2) model of the returns on the equity market neutral hedge fund with the sample period ending on 21 May 2010 (Friday). Generate forecasts of y_{1t} for the next working week, from 24 to 28 May 2010.

(b) Repeat part (a) for S&P 500 returns.

(c) Estimate a VAR(2) containing the returns on the neutral hedge fund (y_{1t}) and the returns on the S&P 500 (y_{2t}), with the sample period ending on 21 May 2010 (Friday),

$$y_{1t} = \alpha_0 + \alpha_1 y_{1t-1} + \alpha_2 y_{1t-2} + \alpha_3 y_{2t-1} + \alpha_4 y_{2t-2} + v_{1t}$$
$$y_{2t} = \beta_0 + \beta_1 y_{1t-1} + \beta_2 y_{1t-2} + \beta_3 y_{2t-1} + \beta_4 y_{2t-2} + v_{2t}.$$

Generate forecasts of y_{1t} for the next working week, from 24 to 28 May 2010.

(d) For the AR(2) and VAR(2) forecasts obtained for the returns on the neutral hedge fund (y_{1t}) and the S&P 500 (y_{2t}), compute the RMSE (a total of four RMSEs) for each model. Discuss which model yields the superior forecasts.

(e) Let f_{1t}^{AR} be the forecasts from the AR(2) model of the returns on the neutral hedge fund and f_{1t}^{VAR} be the corresponding VAR(2) forecasts. Restricting the sample period just to the forecast period, 24 to 28 May, estimate the following unrestricted regression that pools the two sets of forecasts

$$y_{1t} = \omega_0 + \omega_1 f_{1t}^{AR} + \omega_2 f_{1t}^{VAR} + \eta_t,$$

where η_t is a disturbance term with zero mean and variance σ_η^2 and $w_1 + w_2 = 1$. Interpret the parameter estimates and discuss whether pooling the forecasts has improved the forecasts of the returns on the neutral hedge fund.

5. Evaluating Forecast Distributions

(a) (*Correct Model Specification*) Simulate $y_1, y_2, \cdots, y_{1000}$ observations $(T = 1000)$ from the true model given by a $N(0,1)$ distribution. Assuming that the specified model is also $N(0,1)$, for each t compute the probability integral transform

$$u_t = \Phi(y_t).$$

Interpret the properties of the histogram of u_t.

(b) *(Mean Misspecification)* Repeat part (a) except that the true model is $N(0.5, 1)$ and the misspecified model is $N(0, 1)$.

(c) *(Variance Misspecification)* Repeat part (a) except that the true model is $N(0, 2)$ and the misspecified model is $N(0, 1)$.

(d) *(Skewness Misspecification)* Repeat part (a) except that the true model is the standardized gamma distribution

$$y_t = \frac{g_t - ba}{\sqrt{b^2 a}},$$

where g_t is a gamma random variable with parameters $\{b = 0.5, a = 2\}$ and the misspecified model is $N(0, 1)$.

(e) *(Kurtosis Misspecification)* Repeat part (a) except that the true model is the standardized Student t distribution

$$y_t = \frac{s_t}{\sqrt{\dfrac{v}{v - 2}}},$$

where s_t is a Student t random variable with degrees of freedom equal to $v = 5$, and the misspecified model is $N(0, 1)$.

6. Predicting the Equity Premium

goyalwelch2003.*

The data are annual observations for the period 1926 to 2002 on the returns to the S&P 500 Index, rm_t, equity premium, EQP_t, the dividend price ratio, DP_t, and the dividend yield, DY_t. The data are identical to those used by Goyal and Welch (2003) in their research on the determinants of the US equity premium.

(a) Compute basic summary statistics for the market return, the equity premium, the dividend-price ratio, and the dividend yield.

(b) Plot these variables and compare the results with Figure 7.5.

(c) Estimate the predictive regressions

$$EQP_t = \alpha_p + \beta_p DP_{t-1} + v_{pt}$$
$$EQP_t = \alpha_y + \beta_y DY_{t-1} + v_{yt},$$

for two different sample periods, 1926 to 1990 and 1926 to 2002, and compare your results with Table 7.3.

(d) Estimate the regressions recursively using data up to 1940 as the starting sample in order to obtain recursive estimates of β_y and β_p together with 95% confidence intervals. Plot and interpret the results.

(e) Estimate the predictive regressions using the sample period 1926 to 1990. Use these models to provide ex post forecasts of EQP_t over the period 1991 to 2002. Evaluate these forecasts employing commonly used forecast evaluation statistics and comment on your results.

7. Simulating VaR for a Single Asset

pv.*

The data are monthly observations on US equity prices from January 1871 to September 2016. Equity returns, expressed as a percentage, are given by

$$re_t = 100 \times (\log P_t - \log P_{t-1}).$$

The aim is to compute the 6-month 99% value at risk for an asset that pays the value of the index.

(a) Assume that the equity returns are generated by an AR(1) model

$$re_t = \phi_0 + \phi_1 re_{t-1} + v_t.$$

Estimate the model and compute the residuals, $\widehat{v}_t$.

(b) Generate 1000 forecasts of the terminal equity price P_{T+6} using stochastic simulation by implementing the following steps.

(i) Forecast $\widehat{re}^s_{T+k}$ using the scheme

$$\widehat{re}^s_{T+k} = \widehat{\phi}_0 + \widehat{\phi}_1 \widehat{re}^s_{T+k-1} + \tilde{v}_{T+k},$$

where $\tilde{v}_{T+k}$ is a random draw from the residuals, $\widehat{v}_t$.

(ii) Compute the simulated equity price

$$\widehat{P}^s_{T+k} = \widehat{P}^s_{T+k-1} \exp(\widehat{re}^s_{T+k}/100).$$

(iii) Repeat (i) and (ii) for $k = 1, 2, \cdots 6$.

(iv) Repeat (i), (ii), and (iii) for $s = 1, 2, \cdots, 1000$.

(c) Compute the 99% value at risk based on the S simulated equity prices at $T + 6$ and the initial value of the index in September 2016.

Methods

CHAPTER 8

Instrumental Variables

In Part I, linear regression is shown to provide a flexible framework for exploring a wide variety of financial theories. Examples include the CAPM, the multifactor Fama–French model, the present value model, and models of the term structure of interest rates. Estimation of these models relies on the principle of ordinary least squares that gives consistent parameter estimates subject to certain conditions, which are outlined in Chapter 3. One of these conditions requires that the explanatory variables in the model be uncorrelated with the disturbance term. This condition is an important one. When it does not hold, the ordinary least squares estimator is no longer consistent.

There are many cases in financial econometrics where this critical assumption breaks down and the explanatory variables and the disturbance term are correlated. Three common situations where such correlation arises are (i) when the explanatory variables are measured with error, (ii) when relevant explanatory variables are omitted, and (iii) when variables are included as explanatory regressors without accounting for the fact they are jointly determined with the dependent variable.

This chapter explores a general methodology for addressing these difficulties. The approach is known as instrumental variables estimation. It was introduced informally in early empirical work in the first half of the twentieth century and received its first general treatment in the work of Denis Sargan (1958, 1959). The methodology has been highly influential in applications throughout the social and business sciences. A key requirement for implementing the method is the availability of additional variables that can serve as *instruments* for the explanatory variables. To qualify as instruments, the variables need to satisfy two vital properties. They must be *relevant* in the sense that they are correlated with the explanatory variables that they are instrumenting for, and they must be uncorrelated with (or *orthogonal* to) the regression equation disturbances. These two conditions are known as the relevance and orthogonality conditions.

8.1 THE EXOGENEITY ASSUMPTION

In the linear regression model of Chapter 3, the dependent variable y_t is expressed as a linear function of a regressor x_t (or a set of regressors in the case of the multiple regression model)

$$y_t = \beta_0 + \beta_1 x_t + u_t, \tag{8.1}$$

where u_t is a disturbance term with mean zero and variance σ_u^2. Under the conditions outlined in Chapter 3, the ordinary least squares estimators of the parameters of this model have some desirable properties. Among these the property of consistency ensures that the estimators converge in probability to the true coefficients as the sample size increases indefinitely. This property of least squares is particularly relevant in financial applications where there are often large numbers of observations to use in applied work.

The conditions under which consistency holds require that there be no change in the true coefficients over the sample and that the regressor x_t be exogenous. The exogeneity assumption is a strong one and can take many different forms. One version of the condition that is fundamental in ensuring consistency of least squares regression is orthogonality (or no correlation) between the regressor x_t and the equation error u_t. This condition is expressed as

$$E(u_t x_t) = 0. \tag{8.2}$$

The orthogonality condition in equation (8.2) is satisfied if the model to be estimated, equation (8.1), is correctly specified and satisfies the standard conditions for least squares regression to perform well. However, many situations arise in applied work with financial data where an alternative (proxy) model is actually estimated because of limitations in the available data or where underlying conditions change because the generating mechanism is more complex. In such cases, a common result is that the orthogonality condition fails and some regressors are correlated with the disturbance term. Examples that give rise to this situation are as follows.

(i) Errors in variables

In models of the risk-return trade-off, expected return is a function of the expected variance of the asset. As the variance of a risky asset is typically unobserved, econometric investigations of this relationship typically use proxies for the variance, such as an index of volatility published on the Chicago Board Options Exchange known as the VIX. Given that the VIX is an imprecise measure of the variance, the no-correlation assumption between the proxy variable and the disturbance of the augmented equation is likely to be violated.

(ii) Omitted variables

The classic example in financial econometrics of omitted variables is the CAPM. Traditionally the CAPM is estimated as a one factor model with the excess return on the market as the only risk factor being priced. More recently, a number of other potential risk factors, such as size, value, and momentum, are proposed. Clearly if these additional factors are indeed important in the pricing of a risky asset, then the β-risk estimated from a single factor model is unlikely to be estimated consistently.

(iii) Simultaneity

In empirical corporate finance, a typical question is whether or not family-owned firms perform better than other firms. This question is usually answered by positing that family ownership is an important explanatory variable for a measure of firm performance. It is quite possible, however, that the reverse is true and that it is the firm's performance that explains the ownership structure. Any single equation study in which a given variable is modeled in terms of a number of regressors runs the risk of the simultaneous determination of the response variable and the regressors. This problem is particularly acute in empirical corporate finance where there are no strong theoretical underpinnings.

Despite the fact that there is more than one fundamental reason for the violation of the no-correlation assumption in a linear regression model, regressors that are correlated with the disturbance term are generally referred to as endogenous variables, while regressors that are uncorrelated with the disturbance term are referred to as being exogenous. For this reason, the violation of the no-correlation assumption is generally referred to as an endogeneity problem and testing a regressor for possible correlation with the disturbance term is known as testing for endogeneity.

The instrumental variables method with which this chapter is concerned provides a mechanism for obtaining consistent estimates of the parameters of a linear regression when the no-correlation assumption of the model is violated.

8.2 ESTIMATING THE RISK-RETURN TRADEOFF

A fundamental idea in finance is that investors require a larger risk premium at times when the stock market is riskier, with the size of the premium related to how risk averse investors are. The inter-temporal CAPM model (Merton, 1973, 1980) provides a formal statement of this relationship in which the expected excess return on the aggregate stock market at time t (r_t) is a linear function of the expected variance at time t (σ_t^2)

$$E_{t-1}(r_t) = \gamma\, E_{t-1}(\sigma_t^2),$$

in which γ is a parameter representing the degree of relative risk aversion of the representative investor and the notation $E_{t-1}(\cdot)$ emphasizing that the expectations are based on information at time $t-1$. In a linear regression framework, the inter-temporal CAPM can be written as

$$r_t = \alpha + \gamma\, E_{t-1}(\sigma_t^2) + u_t. \tag{8.3}$$

For the Merton model to hold, the parameters in equation (8.3) must satisfy the restrictions $\alpha = 0$ and $\gamma > 0$.

Equation (8.3) cannot be estimated in its present form as the expected conditional variance, $E_{t-1}(\sigma_t^2)$, is unobservable. A common approach is to choose an observable proxy for the conditional variance. The Chicago Board Options Exchange (CBOE) publishes an index of the riskiness (volatility) of the S&P 500 stock market index, known as the VIX, which is constructed using the information contained in financial options written on the S&P 500 Index (see Chapter 17). Although the VIX is quoted as an annualized conditional standard deviation, it is easily scaled to reflect a daily conditional variance, denoted h_t.

The relationship between the proxy variance h_t and the true unobserved conditional variance $E_{t-1}(\sigma_t^2)$ is

$$h_t = E_{t-1}(\sigma_t^2) + \epsilon_t, \tag{8.4}$$

where ϵ_t represents the measurement error, which is assumed to be distributed with zero mean and variance σ_ϵ^2. Using this expression to substitute out the unobservable variable $E_{t-1}(\sigma_t^2)$ in equation (8.3) yields the following augmented regression equation in which all variables are now observed

$$r_t = \alpha + \gamma h_t + v_t. \tag{8.5}$$

The disturbance term v_t is

$$v_t = -\gamma \epsilon_t + u_t, \tag{8.6}$$

which represents a composite of two disturbance terms: the disturbance term u_t in equation (8.3), which represents deviations from the inter-temporal CAPM relationship, and the measurement error ϵ_t in equation (8.4), which arises from using a proxy for the unobserved variance. Given the observable proxy h_t, it is tempting to estimate the relative risk aversion parameter, γ, in equation (8.5) by ordinary least squares.

Figure 8.1 provides a scatter plot of the relationship between daily returns to the S&P 500 Index and the proxy for the conditional variance, h_t, for the period 2 January 1990 to 1 June 2012. It is apparent that the relationship is fairly noisy and there is no obvious positive relationship evident in the scatter. Estimating equation (8.5) by ordinary least squares using the returns to the S&P 500 Index and the proxy for the conditional variance yields the following results

$$r_t = \underset{(0.0002)}{0.0018} - \underset{(0.9534)}{9.7202}\, h_t + \widehat{v}_t, \tag{8.7}$$

where standard errors are given in parentheses. The estimate of the coefficient of risk aversion is negative, a result that is markedly at odds with the theory and suggests that something is amiss with the econometrics.

The problem with estimating equation (8.5) by ordinary least squares is that the condition in equation (8.2) is not satisfied. This failure can be formally demonstrated by computing the covariance between h_t and v_t in equation (8.5) using equation (8.4) and equation (8.6), giving

$$\text{cov}(h_t, v_t) = \text{cov}[(E_{t-1}(\sigma_t^2) + \epsilon_t), (-\gamma \epsilon_t + u_t)] = -\gamma \sigma_\epsilon^2 \neq 0. \tag{8.8}$$

To gain insight into the effects of this violation on the least squares estimator of γ using the regression model equation (8.5), the population slope parameter for this model is

$$\frac{\text{cov}(r_t, h_t)}{\text{var}(h_t)} = \frac{\text{cov}(\alpha + \gamma z_t + v_t, h_t)}{\text{var}(h_t)} = \gamma + \frac{\text{cov}(v_t, h_t)}{\text{var}(h_t)} = \gamma - \gamma \frac{\sigma_\epsilon^2}{\text{var}(h_t)}, \tag{8.9}$$

where the second step uses equation (8.5) and the last step uses equation (8.8). Only in the special case where there is no measurement error, $\sigma_\epsilon^2 = 0$, will the slope population parameter of equation (8.5) correspond to the risk aversion parameter γ in the true model given in equation (8.3). When there is measurement error, $\sigma_\epsilon^2 \neq 0$, the slope

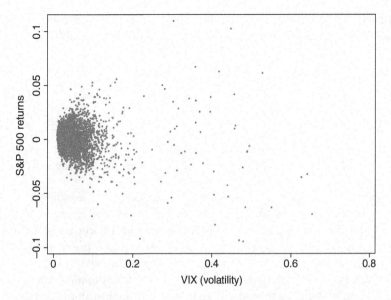

FIGURE 8.1 Scatter plot illustrating the relationship between returns to the S&P 500 Index and the proxy for the conditional variance, h_t, given by the appropriately scaled VIX Index.

population parameter of equation (8.5) is biased downward. The implication is that least squares produces an inconsistent estimator of γ.

To circumvent the problems of least squares estimation of equation (8.5), we suppose that there exists a suitable instrumental variable z_t for the regressor, which satisfies the following two conditions

$$\text{cov}(h_t, z_t) \neq 0, \qquad \text{cov}(z_t, v_t) = 0. \tag{8.10}$$

The first condition ensures that the instrument z_t is correlated with (and hence relevant for) the proxy variable, h_t. The second condition ensures that z_t is uncorrelated with the disturbance term v_t in equation (8.5) and therefore satisfies the orthogonality requirement with respect to the equation error. The covariance between returns, r_t, and the variable z_t is given by

$$\begin{aligned}
\text{cov}(r_t, z_t) &= \text{cov}(\alpha + \gamma h_t + v_t, z_t) \\
&= \text{cov}(\gamma h_t, z_t) + \text{cov}(v_t, z_t) \\
&= \gamma \, \text{cov}(h_t, z_t).
\end{aligned} \tag{8.11}$$

Rearranging equation (8.11) suggests that an alternative expression for the population parameter γ is

$$\gamma = \frac{\text{cov}(r_t, z_t)}{\text{cov}(h_t, z_t)}.$$

When these population quantities are replaced by their sample counterparts, the resulting expression is a new estimator of γ, known as the instrumental variable estimator

$$\widehat{\gamma}_{IV} = \frac{\dfrac{1}{T}\sum_{t=1}^{T}(r_t - \overline{r})(z_t - \overline{z})}{\dfrac{1}{T}\sum_{t=1}^{T}(h_t - \overline{h})(z_t - \overline{z})}. \tag{8.12}$$

Given that the two conditions in equation (8.10) are satisfied, the instrumental variables estimator is consistent. Situations where these properties are not satisfied are discussed in Section 8.5.

To implement this estimation procedure in equation (8.12), a suitable instrumental variable, z_t, must be found that satisfies the two conditions in equation (8.10). In the current context, a solution is readily available because for the current sample, the first-order autocorrelation coefficient of the conditional variance proxy, h_t, is 0.9705, so that $\mathrm{cov}(h_t, z_t) = \mathrm{cov}(h_t, h_{t-1}) \neq 0$. Moreover, at time t, the lagged value h_{t-1} may be taken as given and therefore $\mathrm{cov}(z_t, v_t) = \mathrm{cov}(h_{t-1}, v_t) = 0$. Estimating equation (8.5) by instrumental variables using the lagged variable h_{t-1} as the instrument for h_t gives

$$r_t = \underset{(0.0002)}{-0.0003} + \underset{(0.9975)}{3.0190}\, h_t + \widehat{v}_t, \tag{8.13}$$

where standard errors are given in parentheses. The estimate of the risk-aversion parameter is now positive and significant as predicted by financial theory. In addition, the size of the estimated coefficient, 3.019, matches empirical estimates in the published literature (Ghysels, Santa-Clara, and Valkanov, 2005; Bali and Peng, 2006). Moreover, a comparison of the $\widehat{\gamma}$ and $\widehat{\gamma}_{IV}$ in equations (8.7) and (8.13), respectively, shows that $\widehat{\gamma}$ is biased downward, as predicted by equation (8.9).

The version of the inter-temporal CAPM in equation (8.5) is a regression equation where the dependent variable is the return on an asset and the explanatory variable is a proxy for the conditional variance. This model is characterized by an errors-in-variables problem and is estimated by instrumental variables using h_{t-1} as an instrument for h_t. In Section 8.3, the model structure is extended to allow for additional explanatory variables, which are all exogenous. The aim is to augment the instrumental variables estimator in such a way that information on all of the exogenous variables in the system is combined to provide an improved instrument for the proxy variable.

8.3 THE GENERAL INSTRUMENTAL VARIABLES ESTIMATOR

To highlight how the general instrumental variables estimator is implemented in the case where there are multiple explanatory variables, consider the multi-factor Fama–French model given by

$$r_{it} - r_{ft} = \alpha + \beta_1(r_{mt} - r_{ft}) + \beta_2 \mathrm{SMB}_t + \beta_3 \mathrm{HML}_t + \beta_4 \mathrm{MOM}_t + v_t, \tag{8.14}$$

where $r_{it} - r_{ft}$ is the excess return on the asset i, $r_{mt} - r_{ft}$ is the market factor computed as the excess return on the market, SMB is the size factor measuring the performance of small stocks relative to big stocks, HML is the value factor that measures the performance of value stocks relative to growth stocks, MOM is the momentum factor, and v_t is a disturbance term. The contributions of SMB, HML, and MOM are determined by the parameters β_2, β_3, and β_4, respectively.

For convenience, the ordinary least squares parameter estimates of this model obtained in Chapter 3 using monthly data on a portfolio index for Nondurables in the United States from January 1927 to December 2013 are

$$r_{it} - r_{ft} = \underset{(0.0706)}{0.1786} + \underset{(0.0140)}{0.7674} \, (r_{mt} - r_{ft}) - \underset{(0.0223)}{0.0315} \, \text{SMB}_t$$

$$+ \underset{(0.0211)}{0.0284} \, \text{HML}_t + \underset{(0.0162)}{0.0247} \, \text{MOM}_t + \widehat{v}_t, \qquad (8.15)$$

where standard errors are in parentheses. The Beta-risk estimate is 0.7674, which suggests that Nondurables represents a conservative industry portfolio.

In theory, the market factor in equation (8.14) is defined as the return on all wealth, not just the return on equities. However, the return on all wealth is difficult to measure and in almost all cases, the market return on equities is effectively used as a proxy variable. There is therefore an errors-in-variables problem and estimation of equation (8.15) by ordinary least squares is inappropriate because

$$\text{cov}[(r_{mt} - r_{ft}), v_t] \neq 0, \qquad (8.16)$$

leading to a violation of the conditions needed for the ordinary least squares estimator applied to equation (8.14) to be consistent.

To re-estimate the model in equation (8.14) by instrumental variables, the following strategy is employed. A potential instrument for the market factor, $(r_{mt} - r_{ft})$, is lagged returns on the market factor, $(r_{mt-1} - r_{ft-1})$. However, to incorporate information from the exogenous variables $\{\text{SMB}_t, \text{HML}_t, \text{MOM}_t\}$ in equation (8.14) so as to improve the overall quality of the instrument for the market factor, all of the exogenous variables are now combined together with the lagged market factor instrument (which is called a predetermined variable) by specifying the following regression equation

$$r_{mt} - r_{ft} = \pi_0 + \pi_1 (r_{mt-1} - r_{ft-1}) + \pi_2 \, \text{SMB}_t + \pi_3 \, \text{HML}_t + \pi_4 \, \text{MOM}_t + e_t, \qquad (8.17)$$

where e_t is a disturbance term that is independent of all of the explanatory variables in equation (8.17). This equation is often referred to as the reduced form, which expresses an endogenous variable as a function of all of the exogenous and predetermined variables in the system. The ordinary least squares estimates of equation (8.17), with standard errors in parentheses, are

$$r_{mt} - r_{ft} = \underset{(0.1560)}{0.6806} + \underset{(0.0287)}{0.0113} \, (r_{mt-1} - r_{ft-1}) + \underset{(0.0484)}{0.4719} \, \text{SMB}_t$$

$$+ \underset{(0.0466)}{0.1223} \, \text{HML}_t - \underset{(0.0347)}{0.2970} \, \text{MOM}_t + \widehat{e}_t, \qquad (8.18)$$

where $\widehat{e}_t$ is the ordinary least squares residual. Although the lagged market factor is statistically insignificant in this reduced form regression and is therefore not a good choice of instrumental variable, this example does serve to demonstrate the general procedure.

The instrument for the market factor is computed as the predictor from this equation

$$\widehat{r_{mt} - r_{ft}} = 0.6806 + 0.0113\,(r_{mt-1} - r_{ft-1}) + 0.4719\,\mathrm{SMB}_t$$
$$+ 0.1223\,\mathrm{HML}_t - 0.2970\,\mathrm{MOM}_t. \tag{8.19}$$

The estimated reduced form equation represents a weighted average of the four exogenous and predetermined variables. The weights are determined optimally in the sense that the estimated equation provides the best predictor of the endogenous variable $(r_{mt} - r_{ft})$ from a conditional expectations point of view. A plot of the instrument in equation (8.19) is given in Figure 8.2.

Estimating equation (8.14) by instrumental variables is achieved by regressing $r_{it} - r_{ft}$ on $\{1, \widehat{r_{mt} - r_{ft}}, \mathrm{SMB}_t, \mathrm{HML}_t, \mathrm{MOM}_t\}$ where $\widehat{r_{mt} - r_{ft}}$ is defined in equation (8.19). The instrumental variables estimates, with standard errors in parentheses, are given in the displayed equation

$$r_{it} - r_{ft} = \underset{(0.87290)}{0.0303} + \underset{(1.2651)}{0.9833}\,(r_{mt} - r_{ft}) - \underset{(0.6030)}{0.1343}\,\mathrm{SMB}_t$$
$$+ \underset{(0.1568)}{0.0020}\,\mathrm{HML}_t + \underset{(0.3771)}{0.0890}\,\mathrm{MOM}_t + \widehat{v}_t. \tag{8.20}$$

Again notice that the estimated model is expressed in terms of the original regressors in the model even though estimation is based on replacing $(r_{mt} - r_{ft})$ by its instrument. Unlike the parameter estimates in equation (8.15), the parameter estimates in equation (8.20) are statistically consistent when $T \to \infty$. The requirement that all the regressors used to estimate the model are uncorrelated with the disturbance term is now satisfied because

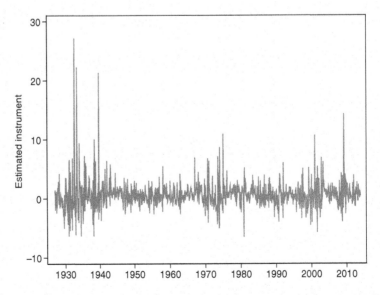

FIGURE 8.2 The estimated market factor instrument computed using equation (8.19) for the Fama–French model. Data are monthly excess returns on a nondurables portfolio index for the United States, and the sample period is January 1927 to December 2013.

$$\text{cov}[\widehat{r_{mt} - r_{ft}}, v_t] = 0, \tag{8.21}$$

which follows from the fact that $\widehat{r_{mt} - r_{ft}}$ is simply a linear function of the predetermined and exogenous variables $\{1, r_{mt-1} - r_{ft-1}, \text{SMB}_t, \text{HML}_t, \text{MOM}_t\}$, which by construction and definition are individually uncorrelated with v_t. A comparison of the ordinary least squares parameter estimates in equation (8.15) and the instrumental variables estimates in equation (8.20) show that the estimate of β-risk has increased from 0.7674 to 0.9833, suggesting that this asset is not necessarily a conservative stock. A formal test of the hypothesis that β-risk is unity is given by the t statistic

$$t = \frac{0.9833 - 1.000}{1.2681} = -0.0132.$$

The p value is 0.9895, showing a failure to reject the null hypothesis that the β-risk is unity at the 5% level. Of course, this result is to be expected given the statistical insignificance of the coefficient on the market factor in the second stage regression reported in equation (8.20).

The Fama–French model is characterized by a single endogenous regressor and multiple exogenous explanatory variables. The instrumental variables estimator is easily extended to the class of models where there are multiple endogenous explanatory variables and multiple exogenous explanatory variables in the regression specification. Suppose that there are N endogenous variables, $x_{1t}, \cdots, x_{Nt}$, and K exogenous variables, $w_{1t}, \cdots, w_{Kt}$, so that the model is specified as

$$y_t = \beta_0 + \sum_{i=1}^{N} \beta_i x_{it} + \sum_{i=k}^{K} \phi_k w_{kt} + v_t. \tag{8.22}$$

In order to identify the parameters $\beta_1, \cdots, \beta_N$, there must be at least L instruments $z_1, \cdots, z_L$, where $L \geq N$, which are not included in the model. This condition, known as the *order condition*, is a necessary but not sufficient condition to identify all of the parameters of the structural model in equation (8.22). If the number of instruments matches the number of endogenous variables ($L = N$), the model is referred to as being just identified. If there are more instruments available than endogenous variables ($L > N$), the model is said to be overidentified. If there are insufficient instruments ($L < N$), the model is underidentified and cannot be estimated using instrumental variables.

The general instrumental variables estimator is computed as follows

Step 1: Estimate the reduced form by regressing each of the N endogenous regressors on all of the L instruments and K exogenous variables in the following sequence of N ordinary least squares regressions,

$$x_{it} = \pi_{i0} + \sum_{j=1}^{L} \pi_{ij} z_{jt} + \sum_{k=1}^{K} \psi_{ik} w_{kt} + e_{it}, \qquad i = 1, 2, \cdots, N.$$

Let the predicted values from each of these N regressions be $\widehat{x}_{1t}, \cdots, \widehat{x}_{Nt}$.

Step 2: Regress y_t on the N predicted values of the endogenous regressors and the exogenous variables in the equation

$$y_t = \beta_0 + \sum_{i=1}^{N} \beta_i \widehat{x}_{it} + \sum_{k=1}^{K} \phi_k w_{kt} + v_t,$$

to obtain the estimator $\widehat{\theta}_{IV} = \{\widehat{\beta}_0, \cdots, \widehat{\beta}_N, \widehat{\phi}_1, \cdots, \widehat{\phi}_K\}$.

8.4 TESTING FOR ENDOGENEITY

The advantage of using an instrumental variables estimator is that it yields consistent parameter estimates in the presence of endogenous explanatory variables. Even if there is no endogeneity problem, and ordinary least squares yields consistent parameter estimates anyway, the instrumental variables estimator is still a consistent estimator. This observation suggests that the instrumental variables estimator is robust to various types of misspecification and delivers consistent estimates of the parameters in many situations.

There is a cost to using the instrumental variables estimator when it is not needed because there is a loss of information from using an instrument for an explanatory variable in regression. The instrument is a fitted value from an auxiliary regression, and necessarily therefore an imprecise measure of the variable it is instrumenting. This reduction in information about the regressor translates into reduced efficiency in instrumental variables estimation relative to ordinary least squares, which, in turn, translates into standard errors that are larger than the ordinary least squares standard errors, so that

$$\text{var}(\widehat{\theta}_{OLS}) < \text{var}(\widehat{\theta}_{IV}). \tag{8.23}$$

This result may be established from the fact that the variances of the ordinary least squares and instrumental variables estimators are approximately[1]

$$\text{var}(\widehat{\theta}_{OLS}) \approx \frac{1}{T} \frac{\sigma_u^2}{\sigma_x^2}, \qquad \text{var}(\widehat{\theta}_{IV}) \approx \frac{1}{T} \frac{\sigma_u^2}{\rho_{xz}^2 \sigma_x^2}, \tag{8.24}$$

where $0 < \rho_{xz}^2 < 1$ is the squared correlation between the endogenous regressor x_t and the instrument z_t. Since $0 < \rho_{xz}^2 < 1$, the result in equation (8.23) follows immediately.

To check whether instrumental variables regression is needed and to guard against the loss of efficiency, it is often appropriate to perform a preliminary test of endogeneity. To show how to construct such a test, consider the model

$$y_t = \beta_0 + \beta_1 x_t + v_t, \qquad v_t \sim N(0, \sigma^2). \tag{8.25}$$

A test of the endogeneity of x_t is formulated in terms of the following hypotheses,

$$H_0 : \text{cov}(x_t, v_t) = 0 \qquad [x_t \text{ Exogenous}]$$
$$H_1 : \text{cov}(x_t, v_t) \neq 0. \qquad [x_t \text{ Endogenous}]$$

---

[1] The variance expressions given in equation (8.24) hold approximately as $T \to \infty$ in the general case where the regressors and instruments may include predetermined variables and all variables in the model are stationary.

If the null hypothesis is rejected, then x_t is endogenous, and an instrumental variables estimator may be used to achieve consistency. If there is a failure to reject the null hypothesis, then in this case, x_t is exogenous and there is no need to employ instrumental variables estimation.

To construct a test of endogeneity, an auxiliary regression approach proposed by Davidson and MacKinnon (1989, 1993) may be employed. Suppose that a valid instrument for x_t in equation (8.25) exists so that the relevance and orthogonality conditions both hold, namely,

$$x_t = \pi_0 + \pi_1 z_t + e_t, \qquad \pi_1 \neq 0, \tag{8.26}$$

and

$$\text{cov}(x_t, v_t) = 0.$$

It follows that

$$\text{cov}(x_t, v_t) = \text{cov}(\pi_0 + \pi_1 z_t + e_t, v_t) = \text{cov}(e_t, v_t),$$

and thus

$$\text{cov}(x_t, v_t) = 0 \Rightarrow \text{cov}(e_t, v_t) = 0. \tag{8.27}$$

The condition in expression (8.27) may be written in a slightly different way by requiring that the coefficient α is zero in the linear regression

$$v_t = \alpha e_t + \eta_t, \tag{8.28}$$

where η_t is a disturbance term that is uncorrelated with e_t. Since v_t and e_t are disturbance terms, they are unobserved and equation (8.28) cannot be estimated as it stands, and a test of $\alpha = 0$ cannot be conducted based on this equation alone. But substituting equation (8.28) for v_t into the original model in equation (8.25) gives

$$y_t = \beta_0 + \beta_1 x_t + \alpha e_t + \eta_t,$$

a result that suggests the following auxiliary regression-based test of endogeneity of x_t.

Step 1: Estimate the regression

$$x_t = \pi_0 + \pi_1 z_t + e_t,$$

by ordinary least squares to obtain the estimates $\widehat{\pi}_0$ and $\widehat{\pi}_1$ and then compute the residuals $\widehat{e}_t$.

Step 2: Estimate the regression

$$y_t = \beta_0 + \beta_1 x_t + \alpha \widehat{e}_t + \eta_t,$$

by ordinary least squares and test $H_0 : \alpha = 0$ using a t test. Failure to reject the null hypothesis will indicate that the condition in equation (8.27) is not satisfied and that there is a potential endogeneity problem.

This simple regression-based test of endogeneity may be illustrated by returning to the risk-return trade-off application estimated in Section 8.2. The first step is to regress

h_t, the proxy for the conditional variance given by the appropriately scaled VIX Index, on the instrumental variable, in this case its own lag, giving

$$h_t = \underset{(0.0000)}{0.0000} + \underset{(0.0032)}{0.9705} \, h_{t-1} + \widehat{e}_t,$$

in which $\widehat{e}_t$ are the ordinary least squares residuals. The second stage regression yields

$$r_t = \underset{(0.0002)}{-0.0003} + \underset{(0.6869)}{3.0190} \, h_t - \underset{(2.8475)}{218.802} \, \widehat{e}_t + \widehat{\eta}_t.$$

The test statistic is now constructed as

$$t = -\frac{218.802}{2.8475} = -76.84,$$

which gives a p value of 0.000. The null hypothesis of no endogeneity is easily rejected, a result that validates the use of instrumental variables to estimate the risk-return relationship.

This test is known as the Durbin–Wu–Hausman test after the three people who developed its original versions (Durbin, 1954; Wu, 1973; Hausman, 1978). It is readily extended to the case of multiple instruments and multiple endogenous variables. All that is required is that multiple estimated residual terms be included in the regression in Step 2 and each of these are tested separately for a zero coefficient. Another of the advantages of the auxiliary regression based test of endogeneity is that it can be used when the disturbances in the original regression model in equation (8.12) are not identically and independently distributed. In this situation, the t test used to test zero restrictions in Step 2 should be based on robust estimates of the standard errors.

8.5 WEAK INSTRUMENTS

One of the two conditions required for z_t to be a valid instrument of x_t is that the two variables indeed be correlated. This condition is made explicit using the reduced form equation (8.26) where correlation between z_t and x_t requires the condition $\pi_1 \neq 0$. If this condition is not satisfied and $\pi_1 = 0$, the link between the two variables is broken, so the instrument z_t carries no information about the endogenous regressor x_t. In this situation, the instrumental variables estimator of θ breaks down as it now provides no information on the unknown parameters of the true model.[2]

This discussion suggests two extreme situations—one where z_t is a good instrument with $\pi_1 \neq 0$ and one where it is a bad instrument with $\pi_1 = 0$. However, there is an important intermediate case where the instrument does exhibit some correlation with x_t so $\pi_1 \neq 0$, but this correlation is relatively low. In this situation, the instrument z_t is referred to as a weak instrument. In particular, it has been shown—for example, by Bound, Jaeger, and Baker (1995), and Staiger and Stock (1997)—that the weak-instruments problem can arise even when the correlations between endogenous regressors and the instruments are significant at conventional levels (5% or 1%) and the sample size is large. The main

---

[2] When T is large, $\text{var}(\sqrt{T}\widehat{\theta}_{IV}) \approx \sigma_u^2/(\rho_{xz}^2 \sigma_x^2)$. Hence, if $\rho_{xz} \to 0$ and the relevance condition fails (so there is no relationship between the two variables), the variance of the instrumental variables estimator of $\sqrt{T}\,\theta$ approaches infinity as $T \to \infty$.

implication of using weak instruments to estimate θ is that the distribution of the instrumental variables estimator is no longer asymptotically normal.

8.5.1 Illustrating the Effect of Weak Instruments

The problem posed by weak instruments is easy to demonstrate by simulation. Consider the simple model

$$
\begin{aligned}
y_t &= \beta x_t + v_t & \text{[Structural equation]} \\
x_t &= \pi z_t + e_t, & \text{[Reduced form equation]}
\end{aligned} \tag{8.29}
$$

in which y_t and x_t are endogenous variables, z_t is an exogenous variable, and

$$
\begin{bmatrix} v_t \\ e_t \end{bmatrix} \sim iid \left(\begin{bmatrix} 0 \\ 0 \end{bmatrix}, \begin{bmatrix} \sigma_v^2 & \sigma_{ve} \\ \sigma_{ve} & \sigma_e^2 \end{bmatrix} \right).
$$

The instrumental variables estimator of β is

$$
\widehat{\beta}_{IV} = \frac{\widehat{\text{cov}}\left(y_t, z_t\right)}{\widehat{\text{cov}}\left(x_t, z_t\right)},
$$

and if $\widehat{\text{cov}}(x_t, z_t)$ is relatively small, the denominator is nearly zero. The sampling distribution of $\widehat{\beta}_{IV}$ and its t statistic are now poorly approximated by a normal distribution even asymptotically.[3] The intuition is that small changes in $\widehat{\text{cov}}(x_t, z_t)$ from one sample to the next can induce big changes in $\widehat{\beta}_{IV}$. It follows that, when the instruments are weak, the usual methods of inference are potentially unreliable.

The parameter π in equation (8.29) controls the strength of the instrument. A value of $\pi = 0$ means that there is no correlation between x_t and z_t, in which case z_t is not a valid instrument. It is, in fact, irrelevant. The weak instrument problem occurs when the value of π is "small" relative to σ_e^2, the variance of e_t. To highlight the properties of the instrumental variables estimator of β in the presence of a weak instrument, let the parameters of the model in equation (8.29) be $\beta = 0$, $\pi = 0.25$, and

$$
\begin{bmatrix} v_t \\ e_t \end{bmatrix} \sim iid\, N \left(\begin{bmatrix} 0 \\ 0 \end{bmatrix}, \begin{bmatrix} 1 & 0.99 \\ 0.99 & 1 \end{bmatrix} \right).
$$

The sampling distributions of the least squares and instrumental variable estimators of β, computed by Monte Carlo methods for a sample of size $T = 5$ with $10,000$ replications, are shown in Figure 8.3. The sampling distribution of $\widehat{\beta}_{IV}$ is far from being normal or centered on the true value of $\beta = 0$, despite the fact that $\pi \neq 0$. In fact, the sampling distribution is bimodal with neither of the two modes being located near the true value of β.[4]

---

[3] In fact, under certain conditions, the asymptotic distribution of $\widehat{\beta}_{IV}$ and its t statistic as $T \to \infty$ correspond after a simple reparameterization to the finite sample distributions (Phillips, 1989). The upshot is that, with poor instrumentation, the outcome is as if there were no longer an infinite sample of data.

[4] Bimodality in the distribution of the instrumental variables estimator is a common occurrence, especially when there is strong endogeneity in the regressor, as in the present case where $\text{cov}(v_t, e_t) = 0.99$ (Phillips, 2006).

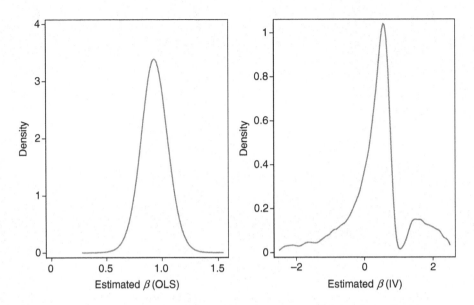

FIGURE 8.3 Sampling distributions of the ordinary least squares (left-hand panel) and instrumental variables (right-hand panel) estimators in the presence of a weak instrument where the true population parameter is $\beta = 0$.

As the quality of the instrument improves in terms of its relevance (here represented by higher values of π), the sampling distribution of the instrumental variables estimator approaches normality with its mean located at the true value of $\beta = 0$. The distribution of the ordinary least squares estimator is biased away from the true parameter value, but it is well behaved in the sense of being unimodal. In fact, the exact finite sample distributions of ordinary least squares and instrumental variables estimators belong to the same family (Phillips, 1980) and they become identical when the number of instruments uses up all the degrees of freedom in the sample.[5] Staiger and Stock (1997) show that in the worst case scenario, weak instruments can result in the bias of the instrumental variables estimator being the same as the bias of the ordinary least squares estimator.

8.5.2 Tests for Weak Instruments
Define the reduced form equation for x_t as

$$x_t = \pi_0 + \pi_1 z_t + \pi_1 w_t + e_t, \qquad (8.30)$$

in which x_t is the endogenous explanatory variable, z_t is an instrument, and w_t is a further exogenous variable that may be included in the structural equation of interest and that appears in the reduced form equation (8.30) for x_t. A natural test of weak instruments is based on using an F test of the joint restrictions

---

[5] The equivalence arises because, in this case, the fitted values that are used to construct instruments are identical to the variables.

$$H_0 : \pi_1 = \pi_1 = 0 \qquad \text{[Weak instruments]}$$
$$H_1 : \text{at least one restriction fails.} \quad \text{[Good instruments]} \tag{8.31}$$

This testing framework is easily extended to the case of $N = 1$ endogenous regressor, L instruments, and K exogenous regressors. To allow for N endogenous regressors, the weak instrument test is based on a joint test of the quality of all possible instruments for the full set of endogenous regressors. These tests are known as reduced rank tests and are a multivariate analogue of the F test. They are available in most econometric software packages.

Implementing these tests for weak instrumentation requires setting critical values for the rejection of H_0. The issue is complicated by the fact (shown in Staiger and Stock, 1997), that weak instruments may still be present even if the hypothesis is rejected at conventional significance levels. A popular rule of thumb is to reject the null hypothesis of weak instruments if the F statistic is greater than 10, a critical value well in excess of the value required by conventional significance levels. Even this rule may not be sufficiently strict and alternative critical values are provided by Stock and Yogo (2005).

8.5.3 Robust Inference in the Structural Equation

Consider the following simple model with $N = 1$ endogenous regressor x_t, $K = 1$ included exogenous regressor w_t, and $L = 1$ instrument z_t:

$$y_t = \beta_0 + \beta_1 x_t + \phi_1 w_t + v_t,$$
$$x_t = \pi_0 + \pi_1 z_t + \pi_2 w_t + e_t. \tag{8.32}$$

Suppose that z_t is a valid instrument for x_t in the sense that it satisfies the orthogonality condition and in the reduced form regression $\pi_1 \neq 0$ even though its value may be small so that weakness in this instrument is not precluded. It turns out that it may still be possible to conduct robust testing and inference on the parameter β_1 in the structural equation notwithstanding the presence of a weak instrument.

Substituting for x_t in the structural equation yields the reduced form equation for y_t given by

$$y_t = \tilde{\pi}_0 + \tilde{\pi}_1 z_t + \tilde{\pi}_2 w_t + \tilde{e}_t, \tag{8.33}$$

with

$$\tilde{\pi}_0 = \beta_0 + \beta_1 \pi_0, \qquad \tilde{\pi}_1 = \beta_1 \pi_1, \qquad \tilde{\pi}_2 = \beta_1 \psi_1 + \phi_1.$$

To perform a significance test on the parameter β_1 in equation (8.32), the approach is indirect and performs a test on the reduced form parameter $\tilde{\pi}_1$ in equation (8.33) instead. This test is known as the Anderson–Rubin test (Anderson and Rubin, 1949). It is a t or F test of the null hypothesis $H_0 : \tilde{\pi}_1 = 0$, which reduces to a test of $\beta_1 = 0$ when $\pi_1 \neq 0$, a condition that applies if z_t is a valid instrument for x_t and the relevance condition is met. If the hypothesis $\tilde{\pi}_1 = 0$ cannot be rejected, then $\beta_1 = 0$ also cannot be rejected.

This test turns out to have some partial robustness to weak instruments. Weak instruments imply that π_1 is small, so that $\tilde{\pi}_1 = \beta_1 \pi_1$ is also small provided that β_1 itself is not too large. In the latter event, β_1 will diverge substantially from its value under the null hypothesis $\beta_1 = 0$. It follows that rejecting the null hypothesis of $\tilde{\pi}_1 = 0$ will be less likely in such cases where π_1 is small. In other words, while the Anderson–Rubin test remains valid in such cases, the presence of a weak instrument will typically reduce the power of this test.

A second weakness of the Anderson–Rubin test is that the dimension of $\tilde{\pi}_1$ may well exceed the dimension of β_1, perhaps substantially. Since the null hypothesis of interest concerns β_1, basing a test on an estimate of a parameter of higher dimension such as $\tilde{\pi}_1$ also typically leads to a loss of power, as discussed in Kleibergen (2002), Chernozukhov and Hansen (2008), and Phillips and Gao (2017), who present alternative formulations of this test with improved properties. Other approaches have been suggested and are surveyed in Andrews and Stock (2005).

The subject of weak instrumentation in regression continues to attract considerable interest, largely because of its relevance to empirical work where the reduced form explanatory power of potential instruments that plausibly satisfy the orthogonality condition is often much lower than is desirable.

8.6 CONSUMPTION CAPM

One of the most celebrated examples of endogeneity and weak instruments in financial econometrics is provided by asset pricing models in which asset prices are related to the consumption and savings decisions of investors. Since deferred consumption is used to finance future portfolio choices, the consumption decision is an important determinant of intertemporal asset prices. The consumption-based Capital Asset Pricing Model (C-CAPM) assumes that a representative agent chooses current and future real consumption $\{C_t, C_{t+1}, C_{t+2}, \cdots\}$ to maximize the expected utility function

$$E_t\left[\sum_{j=0}^{\infty} \delta^j U(C_{t+j})\right], \tag{8.34}$$

subject to the wealth constraint

$$W_{t+1} = (1 + R_{t+1})(W_t - C_t),$$

where $U(\cdot)$ is a utility function, W_t is wealth, R_t is the simple return on an asset (more precisely on wealth), E_t is the conditional expectations operator based on information at time t, and δ is the discount rate.

One of the first-order conditions, known as an Euler equation[6], describing the investor's optimal consumption decision is given by

$$U'(C_t) = E_t[\delta U'(C_{t+1})(1 + R_{t+1})], \tag{8.35}$$

in which the notation $U'(\cdot)$ refers to the first derivative of $U(\cdot)$. The Euler equation encapsulates the condition that the investor should consume to the point at which the marginal utility of one real dollar of current consumption is equal to the discounted

---

[6] Euler equations are named after the great Swiss mathematician Leonhard Euler who initiated the study of differential equations and introduced the concept of a mathematical function, among many other innovations in mathematics.

expected marginal utility of investing the real dollar at the current interest rate and consuming the proceeds. Dividing equation (8.35) by $U'(C_t)$ gives

$$E_t\left[\delta\frac{U'(C_{t+1})(1+R_{t+1})}{U'(C_t)}\right]=1,$$

in which the ratio $\delta U'(C_{t+1})/U'(C_t)$ is an important factor known as the stochastic discount factor.

To implement the model, a functional form for $U(C_t)$ must be specified. A form often used in empirical research is the power utility function

$$U(C_t)=\frac{C_t^{1-\gamma}-1}{1-\gamma},$$

in which γ is the relative risk aversion parameter. Utility functions are concave functions with the measure of curvature, $-U''(C_t)/U'(C_t)$ giving the degree of risk aversion. For this particular utility function

$$U'(C_t)=C_t^{-\gamma},\qquad U''(C_t)=-\gamma C_t^{-\gamma-1},\qquad -C_t\frac{U''(C_t)}{U'(C_t)}=\gamma,$$

so that this function has constant relative risk aversion, γ. Using the power utility function, the Euler equation takes the explicit form

$$E_t\left[\delta\left(\frac{C_{t+1}}{C_t}\right)^{-\gamma}(1+R_{t+1})\right]=1. \tag{8.36}$$

As it stands, the Euler equation is nonlinear in the parameters δ and γ. However, by assuming that the argument in the square brackets is distributed as a lognormal distribution, it is possible to derive a linear model that can be used to estimate the relative risk aversion parameter, γ.

Taking natural logarithms of this equation gives

$$\log E_t\left[\delta\left(\frac{C_{t+1}}{C_t}\right)^{-\gamma}(1+R_{t+1})\right]=0, \tag{8.37}$$

since $\log 1=0$. The left hand side of equation (8.37) is the logarithm of a conditional expectation that may be simplified if some additional assumptions are made, as is now explained.

Let X be lognormally distributed, then by a property of this distribution

$$\log E_t[X]=E_t[\log X]+\frac{1}{2}\text{var}_t(\log X). \tag{8.38}$$

Now define

$$X=\delta(C_{t+1}/C_t)^{-\gamma}(1+R_{t+1}), \tag{8.39}$$

so that the task becomes one of finding the relatively straightforward expressions for the two terms on the right hand side of equation (8.38), based on the assumption that X

does indeed follow a lognormal distribution. Taking the logarithm of the variable X in equation (8.39) yields

$$\log X = \log \delta - \gamma \Delta c_{t+1} + r_{t+1},\qquad(8.40)$$

in which $\Delta c_{t+1} = \log C_{t+1} - \log C_t$ and $r_{t+1} = \log(1 + R_{t+1})$. The two required terms on the right-hand side of equation (8.38) are then given by

$$E_t[\log X] = \log \delta - \gamma\, E_t[\Delta c_{t+1}] + E_t[r_{t+1}]$$
$$\mathrm{var}_t(\log X) = \gamma^2 \sigma_c^2 + \sigma_r^2 - 2\gamma\sigma_{cr},$$

with

$$\sigma_c^2 = \mathrm{var}_t(\Delta c_{t+1}), \quad \sigma_r^2 = \mathrm{var}_t(r_{t+1}), \quad \sigma_{cr} = \mathrm{cov}_t(\Delta c_{t+1}, r_{t+1}).$$

Using these results together with equation (8.38) enables equation (8.37) to be written as

$$\log \delta - \gamma\, E_t[\Delta c_{t+1}] + E_t[r_{t+1}] + \frac{1}{2}(\gamma^2 \sigma_c^2 + \sigma_r^2 - 2\gamma\sigma_{cr}) = 0.\qquad(8.41)$$

Equation (8.41) is of little help because it contains terms representing unobserved expectations. A common modeling approach is to define the following expectations generating equations

$$r_{t+1} = E_t[r_{t+1}] + u_{1\,t+1}$$
$$\Delta c_{t+1} = E_t[\Delta c_{t+1}] + u_{2\,t+1},$$

in which $u_{1\,t+t}$ and $u_{2\,t+1}$ represent errors in forming conditional expectations. Using these expressions in equation (8.41) gives a linear regression model between the log returns of an asset and the growth rate in consumption

$$r_{t+1} = \beta_0 + \beta_1 \Delta c_{t+1} + v_{t+1},\qquad(8.42)$$

where

$$\beta_0 = -\log \delta - \frac{1}{2}(\gamma^2 \sigma_c^2 + \sigma_r^2 - 2\gamma\sigma_{cr}),$$
$$\beta_1 = \gamma,$$
$$v_{t+1} = u_{1\,t+1} - \gamma u_{2\,t+1}.$$

In expression (8.42), the slope parameter is in fact the relative risk aversion coefficient, γ. The expression for the intercept term shows that β_0 is a function of a number of parameters including γ, the discount rate δ, the variance of consumption growth σ_c^2, the variance of log asset returns σ_r^2, and the covariance between the logarithm of asset returns and real consumption growth, σ_{cr}. Note that v_{t+1} is a composite error term that comprises the rational forecasting errors on both r_{t+1} and Δc_{t+1} so that $\mathrm{cov}(v_{t+1}, \Delta c_{t+1}) \neq 0$. This means that the ordinary least squares estimator of β_1 in equation (8.42) and hence the estimator of γ will be inconsistent.

As an illustration of the problems involved in estimating the risk aversion parameter in this framework, Table 8.1 provides estimates of γ based on equation (8.42) using the same data set as that used by Ferson and Harvey (1992). The data are quarterly observations from June 1947 to December 1987 on US seasonally adjusted, real nondurables,

TABLE 8.1   Estimates of the relative risk aversion parameter, γ, based on equation (8.42) using the data set of Ferson and Harvey (1992). The instruments (Inst.) are the lagged growth rate of real consumption, Δc_t, and the lagged return on a Treasury bill, tb_t.

r_{t+1}	$\hat{\gamma}_{OLS}$	p value	$\hat{\gamma}_{IV}$	p value	$\hat{\gamma}_{IV}$	p value
			Inst: Δc_t		Inst: Δc_t, tb_t	
gb_{t+1}	−0.2362	0.963	206.48	0.980	27.908	0.666
cb_{t+1}	0.1429	0.783	260.52	0.980	27.491	0.668
$d1_{t+1}$	2.2861	0.029	290.62	0.980	30.519	0.667
$d10_{t+1}$	1.2879	0.021	286.79	0.980	24.693	0.664

consumption expenditure together with real returns on four portfolios. The portfolios are the value-weighted indices of the smallest decile, $d1_{t+1}$, and the largest decile, $d10_{t+1}$, of common stocks on the New York Stock Exchange; a long-term government bond, gb_{t+1} and a long-term corporate bond, cb_{t+1}.

The ordinary least squares estimates of γ in Table 8.1 are mainly positive, as required by the underlying theory, and the estimates for the $d1$ and $d10$ portfolios are statistically significant. When instrumental variables estimation is used with lagged consumption growth, Δc_t, as the single instrument for Δc_{t+1}, the estimates increase substantially in magnitude and are not significantly different from zero. The results improve only slightly when the lagged Treasury bill rate, tb_t, is added to the instrument list. The estimates of γ now appear more realistic, but the p values continue to show that the estimates are not significant.

The problem with instrumental variables estimation in this context is that Δc_{t+1} is difficult to forecast using historical data and therefore the two instruments, Δc_t and tb_t, are most likely weak instruments. This is confirmed in the single instrument case where the R^2 and the F statistic from the first stage regression are effectively zero, indicating the presence of a severe weak instrument problem. It seems that for this data set at least, the use of instrumental variables to estimate the coefficient of relative risk aversion from the linearized Euler equation is unsatisfactory. An alternative estimation strategy for this model is investigated in Chapter 9.

8.7 ENDOGENEITY AND CORPORATE FINANCE

The problem of endogenous regressors can be particularly acute in empirical corporate finance. The question of whether or not family-owned firms perform better than other firms (Andersen and Reeb, 2003; Adams, Almeida, and Ferreira, 2009) is a typical example. On the one hand, there are a number of perfectly valid reasons why family firms may perform worse than publicly owned firms. Combining ownership and control allows shareholders to exchange profit for private rent or the extraction of private benefits from the firm. Executive management positions are limited to family, and this constricts the talent pool from which management is drawn. On the other hand, there are also strong arguments in favor of the profitability of family-owned firms. Combining ownership and control enhances monitoring and direction of the firm. Family firms may also have longer investment horizons, which will enhance investment efficiency. Against this background, theory provides no clear guidance on the sign of a family ownership variable in a regression model. Moreover, it is also unclear whether firms' performance is driven by ownership structure or whether the ownership structure is determined by the performance of the firm. For these reasons, the variables are best regarded as being jointly determined and endogenous.

Some of the problems encountered when examining endogeneity in an empirical corporate finance setting will now be illustrated using a subset of the data used in Adams et al. (2009). The data are 2254 firm-year observations over the period 1992 to 1999. The logarithm of Tobin's Q is used as a measure of firm performance,[7] which is to be explained in terms of the size of the firm (*assets*), the age of the firm (*age*), the volatility of the operating environment (*vol*) as measured by the standard deviation of the previous 60 month returns, and a dummy variable indicating whether or not the founder of the firm is also its chief executive officer (*CEO*).

Table 8.2 provides the relevant summary statistics stratified by whether or not the firm is a family-owned firm. The evidence from these descriptive statistics seems to support the hypothesis that family firms perform better than their public counterparts, with the mean of $\log Q$ for the family owned firms being larger than that for public companies.

The hypothesis may be addressed more formally by a regression model. In the application, all observations are treated as independent draws from the distribution of all US firms and the fact that there are repeated observations of the same firm in different years is ignored. Dummy variables for each of the years will be included to account for time series differences in the performance of firms. The linear regression model to be estimated is

$$\log(Q_i) = \beta_0 + \beta_1 CEO_i + \beta_2 \log(assets_i) + \beta_3 \log(age_i) + \beta_4 vol_i + v_i. \tag{8.43}$$

TABLE 8.2 Summary statistics for a subset of the data used in Adams, Almeida, and Ferreira (2009) in their study on family firms. The data are 2254 firm-year observations over the period 1992 to1999.

	log Q	log(assets)	log(age)	vol
Non-Family Firms				
Mean	0.560	8.748	3.941	0.279
SD	0.431	1.098	0.814	0.103
Max.	2.772	12.912	4.990	1.052
Min.	−0.174	5.778	0.000	0.115
Family Firms				
Mean	0.749	8.078	2.772	0.390
SD	0.577	0.879	0.747	0.121
Max.	2.953	10.271	4.304	0.810
Min.	−0.181	6.151	0.000	0.190
Total				
Mean	0.584	8.666	3.796	0.293
SD	0.456	1.095	0.893	0.112
Max.	2.953	12.912	4.990	1.052
Min.	−0.181	5.778	0.000	0.115

---

[7] Tobin's Q is the ratio of the market value of a company to the replacement cost of its assets.

A central point at issue here is whether or not the family firm variable, represented here by the binary variable, *CEO*, is endogenous. This may be tested using the Durbin–Wu–Hausman test outlined in Section 8.4 if at least one instrument for *CEO* can be found. The instrument suggested by Adams et al. (2009) is the current age of the founder (*ageF*) regardless of whether the founder works for the company or not (if there are multiple founders, the average age is used). For simplicity, the variable is measured only in 1994 but is used for the whole sample. The motivation for using this variable as an instrument stems from the fact that the age of the founder is unlikely to be driven by firm performance and this then alleviates the endogeneity problem. A possible caveat is that the variable *ageF* may very well be correlated with the age of the firm, which could have an effect on firm performance.

To test for the endogeneity of the *CEO* variable, the auxiliary regression approach is used. The two regressions required to implement the test are

$$CEO_i = \pi_0 + \pi_1 ageF_i + \pi_2 \log(assets_i) + \pi_3 \log(age_i) + \pi_4 vol_i + e_i$$

$$\log(Q_i) = \beta_0 + \beta_1 CEO_i + \beta_2 \log(assets_i) + \beta_3 \log(age_i) + \beta_4 vol_i + \beta_5 \widehat{e}_i + v_i,$$

in which $\widehat{e}_i$ are the ordinary least squares residuals from the first regression. An F test of the restriction that $\beta_5 = 0$ is $F(1, 2237) = 149.21$, with a p value of 0.000. There is therefore strong evidence of endogeneity and the use of instrumental variables estimation is indicated. The regression of the potentially endogenous regressor on the instrument and the other explanatory variables simply ignores the fact that the dependent variable of this regression, *CEO*, is in fact a binary dependent variable. For the moment, this problem is simply ignored; but an adjustment to this simple instrumental variables estimator can be constructed using estimation methods for limited dependent variables (see Chapter 16).

Table 8.3 reports the parameter estimates of the model in equation (8.43) using both ordinary least squares and instrumental variables with *ageF* used as an instrument for *CEO*. The results are unequivocal. The *CEO* coefficient is significant and positive, indicating that family-owned firms perform significantly better than their public counterparts. The large increase in the size of the coefficient on this variable when using instrumental variables, 0.895 as opposed to 0.223, is strongly suggestive of an endogeneity bias

TABLE 8.3 Ordinary least squares (OLS) and instrumental variables (IV) estimates of the model in equation (8.43). The variable *CEO* is instrumented with the mean age of the founder (*ageF*) in 1994 in the instrumental variables regression. Standard errors are in parentheses.

	OLS	IV
CEO	0.223	0.895
	(0.032)	(0.091)
log (*assets*)	−0.026	−0.017
	(0.009)	(0.009)
log (*age*)	−0.036	0.050
	(0.012)	(0.014)
vol	−0.816	−1.186
	(0.099)	(0.115)
Constant	1.127	0.732
	(0.110)	(0.118)

in the ordinary least squares estimate. In this case, it does not lead to rejection of the null hypothesis but the ordinary least squares results seriously understate the importance of this effect.

8.8 EXERCISES

The data required for the exercises are available for download as EViews workfiles (*.wfl), Stata datafiles (*.dta), comma delimited text files (*.csv), and as Excel spreadsheets (*.xlsx).

1. **Properties of the Instrumental Variables Estimator**

   This Monte Carlo experiment demonstrates the inconsistency of the ordinary least squares estimator and the efficacy of instrumental variables estimation for the errors in variables problem. Consider the simple linear model

   $$y_t = \beta_0 + \beta_1 x_t + u_t$$
   $$x_t = z_t + v_t,$$

   with $u_t \sim N(0, 1)$, $z_t \sim N(0, 1)$, $\beta_0 = 10$, and $\beta_1 = 2$.

   (a) Simulate the model for $p = \{0.2, 0.5\}$ and $T = \{50; 100; 200; 400\}$. For each of 1000 repetitions of the simulation, store the estimate of β_1 obtained by ordinary least squares and instrumental variables z_t as an instrument for x_t.

   (b) Summarize the results for the ordinary least squares estimator. What do you conclude about the consistency of ordinary least squares in this problem?

   (c) Repeat part (b) for the instrumental variables estimator. Discuss your results.

   (d) Simulate the model just once with a sample size of $T = 500$.

      (i) Estimate the model by instrumental variables.

      (ii) Estimate the model using the two-step least squares approach and compare the standard errors on the parameters to those obtained in (i). Explain why the two estimates of standard error are not the same.

2. **Risk-Return Relationship**

spvol.*

   The intertemporal CAPM is expressed as

   $$r_t = \alpha + \gamma \, \mathrm{E}_{t-1}(\sigma_t^2) + u_t,$$

   in which r_t is a return, σ_t^2 is the unobserved conditional variance of r_t, and u_t is a disturbance term. The intertemporal CAPM requires that $\alpha = 0$ and $\gamma > 0$. The model is to be estimated using daily returns on the S&P 500 Index and a proxy for the conditional variance based on the suitably scaled VIX Index for the period 2 January 1990 to 1 June 2012.

   (a) Draw a scatter plot of the relationship between daily returns, r_t, on the S&P 500 Index and the proxy for the conditional variance, h_t, based on the VIX.

(b) Estimate the risk aversion parameter γ by ordinary least squares based on the equation

$$r_t = \alpha + \gamma h_t + v_t,$$

where v_t is a disturbance term. Discuss the properties of this estimator.

(c) Now estimate γ by instrumental variables using h_{t-1} as an instrument for h_t. Discuss the results.

(d) Test for the endogeneity of h_t. What do you conclude?

3. Weak Instruments

Consider the model

$$\begin{array}{cc} y_t = \beta x_t + v_t \\ x_t = \pi z_t + e_t, \end{array} \qquad \left[\begin{array}{c} v_t \\ e_t \end{array} \right] \sim iid\,N\left(\left[\begin{array}{c} 0 \\ 0 \end{array} \right], \left[\begin{array}{cc} 1.00 & 0.99 \\ 0.99 & 1.00 \end{array} \right] \right).$$

The sample size is $T = 5$ and 10000 replications are used to generate the sampling distribution of the estimator.

(a) Generate the sampling distribution of the instrumental variables estimator for the parameter values $\beta = 0.0$ and $\pi = \{0, 0.25, 0.5, 1.0\}$. Discuss the sampling properties of the instrumental variables estimator in each case. Also compute the sampling distributions of the ordinary least squares estimator for each case.

$$\text{plim}(\widehat{\beta}_{OLS}) = \frac{\sigma_{12}}{\sigma_{22}} = 0.99.$$

(b) Repeat part (a) for samples of size $T = \{50, 500\}$. Comment on the results.

4. Consumption CAPM

ccapm.*

The data are quarterly observations from June 1947 to December 1987 on US seasonally adjusted, nondurables consumption deflated by the personal consumption deflator together with real returns on four portfolios; namely, value-weighted indices of the smallest, $d1_{t+1}$, and largest deciles, $d10_{t+1}$, common stocks on the New York Stock Exchange, a long-term government bond, gb_{t+1} and a long-term corporate bond, cb_{t+1}.

Consider the linear regression form of the C-CAPM given by

$$r_{t+1} = \beta_0 + \beta_1 \Delta c_{t+1} + v_{t+1},$$

where r_{t+1} is the return on a portfolio, Δc_{t+1} is the growth rate of consumption, and v_{t+1} is a disturbance term. In this expression, the slope parameter of the regression equation, β_1, is in fact the relative risk aversion coefficient, γ.

(a) Estimate β_1 by ordinary least squares using the returns on each of the four portfolios in the data set. What is the problem with using this estimator to compute the parameter estimates of this model?

(b) Estimate β_1 by instrumental variables using the returns on each of the four portfolios in the data set, and with the following configurations:

(i) Δc_t as an instrument for Δc_{t+1}; and

(ii) Δc_t and the lagged Treasury bill rate, tb_t as instruments for Δc_{t+1}.

Comment on the results.

(c) Perform a series of tests for weak instruments on the regressions in part (b). What do you conclude?

5. Performance of Family Firms

familyfirms.*

The data are 2254 firm-year observations over the period 1992 to 1999. The logarithm of Tobin's Q is used as a measure of firm performance, which is to be explained in terms of the size of the firm (*assets*), the age of the firm (*age*), the volatility of the operating environment (*vol*) as measured by the standard deviation of the previous 60 month returns, and a dummy variable indicating whether or not the founder of the firm is also its chief executive officer (*CEO*).

(a) Compute summary statistics for the variables in the data set stratified by whether or not the firm is family-owned. Interpret the results.

(b) Consider the linear regression

$$\log(Q_i) = \beta_0 + \beta_1 CEO_i + \beta_2 \log(assets_i) + \beta_3 \log(age_i) + \beta_4 vol_i + v_i,$$

where v_i is a disturbance term. Test whether the family firm variable, *CEO*, is endogenous or not using the age of the founder, *ageF*, as an instrument.

(c) Irrespective of your results in part (b), estimate the equation by ordinary least squares and instrumental variables using *ageF* as the instrument for *CEO*. Compare and contrast the results.

CHAPTER 9

Generalized Method
of Moments

As seen in Chapter 8, the instrumental variables approach is a powerful method of dealing with the presence of endogenous explanatory variables in regression. The approach was developed originally for the estimation of linear equations. But the idea extends to more complex models. The most important extension of the methodology is to generalized method of moments (GMM) estimation.

GMM estimation is a flexible mechanism for estimating parameters in a broad range of models in finance. Akin to the instrumental variables approach, which relies heavily on the relevance and orthogonality of the instruments, GMM has its genesis in the presence of orthogonality conditions that embody some of the fundamental properties of an underlying behavioral model. The class of GMM estimators nests many other statistical procedures, including ordinary least squares, instrumental variables, method of moments estimation, and under certain conditions even maximum likelihood estimation, which is another general approach to estimation that is presented in Chapter 10.

The main requirement for using GMM is that the model, or certain aspects of the model, be expressed in terms of population moments. An important and useful feature of the GMM approach is that it is not necessary to prescribe the form of the distributions that give rise to the moment expressions. Only the moment equalities (or in even more general cases, moment inequalities) need to be specified. This requirement is satisfied by most, if not all, models in finance. Included within this compass are the capital asset pricing model, models that are represented by the first-order conditions of an intertemporal dynamic optimization problem such as the consumption based capital asset pricing model, the Black–Scholes option pricing model, latent factor models, short-term interest rates models, and models of trade durations, among many others.

The GMM approach was introduced by Lars Hansen (1982) who shared the 2013 Nobel Prize in Economics for this contribution to the study of financial economics.[1] The method's generality quickly led to its extensive adoption as a tool of empirical estimation in both economics and finance. Its use is now widespread throughout these disciplines

---

[1] The other recipients of the 2013 Nobel Prize in Economics were Robert Shiller and Eugene Fama.

and continues to be developed. In implementing GMM in financial model applications, it is helpful to distinguish cases where analytical solutions are available, such as in instrumental variable estimation, and cases where numerical solutions are needed. The latter fall under the more general category of extremum estimation problems.

9.1 SINGLE PARAMETER MODELS

This section deals with financial models where there is a single unknown parameter that needs to be estimated from the data. An important feature of the models considered here is that they are characterized by one population moment and one unknown parameter. This matching of the number of moments and parameters represents the GMM version of a just-identified situation in instrumental variables estimation where the number of instruments is the same as the number of endogenous regressors that these variables are instrumenting.

9.1.1 Present Value Model

To motivate the GMM estimator in the single parameter case, consider the present value model where the price of an asset P_t is equated to the discounted flow of future dividend payments D_t, with constant discount rate δ

$$P_t = E_t \sum_{i=1}^{\infty} \frac{D_{t+i}}{(1+\delta)^i}, \tag{9.1}$$

where E_t is the conditional expectations operator based on information available at time t.

Consider the monthly data on US equity prices and dividends for the period January 1871 to September 2016, used extensively in Part I of the book. The aim is to estimate the unknown discount rate δ in equation (9.1) implied by the data on P_t and D_t. Assuming that dividend payments follow a random walk, the conditional expectations of future dividend payments are given by

$$E_t D_{t+i} = D_t, \qquad i \geq 0. \tag{9.2}$$

Using the condition in equation (9.1) and rearranging the equation simplifies the present value relationship to

$$P_t = \frac{D_t}{\delta}, \tag{9.3}$$

or to

$$\frac{D_t}{P_t} = \delta. \tag{9.4}$$

This expression shows that the present value model is characterized by the equilibrium condition that the dividend-price ratio at time t, that is, the dividend yield at time t, equals the discount parameter δ.

To derive the GMM estimator of $\theta = \{\delta\}$, equation (9.4) is re-expressed in terms of a moment relation m_t according to the specification

$$m_t = \frac{D_t}{P_t} - \theta. \tag{9.5}$$

A plot of m_t at each t with the unknown parameter chosen as $\theta = 0.05$ is given in Figure 9.1.

To derive the GMM estimator of θ for the present value model, consider taking the sample average of m_t in equation (9.5)

$$\overline{m}_T(\theta) = \frac{1}{T}\sum_{t=1}^{T} m_t. \tag{9.6}$$

The GMM estimator $\widehat{\theta}$ in this case is the solution of the following simple equation

$$\overline{m}_T(\theta) = 0, \tag{9.7}$$

which sets the sample moment to zero. Substituting the moment expression (9.5) in equation (9.7) shows that the GMM estimator is determined by solving

$$\overline{m}_T(\widehat{\theta}) = \frac{1}{T}\sum_{t=1}^{T}\left(\frac{D_t}{P_t} - \widehat{\theta}\right) = 0. \tag{9.8}$$

Upon rearranging this expression, the GMM estimator is

$$\widehat{\theta} = \frac{1}{T}\sum_{t=1}^{T}\frac{D_t}{P_t}, \tag{9.9}$$

which is the sample mean of the dividend yields over the sample period. Using the US price and dividend data for January 1871 to September 2016 gives a GMM estimate of the discount parameter of $\widehat{\theta} = \widehat{\delta} = 0.0438$, or 4.4% per annum.

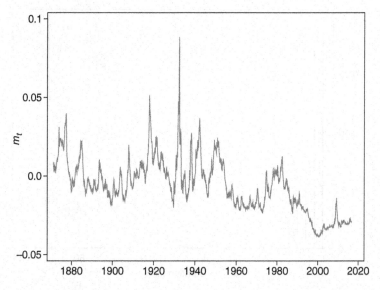

FIGURE 9.1 Time series plot of the GMM moment, m_t, for the present value model in equation (9.5) with $\theta = 0.05$. The data are US price and dividend data for the period January 1871 to September 2016.

9.1.2 Model of Trade Durations

As an alternative class of financial models, consider the following model of durations between trades, y_t, based on the exponential distribution

$$f(y_t; \theta) = \frac{1}{\gamma} \exp\left(-\frac{y_t}{\gamma}\right), \tag{9.10}$$

where γ is an unknown parameter. Figure 9.2 gives the empirical distribution of the time between trades (in seconds) for American Airlines (AMR) on 1 August 2006 from 09:30 to 16:00. The empirical distribution provides support for the choice of an exponential distribution as it is positively skewed with a peak at the shortest duration of 1 second.

A property of the exponential distribution in equation (9.10) is that the population mean of durations is

$$E(y_t) = \gamma. \tag{9.11}$$

Letting $\theta = \{\gamma\}$ represent the unknown parameter, this suggests that the GMM moment relation may be defined as

$$m_t = y_t - \theta. \tag{9.12}$$

This moment is plotted in Figure 9.3 for the case where $\theta = 10$.

To find the GMM estimator of θ the condition in equation (9.7) is used, which shows that the estimator is determined by solving

$$\overline{m}_T(\widehat{\theta}) = \frac{1}{T} \sum_{t=1}^{T} (y_t - \widehat{\theta}) = 0. \tag{9.13}$$

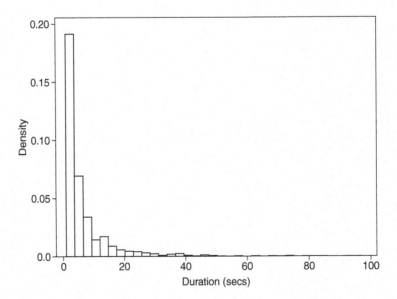

FIGURE 9.2 Time between trades (in seconds) for American Airlines (AMR) on 1 August 2006 from 09:30 to 16:00, based on a total of 3643 durations.

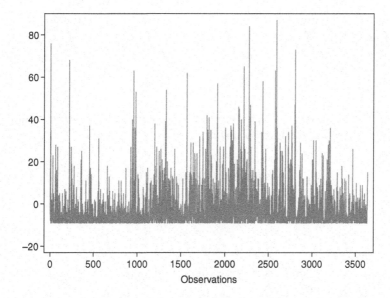

FIGURE 9.3 A time series plot of the GMM moment equation for the time between trades (in seconds) in equation (9.10) using $\theta = 10$. The data are for American Airlines (AMR) on 1 August 2006 from 09:30 to 16:00 and there are 3643 durations.

The GMM solution is the sample mean of the observed durations

$$\widehat{\theta} = \frac{1}{T} \sum_{t=1}^{T} y_t = \bar{y},$$ (9.14)

which, for the AMR trade durations, yields an estimate of $\widehat{\theta} = \widehat{\gamma} = 6.421$, indicating that on this trading day there were approximately 6 seconds between trades.

9.2 MULTIPLE PARAMETER MODELS

This simple GMM framework is extended to financial models with more than a single unknown parameter and where the model is represented by a number of moment conditions that just matches the number of unknown parameters—the just-identified case again. Let the number of unknown parameters be K so θ is a $(K \times 1)$ vector. As there are K moments, then m_t is a $(K \times 1)$ vector given by

$$m_t = \begin{bmatrix} m_{1t} \\ m_{2t} \\ \vdots \\ m_{Kt} \end{bmatrix},$$ (9.15)

where m_{it} represents the ith moment relation at time t. Correspondingly, the GMM condition in equation (9.7) is a $(K \times 1)$ vector, which is given by

$$\overline{m}_T(\theta) = \frac{1}{T} \sum_{t=1}^{T} m_t(\theta), \tag{9.16}$$

where $\overline{m}(\theta)$ is now a $(K \times 1)$ vector of sample moments. For this class of models, the GMM estimator of θ is obtained by solving for $\widehat{\theta}$

$$\overline{m}_T(\widehat{\theta}) = \frac{1}{T} \sum_{t=1}^{T} m_t(\widehat{\theta}) = 0, \tag{9.17}$$

which is a set of K simultaneous equations in the K elements of $\widehat{\theta}$.

9.2.1 CAPM

Consider the CAPM where y_t is the excess return on an asset, and x_t is the excess return on the market portfolio

$$y_t = \alpha + \beta x_t + u_t, \qquad u_t \sim iid(0, \sigma^2). \tag{9.18}$$

The unknown parameters are $\theta = \{\alpha, \beta, \sigma\}$, where α is a measure of abnormal returns, β represents the β-risk of the asset, and σ is the standard deviation of the disturbances that measures the idiosyncratic risk of the asset. The CAPM is a linear regression model— see Chapter 3—which can be estimated by ordinary least squares. For the ordinary least squares estimator to have desirable properties, the linear regression model needs to satisfy the following three population moment conditions:

$$E(u_t) = 0, \qquad E(u_t x_t) = 0, \text{ and } \qquad E(u_t^2) = \sigma^2. \tag{9.19}$$

The first condition is that the mean of the idiosyncratic term u_t is zero. The second condition is that the excess return on the market given by x_t needs to be uncorrelated with the idiosyncratic risk term u_t. The third and final condition is that the variance of the idiosyncratic risk is constant and equals σ^2.

The three population moments in equation (9.19) suggest the following GMM moment relations

$$\begin{aligned} m_{1t} &= u_t - 0, \\ m_{2t} &= u_t x_t - 0, \\ m_{3t} &= u_t^2 - \sigma^2. \end{aligned} \tag{9.20}$$

As $u_t = y_t - \alpha - \beta x_t$, the vector of moments m_t in equation (9.15) is the following (3×1) vector,

$$m_t = \begin{bmatrix} m_{1t} \\ m_{2t} \\ m_{3t} \end{bmatrix} = \begin{bmatrix} y_t - \alpha - \beta x_t \\ (y_t - \alpha - \beta x_t) x_t \\ (y_t - \alpha - \beta x_t)^2 - \sigma^2 \end{bmatrix}. \tag{9.21}$$

Using the GMM moment condition in equation (9.17), the GMM estimator $\widehat{\theta} = \{\widehat{\beta_0}, \widehat{\beta_1}, \widehat{\sigma}^2\}$ is obtained by solving the following (3×1) system of equations:

$$\overline{m}_T(\widehat{\theta}) = \frac{1}{T} \sum_{t=1}^{T} \begin{bmatrix} y_t - \widehat{\alpha} - \widehat{\beta} x_t \\ (y_t - \widehat{\alpha} - \widehat{\beta} x_t) x_t \\ (y_t - \widehat{\alpha} - \widehat{\beta} x_t)^2 - \widehat{\sigma}^2 \end{bmatrix} = \begin{bmatrix} 0 \\ 0 \\ 0 \end{bmatrix}. \tag{9.22}$$

The resulting GMM estimators are

$$\widehat{\beta} = \frac{\sum_{t=1}^{T} (x_t - \overline{x})(y_t - \overline{y})}{\sum_{t=1}^{T} (x_t - \overline{x})^2},$$

$$\widehat{\alpha} = \overline{y} - \widehat{\beta}\overline{x}, \tag{9.23}$$

$$\widehat{\sigma}^2 = \frac{1}{T} \sum_{t=1}^{T} (y_t - \widehat{\alpha} - \widehat{\beta} x_t)^2,$$

which are equivalent to the solutions obtained for the ordinary least squares estimator of the CAPM in Chapter 3. This result is important since it shows the equivalence of the GMM and ordinary least squares estimators not just for the CAPM but for all linear regression models satisfying the population moment properties in equation (9.19).

Data on the excess returns for Exxon, y_t, and the market, x_t, are given in Figure 9.4 for the period May 1990 to July 2004. The GMM estimates are computed using equation (9.23), with the result that

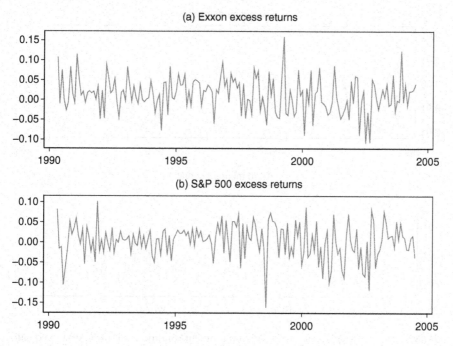

FIGURE 9.4 Monthly excess returns on Exxon (a) and the S&P 500 (b) for the period May 1990 to July 2004.

$$\widehat{\theta} = \{\widehat{\alpha}, \widehat{\beta}, \widehat{\sigma}\} = \{0.012, 0.502, 0.038\}. \tag{9.24}$$

The three GMM moment equations in equation (9.21), evaluated at the GMM parameter estimates $\widehat{\theta}$ in equation (9.24), are plotted in Figure 9.5. The sample means of m_{1t}, m_{2t}, and m_{3t} are by construction

$$\overline{m}_1 = \frac{1}{T}\sum_{t=1}^{T} m_{1t}(\widehat{\theta}) = 0, \qquad \overline{m}_2 = \frac{1}{T}\sum_{t=1}^{T} m_{2t}(\widehat{\theta}) = 0, \qquad \overline{m}_3 = \frac{1}{T}\sum_{t=1}^{T} m_{3t}(\widehat{\theta}) = 0.$$

The bivariate CAPM can also be extended to allow for multiple factors, as was done in Chapter 3, in which case the model is represented as a multiple linear regression model.

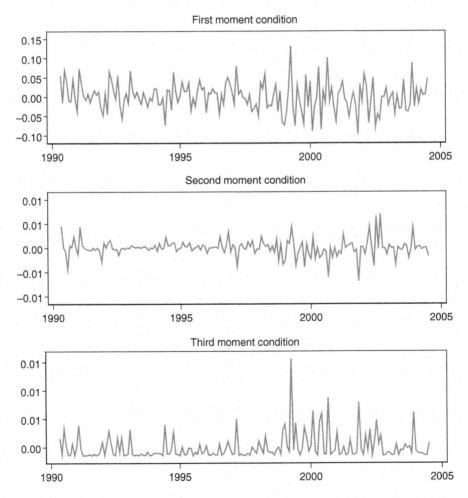

FIGURE 9.5 Time series plots of the three GMM moment conditions for the CAPM in equation (9.21) using monthly excess returns on Exxon and the S&P 500 Market Index for the period May 1990 to July 2004. The moments are evaluated at the GMM parameter estimates $\widehat{\theta}$.

9.2.2 A Gamma Model of Asset Prices

Table 9.1 provides annual prices for General Electric over the period 1991 to 2003. Also given are the second uncentered moment of prices, P_t^2 and the price reciprocal, $1/P_t$. As the price of General Electric shares is constrained to be positive, the specified price model is chosen to be the gamma distribution

$$f(P_t; \theta) = \frac{\beta^\alpha}{\Gamma(\alpha)} P_t^{\alpha-1} \exp(-\beta P_t), \qquad P_t > 0, \tag{9.25}$$

with $\theta = \{\alpha, \beta\}$ as the unknown parameters that satisfy the properties $\alpha, \beta > 0$. The parameter α is known as the shape parameter and β is known as the rate parameter. The function $\Gamma(\alpha)$ is the gamma function, which is defined by the integral

$$\Gamma(\alpha) = \int_0^\infty s^{\alpha-1} e^{-s} ds.$$

The first two population moments of the gamma distribution are

$$E(P_t) = \frac{\alpha}{\beta}, \qquad E(P_t^2) = \frac{\alpha(\alpha+1)}{\beta^2}. \tag{9.26}$$

This suggests that the GMM estimator of θ may be based on simple moment equations involving the centered quantities

$$\begin{aligned} m_{1t} &= P_t - \frac{\alpha}{\beta} \\ m_{2t} &= P_t^2 - \frac{\alpha(\alpha+1)}{\beta^2}. \end{aligned} \tag{9.27}$$

TABLE 9.1 Average annual stock price of General Electric, P_t, for the years 1991 to 2003.

Year	P_t	P_t^2	P_t^{-1}
1991	1.12	1.2544	0.8928
1992	1.76	3.0976	0.5681
1993	3.07	9.4249	0.3257
1994	4.30	18.4900	0.2325
1995	6.29	39.5641	0.1589
1996	10.52	110.6704	0.0950
1997	16.88	284.9344	0.0592
1998	24.44	597.3136	0.0409
1999	34.55	1193.7020	0.0289
2000	47.27	2234.4530	0.0211
2002	40.03	1602.4010	0.0249
2002	29.07	845.0649	0.0344
2003	27.31	745.8361	0.0366
Average:	18.97	591.2467	0.1938

Using equation (9.17), the GMM estimator $\widehat{\theta} = \{\widehat{\alpha}, \widehat{\beta}\}$ is the solution of

$$\overline{m}_T(\widehat{\theta}) = \frac{1}{T} \sum_{t=1}^{T} \begin{bmatrix} P_t - \dfrac{\widehat{\alpha}}{\widehat{\beta}} \\[2mm] P_t^2 - \dfrac{\widehat{\alpha}(\widehat{\alpha}+1)}{\widehat{\beta}^2} \end{bmatrix} = \begin{bmatrix} 0 \\ 0 \end{bmatrix}, \tag{9.28}$$

and solving for $\widehat{\theta}$ yields

$$\widehat{\alpha} = \frac{\left(T^{-1}\sum_{t=1}^{T} P_t\right)^2}{T^{-1}\sum_{t=1}^{T} P_t^2 - \left(T^{-1}\sum_{t=1}^{T} P_t\right)^2}, \quad \widehat{\beta} = \frac{T^{-1}\sum_{t=1}^{T} P_t}{T^{-1}\sum_{t=1}^{T} P_t^2 - \left(T^{-1}\sum_{t=1}^{T} P_t\right)^2}.$$

Calculating with the sample moments of the data in Table 9.1 gives the estimates

$$\widehat{\alpha} = \frac{18.97^2}{591.2467 - 18.97^2} = 1.5552, \quad \widehat{\beta} = \frac{18.97}{591.2467 - 18.97^2} = 0.0820. \tag{9.29}$$

The estimate of the shape parameter $\widehat{\alpha} = 1.5552 > 1$ implies that the price distribution is hump-shaped with positive skewness.

The population moments of the gamma distribution given in equation (9.26) are not the only moments of the gamma distribution. Another population moment is given by

$$E\left[\frac{1}{P_t}\right] - \frac{\beta}{\alpha - 1} = 0. \tag{9.30}$$

If this population moment is used with the first population moment in equation (9.26), then (just-identified) GMM estimates may also be based on the two centered quantities

$$\begin{aligned} m_{1t} &= P_t - \frac{\alpha}{\beta} \\[2mm] m_{2t} &= \frac{1}{P_t} - \frac{\beta}{\alpha - 1}. \end{aligned} \tag{9.31}$$

In this case, the estimates $\widehat{\theta} = \{\widehat{\alpha}, \widehat{\beta}\}$ are obtained by using equation (9.17) to solve

$$\overline{m}_T(\widehat{\theta}) = \frac{1}{T} \sum_{t=1}^{T} \begin{bmatrix} P_t - \dfrac{\widehat{\alpha}}{\widehat{\beta}} \\[2mm] \dfrac{1}{P_t} - \dfrac{\widehat{\beta}}{\widehat{\alpha} - 1} \end{bmatrix} = \begin{bmatrix} 0 \\ 0 \end{bmatrix}, \tag{9.32}$$

which yields the solutions

$$\widehat{\alpha} = \frac{T^{-1}\sum_{t=1}^{T} P_t}{T^{-1}\sum_{t=1}^{T} P_t - \left(T^{-1}\sum_{t=1}^{T} 1/P_t\right)^{-1}}, \quad \widehat{\beta} = \frac{\widehat{\alpha}}{T^{-1}\sum_{t=1}^{T} P_t}.$$

Using the data in Table 9.1, the GMM estimates are

$$\widehat{\alpha} = \frac{18.97}{18.97 - 0.1938^{-1}} = 1.3736, \quad \widehat{\beta} = \frac{1.3736}{18.97} = 0.0724. \tag{9.33}$$

A comparison of the gamma distribution parameter estimates in equations (9.29) and (9.33) shows that the estimates are clearly not unique. In fact, a third set of GMM estimates could be obtained by using another combination of two population moments.

Choosing different moments to estimate the unknown parameters uses different summary information in the data and this leads to different estimates. The outcome is analogous to using different instruments for an endogenous regressor in the instrumental variable procedure. This type of indeterminacy is a characteristic of both GMM and IV estimation, and it raises the question of which moment information is more reliable in estimating the parameter vector θ. In the present example, the question may be translated into identifying the moments of the centered quantities m_t that are more important in modeling the price distribution. A useful general solution to this problem is to avoid making a specific choice of a subset of m_t but to use all of its elements and to rely on the data to weight their relative importance. To do so, it is necessary to construct a criterion for finding a GMM estimator that embodies the relative importance of the different moments. One way of achieving this is to weight the elements of m_t in terms of their precision in estimating the parameters of the price distribution.

9.3 OVERIDENTIFIED MODELS

The estimators discussed so far in this chapter are obtained using a system of equations where the number of moment equations used in estimation matches the number of unknown parameters. A more general situation was illustrated in the gamma asset price model where there were two unknown parameters and three population moments. Taking the moments two at a time led to different (just-identified) parameter estimates depending on the moments selected for estimation. Combining all three moments results in a system with more equations than unknown parameters, a model property that is called overidentification.[2] This section extends the principle of GMM estimation for just-identified models based on equation (9.17) to overidentified models where there are N moment equations and K unknown parameters. The degree of overidentification in this case is measured by the difference $N - K > 0$.

GMM estimation of overidentified models employs all the moment relations, weighting each of them so that the moments with greatest precision are accorded the most influence. To motivate the approach consider the trade durations model studied in Section 9.1.2 where $N = 2$ population moments given by the mean and the variance

$$E(y_t) = \gamma, \qquad \text{var}(y_t) = \gamma^2, \tag{9.34}$$

---

[2] Models where the number of moment equations is less than the number of parameters are referred to as underidentified models. In such cases, there is insufficient information to identify all of the unknown parameters, although some parameters may still be identified. This chapter focuses on financial models that are either just-identified or overidentified.

are employed, each depending on the single unknown parameter γ. Letting $\theta = \{\gamma\}$ be the ($K = 1$) unknown parameter, so that the corresponding moment relations are

$$
\begin{aligned}
m_{1t} &= y_t - \theta \\
m_{2t} &= (y_t - \theta)^2 - \theta^2,
\end{aligned}
\tag{9.35}
$$

leading to the sample moment vector

$$
\bar{m}_T(\theta) = \frac{1}{T} \sum_{t=1}^{T} m_t = \frac{1}{T} \sum_{t=1}^{T} \left[\begin{array}{c} y_t - \theta \\ (y_t - \theta)^2 - \theta^2 \end{array} \right] = \left[\begin{array}{c} \bar{y} - \theta \\ s^2(\theta) - \theta^2 \end{array} \right],
\tag{9.36}
$$

where

$$
\bar{y} = \frac{1}{T} \sum_{t=1}^{T} y_t, \qquad s^2(\theta) = \frac{1}{T} \sum_{t=1}^{T} (y_t - \theta)^2.
\tag{9.37}
$$

The estimators considered so far require finding $\widehat{\theta}$ by solving the moment condition in equation (9.17). For the trade durations model, this would involve solving the simultaneous system

$$
\left[\begin{array}{c} \bar{y} - \widehat{\theta} \\ s^2 - \widehat{\theta}^2 \end{array} \right] = \left[\begin{array}{c} 0 \\ 0 \end{array} \right].
\tag{9.38}
$$

Even if the true distribution were exponential and the population moments in equation (9.34) were indeed the correct moments, the condition in equation (9.38) requires that $\widehat{\theta} = \bar{y} = s$ holds exactly, which places a restriction on the data that the sample mean and sample standard deviation be the same, an event that has probability zero.

In such overidentified models, the GMM approach is to combine the moments into a single criterion for estimation that has a well-defined unique solution. The method of combining the moment equations formally involves weighting the individual moment conditions and constructing an extremum estimation criterion that embodies these weighted moments.

9.3.1 Choosing the Weights

Each element of the moment relation m_t plays a role in identifying the unknown parameters of θ. Some moments are inevitably more informative than others with regard to particular elements of θ, thereby utilizing the data more effectively and producing greater precision in estimating these parameters. A natural approach is to assign weights for the relative importance of each moment according to the variances of the elements of m_t. Moments with smaller variances display greater precision and are therefore assigned greater weight in computing the GMM estimator.

Diagonal Weights

Let $W_T(\theta)$ be a diagonal weight matrix constructed from the variances, var(m_{it}), of the individual moment relations m_{it}. Since these variances each depend on θ, the weight matrix has the following general form,

$$W_T(\theta) = \begin{bmatrix} \text{var}(m_{1t}) & 0 & \cdots & 0 \\ 0 & \text{var}(m_{2t}) & \cdots & 0 \\ \vdots & \vdots & \ddots & \vdots \\ 0 & 0 & \cdots & \text{var}(m_{Nt}) \end{bmatrix}. \tag{9.39}$$

Evaluating this matrix at the GMM estimator $\widehat{\theta}$, gives

$$W_T(\widehat{\theta}) = \begin{bmatrix} \text{var}(m_{1t}) & 0 & \cdots & 0 \\ 0 & \text{var}(m_{2t}) & \cdots & 0 \\ \vdots & \vdots & \ddots & \vdots \\ 0 & 0 & \cdots & \text{var}(m_{Nt}) \end{bmatrix}. \tag{9.40}$$

Prior to estimation the parameter θ is, of course, unknown. As discussed below, preliminary estimates of θ may be used based on a specific setting of the weight matrix, such as the identity matrix $W_T = I_N$ that ascribes equal weights to each moment. The resulting estimates may then be used to construct a weight matrix of the form in equation (9.40).

For the CAPM model in Section 9.2.1, there are three parameters $\theta = \{\alpha, \beta, \sigma^2\}$ with respective moment relations

$$m_t = \begin{bmatrix} m_{1t} \\ m_{2t} \\ m_{3t} \end{bmatrix} = \begin{bmatrix} y_t - \alpha - \beta x_t \\ (y_t - \alpha - \beta x_t) x_t \\ (y_t - \alpha - \beta x_t)^2 - \sigma^2 \end{bmatrix}, \tag{9.41}$$

where y_t is the monthly excess return on Exxon, and x_t is the monthly excess return on the market based on the S&P 500 stock index. Using the GMM parameter estimates of $\widehat{\theta}$ given in equation (9.24), the sample variances of the GMM moment equations are

$$\text{var}(m_{1t}) = \frac{1}{T}\sum_{t=1}^{T} m_{1t}^2 = \frac{1}{T}\sum_{t=1}^{T}(y_t - \widehat{\alpha} - \widehat{\beta}x_t)^2 = 0.001456$$

$$\text{var}(m_{2t}) = \frac{1}{T}\sum_{t=1}^{T} m_{2t}^2 = \frac{1}{T}\sum_{t=1}^{T}((y_t - \widehat{\alpha} - \widehat{\beta}x_t)x_t)^2 = 3.15 \times 10^{-6} \tag{9.42}$$

$$\text{var}(m_{3t}) = \frac{1}{T}\sum_{t=1}^{T} m_{3t}^2 = \frac{1}{T}\sum_{t=1}^{T}((y_t - \widehat{\alpha} - \widehat{\beta}x_t)^2 - \widehat{\sigma}^2)^2 = 5.22 \times 10^{-6}.$$

Using the variance estimates in equation (9.42) for the CAPM model, $W_T(\widehat{\theta})$ is computed as

$$W_T(\widehat{\theta}) = \begin{bmatrix} 0.001456 & 0 & 0 \\ 0 & 3.15 \times 10^{-6} & 0 \\ 0 & 0 & 5.22 \times 10^{-6} \end{bmatrix}.$$

Covariance Weights: Heteroskedasticity

The diagonal form of the weight matrix in equation (9.39) focuses just on the variances, but in general there are covariances among the moments that can also be taken into account in weighting moments. For this more general case, the weight matrix is defined as

$$W_T(\theta) = \begin{bmatrix} \text{var}(m_{1t}) & \text{cov}(m_{1t}, m_{2t}) & \cdots & \text{cov}(m_{1t}, m_{Nt}) \\ \text{cov}(m_{2t}, m_{1t}) & \text{var}(m_{2t}) & \cdots & \text{cov}(m_{2t}, m_{Nt}) \\ \vdots & \vdots & \ddots & \vdots \\ \text{cov}(m_{Nt}, m_{1t}) & \text{cov}(m_{Nt}, m_{2t}) & \cdots & \text{var}(m_{Nt}) \end{bmatrix}$$

$$= \frac{1}{T} \sum_{t=1}^{T} \begin{bmatrix} m_{1t}^2 & m_{1t}m_{2t} & \cdots & m_{1t}m_{Nt} \\ m_{2t}m_{1t} & m_{2t}^2 & \cdots & m_{2t}m_{Nt} \\ \vdots & \vdots & \ddots & \vdots \\ m_{Nt}m_{1t} & m_{Nt}m_{2t} & \cdots & m_{Nt}^2 \end{bmatrix}$$

$$= \frac{1}{T} \sum_{t=1}^{T} m_t m_t'. \tag{9.43}$$

The weight matrix evaluated at the GMM parameter estimates of the CAPM model is computed as the (3×3) matrix

$$W_T(\widehat{\theta}) = \begin{bmatrix} 0.001456 & 6.47 \times 10^{-6} & 9.33 \times 10^{-6} \\ 6.47 \times 10^{-6} & 3.15 \times 10^{-6} & 3.65 \times 10^{-8} \\ 9.33 \times 10^{-6} & 3.65 \times 10^{-8} & 5.22 \times 10^{-6} \end{bmatrix}.$$

Covariance Weights: Heteroskedasticity and Autocorrelation

The form of the weight matrix in equation (9.43) takes account of contemporaneous but not temporal correlation of the moments. To allow for autocorrelation in m_t, the weight matrix may be defined as

$$W_T(\theta) = \frac{1}{T} \sum_{t=1}^{T} m_t m_t' + \sum_{i=1}^{P} w_i \left(\frac{1}{T} \sum_{t=i+1}^{T} \left(m_t m_{t-i}' + m_{t-i} m_t' \right) \right). \tag{9.44}$$

The first term on the right-hand side represents the heteroskedastic weighting matrix given in equation (9.43). The second term allows for autocorrelations of length P in the moment relations. The factors w_i that appear in the second term of equation (9.44) are themselves weights that control the contributions from autocorrelation at each lag i. These weights are prescribed in a manner that leads to a positive definite weight matrix $W_T(\theta)$. A common choice of the weights in econometric work follows the triangular decay system

$$w_i = 1 - \frac{i}{P+1}, \qquad i = 1, 2, \cdots, P, \tag{9.45}$$

known as Bartlett or Newey–West weights, although other choices exist. These weights have the effect of dampening the contributions of autocorrelations on $W_T(\theta)$ from longer lags. In the special case where there is no autocorrelation

$$w_1 = w_2 = \cdots = w_P = 0, \tag{9.46}$$

the weight matrix in equation (9.44) reverts to equation (9.43).

For instance, if there is autocorrelation of order 2, so that $P = 2$, the corresponding weight matrix has explicit form

$$W_T(\theta) = \frac{1}{T} \sum_{t=1}^{T} m_t m_t' + w_1 \left(\frac{1}{T} \sum_{t=2}^{T} (m_t m_{t-1}' + m_{t-1} m_t') \right)$$

$$+ w_2 \left(\frac{1}{T} \sum_{t=3}^{T} (m_t m_{t-2}' + m_{t-2} m_t') \right), \tag{9.47}$$

with weights chosen as

$$w_1 = 1 - \frac{1}{3} = \frac{2}{3}, \qquad w_2 = 1 - \frac{2}{3} = \frac{1}{3}.$$

The choice of the maximum lag P can be determined by theory in some cases where the value of P follows directly from the properties of the model. An example is given by models of forward market efficiency where an overlapping data problem arises in which the expectations horizon has a different frequency from the observation interval of the data (see Martin, Hurn, and Harris, 2013). If there are no helpful guidelines from theory, an alternative approach is to choose P according to a statistical criterion such as

$$P = \text{int} \left[4 \left(\frac{T}{100} \right)^{2/9} \right], \tag{9.48}$$

where $[\cdot]$ denotes the smallest integer of the term in brackets. This rule is based on asymptotic arguments and has been found to perform well in Monte Carlo simulations.

9.3.2 Objective Function

A general formulation of the GMM principle of estimation makes use of an objective function that embodies a vector of relevant moments and a system of weights. The objective function is a quadratic form in the moments, with the matrix of this form given by a weight matrix constructed according to the various formulations defined above. The GMM estimator is then the solution that minimizes the following weighted quadratic form

$$\widehat{\theta} = \arg\min_{\theta} Q_T(\theta), \tag{9.49}$$

where

$$Q_T(\theta) = \overline{m}_T(\theta)' W_T^{-1} \overline{m}_T(\theta), \tag{9.50}$$

and θ is the $(K \times 1)$ vector of unknown parameters. The $(N \times 1)$ vector of sample moments, $\overline{m}_T(\theta)$, is

$$\overline{m}_T(\theta) = \frac{1}{T} \sum_{t=1}^{T} m_t, \tag{9.51}$$

while $W_T = W_T(\theta)$ is an $(N \times N)$ weight matrix that measures the precision of each moment in m_t.

The GMM estimator satisfies first-order conditions for optimization of equation (9.49), which are obtained by matrix differentiation, giving

$$G_T(\theta) = \frac{\partial Q_T}{\partial \theta} = 2D_T(\theta)'W_T^{-1}\overline{m}_T(\theta), \qquad (9.52)$$

where

$$D_T(\theta) = \frac{\partial \overline{m}_T(\theta)}{\partial \theta'}, \qquad (9.53)$$

is an $(N \times K)$ matrix of derivatives of the GMM moment function $\overline{m}_T(\theta)$, and where the weight matrix W_T is treated here as given and not dependent on θ, although possibly dependent on the sample size T. The GMM estimator $\widehat{\theta}$ satisfies the equation obtained by setting the gradient in equation (9.52) to zero at $\theta = \widehat{\theta}$, that is,

$$D_T(\widehat{\theta})'W_T^{-1}\overline{m}_T(\widehat{\theta}) = 0. \qquad (9.54)$$

Equation (9.54) is a nonlinear set of K equations in $\widehat{\theta}$ and requires numerical methods to find the solution.

The dimension of the first-order system in equation (9.54) is K as $D_T(\widehat{\theta})'$ is a $(K \times N)$ matrix, which combines with the $(N \times N)$ weight matrix W_T and the $(N \times 1)$ vector $\overline{m}_T(\widehat{\theta})$ to yield a $(K \times 1)$ vector, which matches the number of unknown parameters in θ. Thus, use of the objective function in equation (9.50) reduces the dimension of the overidentified system of equations in equation (9.51) where $\overline{m}_T(\widehat{\theta})$ is an $(N \times 1)$ vector involving the estimate $\widehat{\theta}$ of K unknown parameters. The weight matrix W_T plays a key role in this reduction to a system of K equations in K unknowns, which makes the system analogous to a just-identified model. The new system of K equations is constructed from the initial $N > K$ equations by using what is, in effect, a weighted sum of the original moment relations m_t.

To see this formally, consider the trade durations model where the sample moments are given by equation (9.37). To derive the GMM estimator using equation (9.54), the following terms are needed

$$\overline{m}_T(\widehat{\theta}) = \begin{bmatrix} \overline{m}_1 \\ \overline{m}_2 \end{bmatrix} = \begin{bmatrix} \overline{y} - \widehat{\theta} \\ s^2(\widehat{\theta}) - \widehat{\theta}^2 \end{bmatrix}, \qquad (9.55)$$

and

$$D_T(\theta) = \frac{\partial \overline{m}_T(\theta)}{\partial \theta'} = \frac{\partial}{\partial \theta'}\begin{bmatrix} \overline{y} - \theta \\ s^2(\theta) - \theta^2 \end{bmatrix} = \begin{bmatrix} -1 \\ -2(\overline{y} - \theta) - 2\theta \end{bmatrix}, \qquad (9.56)$$

as $\partial s^2(\theta)/\partial \theta = -2(\overline{y} - \theta)$, which, upon evaluation at $\widehat{\theta}$, leads to

$$D_T(\widehat{\theta}) = \begin{bmatrix} -1 \\ -2\overline{y} \end{bmatrix}. \qquad (9.57)$$

Substituting equations (9.55) and (9.57) in equation (9.54) and using a diagonal weighting matrix, the GMM estimator is the solution of the following equation from the first-order condition

$$D_T(\widehat{\theta})'W_T^{-1}\overline{m}_T(\widehat{\theta}) = \begin{bmatrix} -1 \\ -2\overline{y} \end{bmatrix}' \begin{bmatrix} \mathrm{var}(m_{1t}) & 0 \\ 0 & \mathrm{var}(m_{2t}) \end{bmatrix}^{-1} \begin{bmatrix} \overline{y}-\widehat{\theta} \\ s^2-\widehat{\theta}^2 \end{bmatrix}$$

$$= -\frac{(\overline{y}-\widehat{\theta})}{\mathrm{var}(m_{1t})} - \frac{2\overline{y}(s^2-\widehat{\theta}^2)}{\mathrm{var}(m_{2t})} = 0. \tag{9.58}$$

This expression shows that the GMM criterion compresses the two moment conditions into a single equation by taking a weighted average of these two moment conditions, with the weights based on the corresponding elements of the weight matrix. In effect, the overidentified model of two equations and one unknown parameter is converted into a just-identified model with one equation and one unknown parameter by using the variances of the respective moments m_{1t} and m_{2t} to produce a weighted average of these moments.

Explicit expressions of the weights in equation (9.58), as given by $\mathrm{var}(m_{1t})$ and $\mathrm{var}(m_{2t})$, are obtained for the durations model by evaluating these variances at a preliminary estimate of θ. Such an estimate might be obtained by using the objective criterion in equation (9.49) with equal weights and the diagonal weight matrix $W_T = I_N$, leading to $\widetilde{\theta}$. The resulting expressions are

$$\mathrm{var}(m_{1t}) = \frac{1}{T}\sum_{t=1}^{T} m_{1t}^2 = \frac{1}{T}\sum_{t=1}^{T}(y_t-\widetilde{\theta})^2 = s^2$$

$$\mathrm{var}(m_{2t}) = \frac{1}{T}\sum_{t=1}^{T} m_{2t}^2 = \frac{1}{T}\sum_{t=1}^{T}\left((y_t-\widetilde{\theta})^2 - \widetilde{\theta}^2\right)^2. \tag{9.59}$$

The first weight represents the sample variance of y_t evaluated at $\widetilde{\theta}$, whereas the second weight represents the fourth moment or the kurtosis coefficient of y_t, again evaluated at $\widetilde{\theta}$. Inspection of equation (9.58) shows that the smaller the sample variance of y_t, the greater the weight placed on the first moment m_{1t} relative to the second moment m_{2t} in the estimation of θ.

9.4 ESTIMATION

To compute GMM estimates numerically using the criterion in equation (9.49), it is necessary to use an iterative numerical algorithm. In fact, numerical methods are generally needed in just-identified cases as well because the moment equations often involve nonlinear functions of the unknown parameters.

To shed light on the features of an iterative GMM estimation algorithm, consider the weighted moment equation (9.58) corresponding to the trade durations model. Let the starting parameter value in the iteration be

$$\theta_{(0)} = \gamma_{(0)} = 0.0.$$

Using this value in the GMM moment relations in equation (9.35) gives

$$m_{1t} = y_t - \theta_{(0)} = y_t$$
$$m_{2t} = (y_t - \theta_{(0)})^2 - \theta_{(0)}^2 = y_t^2.$$

Then, from equation (9.35), setting $\theta = \theta_{(0)} = 0$ gives

$$\overline{m}_T(\theta_{(0)}) = \begin{bmatrix} \overline{m}_1 \\ \overline{m}_2 \end{bmatrix} = \frac{1}{T} \sum_{t=1}^{T} \begin{bmatrix} y_t - \theta_{(0)} \\ (y_t - \theta_{(0)})^2 - \theta_{(0)}^2 \end{bmatrix} = \begin{bmatrix} 6.421 \\ 120.521 \end{bmatrix}.$$

Also from equation (9.59), the variance weights are

$$\text{var}(m_{1t}) = \frac{1}{T} \sum_{t=1}^{T} (y_t - \theta_{(0)})^2 = \frac{1}{T} \sum_{t=1}^{T} y_t^2 = 79.316$$

$$\text{var}(m_{2t}) = \frac{1}{T} \sum_{t=1}^{T} \left((y_t - \theta_{(0)})^2 - \theta_{(0)}^2 \right)^2 = \frac{1}{T} \sum_{t=1}^{T} y_t^2 = 215289.795,$$

leading to the diagonal weight matrix

$$W_T(\theta_{(0)}) = \begin{bmatrix} \text{var}(m_{1t}) & 0 \\ 0 & \text{var}(m_{2t}) \end{bmatrix} = \begin{bmatrix} 79.316 & 0 \\ 0 & 215289.795 \end{bmatrix},$$

based on the starting value for θ. Finally, from equation (9.57)

$$D_T(\theta_{(0)}) = \begin{bmatrix} -1 \\ -2\overline{y} \end{bmatrix} = \begin{bmatrix} -1 \\ -2 \times 6.4208 \end{bmatrix} = \begin{bmatrix} -1 \\ -12.8416 \end{bmatrix}.$$

Using all of these terms in the gradient function in equation (9.52) gives

$$G(\theta_{(0)}) = 2D_T(\theta_{(0)})' W_T^{-1} \overline{m}_T(\theta_{(0)})$$

$$= 2 \begin{bmatrix} -1 \\ -12.8416 \end{bmatrix}' \begin{bmatrix} 79.316 & 0 \\ 0 & 215289.795 \end{bmatrix}^{-1} \begin{bmatrix} 6.421 \\ 120.521 \end{bmatrix}$$

$$= -0.1763.$$

Since the gradient is negative, increases in the θ value will lower the value of the objective criterion. Thus, the starting value $\theta_{(0)} = 0$ is below the GMM estimate $\widehat{\theta}$ that minimizes the objective function in equation (9.49), which suggests performing the same calculations for a larger trial value of θ. Table 9.2 summarizes the calculations for $\theta_{(0)} = 0$ and a grid of possible values of θ based on increasing trial values of θ in steps of unity.

TABLE 9.2   GMM parameter estimates of the overidentified trade durations model based on a grid search algorithm, using the moments in equation (9.35) and a diagonal weighting matrix.

θ	$\overline{m}_1$	$\overline{m}_2$	var(m_{1t})	var(m_{2t})	G
0	6.421	120.521	79.316	215289.795	−0.176
1	5.421	107.680	79.316	201174.616	−0.148
2	4.421	94.838	79.316	187693.968	−0.120
3	3.421	81.996	79.316	174847.850	−0.093
4	2.421	69.155	79.316	162636.263	−0.065
5	1.421	56.313	79.316	151059.205	−0.038
6	0.421	43.472	79.316	140116.678	−0.011
7	−0.579	30.630	79.316	129808.681	0.015
8	−1.579	17.788	79.316	120135.215	0.041
9	−2.579	4.947	79.316	111096.278	0.065
10	−3.579	−7.895	79.316	102691.872	0.089

Increasing the parameter value in the next step to $\theta_{(1)} = 1$ shows that the gradient is now smaller, suggesting that the updated value is closer to $\widehat{\theta}$. Examining the results for all the trial values of θ reveals that $\widehat{\theta}$ falls within the range of θ given by the interval $[6, 7]$. In this interval, the gradient changes sign from negative to positive, suggesting by continuity that the solution value will lie within this interval by virtue of continuity. This range of values happens also to be consistent with the estimate of $\widehat{\theta} = 6.421$ that uses only the moment condition m_t in equation (9.12).

Values of the gradient function for θ in the interval $[0, 10]$ are shown in Figure 9.6. The gradient function rises over this interval, crossing zero at the estimated value $\widehat{\theta} = 6.421$ and continuing to rise for higher values of θ. This behavior of the gradient function shows that the extremum objective function is nonlinear over this range of θ, reaching a minimum value at the estimate $\widehat{\theta} = 6.421$.

The estimation method outlined above for the trade durations model provides a fairly crude updating method based on the sign of the gradient with the step lengths arbitrarily chosen to be equal to unity. More computationally efficient procedures exist that make use of both the first and second derivatives of equation (9.49) to provide optimal step lengths. Appendix D provides a discussion of some of the more well-known numerical optimization algorithms. When applying these algorithms to solve the extremum problem in equation (9.49), some choices are available that depend on how the weight matrix $W_T(\theta)$ is treated during the iterations. Four of the most commonly adopted methods are summarized below.

1. One-step estimator

The one-step GMM estimator, which is denoted as $\widehat{\theta}_{(1)}$, involves setting $W_T(\theta)$ equal to the identity matrix I_N in the objective criterion equation (9.49), giving

$$\widehat{\theta}_{(1)} = \arg\min_{\theta} \overline{m}_T(\theta)' \overline{m}_T(\theta). \tag{9.60}$$

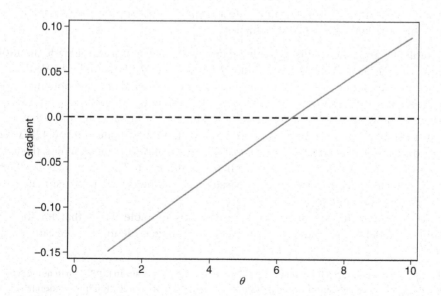

FIGURE 9.6 The gradient function for the overidentified trade duration model.

While convenient for implementation, the one-step estimator suffers a lack of precision stemming from the fact that informative and less informative moment conditions are given equal weight in the GMM criterion function $Q_T(\theta)$.

2. **Two-step estimator**

An improvement over the one-step approach is to first compute $\widehat{\theta}_{(1)}$ and then utilize this estimate to compute the fitted covariance matrix of the moment conditions, $W_T(\widehat{\theta}_{(1)})$. The two-step GMM estimator is obtained by using $W_T(\widehat{\theta}_{(1)})^{-1}$ as the weight matrix in the criterion function. The resultant parameter estimates are denoted $\widehat{\theta}_{(2)}$ and satisfy

$$\widehat{\theta}_{(2)} = \arg\min_{\theta} \overline{m}_T(\theta)' W_T(\widehat{\theta}_{(1)})^{-1} \overline{m}_T(\theta). \tag{9.61}$$

3. **Iterative estimator**

A natural extension of the two-step estimator is to further update the weight matrix using $W_T(\widehat{\theta}_{(2)})^{-1}$ and to compute the GMM estimator with this weight matrix in the criterion function. This process gives rise to a sequence of estimators, commonly referred to as the iterative estimator, of the form

$$\widehat{\theta}_{(j+1)} = \arg\min_{\theta} \overline{m}_T(\theta)' W_T(\widehat{\theta}_{(j)})^{-1} \overline{m}_T(\theta), \tag{9.62}$$

for $j = 1, 2, \cdots$. The iteration can be continued until the estimators and the weight matrix converge within some assigned level of tolerance.

4. **Continuous updating estimator**

Rather than switching between the separate estimation of θ and $W_T(\theta)$, an alternative strategy is to estimate them jointly using

$$\widehat{\theta} = \arg\min_{\theta} \overline{m}_T(\theta)' W_T(\theta)^{-1} \overline{m}_T(\theta). \tag{9.63}$$

This method is referred to as the continuous updating estimator or CUE. Hansen, Heaton, and Yaron (1996) provide a useful comparison on the performance of these variants of the GMM estimator.[3]

Table 9.3 gives the results of applying the iterated estimator to the trade durations model in equation (9.35) based on a full weight matrix that allows for heteroskedasticty. The point estimate is $\widehat{\theta} = 5.683$, which is slightly smaller than that obtained using the diagonal weighting matrix given in Table 9.2, where the estimate was found to lie within the range of $\theta = \{6, 7\}$. Also given in Table 9.3 is the GMM estimate based on the just-identified model using m_{1t} as the moment. This estimate is $\widehat{\theta} = 6.421$, which from equation (9.14) corresponds to the sample mean of y_t. For completeness, the GMM estimate based on use of the single moment m_{2t} is also given. This estimate is $\widehat{\theta} = 9.385$, which is much higher than the estimate based on m_{1t} alone as well as the estimate based on joint use of m_{1t} and m_{2t}.

An important feature of the numerical results in Table 9.3 is that for the just-identified model based on the moment m_{1t}, the estimate is identical to the earlier result

---

[3] The original idea behind CUE estimation goes back to early work by Durbin (1988) on iterating versions of three-stage least squares and instrumental variables methods to deliver the full information maximum likelihood estimator in simultaneous equations models.

TABLE 9.3 GMM parameter estimates of the trade durations model using the iterated estimator. The moments are based on equation (9.35) and a heteroskedastic weighting matrix.

Moments	Estimate	Std. Err.	t stat.	p value	Q	J = TQ
m_{1t}, m_{2t}	5.683	0.113	50.26	0.000	0.016	59.647
m_{1t}	6.421	0.148	43.52	0.000	0.000	0.000
m_{2t}	9.385	0.424	22.16	0.000	0.000	0.000

following from equation (9.14) where the weighting matrix W_T was not used to compute the GMM estimate. This result illustrates the point that for the just-identified model with $N = K$, the GMM estimator $\widehat{\theta}$ is independent of W_T. This property is explained by the first-order condition in equation (9.54). Under just-identification, the matrices $D_T(\widehat{\theta})'$ and W_T are both $(K \times K)$, so that $D_T(\widehat{\theta})' W_T^{-1}$ is a $(K \times K)$ nonsingular matrix. The first-order condition therefore reduces to $\overline{m}_T(\widehat{\theta}) = 0$, which is the GMM solution for the just-identified model.

This property of an exactly identified model is evident in Table 9.3 where the value of the GMM objective function $Q_T(\theta)$ is zero for the two just-identified cases because $\overline{m}_T(\widehat{\theta}) = 0$ must hold. However, for the overidentified model in Table 9.2, the value of the objective function is $Q_T(\widehat{\theta}) = 0.01642$, indicating that $\overline{m}_T(\widehat{\theta}) \neq 0$ in this case.

9.5 PROPERTIES OF THE GMM ESTIMATOR

In extremum estimation problems such as equation (9.49) where the criterion is being optimized with respect to the parameter vector θ, it is convenient to use a special notation to distinguish the true value of the parameter. In the present case, the true value of the parameter is denoted θ_0. The properties of the GMM estimator $\widehat{\theta}$ may then be examined in relation to this true value θ_0. As seen earlier, GMM estimation typically involves nonlinear optimization methods, and therefore no explicit formula for the estimator $\widehat{\theta}$ is available. Moreover, with few exceptions, the known properties of the estimator $\widehat{\theta}$ are based on large sample asymptotics where $T \to \infty$. These properties have been developed under certain conditions that are assumed to apply to the primary ingredients of the model, namely, the objective function $Q_T(\theta)$, the moment functions $\overline{m}_T(\theta)$, and the data on which these quantities depend.

The conditions under which the asymptotic theory is developed are generally known as regularity conditions. These conditions impose regular features on the components of the model that may be expected to hold for certain wide classes of models and data. For instance, assumptions of stationarity in the data or prescribed forms of heterogeneity may be imposed; the required population moment functions will be required to exist and be finite; the functions may be assumed to be continuously differentiable to the second order; and upon suitable normalization, the objective function may be assumed to have a well-defined limit function whose (typically convex) shape assists in identifying the true parameter vector θ_0, which is usually assumed to lie in the interior of a compact parameter space.

Regularity conditions are often stated at a high level of generality, and additional, more specific conditions are required to justify them in terms of the specific components of the model. The following discussion does not go into those technical details, which are readily available in advanced references on GMM estimation such as Hall (2005). Instead, we simply outline the impact that these conditions have on the asymptotic properties of the GMM estimator $\widehat{\theta}$ of θ_0 as the sample size $T \to \infty$.

Population Moments

Let $E[m_t(\theta)]$ represent the GMM population moment, which under stationarity and provided the moment exists, will be a well-defined function of θ. The relationship between this population moment and sample moments relies on the operation of a law of large numbers, which ensures that the sample mean of $m_t(\theta)$ approaches the population mean as $T \to \infty$, namely,

$$\overline{m}_T(\theta) = \frac{1}{T}\sum_{t=1}^{T} m_t(\theta) \xrightarrow{p} E[m_t(\theta)], \tag{9.64}$$

where $\xrightarrow{p}$ represents convergence in probability. The convergence property in equation (9.64) holds under a wide variety of more fundamental conditions on the data and the form of the function m_t (Hansen, 1982).

Similar asymptotic behavior applies to the objective function in equation (9.50), which is a quadratic function of $\overline{m}_T(\theta)$. The regularity conditions established by Hansen (1982) ensure the related convergence property

$$Q_T(\theta) = \overline{m}_T(\theta)' W_T^{-1} \overline{m}_T(\theta) \xrightarrow{p} Q(\theta). \tag{9.65}$$

Another important property of the population moment $E[m_t(\theta)]$ is that evaluation at the true parameter value θ_0 gives

$$E[m_t(\theta_0)] = 0. \tag{9.66}$$

It follows from equations (9.64) and (9.66) that the function $Q(\theta)$ has an identifiable minimum at θ_0, and in view of the zero value of equation (9.66)

$$Q(\theta_0) = 0. \tag{9.67}$$

Comparison of equation (9.66) and the GMM condition in equation (9.17) reveals that the latter represents the sample analogue of the former, but with θ_0 replaced by the estimator $\widehat{\theta}$. This relationship is suggestive of one of the key properties of the GMM estimator $\widehat{\theta}$.

Consistency

If the model is correctly specified and the sample moments $\overline{m}_T(\theta)$ accurately reflect the population model in the sense that equations (9.64) and (9.65) hold, a further technical argument[4] reveals that

$$\widehat{\theta} = \arg\min_{\theta} Q_T(\theta) \xrightarrow{p} \arg\min_{\theta} Q(\theta) = \theta_0, \tag{9.68}$$

---

[4] The argument relies on the argmax continuous mapping theorem (see Van der Vaart and Wellner, 1996), which gives conditions under which the argmin and argmax functionals are continuous and ensures the result stated in equation (9.68).

showing that

$$\text{plim}(\widehat{\theta}) = \theta_0, \tag{9.69}$$

and the GMM estimator $\widehat{\theta}$ is a consistent estimator of θ_0. Hence, in large samples, the GMM estimator $\widehat{\theta}$ is expected to be well-centered on the population parameter θ_0. The consistency property does not depend on the specific choice of the weight matrix $W_T(\theta)$, provided only that this matrix is positive definite in the limit and equation (9.68) holds. For this reason, the one-step GMM estimator in equation (9.60) where the weight matrix $W_T = I_N$ is employed still delivers a consistent estimator of θ_0.

A simple illustration of consistency in a practical case is given in Figure 9.7 where the GMM estimator $\widehat{\theta}$ is shown to approach the true population parameter $\theta_0 = 10$, with the realized fluctuations between $\widehat{\theta}$ and θ_0 steadily decreasing as T increases.

Asymptotic Efficiency

The asymptotic covariance matrix of $\widehat{\theta}$ has the form

$$\Omega_T = \left[D_T(\theta_0)' W_T(\theta_0)^{-1} D_T(\theta_0) \right]^{-1}, \tag{9.70}$$

where

$$D_T(\theta_0) = \frac{1}{T} \sum_{t=1}^{T} \left. \frac{\partial m_t(\theta)}{\partial \theta'} \right|_{\theta=\theta_0} \tag{9.71}$$

is the $(N \times K)$ matrix of first derivatives of the moment conditions with respect to the parameters evaluated at the population parameter vector θ_0. $W_T(\theta_0)$ is the weight matrix evaluated at θ_0 and is the sample covariance matrix of the chosen moments m_t, namely,

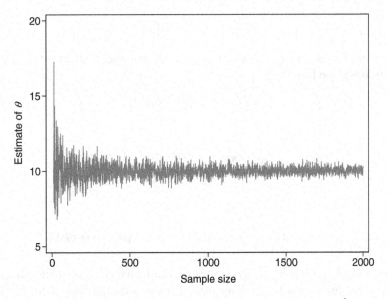

FIGURE 9.7 Demonstration of the consistency property of the GMM estimator $\widehat{\theta}$. The population distribution is exponential, with true parameter $\theta_0 = 10$, and the GMM estimator is the sample mean.

$$W_T(\theta_0) = \frac{1}{T} \sum_{t=1}^{T} m_t(\theta_0) m_t'(\theta_0). \tag{9.72}$$

Under certain conditions, this choice of weight matrix is asymptotically optimal in the sense that it delivers, at least in large samples, the smallest covariance matrix based on the given set of moments m_t. That is, compared to a covariance matrix Ω_T^* that is based on any other weight matrix, the difference $\Omega_T^* - \Omega_T$ is a positive semi-definite matrix (Hansen, 1982).

When interpreting this form of asymptotic efficiency it is important to remember that it is restricted to the given set of moments in m_t. Changing this set of moments will result in a different asymptotically efficient GMM estimator. Moreover, as the two-step, iterative and continuous GMM estimators in equations (9.61) to (9.63) use the weight matrix in the updating schemes, these estimators are consistent and asymptotically efficient compared with the one-step estimator in equation (9.60), which is consistent but not asymptotically efficient, as it is not based on the optimal weight matrix. This relation may be exhibited formally as

$$\text{var}(\widehat{\theta}_{(1)}) > \{\text{var}(\widehat{\theta}_{(2)}), \text{var}(\widehat{\theta}_{(j+1)}), \text{var}(\widehat{\theta})\}. \tag{9.73}$$

In terms of asymptotic behavior, the two-step, iterative, and continuous estimators are all equivalent. The potential gains from adopting the iterative and continuous estimators are that these estimators often tend to exhibit better small sample properties than the two-step estimator.

Asymptotic Normality
The asymptotic distribution of the GMM estimator is

$$\sqrt{T}\left(\widehat{\theta} - \theta_0\right) \xrightarrow{d} N(0, \Omega), \tag{9.74}$$

where $\xrightarrow{d}$ denotes convergence in distribution. The covariance matrix Ω of the asymptotic distribution is given by

$$\Omega = \left[D(\theta_0)' W(\theta_0)^{-1} D(\theta_0)\right]^{-1}, \tag{9.75}$$

where

$$D(\theta_0) = \plim_{T \to \infty} \frac{1}{T} \sum_{t=1}^{T} \frac{\partial m_t(\theta)}{\partial \theta'} \bigg|_{\theta=\theta_0} = E\left[\frac{\partial m_t(\theta_0)}{\partial \theta'}\right], \tag{9.76}$$

and

$$W_T(\theta_0) = \plim_{T \to \infty} \frac{1}{T} \sum_{t=1}^{T} m_t(\theta_0) m_t(\theta_0)' = E[m_t(\theta_0) m_t(\theta_0)']. \tag{9.77}$$

These results follow from regularity conditions on the data and moment functions that permit the operation of a law of large numbers and a central limit theorem (Hansen, 1982).

Figure 9.8 provides a demonstration of asymptotic normality that gives the sampling distributions of the one-step and two-step estimators. This figure also reveals the asymptotic efficiency of the two-step estimator over the one-step estimator given in equation (9.73), with the former clearly exhibiting a smaller variance.

An important practical implication of the asymptotic normality of the GMM estimator is that hypothesis tests may be conducted with p values based on the (asymptotic) normal distribution. To perform hypothesis tests in applications the covariance matrix of $\widehat{\theta}$ needs to be estimated. This is achieved by replacing the unknown population parameter θ_0 by the GMM estimator $\widehat{\theta}$, yielding

$$\mathrm{var}(\widehat{\theta}) = \frac{1}{T}\left[D_T(\widehat{\theta})'W_T(\widehat{\theta})^{-1}D_T(\widehat{\theta})\right]^{-1}. \tag{9.78}$$

Standard errors are computed as the square roots of the diagonal elements of $\mathrm{var}(\widehat{\theta})$. For the trade durations model, the pertinent standard errors are reported in Table 9.3.

Relationships to Other Estimators
The GMM estimator nests a number of well-known estimators used in empirical finance. It has already been shown that the GMM estimator is equivalent to the ordinary least squares estimator of the linear regression model in the context of the capital asset pricing model for the case where the population moments are given by equation (9.19). The GMM estimator also nests the instrumental variables estimator, which was discussed in Chapter 8.

To demonstrate this point, consider the following moment equations

$$\mathrm{E}(u_t) = 0, \qquad \mathrm{E}(u_t z_t) = 0, \qquad \mathrm{E}(u_t^2) = \sigma^2, \tag{9.79}$$

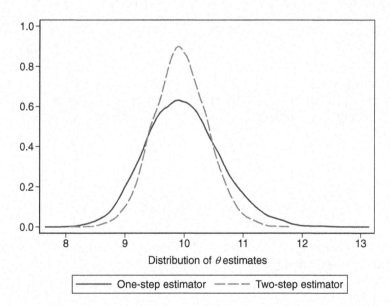

Distribution of θ estimates

———— One-step estimator   — — — Two-step estimator

FIGURE 9.8 Demonstration of the asymptotic normality property of the GMM estimator $\widehat{\theta}$. The population distribution is an exponential distribution with true parameter value $\theta_0 = 10$. The distributions of the one-step and two-step GMM estimators are computed from samples of size 500 using 10000 replications.

where u_t is a disturbance term and z_t is the instrument. For the CAPM, these GMM moment equations are

$$m_t = \begin{bmatrix} m_{1t} \\ m_{2t} \\ m_{3t} \end{bmatrix} = \begin{bmatrix} y_t - \alpha - \beta x_t \\ (y_t - \alpha - \beta x_t)z_t \\ (y_t - \alpha - \beta x_t)^2 - \sigma^2 \end{bmatrix}, \qquad (9.80)$$

and the GMM estimator is the solution of the following system of equations

$$\overline{m}_t(\widehat{\theta}) = \frac{1}{T}\sum_{t=1}^{T} \begin{bmatrix} y_t - \widehat{\beta}_0 - \widehat{\beta}_1 x_t \\ (y_t - \widehat{\beta}_0 - \widehat{\beta}_1 x_t)z_t \\ (y_t - \widehat{\beta}_0 - \widehat{\beta}_1 x_t)^2 - \widehat{\sigma}^2 \end{bmatrix} = \begin{bmatrix} 0 \\ 0 \\ 0 \end{bmatrix}. \qquad (9.81)$$

Solving for $\widehat{\theta} = \{\widehat{\alpha}, \widehat{\beta}, \widehat{\sigma}^2\}$ yields the GMM estimators

$$\widehat{\beta}_1 = \frac{\sum_{t=1}^{T}(z_t - \overline{z})(y_t - \overline{y})}{\sum_{t=1}^{T}(z_t - \overline{z})(x_t - \overline{x})},$$

$$\widehat{\beta}_0 = \overline{y} - \widehat{\beta}_1 \overline{x}, \qquad (9.82)$$

$$\widehat{\sigma}^2 = \frac{1}{T}\sum_{t=1}^{T}(y_t - \widehat{\beta}_0 - \widehat{\beta}_1 x_t)^2,$$

which are equivalent to the instrumental variables estimators presented in Chapter 8.

9.6 TESTING

The focus in the discussion so far has been on specifying a model in terms of a set of moment equations and estimation of the unknown parameters of this model by GMM. This approach presupposes that the model is correctly specified in the sense that the moment equations accurately characterize properties of the variable y_t under study. To explore the adequacy of the model specification, three broad classes of tests are investigated. The first provides an overall test of the adequacy of the model. The second identifies the role of the explanatory variables in the model. The third is a diagnostic test to identify if any features of y_t have been excluded from the model.

9.6.1 An Overall Specification Test

An overall test of the adequacy of the specified model is given by the J test.[5] The null and alternative hypotheses are

$$\begin{aligned} &H_0: \text{Model is correctly specified} \\ &H_1: \text{Model is not correctly specified.} \end{aligned} \qquad (9.83)$$

The J test statistic has a simple form and is obtained by scaling the fitted GMM objective function $Q_T(\widehat{\theta})$ in equation (9.50) by the sample size, giving

---

[5] In recognition of the fundamental contributions to method of moments estimation made by Denis Sargan and Lars Hansen, this test is commonly referred to as the Hansen–Sargan J test.

$$J = TQ_T(\widehat{\theta}) = T\overline{m}_T(\widehat{\theta})'W_T^{-1}\overline{m}_T(\widehat{\theta})$$

$$= \left(\frac{1}{\sqrt{T}}\sum_{t=1}^{T}m_t(\widehat{\theta})\right)' W_T^{-1}\left(\frac{1}{\sqrt{T}}\sum_{t=1}^{T}m_t(\widehat{\theta})\right). \tag{9.84}$$

The model is assumed to be specified correctly under the null hypothesis, and this implies that the sample moments based on y_t match the population moments of the specified model. The fitted GMM sample moment $\overline{m}_T(\widehat{\theta})$ provides a measure of the distance between the sample and population moment, which is zero under the null hypothesis. So this distance should be small in a statistical sense, which in turn should yield a small value of the GMM objective function $Q_T(\widehat{\theta})$. When the model is improperly specified there will be a mismatch between the sample and the population moments, resulting in a large value of $\overline{m}_T(\widehat{\theta})$ and hence J.

This behavioral difference between the null and alternative hypotheses forms the basis of the test. The scaling by the sample size in the J test statistic of equation (9.84) ensures that the statistic has a well-defined asymptotic distribution under the null hypothesis, which follows from the asymptotic behavior of the scaled sample moment function $\frac{1}{\sqrt{T}}\sum_{t=1}^{T}m_t(\widehat{\theta})$.

To implement the J test the distribution of the test statistic is needed. Under the null hypothesis, the J statistic in equation (9.84) is distributed asymptotically as χ^2_{N-K}, where the number of overidentifying restrictions $N-K$ represents the degrees of freedom. The null hypothesis H_0 is rejected for values of J larger than the critical value from the χ^2_{N-K} distribution for a chosen level of significance.

A test of the overall specification of the trade durations model is given in Table 9.3. The value of the J statistic to test the 2-moment version of the model specification is $J = 59.6471$. As there are $N = 2$ moments and $K = 1$ unknown parameter, the excess moment condition is $N - K = 1$. From the chi-square distribution with 1 degree of freedom and a size of 5%, the critical value is 3.8410. As J clearly exceeds the critical value, the model specification is strongly rejected at the 5% level.

Table 9.3 also provides the GMM estimates of the trade durations model based on alternative single moment GMM equations. In both cases, the objective function is $Q_T(\widehat{\theta}) = 0$, with a corresponding zero value, $J = 0$, for the test statistic. However, for this case the zero outcome does not imply that the chosen model is necessarily correctly specified, as both models are just-identified, so a value of zero for the GMM objective function is an inevitable consequence of the form of the test statistic in the just-identified case. The implication of this result is that the J test is only relevant in overidentified models. The J test may therefore be interpreted as a test of the validity of the overidentifying moment equations in the model.

9.6.2 Tests of Significance
Instead of testing the overall specification of the model, t tests can be used to test hypotheses about particular parameter values. The t statistic on a single parameter tests the following null and alternative hypotheses

$$\begin{aligned} H_0&: \theta = \theta_0 \\ H_1&: \theta \neq \theta_0. \end{aligned} \tag{9.85}$$

The t statistic is constructed as

$$t = \frac{\widehat{\theta} - \theta_0}{\text{se}(\widehat{\theta})}, \tag{9.86}$$

which under the null hypothesis is distributed asymptotically as $N(0,1)$. For the trade durations model, t statistics for the case of $\theta_0 = 0$ are given in Table 9.3 together with p values based on asymptotic normality.[6] For all the reported models, the estimate of $\theta = \{\gamma\}$ is statistically significant.

Other types of significance tests can be performed that involve joint testing of subsets of the parameters. These tests are known as Wald tests, and they will be formally introduced in Chapter 10.

9.6.3 Diagnostic Tests

Diagnostic tests aim to detect model misspecification by identifying potential patterns in the disturbance terms. In the case of the GMM model, the disturbance is represented by the gap between the sample moments and the population moments. For a correctly specified model, this suggests that $E[m_t(\theta_0)] = 0$, which implies that a test of the model can be based on the following respective null and alternative hypotheses:

$$\begin{aligned} H_0 &: E[m_t(\theta_0)] = 0 \\ H_1 &: E[m_t(\theta_0)] \neq 0. \end{aligned} \tag{9.87}$$

This means that the disturbance corresponding to each moment should have zero mean under the null hypothesis.

To implement the diagnostic test, reconsider the trade durations model based on the $N = 2$ moments in equation (9.35). Evaluating these moments at the GMM estimator $\widehat{\theta}$ gives the fitted moment relations

$$\begin{aligned} m_{1t} &= y_t - \widehat{\theta} \\ m_{2t} &= (y_t - \widehat{\theta})^2 - \widehat{\theta}. \end{aligned} \tag{9.88}$$

In the present context these may also be interpreted as residuals. If the model is correctly specified, the sample means should be zero under the null hypothesis. To test this hypothesis in the case of the first moment consider estimating the following regression equation

$$m_{1t} = \beta + u_t, \tag{9.89}$$

where u_t is a disturbance term distributed as $(0, \sigma_u^2)$. The null hypothesis is $\beta = 0$, which is tested using a simple t test. The results from estimating this regression equation by ordinary least squares, with standard errors in parentheses, are

$$m_{1t} = \underset{(0.1476)}{0.7379} + \widehat{u}_t.$$

---

[6] Strictly speaking, the t statistics in Table 9.3 do not have an asymptotic normal distribution in this case, as the null hypothesis falls on the boundary of the feasible parameter space, which is $\theta = 0$ for the exponential distribution. Tests on the boundary of a parameter space need to take account of the different behavior of estimates in the immediate vicinity of the boundary. Readers are referred to Andrews (2001) for details.

A t test is based on

$$t = \frac{0.7379 - 0.0000}{0.1476} = 5.00,$$

which is distributed asymptotically as $N(0, 1)$ under the null hypothesis. The p value is 0.000, resulting in a rejection of the null at the 5% and 1% levels, thereby producing evidence of misspecification in the first moment relation.

Repeating the diagnostic test for the second moment, the regression equation is similarly specified as

$$m_{2t} = \beta + u_t, \tag{9.90}$$

where u_t is again a disturbance term distributed as $(0, \sigma_u^2)$. Estimating this regression equation by ordinary least squares gives

$$m_{2t} = 47.5439 + \widehat{u}_t.$$
$$\underset{(6.2766)}{}$$

The t statistic is computed as

$$t = \frac{47.5439 - 0.0000}{6.2766} = 7.57.$$

The p value is 0.000, yielding evidence of misspecification in the second moment relation at the 5% and 1% levels as well.

The diagnostic tests performed immediately above relate to the mean of the moments m_t. Other types of tests can be designed. For example, a test of excess kurtosis (beyond that of a normal distribution) can be performed by setting the dependent variable in the test equation (9.89) to be $v_t^4 - 3$, where v_t is the standardized moment of m_t, which has zero mean and unit variance. Alternatively, a test of first-order autocorrelation may be based on defining the dependent variable as $v_t v_{t-1}$. In both cases, the dependent variable is regressed on a constant, which is tested to be zero under the null hypothesis.

Another class of tests that are known as conditional moment tests is based on augmenting the test equation (9.89) by a set of variables that are already included in the model. These tests still focus on testing for a zero intercept but now do so in the presence of a set of conditioning variables. Conditional moment tests are also investigated in Chapter 10, where an alternative class of estimators based on maximum likelihood methods is presented and where augmentation is based on the gradients of the log-likelihood function rather than auxiliary variables.

9.7 CONSUMPTION CAPM REVISITED

The consumption-based capital asset pricing model (C-CAPM) as already discussed in Chapter 8 represents an important application of GMM in empirical finance, as it is one of the earliest applications of this estimation framework. The C-CAPM model is based on the assumption that a representative agent maximizes the intertemporal utility function

$$\sum_{i=0}^{\infty} \delta^i \, \mathrm{E}_t \left[\frac{C_{t+i}^{1-\gamma} - 1}{1 - \gamma} \right], \tag{9.91}$$

subject to the wealth constraint

$$W_{t+1} = (1 + R_{t+1})(W_t - C_t),$$ (9.92)

where C_t is real consumption, W_t is wealth, R_t is the simple return on an asset (more precisely on wealth), and E_t is the conditional expectations operator where conditioning is taken on all relevant variables available at time t. The unknown parameters are the discount rate δ and the relative risk aversion parameter γ, which are summarized in the $K = 2$ parameter vector $\theta = \{\delta, \gamma\}$.

The first-order condition is

$$E_t\left[\delta\left(\frac{C_{t+1}}{C_t}\right)^{-\gamma}(1 + R_{t+1}) - 1\right] = 0.$$ (9.93)

It is illuminating to re-express the model by defining

$$u_{t+1} = \delta\left(\frac{C_{t+1}}{C_t}\right)^{-\gamma}(1 + R_{t+1}) - 1,$$ (9.94)

which may also be interpreted as a disturbance term. Using equation (9.94) in equation (9.93) simplifies the formulation of the population moment of the model as

$$E_t[u_{t+1}] = 0.$$ (9.95)

Equation (9.95) represents the population moment characterizing the C-CAPM with $K = 2$ unknown parameters. Before deriving the GMM parameter estimators for θ, two issues need to be addressed. The first is that the expectation in equation (9.95) is a conditional expectation, whereas the population expectations used in the discussion so far have been expressed as unconditional expectations.[7] The second is that there is just one moment equation and two unknown parameters, resulting in an underidentified model without further information.

The first issue is solved by using the law of iterated expectations, which converts a conditional expectation into an unconditional expectation by taking a further expectation operation. In the case of equation (9.95), the operation leads to

$$E[E_t(u_{t+1})] = E(u_{t+1}).$$ (9.96)

The intuition behind this result is that by virtue of its definition, a conditional expectation implies that the conditional expected value of u_{t+1} varies across all possible values of the information set. Averaging over all of these conditional expectations corresponding to each potential value of the information set then averages out the role of the information set, thereby yielding the unconditional expectation of u_{t+1}.[8]

---

[7] One exception is the present value model in Section 9.1.1 where the pertinent moment condition is expressed in terms of a conditional expectation of future dividends. There the solution is to assume that dividends follow a random walk, so the conditional expectation based on information at time t of future dividends simply equals the current dividend D_t.

[8] To prove the law of iterated expectations in the simplest case, let y be the random variable of interest and x represent the information set with density $f(x)$. Using the definitions of unconditional and conditional expectations

$$E_x[E[y|x]] = \int [E[y|x]]f(x)\,dx = \int \left[\int yf(y|x)\,dy\right]f(x)\,dx,$$

The second issue is solved by using the properties of instrumental variables as discussed in Chapter 8. Here the instruments are chosen to be the information set underlying the conditional expectation in equations (9.91) or (9.95). For example, let the information set be represented by a constant and C_t/C_{t-1}, the lagged real consumption ratio, giving

$$z_t = \{1, C_t/C_{t-1}\}. \tag{9.97}$$

From the properties of the instrumental variables estimator, u_{t+1} is independent of z_t since the following condition is satisfied

$$E[u_{t+1}z_t] = 0,$$

or upon using equation (9.97)

$$E[u_{t+1}] = 0, \qquad E[u_{t+1}C_t/C_{t-1}] = 0. \tag{9.98}$$

There are now two population moments characterizing the C-CAPM from which it is possible to derive the GMM estimators for the two population parameters $\theta = \{\delta, \gamma\}$. As there are $N = 2$ population moments and $K = 2$ unknown parameters, this form of the model is just-identifed.

To derive the GMM estimator of θ, the two population moments in equation (9.98) imply the following explicit GMM moment relations,

$$m_{1t} = \delta \left(\frac{C_{t+1}}{C_t}\right)^{-\gamma} (1 + R_{t+1}) - 1$$
$$m_{2t} = \left(\delta \left(\frac{C_{t+1}}{C_t}\right)^{-\gamma} (1 + R_{t+1}) - 1\right) \frac{C_t}{C_{t-1}}. \tag{9.99}$$

Upon using equation (9.17), the GMM estimator $\widehat{\theta} = \{\widehat{\delta}, \widehat{\gamma}\}$ satisfies

$$\frac{1}{T} \sum_{t=1}^{T} \left(\widehat{\delta}\left(\frac{C_{t+1}}{C_t}\right)^{-\widehat{\gamma}} (1 + R_{t+1}) - 1\right) = 0$$
$$\frac{1}{T} \sum_{t=1}^{T} \left(\widehat{\delta}\left(\frac{C_{t+1}}{C_t}\right)^{-\widehat{\gamma}} (1 + R_{t+1}) - 1\right) \frac{C_t}{C_{t-1}} = 0. \tag{9.100}$$

These two equations represent a nonlinear system with two unknowns, which may be estimated using an iterative algorithm.

This C-CAPM is estimated using monthly data for the United States beginning February 1959 and ending December 1978. The data consist of seasonally adjusted

---

where the subscript on $E_x[\cdot]$ emphasizes that the expectation is taken with respect to x and where $f(y|x)$ is the conditional density of y given x. From the definition of the conditional density $f(y|x) = f(y,x)/f(x)$, where $f(y,x)$ is the joint density of (y,x), this expression becomes, after rearranging

$$E_x[E[y|x]] = \int \left[\int y \frac{f(y,x)}{f(x)} dy\right] f(x) dx = \int y \left[\int f(y,x) dx\right] dy.$$

From the definition of the marginal density $f(y)$, namely, $\int f(y,x) dx = f(y)$, it follows that $E_x[E[y|x]] = \int yf(y) dy = E[y]$.

real consumption C_t, the real Treasury bill rate R_t, and real value weighted returns r_t. Forming the consumption ratio C_t/C_{t-1} means that the effective sample begins in March 1959. The data are a revised version of the original data used by Hansen and Singleton (1982). The GMM parameter estimates based on an iterated estimator are given in Table 9.4 for various choices of instruments.

The first instrument set consists of $z_t = \{1, C_t/C_{t-1}\}$, which yields a just-identified model resulting in the fitted GMM objective function taking the value $Q_T(\widehat{\theta}) = 0$. The second instrument set is $z_t = \{1, C_t/C_{t-1}, R_t\}$, resulting in an overidentified system with degree of overidentification equal to $N - K = 1$. The third and final instrument set is $z_t = \{1, C_t/C_{t-1}, R_t, r_t\}$, which leads to $N - K = 2$ overidentifying restrictions. An overall test of the model using the J test shows support for the C-CAPM specification, as the overidentifying restrictions in the case of the second and third instrument sets are not rejected at the 5% level.

The discount parameter estimates in Table 9.4 are robust across all instrument sets with values of around 0.998. As $\delta = 1/(1 + r)$, where r is the constant real discount rate, it follows that

$$r = \frac{1}{\delta} - 1 = \frac{1}{0.998} - 1 = 0.002,$$

or 0.2%, an estimate that appears to be very low. The estimates of the relative risk aversion parameter, γ, range from 0.554 to 1.0246. These estimates reveal that relative risk aversion is also low over the sample period considered. However, the standard errors are large relative to the point estimates, so that γ is estimated imprecisely.

9.8 THE CKLS MODEL OF INTEREST RATES

As discussed in Chapter 6, the short-term interest rate (or short maturity bond yield) plays an important role in financial markets because of the expectations hypothesis of the term structure of interest rates, which posits that long rates are simply a weighted average of expected future short rates. Consequently, modeling the dynamics of the short-term interest rate has received a lot of attention in the financial econometrics literature. One of

TABLE 9.4 GMM parameter estimates of the C-CAPM using the GMM moment relations in equation (9.99) for alternative instrument sets. The data are monthly US data for the period March 1959 to December 1978. The estimates are obtained using the iterated updating algorithm and a heteroskedastic weighting matrix. Standard errors are in parentheses.

Parameter	Instrument Set (z_t)		
	$\{1, C_t/C_{t-1}\}$	$\{1, C_t/C_{t-1}, R_t\}$	$\{1, C_t/C_{t-1}, R_t, r_t\}$
δ	0.9983	0.9982	0.9977
	(0.0045)	(0.0044)	(0.0043)
γ	0.5540	1.0246	0.7241
	(1.9390)	(1.8613)	(1.7599)
Q	0.0000	0.0045	0.0053
J	0.0000	1.0679	1.2796
p value		0.3014	0.5274

the most popular models of the short-term interest rate is the CKLS model due to Chan et al. (1992), given by

$$\Delta r_{t+1} = \alpha + \beta r_t + \sigma r_t^{\gamma} z_{t+1}, \qquad z_{t+1} \sim iid(0,1), \tag{9.101}$$

in which r_t is the short-term interest rate, z_{t+1} is a disturbance term, and $\theta = \{\alpha, \beta, \sigma, \gamma\}$ are parameters. This model relates the change in interest rates at time $t+1$ to the level of the interest rate in period t. The variance of the change in interest rates is also related to the level of the interest rate in period t because z_{t+1} is scaled by the factor σr_t^{γ}. Consequently, the parameter γ is commonly referred to as the levels effect parameter.

Figure 9.9 plots the levels and differences of the 1- and 12-month US zero-coupon bond yields for the period December 1946 to February 1991. It is apparent from the behavior of the yields, particularly in the early 1980s, that there is a relationship between the high levels of interest rates and increased volatility in the interest rate changes.

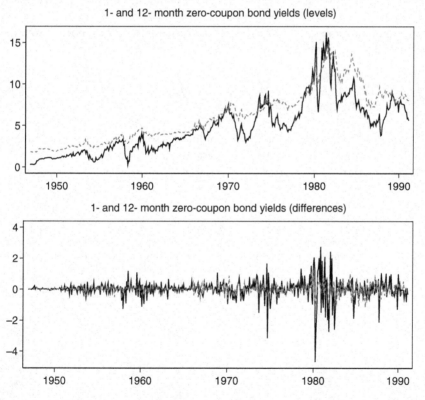

FIGURE 9.9 Monthly US zero-coupon bond yields for the period December 1946 to February 1991. The top panel shows the levels of 1 month (solid line) and 12 month (short dashed line) bond yields, while the lower panel shows the differences in these yields.

This period corresponds to a change in the stance of monetary policy during this period known as the Volcker experiment.[9]

To estimate this model by GMM, use the model in equation (9.101) to define the following moment relations

$$
m_t = \begin{bmatrix} m_{1t} \\ m_{2t} \\ m_{3t} \\ m_{4t} \end{bmatrix} = \begin{bmatrix} (\Delta r_{t+1} - \alpha - \beta r_t) \\ (\Delta r_{t+1} - \alpha - \beta r_t) r_t \\ (\Delta r_{t+1} - \alpha - \beta r_t)^2 - \sigma^2 r_t^{2\gamma} \\ ((\Delta r_{t+1} - \alpha - \beta r_t)^2 - \sigma^2 r_t^{2\gamma}) r_t \end{bmatrix}, \tag{9.102}
$$

where the first two moment conditions relate to the mean of Δr_{t+1}, and the second two moment conditions relate to the variance of Δr_{t+1}. As there are four parameters and four moment conditions, the model is just-identified.

The GMM estimates for θ obtained when using the US zero-coupon bond yield data for maturities of 1, 3, 6, 9, and 12 months are reported in Table 9.5. The model is estimated using a one-step estimator with a heteroskedastic weighting matrix. The results show a strong levels effect in US interest rates that changes over the maturity of the asset. The estimates of γ increase in magnitude as maturity increases from 0 to 6 months, reach a peak at 6 months, and then taper off thereafter.

An important property of the CKLS model is that it nests a number of well-known interest rate models as special cases.

1. $H_0 : \gamma = 0.5$:

   The CKLS model with $\gamma = 0.5$ corresponds to the square-root or CIR model proposed by Cox, Ingersoll, and Ross (1985). The importance of this restriction stems from the fact that the CIR model is more analytically tractable than the CKLS model and allows for the development of some important theoretical results relating to the term structure of interest rates and the pricing of bonds.

2. $H_0 : \gamma = 1.0$:

   The CKLS model with $\gamma = 1.0$ corresponds to the model proposed by Brennan and Schwartz (1980).

TABLE 9.5   GMM estimation of the CKLS interest rate model. A one-step estimator is used, and standard errors are reported in parentheses. Data are monthly US zero-coupon bond yields (with maturities of 1, 3, 6, 9, and 12 months) for the period December 1946 to February 1991.

Parameter	1 month	3 month	6 month	9 month	12 month
α	0.1057	0.0896	0.0894	0.0907	0.0462
	(0.0587)	(0.0538)	(0.0568)	(0.0563)	(0.0267)
β	−0.0198	−0.0154	−0.0147	−0.0147	−0.0056
	(0.0159)	(0.0137)	(0.0137)	(0.0133)	(0.0056)
σ	0.0494	0.0352	0.0260	0.0266	0.0286
	(0.0185)	(0.0166)	(0.0153)	(0.0153)	(0.00673)
γ	1.3518	1.4248	1.5333	1.5173	1.1779
	(0.1882)	(0.2314)	(0.2833)	(0.2777)	(0.1136)

[9] Paul Volcker, Federal Reserve Chair from 1979–1987, raised federal funds rate to a record 20% in a bid to end inflation. This period has subsequently become known as the Volcker experiment.

TABLE 9.6 GMM tests of the restrictions $\gamma = 0.5$ and $\gamma = 1.0$ imposed on the CKLS model. A two-step estimator is used with a heteroskedastic weighting matrix. Data are monthly US zero-coupon bond yields (with maturities of 1, 3, 6, 9, and 12 months) for the period December 1946 to February 1991.

	1 month	3 month	6 month	9 month	12 month
γ	1.350	1.424	1.525	1.510	1.178
	(0.188)	(0.232)	(0.285)	(0.279)	(0.114)
$H_0 : \gamma = 0.5$:					
$Q_T(\hat{\theta})$	0.021	0.017	0.013	0.014	0.045
J_{HS}	11.04	8.859	7.043	7.159	23.84
p value	0.001	0.003	0.008	0.008	0.000
$H_0 : \gamma = 1.0$:					
$Q_T(\hat{\theta})$	0.005218	0.004930	0.004732	0.004691	0.004467
J_{HS}	2.7657	2.6131	2.5081	2.4862	2.3675
p value	0.09631	0.1060	0.1133	0.1148	0.1239

There are two ways to test these hypotheses. The first is to perform a t test using the estimated parameters and associated standard errors from Table 9.5. The second is to estimate the model imposing the restriction and then test the overidentifying restrictions using the Hansen–Sargan J test. The tests statistics from the latter approach, together with the estimate of γ in the unrestricted model for comparative purposes, are reported in Table 9.6. These estimates are produced using a two-step GMM estimator with a heteroskedastic weighting matrix. On the evidence provided by these results, there is a strong rejection of the CIR square-root model, $H_0 : \gamma = 0.5$. Simple inspection of the point estimates of γ and their standard errors indicate that this restriction will not be supported and this intuition is borne out in every case by the value of the Hansen–Sargent J test. A completely different picture emerges for the Brennan and Schwartz model, $H_0 : \gamma = 1.0$. In every case, the null hypothesis cannot be rejected, giving a set of results that is strongly supportive of this model for these data.

9.9 EXERCISES

The data required for the exercises are available for download as EViews workfiles (*.wf1), Stata datafiles (*.dta), comma delimited text files (*.csv), and as Excel spreadsheets (*.xlsx).

1. Present Value Model

> pv.*

The data are monthly observations on US equity prices and dividends for the period January 1871 to September 2016. The present value model equates the price of an asset with the discounted flow of future dividend payments,

$$P_t = E_t \sum_{i=1}^{\infty} \frac{D_{t+i}}{(1+\delta)^i} = \frac{D_t}{\delta},$$

where δ is the discount rate and $E_t(D_{t+i}) = D_t$ for all $i \geq 0$.

(a) Plot the monthly data on US equity prices, dividend payments, and the dividend yield, calculated as D_t/P_t, from January 1871 to June 2004.

(b) The moment relation for estimating the discount rate, δ, is

$$m_t = \frac{D_t}{P_t} - \delta.$$

Setting $\delta = 0.05$, plot m_t and comment on the result.

(c) Use the moment relation in part (b) to estimate δ by GMM.

2. Durations

$$\boxed{\text{amr.}^*}$$

The data are high-frequency (in seconds) data for American Airlines (AMR) on 1 August 2006 from 09:30 to 16:00.

(a) From the data, construct a record of the 3643 unique times between trades. Ensure that the first duration is 27 seconds, which represents the time from the opening of the market to the first recorded transaction in AMR.

(b) Plot a histogram of the duration data and interpret the shape of the empirical distribution.

(c) The GMM moment relation for estimating the parameter of the exponential distribution, θ, is given by

$$m_t = y_t - \theta.$$

Plot m_t for $\theta = 10$ and comment on the result.

(d) Use the moment relation in part (c) to estimate θ by GMM.

3. Estimating Parameters of Univariate Distributions

(a) **Normal distribution**

Simulate $T = 1000$ observations from the normal distribution

$$f(y; \mu, \sigma^2) = \frac{1}{\sqrt{2\pi\sigma^2}} \exp\left[-\frac{1}{2}\left(\frac{y-\mu}{\sigma}\right)^2\right],$$

with mean $\mu = 0$ and standard deviation $\sigma = 0.5$. Estimate the parameters $\theta = \{\mu, \sigma\}$ by GMM using the following three moments

$$E[y_t] = \mu, \qquad E[y_t^2] = \sigma^2 + \mu^2, \qquad E[(y_t - \mu)^4] = 3\sigma^4.$$

(b) **Student t distribution**

Simulate $T = 1000$ observations from the t distribution

$$f(y; \nu) = \frac{\Gamma[(\nu+1)/2]}{\sqrt{\pi\nu}\Gamma[\nu/2]}\left[1 + \frac{(y-\mu)^2}{\nu}\right]^{-(\nu+1)/2},$$

with mean $\mu = 0$, degrees of freedom $\nu = 5$, and $\Gamma(\cdot)$ being the gamma function. Estimate the parameters $\theta = \{\mu, \nu\}$ by GMM using the following three moments

$$E[y_t] = \mu, \quad E[(y_t - \mu)^2] = \frac{\nu}{\nu - 2}, \quad E[(y_t - \mu)^4] = 3\frac{\nu^2}{(\nu - 2)(\nu - 4)}.$$

(c) Gamma distribution

Simulate $T = 1000$ observations from the gamma distribution

$$f(y; \theta) = \frac{\beta^\alpha}{\Gamma(\alpha)} \exp[-\beta y] y^{\alpha - 1}, \qquad y \geqslant 0, \alpha > 0, \beta > 0,$$

with scale parameter $\alpha = 2$ and rate parameter $\beta = 1$. Estimate the parameters $\theta = \{\alpha, \beta\}$ by GMM using the following three moments

$$E[y_t] = \alpha/\beta, \quad E[y_t^2] = \frac{\alpha(\alpha + 1)}{\beta^2}, \quad E[1/y_t] = \frac{\beta}{\alpha - 1}.$$

4. Capital Asset Pricing Model

```
capm.*
```

The data are monthly excess returns for Exxon, y_t, and the S&P 500 index, x_t, for the period May 1990 to July 2004. The CAPM is given by

$$y_t = \alpha + \beta x_t + u_t, \qquad u_t \sim iid(0, \sigma^2).$$

(a) Plot the excess returns to Exxon and the market index and discuss their time series properties.

(b) Estimate the parameters $\theta = \{\alpha, \beta, \sigma\}$ by ordinary least squares.

(c) Estimate $\theta = \{\alpha, \beta, \sigma\}$ by GMM using the following three moments

$$m_t = \begin{bmatrix} m_{1t} \\ m_{2t} \\ m_{3t} \end{bmatrix} = \begin{bmatrix} y_t - \alpha - \beta x_t \\ (y_t - \alpha - \beta x_t) x_t \\ (y_t - \alpha - \beta x_t)^2 - \sigma^2 \end{bmatrix}.$$

Compare these estimates with those obtained in part (b).

5. Gamma Model of Asset Prices

```
capm.*
```

The file contains monthly price data on General Electric and the S&P 500 index for the period May 1990 to July 2004. Assume that prices follow the gamma distribution

$$f(P_t; \theta) = \frac{\beta^\alpha}{\Gamma(\alpha)} P_t^{\alpha - 1} \exp(-\beta P_t), \qquad P_t > 0,$$

with $\theta = \{\alpha, \beta\}$ and $\alpha, \beta > 0$.

(a) Estimate θ by GMM using the following three population moments of the gamma distribution

$$E(P_t) = \frac{\alpha}{\beta}, \quad E(P_t^2) = \frac{\alpha(\alpha + 1)}{\beta^2}, \quad E\left(\frac{1}{P_t}\right) - \frac{\beta}{\alpha - 1} = 0,$$

using the one-step GMM estimator.

(b) Redo part (a) using the two-step GMM estimator. Compare your results with those obtained in part (a).

(c) Redo part (a) using the iterated GMM estimator. Observe how many iterations are required to achieve convergence and comment on the results.

6. The Consumption Capital Asset Pricing Model

> ccapm_hs.*

The data are observations on the US real consumption ratio, c_{t+1}/c_t (*CRATIO*), the real Treasury bill rate, r_{t+1} (*R*), and the real value weighted returns to the market, e_{t+1} (*VWR*). The first-order condition of the C-CAPM is given by

$$E_t[\beta(c_{t+1}/c_t)^{-\gamma}(1+r_{t+1}) - 1] = 0,$$

where c_t is real consumption, and r_t is the real interest rate. The parameters are the discount factor, β, and the relative risk aversion coefficient, γ.

(a) Estimate the parameters $\theta = \{\beta, \gamma\}$ by GMM using $w_t = \{1, c_t/c_{t-1}\}$ as instruments and starting values $\theta_{(0)} = \{\beta = 1.0, \gamma = 1.0\}$. Interpret the parameter estimates.

(b) Repeat part (a) using the following instrument sets.

   (i) $w_t = \{1, c_t/c_{t-1}, r_t\}$.
   (ii) $w_t = \{1, c_t/c_{t-1}, r_t, e_t\}$.
   (iii) $w_t = \{1, c_t/c_{t-1}, r_t, e_t, e_{t-1}\}$.

   In each case, test the overidentifying restrictions.

(c) Compare the parameter estimates across the four sets of instruments in parts (a) and (b).

7. Level Effects in US Interest Rates

> leveleffect.*

The data are monthly yields data on US Treasury zero-coupon bonds for the period December 1946 to February 1991. The zero-coupon bonds have maturities of 1, 3, 6, 9, and 12 months.

(a) For each yield, estimate the following interest rate equation using a one-step GMM estimator

$$r_{t+1} - r_t = \alpha + \beta r_t + \sigma r_t^{\gamma} z_{t+1},$$

where z_t is *iid* $(0, 1)$, and the instrument set is $w_t = \{1, r_t\}$.

(b) For each yield, test the following restrictions: $\gamma = 0.0$, $\gamma = 0.5$, and $\gamma = 1.0$.

(c) Repeat parts (a) and (b) using the iterative GMM estimator with heteroskedastic weighting matrix. Are there any significant differences in the results?

(d) If the level effect model of the interest rate captures time-varying volatility and $\alpha, \beta \simeq 0$, then

$$E\left[\left(\frac{r_{t+1} - r_t}{r_t^\gamma}\right)^2\right] \simeq \sigma^2.$$

Plot the series

$$\frac{r_{t+1} - r_t}{r_t^\gamma},$$

for $\gamma = 0.0, 0.5, 1.0$, and 1.5, and discuss the properties of the series.

8. **Decomposing International Equity Returns**

| equities.* |

The data file contains daily equity prices, P_t, on the S&P 500, FTSE100, and the EURO50 stock indices for the period 29 July 2004 to 3 March 2009.

(a) Compute and plot the centered daily percentage log-returns for the three equity indices. Let the log-returns be, respectively, r_{1t} (S&P 500), r_{2t} (FTSE100), and r_{3t} (EURO50).

(b) Consider the latent factor model

$$r_{it} = \lambda_i w_t + \sigma_i v_{it}, \qquad i = 1, 2, 3,$$

where r_{it} is assumed to have zero mean, and the latent factors $\{w_t, v_{1t}, v_{2t}, v_{3t}\}$ are $iid\,(0, 1)$. The loadings on the world factor and the idiosyncratic factor for country i, are, respectively, λ_i and σ_i. Show that the theoretical moments of r_{it} are

$$\mathrm{var}(r_{it}) = \lambda_i^2 + \sigma_i^2, \quad i = 1, 2, 3,$$
$$\mathrm{cov}(r_{it} r_{jt}) = \lambda_i \lambda_j, \quad i \neq j.$$

(c) The moment structure in part (b) gives rise to the following moment equations

$$m_{1t} = r_{1t}^2 - \lambda_1^2 - \sigma_1^2$$
$$m_{2t} = r_{2t}^2 - \lambda_2^2 - \sigma_2^2$$
$$m_{3t} = r_{3t}^2 - \lambda_3^2 - \sigma_3^2$$
$$m_{4t} = r_{1t} r_{2t} - \lambda_1 \lambda_2$$
$$m_{5t} = r_{1t} r_{3t} - \lambda_1 \lambda_3$$
$$m_{6t} = r_{2t} r_{3t} - \lambda_2 \lambda_3.$$

Estimate the parameters $\theta = \{\lambda_1, \lambda_2, \lambda_3, \sigma_1, \sigma_2, \sigma_3\}$ by GMM using the iterative GMM estimator with the heteroskedasticity robust weighting matrix.

(d) Interpret the parameter estimates by computing the relative contributions to volatility of the world factor (w_t) and the idiosyncratic factors ($v_{1,t}, v_{2,t}, v_{3,t}$) given by

$$\frac{\lambda_i^2}{\lambda_i^2 + \sigma_i^2}, \qquad \frac{\sigma_i^2}{\lambda_i^2 + \sigma_i^2}, \qquad i = 1, 2, 3.$$

(e) Show that the factor decomposition in part (b) gives an exact decomposition of the empirical covariance matrix of r_{it}.

(f) Re-estimate the model imposing the restriction $\lambda_i = \lambda$ for all i. Test the over-identifying restriction using the Hansen–Sargan J test.

9. **Spillover Effects of US Shocks on the Eurozone**

> eurozone.*

The data file contains weekly data on the equity prices of 10 Eurozone countries and the United States, all expressed in \$US. The data are weekly from 5 January 1990 to 5 May 2017.

(a) For 5 countries—France, Germany, the Netherlands, Spain, and the US—compute and plot the centered weekly percentage equity log-returns. Let these series be named, respectively, as $r_{1t}, r_{2t}, r_{3t}, r_{4t}$, and r_{5t}, where the last return corresponds to the US.

(b) Consider the following latent factor model

$$r_{it} = \lambda_i w_t + \sigma_i v_{it}, \qquad i = 1, 2, 3, 4, 5,$$

where w_t is a world factor and $v_{1t}, v_{2t}, \cdots, v_{5t}$ are all idiosyncratic factors, which are assumed to be independently and identically distributed with mean zero and variance 1. The loadings on the world factor and the idiosyncratic factor for country i are, respectively, λ_i and σ_i.

(i) Derive expressions for the variances $\text{var}(r_{it})$ and the covariances $\text{cov}(r_{it} r_{jt})$.
(ii) Use these expressions to estimate the model by GMM. Choose 0.1 as the starting value for all unknown parameters.
(iii) Perform a test of the model using the Hansen–Sargan J test.
(iv) Compute the relative contributions to volatility of the common factor, (w_t).

(c) Now consider the following factor latent structure where shocks from the US (v_{5t}) directly affect France, Germany, and the Netherlands, but not Spain, given by

$$r_{1t} = \lambda_1 w_t + \sigma_1 v_{1t} + \gamma_1 v_{5t}$$
$$r_{2t} = \lambda_2 w_t + \sigma_2 v_{2t} + \gamma_2 v_{5t}$$
$$r_{3t} = \lambda_3 w_t + \sigma_3 v_{3t} + \gamma_3 v_{5t}$$
$$r_{4t} = \lambda_4 w_t + \sigma_4 v_{4t}$$
$$r_{5t} = \lambda_5 w_t + \sigma_5 v_{5t},$$

where γ_1, γ_2, and γ_3 represent the effects of shocks in the US on France, Germany, and the Netherlands, respectively.

(i) Derive expressions for the variances $\text{var}(r_{it})$ and the covariances $\text{cov}(r_{it})$.
(ii) Use these expressions to estimate the model by GMM. Choose 0.1 as the starting values for γ_1, γ_2, and γ_3; and for the remaining parameters, choose the estimates obtained in part (b).
(iii) Construct a test of the hypotheses $\gamma_1 = \gamma_2 = \gamma_3 = 0$ and interpret the result.

CHAPTER 10

Maximum Likelihood

Maximum likelihood estimation is a general method of statistical estimation with a long history that dates back over a century to the research of the economist and statistician, Francis Ysidro Edgeworth. The method was systematically explored and championed by Sir Ronald Fisher, who became its principal exponent during the first part of the twentieth century and who formulated many of its properties. Harald Cramér (1946) provided a full development of the approach and its properties in a classic treatise on the mathematical methods of statistics.[1]

Maximum likelihood provides an alternative general framework to the GMM approach discussed in Chapter 9. Like GMM, the method is applicable to a broad range of financial econometric models and is convenient when full specification of the probability distribution of the data forms part of the underlying model. The maximum likelihood estimator is obtained by finding the value of the unknown parameter vector that is *most likely* to have generated the observed data, where the phrase is interpreted in the probabilistic sense that the maximum likelihood estimator is that value of the parameter that maximizes the probability density function of the data, given the actual observations. Consequently, the method requires that the probability distribution of the stochastic process generating the observed data be fully specified. This requirement is more stringent than what is needed for other estimators such as ordinary least squares, instrumental variables, and GMM. But the approach is attractive because the maximum likelihood estimator possesses a number of highly desirable, large-sample properties under very general conditions. Moreover, the method is often used under the presumption of a convenient probability distribution such as the normal (Gaussian), in which event the method is sometimes referred to as Gaussian estimation or quasi-maximum likelihood.

This chapter develops the maximum likelihood approach, presents some of the properties of maximum likelihood estimators, and details fundamental testing procedures

---

[1] Readers are referred to the essays by Stigler (1978) and Aldrich (1997) for histories that describe some of the origins and phases of development of the maximum likelihood method and the work of its principal protagonists. Pratt (1976) clarifies the contributions of Edgeworth to the genesis of maximum likelihood and its statistical properties in a series of contributions over 1908–1909, which are antecedent to the work of Fisher.

that are based on the likelihood principle, such as the likelihood ratio test and the Lagrange multiplier or score test, as well as the closely related and commonly used Wald test.

10.1 DISTRIBUTIONS IN FINANCE

This section discusses some of the links between financial theory, observed financial data, and the probability distributions from which these data are drawn.

10.1.1 Returns

A common assumption adopted in finance is that the returns (r_t) on an asset are normally distributed with mean μ and variance σ^2. The distribution of returns is then formally written in terms of the normal probability density as

$$f(r_t; \mu, \sigma^2) = \frac{1}{\sqrt{2\pi\sigma^2}} \exp\left[-\frac{(r_t - \mu)^2}{2\sigma^2}\right],$$

or more compactly as

$$r_t \sim N(\mu, \sigma^2).$$

The assumption of a normal distribution often relates to the disturbance terms that appear in the formulation of a financial model. In linear models, this assumption implies that returns themselves are normally distributed. There are two important models of financial returns that adopt the assumption of normality.

   (i) Constant mean model

$$r_t = \mu + u_t, \qquad u_t \sim iid\, N(0, \sigma^2).$$

It follows directly from the distributional assumption on the disturbance term that the distribution of r_t is

$$f(r_t; \theta) = \frac{1}{\sqrt{2\pi\sigma^2}} \exp\left[-\frac{(r_t - \mu)^2}{2\sigma^2}\right],$$

where $\theta = \{\mu, \sigma^2\}$ is the parameter vector.

   (ii) CAPM

$$r_t - r_{ft} = \alpha + \beta(r_{mt} - r_{ft}) + u_t, \qquad u_t \sim iid\, N(0, \sigma^2).$$

In this instance, the distribution of r_t is

$$f(r_t | r_{mt}, r_{ft}; \theta) = \frac{1}{\sqrt{2\pi\sigma^2}} \exp\left[-\frac{(r_t - r_{ft} - \alpha - \beta(r_{mt} - r_{ft}))^2}{2\sigma^2}\right],$$

with parameter vector $\theta = \{\alpha, \beta, \sigma^2\}$.

Figure 10.1 gives histograms for the monthly log returns on six assets. Superimposed on each histogram is the normal distribution with μ and σ^2 replaced by their sample estimates. All six log-return distributions are reasonably well represented by the normal distribution. The main distributional characteristic not captured by the normal distribution is the peakedness of the distribution, with the normal distribution tending to

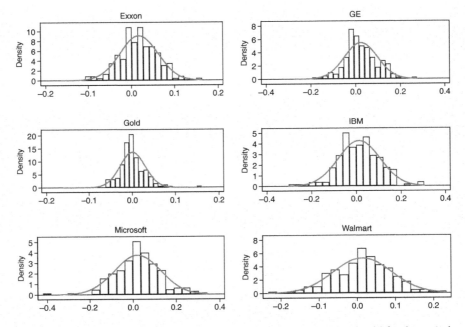

FIGURE 10.1 Histograms of the monthly log returns on five US stocks and gold for the period May 1990 to July 2004. Overlaid on the histograms are normal distributions with maximum likelihood estimates of μ and σ^2.

underestimate the observed mode. A formal test of normality is given in Table 10.1 based on the Jarque–Bera test. Four of the six log-returns pass the normality test, whereas gold and Microsoft do not.

To capture potential non-normal asset returns, the assumption of a normal distribution is sometimes replaced by the assumption that returns follow a t distribution whose probability density is given by

$$f(r_t; \mu, \sigma^2, v) = \frac{\Gamma\left(\frac{v+1}{2}\right)}{\sqrt{\pi \sigma^2 v}\,\Gamma\left(\frac{v}{2}\right)} \left(1 + \frac{(r_t - \mu)^2}{\sigma^2 v}\right)^{-\left(\frac{v+1}{2}\right)}, \tag{10.1}$$

where v represents the degrees of freedom parameter and $\Gamma(\cdot)$ is the gamma function as defined in Chapter 9. The parameter v provides additional flexibility (compared

TABLE 10.1 Jarque–Bera test of normality on the monthly log returns on five US stocks and gold for the period May 1990 to July 2004.

Stock	Mean	Std. Dev.	Skew	Kurt	J–B stat	p value
Exxon	0.017	0.044	0.039	3.498	1.80	0.407
General Electric	0.023	0.074	0.128	3.508	2.29	0.318
Gold	0.000	0.030	1.144	7.576	185.36	0.000
IBM	0.012	0.094	−0.081	3.766	4.35	0.114
Microsoft	0.021	0.107	−0.161	4.538	17.49	0.000
Walmart	0.013	0.076	−0.165	3.228	1.14	0.565

with the normal distribution) in modeling empirical distributions. In the special case where $v \rightarrow \infty$, the t distribution becomes the normal distribution. The form of the t distribution given in equation (10.1) is a location-scale version of the distribution in which μ characterizes central location (not necessarily the mean, because the mean does not exist when $v = 1$), and σ characterizes dispersion (not necessarily variance because the variance does not exist when $v \leq 2$).

The plots in Figure 10.2 illustrate how the t distribution does a slightly better job of capturing the distributional features of returns than the normal distribution, particularly in terms of the peakedness of the distribution.

The value of the parameter v in the t distribution determines the number of integer moments of the distribution that exist. Specifically, integer moments lower than v exist. Thus, the mean or first moment of the t_v distribution exists provided $v > 1$; the second moment exists if $v > 2$ and in that case, the variance is given by $\sigma^2 \frac{v}{v-2}$; the first three moments exist if $v > 3$; and for $v > 4$, the first four moments all exist. For the special case where $v = 1$, no integer moments exist (moments of fractional order less than unity do exist). This distribution is an extreme form of heavy-tailed distribution that is known as the Cauchy distribution. Setting $v = 1$ in equation (10.1) gives the density

$$f(r_t; \mu, \sigma^2) = \frac{1}{\pi\sigma} \left(1 + \frac{(r_t - \mu)^2}{\sigma^2} \right)^{-1}, \tag{10.2}$$

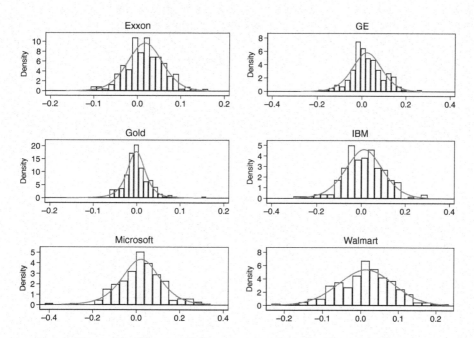

FIGURE 10.2 Histograms of the monthly log returns on five US stocks and gold for the period May 1990 to July 2004. Overlaid on the histograms are t distributions with maximum likelihood estimates of μ, σ^2, and v.

which reduces to the familiar standard Cauchy form

$$f(r_t) = \frac{1}{\pi \left(1 + r_t^2\right)},$$ (10.3)

when $\mu = 1$ and $\sigma = 0$. In this case, the probability of observing a return greater than 20 is approximately $\frac{1}{\pi t}|_{r=20} \approx \frac{1}{63}$. Thus, one draw in 63 from the standard Cauchy distribution can be expected to be as large as 20. For a standard normal distribution, this probability would be effectively zero, and such a draw would be inconceivably rare.

10.1.2 Asset Prices

By definition, log-returns are computed as the change over time in the natural logarithm of the price P_t of an asset, namely,

$$r_t = \log P_t - \log P_{t-1}.$$

The assumption that r_t is normally distributed with mean μ and variance σ^2 implies that P_t, conditional on the lagged price P_{t-1}, is lognormally distributed with density

$$f(P_t | P_{t-1}; \mu, \sigma^2) = \frac{1}{\sqrt{2\pi\sigma^2}P_t} \exp\left[-\frac{(\log P_t - (\mu + \log P_{t-1}))^2}{2\sigma^2} \right].$$

A plot of the distribution of P_t based on lognormality is given in Figure 10.3 with parameters $\mu = 1, \sigma^2 = 0.4$, and $P_{t-1} = 1$. An important feature of this distribution is that it is defined only over the non-negative region. The support of the distribution is therefore said to be the non-negative part of the real line. In the present case, this results in the distribution exhibiting positive skewness with a long right-hand tail.

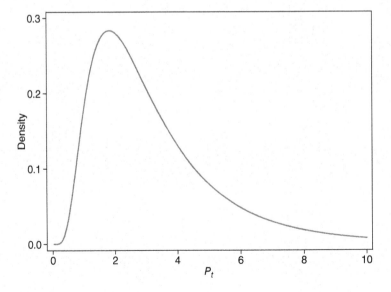

FIGURE 10.3 A plot of the lognormal distribution for equity prices, P_t, with parameters $\mu = 1$, $\sigma^2 = 0.4$, and $P_{t-1} = 1$.

Two important examples of the incidence of the lognormal distribution in finance are the following.

(i) **Simple gross returns on an asset, R_{gt}**

Log-returns are defined as

$$r_t = \log\left(\frac{P_t}{P_{t-1}}\right) = \log\left(1 + \frac{P_t - P_{t-1}}{P_{t-1}}\right) = \log(1 + R_t) = \log(R_{gt}).$$

It follows that if r_t is normally distributed with mean, μ, and variance, σ^2, then $R_{gt} = P_t/P_{t-1}$ is lognormally distributed with density

$$f(R_{gt}; \mu, \sigma^2) = \frac{1}{\sqrt{2\pi\sigma^2}R_{gt}} \exp\left[-\frac{(\log R_{gt} - \mu)^2}{2\sigma^2}\right].$$

(ii) **Black–Scholes option pricing model**

In the Black–Scholes model, it is assumed that the price P_t of an asset is determined by the equation

$$\log P_t - \log P_{t-1} = \mu + u_t, \qquad u_t \sim N(0, \sigma^2),$$

which implies that logarithms of prices follow a Gaussian random walk with drift. The use of cumulative normal distribution functions then arises naturally in computing the option price formula and follows directly from this lognormality assumption.

10.1.3 Yields and Interest Rates

An important distributional property of a bond yield is that it must be positive. In view of this feature of bond yields, the assumption of normality is potentially inappropriate as it necessarily assigns non-zero probability to negative yields. The property is especially relevant when yields come close to the zero boundary as happened during the recent global financial crisis.

To capture the fact that yields and nominal interest rates are positive random variables, two possible distributions for such a variable, y_t are the following

(i) Lognormal distribution with parameter vector $\theta = \{\mu, \sigma^2\}$ and density

$$f(y_t; \theta) = \frac{1}{\sqrt{2\pi\sigma^2}y_t} \exp\left[-\frac{(\log y_t - \mu)^2}{2\sigma^2}\right].$$

(ii) Gamma distribution with parameter vector $\theta = \{\alpha, \beta\}$ and density

$$f(y_t; \theta) = \frac{\alpha^\beta}{\Gamma(\beta)} y_t^{\beta-1} e^{-\alpha y_t},$$

where α and β are the shape and rate parameters of the distribution, respectively.

Figure 10.4 provides a plot of the histogram of daily observations on the monthly Eurodollar rate from 4 January 1971 to 31 December 1991. Leakage of the density into the negative region under the assumption that interest rates are normally distributed is clearly shown in the fitted normal density. The gamma distribution appears more satisfactory in this regard. Both the gamma and normal distributions fail to capture the bimodality that is present in the histogram plot. The assumption of a gamma distribution underlies the continuous time model of interest rates proposed by Cox, Ingersoll, and Ross (1985).

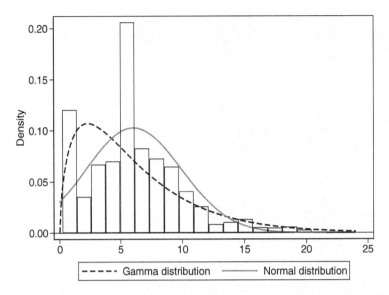

FIGURE 10.4 Histogram of the daily Eurodollar rate from 4 January 1971 to 31 December 1991. Superimposed on the histogram are plots of the best-fitting normal and gamma distributions.

10.1.4 Durations

Figure 9.2 in Chapter 9 gives a histogram of the duration between trades on the US stock AMR, the parent company of American Airlines. The data are recorded at second intervals from 9:30am to 4:00pm on 1 August 2006. The shape of the empirical distribution suggests that a suitable choice is an exponential distribution,[2] whose density is given by

$$f\left(y_t; \alpha\right) = \alpha e^{-\alpha y_t}, \qquad \alpha > 0.$$

Other appropriate choices of distributions to model the time duration between trades are as follows.

(i) Weibull distribution

$$f\left(y_t; \alpha, \beta\right) = \alpha \beta y_t^{\beta-1} e^{-\alpha y_t^{\beta}}, \qquad \alpha, \beta > 0.$$

The exponential distribution is a special case of the Weibull distribution with $\beta = 1$.

(ii) Gamma distribution

$$f\left(y_t; \mu, \alpha, \beta\right) = \frac{\alpha^{\beta}}{\Gamma\left(\beta\right)} \left(y_t - \mu\right)^{\beta-1} e^{-\alpha\left(y_t - \mu\right)}.$$

The exponential distribution is a special case of the gamma distribution with $\mu = 0$ and $\beta = 1$.

---

[2] Note that this specification of the exponential distribution is different to that used in Chapter 9 in the sense that the parameter α is the reciprocal of the parameter γ.

10.2 ESTIMATION BY MAXIMUM LIKELIHOOD

This section introduces the likelihood function and the maximum likelihood estimator. Several cases are considered, which differ according to the properties of the data. In each case, it is assumed that the form of the probability distribution of the data is known up to certain parameters that are to be estimated.

10.2.1 The Log Likelihood Function

The likelihood function and log likelihood function are constructed from the assumed form of the probability density of the data. This distribution is formulated to depend on a set of unknown parameters that are embodied in a parameter vector θ that is to be estimated from a given sample of T observations $\{y_1, y_2, \cdots, y_T\}$. Just as in the case of GMM, the maximum likelihood estimator of θ is obtained by means of extremum estimation. But for maximum likelihood the objective function is the logarithm of the probability distribution of the data. This objective function is known as the log likelihood function.

Four types of log likelihood functions are presented here depending on the properties of the sample data and the nature of the probability distribution associated with the generating mechanism of y_t.

Case 1. Independent and Identically Distributed Observations

$$\log L(\theta) = \frac{1}{T} \sum_{t=1}^{T} \log f(y_t; \theta). \tag{10.4}$$

This is the simplest of the four cases. The random variables (y_t) are independent and identically distributed across all observations $t = 1, \cdots, T$. The likelihood function is then the product of the probability densities

$$L(\theta) = \prod_{t=1}^{T} f(y_t; \theta),$$

and the log likelihood function is the logarithm of this product, leading to equation (10.4). Both the likelihood function and the log likelihood function are considered as functions of the parameter θ once the observed values $\{y_1, y_2, \cdots, y_T\}$ are used in constructing $L(\theta)$.

Case 2. Non-identically Distributed Observations

$$\log L(\theta) = \frac{1}{T} \sum_{t=1}^{T} \log f(y_t | x_t; \theta).$$

This case allows for each of the component densities $f(y_t | x_t; \theta)$ of y_t to be conditional on a set of given explanatory variables x_t. This dependence has the effect of making the distribution of y_t evolve over time according to the nature of its dependence on the covariates x_t. Again, the likelihood function is constructed using the observed data $\{y_t, x_t : t = 1, \cdots, T\}$ and is treated as a function of the unknown parameter vector θ.

Case 3. Dependently Distributed Observations

$$\log L(\theta) = \frac{1}{T-1} \sum_{t=2}^{T} \log f(y_t | y_{t-1}; \theta). \tag{10.5}$$

In this case, the random variables $\{y_t : t = 1, \cdots, T\}$ are dependent and the distribution of each y_t depends on the past value y_{t-1}. So the component densities $f(y_t | y_{t-1}; \theta)$ in equation (10.5) are conditional probability densities given the immediately preceding past value. To take account of this dependence on past values, the likelihood is expressed in terms of the joint density of $\{y_t : t = 2, \cdots, T\}$ given the initial value y_1. As a result, there are only $T - 1$ components in the sum equation (10.5) and, correspondingly, the simple average of the logarithms of the densities is taken over these values, thereby scaling the sum by $1/(T-1)$.

This case may be extended to allow for more general forms of dependence. For instance, the component densities may be conditional densities depending on several past values such as $\{y_{t-1}, y_{t-2}, \cdots, y_{t-p}\}$, in which case the average is restricted to the last $T - p$ observations and is conditioned on p initial values.

Case 4. Dependent and Non-identically Distributed Observations

$$\log L(\theta) = \frac{1}{T-1} \sum_{t=2}^{T} \log f(y_t | x_t, y_{t-1}; \theta).$$

In this case, the probability density of y_t depends on a set of explanatory variables x_t as well as its own past value y_{t-1}.

The maximum likelihood estimator of θ, denoted $\widehat{\theta}$, is obtained by finding the value of the parameter that maximizes the log likelihood function, $\log L(\theta)$, that is, by solving the extremum problem

$$\widehat{\theta} = \arg\max_{\theta} \log L(\theta).$$

The simple but powerful motivation underlying this estimator is that $\widehat{\theta}$ is the value that maximizes the likelihood function $L(\theta)$, so that $\widehat{\theta}$ may be interpreted as the value of θ that is *most likely* to have generated the observed data, as represented by this optimizing value $L(\widehat{\theta}) > L(\theta)$ for all $\theta \neq \widehat{\theta}$. Numerical methods are typically needed to calculate this maximizing value, and only in special cases are analytic formulae available.

10.2.2 The Maximum Likelihood Estimator

First order conditions for the maximum likelihood estimator are obtained by calculus when the likelihood function is a smooth continuously differentiable function, as it is in cases of regular density functions. The $\log L(\theta)$ function is then optimized by taking the first derivative with respect to θ, which is known as the *gradient* (or *score*, in the present case of the log likelihood) and denoted here by $G(\theta)$. For a single parameter ($K = 1$) likelihood, the gradient is simply the scalar derivative

$$G(\theta) = \frac{d \log L(\theta)}{d\theta}.$$

In the case of K parameters, the $K \times 1$ gradient vector is the vector of partial derivatives

$$G(\theta) = \frac{\partial \log L(\theta)}{\partial \theta}.$$

The maximum likelihood estimator $\widehat{\theta}$ satisfies the zero gradients condition

$$G(\widehat{\theta}) = \frac{\partial \log L(\theta)}{\partial \theta}\bigg|_{\theta=\widehat{\theta}} = 0, \tag{10.6}$$

for an optimum. Equation (10.6) is known as the likelihood equation.

To establish that the maximum likelihood estimator maximizes $\log L(\theta)$ (as opposed to finding a turning point that is not a maximum), the second derivative of the log likelihood function, known as the *Hessian*[3] and denoted $H(\theta)$, is needed. For the single ($K = 1$) parameter case, the Hessian is

$$H(\theta) = \frac{d^2 \log L(\theta)}{d\theta^2}.$$

For the K-parameter case, the Hessian is the ($K \times K$) matrix of second derivatives

$$H(\theta) = \frac{\partial^2 \log L(\theta)}{\partial\theta\partial\theta'}.$$

The condition required for the maximum likelihood estimator to maximize $\log L(\theta)$ is that the Hessian be negative definite at $\widehat{\theta}$, that is,

$$H(\widehat{\theta}) = \frac{\partial^2 \log L(\theta)}{\partial\theta\partial\theta'}\bigg|_{\theta=\widehat{\theta}} < 0.$$

For example, the conditions for negative definiteness in the one- and two-parameter cases are

$$\begin{aligned}
&\text{1-parameter} &:\quad& H_{11} < 0 \\
&\text{2-parameters} &:\quad& H_{11} < 0, H_{11}H_{22} - H_{12}H_{21} > 0,
\end{aligned}$$

where H_{ij} is the ijth element of $H(\widehat{\theta})$.

The negative definite Hessian condition ensures that $\widehat{\theta}$ delivers a local maximum of $L(\theta)$ and is necessary, not sufficient, for a global maximum of the likelihood. With very few exceptions, it is the global maximum of the likelihood function that delivers the maximum likelihood estimator. It is therefore necessary in practical work to check that the solution obtained for the likelihood equation (10.6) is not just a local maximum.[4]

10.3 APPLICATIONS

This section illustrates the principle of maximum likelihood estimation in a series of models that commonly appear in financial econometric work.

---

[3] The Hessian matrix of second order partial derivatives was developed in the mid-nineteenth century and is named after the German mathematician Ludwig Otto Hesse who introduced it.

[4] This is often achieved by using several different starting values in the iterative procedure employed in the numerical calculations or by using a grid search method to explore the form of the likelihood surface to check for the existence of multiple maxima and to select the maximum maximorum (largest of the maxima).

10.3.1 Duration Model of Trades

The duration model of trades, y_t, is given by the exponential distribution

$$f\left(y_t;\alpha\right) = \alpha e^{-\alpha y_t}, \qquad \alpha > 0,$$

where the observations y_t are assumed to be *iid*. To derive the maximum likelihood estimator of the single parameter $\theta = \{\alpha\}$, the construction of the log likelihood function $\log L(\theta)$ follows Case 1, giving

$$\log L(\theta) = \frac{1}{T}\sum_{t=1}^{T}\log f(y_t;\theta) = \frac{1}{T}\sum_{t=1}^{T}\log\left(\theta\exp[-\theta y_t]\right)$$

$$= \frac{1}{T}\sum_{t=1}^{T}\log\theta - \frac{1}{T}\sum_{t=1}^{T}\theta y_t = \log\theta - \theta\frac{1}{T}\sum_{t=1}^{T}y_t.$$

Using the durations between trades data for the company AMR measured at 1-second intervals on 1 August 2006, the log likelihood function $\log L(\theta)$ is plotted in Figure 10.5 for $\theta = \alpha$ over the range $0 < \theta \leq 1$. Evidently from this graph, the likelihood function has its highest values for θ in the range $0.1 \leq \theta \leq 0.2$.

To derive the maximum likelihood estimator, the gradient function is calculated as

$$G(\theta) = \frac{d\log L(\theta)}{d\theta} = \frac{1}{\theta} - \frac{1}{T}\sum_{t=1}^{T}y_t,$$

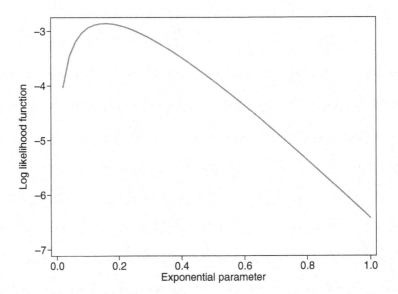

FIGURE 10.5 The log likelihood function with respect to the parameter θ of the exponential model of durations. The data are durations between AMR trades measured in intervals of 1 second from 9:30 to 16:00 on 1 August 2006.

and setting $G(\widehat{\theta}) = 0$ gives

$$\frac{1}{\widehat{\theta}} - \frac{1}{T}\sum_{t=1}^{T} y_t = 0.$$

Solving this equation for $\widehat{\theta}$ yields the maximum likelihood estimator

$$\widehat{\theta} = \frac{T}{\sum_{t=1}^{T} y_t} = \frac{1}{\bar{y}},$$

which is the reciprocal of the sample mean of the durations data.

Since the sample mean is $\bar{y} = 6.4208$, the maximum likelihood estimator has the value

$$\widehat{\theta} = \frac{1}{6.4208} = 0.1557,$$

corroborating the graphical plot of $\log L(\theta)$ in Figure 10.5.

To check the second order condition for a maximum, the Hessian is

$$H(\theta) = \frac{d^2 \log L(\theta)}{d\theta^2} = -\frac{1}{\theta^2}.$$

Evaluating this expression at $\widehat{\theta}$ shows that

$$H(\widehat{\theta}) = -\frac{1}{\widehat{\theta}^2} = -\frac{1}{0.1557^2} = -41.2268 < 0,$$

and the second order condition for a maximum is satisfied. Moreover, the Hessian for this model has the analytic form $-1/\theta^2$ and is therefore negative for all values of θ. In consequence, the log likelihood function is globally concave, which assures the local maximum is a global maximum in this case.

10.3.2 Constant Mean Model

The constant mean model of returns is

$$r_t = \mu + u_t, \qquad u_t \sim iid\,N(0,\sigma^2). \tag{10.7}$$

By transposition of equation (10.7)

$$u_t = (r_t - \mu) \sim iid\,N(0,\sigma^2) \Rightarrow r_t \sim iid\,N(\mu,\sigma^2),$$

so that the sample data, r_t, are independent drawings from a normal distribution with mean μ and variance σ^2. The distribution of r_t is therefore given by

$$f(r_t;\theta) = \frac{1}{\sqrt{2\pi\sigma^2}}\exp\left[-\frac{(r_t - \mu)^2}{2\sigma^2}\right],$$

with parameter vector $\theta = \{\mu,\sigma^2\}$.

To derive the maximum likelihood estimator of θ, the log likelihood function follows Case 1 and has the form

$$\log L(\theta) = \frac{1}{T} \sum_{t=1}^{T} \log f(r_t; \theta) = \frac{1}{T} \sum_{t=1}^{T} \log\left(\frac{1}{\sqrt{2\pi\sigma^2}} \exp\left[-\frac{(r_t - \mu)^2}{2\sigma^2}\right]\right)$$

$$= \frac{1}{T} \sum_{t=1}^{T} \log \frac{1}{\sqrt{2\pi\sigma^2}} - \frac{1}{T} \sum_{t=1}^{T} \frac{(r_t - \mu)^2}{2\sigma^2}$$

$$= -\frac{1}{2}\log 2\pi - \frac{1}{2}\log\sigma^2 - \frac{1}{2\sigma^2}\frac{1}{T}\sum_{t=1}^{T}(r_t - \mu)^2,$$

with the (2×1) gradient vector given by

$$G(\theta) = \begin{bmatrix} \dfrac{\partial \log L(\theta)}{\partial \mu} \\[2ex] \dfrac{\partial \log L(\theta)}{\partial \sigma^2} \end{bmatrix} = \begin{bmatrix} \dfrac{1}{\sigma^2 T} \sum_{t=1}^{T} (y_t - \mu) \\[2ex] -\dfrac{1}{2\sigma^2} + \dfrac{1}{2\sigma^4 T} \sum_{t=1}^{T} (y_t - \mu)^2 \end{bmatrix}.$$

The maximum likelihood estimator is found by setting $G(\widehat{\theta}) = 0$, which requires solving the two equations

$$\frac{1}{\widehat{\sigma}^2 T} \sum_{t=1}^{T} (y_t - \widehat{\mu}) = 0$$

$$-\frac{1}{2\widehat{\sigma}^2} + \frac{1}{2\widehat{\sigma}^4 T} \sum_{t=1}^{T} (y_t - \widehat{\mu})^2 = 0,$$

for $\widehat{\mu}$ and $\widehat{\sigma}^2$. Solving for $\widehat{\mu}$ using the first expression yields

$$\frac{1}{\widehat{\sigma}^2 T} \sum_{t=1}^{T} (y_t - \widehat{\mu}) = \sum_{t=1}^{T} (y_t - \widehat{\mu}) = \sum_{t=1}^{T} y_t - T\widehat{\mu} = 0,$$

so that the maximum likelihood estimator is given by the sample mean of y_t

$$T\widehat{\mu} = \sum_{t=1}^{T} y_t \Rightarrow \widehat{\mu} = \frac{1}{T} \sum_{t=1}^{T} y_t = \bar{y}.$$

Solving for $\widehat{\sigma}^2$ using the second expression in gives

$$-\frac{1}{2\widehat{\sigma}^2} + \frac{1}{2\widehat{\sigma}^4 T} \sum_{t=1}^{T} (y_t - \widehat{\mu})^2 = 0,$$

which leads to the solution

$$\widehat{\sigma}^2 = \frac{1}{T} \sum_{t=1}^{T} (y_t - \widehat{\mu})^2.$$

This expression is the sample variance of y_t with the full sample size T appearing in the denominator.

Differentiating $G(\theta)$ with respect to θ yields the (2×2) Hessian matrix

$$
H(\theta) = \begin{bmatrix} \dfrac{\partial^2 \log L(\theta)}{\partial \mu^2} & \dfrac{\partial^2 \log L(\theta)}{\partial \mu \partial \sigma^2} \\[2ex] \dfrac{\partial^2 \log L(\theta)}{\partial \sigma^2 \partial \mu} & \dfrac{\partial^2 \log L(\theta)}{\partial (\sigma^2)^2} \end{bmatrix}
$$

$$
= \begin{bmatrix} -\dfrac{1}{\sigma^2} & -\dfrac{1}{\sigma^4 T} \sum_{t=1}^{T} (y_t - \mu) \\[2ex] -\dfrac{1}{\sigma^4 T} \sum_{t=1}^{T} (y_t - \mu) & \dfrac{1}{2\sigma^4} - \dfrac{1}{\sigma^6 T} \sum_{t=1}^{T} (y_t - \mu)^2 \end{bmatrix}.
$$

Evaluating this matrix at $\widehat{\theta}$

$$
H(\widehat{\theta}) = \begin{bmatrix} H_{11} & H_{12} \\[1ex] H_{21} & H_{22} \end{bmatrix} = \begin{bmatrix} -\dfrac{1}{\widehat{\sigma}^2} & 0 \\[2ex] 0 & -\dfrac{1}{2\widehat{\sigma}^4} \end{bmatrix},
$$

which uses the following

$$
\frac{1}{T} \sum_{t=1}^{T} (y_t - \widehat{\mu}) = 0, \qquad \frac{1}{T} \sum_{t=1}^{T} (y_t - \mu)^2 = \widehat{\sigma}^2,
$$

where the first condition is based on $G(\widehat{\theta})$, and the second condition is based on the maximum likelihood estimator of σ^2.

The relevant second order conditions for a maximum are satisfied because

$$
H_{11} = -\frac{1}{\widehat{\sigma}^2} < 0,
$$

$$
H_{11} H_{22} - H_{12} H_{21} = \left(-\frac{1}{\widehat{\sigma}^2} \right) \left(-\frac{1}{2\widehat{\sigma}^4} \right) - (0)(0) = \frac{1}{2\widehat{\sigma}^6} > 0.
$$

10.3.3 The CAPM Model

The CAPM regression equation is given by

$$
y_t = \alpha + \beta x_t + u_t, \qquad u_t \sim iid\, N(0, \sigma^2), \tag{10.8}
$$

where $y_t = r_t - r_{ft}$ is the excess return on the asset, and $x_t = r_{mt} - r_{ft}$ is the excess return on the market. It follows from equation (10.8) that

$$
y_t - \alpha - \beta x_t \sim iid\, N(0, \sigma^2) \quad \Longrightarrow \quad y_t \sim iid\, N(\alpha + \beta x_t, \sigma^2).
$$

Taking $r_{mt} - r_{ft}$ as given, the distribution of r_t with parameter vector $\theta = \{\alpha, \beta, \sigma^2\}$ is

$$
f(r_t | r_{mt}, r_{ft}; \theta) = \frac{1}{\sqrt{2\pi\sigma^2}} \exp\left[-\frac{(r_t - r_{ft} - \alpha - \beta(r_{mt} - r_{ft}))^2}{2\sigma^2} \right].
$$

To derive the maximum likelihood estimator of $\theta = \{\alpha, \beta, \sigma^2\}$, the log likelihood function $\log L(\theta)$ is constructed based on Case 2, giving

$$
\begin{aligned}
\log L(\theta) &= \frac{1}{T} \sum_{t=1}^{T} \log f(y_t | x_t; \theta) = \frac{1}{T} \sum_{t=1}^{T} \log \left(\frac{1}{\sqrt{2\pi\sigma^2}} \exp\left[-\frac{(y_t - \alpha - \beta x_t)^2}{2\sigma^2} \right] \right) \\
&= \frac{1}{T} \sum_{t=1}^{T} \log \frac{1}{\sqrt{2\pi\sigma^2}} - \frac{1}{T} \sum_{t=1}^{T} \frac{(r_t - \alpha - \beta x_t)^2}{2\sigma^2} \\
&= -\frac{1}{2} \log 2\pi - \frac{1}{2} \log \sigma^2 - \frac{1}{2\sigma^2} \frac{1}{T} \sum_{t=1}^{T} (r_t - \alpha - \beta x_t)^2 .
\end{aligned}
$$

The (3×1) gradient vector is

$$
G(\theta) = \begin{bmatrix} \dfrac{\partial \log L(\theta)}{\partial \alpha} \\[2ex] \dfrac{\partial \log L(\theta)}{\partial \beta} \\[2ex] \dfrac{\partial \log L(\theta)}{\partial \sigma^2} \end{bmatrix} = \begin{bmatrix} \dfrac{1}{\sigma^2 T} \sum_{t=1}^{T} (y_t - \alpha - \beta x_t) \\[2ex] \dfrac{1}{\sigma^2 T} \sum_{t=1}^{T} (y_t - \alpha - \beta x_t) x_t \\[2ex] -\dfrac{1}{2\sigma^2} + \dfrac{1}{2\sigma^4 T} \sum_{t=1}^{T} (y_t - \alpha - \beta x_t)^2 \end{bmatrix} .
$$

Setting $G(\widehat{\theta}) = 0$ requires that

$$
G(\widehat{\theta}) = \begin{bmatrix} \dfrac{1}{\widehat{\sigma}^2 T} \sum_{t=1}^{T} (y_t - \widehat{\alpha} - \widehat{\beta} x_t) \\[2ex] \dfrac{1}{\widehat{\sigma}^2 T} \sum_{t=1}^{T} (y_t - \widehat{\alpha} - \widehat{\beta} x_t) x_t \\[2ex] -\dfrac{1}{2\widehat{\sigma}^2} + \dfrac{1}{2\widehat{\sigma}^4 T} \sum_{t=1}^{T} (y_t - \widehat{\alpha} - \widehat{\beta} x_t)^2 \end{bmatrix} = \begin{bmatrix} 0 \\ 0 \\ 0 \end{bmatrix} .
$$

This is a linear system of three equations and three unknowns with the following solution

$$
\widehat{\alpha} = \bar{y} - \widehat{\beta} \bar{x}
$$

$$
\widehat{\beta} = \frac{\sum_{t=1}^{T} (y_t - \bar{y})(x_t - \bar{x})}{\sum_{t=1}^{T} (x_t - \bar{x})^2}
$$

$$
\widehat{\sigma}^2 = \frac{1}{T} \sum_{t=1}^{T} (y_t - \widehat{\alpha} - \widehat{\beta} x_t)^2 .
$$

The expressions for $\widehat{\alpha}$ and $\widehat{\beta}$ are in fact the ordinary least squares estimators from Chapter 3, demonstrating that for this class of models, the ordinary least squares estimator is equivalent to the maximum likelihood estimator, at least under Gaussianity. The expression for $\widehat{\sigma}^2$ shows that the maximum likelihood estimator is equivalent to the ordinary least squares estimator apart from the degrees of freedom correction given by $T - 2$ for the bivariate model in the case of ordinary least squares.

Differentiating $G(\theta)$ with respect to θ yields a (3×3) Hessian matrix given by

$$H(\theta) = \begin{bmatrix} \dfrac{\partial^2 \log L(\theta)}{\partial \alpha^2} & \dfrac{\partial^2 \log L(\theta)}{\partial \alpha \partial \beta} & \dfrac{\partial^2 \log L(\theta)}{\partial \alpha \partial \sigma^2} \\[2mm] \dfrac{\partial^2 \log L(\theta)}{\partial \beta \partial \alpha} & \dfrac{\partial^2 \log L(\theta)}{\partial \beta^2} & \dfrac{\partial^2 \log L(\theta)}{\partial \beta \partial \sigma^2} \\[2mm] \dfrac{\partial^2 \log L(\theta)}{\partial \sigma^2 \partial \alpha} & \dfrac{\partial^2 \log L(\theta)}{\partial \sigma^2 \partial \beta} & \dfrac{\partial^2 \log L(\theta)}{\partial (\sigma^2)^2} \end{bmatrix}$$

$$= \begin{bmatrix} -\dfrac{1}{\sigma^2} & -\dfrac{1}{\sigma^2 T}\sum_{t=1}^{T} x_t & -\dfrac{1}{\sigma^4 T}\sum_{t=1}^{T} u_t \\[3mm] -\dfrac{1}{\sigma^2 T}\sum_{t=1}^{T} x_t & -\dfrac{1}{\sigma^2 T}\sum_{t=1}^{T} x_t^2 & -\dfrac{1}{\sigma^4 T}\sum_{t=1}^{T} u_t x_t \\[3mm] -\dfrac{1}{\sigma^4 T}\sum_{t=1}^{T} u_t & -\dfrac{1}{\sigma^4 T}\sum_{t=1}^{T} u_t x_t & \dfrac{1}{2\sigma^4} - \dfrac{1}{\sigma^6 T}\sum_{t=1}^{T} u_t^2 \end{bmatrix},$$

where $u_t = y_t - \alpha - \beta x_t$ is the disturbance term. Evaluating this expression at $\widehat{\theta}$ gives

$$H(\widehat{\theta}) = \begin{bmatrix} -\dfrac{1}{\widehat{\sigma}^2} & -\dfrac{1}{\widehat{\sigma}^2 T}\sum_{t=1}^{T} x_t & -\dfrac{1}{\widehat{\sigma}^4 T}\sum_{t=1}^{T} \widehat{u}_t \\[3mm] -\dfrac{1}{\widehat{\sigma}^2 T}\sum_{t=1}^{T} x_t & -\dfrac{1}{\widehat{\sigma}^2 T}\sum_{t=1}^{T} x_t^2 & -\dfrac{1}{\widehat{\sigma}^4 T}\sum_{t=1}^{T} \widehat{u}_t x_t \\[3mm] -\dfrac{1}{\widehat{\sigma}^4 T}\sum_{t=1}^{T} \widehat{u}_t & -\dfrac{1}{\widehat{\sigma}^4 T}\sum_{t=1}^{T} \widehat{u}_t x_t & \dfrac{1}{2\widehat{\sigma}^4} - \dfrac{1}{\widehat{\sigma}^6 T}\sum_{t=1}^{T} \widehat{u}_t^2 \end{bmatrix},$$

where $\widehat{u}_t = y_t - \widehat{\alpha} - \widehat{\beta} x_t$ is the residual from the fitted equation.

The Hessian simplifies to

$$H(\widehat{\theta}) = \begin{bmatrix} -\dfrac{1}{\widehat{\sigma}^2} & -\dfrac{1}{\widehat{\sigma}^2 T}\sum_{t=1}^{T} x_t & 0 \\[3mm] -\dfrac{1}{\widehat{\sigma}^2 T}\sum_{t=1}^{T} x_t & -\dfrac{1}{\widehat{\sigma}^2 T}\sum_{t=1}^{T} x_t^2 & 0 \\[3mm] 0 & 0 & -\dfrac{1}{2\widehat{\sigma}^4} \end{bmatrix},$$

which makes use of the results

$$\sum_{t=1}^{T} \widehat{u}_t = 0, \qquad \sum_{t=1}^{T} \widehat{u}_t x_t = 0, \qquad \widehat{\sigma}^2 = \frac{1}{T}\sum_{t=1}^{T} \widehat{u}_t^2,$$

where the first two are based on the first order conditions, and the third is based on the solution of $\widehat{\sigma}^2$. It is easy to verify that this matrix is negative definite, thereby satisfying the second order conditions for a maximum.

10.3.4 Vasicek Interest Rate Model

The discrete time model of the interest rate, r_t, proposed by Vasicek (1977) assumes that the dynamics of the interest rate obey the AR(1) equation

$$r_t = \alpha + \rho r_{t-1} + u_t, \qquad u_t \sim iid\, N(0, \sigma^2),$$

resulting in the distribution of r_t with parameter vector $\theta = \{\alpha, \rho, \sigma^2\}$ given by

$$f(r_t \mid r_{t-1}; \alpha, \rho, \sigma^2) = \frac{1}{\sqrt{2\pi\sigma^2}} \exp\left[-\frac{(r_t - \alpha - \rho r_{t-1})^2}{2\sigma^2} \right].$$

Examples of the conditional distribution of r_t are given in Figure 10.6 with the conditional mean, $\alpha + \rho r_{t-1}$, taking the values 5%, 10%, and 15%, respectively, and setting $\sigma^2 = 0.5$. The data are daily Eurodollar interest rates first used by Aït-Sahalia (1996).

To derive the maximum likelihood estimator of $\theta = \{\alpha, \rho, \sigma^2\}$, the log likelihood function is based on Case 3,

$$\log L(\alpha, \rho, \sigma^2) = -\frac{1}{2}\log 2\pi - \frac{1}{2}\log\sigma^2 - \frac{1}{2\sigma^2}\frac{1}{T-1}\sum_{t=2}^{T}(r_t - \alpha - \rho r_{t-1})^2.$$

This expression is equivalent to the form of $\log L(\theta)$ for the CAPM, with r_{t-1} replacing x_t, and corresponds to the likelihood function for a Gaussian AR(1) model with data $[r_t : t = 1, \cdots, T]$ generated from a fixed initial observation r_1. The maximum likelihood estimators are given by the following explicit formulae

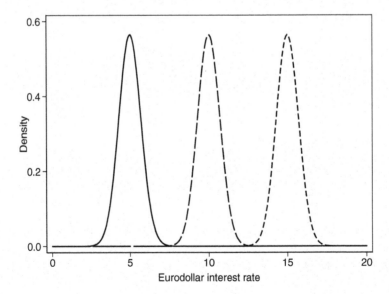

FIGURE 10.6 Conditional distributions of the Vasicek model, with the conditional mean, $\alpha + \rho r_{t-1}$, taking the values 5% (solid line), 10% (long-dashed line), and 15% (dashed line), respectively.

$$\widehat{\alpha} = \overline{r}_t - \widehat{\rho}\overline{r}_{t-1}$$

$$\widehat{\rho} = \frac{\sum_{t=2}^{T} (r_t - \overline{r}_t)(r_{t-1} - \overline{r}_{t-1})}{\sum_{t=2}^{T} (r_{t-1} - \overline{r}_{t-1})^2}$$

$$\widehat{\sigma}^2 = \frac{1}{T-1} \sum_{t=2}^{T} (r_t - \widehat{\alpha} - \widehat{\rho}r_{t-1})^2,$$

where

$$\overline{r}_t = \frac{1}{T-1} \sum_{t=2}^{T} r_t, \qquad \overline{r}_{t-1} = \frac{1}{T-1} \sum_{t=2}^{T} r_{t-1}.$$

10.4 NUMERICAL METHODS

In many financial econometric applications, the system of first order conditions $G(\widehat{\theta}) = 0$ for maximum likelihood does not have an analytical solution. In these cases, a numerical procedure is used to locate the maximum of the likelihood function. Such procedures are typically iterative but may also involve systematic searching over a grid of possible values. Iterative methods work from some starting value for θ, denoted $\theta_{(0)}$, and at each stage produce a new potential value $\widehat{\theta}_{(k)}$ proceeding sequentially until convergence. Convergence is deemed to occur where $G(\widehat{\theta}_{(k)}) \simeq 0$, and $\widehat{\theta}_{(k+1)} \simeq \widehat{\theta}_{(k)}$, up to some specified level of numerical tolerance in terms of significant digits. This process is known as numerical optimization. A general description of the problem and various commonly used optimization algorithms used in this context are given in Appendix D.

An example of the use of numerical methods to compute the maximum likelihood estimator is provided by the CAPM with disturbances that follow the t distribution. The heavy-tailed t distribution helps to accommodate the presence of outliers in the data. Unfortunately, closed-form expressions for the maximum likelihood estimators of the parameters of the model are no longer available in this case. This model, which is known as the robust CAPM, is

$$y_t = \alpha + \beta x_t + u_t, \qquad u_t \sim iid\ St(0, \sigma^2, \nu),$$

where $y_t = r_t - r_{ft}$ is the excess return on the asset, and $x_t = r_{mt} - r_{ft}$ is the excess return on the market. The notation $St(0, \sigma^2, \nu)$ represents a standardized form of t distribution in which the density is given by

$$f(u_t) = \frac{\Gamma\left(\dfrac{\nu+1}{2}\right)}{\sqrt{\pi\sigma^2(\nu-2)}\Gamma\left(\dfrac{\nu}{2}\right)} \left(1 + \frac{u_t^2}{\sigma^2(\nu-2)}\right)^{-\left(\frac{\nu+1}{2}\right)}, \tag{10.9}$$

where the degrees of freedom parameter ν is assumed to satisfy $\nu > 2$, a condition that ensures the variance is finite. In fact, the variance[5] of the standardized distribution $St(0, \sigma^2, \nu)$ is the squared scale coefficient σ^2, which is convenient in many applications. This form of the t distribution differs slightly from that given earlier in equation (10.1)

---

[5] When $\nu > 2$, the variance of the standard t distribution with density given in the earlier expression in equation (10.1) is $\sigma^2 \frac{\nu}{\nu-2}$.

because it allows u_t to have dispersion measured directly by the scale parameter σ. As before in equation (10.1), the parameter ν determines how heavy the tails of the distribution are, thereby capturing the effects of outliers.

Transforming to the implied distribution of the observations y_t gives the density

$$f\left(y_t \mid x_t; \theta\right) = \frac{\Gamma\left(\dfrac{\nu+1}{2}\right)}{\sqrt{\pi \sigma^2 (\nu-2)}\, \Gamma\left(\dfrac{\nu}{2}\right)} \left(1 + \frac{(y_t - \alpha - \beta x_t)^2}{\sigma^2 (\nu-2)}\right)^{-\left(\frac{\nu+1}{2}\right)}. \tag{10.10}$$

To derive the maximum likelihood estimator of $\theta = \{\alpha, \beta, \sigma^2, \nu\}$, the likelihood function $\log L(\theta)$ is based on Case 2 in Section 10.2 and has the form

$$\begin{aligned}
\log L(\theta) &= \frac{1}{T} \sum_{t=1}^{T} \log f\left(y_t \mid x_t; \theta\right) \\
&= \log \Gamma\left(\frac{\nu+1}{2}\right) - \frac{1}{2}\log \sigma^2 - \frac{1}{2}\log\left(\pi(\nu-2)\right) \\
&\quad - \log \Gamma\left(\frac{\nu}{2}\right) - \left(\frac{\nu+1}{2}\right)\frac{1}{T}\sum_{t=1}^{T}\log\left(1 + \frac{(y_t - \alpha - \beta x_t)^2}{\sigma^2(\nu-2)}\right).
\end{aligned}$$

Since this expression for the log likelihood function is nonlinear in the parameters, a numerical approach is adopted to compute the maximum likelihood estimator, $\widehat{\theta}$.

The results of estimating this robust version of the CAPM by maximum likelihood using a numerical optimization algorithm are given in Table 10.2. For comparison, the CAPM estimates based on the assumption that the disturbances are normally distributed are also presented. The estimates of the degrees of freedom parameter, $\widehat{\nu}$, suggest the presence of outliers especially for gold ($\widehat{\nu} = 4.250$), IBM ($\widehat{\nu} = 5.680$), and Microsoft ($\widehat{\nu} = 4.710$). A comparison of the estimates of the β-risk ($\widehat{\beta}$), for both normal and t disturbances, suggests that the effect of outliers on the estimation of this parameter is minimal.

10.5 PROPERTIES

In this section, the properties of maximum likelihood estimators are discussed following the approach adopted in Chapter 3 for the ordinary least squares estimator and Chapter 9 for the generalized method of moments estimator. These properties hold under regularity conditions that are quite weak and allow for a very general class of distributions as discussed in many statistical textbooks following Cramér's (1946) original treatise.[6]

Consistency
An important property of the maximum likelihood estimator $\widehat{\theta}_T$ is that it is, with very few exceptions, a consistent estimator of the population parameter θ_0. As usual, consistency is formally expressed by writing

$$\text{plim}(\widehat{\theta}_T) = \theta_0.$$

---

[6] A pragmatic recent treatment of maximum likelihood estimation is given in Millar (2011). A rigorous development of the asymptotic statistical properties of maximum likelihood and related extremum estimators is provided in the advanced text by van de Vaart (2000).

TABLE 10.2 Parameter estimates of the CAPM model based on the t and normal distributions for the monthly excess log-returns on five US financial assets and gold for the period May 1990 to July 2004. Standard errors are in parentheses.

Stock	Distribution	$\hat{\alpha}$	$\hat{\beta}$	$\hat{\sigma}$	$\hat{\nu}$	log L
Exxon	Normal	0.012 (0.003)	0.502 (0.502)	0.038 (0.002)		3.685
	Student t	0.012 (0.003)	0.502 (0.069)	0.038 (0.002)	11.707 (10.733)	1.852
GE	Normal	0.016 (0.004)	1.143 (0.098)	0.054 (0.003)		3.327
	Student t	0.014 (0.004)	1.163 (0.102)	0.054 (0.003)	13.671 (15.423)	1.492
Gold	Normal	−0.003 (0.002)	−0.098 (0.053)	0.029 (0.002)		3.942
	Student t	−0.005 (0.002)	−0.111 (0.050)	0.030 (0.003)	4.250 (1.491)	2.171
IBM	Normal	0.004 (0.006)	1.205 (0.140)	0.078 (0.004)		2.966
	Student t	0.006 (0.006)	1.214 (0.129)	0.079 (0.007)	5.680 (2.299)	1.160
Microsoft	Normal	0.012 (0.007)	1.447 (0.155)	0.087 (0.005)		2.865
	Student t	0.013 (0.006)	1.354 (0.139)	0.088 (0.009)	4.710 (1.716)	1.072
Walmart	Normal	0.007 (0.005)	0.868 (0.119)	0.066 (0.004)		3.136
	Student t	0.008 (0.005)	0.893 (0.120)	0.066 (0.004)	11.674 (9.782)	1.303

Efficiency

Asymptotic efficiency concerns the degree of dispersion (scatter or variation) of $\widehat{\theta}_T$ around θ_0 as the sample size T increases. For maximum likelihood estimators, the spread of scatter decreases as T increases in line with the consistency property. This reduction can be measured by means of the covariance matrix of $\widehat{\theta}_T$, which in typical cases that satisfy the regularity conditions mentioned earlier takes the following asymptotic form

$$E[(\widehat{\theta}_T - \theta_0)(\widehat{\theta}_T - \theta_0)'] \overset{a}{\sim} \frac{1}{T}\Omega(\theta_0).$$

In this expression, $\Omega(\theta_0)$ is a fixed matrix and the factor T^{-1} shows that for increasing sample sizes the dispersion of $\widehat{\theta}_T$ becomes smaller.[7]

An important asymptotic property of the maximum likelihood estimator is that under certain general conditions (the regularity conditions again), this estimator is more efficient than any other estimator. Achieving this efficiency level corresponds to achieving the smallest possible asymptotic variance, which is commonly known as the Cramér–Rao lower bound.

---

[7] The property is an asymptotic one as $T \to \infty$. In finite samples, there is no assurance that the covariance matrix of the maximum likelihood estimator is finite.

Two common choices for estimating the (asymptotic) covariance matrix $\Omega(\theta_0)$ are as follows.

(i) An estimate based on the Hessian matrix

$$\Omega(\widehat{\theta}_T) = -H(\widehat{\theta}_T)^{-1},$$

where

$$H(\widehat{\theta}_T) = \frac{1}{T} \sum_{t=1}^{T} \frac{\partial^2 \log f(y_t; \theta)}{\partial \theta \partial \theta'} \bigg|_{\theta = \widehat{\theta}_T}.$$

(ii) An estimate based on the Outer Product of Gradients (OPG) matrix

$$\Omega(\widehat{\theta}_T) = J(\widehat{\theta}_T)^{-1},$$

where

$$J(\widehat{\theta}_T) = \frac{1}{T} \sum_{t=1}^{T} \frac{\partial \log f(y_t; \theta)}{\partial \theta} \frac{\partial \log f(y_t; \theta)}{\partial \theta'} \bigg|_{\theta = \widehat{\theta}_T}.$$

The covariance matrix of $\widehat{\theta}_T$ may therefore be estimated via two formulae as

$$\text{cov}(\widehat{\theta}_T) = \begin{cases} -\dfrac{1}{T} H(\widehat{\theta}_T)^{-1} & : \quad \text{Hessian} \\[2mm] \dfrac{1}{T} J(\widehat{\theta}_T)^{-1} & : \quad \text{OPG}. \end{cases} \tag{10.11}$$

Standard errors of $\widehat{\theta}_T$ are given by the square roots of the diagonal elements of this matrix.

Asymptotic Normality
In a wide range of applications (typically those involving stationary data), the asymptotic distribution of $\widehat{\theta}_T$ is given by

$$\widehat{\theta}_T \overset{a}{\sim} N\left(\theta_0, \frac{1}{T}\Omega(\theta_0)\right), \qquad \sqrt{T}(\widehat{\theta}_T - \theta_0) \overset{d}{\longrightarrow} N(0, \Omega(\theta_0)).$$

The first expression shows the asymptotic approximation to the finite sample distribution of $\widehat{\theta}_T$ and the second shows the precise form of the limiting distribution as $T \to \infty$. This result plays an important role in facilitating inference concerning the unknown parameter vector θ_0 once the asymptotic covariance matrix $\Omega(\theta_0)$ is estimated using $\text{cov}(\widehat{\theta}_T)$.

Invariance
These properties of consistency, efficiency, and asymptotic normality are all large sample properties. Maximum likelihood estimation also has the property of invariance. This property means that for any monotonic nonlinear function $\tau(\cdot)$, the maximum likelihood estimator of $\tau(\theta_0)$ is given by $\tau(\widehat{\theta}_T)$. The invariance property is particularly useful in situations when an analytical expression for the maximum likelihood estimator is not available but can be computed by substitution.

For example, the variance of the returns on a financial asset is denoted σ^2. The maximum likelihood estimator is

$$\widehat{\sigma}^2 = \frac{1}{T} \sum_{t=1}^{T} (r_t - \overline{r})^2,$$

where r_t is the return with sample mean $\bar{r}$. The volatility or risk of the asset is represented by the population standard deviation σ, and the maximum likelihood estimator of volatility is the corresponding function of $\hat{\sigma}$, namely,

$$\hat{\sigma} = \sqrt{\hat{\sigma}^2},$$

because of the invariance principle. In this case, $\tau(\cdot)$ is simply the square root function.

Another example relates to the estimation of the weights of the assets in the construction of the minimum variance portfolio. Let the population variances of the returns on two assets be given by σ_1^2 and σ_2^2 and the covariance by $\sigma_{1,2}$. The corresponding maximum likelihood estimators for a sample of size T are

$$\hat{\sigma}_1^2 = \frac{1}{T}\sum_{t=1}^{T}(r_{1t} - \bar{r}_1)^2,$$

$$\hat{\sigma}_2^2 = \frac{1}{T}\sum_{t=1}^{T}(r_{2t} - \bar{r}_2)^2,$$

$$\hat{\sigma}_{12} = \frac{1}{T}\sum_{t=1}^{T}(r_{1t} - \bar{r}_1)(r_{2t} - \bar{r}_2),$$

where r_{it} is the return on the ith asset with sample mean $\bar{r}_i$. Since the optimal weight on the first asset is

$$w_1 = \frac{\sigma_2^2 - \sigma_{12}}{\sigma_1^2 + \sigma_2^2 - 2\sigma_{12}},$$

the maximum likelihood estimator of the population parameter w_1 is given by the corresponding function of the estimates, namely,

$$\hat{w}_1 = \frac{\hat{\sigma}_2^2 - \hat{\sigma}_{12}}{\hat{\sigma}_1^2 + \hat{\sigma}_2^2 - 2\hat{\sigma}_{12}},$$

by invoking the invariance principle.

10.6 QUASI MAXIMUM LIKELIHOOD ESTIMATION

The models discussed so far and the corresponding likelihood functions are all founded on the assumption that the models are specified correctly. Some of the properties of maximum likelihood continue to hold under model and likelihood misspecification. For some misspecified models it may, for example, be possible to estimate a subset of parameters for which consistency and asymptotic normality still hold even when the log likelihood function for these models is misspecified. In such cases, the log likelihood is referred to as the quasi log likelihood and the estimator is correspondingly known as a quasi maximum likelihood estimator. One consequence of misspecification of the likelihood is that the quasi maximum likelihood estimator does not achieve the same efficiency level as the maximum likelihood estimator.

Under general conditions the asymptotic distribution of the quasi maximum likelihood estimator, written as $(\hat{\theta}_Q)$, has the form

$$\sqrt{T}(\hat{\theta}_Q - \theta_0) \xrightarrow{d} N(0, \Omega_Q), \tag{10.12}$$

whose asymptotic variance Ω_Q depends on the type of misspecification introduced into the model and likelihood. The linear regression model can be used to illustrate. Suppose

$$y_t = \alpha + \beta x_{1t} + u_t, \qquad u_t \sim N(0, \sigma_u^2), \tag{10.13}$$

where y_t is the dependent variable, x_{1t} is the explanatory variable, u_t is the disturbance term, and the unknown parameters are taken as the mean parameters in the regression equation $\theta = \{\alpha, \beta\}$. Three types of misspecification, are now considered.

Nonnormality

A common type of misspecification occurs when u_t is assumed to be normally distributed when in fact it is not. This situation occurs so frequently that it has the special name of Gaussian estimation. Gaussian estimation leads in the linear regression model to simple least squares estimation, in which case the asymptotic covariance matrix is given by the usual least squares formula. For a sample of T observations, the quasi maximum likelihood standard errors are therefore the square roots of the diagonal elements of the matrix

$$\frac{1}{T}\widehat{\Omega}_Q = \frac{\widehat{\sigma}_u^2}{T}\left(\frac{1}{T}\sum_{t=1}^{T} x_t x_t'\right)^{-1}, \tag{10.14}$$

where $\widehat{\sigma}_u^2$ is the residual variance and $x_t = [1 x_{1t}]'$. Thus, inference may be conducted in the usual way for ordinary least squares estimation.

Heteroskedasticity

The second type of misspecification is that the disturbance variance is assumed to be constant when the true variance is time varying. The asymptotic covariance matrix of the quasi maximum likelihood estimator is constructed using the signal matrix of the regressors (H) and the outer product of the gradients, given by $\Omega_Q = H^{-1}JH^{-1}$, which is commonly known as the sandwich estimator. The standard errors of the quasi maximum likelihood estimator are then given by the square roots of the diagonal components of this matrix. In the simple case of the linear regression with a single regressor, an estimate of the asymptotic variance of $\widehat{\theta}_Q$ takes the following form,

$$\frac{1}{T}\widehat{\Omega}_Q = \frac{1}{T}\left(\frac{1}{T}\sum_{t=1}^{T} X_t X_t'\right)^{-1}\left(\frac{1}{T}\sum_{t=1}^{T}\widehat{u}_t^2 X_t X_t'\right)\left(\frac{1}{T}\sum_{t=1}^{T} X_t X_t'\right)^{-1}. \tag{10.15}$$

Standard errors based on this expression are also known as White standard errors (White, 1980). The squared residual $\widehat{u}_t^2$ represents a crude estimate of the disturbance variance at time t. If the true disturbance variance were constant, an appropriate estimator would be to replace $\widehat{u}_t^2$ with $\widehat{\sigma}_u^2$ for each t, with the result that equation (10.15) reduces to equation (10.14).

Autocorrelation

The third and final type of misspecification considered here is when the disturbance is assumed to be independent when in fact it is autocorrelated of unknown order. The asymptotic covariance matrix of the quasi maximum likelihood estimator is still of the same form as it is for the case where misspecification occurs because of heteroskedasticity, with the exception that the outer product of the gradients matrix, J, in the sandwich estimator also takes into account the autocorrelation in the disturbances. The standard errors of the quasi maximum likelihood estimator are now computed as the square roots of the diagonal components of this sandwich matrix. In the case of the linear regression model with a single regressor, the estimated asymptotic variance of $\widehat{\theta}_Q$ is

$$\frac{1}{T}\widehat{\Omega}_Q = \frac{1}{T}\left(\frac{1}{T}\sum_{t=1}^{T}X_tX_t'\right)^{-1}\left(\widehat{\Gamma}_0 + \sum_{i=1}^{p}w_i\left(\widehat{\Gamma}_i + \widehat{\Gamma}_i'\right)\right)\left(\frac{1}{T}\sum_{t=1}^{T}X_tX_t'\right)^{-1}, \qquad (10.16)$$

where the lag length p and weights w_i are chosen according to some decision rule, and $\widehat{\Gamma}_i$ is the estimated autocovariance

$$\widehat{\Gamma}_i = \frac{1}{T}\sum_{t=i+1}^{T}\widehat{u}_t\widehat{u}_{t-i}x_tx_{t-i}', \; i = 0, 1, 2, \cdots. \qquad (10.17)$$

Standard errors based on this expression are also known as Bartlett–Newey–West standard errors (Bartlett, 1950; Newey and West, 1987).

10.7 TESTING

The likelihood function provides a simple and intuitive approach to inference, the most common form of which is to test whether the parameter of the model has a certain hypothesized value, θ_0. If this value differs from the maximum likelihood estimate $\widehat{\theta}$, then by virtue of the construction of $\widehat{\theta}$, the hypothesized value θ_0 must correspond to a lower value of the log likelihood function. The crucial statistical question is how significant the decrease in the likelihood is in moving between these two values. Determining the significance of this reduction in the log likelihood function leads to one of the most fundamental approaches to hypothesis testing in statistics. The resulting procedure is known as the likelihood ratio test. In addition to this test, several other procedures are available that utilize the maximum likelihood estimate and these will be discussed briefly in what follows.

10.7.1 Testing Framework and Test Statistics

The simplest versions of the null and alternative hypotheses to be tested may be stated in terms of the full parameter vector θ in the form

$$H_0 : \theta = \theta_0, \quad H_1 : \theta \neq \theta_0.$$

In more general cases, the null hypothesis H_0 may involve certain posited restrictions on the true value θ_0. For instance, certain elements of θ may take specific values or may be hypothesized to satisfy certain linear or nonlinear relations.

Three commonly used tests may be constructed for such hypotheses: the likelihood ratio test (LR), the Wald test (WD), and the Lagrange multiplier test (LM). These tests are distinguished by whether estimation takes place under the null hypothesis, the alternative hypothesis, or both hypotheses. Accordingly, there are two types of estimators to consider, namely,

$\widehat{\theta}_0$: parameters estimated under the restrictions of H_0
$\widehat{\theta}_1$: parameters estimated with no such restrictions H_1.

The following forms symbolize the construction of these three tests, which involve use of the restricted and unrestricted estimates of θ

Likelihood ratio : $\quad LR = -2T\left(\log L(\widehat{\theta}_0) - \log L(\widehat{\theta}_1)\right)$

Wald : $\quad WD = T[\widehat{\theta}_1 - \widehat{\theta}_0]'[\Omega(\widehat{\theta}_1)]^{-1}[\widehat{\theta}_1 - \widehat{\theta}_0]$

Lagrange multiplier : $\quad LM = TG(\widehat{\theta}_0)'[\Omega(\widehat{\theta}_0)]G(\widehat{\theta}_0).$

In the expressions for the WD and LM test statistics, the choice of the estimate of the covariance matrix $\Omega(\widehat{\theta})$ depends on the configuration of the null and alternative hypotheses. The LM test involves estimation under the null hypothesis alone, and the covariance matrix may then be delivered as in expression (10.11) for estimation under the null. An important feature of all three tests is that in large samples, they are distributed as chi-squared, with degrees of freedom equal to the number of restrictions (M) associated with the null hypothesis, χ^2_M.

In the special case where the null hypothesis restricts all elements of the parameter vector, so that $H_0 : \theta = \theta_0$, the restrictions under the null then imply that the restricted maximum likelihood estimate is simply $\widehat{\theta}_0 = \theta_0$. In this case, if the dimension of θ is N, then $M = N$ and under the null hypothesis the tests are asymptotically χ^2_N. If restrictions are imposed only on a subset of the parameters, so that $M < N$, the forms of LR and LM remain the same but the WD statistic is redefined in terms of those parameters that are restricted under the null hypothesis (for details, see Martin, Hurn, and Harris, 2013).

Likelihood Ratio Test

The LR statistic measures the distance between the value of the log likelihood under the null hypothesis, $\log L(\widehat{\theta}_0)$, and its value under the alternative hypothesis, $\log L(\widehat{\theta}_1)$. A small difference between these likelihoods tends to favor the null hypothesis because relaxation of the null hypothesis restrictions only leads to a marginal improvement in the likelihood value. A large difference between the likelihood values indicates that the data favor the less restrictive hypothesis and therefore suggest a rejection of the null hypothesis. The statistical test measures the significance of these departures using the large sample distribution of the test statistic.

Wald Test

The WD test is based on the distance between the parameter estimate under the alternative hypothesis, $\widehat{\theta}_1$, and the value of the parameter under the null hypothesis, $\widehat{\theta}_0$. In computing the test, this distance is weighted by the inverse of the covariance matrix of the estimate evaluated under the alternative hypothesis, $\Omega(\widehat{\theta}_1)$. This covariance matrix uses a measure of the curvature of log likelihood function. In particular, sharper log likelihood functions at the unrestricted estimate $\widehat{\theta}_1$ correspond to smaller variances and these typically lead to tighter inferences. The opposite is the case for nearly flat likelihood functions around $\widehat{\theta}_1$.

Lagrange Multiplier Test

The LM test is based on the distance between the gradient of the log likelihood function under the null hypothesis, $G(\widehat{\theta}_0)$, and the gradient of the log likelihood function under the alternative hypothesis. By virtue of the optimizing property of the unrestricted maximum likelihood estimator, this estimator satisfies first order conditions and it follows that $G(\widehat{\theta}_1) = 0$.

The test statistic is weighted by the covariance matrix $\Omega(\widehat{\theta}_0)$, which is the inverse of the covariance matrix of $G(\widehat{\theta}_0)$, as defined previously. A convenient expression for computing the LM statistic is where $\Omega(\widehat{\theta}_0)$ is based on the outer product of gradients matrix, $J(\widehat{\theta})$, so that

$$LM = TG(\widehat{\theta}_0)'[T^{-1}J(\widehat{\theta}_0)^{-1}]G(\widehat{\theta}_0),$$

where

$$G(\widehat{\theta}_0) = \frac{1}{T}\sum_{t=1}^{T} g_t, \quad J(\widehat{\theta}_0) = \frac{1}{T}\sum_{t=1}^{T} g_t g_t',$$

and all gradients are evaluated at the restricted estimate $\widehat{\theta}_0$.

An alternative form of the LM statistic, which is convenient for a broad class of models is

$$LM = T\left(\frac{1}{T}\sum_{t=1}^{T} g_t\right)' \frac{1}{T}\left(\frac{1}{T}\sum_{t=1}^{T} g_t g_t'\right)^{-1}\left(\frac{1}{T}\sum_{t=1}^{T} g_t\right)$$

$$= \left(\sum_{t=1}^{T} g_t\right)'\left(\sum_{t=1}^{T} g_t g_t'\right)^{-1}\left(\sum_{t=1}^{T} g_t\right) = TR^2,$$

where R^2 is the coefficient of determination from regressing a vector of ones on the gradient variates g_t (without an intercept).

Computing the LM test involves the following steps.

Step 1: Estimate the restricted model and compute $\widehat{\theta}_0$.

Step 2: Estimate the auxiliary regression where the dependent variable is a vector of ones and the explanatory variables are the gradients in g_t, all evaluated at $\widehat{\theta}_0$.

Step 3: Compute the statistic $LM = TR^2$, where R^2 is the coefficient of determination in the auxiliary regression of Step 2.

A vast number of diagnostic tests that are used in empirical work to determine the validity of an estimated regression model are constructed using the LM test principle via the TR^2 formula. The following tests are especially popular.

(i) The regression error autocorrelation test involves estimating the model without autocorrelation (the restricted model) and then estimating an auxiliary regression equation with the appropriate gradient function variables evaluated under the null, leading to the test statistic based on TR^2.

(ii) The White test for heteroskedasticity involves estimating the model without heteroskedasticity (the restricted model) and then estimating an auxiliary regression equation with the appropriate gradient function variables evaluated under the null and the test statistic computed as TR^2.

10.7.2 Testing the Duration Model of Trades

Consider again the AMR duration between trades data for 1 August 2006. Assume now that these durations follow the Weibull distribution

$$f(y_t; \alpha, \beta) = \alpha \beta y_t^{\beta-1} e^{-\alpha y_t^\beta}, \qquad \alpha, \beta > 0.$$

A natural test of this model is represented by the two hypotheses

$$H_0 : \beta = 1, \quad H_1 : \beta \neq 1,$$

so that under the null hypothesis, the Weibull distribution reduces to an exponential distribution.

To perform a likelihood ratio test, both the unrestricted and restricted models are estimated by maximum likelihood method. Using the Weibull distribution, the unrestricted log likelihood function based on Case 1 is

$$\log L(\theta) = \log(\alpha) + \log(\beta) + (\beta - 1)\frac{1}{T}\sum_{t=1}^{T}\log y_t - \alpha\frac{1}{T}\sum_{t=1}^{T}y_t^\beta.$$

The gradients are

$$\frac{\partial \log L(\theta)}{\partial \alpha} = \frac{1}{\alpha} - \frac{1}{T}\sum_{t=1}^{T}y_t^\beta,$$

$$\frac{\partial \log L(\theta)}{\partial \beta} = \frac{1}{\beta} + \frac{1}{T}\sum_{t=1}^{T}\log y_t - \alpha\frac{1}{T}\sum_{t=1}^{T}\log(y_t)y_t^\beta,$$

where the second expression uses logarithmic differentiation.

Setting these two derivatives to zero the maximum likelihood estimator $\widehat{\theta} = \{\widehat{\alpha}, \widehat{\beta}\}$ is the solution of

$$0 = \frac{1}{\widehat{\alpha}} - \frac{1}{T}\sum_{t=1}^{T}y_t^{\widehat{\beta}},$$

$$0 = \frac{1}{\widehat{\beta}} + \frac{1}{T}\sum_{t=1}^{T}\log y_t - \widehat{\alpha}\frac{1}{T}\sum_{t=1}^{T}\log(y_t)y_t^{\widehat{\beta}}.$$

This is a nonlinear system of equations that is solved using an iterative algorithm.

The unrestricted maximum likelihood estimates, $\widehat{\theta}_1 = \{\widehat{\alpha}_1, \widehat{\beta}_1\}$, are found to be

$$\widehat{\alpha}_1 = 0.1904, \qquad \widehat{\beta}_1 = 0.9166.$$

The unrestricted log likelihood value is $\log L(\widehat{\theta}_1) = -2.8517$. The restricted maximum likelihood estimates, $\widehat{\theta}_0 = \{\widehat{\alpha}_0, \widehat{\beta}_0\}$, are

$$\widehat{\alpha}_0 = 0.15575, \qquad \widehat{\beta}_0 = 1.0000.$$

Note the restricted estimate for α is also obtained directly by using the analytical result that the parameter estimate is the reciprocal of the sample mean of durations. The restricted log likelihood value is $\log L(\widehat{\theta}_0) = -2.8595$.

The likelihood ratio statistic is computed as

$$LR = -2T\left(\log L(\widehat{\theta}_0) - \log L(\widehat{\theta}_1)\right)$$
$$= -2 \times 3643 \times (-2.859 + 2.8517) = 57.3311.$$

Under the null hypothesis, LR is distributed, as χ_1^2, resulting in a p value of 0.0000. There is therefore a strong rejection at the 5% level that the durations between trades are exponentially distributed.

To perform a Wald test of the hypotheses, the unrestricted model is estimated and the restriction $\beta = 1$ is tested. The value of the Wald statistic is $WD = 59.32$ and under the null hypothesis, WD is distributed as χ_1^2, resulting in a p value of 0.000 and indicating a clear rejection of the null hypothesis at the 5% level.

Since the Wald test involves just the one restriction, an alternative way of performing the test is to perform a simple t test. The t statistic is

$$t = \frac{0.9166 - 1.0000}{0.01083} = -7.7020.$$

Squaring the result of the t test gives the value of the Wald statistic computed earlier, $WD = (-7.7020)^2 = 59.32$. This result highlights that t tests are closely related to simple Wald tests. As in Wald tests, the parameters are estimated under the alternative hypothesis in constructing a t test. However, in focusing on a single parameter, t tests also allow for directional alternatives so that a null hypothesis such as $H_0 : \theta = \theta_0$ may be tested against either the alternatives $H_1 : \theta > \theta_0$ or $H_1 : \theta < \theta_0$.

To perform a Lagrange multiplier test of the restrictions, the gradients of the log likelihood function must be evaluated under the null hypothesis. The gradients at each t are given by

$$g_{1t} = \frac{\partial \log f(y_t; \alpha, \beta)}{\partial \alpha} = \frac{1}{\alpha} - y_t^\beta$$
$$g_{2t} = \frac{\partial \log f(y_t; \alpha, \beta)}{\partial \beta} = \frac{1}{\beta} + \log y_t - \alpha \log(y_t) y_t^\beta.$$

Evaluating these expressions at the restricted parameter estimates, $\widehat{\theta}_0 = \{0.15575, 1.0000\}$, gives

$$g_{1t} = \frac{1}{0.15575} - y_t$$
$$g_{2t} = 1 + \log y_t - 0.15575 \log(y_t) y_t.$$

Performing the auxiliary regression with unity as the dependent variable and g_{1t} and g_{2t} as explanatory variables yields a coefficient of determination given by $R^2 = 0.1706$. The value of the LM statistic is then

$$LM = TR^2 = 3643 \times 0.1706 = 62.1564.$$

Under the null hypothesis, the statistic LM is distributed as χ_1^2 resulting in a p value of 0.0000, once again indicating strong rejection of the null hypothesis at the 5% level. This is the same qualitative result as those obtained using the LR and WD tests.

An important feature of the LM test in testing for durations is that it is not necessary in this case to estimate the model using an iterative optimization algorithm. Since the test is constructed under the null hypothesis, analytical expressions for the estimators are available. In this instance, α is estimated as the inverse of the sample mean of the durations data and β is simply set equal to its value under the null hypothesis, namely, unity. This facility contrasts with the LR and WD tests, which both require use of an iterative algorithm because both these tests involve estimation of the model under the alternative hypothesis where no analytical expressions for the estimators exist.

As all three testing procedures are equivalent in large samples, the choice is sometimes a matter of convenience, which, for the present example, would be the LM test since it is relatively simple to implement. It is not always the LM statistic that is most convenient or appropriate. As demonstrated in the next example involving the CAPM model, the WD test is found there to be more convenient. Moreover, even though the three tests may have equivalent asymptotic properties, the tests often have very different finite sample properties, which may bias the tests toward one or other of the hypotheses.

10.7.3 Testing the CAPM
The CAPM is given by

$$r_{it} - r_{ft} = \alpha + \beta(r_{mt} - r_{ft}) + u_t,$$

where the dependent variable is the excess return on an asset $(r_{it} - r_{ft})$, the explanatory variable is the excess return on the market $(r_{mt} - r_{ft})$, and u_t is a disturbance term. Consider testing the following joint restrictions

$$H_0 : \alpha = 0, \beta = 1; \quad H_1 : \text{at least one restriction is not satisfied.}$$

Under the null hypothesis, the model becomes

$$r_{it} - r_{ft} = 0 + (r_{mt} - r_{ft}) + u_t,$$

or more simply

$$r_{it} - r_{mt} = u_t,$$

so that the test of the restrictions is equivalent to testing that the excess return of the asset relative to the market is random.

The unrestricted model is easily estimated by ordinary least squares and it is therefore convenient to perform a Wald test of the restrictions. The Wald test of the hypotheses may use either the Hessian $H(\widehat{\theta}_1)$ or the $J(\widehat{\theta}_1)$ matrix to compute the covariance matrix of the estimates. The three sets of Wald tests on the CAPM for the six assets are summarized in Table 10.3. The parameter estimates are the unrestricted maximum likelihood estimates based on the assumption that the disturbances are normally distributed which makes them equivalent to the ordinary least squares estimates, which are reported in Table 10.2. The covariance matrix of the disturbances is computed using the Hessian matrix of the unrestricted model, $H(\widehat{\theta}_1)$.

In the case of Exxon, the value of the Wald test of the null hypothesis $H_0 : \alpha = 0, \beta = 1$ yields a test statistic of $WD = 64.5067$. Under the null hypothesis, WD is distributed as χ_2^2 resulting in a p value of 0.0000 and showing strong rejection of the null hypothesis at the 5% level. As the null hypothesis is rejected, the two restrictions in the null hypothesis are tested separately. A test that the intercept is zero is represented by the hypotheses

$$H_0 : \alpha = 0, \quad H_1 : \alpha \neq 0.$$

TABLE 10.3   Wald tests of restrictions on the CAPM equations for the monthly excess log-returns on five US financial assets and gold for the period May 1990 to July 2004, with p values based on the Hessian in parentheses.

Stock	Null Hypothesis		
	$H_0 : \alpha = 0$	$H_0 : \beta = 1$	$H_0 : \alpha = 0, \beta = 1$
Exxon	16.6479	52.3976	64.5067
	(0.0000)	(0.0000)	(0.0000)
GE	13.9334	2.1270	17.1048
	(0.0002)	(0.1447)	(0.0002)
Gold	1.4016	426.2581	434.9162
	(0.2365)	(0.0000)	(0.0000)
IBM	0.5154	2.1061	2.8182
	(0.4728)	(0.1467)	(0.2444)
Microsoft	3.3414	8.2005	12.5180
	(0.0676)	(0.0042)	(0.0019)
Walmart	1.8494	1.2177	2.8333
	(0.1739)	(0.2698)	(0.2425)

The value of the Wald statistic is

$$WD = \left(\frac{0.012018 - 0.0}{0.002945} \right)^2 = 16.6479.$$

Using χ_1^2, the p value is 0.0000, once again showing a strong rejection of the null hypothesis at the 5% level. Taking the square root of the Wald statistic gives

$$t = \frac{0.012018 - 0.0}{0.002945} = 4.0802,$$

which is the corresponding t statistic, whose value is significantly positive, confirming a strong directional rejection of the null hypothesis in favor of a positive intercept $\alpha > 0$.

To test whether the slope is unity, the relevant hypotheses are

$$H_0 : \beta = 1, \quad H_1 : \beta \neq 1.$$

The value of the Wald statistic is

$$WD = \left(\frac{0.501768 - 1.0}{0.068830} \right)^2 = 52.3976.$$

Using χ_1^2, the p value is also 0.0000 and the null hypothesis is rejected at the 5% level. Taking the square root of the Wald statistic gives

$$t = \frac{0.501768 - 1.0}{0.068830} = -7.2386,$$

which is the corresponding t statistic, showing that the slope is significantly less than unity.

10.8 EXERCISES

The data required for the exercises are available for download as EViews workfiles (*.wf1), Stata datafiles (*.dta), comma delimited text files (*.csv), and as Excel spreadsheets (*.xlsx).

1. Univariate Distributions

capm.*

The data are monthly prices for Exxon, GE, gold, IBM, Microsoft, Walmart, and the S&P 500 index, together with the 3-month US Treasury Bill rate. The sample period is from April 1990 to July 2004.

(a) Compute the percentage monthly log returns on each of the assets given by

$$r_{it} = 100 \times (\log P_{it} - \log P_{it-1}),$$

where P_{it} is the relevant asset price at time t. For each of the log returns series, compute the sample skewness, kurtosis, and Jarque–Bera test of normality. Interpret the results.

(b) Assume that log returns follow a normal distribution given by

$$f(r_t; \mu, \sigma^2) = \frac{1}{\sqrt{2\pi\sigma^2}} \exp\left[-\frac{(r_t - \mu)^2}{2\sigma^2}\right].$$

For each asset, estimate the parameters of the distribution, μ and σ, and comment on the results.

(c) Now assume that the log returns follow a t distribution given by

$$f(r_t; \mu, \sigma^2, v) = \frac{\Gamma\left(\frac{v+1}{2}\right)}{\sqrt{\pi\sigma^2 v}\, \Gamma\left(\frac{v}{2}\right)} \left(1 + \frac{(r_t - \mu)^2}{\sigma^2 v}\right)^{-\left(\frac{v+1}{2}\right)},$$

where v represents the degrees of freedom parameter. Estimate the parameters of the distribution, μ, σ, and v, and comment on the results.

(d) On the same graph, plot the histogram of the returns together with the best fitting normal and t distributions. Interpret the results.

2. International Stock Indices

stockindices.*

The data are daily observations on the S&P 500 (SPX), Dow Jones (DJX), Hang Seng (HSX), Nikkei (NKX), Deutsche Aktien (DAX), and FTSE (UKX) stock indices for period 4 January 1999 to 2 April 2014.

(a) Compute the log return to the ith market index as

$$r_{it} = \log P_{it} - \log P_{it-1}.$$

Plot the histogram in each case and comment briefly on your results.

(b) Assume that stock market log returns follow a normal distribution given by

$$f(r_t; \mu, \sigma^2) = \frac{1}{\sqrt{2\pi\sigma^2}} \exp\left[-\frac{(r_t - \mu)^2}{2\sigma^2} \right].$$

For each stock market, estimate the parameters of the normal distribution, μ and σ, and comment on the results.

(c) Now assume that the log returns follow a t distribution given by

$$f(r_t; \mu, \sigma^2, \nu) = \frac{\Gamma\left(\dfrac{\nu+1}{2}\right)}{\sqrt{\pi\sigma^2\nu}\,\Gamma\left(\dfrac{\nu}{2}\right)} \left(1 + \frac{(r_t - \mu)^2}{\sigma^2\nu} \right)^{-\left(\frac{\nu+1}{2}\right)},$$

where ν represents the degrees of freedom parameter. Estimate the parameters of the distribution, μ, σ, and ν and comment on the results.

(d) Compare and contrast the results in parts (b) and (c).

3. Eurodollar Interest Rates

eurodata.*

The data are daily Eurodollar rates from 4 January 1971 to 31 December 1991, $T = 11049$.

(a) Plot the time series of Eurodollar rates and comment briefly on the results.

(b) Assume that interest rates follow a lognormal distribution with parameter vector $\theta = \{\mu, \sigma^2\}$ given by

$$f(y_t; \theta) = \frac{1}{\sqrt{2\pi\sigma^2}y_t} \exp\left[-\frac{(\log y_t - \mu)^2}{2\sigma^2} \right].$$

Estimate $\theta = \{\mu, \sigma^2\}$ by maximum likelihood.

(c) Assume that interest rates follow a gamma distribution with parameter vector $\theta = \{\alpha, \beta\}$ given by

$$f(y_t; \theta) = \frac{\alpha^\beta}{\Gamma(\beta)} y_t^{\beta-1} e^{-\alpha y_t}.$$

Estimate $\theta = \{\alpha, \beta\}$ by maximum likelihood.

(d) Plot a histogram of the interest rates and superimpose the lognormal and gamma distributions using the parameter estimates obtained in parts (b) and (c), respectively.

4. Modeling Durations

amr.*

The data are high frequency (1-second intervals) observations on the trades recorded by American Airlines (AMR) from 9:30 to 16:00 on 1 August 2006.

(a) Create a series of durations by recording the integer duration (variable u) when a trade occurs (variable $y = 1$). Force the first observation of the series to be the number of seconds from the start of the day's trading ($u_1 = 27$).

(b) Assume that durations between trades follow an exponential distribution with parameter $\theta = \{\alpha\}$ given by

$$f(y_t; \theta) = \alpha e^{-\alpha y_t}, \qquad \alpha > 0.$$

(i) Compute the values of the log likelihood function for values of $\theta = \{\alpha\}$ in the range $0 < \theta < 1$.

(ii) Now estimate the value of $\theta = \{\alpha\}$ by maximum likelihood. Verify that the result is consistent with the plot obtained in (i) and also that the second-order condition for a maximum is satisfied.

(iii) Using the results from (ii), draw a histogram of the durations with the exponential distribution superimposed on it.

(c) Now assume that the durations between trades follow a Weibull distribution given by

$$f(y_t; \alpha, \beta) = \alpha \beta y_t^{\beta-1} e^{-\alpha y_t^\beta}, \qquad \alpha, \beta > 0.$$

Since the Weibull distribution reduces to an exponential distribution if $\beta = 1$, test the null hypothesis $H_0 : \beta = 1$ using the likelihood ratio, Wald and Lagrange multiplier tests: Interpret the results.

5. **Testing the CAPM**

capm.*

The data are monthly prices for Exxon, GE, gold, IBM, Microsoft, Walmart, and the S&P 500 index, together with the 3-month US Treasury Bill rate expressed as an annual return. The sample period is from April 1990 to July 2004.

(a) Compute the monthly excess log returns on each asset and the market index given by

$$r_{it} = \log P_{it} - \log P_{it-1} - r_{ft}/12,$$

where P_{it} is the relevant asset price (or market index) at time t, and r_{ft} is the Treasury Bill rate, which is quoted as an annual percentage rate.

(b) The CAPM model is

$$y_t = \alpha + \beta x_t + u_t,$$

where y_t is the excess return on the asset, and x_t is the excess return on the market. Estimate this model based on the following assumptions.

(i) The disturbances are distributed normally, $u_t \sim iid\ N(0, \sigma^2)$.

(ii) The disturbances follow a t distribution with v degrees of freedom, $u_t \sim iid\ St(0, \sigma^2, v)$.

Discuss the results.

(c) Using the estimates based on the assumption that the disturbances are normally distributed, test the following hypotheses using Wald tests.

   (i) $\alpha = 0$.
   (ii) $\beta = 1$.
   (iii) $\alpha = 0$, $\beta = 1$.

6. **Cauchy Distribution**

   The Cauchy distribution is an extreme case of the t distribution, as none of its moments exist. The probability density function of the Cauchy distribution is given by

   $$f(y_t; \theta) = \frac{\gamma}{\pi} \left(\frac{1}{\gamma^2 + (y_t - \alpha)^2} \right),$$

   in which $\theta = \{\alpha, \gamma\}$ are unknown parameters, with α being the location parameter and γ the scale parameter.

   (a) Demonstrate by simulation that the sample mean is not a consistent estimator of the location parameter, α, of the Cauchy distribution, with $\alpha = 0$ and $\gamma = 1$, but that the median is. [Hint: To draw from this distribution, recognize that this Cauchy distribution is related to the t family of distributions].

   (b) Generate 1000 observations $y_t = \{y_1, y_2, \cdots, y_{1000}\}$ from the Cauchy distribution, with $\alpha = 0$ and $\gamma = 1$, and estimate α and γ by maximum likelihood.

   (c) Test the null hypothesis $H_0 : \gamma = 1$ using the likelihood ratio, Wald and Lagrange multiplier tests.

   (d) Test the joint hypothesis $H_0 : \alpha = 0, \gamma = 1$ using a Wald test.

7. **A Model of Global Financial Crises**

   ┌───┐
   │   crisis. *   │
   └───┘

   The data file contains the number of countries (from a total of 215) that experienced a banking crisis (banking) or currency crisis (currency) within each of the years 1880 to 2010 (see Reinhart and Rogoff, 2009). The total number of countries considered is 21.

   An important area of research in empirical finance is understanding the spread of financial crises across national borders. Let the number of financial crises experienced by countries each year be represented by y_t, which is assumed to have a geometric distribution

   $$f(y_t; \theta) = \theta (1 - \theta)^{y_t}, \qquad y_t = 0, 1, 2, \cdots,$$

   where the unknown parameter $0 < \theta < 1$, represents the probability of a financial crisis occurring in a year. If in a given year there are no countries in crisis, then $y_t = 0$; otherwise, y_t takes the value of a positive integer corresponding to the number of crises that occurred globally that year.

(a) For a sample of $\{y_1, y_2, \cdots, y_T\}$ *iid* observations, derive the log likelihood function

$$\log L(\theta) = \frac{1}{T} \sum_{t=1}^{T} \log f(y_t; \theta).$$

Derive an expression for the expected value of the log likelihood function, $E[\log L(\theta)]$, using the following property of the geometric distribution,

$$E(y_t) = \frac{1-\theta}{\theta}.$$

(b) Derive expressions for the gradient, $G(\theta)$, the Hessian, $H(\theta)$, and the information matrix

$$I(\theta) = -E[H(\theta)].$$

(c) Find $\widehat{\theta}$, the maximum likelihood estimator of θ, and check that it is a maximum.

(d) Use the data on banking crises from 1880 to 2010, $T = 211$, to answer the following questions.

(i) Compute the maximum likelihood estimate and interpret the result.

(ii) Compute the value of the log likelihood function evaluated at the maximum likelihood estimate computed in part (i).

(iii) Test the following null and alternative hypotheses

$$H_0 : \theta = 0.5$$
$$H_1 : \theta \neq 0.5,$$

using an LR test. Choose a 5% level of significance.

(e) Repeat part (d) using the data on currency crises and compare the two sets of results.

CHAPTER 11

Panel Data Models

The methods with which this book has so far been concerned involve two types of data: time series, with an ordered temporal sequence of T observations; and cross section, with an unordered collection of observations associated with N individuals. Such data are unidimensional, representing only a single dimension in which measurements may be taken over time or across individual units. The process of financial data collection that is undertaken daily by central banks and other statistical agencies reflects a very different reality—the underlying multidimensional nature of the modern financial world.

In a similar way, the estimation methods have so far focused on either time series or cross section data. This chapter widens the study and the corresponding methodology to take account of multidimensional data and to build and estimate models in which the observations are taken over time as well as across units or individuals. Combined data sets of this form are known as panel data or longitudinal data, with the number of combined measurements amounting to $N \times T$ observations, describing N individual units observed longitudinally over T time periods.

Such panels of data represent a rich source of information because they combine cross section information on the impact of individual characteristics often described as heterogeneity over individuals with time series information on adjustment dynamics or the evolution over time of each individual unit. Two-dimensional panels of this sort are a special case of more general multi dimensional data that allow for additional directions of variation. For instance, three-dimensional data might detail the purchases of each individual investor $i = 1, \cdots, N$ over a certain time period $t = 1, \cdots, T$ of a collection of different financial products $j = 1, \cdots, J$. In this case, the number of combined measurements amounts to $N \times T \times J$ observations. An econometric model describing the evolution of such data over time may then allow for heterogeneity across individual investors according to risk preferences and across different financial assets according to their characteristic features.

Multidimensional panels involve a substantial increase in the number of observations. But panels also involve an increase in model complexity arising from the additional variation in the data that needs to be explained. The changes in the models and the nature of the data from the unidimensional case lead to corresponding changes in methods of estimation. Methods such as least squares, instrumental variables, and generalized method of moments are still commonly used. But these methods require modifications or innovations that are tailored to the special requirements necessitated by particular features of the data. Examples involve dealing with the heterogeneity across individuals or the availability of a very small number of time series observations (T) relative to the number of individual units (N) in the sample.

11.1 TYPES OF PANEL DATA

Panel data are often classified into *long* panels where the time series sample size T is large and *wide* panels where the cross section sample size N is large. Panels with T small and N large are called short wide panels. Similarly, long narrow panels have large T and small N. Both types of panels occur in financial data.

Empirical research on asset pricing and investments makes use of an abundance of time series data usually on a representative but limited group of stocks. The typical data set in asset pricing problems is therefore a long narrow panel with large T and small N. An example of such a panel is given in Table 11.1, which comprises a snapshot of $T = 288$ monthly excess returns from January 1992 to December 2013 for $N = 5$ US pharmaceutical and allied health stocks that are contained in the Dow Jones index: Johnson and Johnson (JNJ), Merck (MRK), Pfizer (PFE), Proctor and Gamble (PG), and the United Health Group (UNH). For comparison, the excess returns on the Dow Jones are also given.

Data availability, on the other hand, is a major issue in empirical corporate finance research. Very often data are publicly available only when published in annual reports. However, a collection of time series data for as little as 5 years becomes much more powerful when combined with a very large number of firms, resulting in a short wide panel with small T and large N. An example of such a wide panel is given in Table 11.2,

TABLE 11.1 A long panel containing data on monthly excess returns on the US stocks Johnson and Johnson, Merck, Pfizer, Proctor and Gamble, and the United Health Group as representative stocks for the pharmaceutical and allied health sector in the Dow Jones Industrial Average for the period January 1992 to December 2013. Also shown is the market excess return on the Dow Jones.

Dates	JNJ	MRK	PFE	PG	UNH	Dow
Jan-1992	−0.071	−0.061	−0.147	0.097	0.108	0.014
Feb-1992	−0.058	−0.000	0.018	−0.024	−0.043	0.011
Mar-1992	−0.041	−0.072	−0.073	0.003	−0.013	−0.013
Apr-1992	−0.030	−0.018	0.025	0.007	−0.039	0.034
May-1992	0.018	0.036	0.038	−0.008	0.146	0.008
Jun-1992	−0.082	−0.036	−0.024	−0.114	−0.070	−0.027
Jul-1992	0.095	0.059	0.066	0.093	0.100	0.019
Aug-1992	−0.005	−0.065	−0.015	−0.082	−0.079	−0.044
Sep-1992	−0.047	−0.094	−0.035	0.052	0.162	0.002
Oct-1992	0.057	−0.014	0.008	0.066	0.032	−0.016
Nov-1992	0.005	0.026	0.032	0.023	0.042	0.022
Dec-1992	−0.005	−0.039	−0.078	−0.012	0.042	−0.004
⋮	⋮	⋮	⋮	⋮	⋮	⋮
Dec-2013	−0.033	0.004	−0.035	−0.034	0.011	0.030

which contains a snapshot of data on Tobin's Q for $T = 8$ years from 1992 to 1999 on $N = 330$ firms, as identified by their respective firm numbers {1045, 1078, 1164, 1209, 1213, 1240, ..., 65399, 65417}.

Panel data can be also classified into *balanced* panels and *unbalanced* panels. A balanced panel is one with no missing observations, as is the case for the panel data given in Table 11.1 where every cell of the $T \times N$ matrix contains an observed data point. The presence of cells with missing (time series) observations yields an unbalanced panel, as the sample sizes for each cross section member are no longer the same. The corporate finance data in Table 11.2 exhibit an unbalanced panel: Observations on Tobin's Q are recorded for all years for the three firms (1045, 1078, 1209), whereas the three firms (1164, 1213, 1240) are missing the 1992 observations; while the last two firms (65399, 65417) have observations available for only the last 2 years.

When using panel data, a complete set of equations for the system comprises an equation specified for each of the N cross sections. Such a complete system may be estimated jointly. In the case of the empirical asset pricing data in Table 11.1, this scheme might involve estimating $N = 5$ different CAPMs, one for each of the 5 stocks. For the corporate finance data in Table 11.2, it would involve specifying $N = 330$ equations where the performance of each firm is determined by some suitable set of explanatory variables. Even though the combination of time series and cross section data produces a large number, $N \times T$, of observations, panel models also involve a large number of unknown parameters, many of which relate to the specific characteristics of each unit or individual in the cross section. Other parameters, such as those that represent common forms of financial agent responses, may be common—or homogeneous—across equations. The ability to estimate financial econometric models of this type involves dealing at once with the heterogeneity of individual characteristics and the homogeneity of common behavior. These features of panel data models lead to large numbers of potentially nuisance parameters—called *incidental* parameters—and a much smaller number of homogeneous parameters that result from commonality restrictions that apply across the parameters of the N equations for each cross section unit.

Panel models are often classified according to restrictions that are imposed on the parameters. Two extreme forms are the no common effects model, where no restrictions at all are imposed on the coefficients, and the common effects model, which is the

TABLE 11.2   A wide panel containing data on Tobin's Q for $T = 8$ years from 1992 to 1999 on $N = 330$ firms, as identified by their firm number.

Year	Firm								
	1045	1078	1164	1209	1213	1240	...	65399	65417
1992	1.0930	4.1763	.	1.6530	.	.	...	.	.
1993	1.0975	3.6859	1.4993	1.4875	1.3592	2.6356		.	.
1994	1.0380	3.5995	1.3720	1.6146	1.0394	2.6290		.	.
1995	1.1038	4.0146	1.6970	1.5886	1.1273	2.5912	...	.	.
1996	1.1147	4.0994	1.5089	1.5924	1.0506	2.3844		.	.
1997	1.2348	4.7351	1.6250	1.8921	1.6437	2.7849		.	.
1998	1.1851	6.1944	2.0017	1.5632	1.6474	2.9523	...	1.3709	2.9476
1999	1.1257	4.3443	2.0932	1.4548	1.1290	1.4598		1.3916	2.6447

most restrictive. Intermediate cases are the fixed effects model, where individual specific incidental parameters—usually the intercept coefficients in the equations—are treated as fixed coefficients to be estimated; and the random effects model, where the incidental parameters are treated as random variables from a distribution with some given mean and variance. Both types of model are widely used in empirical finance; and both models may be extended to allow for dynamics and nonstationarity.

11.2 REASONS FOR USING PANEL DATA

There are a number of advantages to be obtained from combining time series and cross section data in studying financial markets. To the extent that characteristics are common in governing financial behavior, there is substantial benefit in estimating the parameters of financial models that describe such behavior using all available data. In particular, methods of estimating panel models are designed to take advantage of the statistical power involved in cross section averaging whenever commonality is present. This typically leads to greater efficiency and higher rates of consistency in estimation. Longitudinal data also enable analysts to monitor performance in financial assets over time and compare time profiles of different assets.

While recognizing these advantages in the use of panel data, attention must also be given to the reliability and availability of the data. Econometric methods may be able to mitigate or control for the effects of low quality or missing data, but they cannot completely overcome such shortcomings and their effects are inevitably present in empirical findings.

Data Reliability

Recorded financial data are not always measured without error. The quality of data depends on accounting conventions, institutional arrangements, and the statistical methods that are adopted in compiling databases. Data extracted from company reports may be reported or entered with errors. The accounting standards used to compile statistics can vary across firms and across countries. For many financial firms, national auditing standards require companies to report accurately key performance and cost statistics. But this is not always the case for hedge funds, where statistics reported on the returns of hedge funds are based on self-reporting by the funds themselves.

An advantage of combining data into a panel is that it may improve reliability in estimation and inference by mitigating the effects of some poor data that may be present in the panel by virtue of the averaging process that includes both high and low quality data. Such improvement stems from an assumption that is often implicit in the averaging process that errors in firm data will tend to negate each other by virtue of the action of the law of large numbers. In the limit, the combination of data from a wide cross section results in the data errors being averaged out.

To illustrate this process, let $r_{jt} - r_{ft}$ be the excess return on the jth stock at time t. An estimate of the expected excess return for the jth stock over time is given by the sample mean of the times series of excess returns on this stock

$$\widehat{\mu}_j = \frac{1}{T}\sum_{t=1}^{T}(r_{jt} - r_{ft}), \qquad j = 1, 2, \cdots, N. \tag{11.1}$$

Now consider an equal weighted portfolio where all N stocks are held in equal amounts in the portfolio. An estimate of the expected excess return at time t is obtained by computing the sample mean of the excess returns of the N stocks at t according to the cross section average

$$\widehat{\mu}_t = \frac{1}{N} \sum_{j=1}^{N} (r_{jt} - r_{ft}), \qquad t = 1, 2, \cdots, T. \tag{11.2}$$

An overall estimate of the expected return on the portfolio is obtained by averaging over time as in equation (11.1) and over cross section (stocks) as in equation (11.2), leading to

$$\widehat{\mu} = \frac{1}{NT} \sum_{j=1}^{N} \sum_{t=1}^{T} (r_{jt} - r_{ft}). \tag{11.3}$$

Even if the excess returns for some stocks contain errors, these errors will be mitigated when computing the sample average excess returns $\widehat{\mu}_j$ and $\widehat{\mu}_t$ given in equations (11.1) and (11.2), and even more so when estimating the overall expected return $\widehat{\mu}$ in equation (11.3).

Data Availability
For the corporate finance data on firm performance in Table 11.2, it is not feasible with only $T = 8$ years of data to explain the performance of each of the $N = 330$ firms by a large number of explanatory variables using time series data alone. This difficulty is partly circumvented by pooling the cross section observations in a way that facilitates estimation of time series features, such as dynamic responses, that might reasonably be assumed to be common across the panel. In contrast, data on excess returns reported for the $N = 5$ stocks in Table 11.1 constitute a long narrow panel, which enables multiple explanatory variables to be used to explain firm performance by using time series data alone. The panel model may then be interpreted as a multiple equation model with a fixed number of equations N.

A more extreme situation occurs when some explanatory variables are either unavailable or cannot be measured accurately, a phenomenon that can result in biased and inconsistent parameter estimates. Consider the following 2-factor CAPM that relates excess returns on the jth asset $(r_{jt} - r_{ft})$ to the market excess return $(r_{mt} - r_{ft})$ and an additional factor w_{jt}, so that

$$r_{jt} - r_{ft} = \alpha + \beta(r_{mt} - r_{ft}) + \gamma w_{jt} + u_{jt}. \tag{11.4}$$

If w_{jt} is measured with error (or is unobserved), the ordinary least squares parameter estimates of equation (11.4) are biased and inconsistent whenever the two factors $r_{mt} - r_{ft}$ and w_{jt} are correlated (see also Chapter 8). Now suppose that w_{jt} is unobserved and varies across section but is constant over time so that $w_{jt} = w_j$, resulting in the model

$$r_{jt} - r_{ft} = \alpha + \beta(r_{mt} - r_{ft}) + \gamma w_j + u_{jt}. \tag{11.5}$$

Using the difference operator $\Delta x_t \equiv x_t - x_{t-1}$ to take first differences of equation (11.5) results in the following first differenced version of the model,

$$\Delta(r_{jt} - r_{ft}) = \beta \Delta(r_{mt} - r_{ft}) + \Delta u_{jt}. \tag{11.6}$$

In this equation, the effect of w_j is no longer present because it is eliminated by differencing. In consequence, the parameter β can be estimated consistently by ordinary least squares regression provided the regressor $\Delta(r_{mt} - r_{ft})$ is uncorrelated with the equation disturbances Δu_{jt}.

Statistical Efficiency

Combining time series data (of length T) and cross section data (of length N) into a panel offers the prospect of improved accuracy in parameter estimation due to the augmented sample size (of magnitude $N \times T$). The improvement in statistical efficiency from having a larger sample size is reflected in smaller variances, sharper (more powerful) tests, and shorter confidence intervals. These improvements in statistical efficiency and inference are achieved by restrictions on the model that are delivered by virtue of a panel structure that imposes commonalities in the parameters across equations. The gains depend on the validity of the restrictions and the nature of the restrictions determine the type of panel model.

In some situations, the augmented data sets arising from the combination of cross section and time series data lead to simplifications in statistical analysis. In such cases, panel analysis and inference can be conducted in a more straightforward manner than is possible with a time series sample alone. An important example occurs in nonstationary models such as those considered in Chapters 5 and 6, where the presence of unit root nonstationarity leads to nonstandard limit distributions for statistical tests based solely on time series samples. By using all of the data in a nonstationary panel, the effect of cross section averaging enables the use of central limit arguments when the cross section sample size $N \to \infty$. Panel estimators and test statistics then typically have asymptotic normal and chi squared distributions, which facilitate the use of conventional inference procedures.

Testing Hypotheses

Rich data sets that come with panels also lead to an expanded range of hypotheses of interest. Certain hypotheses may be tested using panel data that are not possible with time series or cross section data alone. For example, consider the capital asset pricing model for N different stocks

$$r_{jt} - r_{ft} = \alpha_j + \beta_j(r_{mt} - r_{ft}) + u_{jt}, \qquad j = 1, 2, \cdots, N, \tag{11.7}$$

where $r_{jt} - r_{ft}$ represents the excess return at time t on the jth stock, $r_{mt} - r_{ft}$ is the market excess return at time t, and u_{jt} is a disturbance at time t on the jth equation. Estimation of this equation for all N stocks yields N estimates of the α-risk parameters and N estimates of the β-risk parameters. One interesting set of restrictions involves testing whether all of the stocks track the market index in exactly the same way. This involves determining if the β-risks for the N firms are all the same, namely,

$$\beta_1 = \beta_2 = \cdots = \beta_N = \beta. \tag{11.8}$$

A second set of restrictions involves determining if the α-risks for the N firms are all the same. The restrictions are

$$\alpha_1 = \alpha_2 = \cdots = \alpha_N = \alpha. \tag{11.9}$$

A special case of these restrictions is where there are no abnormal returns, and the common α-risk parameter is $\alpha = 0$ a test of the validity of this special case is known as the Gibbons–Ross–Shanken test. Finally, a combination of the restrictions in equations (11.8) and (11.9) amounts to testing whether the stocks are equivalent to each other in that they all share the same α- and β-risks.

Recent research has considered the more ambitious case where there may be subgroups of assets with the same α- and β-risks. If those subgroups were known in advance, then the parameters may be estimated and the hypothesis of homogeneity in those subgroups may be tested directly. But if the subgroups are not known in advance, then the subgroups in which there is homogeneity also need to be estimated. Such econometric procedures are known as classification methods, and techniques for conducting this type of analysis are now available. Bonhomme and Manresa (2015) and Su, Shi, and Phillips (2016) provide methodologies for performing estimation and inference along these lines.

11.3 TWO INTRODUCTORY PANEL MODELS

11.3.1 No Common Effects

The most unrestricted panel model is the no common effects model

$$y_{jt} = \alpha_j + \beta_j x_{jt} + u_{jt}, \qquad u_{jt} \sim (0, \sigma_j^2), \tag{11.10}$$

where y_{jt} and x_{jt} are, respectively, the dependent and explanatory variables associated with the jth cross section at time t. The disturbance term u_{jt} is assumed to be distributed with zero mean and variance that varies over the cross sections. This model can also be extended to allow for multiple explanatory variables. The no common effects model is the most unrestricted form within this class of panel model as the intercepts α_j, slopes β_j, and variances σ_j^2 are all allowed to vary overcross sections, thereby providing a framework that accommodates full heterogeneity over individuals in the cross section.

An important example of the no common effects model is the single factor CAPM given in equation (11.7), which links the excess return on a financial asset to its exposure to a single risk factor where $y_{jt} = r_{jt} - r_{ft}$ is the excess return on the jth asset at time t, and $x_{jt} = r_{mt} - r_{ft}$ is the corresponding market excess return at time t. The CAPM equation is given again for convenience as

$$r_{jt} - r_{ft} = \alpha_j + \beta_j(r_{mt} - r_{ft}) + u_{jt}, \tag{11.11}$$

where u_{jt} represents the idiosyncratic risk of the jth asset. The intercepts and the slope parameters represent, respectively, the α-risks and the β-risks for each of the N assets.

The no common effects CAPM in equation (11.11) means that the model is specified for each stock as follows

$$
\begin{aligned}
\text{Stock 1:} \quad & r_{1t} - r_{ft} = \alpha_1 + \beta_1(r_{mt} - r_{ft}) + u_{1t}, & u_{1t} &\sim (0, \sigma_1^2), \\
\text{Stock 2:} \quad & r_{2t} - r_{ft} = \alpha_2 + \beta_2(r_{mt} - r_{ft}) + u_{2t}, & u_{2t} &\sim (0, \sigma_2^2), \\
& \qquad\qquad \vdots \\
\text{Stock N:} \quad & r_{Nt} - r_{ft} = \alpha_N + \beta_N(r_{mt} - r_{ft}) + u_{Nt}, & u_{Nt} &\sim (0, \sigma_N^2).
\end{aligned}
$$

This decomposition of the no common effects CAPM means that the parameters of the model can be estimated by applying ordinary least squares to each equation separately. This indeed was the strategy adopted in Chapter 3 where the CAPM was estimated by least squares for each stock.

The parameter estimates, standard errors, and residual sum of squares (RSS) of the no common effects CAPM in equation (11.11) for the $N = 5$ stocks given in Table 11.1 are

$$r_{1t} - r_{ft} = \underset{(0.0030)}{0.0022} + \underset{(0.0725)}{0.6212} (r_{mt} - r_{ft}) + \widehat{u}_{1t}, \qquad RSS = 0.6369, \qquad (11.12)$$

$$r_{2t} - r_{ft} = \underset{(0.0043)}{-0.0028} + \underset{(0.1027)}{0.7264} (r_{mt} - r_{ft}) + \widehat{u}_{2t}, \qquad RSS = 1.2766, \qquad (11.13)$$

$$r_{3t} - r_{ft} = \underset{(0.0037)}{0.0005} + \underset{(0.0873)}{0.6862} (r_{mt} - r_{ft}) + \widehat{u}_{3t}, \qquad RSS = 0.9220, \qquad (11.14)$$

$$r_{4t} - r_{ft} = \underset{(0.0034)}{0.0031} + \underset{(0.0821)}{0.4812} (r_{mt} - r_{ft}) + \widehat{u}_{4t}, \qquad RSS = 0.8165, \qquad (11.15)$$

$$r_{5t} - r_{ft} = \underset{(0.0053)}{0.0072} + \underset{(0.1264)}{0.9158} (r_{mt} - r_{ft}) + \widehat{u}_{5t}, \qquad RSS = 1.9327, \qquad (11.16)$$

where the stocks are arranged in the order JNJ $(j = 1)$, MRK $(j = 2)$, PFE $(j = 3)$, PG $(j = 4)$, and UNH $(j = 5)$. The number of estimated coefficient parameters here is 10. The estimates of β-risk suggest that all pharmaceutical stocks are conservative since all estimates are positive but less than unity. The α-risk estimates are all positive with the exception of MRK, although the standard errors reveal that the statistical significance of these risk coefficients is marginal.

The idiosyncratic risks σ_j are estimated by

$$\widehat{\sigma}_j = \sqrt{\frac{1}{T} \sum_{t=1}^{T} \widehat{u}_{jt}^2}. \qquad (11.17)$$

Using the RSS in equations (11.12) to (11.16) gives the following idiosyncratic risk estimates

$$\widehat{\sigma}_1 = \sqrt{\frac{0.6369}{264}} = 0.0493, \quad \widehat{\sigma}_2 = \sqrt{\frac{1.2766}{264}} = 0.0698, \quad \widehat{\sigma}_3 = \sqrt{\frac{0.9220}{264}} = 0.0593,$$

$$\widehat{\sigma}_4 = \sqrt{\frac{0.8165}{264}} = 0.0558, \quad \widehat{\sigma}_5 = \sqrt{\frac{1.9327}{264}} = 0.0859.$$

The standard errors reported for the parameter estimates in equations (11.12) to (11.16) are based on these estimates of the residual standard deviation for each estimated equation. As the residual standard deviations are allowed to vary over the cross sections, these standard errors are sometimes referred to as panel robust standard errors.

11.3.2 Common Effects
At the other end of the panel spectrum is the case of common effects in which there is extreme pooling of information. Each equation of this model is assumed to have the same intercept and same slope coefficients. Imposing these restrictions yields the common effects model

$$y_{jt} = \alpha + \beta x_{jt} + u_{jt}, \qquad u_{jt} \sim (0, \sigma_j^2), \qquad (11.18)$$

where the regression coefficients are the same for each equation $j = 1, \cdots, N$, but equation error variances σ_j^2 are heterogeneous.

In the case of the common effects CAPM, $y_{jt} = r_{jt} - r_{ft}$ is the excess return on the jth asset, and $x_{jt} = r_{mt} - r_{ft}$ is the excess return on the market portfolio, so equation (11.18) has the explicit form

$$r_{jt} - r_{ft} = \alpha + \beta(r_{mt} - r_{ft}) + u_{jt}, \tag{11.19}$$

with u_{jt} representing the idiosyncratic risk of the jth stock at time t. For this model, both the α-risks and the β-risks are assumed to be the same across all N stocks, although the model still allows for differing idiosyncratic risks σ_j^2. As all stocks in this model are assumed to have the same risk characteristics, the equation might be regarded as an industry-wide CAPM in which the stocks of this industry share common determining regression effects relative to the market while retaining differences in idiosyncratic risk effects via the equation errors.

The common effects CAPM in equation (11.19) has only two regression parameters, α and β. By comparison, the number of unknown parameters in the no common effects model in equation (11.11) is $2N$. The difference of $R = 2N - 2$, parameters represents the number of restrictions that the common effects model imposes on the no common effects model.

To estimate the common effects model with the restrictions imposed, the approach adopted is to stack the data as in Table 11.3. For the dependent variable $r_{jt} - r_{ft}$, the time series of each stock are stacked on top of each other to produce a new variable that is an $(NT \times 1)$ vector of excess returns on all N stocks over all time periods. Stacking the explanatory variable is achieved in exactly the same way except that the excess returns on the market are the same for all stocks, so the stacked explanatory variable simply stacks

TABLE 11.3   The excess returns to the US stocks Johnson and Johnson (JNJ), Merck (MRK), Pfizer (PFE), Proctor and Gamble (PG), and the United Health Group (UNH) in the Dow Jones Industrial Average. Also shown is the market excess return on the Dow Jones. This is an example of panel data in long or stacked form.

Dates	Stocks	$r_{jt} - r_{ft}$	$r_{mt} - r_{ft}$
Jan-1992	JNJ	−0.071	0.014
Feb-1992	JNJ	−0.058	0.011
⋮	⋮	⋮	⋮
	JNJ	−0.033	0.030
Jan-1992	MRK	−0.061	0.014
Feb-1992	MRK	−0.000	0.011
⋮	⋮	⋮	⋮
	MRK	−0.033	0.030
Jan-1992	PFE	−0.147	0.014
Feb-1992	PFE	0.018	0.011
⋮	⋮	⋮	⋮
	PFE	−0.033	0.030
Jan-1992	PG	0.097	0.014
Feb-1992	PG	−0.024	0.011
⋮	⋮	⋮	⋮
	PG	−0.033	0.030
Jan-1992	UNH	0.108	0.014
Feb-1992	UNH	−0.043	0.011
⋮	⋮	⋮	⋮
Dec-2013	UNH	0.011	0.030

the same variable on itself N times to produce an $(NT \times 1)$ vector of excess returns of the market.

Estimation then involves a linear regression of the stacked dependent variable on a constant vector—represented by an $(NT \times 1)$ vector of ones—and the stacked explanatory variable. This process of stacking the data and applying least squares to the stacked system imposes the cross-equation restrictions that the α-risks and the β-risks are the same across all N stocks.

The common effects estimates of the CAPM parameters for the excess returns in Table 11.3 are given in the fitted equation system

$$r_{jt} - r_{ft} = \underset{(0.0018)}{0.0021} + \underset{(0.0557)}{0.6862} \, (r_{mt} - r_{ft}) + \widehat{u}_{jt}, \qquad RSS = 5.6473, \qquad (11.20)$$

for $j = 1, 2, \cdots, N$. The standard errors given in parentheses are the panel robust standard errors. These are based on extracting the residuals for each stock and computing the respective estimated idiosyncratic risk parameters $\widehat{\sigma}_j$, which are used to weight the explanatory variable $r_{mt} - r_{ft}$ associated with each cross section unit in estimating the required standard errors.

The fitted slope coefficient $\widehat{\beta} = 0.6862$ gives an overall estimate of the β-risk of the $N = 5$ stocks and thus provides an estimate of the collective β-risk of the pharmaceutical industry. The estimate is positive but less than unity, suggesting that pharmaceutical stocks overall are conservative stocks. Comparison with the no common effects β-risk estimates for each stock given in equation (11.12) shows that the common effects β-risk falls within the range of the individual stock estimates, which have a minimum of 0.4812 and maximum of 0.9158, highlighting the property that the common effects estimate 0.6862 delivers an estimate of the overall β-risk for the pharmaceutical industry.

The common effects model in equation (11.19) is a restricted version of the no common effects model in equation (11.11), and these restrictions may be tested. The null and alternative hypotheses are

$$H_0 : \alpha_1 = \alpha_2 = \cdots = \alpha_N = \alpha \text{ and } \beta_1 = \beta_2 = \cdots = \beta_N = \beta$$
$$H_1 : \text{at least one restriction fails.}$$

Under the null hypothesis there are two unknown parameters given by α and β compared to the $2N$ unknown parameters in the no common effects model. This difference $R = 2N - 2$ represents the total number of restrictions imposed by the common effects model. To test these restrictions, the F statistic is calculated according to the formula

$$F = \frac{RSS_R - RSS_U}{RSS_U} \times \frac{N(T-2)}{R}, \qquad (11.21)$$

where RSS_U is the unrestricted residual sum of squares from the no common effects model, and RSS_R is the restricted residual sum of squares from the common effects model. This statistic is distributed under the null hypothesis and under Gaussian assumptions as $F_{R,N(T-2)}$.

To apply this test to the pharmaceutical stocks, RSS_U is obtained by summing the RSS for each of the $N = 5$ stocks in equations (11.12) to (11.16). RSS_R is given by the RSS for the common effects model in equation (11.20). As $N = 5$, $T = 264$, and $R = 2(N - 1) = 8$, the resultant F test statistic is

$$F = \frac{5.6473 - 5.5848}{5.5848} \times \frac{5(264 - 2)}{8} = 1.8336.$$

As this statistic is distributed as $F_{R,N(T-2)} = F_{8,1310}$, the p value is 0.0669, resulting in the restrictions of the common effects model not being rejected at the 5% level. The outcome is marginal because the p value is close to the 5% level and the test would reject the hypothesis of common effects at the 10% level.

An asymptotic version of the F test is the chi-square test, which is simply obtained by multiplying both sides of the F statistic in equation (11.21) by the number of restrictions R, which yields

$$RF = \frac{RSS_R - RSS_U}{RSS_U} \times N(T - 2). \tag{11.22}$$

This statistic is distributed asymptotically under the null hypothesis as χ_R^2. The asymptotic χ^2 version of the test is

$$RF = 8 \times 1.8336 = 14.6695,$$

which is distributed asymptotically under the null hypothesis as χ_8^2. The associated p value is 0.0659, which leads to the same conclusion as for the F test.

A more restrictive version of the common effects model is to assume that the disturbance variance is constant over time and across section so that $u_{jt} \sim (0, \sigma^2)$. If the idiosyncratic risks are assumed to be the same across stocks, then an estimate of the overall idiosyncratic risk is obtained by using the residual sum of squares in equation (11.20), giving

$$\hat{\sigma} = \sqrt{\frac{1}{NT} \sum_{j=1}^{N} \sum_{t=1}^{T} \hat{u}_{jt}^2} = \sqrt{\frac{5.6473}{5 \times 264}} = 0.0655.$$

This quantity is simply the standard deviation of the residuals from the ordinary least squares regression of the stacked dependent variable on the stacked explanatory variables.

11.4 FIXED AND RANDOM EFFECTS PANEL MODELS

The no common effects model in equation (11.10) and the common effects model in equation (11.18) are two extremes in the panel model spectrum. Between these two extremes are found the primary workhorses of panel data modeling—the fixed effects model and the random effects model. The distinguishing feature of these two models is that the cross sectional units have heterogeneous intercepts but homogeneous slope coefficients of the explanatory variables.

11.4.1 The Fixed Effects Model

In the fixed effects model, the intercepts vary across individual units and are treated as fixed coefficients to be estimated, while the slope coefficients are assumed to be the same in each equation. The simple bivariate panel regression then has the following form

$$y_{jt} = \alpha_j + \beta x_{jt} + u_{jt}, \qquad u_{jt} \sim (0, \sigma^2), \tag{11.23}$$

where the simplifying assumption of constant equation error variance over the cross sections is made, so that $\sigma_1^2 = \sigma_2^2 = \cdots = \sigma_N^2 = \sigma^2$. In this specification the α_j are considered fixed parameters by assumption, thereby giving the model its name. The fixed effects model is characterized by N intercepts $(\alpha_j : j = 1, \cdots, N)$ and 1 slope parameter (β). As discussed earlier, the intercepts are known as incidental parameters.

A comparison of the no common effects model in equation (11.10) and the fixed effects model in equation (11.23) suggests that the fixed effects model imposes $N-1$ restrictions on the no common effects model by requiring the slope coefficient β to be common in each equation. Alternatively, a comparison of the fixed effects model and the common effects model in equation (11.18) suggests that the common effects model imposes $N-1$ restrictions on the fixed effects model by requiring the constant term α to be common across all equations.

An alternative way to specify the fixed effects model is to define a set of dummy variables as

$$D_{jt} = \begin{cases} 1 & \text{cross section } j \\ 0 & \text{otherwise.} \end{cases} \tag{11.24}$$

The first two stacked dummy variables are

$$D_{1t} = \begin{bmatrix} 1 \\ 1 \\ \vdots \\ 1 \\ 0 \\ 0 \\ \vdots \\ 0 \\ \vdots \\ 0 \\ 0 \\ \vdots \\ 0 \end{bmatrix} \begin{matrix} \left.\begin{matrix} \\ \\ \\ \end{matrix}\right\} j=1 \\ \left.\begin{matrix} \\ \\ \\ \end{matrix}\right\} j=2 \\ \\ \left.\begin{matrix} \\ \\ \\ \end{matrix}\right\} j=N \end{matrix} \qquad D_{2t} = \begin{bmatrix} 0 \\ 0 \\ \vdots \\ 0 \\ 1 \\ 1 \\ \vdots \\ 1 \\ \vdots \\ 0 \\ 0 \\ \vdots \\ 0 \end{bmatrix} \begin{matrix} \left.\begin{matrix} \\ \\ \\ \end{matrix}\right\} j=1 \\ \left.\begin{matrix} \\ \\ \\ \end{matrix}\right\} j=2 \\ \\ \left.\begin{matrix} \\ \\ \\ \end{matrix}\right\} j=N \end{matrix} .$$

Equation (11.23) is now rewritten as

$$y_{jt} = \alpha_1 D_{1t} + \alpha_2 D_{2t} + \cdots + \alpha_N D_{Nt} + \beta x_{jt} + u_{jt}, \tag{11.25}$$

or more compactly

$$y_{jt} = \sum_{j=1}^{N} \alpha_j D_{jt} + \beta x_{jt} + u_{jt}. \tag{11.26}$$

Estimation of this model proceeds in a similar way to the estimation of the common effects model in equation (11.18) where the dependent and explanatory variables are stacked into vectors of dimension $(NT \times 1)$. To allow for the fixed effects, dummy variables associated with each cross section are also generated, with each representing an $(NT \times 1)$ vector.

The fixed effects model is estimated by an ordinary least squares regression of the $(NT \times 1)$ stacked dependent variable y_{jt} on the $(NT \times 1)$ stacked explanatory variable x_{jt} and the N stacked dummy variables, $D_{1t}, D_{2t}, \cdots, D_{Nt}$. Alternatively, if a constant is included in the regression equation, then one of the dummy variables is excluded to avoid the dummy variable trap of collinear regressors.

In many practical situations where N is large, the dummy variable form of the regression equation appears infeasible due to loss of degrees of freedom from having to specify a large number of dummy variables to capture all of the fixed effects in equation (11.23). For the long panel in Table 11.1, there would be only $N = 5$ dummy variables and estimation of equation (11.26) by ordinary least squares is straightforward. But for the wide panel in Table 11.2, there would be $N = 330$ dummy variables in the form of equation (11.26), making the regression appear infeasible. The following simple computational procedure is available in such cases.

(i) Express the equation for the jth cross section in time-averaged form as

$$\frac{1}{T}\sum_{t=1}^{T} y_{jt} = \alpha_j + \beta \frac{1}{T}\sum_{t=1}^{T} x_{jt} + \frac{1}{T}\sum_{t=1}^{T} u_{jt}$$

$$\bar{y}_j = \alpha_j + \beta \bar{x}_j + \bar{u}_j. \tag{11.27}$$

(ii) Subtract equation (11.27) from equation (11.23) to yield the data in deviation-from-the-mean form, given by

$$y_{jt} - \bar{y}_j = \beta(x_{jt} - \bar{x}_j) + u_{jt} - \bar{u}_j, \tag{11.28}$$

in which the fixed effects α_j have been eliminated.

(iii) Estimate equation (11.28) by ordinary least squares to obtain $\widehat{\beta}$.

(iv) The estimates of the fixed effects for each of the j assets are recovered from equation (11.27) given that $\bar{u}_j = 0$. These estimates are

$$\widehat{\alpha}_j = \bar{y}_i - \widehat{\beta}\bar{x}_j, \tag{11.29}$$

where $\widehat{\beta}$ is the least squares estimator from Step 3.

Estimation of the fixed effects model using either the dummy variable regression approach or by subtracting time-average means to remove fixed effects first yields exactly the same estimates of the parameters α_j and β. Moreover, the residuals obtained from these two procedures are also identical, so that inference is unaffected. Computer software routinely uses the second approach to obtain the estimates in practice.

11.4.2 The Random Effects Model

A key feature of the fixed effects model is that the intercepts α_j in equation (11.23) are assumed to be constant. An alternative approach is to assume that the differences in the cross section elements involve random variable intercepts so that

$$\alpha_j = \alpha + v_j, \qquad v_j \sim (0, \sigma_v^2). \tag{11.30}$$

The v_j are assumed to be distributed with zero mean and constant variance, so that the random intercepts in each equation all have the same mean α. More importantly, the random errors v_j in these intercepts are typically assumed to be independent of the equation disturbances u_{jt}.

Using equation (11.30) in equation (11.23) yields the random effects model

$$y_{jt} = \alpha + v_j + \beta x_{jt} + u_{jt}, \qquad u_{jt} \sim (0, \sigma^2), \tag{11.31}$$

where, once again, the assumption of constant variance over the cross sections is used. The random effects, v_j, are assumed to be independent of the disturbances u_{jt}, so that $E(v_j u_{jt}) = 0$, and the explanatory variable x_{jt}, so that $E(v_j x_{jt}) = 0$, for all j and t.

The random effects model may be written in terms of a single disturbance as

$$y_{jt} = \alpha + \beta x_{jt} + w_{jt}, \tag{11.32}$$

where the composite disturbance w_{jt} is

$$w_{jt} = u_{jt} + v_j. \tag{11.33}$$

Estimation of the random effects model is somewhat more involved than the fixed effects model. The complexity arises from the composite form of the equation disturbance term w_{jt} in equation (11.33). The covariance structure of w_{jt} is

$$E(w_{jt}) = E(u_{jt} + v_j) = E(u_{jt}) + E(v_j) = 0$$
$$\mathrm{var}(w_{jt}^2) = E[(u_{jt} + v_j)^2] = E(u_{jt}^2) + E(v_j^2) + 2E(u_{jt}v_j) = \sigma^2 + \sigma_v^2$$
$$\mathrm{cov}(w_{jt}w_{js}) = E[(u_{jt} + v_j)(u_{js} + v_j)] = E(u_{jt}u_{js}) + E(u_{jt}v_j) + E(u_{js}v_j) + E(v_j^2)$$
$$= \sigma_v^2,$$

by using the assumption that $E(u_{jt}v_j) = 0$. Letting $w_j = (w_{j1}, w_{j2}, \cdots, w_{jT})'$ be the $(T \times 1)$ vector of disturbances for the jth cross section, the structure of the $(T \times T)$ covariance matrix of w_j is

$$\Omega_j = E(w_j w_j') = \begin{bmatrix} \sigma^2 + \sigma_v^2 & \sigma_v^2 & \sigma_v^2 & \cdots & \sigma_v^2 \\ \sigma_v^2 & \sigma^2 + \sigma_v^2 & \sigma_v^2 & \cdots & \sigma_v^2 \\ \sigma_v^2 & \sigma_v^2 & \ddots & & \vdots \\ \vdots & \vdots & & \ddots & \vdots \\ \sigma_v^2 & \sigma_v^2 & \cdots & \cdots & \sigma^2 + \sigma_v^2 \end{bmatrix}. \tag{11.34}$$

This matrix has a specific correlation structure that is constant through time

$$\rho_{ts} = \frac{\mathrm{cov}(w_{jt}w_{js})}{\sqrt{\mathrm{var}(w_{jt})\mathrm{var}(w_{js})}} = \frac{\sigma_v^2}{\sigma^2 + \sigma_v^2}. \tag{11.35}$$

Combining all disturbances into the $(NT \times NT)$ composite disturbance vector $w = (w_1, w_2, \cdots, w_N)'$, the full covariance matrix of w has the form

$$\Omega = E(ww') = \begin{bmatrix} \Omega_1 & 0 & 0 & 0 \\ 0 & \Omega_2 & 0 & 0 \\ \vdots & \vdots & \ddots & \vdots \\ 0 & 0 & \cdots & \Omega_N \end{bmatrix}. \tag{11.36}$$

This matrix is block diagonal with zero off-diagonal blocks because the random effects are independent for different cross section elements.

The steps involved to estimate the parameters of the random effects model in this more general case are as follows.

(i) Choose starting values for σ^2 and σ_v^2.

(ii) Define the quasi-difference parameter

$$\lambda = 1 - \frac{\sigma}{\sqrt{\sigma^2 + T\sigma_v^2}}, \tag{11.37}$$

and compute the quasi-differenced data

$$\tilde{y}_{jt} = y_{jt} - \lambda \bar{y}_j, \qquad \tilde{x}_{jt} = x_{jt} - \lambda \bar{x}_{jt}, \tag{11.38}$$

where $\bar{y}_j$ and $\bar{x}_j$ are time averages as in the fixed effects estimation described previously.

(iii) The generalized least squares estimator based on the starting values for (σ^2, σ_v^2) is obtained by estimating the following transformed equation by ordinary least squares

$$\tilde{y}_{jt} = \alpha(1 - \lambda) + \beta \tilde{x}_{jt} + \tilde{w}_{jt}, \tag{11.39}$$

in which $\tilde{w}_{jt}$ is a disturbance term.

An important special case of the generalized least squares estimator is where there are no random effects and $\sigma_v^2 = 0$. In this situation, the quasi-differencing parameter in equation (11.37) is $\lambda = 0$, so there is no need to quasi-difference the data. The estimates of α and β are simply obtained from the common effects model by regressing y_{jt} on a constant and x_{jt}.

The other extreme occurs when $\lambda = 1$. In this case the quasi-differenced regression equation in (11.39) is equivalent to equation (11.28), which is used to estimate the fixed effects model by ordinary least squares so that the fixed and random effects models are equivalent with $\alpha_j = v_j$. This special case arises, for example, when $T \to \infty$ because from equation (11.37)

$$\lim_{T \to \infty} \lambda = 1.$$

This property of the random effects estimator suggests that an approximate large T asymptotic strategy to estimate random effects, v_j, is to estimate β by generalized least squares and use equation (11.29) to extract estimates of v_j as is done for the fixed effects model.

To investigate some of the differences that can arise between fixed and random effects estimates in practical work, a typical corporate finance setting with a wide panel data set is adopted for illustration. The data were used in Adams, Almeida, and Ferreira (2009) to explore the performance of family owned firms and were introduced in Chapter 8. The data comprise 2254 firm-year observations over the 1992–1999 period, a snapshot of which appears in Table 11.2. Tobin's Q is used as a measure of firm performance, which is to be explained in terms of a dummy variable indicating whether or not the founder of the firm is also its chief executive officer, CEO, the size of the firm, (*assets*), the age of the firm, (*age*), and the volatility of the operating environment, (*vol*) as measured by the standard deviation of the previous 60-month returns.

Table 11.4 reports the results obtained by estimating the following fixed and random effects models

$$\log Q_t = \alpha_j + \beta_1 CEO_{jt} + \beta_2 \log assets_{jt} + \beta_3 \log age_{jt} + \beta_4 vol_{jt} + u_{jt}$$
$$\log Q_t = \alpha + \beta_1 CEO_{jt} + \beta_2 \log assets_{jt} + \beta_3 \log age_{jt} + \beta_4 vol_{jt} + v_j + u_{jt}.$$

The results reveal significant differences between the fixed and random effects parameter estimates. These differences involve both the sign and the significance of the coefficients. Most notably, the coefficient on the CEO dummy variable is insignificant in the fixed effects model but is positive and significant in the random effects model. These differences produce a different outcome in testing a key hypothesis under study concerning the impact of the background of CEO on firm performance, implying no impact from fixed effects estimation but significant positive impact in random effects estimation. The only estimated parameter that appears compatible across the two fitted models is that relating to the volatility of the operating environment of the firm. A statistically significant and negative coefficient estimate is found in both cases, indicating that increased volatility hampers firm performance. It appears, therefore, that in corporate finance applications exactly how individual heterogeneity is treated in panel data can well turn out to be a crucial issue in the empirical findings.

The difference between the estimated fixed and random effects for the family firms panel is illustrated in Figure 11.1. The figure displays a histogram of the estimated fixed effects with a normal density superimposed showing the random effects distribution $N(0, \widehat{\sigma}_v^2)$. Both the fixed and random effects are normalized to have mean zero. The main difference between the two models is apparent: The distribution of fixed effects is asymmetric with a long right-hand tail, whereas the random effects are symmetrically distributed with thin tails. These results reveal some big differences in firm performance: There are firms with very large positive intercepts affecting performance as well as a concentration of firms with small negative intercepts. These empirical differences are not captured by the random effects model estimates, indicating a shortcoming in that model's formulation. The implication is that the assumption underlying the random effects model may not be appropriate for this application.

11.4.3 Fixed versus Random Effects: The Hausman Test

A formal test of fixed effects versus random effects in modeling panel data can be based on the fundamental assumption that the random effects, v_j, are considered to be independent of the explanatory variables, x_{jt}, that is

TABLE 11.4 Estimates of the fixed and random effects panel models for the family firms data.

	Fixed Effects		Random Effects	
	Coefficient	Standard Error	Coefficient	Standard Error
CEO	0.035	0.046	0.093	0.039
assets	−0.009	0.016	0.020	0.012
age	0.277	0.052	0.002	0.022
vol	−0.697	0.104	−0.562	0.094
constant	−0.188	0.178	0.556	0.125

$$E(v_j x_{jt}) = 0.$$

If this condition fails then the fixed effects model is preferred as this estimator is still consistent in this case, although not efficient if randomness in the intercepts is a maintained assumption. Formally, the hypotheses are

$$H_0 : \text{random effects}$$
$$H_1 : \text{fixed effects.}$$

To perform the test, let $\widehat{\beta}_{FE}$ and $\widehat{\beta}_{RE}$ represent, respectively, the fixed and random effects estimates of the slope parameters. The general form of the test is based on the Wald statistic

$$WD = \left[\widehat{\beta}_{FE} - \widehat{\beta}_{RE}\right]' \left[\text{cov}(\widehat{\beta}_{FE}) - \text{cov}(\widehat{\beta}_{RE})\right]^{-1} \left[\widehat{\beta}_{FE} - \widehat{\beta}_{RE}\right], \qquad (11.40)$$

where $\text{cov}(\widehat{\beta}_{FE})$ and $\text{cov}(\widehat{\beta}_{RE})$ are estimates of the covariance matrices of $\widehat{\beta}_{FE}$ and $\widehat{\beta}_{RE}$. The test statistic WD is distributed asymptotically under the null hypothesis as χ^2_R, where R represents the number of explanatory variables in the model excluding the constant. Intuitively, under the null hypothesis, the random and fixed effects estimators are both consistent and should not be statistically different from each other. In this case, the Wald statistic will not be significant and the random effects estimator, which is also an efficient estimator being based on the generalized least squares principle, is to be preferred. Under the alternative, the random effects estimator is no longer consistent, resulting in a significant Wald statistic, and the fixed effects model is preferred.

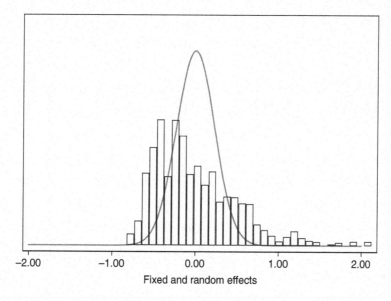

FIGURE 11.1 Illustration of the difference between the estimated fixed and random effects for the family firms panel data set. The histogram represents the distribution of the estimated fixed effects, while the random effects are drawings from a normal distribution with variance $\widehat{\sigma}^2_v = 0.23^2$. Both the fixed and random effects are normalized to have a mean of zero.

This form of the Wald test is due to Hausman (1978) who showed the convenient relationship

$$\text{cov}(\widehat{\beta}_{FE} - \widehat{\beta}_{RE}) = \text{cov}(\widehat{\beta}_{FE}) - \text{cov}(\widehat{\beta}_{RE}),$$

which facilitates estimation of the covariance weighting matrix that is used in the WD statistic to measure differences between the estimates $\text{cov}(\widehat{\beta}_{FE})$ and $\text{cov}(\widehat{\beta}_{RE})$.

A Hausman test for fixed versus random effects using the statistic in equation (11.40) is now performed using the family firms data. The differences in the fixed and random effects parameter estimates in Table 11.4 associated with the $R = 4$ explanatory variables are

$$\widehat{\beta}_{FE} - \widehat{\beta}_{RE} = \begin{bmatrix} 0.035 & - & 0.093 \\ -0.009 & - & 0.020 \\ 0.277 & - & 0.002 \\ -0.697 & - & -0.562 \end{bmatrix} = \begin{bmatrix} -0.058 \\ -0.029 \\ 0.275 \\ -0.135 \end{bmatrix},$$

with covariance matrix

$$\text{cov}(\widehat{\beta}_{FE} - \widehat{\beta}_{RE}) = \begin{bmatrix} 0.0022 & 0.0001 & 0.0002 & 0.0002 \\ 0.0001 & 0.0002 & -0.0004 & 0.0003 \\ 0.0002 & -0.0004 & 0.0027 & -0.0007 \\ 0.0002 & 0.0003 & -0.0007 & 0.0107 \end{bmatrix}$$

$$- \begin{bmatrix} 0.0016 & 0.0000 & 0.0002 & -0.0000 \\ 0.0000 & 0.0001 & -0.0000 & 0.0002 \\ 0.0002 & -0.0000 & 0.0005 & 0.0002 \\ -0.0000 & 0.0002 & 0.0002 & 0.0088 \end{bmatrix}$$

$$= \begin{bmatrix} 0.0006 & 0.0000 & 0.0000 & 0.0003 \\ 0.0000 & 0.0001 & -0.0004 & 0.0001 \\ 0.0000 & -0.0004 & 0.0023 & -0.0009 \\ 0.0003 & 0.0001 & -0.0009 & 0.0020 \end{bmatrix}.$$

The value of the Wald statistic is

$$WD = \left[\widehat{\beta}_{FE} - \widehat{\beta}_{RE}\right]' \left[\text{cov}(\widehat{\beta}_{FE}) - \text{cov}(\widehat{\beta}_{RE})\right]^{-1} \left[\widehat{\beta}_{FE} - \widehat{\beta}_{RE}\right]$$

$$= \begin{bmatrix} -0.058 \\ -0.029 \\ 0.275 \\ -0.135 \end{bmatrix}' \begin{bmatrix} 0.0006 & 0.0000 & 0.0000 & 0.0003 \\ 0.0000 & 0.0001 & -0.0004 & 0.0001 \\ 0.0000 & -0.0004 & 0.0023 & -0.0009 \\ 0.0003 & 0.0001 & -0.0009 & 0.0020 \end{bmatrix}^{-1} \begin{bmatrix} -0.058 \\ -0.029 \\ 0.275 \\ -0.135 \end{bmatrix}$$

$$= 44.78,$$

which is distributed as χ_4^2 under the null hypothesis that the random effects model is the correct specification. The corresponding p value is 0.000, showing strong rejection of the random effects model in favor of the fixed effects model. This rejection is completely consistent with the intuition provided by Figure 11.1.

11.5 DYNAMIC PANEL MODELS

The panel data models discussed so far are static models, specifying a relationship between the dependent variable, y_{jt}, and the explanatory variable, x_{jt}, both at time t.

Following the approach of Chapter 4, dynamics may be introduced into the model by including lags of both y_{jt} and x_{jt}.

The case where a lagged dependent variable is included in the model is particularly important because it enables dynamic responses over time to the past history of the variable as in an autoregression. The respective fixed effects and random effects versions of the so-called panel autoregressive model are as follows

$$
\begin{aligned}
\text{Fixed effects} \quad &: \quad y_{jt} = \alpha_j + \beta x_{jt} + \rho y_{jt-1} + u_{jt} \\
\text{Random effects} &: \quad y_{jt} = \alpha + v_j + \beta x_{jt} + \rho y_{jt-1} + u_{jt},
\end{aligned}
\tag{11.41}
$$

where u_{jt} is the disturbance term that is assumed to be independent over time $E(u_{jt}u_{js}) = 0$, for all $t \neq s$.

The autoregressive parameter ρ controls the strength of the dynamics. In the special case $\rho = 0$, the model reduces to the non-dynamic or static panel data model discussed earlier in the chapter. For the case where $-1 < \rho < 1$, the autoregressive dynamics are stationary with the successive effects of shocks on the dependent variable dissipating over time, as discussed in Chapter 4. For the unit root case where $\rho = 1$, the shocks have persistent effects and do not dissipate over time, just as in Chapter 6, resulting in a nonstationary panel model. That model will be discussed later in Section 11.6.

11.5.1 Nickell Bias

Estimating the parameters of panel autoregressive models involves new complications. The most important of these occurs as a result of the presence of incidental parameters— usually the intercept coefficients in the individual equations. These parameters— incidental to each equation and as numerous as there are equations—are a new feature that needs to be considered when the cross section sample size $N \to \infty$.

Elimination of the fixed effect intercepts from each equation by transformation of the system, as in equation (11.28) where time averages are removed, produces a form of endogeneity in the regressor that influences estimation by introducing a new form of bias. The bias arises from the correlation of the lagged regressor with the equation disturbance. In particular, as is apparent from the form of equation (11.28), the transformed lagged dependent variable $y_{jt-1} - \bar{y}_{jt-1}$ is correlated with the transformed disturbance term $u_{jt} - \bar{u}_j$ because

$$
\text{cov}(\bar{y}_{jt-1}, u_{jt}) = \frac{\sigma^2}{T} \neq 0, \text{ for all } t.
\tag{11.42}
$$

This correlation violates one of the key conditions needed for the validity of least squares. In particular, this condition is needed to ensure consistent estimation of the autoregressive coefficient ρ as $N \to \infty$ with finite time series sample size T. Unlike the case in Chapter 4, this non-zero correlation is present even when the disturbance term, u_{jt}, is itself not autocorrelated. The resultant bias in estimating ρ is commonly referred to as Nickell bias, following its original analysis by Nickell (1981).

The condition in equation (11.42) reveals that the bias complication arises because the explanatory variable in the equation is a lagged dependent variable (not an exogenous variable). This complication occurs for both the fixed and random effects panel models given in equation (11.41).

To see how the problem arises in the case of the dynamic random effects model, rewrite the model in the form

$$y_{jt} = \alpha + \beta x_{jt} + \rho y_{jt-1} + w_{jt}, \tag{11.43}$$

where $w_{jt} = u_{jt} + v_j$ represents, as before, the composite disturbance term. As the dependent variable y_{jt} by construction is correlated with w_{jt}, it is also correlated with its individual components u_{jt} and v_j. But the correlation between y_{jt} and v_j holds at any point in time t, because v_j has the same effect on y_{jt} regardless of what point in time this shock occurs. It follows that

$$\text{cov}(y_{jt-1}, w_{jt}) = \text{cov}(y_{jt-1}, u_{jt} + v_j) = \text{cov}(y_{jt-1}, u_{jt}) + \text{cov}(y_{jt-1}, v_j)$$
$$= \text{cov}(y_{jt-1}, v_j) \neq 0, \text{ for all } t. \tag{11.44}$$

In the case of the fixed effects model, suppose that estimation is based on re-centering about the time series means so as to eliminate the fixed effects α_j as in equation (11.28). The relevant form of the model in this case is

$$y_{jt} - \bar{y}_j = \beta(x_{jt} - \bar{x}_{jt}) + \rho(y_{jt-1} - \bar{y}_{jt-1}) + u_{jt} - \bar{u}_j, \tag{11.45}$$

where $\bar{y}_j = T^{-1} \sum_{t=1}^{T} y_{jt}$, and $\bar{y}_{j,-1} = T^{-1} \sum_{t=2}^{T} y_{jt-1}$ are the sample means of y_{jt} and y_{jt-1}. As $\bar{y}_{jt-1}$ involves observations up to $T-1$ on y_{jt} and hence depends on values of u_{js} for $s = t, \cdots, T-1$, there is inevitable correlation between the regressor and the error in equation (11.45). In particular,

$$\text{cov}(\bar{y}_{j,-1}, u_{jt}) = \text{cov}\left(\frac{y_{j0} + y_{j1} + \cdots + y_{jT-1}}{T}, u_{jt}\right)$$
$$= \text{cov}\left(\frac{y_{jt} + \cdots + y_{jT-1}}{T}, u_{jt}\right)$$
$$= \frac{\sum_{s=0}^{\infty} \sum_{k=0}^{T-1-t} \rho^s E(u_{jt+k-s} u_{jt})}{T} \simeq \frac{\sigma^2}{(1-\rho)T} \neq 0. \tag{11.46}$$

The resulting covariance in equation (11.46) creates a bias in the estimate of the coefficient of the lagged dependent variable that is not mitigated by increasing N. The bias in $\hat{\rho}$ as $N \to \infty$ is inherited from equation (11.46) and is of order $1/T$, which is non-negligible in a small T context, especially when the cross section sample size N is large. In particular, the bias has the following explicit asymptotic form

$$\plim_{N \to \infty} (\hat{\rho} - \rho) \simeq -\frac{\text{cov}(\bar{y}_{jt-1}, u_{jt})}{\text{var}(y_{jt-1} - \bar{y}_{jt-1})} \simeq -\frac{\frac{\sigma^2}{(1-\rho)T}}{\frac{\sigma^2}{(1-\rho^2)}} \simeq -\frac{1+\rho}{T}, \tag{11.47}$$

which holds with an error of smaller order in T. Nickell (1981) derived the exact form of the asymptotic bias as well as the simple approximate representation in equation (11.47).

For $\rho > 0$, the bias is negative so that the autoregressive estimate is biased downward, and shock persistence on the dependent variable is thereby underestimated. It is apparent that when T is small, the bias can be substantial. For instance, if $T = 4$ and $\rho = 0.6$, the approximate downward bias is -0.4 or 67% of the true value of ρ. In this case, when N is large, almost all the distribution of $\hat{\rho}$ is located below the true value of ρ.

Table 11.5 reports the result of a simple simulation experiment with a dynamic panel model to illustrate the impact of the Nickell bias. The data generating process is (see Judson and Owen, 1996; Flannery and Hankins, 2013)

$$y_{jt} = \alpha_j + \beta x_{jt} + \rho y_{jt-1} + u_{jt}, \qquad u_{jt} \sim N(0, \sigma^2),$$
$$x_{jt} = \gamma x_{jt-1} + e_{jt}, \qquad e_{jt} \sim N(0, \sigma_e^2),$$

with population parameters $\rho = \{0.2, 0.8\}$, $\beta = 0.8$, $\gamma = 0.5$, and $\sigma^2 = 1.0$. Following Kiviet (1995), σ_e^2 is determined by specifying a value for the signal-to-noise ratio defined as

$$\sigma_s^2 = \text{var}\left(y_{jt} - \frac{1}{1-\rho}\alpha_j\right)$$
$$= \beta^2 \sigma_e^2 \left[1 + \frac{(\gamma + \rho)^2}{1 + \rho\gamma}(\rho\gamma - 1) - (\rho\gamma)^2\right]^{-1} + \frac{\rho^2}{1 - \gamma\rho^2}\sigma^2.$$

The higher the value of σ_s^2, the more useful x_{jt} is in explaining y_{jt}. In the simulation, the setting $\sigma_s^2 = 2$ is used, which, in turn, determines σ_e^2 given the choices of the other parameters. The sample sizes are as follows. The settings $T = \{10, 20, 30\}$ reveal the performance of the fixed effects estimator in short, medium, and long panels; and the settings $N = \{20, 100\}$ illustrate estimator performance in narrow and wide panels. Each parameter combination is assessed using 1000 replications.

The simulation results in Table 11.5 confirm that the fixed effects estimator of ρ suffers from significant bias. As the bias formula in equation (11.47) predicts, the bias of the fixed effects estimator increases with ρ and decreases as T increases.

11.5.2 Estimation

To avoid Nickell bias in estimation of a dynamic panel model, a two-step approach can be adopted. In the first step, the fixed effects (α_j) or random effects (v_j) are removed from the model by taking first differences of the relevant equation in (11.41) giving

$$\Delta y_{jt} = \beta \Delta x_{jt} + \rho \Delta y_{jt-1} + \Delta u_{jt}. \tag{11.48}$$

While this equation removes intercepts, the differencing operation induces correlation between the lagged differenced regressor Δy_{jt-1} and the equation error Δu_{jt}. In particular, $E(\Delta y_{jt-1}\Delta u_{jt}) = -E(y_{jt-1}u_{jt-1}) = -\sigma^2$. Thus, least squares estimation of equation (11.48) leads to biased and inconsistent estimates of the remaining parameters $\{\beta, \rho\}$.

TABLE 11.5 Illustrating the Nickell bias of the fixed effects estimator of ρ in a dynamic panel model using simulated data.

N	T	$\rho = 0.2$		$\rho = 0.8$	
		Mean	Std. Dev.	Mean	Std. Dev.
20	10	0.138	0.051	0.560	0.070
20	20	0.175	0.034	0.693	0.040
20	30	0.181	0.027	0.731	0.029
100	10	0.140	0.023	0.567	0.030
100	20	0.172	0.015	0.694	0.018
100	30	0.182	0.012	0.733	0.013

To correct the bias and inconsistency of least squares estimation, instrumental variable or GMM methods may be employed along the lines discussed in Chapter 9. Suitable instruments may be constructed using carefully chosen lagged values of the dependent variable and exogenous regressors. If K instruments are used at time t for each cross section j observation, giving the $(1 \times K)$ instrument vector z_{jt}, then the corresponding moment conditions at time t are

$$m_t = \frac{1}{N} \sum_{j=1}^{N} \Delta u_{jt} z_{jt} = \frac{1}{N} \sum_{j=1}^{N} (\Delta y_{jt} - \beta \Delta x_{jt} - \rho \Delta y_{jt-1}) z_{jt}, \tag{11.49}$$

which represents the cross section sample average of the vector $\Delta u_{jt} z_{jt}$ over N observations at each point in time. In general, there are approximately T such sets of moment conditions, one set for each point in time.

In choosing the set of instruments to employ at each time period t, there are three commonly used approaches, which are summarized in Table 11.6. Note that the instrument sets begin in period $t = 3$, as 2 observations are automatically lost: one through first differencing the data and the second from the inclusion of the lagged dependent variable on the right-hand side of equation (11.48).

Anderson and Hsiao (1981) suggest the use of lagged levels of the dependent variable as suitable instruments for the regressor Δy_{jt-1}. For instance, the following instruments may be used at each time t

$$z_{jt} = \{\Delta x_{jt}, y_{jt-2}, y_{jt-3}\},$$

TABLE 11.6 **Sets of instruments used by various dynamic panel estimators.**

Period	Anderson–Hsiao
3	$z_{j3} = \{\Delta x_{j3}, y_{j1}\}$
4	$z_{j4} = \{\Delta x_{j4}, y_{j2}, y_{j1}\}$
5	$z_{j5} = \{\Delta x_{j5}, y_{j3}, y_{j2}\}$
$\vdots$	$\vdots$
T	$z_{jT} = \{\Delta x_{jT}, y_{jT-2}, y_{jT-3}\}$

Period	Arellano–Bond
3	$z_{j3} = \{\Delta x_{j3}, y_{j1}\}$
4	$z_{j4} = \{\Delta x_{j4}, y_{j2}, y_{j1}\}$
5	$z_{j5} = \{\Delta x_{j5}, y_{j3}, y_{j2}, y_{j1}\}$
$\vdots$	$\vdots$
T	$z_{jT} = \{\Delta x_{jT}, y_{jT-2}, y_{jT-3}, \cdots, y_{j1}\}$

Period	Arellano–Bover–Blundell–Bond
3	$z_{j3} = \{\Delta x_{j3}, y_{j1}\}$
4	$z_{j4} = \{\Delta x_{j4}, y_{j2}, y_{j1}, \Delta y_{j2}\}$
5	$z_{j5} = \{\Delta x_{j5}, y_{j3}, y_{j2}, y_{j1} \Delta y_{j3}\}$
$\vdots$	$\vdots$
T	$z_{jT} = \{\Delta x_{jT}, y_{jT-2}, y_{jT-3}, \cdots, y_{j1}, \Delta y_{jT-2}\}$

with Δx_{jt} acting as its own instrument and y_{jt-2} and y_{jt-3} acting as instruments for Δy_{jt-1}. The choice of y_{jt-2} is a natural one as it is, by construction, correlated with Δy_{jt-1} since $\Delta y_{jt-1} = y_{jt-1} - y_{jt-2}$. This instrument is also independent of the disturbance term $\Delta u_{jt} = u_{jt} - u_{jt-1}$ in equation (11.48) by virtue of the assumed serial independence of the u_{jt}. Similarly, the instrument y_{jt-3} is correlated with Δy_{jt-1} as a result of the autoregressive dependence in the dynamic process of the model in equation (11.48), and y_{jt-3} is also independent of the equation error $\Delta u_{jt} = u_{jt} - u_{jt-1}$.

The first time period for which sufficient instruments are defined is period $t = 3$, the available observations being Δx_{j3} and y_{j1}. Subsequent observations involve all three instruments. The full set of available moments is therefore given by

$$m_3 = \left(\frac{1}{N} \sum_{j=1}^{N} \Delta u_{j3} \Delta x_{j3}, \frac{1}{N} \sum_{j=1}^{N} \Delta u_{j3} y_{j1} \right)$$

$$m_4 = \left(\frac{1}{N} \sum_{j=1}^{N} \Delta u_{j4} \Delta x_{j4}, \frac{1}{N} \sum_{j=1}^{N} \Delta u_{j4} y_{j2}, \frac{1}{N} \sum_{j=1}^{N} \Delta u_{j4} y_{j1} \right)$$

$$\vdots \qquad \vdots \qquad \vdots$$

$$m_T = \left(\frac{1}{N} \sum_{j=1}^{N} \Delta u_{jT} \Delta x_{jT}, \frac{1}{N} \sum_{j=1}^{N} \Delta u_{jT} y_{jT-2}, \frac{1}{N} \sum_{j=1}^{N} \Delta u_{j4} y_{jT-3} \right).$$

In order to improve the asymptotic efficiency of the GMM estimator, Arellano and Bond (1991) extended the Anderson–Hsiao choice of instruments by including all available lags of the dependent variable. For periods $t = 3$ and $t = 4$, the instrument set is the same as it is for the Anderson–Hsiao estimator above. For $t = 5$, however, the instrument set is $z_{j5} = \{\Delta x_{j5}, y_{j3}, y_{j2}, y_{j1}\}$, with the addition of y_{j1} to the earlier set of instruments. Similarly, for $t = 6$, the instrument set is $z_{j6} = \{\Delta x_{j6}, y_{j4}, y_{j3}, y_{j2}, y_{j1}\}$, with both y_{j2} and y_{j1} being added to the earlier instrument set.

Arellano and Bover (1995) and Blundell and Bond (1998) suggested a further improvement in estimator efficiency by adding Δy_{jt-2} and similar higher order lagged differences to the Arellano–Bond set of instruments at time t. This extension is partly motivated by the possibility that the levels of the lagged dependent variables may be weak instruments for first differenced variables—as they are when $\rho \simeq 1$. In the case of a random effects dynamic panel model, Blundell and Bond (1998) suggested stacking the differenced equation system in equation (11.48) with a further set of levels equations and using suitably lagged differences as instruments for the regressors in these additional equations. Estimation of dynamic panel models using this technique is known as System GMM (S-GMM) estimation and is designed to assist estimation in cases where lagged levels are weak instruments, as in models with substantial persistence where values of the autoregressive coefficient ρ are in the vicinity of unity.

The instrument set selected in Arellano–Bond and Arellano–Bover–Blundell–Bond estimation depends on the time series dimension T of the panel. In long panels with a large T dimension, there is potential for a very large number of moment conditions, a feature that can reduce estimation efficiency in finite samples. In long panel model estimation, it is therefore common to restrict the number of instruments employed and software packages typically allow some flexibility of this type in implementation.

11.5.3 Capital Structure

A commonly held view in corporate finance is that firms behave as if there is an optimal leverage ratio. In a frictionless world, firms would always maintain their target leverage. But in reality, adjustment costs and other frictions may prevent firms from achieving this target. Dynamic panel models may be used to explore the manner in which firms make these adjustments.

Let y_{jt} be the actual leverage ratio of firm j and y_{jt}^* be its target leverage ratio. It is assumed that the target leverage ratio is a linear function of a set of explanatory variables given by

$$y_{jt}^* = \alpha_j + \beta_1 x_{1jt} + \cdots \beta_k x_{kjt}. \tag{11.50}$$

A common assumption in practical work is that the actual ratio adjusts to the target ratio in terms of an adjustment mechanism such as

$$y_{jt} - y_{jt-1} = \gamma(y_{jt}^* - y_{jt-1}) + u_{jt},$$

or

$$y_{jt} = \gamma y_{jt}^* + (1 - \gamma)y_{jt-1} + u_{jt}, \tag{11.51}$$

in which the parameter γ measures the speed of adjustment toward the target leverage ratio. There are three possible scenarios,

$$
\begin{aligned}
\gamma &= 0 && \text{[No Adjustment]} \\
0 &< \gamma < 1 && \text{[Partial Adjustment]} \\
\gamma &= 1. && \text{[Full Adjustment]}
\end{aligned}
$$

Substituting equation (11.50) into equation (11.51) yields the dynamic panel model

$$y_{jt} = \gamma \alpha_j + \gamma \beta_1 x_{1jt} + \cdots + \gamma \beta_k x_{kj} + (1 - \gamma)y_{jt-1} + u_{jt}. \tag{11.52}$$

For the special case of no adjustment the parameter setting is $\gamma = 0$, and the dynamic target leverage model reduces to a panel random walk with unit autoregressive coefficient. At the other extreme where $\gamma = 1$, there is no lagged dependent variable in the regression equation and the relationship between the leverage ratio and the determinants of the target leverage is a contemporaneous one.

The following three empirical measures of leverage are commonly used as the dependent variable y_{jt}.

(i) The ratio of long-term debt plus current debt to the market value of total assets, $lv1_{jt}$.

(ii) The ratio of long-term debt plus current debt to the book value of total assets, $lv2_{jt}$.

(iii) The ratio of long-term debt to the book value of total assets, $lv3_{jt}$.

Leverage measures based on the book value of assets, as in (ii) and (iii), are often used instead of market leverage because the latter can be very sensitive to the market value of equity. Market value can change substantially due to movements in equity markets even if firms do not alter their actual borrowing behavior. While (i) is less commonly used in empirical work, all three leverage measures will be used in the empirical application presented here.

There is a large literature on the variables, x_{kjt}, that best explain target leverage. Following Rajan and Zingales (1995), the following application uses four key variables: collateral as measured by the value of tangible assets, tan_{jt}; the size of the firm measured by the logarithm of the value of total assets, $size_{jt}$; growth opportunities defined as the market-to-book value of assets, mb_{jt}; and operating income before depreciation, $profit_{jt}$.

To test the model of target leverage and dynamic adjustment, a panel data set is constructed comprising observations for target leverage, $lv1_{jt}$, $lv2_{jt}$, and $lv3_{jt}$, together with the financial variables used to model leverage. The panel comprises $N = 5658$ US firms (including all those listed previously) for the period 1971–2014, $T = 44$. Table 11.7 provides coefficient estimates of the partial adjustment model for the leverage ratio in equation (11.52) using the GMM and S-GMM estimators. All fitted coefficients are statistically significant in all models regardless of which empirical measures of leverage are used. The estimates of the speed of adjustment parameter, γ, are all significant, ranging from $1 - 0.686 = 0.314$ to $1 - 0.437 = 0.563$. Overall, these results provide support for the partial adjustment hypothesis. A further implication is that slower adjustment is indicated when using the empirical measure of leverage (i) than when using measures (ii) and (iii).

11.6 NONSTATIONARY PANEL MODELS

The discussion of dynamic panel models has focused so far on models with stationary variables so that the autoregressive parameter ρ satisfies the stability restriction $|\rho| < 1$ in equation (11.41). Important extensions relate to the cases where the variables for

TABLE 11.7 Estimating a partial adjustment model for the leverage ratio using the Arellano–Bond (GMM) and system GMM (S-GMM) estimators, with t statistics in parentheses. The four variable Ranjan and Zingales (1995) specification is used.

	lv1		lv2		lv3	
	GMM	S-GMM	GMM	S-GMM	GMM	S-GMM
tan	0.181 (26.992)	0.189 (29.330)	0.193 (25.189)	0.209 (26.246)	0.119 (15.871)	0.118 (15.383)
size	0.047 (37.437)	0.025 (26.755)	0.024 (17.564)	0.029 (22.849)	0.016 (12.210)	0.019 (15.024)
mb	−0.015 (−38.998)	−0.017 (−43.167)	−0.002 (−5.538)	−0.002 (−4.793)	−0.003 (−7.148)	−0.003 (−5.686)
profit	−0.152 (−37.411)	−0.148 (−36.583)	−0.225 (−48.335)	−0.259 (−55.232)	−0.125 (−27.204)	−0.155 (−33.259)
$lv1_{t-1}$	0.685 (88.949)	0.686 (153.871)				
$lv2_{t-1}$			0.437 (57.035)	0.572 (128.030)		
$lv3_{t-1}$					0.518 (64.174)	0.603 (120.303)
constant	−0.240 (−26.646)	−0.120 (−17.211)	−0.067 (−6.741)	−0.128 (−14.040)	−0.039 (−4.130)	−0.064 (−7.326)

each cross section are nonstationary and may be cointegrated with common long-run parameters.

A primary example of time series cointegration in financial econometrics involves the present value model. The concept of cointegration in that context was discussed in Chapter 6 and applies only for a single cross section that involves the United States. The approach is now extended to investigate this present value relationship for a range of different countries and to determine whether these countries have a common cointegrating vector that embodies the same present value relationship.

A general specification of the present value model for a set of N countries is written as

$$p_{jt} = \alpha_j + \beta_j d_{jt} + u_{jt}, \quad j = 1, 2, \cdots, N, \tag{11.53}$$

where p_{jt} is the log equity price of country j, d_{jt} is the log dividend payment of country j, and u_{jt} is a disturbance term. Assuming that p_{jt} and d_{jt} are nonstationary time series, and u_{jt} is stationary, the parameters α_j and β_j represent the cointegrating parameters that in this formulation may vary for each country. The parameter α_j is a function of the relevant discount factor that relates to country j (for details, see the discussion of the present value model in Chapter 2). The model in equation (11.53) is comparable to the no common effects panel model discussed previously, with the parameters for each cross section being estimated separately using the techniques discussed in Chapter 6.

In the case of the pure form of the present value model, wherein the log dividend yield $(p_{jt} - d_{jt})$ for country j is stationary, the slope coefficient is correspondingly set to $\beta_j = 1$. This restriction on the slope implies cross equation parameter restrictions in the panel model in equation (11.53). A milder form of this restriction is that the slope coefficients are homogeneous and satisfy $\beta_j = \beta$ for some constant β and all $j = 1, 2, \cdots, N$.

Figure 11.2 provides scatter plots of the log prices and log dividends for $N = 12$ countries from January 2002 to March 2016. All prices and dividends are expressed in \$US. All countries depict positive relationships between prices and dividends. For most countries, the scatter plots appear tight and therefore indicate support for the present value model. The exceptions are China and to a lesser extent France, where the scatter plots are more dispersed.

Restricting the slope parameters in equation (11.53) to be the same across the N countries

$$\beta_1 = \beta_2 = \cdots = \beta_N = \beta, \tag{11.54}$$

imposes a common long-run relationship between equity prices and dividends. Using these restrictions in equation (11.53) results in a present value, fixed effects, cointegrating model with homogeneous slopes of the form

$$p_{jt} = \alpha_j + \beta d_{jt} + u_{jt}. \tag{11.55}$$

The fixed effects are given by the parameters $\{\alpha_1, \alpha_2, \cdots, \alpha_N\}$, which allow the discount factor for each country to differ. A further set of restrictions is to assume that the discount factors are also the same across all N countries by imposing the restrictions

$$\alpha_1 = \alpha_2 = \cdots = \alpha_N = \alpha. \tag{11.56}$$

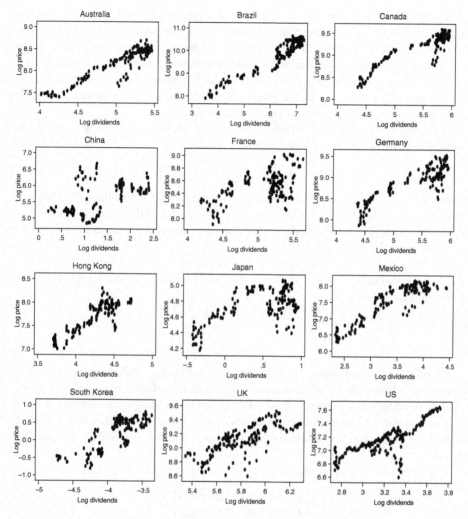

FIGURE 11.2 Scatter plots of monthly log share prices and log dividends for 12 countries for the period January 2002 to March 2016.

Using these restrictions on equation (11.55) now results in the present value common effects cointegrating model

$$p_{jt} = \alpha + \beta d_{jt} + u_{jt}. \tag{11.57}$$

11.6.1 Panel Unit Roots

The existence of a cointegrating relationship between equity prices and dividends for a set of N countries presupposes that these variables for all countries are themselves unit root nonstationary. Tests for unit root nonstationarity are discussed in Chapter 5, but these are constructed for a single time series and would therefore apply only to a single cross section in a panel model.

In this example, equity prices and dividends represent a panel of $N = 12$ countries, and it is natural to consider unit root tests that preserve the panel features of the data and treat the panel jointly. This means that rather than testing each variable separately for a unit root, a test statistic is constructed to assess the presence of a unit root jointly among all N variables (or cross sections) simultaneously. This strategy can be interpreted as an efficient procedure of testing for the presence of a time series unit root in a variable that varies not only over time but also over N cross sections.

To motivate the form of panel unit root tests, consider the fixed effects dynamic panel model in equation (11.41) with no exogenous variables

$$y_{jt} = \alpha_j + \rho y_{jt-1} + u_{jt}, \tag{11.58}$$

in which u_{jt} is a disturbance term, and ρ is the parameter controlling the time series dynamics of all variables in the cross section. Under the null hypothesis of joint unit root nonstationarity, all N processes have common autoregressive parameter $\rho = 1$, so all variables have unit roots.

Just as with time series unit root testing in the case of a single variable, there are a number of panel unit root tests. The Levin, Lin, and Chu (2002) test is based on the panel unit root regression equation

$$\Delta y_{jt} = \alpha_j + \beta y_{jt-1} + \sum_{k=1}^{L} \gamma_{jk} \Delta y_{jt-k} + u_{jt}. \tag{11.59}$$

This model is the panel analogue of the augmented Dickey–Fuller regression equation with $\beta = \rho - 1$ and, like the ADF equation, includes L lagged differences of the dependent variable to address the presence of autocorrelation in the stationary components of the system. The panel form of this unit root test derives from the fact that β is restricted to be the same parameter for all N variables, while the equation intercepts α_j allow for fixed effects.

The null and alternative hypotheses of the panel unit root test are given by

$$\begin{aligned} H_0 &: \beta = 0 \quad \text{[unit root]} \\ H_1 &: \beta < 0. \quad \text{[stationary]} \end{aligned}$$

Note that the null hypothesis requires that all time series in the panel have unit roots ($\rho = 1$) and the alternative similarly requires that all time series have stationary roots ($|\rho| < 1$).

The test is implemented by stacking the N variables, estimating equation (11.59) by least squares and basing the unit root test statistic on a (modified form of) t statistic. In contrast to the nonstandard distribution of time series unit root statistics presented in Chapter 5, the panel unit root t statistic is asymptotically distributed as $N(0, 1)$ under the null hypothesis. This convenient limit result arises because of the power of cross section averaging. Given an assumption of cross section independence, as the cross section sample size $N \to \infty$ a suitably centered t statistic satisfies a central limit theorem, which leads to a limiting normal distribution. Appropriate standardization in the construction of the statistic, and controls on the expansion rate of the respective cross section and time series sample sizes, ensure that the asymptotic distribution is the standard normal $N(0, 1)$ under the null hypothesis.

A less restrictive panel unit root test that allows for some stationary and nonstationary elements in the cross section under the alternative hypothesis was proposed by Im, Pesaran, and Shin (2003). This test involves replacing the specification in equation (11.59) by the weaker formulation

$$\Delta y_{jt} = \alpha_j + \beta_j y_{jt-1} + \sum_{k=1}^{L} \gamma_{jk} \Delta y_{jt-k} + u_{jt}, \tag{11.60}$$

in which the slope coefficients β_j are now not restricted to be the same for each cross section. The null and alternative hypotheses for this test are

$$H_0 : \beta_j = 0, \quad j = 1, 2, \cdots, N$$

$$H_1 : \begin{cases} \beta_j < 0 & \text{for} \quad j = 1, \cdots, N_1 \\ \beta_j = 0 & \text{for} \quad j = N_1 + 1, \cdots, N. \end{cases}$$

Under the null hypothesis all cross sections have unit roots as before, whereas under the alternative hypothesis just N_1 of the N cross sections are stationary. An overall panel unit root test is computed by estimating equation (11.60) separately for each cross section and using a t statistic to test that $\beta_j = 0$. An overall statistic is computed by averaging across the N values of these t statistics. As with the Levin–Lin–Chu test, by properly standardizing the averaged t statistic, the asymptotic distribution of the modified panel unit root test is also standard normal. Monto Carlo simulations reveal that the small sample performance of the Im–Pesaran–Shin test tends to improve on the Levin–Lin–Chu test. The allowance for a more general alternative hypothesis is useful because a test rejection may signal that only some of the cross section elements are stationary.

Applying these panel unit root tests to the log share prices of the 12 countries represented in Figure 11.2 yields the following values of the panel unit root test statistics, together with their p values in parentheses

$$\begin{array}{lll}
\text{Levin–Lin–Chu} & : & -0.7589 \quad (0.2240) \\
\text{Im–Pesaran–Shin} & : & 0.5264 \quad (0.7007).
\end{array}$$

The corresponding results of panel unit root tests applied to the log dividend series shown in Figure 11.2 are given, with p values in parentheses, by

$$\begin{array}{lll}
\text{Levin–Lin–Chu} & : & -3.0755 \quad (0.0011) \\
\text{Im–Pesaran–Shin} & : & -0.9781 \quad (0.1640).
\end{array}$$

Both panel unit root tests in equations (11.59) and (11.60) are computed assuming zero lags ($L = 0$). The panel unit root tests both show log equity prices to be nonstationary. The evidence for log dividends is mixed. The Levin–Lin–Chu test rejects unit roots and finds the variables to be stationary. But the Im–Pesaran–Shin test does not reject the null in favor of the hypothesis that some variables are stationary.

11.6.2 Panel Cointegration

The panel unit root tests for log prices, p_{jt}, and log dividends, d_{jt}, provide supportive evidence that these series are integrated processes of order one. The further step may be taken to assess whether there is empirical evidence in the panel for cointegration as in the fixed effects panel cointegrating regression given in equation (11.55).

As with cointegration testing in non-panel data models, there exists a range of test procedures for cointegration in dynamic panel models. Many of these tests rely on Fisher's (1932) idea of combining individual tests to produce a meta-analysis test. Two examples are the Johansen–Fisher panel cointegration test in Maddala and Wu (1999) and the Choi (2001) panel unit root test. The strategy is simply to apply the tests separately to each time series in the cross section and then combine them using the p value outcomes for these individual tests.

In testing for panel cointegration, the procedure is to apply (for instance) the Johansen cointegration test outlined in Chapter 6 to each cross sectional unit separately. If π_j is the p value of the test for cross section j for a particular hypothesis, the joint statistic based on the N cross section outcomes is constructed as

$$-2\sum_{j=1}^{N}\log\left(\pi_j\right) \to \chi^2_{2N}, \tag{11.61}$$

which is asymptotically distributed as chi square with $2N$ degrees of freedom when $T \to \infty$. The test was called the inverse chi-squared test by Fisher (1932). The asymptotic theory relies on a large time series sample and allows for unbalanced panels with different time series sample sizes T_j provided $T_j \to \infty$ for all $j = 1, \cdots, N$.

The Johansen trace test and associated p values for the cointegrating rank of the relationship between share prices and dividends applied to each of the 12 countries in the panel individually are reported in Table 11.8. At the 5% level of significance, the present value model is supported by 4 of the 12 countries (Australia, Canada, Mexico, and the United States) in which there is one cointegrating vector. If the level of significance is relaxed to 10%, 3 additional countries (France, Hong Kong, and the United Kingdom) also have one cointegrating vector.

TABLE 11.8   The Johansen trace test for the cointegrating rank of the present value relationship in $N = 12$ countries. The test is based on a VECM model with a constant in the cointegrating vector but not in the VAR (restricted constant model) with 1 lag in the underlying VAR. The data are monthly for the period January 2002 to March 2015.

	Cointegrating rank = 0		Cointegrating rank = 1	
	Trace test	p value	Trace test	p value
Australia	31.273	0.0001	3.1188	0.5588
Brazil	14.285	0.2703	3.1805	0.5476
Canada	31.580	0.0009	3.6620	0.4648
China	10.240	0.6162	2.4299	0.6915
France	19.666	0.0602	3.8298	0.4380
Germany	14.513	0.2556	2.2073	0.7362
Hong Kong	18.217	0.0933	6.6356	0.1470
Japan	17.213	0.1247	4.1986	0.3833
Mexico	20.788	0.0423	2.8156	0.6157
South Korea	16.243	0.1633	3.0181	0.5773
United Kingdom	18.965	0.0746	3.5190	0.4884
United States	65.445	0.0000	2.4784	0.6818

Applying the panel cointegration test in equation (11.61) using the p values reported in Table 11.8 yields a test statistic of 102.13 under the null hypothesis of no cointegration. The p value is 0.000, showing strong rejection of this hypothesis. Performing the test on the next stage where the null hypothesis represents a single cointegrating vector yields a test statistic of 16.92. The p value is 0.85, providing strong support for cointegration and hence strong support for the present value model across all 12 countries in the panel.

Having established cointegration in the panel, the cointegrating parameter vector β in equation (11.55), together with the fixed effects α_j, are estimated by modified methods based on least squares (see Chapter 6 for a discussion of fully modified estimators in a time series context). Two popular methods are the fully modified estimator of Phillips and Moon (1999) and the dynamic least squares estimator of Lao and Chiang (1999). See also Baltagi and Kao (2000) for a review and extension of these estimators. In the case of the dynamic least squares panel estimator, equation (11.55) is augmented to include leads and lags of Δd_{jt} as follows

$$p_{jt} = \alpha_j + \beta d_{jt} + \sum_{k=-L}^{L} \gamma_{jk} \Delta d_{jt-k} + u_{jt}, \tag{11.62}$$

which is estimated by ordinary least squares. As with the estimator of the cointegrating parameter vector β for the non-panel case in Chapter 6, the fully modified and dynamic ordinary least squares cointegrating panel estimators have appropriately constructed t ratio statistics that are asymptotically distributed as $N(0, 1)$ under the assumption that there is cointegration.

Given the results of the panel cointegration tests between log share prices and log dividends, the panel dynamic ordinary least squares estimator is used to estimate the panel present value model with lag/lead setting $L = 1$ in equation (11.62). The long-run parameter estimate is $\widehat{\beta} = 0.667$, with a standard error of 0.022. This estimate is significantly less than $\beta = 1$ and therefore represents a rejection of the pure form of the present value model discussed in Chapter 2.

11.7 EXERCISES

The data required for the exercises are available for download as EViews workfiles (*.wf1), Stata datafiles (*.dta), comma delimited text files (*.csv), and as Excel spreadsheets (*.xlsx).

1. **Estimating Simple Panel Models**

> DJindexstocks.*

The data required are the monthly excess returns, $r_{jt} - r_{ft}$, on the US stocks Johnson and Johnson, Merck, Pfizer, Proctor and Gamble, and the United Health Group, and the market excess return, $r_{mt} - r_{ft}$, on the Dow Jones for the period January 1926 to December 2013.

(a) Compute descriptive statistics for the excess returns to the 5 pharmaceutical stocks given in the data.

(b) Estimate the no common effects model

$$r_{jt} - r_{ft} = \alpha_j + \beta_j(r_{mt} - r_{ft}) + u_{jt}, \qquad j = 1, \cdots, 5,$$

for each of the 5 stocks by ordinary least squares and comment on the results.

(c) Estimate the common effects model

$$r_t - r_{ft} = \alpha + \beta(r_{mt} - r_{ft}) + u_{jt},$$

by ordinary least squares and interpret the results.

(d) Test the restrictions involved in moving from the no common effects to the common effects model using an F test.

(e) Estimate the fixed effects and random effects models given by

$$r_{jt} - r_{ft} = \alpha_j + \beta(r_{mt} - r_{ft}) + u_{jt}$$
$$r_{jt} - r_{ft} = \alpha + \beta(r_{mt} - r_{ft}) + v_j + u_{jt},$$

respectively. Comment on the results.

2. **CAPM Model with Different Market Indices**

> djcomposite_monthly.*

The data are monthly prices for the US stocks Exxon Mobil (XOM), General Electric (GE), the Excelon Corporation (EXC), CenterPoint Energy (CNP), FedEx Corporation (FDX), and United Pacific Corporation (UNP) and their associated sector index within the Dow Jones, namely, the Industrial Average (XOM and GE), the Utilities Average (EXC and CNP), and the Transportation Average Indices (FDX and UNP), respectively. Also included is the monthly risk-free interest rate (expressed as a percentage) and the Dow Jones Composite Index, which can be used as a common market index for all the stocks. The sample period is January 1926 to December 2013.

(a) Compute excess returns for each of the 6 stocks and for the 4 different Dow Jones sector indices.

(b) Estimate the fixed effects and random effects models given by

$$r_{jt} - r_{ft} = \alpha_j + \beta(r_{mt} - r_{ft}) + u_{jt}$$
$$r_{jt} - r_{ft} = \alpha + \beta(r_{mt} - r_{ft}) + v_j + u_{jt},$$

respectively, where r_{mt} is the common market index given by the Dow Jones Composite Average. Verify that the two estimators are identical for this model.

(c) Repeat part (b) where the market index for each stock is the appropriate sectoral market index, r_{jmt}. Comment on the results.

3. **A Multifactor Panel Model of the Dow Jones Index**

> dowpanel.*

The data are monthly stock prices of the 30 companies in the Dow Jones for the period March 2008 to June 2013. Also included are the Dow Jones, the risk-free rate expressed as a monthly percentage, a momentum variable (*mom*) representing the cumulated returns for each company from $t-1$ to $t-13$, and a volatility variable (*vol*) representing the standard deviation of the monthly returns on each company from $t-1$ to $t-13$.

(a) Estimate the multifactor fixed effects CAPM given by

$$r_{jt} - r_{ft} = \alpha_j + \beta_1(r_{mt} - r_{ft}) + \beta_2 mom_{jt} + \beta_3 vol_{jt} + u_{jt},$$

where r_{jt} is the monthly log return of company j, r_{ft} is the risk-free rate expressed in standard units at a monthly rate, r_{mt} is the log return on the Dow Jones, and u_{jt} is the disturbance term representing idiosyncratic risk.

   (i) Interpret the parameter estimates of β_1, β_2, and β_3.
   (ii) Interpret the estimates of the fixed effects parameters $\{\alpha_1, \alpha_2, \cdots, \alpha_{30}\}$.
   (iii) Perform a test of the 1-factor CAPM by testing the restrictions $\beta_2 = \beta_3 = 0$.
   (iv) Perform a test of the restriction $\beta_1 = 1$ and interpret the result.

(b) Estimate the multifactor common effects CAPM given by

$$r_{jt} - r_{ft} = \alpha + \beta_1(r_{mt} - r_{ft}) + \beta_2 mom_{jt} + \beta_3 vol_{jt} + u_{jt}.$$

Use a likelihood ratio statistic to test this model against the multifactor fixed effects CAPM in part (a) and interpret the result.

(c) Estimate the multifactor random effects CAPM given by

$$r_{jt} - r_{ft} = \alpha + \beta_1(r_{mt} - r_{ft}) + \beta_2 mom_{jt} + \beta_3 vol_{jt} + v_j + u_{jt},$$

where $v_j \sim (0, \sigma_v^2)$. Compare the parameter estimates of this model and the estimates obtained for the common effects model in part (c). Discuss the results.

4. Gibbons–Ross–Shanken Test

fama_french.*

The data are monthly returns, r_{jt}, for $N = 10$ industry portfolios for the period July 1926 to December 2013, together with the excess return on the market, $r_{mt} - r_{ft}$.

(a) Compute the excess returns on the monthly industry portfolios.
(b) Pool the data and generate dummy variables, D_{jt}, associated with each cross sectional unit (industry portfolio). Estimate the no common effects model

$$r_{jt} - r_{ft} = \sum_{j=1}^{N} \alpha_j D_{jt} + \sum_{j=1}^{N} \beta_j D_{jt}(r_{mt} - r_{ft}) + u_{jt},$$

and interpret the results.
(c) Test for constant α-risk by testing the hypothesis

$$H_0 : \alpha_1 = \alpha_2 = \cdots = \alpha_{10} = \alpha$$
$$H_1 : \text{at least one restrictions fails.}$$

(d) Test for zero α-risk by testing the hypothesis

$$H_0 : \alpha_1 = \alpha_2 = \cdots = \alpha_N = 0$$
$$H_1 : \text{at least one restrictions fails.}$$

This test is known as the Gibbons, Ross, and Shanken (1989) test.

5. Fama–Macbeth Regressions

> fama_french.*

The data are monthly returns, r_{jt}, for $N = 10$ industry portfolios for the period July 1926 to December 2013, together with the excess return on the market, $r_{mt} - r_{ft}$. The single factor CAPM is

$$E(r_{jt} - r_{ft}) = \beta_j E(r_{mt} - r_{ft}) = \beta_j \lambda,$$

where λ is the market price of risk. Fama and MacBeth (1973) propose a three-step approach to estimate λ based on time series and cross section regressions.

(a) First step: time series regression:
Estimate the no common effects CAPM

$$r_{jt} - r_{ft} = \alpha_j + \beta_j(r_{mt} - r_{ft}) + u_{jt}, \qquad j = 1, 2, \cdots, 10,$$

for each of the 10 industry portfolios. Save the estimates of α-risk, $\widehat{\alpha}_j$, and β-risk, $\widehat{\beta}_j$, for each of the 10 stocks.

(b) Second step: cross section regression:
For each point in time t, the following cross section regression model is estimated

$$r_{jt} - r_{ft} = \gamma_t + \beta_j \lambda_t + e_{jt}, \qquad t = 1, 2, \cdots, T, \tag{11.63}$$

in which e_{jt} is a disturbance and where β_j is replaced by $\widehat{\beta}_j$ from the time series regressions. The cross sectional regression disturbances e_{jt} represent the pricing errors for each cross section at a particular point in time. This step yields time series of length T on the respective estimated intercepts and risk prices

$$\{\widehat{\gamma}_1, \widehat{\gamma}_2, \cdots, \widehat{\gamma}_T\}, \qquad \{\widehat{\lambda}_1, \widehat{\lambda}_2, \cdots, \widehat{\lambda}_T\}. \tag{11.64}$$

(c) Third step: calculation of the market price of risk:
The market price of risk is estimated as the sample mean of the time series of risk prices

$$\overline{\lambda} = \frac{1}{T} \sum_{t=1}^{T} \widehat{\lambda}_t,$$

with variance

$$\widehat{\sigma}^2(\overline{\lambda}) = \frac{\widehat{\sigma}^2(\lambda)}{T} = \frac{1}{T^2} \sum_{t=1}^{T} (\widehat{\lambda}_t - \overline{\lambda})^2.$$

(d) Perform a test of zero market risk using a t test of the null hypothesis $H_0 : \lambda = 0$. Interpret the results of this test.

(e) Perform a test of the hypothesis $H_0 : \gamma = 0$ and interpret the result.

(f) Repeat the Fama–Macbeth procedure using the 25 Fama–French portfolios (R1 to R25) sorted in terms of size and book-to-market.

6. **Performance of Family Firms**

> familyfirms.*

The data are 2254 firm-year observations over the 1992–1999 period. The dependent variable is Tobin's Q, which is used as a measure of firm performance. The explanatory variables are the size of the firm, *assets*, the age of the firm, *age*, the volatility of the operating environment, *vol* measured by the standard deviation of the previous 60-month returns and a dummy variable indicating whether or not the founder of the firm is also its chief executive officer, *CEO*.

(a) Estimate the fixed effects model

$$\log Q_{jt} = \alpha_j + \beta_1 CEO_{jt} + \beta_2 \log assets_{jt} + \beta_3 \log age_{jt} + \beta_4 vol_{jt} + u_{jt},$$

and interpret the results.

(b) Estimate the random effects model

$$\log Q_{jt} = \alpha + \beta_1 CEO_{jt} + \beta_2 \log assets_{jt} + \beta_3 \log age_{jt} + \beta_4 vol_{jt} + v_j + u_{jt},$$

and interpret the results.

(c) On the basis of the results in (a) and (b), which model do you prefer and why? Now provide a formal test for fixed versus random effects using a Hausman test. What do you conclude?

(d) Now estimate the dynamic panel data model

$$\Delta \log Q_{jt} = \beta_1 \Delta \log CEO_{jt} + \beta_2 \Delta \log assets_{jt} + \Delta \beta_3 \log age_{jt}$$
$$+ \Delta \beta_4 vol_{jt} + \rho \Delta \log Q_{jt-1} + \Delta u_{jt},$$

using the Arellano–Bond estimator. Interpret the results.

(e) Repeat part (d) using the system GMM estimator and compare the results with those in (d).

7. **Target Leverage and Partial Adjustment**

> capitalstructure.*

The data consist of observations on a number of financial variables for $N = 5658$ US firms for the period 1971–2014. The variables in the panel data set include three different measures of firm leverage, $lv1$, $lv2$, and $lv3$, together with a number of variables used to model firm leverage, including the value of tangible assets, tan_{it}; firm size, $size_{it}$; the tax shield for non-debt finance defined as total depreciation expense divided by the book value of total asset, dep_{it}; growth opportunities defined as the market-to-book value of assets, mb_{it}; operating income before depreciation, $profit_{it}$; the dividend payout ratio, $payout_{it}$; and the idiosyncratic risk of the company, vol_{it}, as a measure of business risk.

(a) Estimate the dynamic partial adjustment model

$$y_{jt} = \gamma \alpha_j + \gamma \beta_1 x_{1jt-1} + \cdots \gamma \beta_k x_{kjt-1} + (1 - \gamma) y_{jt-1} + u_{jt},$$

using the fixed effects estimator, with $lv1$ as the dependent variable y_{jt} and including all the available explanatory variables in the data set. Interpret your results.

(b) Still using the fixed effects estimator, examine if there is statistical support of the hypothesis of Rajan and Zingales (1995) who claim that only four factors— namely, market-to-book, profitability, tangibility, and size—are required to provide a satisfactory model for target leverage.

(c) Repeat parts (a) and (b) using $lv2$ and $lv3$, respectively, as the dependent variable.

(d) Assume that the Rajan and Zingales four factors are sufficient to model leverage. Re-estimate the partial adjustment model in (a) using the GMM and S-GMM estimators for all three empirical leverage measures. Is there any support for the claim that the estimated adjustment speed varies significantly if different estimators are used (Flannery and Hankins, 2013)?

8. Panel Unit Roots and Cointegration

---
presentvalue_panel.*

The data file contains monthly observations on prices and dividends for $N = 12$ countries for the period January 2002 to March 2016. All prices and dividends are expressed in local currency.

(a) Express prices and dividends in terms of a common currency ($US) using the exchange rate variable given in the data file. Generate scatter plots of log prices against log dividends for each of the 12 countries.

(b) Use the panel unit root tests to test the null hypothesis that all countries have unit roots in log prices and log dividends. Is your conclusion robust to the choice of lag length used in the testing procedure?

(c) Construct the Johansen trace test for cointegration between log prices and log dividends for each country and interpret the results. Use a VECM with no lags and include a constant only in the cointegrating equation (the restricted constant model). Interpret your results. Are the conclusions robust to the VECM specification?

(d) Estimate the panel cointegrating regression

$$p_{jt} = \alpha_j + \beta d_{jt} + \sum_{k=-L}^{L} \gamma_{jk} \Delta d_{jt-k} + u_{jt},$$

by dynamic ordinary least squares with $L = 1, 2, 3$. Is the estimate of the common cointegrating parameter, β, robust to the choice of L?

(e) Test the pure form of the present value model by testing the null hypothesis $H_0 : \beta = 1$.

CHAPTER 12

Latent Factor Models

A distinguishing feature of financial time series is the tendency of many financial variables to display similar behavior over time. The similarities can manifest in the location, variation, dynamics, and the sample trajectories of the time series themselves. Here are some examples.

(i) Location: Interest rates on instruments of different maturities tend to move together in such a way that the spreads between them are stationary.

(ii) Variation: Periods of turbulence and tranquility tend to coincide across asset markets both locally and internationally, with the global financial crisis of 2008–2010 representing a prime example of synchronized turbulence.

(iii) Dynamics: The returns to different financial assets tend to exhibit very similar autocorrelation patterns.

(iv) Trajectories: The sample paths of certain financial variables like stock prices and exchange rates can tend to move together over time, reflecting general movements in economic activity.

These common features in financial data suggest that the behavior of a group of financial time series can often be captured by way of a smaller set of common factors that serve to represent the primary drivers of the common behavior over time. The idea is represented algebraically in the following system of regression equations

$$
\begin{aligned}
r_{1t} &= \alpha_1 + \beta_1 s_t + u_{1t} \\
r_{2t} &= \alpha_2 + \beta_2 s_t + u_{2t} \\
&\vdots \quad \vdots \quad \vdots \\
r_{Nt} &= \alpha_N + \beta_N s_t + u_{Nt},
\end{aligned}
\tag{12.1}
$$

which embody a single factor, s_t, as the driver variable in determining the time series behavior of a group of N financial asset returns ($r_{it} : i = 1, \cdots, N$). The coefficients α_i and β_i are parameters, and u_{it} is a disturbance term representing idiosyncratic movements in r_{it}. The parameters ($\beta_i : i = 1, \cdots, N$) play a special role in equation (12.1) as they measure the extent to which each asset is influenced by the driving factor s_t. The parameter β_i is therefore described as the factor loading of s_t for asset i.

If the factor, s_t, is observable, then time series data are available for s_t and the parameters α_i and β_i are estimated simply by regressing r_{it} on a constant and s_t. Typical examples of this type of model are the CAPM, both the simple variant with only a market factor and the Fama–French three-factor model. But factor variables may be unobserved. If time series data on s_t is unavailable, direct least squares estimation of the parameters α_i and β_i in equation (12.1) is not possible. It is by no means obvious how the system can be estimated when all components on the right-hand side of the equation are unobserved, including the factor s_t, the disturbances $u_{1t}, \cdots, u_{Nt}$, and the unknown parameters α_i and β_i.

One solution to the absence of factor data is to use a proxy variable for the unobserved factor. The CAPM is itself in this category because the market factor is generally unobservable. Instead, the return on some relevant market index is employed as an observed proxy. This solution to the problem of latent factors creates an implicit errors-in-variables problem, analogous to those discussed in Chapter 8.

A statistical solution to the latent factor problem when s_t is unobserved is to introduce additional structural assumptions on the model equations (12.1) to facilitate estimation. Two statistical approaches are explored in this chapter: the method of principal components and the Kalman filter. An alternative approach to the problem of unobservable factors is to use the GMM estimator introduced in Chapter 9.

12.1 MOTIVATION

Figure 12.1 shows percentage annualized US Treasury yields for three maturities (1 month, 1 year, and 5 years) for the period July 2001 to September 2010. Inspection of the plots reveals that the levels of the yields tend to move together over time, with the shorter maturities being more dynamic and showing more variation over time.

In addition to the tendency for yields to move together, another feature of the time series behavior of the yields, which is not immediately evident in Figure 12.1, is that yields on neighboring maturities (such as the 1-month and 1-year yield) move together more closely than yields with greater differences in maturities (such as the 1-month and 5-year yield). This empirical property, which is related to the spread between maturities, is highlighted in the correlation matrix for $N = 9$ yields that is shown below,

1-mth	3-mth	6-mth	1-yr	2-yr	3-yr	5-yr	7-yr	10-yr
1.000	0.998	0.992	0.985	0.960	0.933	0.869	0.787	0.702
0.998	1.000	0.997	0.992	0.968	0.940	0.872	0.787	0.700
0.992	0.997	1.000	0.997	0.974	0.945	0.874	0.784	0.697
0.985	0.992	0.997	1.000	0.987	0.964	0.901	0.816	0.734
0.960	0.968	0.974	0.987	1.000	0.993	0.952	0.885	0.812
0.933	0.940	0.945	0.964	0.993	1.000	0.979	0.929	0.867
0.869	0.872	0.874	0.901	0.952	0.979	1.000	0.984	0.949
0.787	0.787	0.784	0.816	0.885	0.929	0.984	1.000	0.987
0.702	0.700	0.697	0.734	0.812	0.867	0.949	0.987	1.000

As is evident in this matrix, the highest correlation for any particular yield occurs with the immediately neighboring yield, and the correlation decays as the difference in maturity increases. These two characteristics suggest that a potential model to explain the

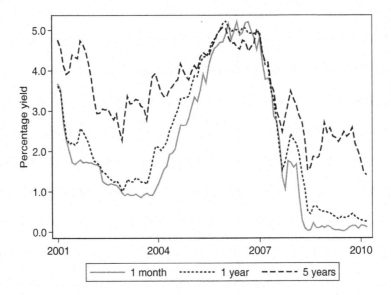

FIGURE 12.1   Plots of the percentage annualized yields on selected maturity zero-coupon US Treasury bonds for the period July 2001 to September 2010.

term structure of interest rates is given by the 2-factor model

$$r_{it} = \alpha_i + \beta_{1i}s_{1t} + \beta_{2i}s_{2t} + u_{it}, \qquad i = 1, 2, \cdots, 9,$$

in which the yield is determined by a level factor, s_{1t}, and a spread factor, s_{2t} in combination with an unobserved disturbance term, u_{it}.

12.2 PRINCIPAL COMPONENTS

The first method for estimating models in which there are latent factors uses principal components[1] to extract the unobserved factors. The method is a practical statistical device and does not rely on any input from financial theory or economics. The idea is to break down the observable variation in the data into orthogonal components that are called principal components because they are constructed to capture the greatest possible contribution to this variation, controlling the number of components to equal the number of posited latent factors. When the number of latent factors is itself unknown, then additional methods are needed to determine that number.

In principal component analysis, the factors and their associated factor loadings are constructed in a manner that assures certain key properties hold.

(i) The factors (or principal components) are constructed sequentially by decomposition of the matrix of observed variation in the data.

---

[1] The concept of principal components originated in early work at the turn of the twentieth century by the English statistician Karl Pearson. It was formally developed later in the 1930s by the American economist and statistician Harold Hotelling.

(ii) Each factor successively accounts for as much remaining variation that is left in the observed data after taking account of the preceding factors.

(iii) Each factor is orthogonal or uncorrelated with every other factor.

12.2.1 Specification

Consider a model containing N asset returns $r_t = \{r_{1t}, r_{2t}, \cdots, r_{Nt}\}$ and $K \leq N$ factors $s_t = \{s_{1t}, s_{2t}, \cdots, s_{Kt}\}$, which is written as

$$
\begin{bmatrix} r_{1t} \\ r_{2t} \\ \vdots \\ r_{Nt} \end{bmatrix} = \begin{bmatrix} \alpha_1 \\ \alpha_2 \\ \vdots \\ \alpha_N \end{bmatrix} + \begin{bmatrix} \beta_{11} & \beta_{12} & \cdots & \beta_{1K} \\ \beta_{21} & \beta_{22} & \cdots & \beta_{2K} \\ \vdots & \vdots & \ddots & \vdots \\ \beta_{N1} & \beta_{N2} & \cdots & \beta_{NK} \end{bmatrix} \begin{bmatrix} s_{1t} \\ s_{2t} \\ \vdots \\ s_{Kt} \end{bmatrix} + \begin{bmatrix} u_{1t} \\ u_{2t} \\ \vdots \\ u_{Nt} \end{bmatrix},
$$

or in matrix notation

$$
r_t = \alpha + \beta s_t + u_t, \tag{12.2}
$$

where α is an $(N \times 1)$ vector containing the intercepts, s_t is a $(K \times 1)$ vector containing the factors, β is an $(N \times K)$ matrix containing the factor loadings, and u_t is an $(N \times 1)$ vector of disturbances.

The vector of latent factors and the disturbance vector are assumed to have the following moment properties

$$
\begin{aligned}
\mathrm{E}(u_t) &= 0, & \mathrm{E}(u_t u_t') &= \Omega, \\
\mathrm{E}(s_t) &= 0, & \mathrm{E}(s_t s_t') &= I, \\
\mathrm{E}(s_t u_t') &= 0,
\end{aligned} \tag{12.3}
$$

where Ω is an $(N \times N)$ covariance matrix representing idiosyncratic risk. Since $\mathrm{E}(s_t) = \mathrm{E}(u_t) = 0$, the mean of the returns is

$$
\mathrm{E}(r_t) = \mathrm{E}(\alpha + \beta s_t + u_t) = \alpha + \beta \, \mathrm{E}(s_t) + \mathrm{E}(u_t) = \alpha.
$$

Given the properties of s_t and u_t in equation (12.3), the covariance structure of r_t can be decomposed into two component sources that embody systematic risk and idiosyncratic risk in the following manner

$$
\begin{aligned}
\mathrm{cov}(r_t) &= \mathrm{E}[(r_t - \alpha)(r_t - \alpha)'] \\
&= \mathrm{E}[(\beta s_t + u_t)(\beta s_t + u_t)'] \\
&= \beta \, \mathrm{E}(s_t s_t')\beta' + \beta \, \mathrm{E}(s_t u_t') + \mathrm{E}(u_t s_t')\beta' + \mathrm{E}(u_t u_t') \\
&= \underbrace{\beta\beta'}_{\text{Systematic Risk}} + \underbrace{\Omega}_{\text{Idiosyncratic Risk}}.
\end{aligned}
$$

In the special case where the number of variables matches the number of factors ($N = K$) and the loading matrix β is nonsingular, there is an exact decomposition of the covariance matrix of r_t into a single component comprised only of the factors. In this special case, $\Omega = 0$ and the covariance matrix of r_t has the form

$$\text{cov}(r_t) = \beta\beta' = \beta_1\beta_1' + \beta_2\beta_2' + \cdots \beta_N\beta_N', \tag{12.4}$$

where β_i is the ith column of β.

12.2.2 Estimation

To estimate the unknown factors (s_t) and associated factor loadings (β_i), the principal components approach uses a matrix orthonormal decomposition of the covariance matrix of r_t that has the following form

$$\text{cov}(r_t) = \sum_{i=1}^{N} \lambda_i P_i P_i' = \lambda_1 P_1 P_1' + \lambda_2 P_2 P_2' + \cdots + \lambda_N P_N P_N'. \tag{12.5}$$

This decomposition expresses $\text{cov}(r_t)$ as a weighted sum of the outer products $P_i P_i'$ of component $(N \times 1)$ vectors P_i with weights λ_i. The vectors P_i and scalars λ_i are the eigenvector/eigenvalue pairs associated with the symmetric positive definite matrix $\text{cov}(r_t)$. This decomposition of the covariance matrix of r_t in equation (12.5) is known as its eigenvector/eigenvalue decomposition. The eigenvectors have the properties of being orthonormal because they satisfy the relations $P_i' P_i = 1$ (unit length) and $P_i P_j = 0$ (orthogonality) $\forall i \neq j$. The eigenvalues $\lambda_i > 0$ yield positive weights because the covariance matrix $\text{cov}(r_t)$ is positive definite. The orthogonal decomposition in equation (12.5) is an explicit representation of the components that diagonalize the covariance matrix $\text{cov}(r_t)$.

A comparison of the decompositions exhibited in equations (12.4) and (12.5) suggests that the loading parameter vector β_i can be chosen as

$$\beta_i = \sqrt{\lambda_i} P_i, \qquad i = 1, 2, \cdots, N. \tag{12.6}$$

To understand the properties of the decomposition in equation (12.5) of the covariance matrix $\text{cov}(r_t)$, consider the explicit form of its diagonal elements, which are the N variances of r_t, namely,

$$\begin{bmatrix} \text{var}(r_{1t}) \\ \text{var}(r_{2t}) \\ \vdots \\ \text{var}(r_{Nt}) \end{bmatrix} = \lambda_1 \begin{bmatrix} P_{11}^2 \\ P_{21}^2 \\ \vdots \\ P_{N1}^2 \end{bmatrix} + \lambda_2 \begin{bmatrix} P_{12}^2 \\ P_{22}^2 \\ \vdots \\ P_{N2}^2 \end{bmatrix} + \cdots + \lambda_N \begin{bmatrix} P_{1N}^2 \\ P_{2N}^2 \\ \vdots \\ P_{NN}^2 \end{bmatrix}. \tag{12.7}$$

Since $P_i' P_i = 1$, the sum of the elements of each of the column vectors on the right-hand side of equation (12.7) all equal unity

$$P_{11}^2 + P_{21}^2 + \cdots + P_{N1}^2 = 1$$
$$P_{12}^2 + P_{22}^2 + \cdots + P_{N2}^2 = 1$$
$$\vdots \qquad\qquad \vdots$$
$$P_{1N}^2 + P_{2N}^2 + \cdots + P_{NN}^2 = 1.$$

This suggests that a measure of the total volatility of all asset returns is obtained by summing each column in equation (12.7) to give

$$\sum_{i=1}^{N} \text{var}(r_{it}) = \lambda_1 + \lambda_2 + \cdots + \lambda_N = \sum_{i=1}^{N} \lambda_i.$$

This important result shows that the total variance of returns can be decomposed in terms of the parameters $\lambda_1, \lambda_2, \cdots, \lambda_N$ and that a measure of the total volatility of the vector of returns r_t is given by the sum of all the eigenvalues of the matrix $\text{cov}(r_t)$. By inspecting the relative magnitudes of the largest K eigenvalues in this decomposition, it is possible to quantify the proportion of the total variation in the data that is explained by these $K < N$ components. In consequence, these components are called the K principal components of $\text{cov}(r_t)$.

Instead of performing an eigen decomposition of the covariance matrix $\text{cov}(r_t)$ the correlation matrix $\text{cor}(r_t)$ can be used instead. The choice of the correlation matrix is useful in circumventing the scaling issues that arise when variables are measured in different units. Since the correlation matrix has unit elements along its main diagonal, the sum of the correlations becomes

$$\sum_{i=1}^{N} \lambda_i = N.$$

To highlight the features of the factor loadings based on principal component analysis, consider the following correlation matrix of the 1-month, 1-year, and 5-year US Treasury yields shown in Figure 12.1

$$\begin{bmatrix} 1.000 & 0.985 & 0.869 \\ 0.985 & 1.000 & 0.901 \\ 0.869 & 0.901 & 1.000 \end{bmatrix}.$$

The estimated eigenvalues and eigenvectors are, respectively,

$$\widehat{\lambda} = \begin{bmatrix} 2.837 \\ 0.151 \\ 0.012 \end{bmatrix}, \quad \widehat{P} = \begin{bmatrix} 0.581 & -0.490 & 0.649 \\ 0.588 & -0.299 & -0.752 \\ 0.563 & 0.819 & 0.114 \end{bmatrix}, \tag{12.8}$$

with the columns of $\widehat{P}$ representing the three eigenvectors

$$\widehat{P}_1 = \begin{bmatrix} 0.581 \\ 0.588 \\ 0.563 \end{bmatrix}, \quad \widehat{P}_2 = \begin{bmatrix} -0.490 \\ -0.299 \\ 0.819 \end{bmatrix}, \quad \widehat{P}_3 = \begin{bmatrix} 0.649 \\ -0.752 \\ 0.114 \end{bmatrix},$$

which correspond in order to that of the three eigenvalues in $\widehat{\lambda}$.

The six unique elements of the correlation matrix are recovered as follows. The main diagonal elements are

$$\text{cor}(r_{1t}) = 2.837 \times (0.581)^2 + 0.151 \times (-0.490)^2 + 0.012 \times (0.649)^2 = 1.000$$
$$\text{cor}(r_{2t}) = 2.837 \times (0.588)^2 + 0.151 \times (-0.299)^2 + 0.012 \times (-0.752)^2 = 1.000$$
$$\text{cor}(r_{3t}) = 2.837 \times (0.563)^2 + 0.151 \times (0.819)^2 + 0.012 \times (0.144)^2 = 1.000,$$

and the off-diagonal elements are

$$\text{cor}(r_{1t}, r_{2t}) = 2.837 \times (0.581) \times (0.588) + 0.151 \times (-0.490) \times (-0.299)$$
$$+ 0.012 \times (0.649) \times (-0.752) = 0.985$$
$$\text{cor}(r_{1t}, r_{3t}) = 2.837 \times (0.581) \times (0.563) + 0.151 \times (-0.490) \times (0.819)$$
$$+ 0.012 \times (0.649) \times (0.144) = 0.869$$
$$\text{cor}(r_{2t}, r_{3t}) = 2.837 \times (0.588) \times (0.563) + 0.151 \times (-0.299) \times (0.819)$$
$$+ 0.012 \times (-0.752) \times (0.144) = 0.901.$$

Some key properties of the parameter estimates are as follows.

(i) *Normalization property of eigenvectors*

$$\widehat{P}_1' \widehat{P}_1 = 0.581^2 + 0.588^2 + 0.563^2 = 1.000$$
$$\widehat{P}_2' \widehat{P}_2 = (-0.490)^2 + (-0.299)^2 + 0.819^2 = 1.000$$
$$\widehat{P}_3' \widehat{P}_3 = 0.649^2 + (-0.752)^2 + 0.114^2 = 1.000.$$

(ii) *Orthogonality of eigenvectors*

$$\widehat{P}_1' \widehat{P}_2 = 0.581 \times (-0.490) + 0.588 \times (-0.299) + 0.563 \times 0.819 = 0$$
$$\widehat{P}_1' \widehat{P}_3 = 0.581 \times 0.649 + 0.588 \times (-0.752) + 0.563 \times 0.114 = 0$$
$$\widehat{P}_2' \widehat{P}_3 = (-0.490) \times (0.649) + (-0.299) \times (-0.752) + 0.819 \times 0.114 = 0.$$

(iii) *Eigenvalues*
As it is the correlation matrix that is being used in the eigen decomposition, the estimated eigenvalues sum to $N = 3$

$$\sum_{i=1}^{3} \widehat{\lambda}_i = 2.837 + 0.151 + 0.012 = 3.$$

The normalized eigenvalues are

$$\frac{2.837}{3} + \frac{0.151}{3} + \frac{0.012}{3} = 0.946 + 0.050 + 0.004 = 1.$$

The first eigenvalue explains 94.6% of the total variance, the second explains an additional 5%, while the contribution of the third and last eigenvalue is 0.4%.

(iv) *Factor loadings*

From equation (12.6) the factor loadings are

$$\widehat{\beta}_1 = \sqrt{\widehat{\lambda}_1}\widehat{P}_1 = \sqrt{2.837}\begin{bmatrix} 0.581 \\ 0.588 \\ 0.563 \end{bmatrix} = \begin{bmatrix} 0.979 \\ 0.990 \\ 0.948 \end{bmatrix}$$

$$\widehat{\beta}_2 = \sqrt{\widehat{\lambda}_2}\widehat{P}_2 = \sqrt{0.151}\begin{bmatrix} -0.490 \\ -0.299 \\ 0.819 \end{bmatrix} = \begin{bmatrix} -0.190 \\ -0.116 \\ 0.318 \end{bmatrix}$$

$$\widehat{\beta}_3 = \sqrt{\widehat{\lambda}_3}\widehat{P}_3 = \sqrt{0.012}\begin{bmatrix} 0.649 \\ -0.752 \\ 0.114 \end{bmatrix} = \begin{bmatrix} 0.071 \\ -0.082 \\ 0.012 \end{bmatrix}.$$

Since the eigen decomposition is based on the correlation matrix, the estimated 1-factor model in equation (12.2) is expressed in terms of standardized yields. The estimated model with loadings based on the vector $\widehat{\beta}_1$ has the following three equations

$$z_{1t} = \widehat{\beta}_{11}s_{1t} + \widehat{u}_{1t} = 0.979\,s_{1t} + \widehat{u}_{1t}$$
$$z_{2t} = \widehat{\beta}_{21}s_{1t} + \widehat{u}_{2t} = 0.990\,s_{1t} + \widehat{u}_{2t}$$
$$z_{3t} = \widehat{\beta}_{31}s_{1t} + \widehat{u}_{3t} = 0.948\,s_{1t} + \widehat{u}_{3t},$$

in which z_{jt} are the standardized yields for $j = 1, 2, 3$. Notice that an increase in the factor s_{1t} results in all 3 yields increasing by similar amounts. This observation suggests that s_{1t} plays the role of the *level* factor.

Since $E(s_{1t}^2) = 1$, the systematic risks are

$$\widehat{h}_1 = \widehat{\beta}_{11}^2 = 0.979^2 = 0.958$$
$$\widehat{h}_2 = \widehat{\beta}_{21}^2 = 0.990^2 = 0.980$$
$$\widehat{h}_3 = \widehat{\beta}_{31}^2 = 0.948^2 = 0.899,$$

and the idiosyncratic risks are

$$\text{var}\,(\widehat{u}_{1t}) = \text{var}\,(r_{1t}) - \widehat{h}_{1t} = 1.000 - 0.958 = 0.042$$
$$\text{var}\,(\widehat{u}_{2t}) = \text{var}\,(r_{2t}) - \widehat{h}_{2t} = 1.000 - 0.980 = 0.020$$
$$\text{var}\,(\widehat{u}_{3t}) = \text{var}\,(r_{3t}) - \widehat{h}_{3,t} = 1.000 - 0.899 = 0.101.$$

The estimated 2-factor model with loadings based on $\widehat{\beta}_1$ and $\widehat{\beta}_2$ is

$$z_{1t} = 0.979s_{1t} - 0.190s_{2t} + \widehat{u}_{1t}$$
$$z_{2t} = 0.990s_{1t} - 0.116s_{2t} + \widehat{u}_{2t}$$
$$z_{3t} = 0.948s_{1t} + 0.318s_{2t} + \widehat{u}_{3t}.$$

The factor s_{2t} represents a *slope* factor, with a positive shock to s_{2t} twisting the yield curve by lowering the short rates (with a negative loading affecting the 1-month and 1-year return) and raising the long rate (with a positive loading affecting the 5-year return).

12.2.3 Factor Extraction

Having obtained the variance matrix decomposition and factor loadings, estimates of the latent factors s_t are obtained as a weighted average of the standardized yields z_t. The factors have the assumed property that they are independent of (or orthogonal to) each other, so a natural choice of the weights is to use in their construction the estimated $(N \times N)$ matrix of eigenvectors $\widehat{P}$ because $\widehat{P}'\widehat{P} = I$. The estimate of the jth factor at time t is given by the transform

$$s_{jt} = \frac{1}{\sqrt{\widehat{\lambda}_j}} \sum_{i=1}^{N} \widehat{P}_{ji} z_{it}. \qquad (12.9)$$

When a full set of $K = N$ factors is employed in conjunction with the loading parameters β_j defined in equation (12.6), this setting of s_{jt} ensures a reciprocal relationship between the factors and the original returns. In particular, the kth element of the vector $\sum_{j=1}^{N} \beta_j s_{jt}$ is

$$\sum_{j=1}^{N} \beta_{kj} s_{jt} = \sum_{j=1}^{N} \sqrt{\widehat{\lambda}_j} \widehat{P}_{kj} \frac{1}{\sqrt{\widehat{\lambda}_j}} \sum_{i=1}^{N} \widehat{P}_{ji} z_{it} = \sum_{i=1}^{N} \left(\sum_{j=1}^{N} \widehat{P}_{kj} \widehat{P}_{ji} \right) z_{it} = z_{kt}, \qquad (12.10)$$

thereby inverting the transform to reproduce the original observation z_{kt}. In practical work, it is usual to select a small number of factors $K < N$ that best represent the overall variation in the observed returns. Hence, in applications, the reciprocal relationship between equation (12.9) and equation (12.10) will not hold.

The representation in equation (12.9) indicates how the jth factor at time t admits the interpretation of a portfolio return because it is constructed as a weighted sum of the yields in the system. From the second key property of the estimates established earlier, the columns of P (eigenvectors) are orthogonal by construction. Therefore, at time t, each of the K factors in $\widehat{s}_t$ that are constructed in this manner are orthogonal to one another.

For the term structure example consisting of the 1-month, 1-year, and 5-year bond yields from July 2001 to September 2010, the estimates of the eigenvalues and eigenvectors are given in equation (12.8). The respective sample means of the three yields are $\{2.038, 2.393, 3.472\}$, with corresponding standard deviations of $\{1.649, 1.584, 0.970\}$. The yields in July 2001 are $\{3.67, 3.62, 4.76\}$ so that the standardized yields are $\{0.989, 0.774, 1.327\}$, and consequently the estimate of the first factor at time $t = 1$ is

$$\widehat{s}_{11} = \frac{0.581}{\sqrt{2.837}} \times 0.989 + \frac{0.588}{\sqrt{0.151}} \times 0.774 + \frac{0.563}{\sqrt{0.012}} \times 1.327 = 1.055.$$

Repeating the calculations for August 2001, $(t = 2)$, the standardized yields are $\{0.905, 0.862, 0.929\}$ and the corresponding estimate of the first factor at time $t = 2$ is now

$$\widehat{s}_{12} = \frac{0.581}{\sqrt{2.837}} \times 0.905 + \frac{0.588}{\sqrt{0.151}} \times 0.862 + \frac{0.563}{\sqrt{0.012}} \times 0.929 = 0.927.$$

Estimates of the factors for the full sample are plotted in Figure 12.2. It is apparent that the first factor (yield level) dominates the second factor (yield slope) in terms of its variability. From mid 2007, at the time of the financial crisis in the United States, the estimated level factor, $\widehat{s}_{1t}$, trends downward, which is representative of the general falls

FIGURE 12.2 Time series plots of the estimated factors $\widehat{s}_{1t}$ (solid line) and $\widehat{s}_{2t}$ (dashed line) obtained from a principal components analysis of the correlation matrix of percentage annualized yields on US Treasuries for 1-month, 1-year, and 5-year maturities for the period July 2001 to September 2010.

experienced by all yields over this period. The estimated factor, $\widehat{s}_{2t}$, determines the slope of the yield curve. A positive slope factor lowers the short yield and increases the long yield. When the slope factor is negative, the yield curve flattens and in some cases an inverted yield curve results.

12.2.4 Selecting the Number of Factors

In addition to the problem of estimating the model and extracting the latent factors, there is the additional question of how many latent factors, K, should be employed in the model. This choice, like that of choosing the lag order in an autoregression or cointegrating rank in a nonstationary system, involves the dual elements of adequately describing a system of N yields with K factors while ensuring that the system is not overfitted by making K too large.

Bai and Ng (2002) propose a formal mechanism for selecting an appropriate number of factors based on an information criterion. The approach consists of estimating the factor model for an increasing number of factors beginning with $K = 1$ and comparing the goodness of fit of each factor model adjusted for the number of estimated factors in that model relative to the total number of observations $N \times T$.

The information statistic in the case of K factors

$$IC_K = \log(\widehat{V}_K) + K\left(\frac{N+T}{NT}\right)\log\left(\frac{NT}{N+T}\right), \qquad (12.11)$$

where

$$\widehat{V}_K = \frac{1}{NT} \sum_{i=1}^{N} \sum_{t=1}^{T} \widehat{u}_{it}^2 \tag{12.12}$$

represents the average of the N residual variances for a K factor model. The second term on the right-hand side of equation (12.11) is a penalty term that takes into account the number of factors, K, the sample size, T, and the dimension of the factor model, N. The optimal number of factors according to this criterion is obtained by minimizing equation (12.11) with respect to K.

To calculate the statistic in equation (12.11) in the term structure example containing $N = 3$ yields with sample size $T = 111$, the residuals in equation (12.12) are computed for each choice of K. For the 1-factor model, these are

$$\widehat{u}_{1t} = z_{1t} - 0.979\widehat{s}_{1t} \qquad \widehat{u}_{2t} = z_{2t} - 0.990\widehat{s}_{1t} \qquad \widehat{u}_{3t} = z_{3t} - 0.948\widehat{s}_{1t}.$$

The average variance for the $K = 1$ factor model is then given by averaging the $N = 3$ residual variances to get

$$\widehat{V}_1 = \frac{0.042 + 0.020 + 0.101}{3} = 0.054.$$

Repeating the calculations for the 2-factor model, the residuals become

$$\widehat{u}_{1t} = r_{1t} - 0.979\widehat{s}_{1t} + 0.190\widehat{s}_{2t}$$
$$\widehat{u}_{2t} = r_{2t} - 0.990\widehat{s}_{1t} + 0.116\widehat{s}_{2t}$$
$$\widehat{u}_{3t} = r_{3t} - 0.948\widehat{s}_{1t} - 0.318\widehat{s}_{2t},$$

resulting in an average variance for the $K = 2$ model of

$$\widehat{V}_2 = \frac{(0.0050 + 0.00666 + 0.0002)}{3} = 0.004.$$

Computing the information criterion in equation (12.11) for each of the two factor models gives the following values

$$IC_1 = \log(0.054) + 1 \times \left(\frac{3 + 111}{3 \times 111}\right) \log\left(\frac{3 \times 111}{3 + 111}\right) = -2.55$$

$$IC_2 = \log(0.004) + 2 \times \left(\frac{3 + 111}{3 \times 111}\right) \log\left(\frac{3 \times 111}{3 + 111}\right) = -4.80,$$

a result that favors the 2-factor model.

12.3 A LATENT FACTOR CAPM

The single-factor CAPM is given by

$$r_{it} - r_{ft} = \alpha_i + \beta_i(r_{mt} - r_{ft}) + u_{it}, \qquad i = 1, 2, \cdots, N, \tag{12.13}$$

in which u_{it} is a disturbance term with zero mean and variance σ_i^2. In the single-factor CAPM β_i is the β-risk of the ith asset measured in terms of exposure to the market factor, which is given by the excess return on the market $r_{mt} - r_{ft}$. From a theory perspective, the use of r_{mt} in equation (12.13) serves as a specific proxy for the excess return on all invested wealth. This broader interpretation of the model may be represented by the alternative specification

$$r_{it} - r_{ft} = \alpha_i + \beta_i s_t + u_{it}, \qquad i = 1, 2, \cdots, N, \tag{12.14}$$

in which s_t is now a latent factor representing the excess return on all invested wealth.

Consider the data set comprising the monthly excess returns on Exxon, GE, gold, IBM, Microsoft, and Walmart for the period April 1990 to July 2004, which was used in Chapter 3.

The covariance matrix (which is not corrected for degrees of freedom) for the six excess returns is

$$\begin{bmatrix}
0.0019 & 0.0009 & -0.0002 & 0.0014 & 0.0009 & 0.0006 \\
0.0009 & 0.0053 & -0.0004 & 0.0020 & 0.0032 & 0.0018 \\
-0.0002 & -0.0004 & 0.0009 & -0.0005 & -0.0006 & -0.0004 \\
0.0014 & 0.0020 & -0.0005 & 0.0088 & 0.0048 & 0.0011 \\
0.0009 & 0.0032 & -0.0006 & 0.0048 & 0.0113 & 0.0024 \\
0.0006 & 0.0018 & -0.0004 & 0.0011 & 0.0024 & 0.0057
\end{bmatrix}.$$

The $N = 6$ eigenvalues of the covariance matrix ordered from highest to lowest are

$$\widehat{\lambda} = \{0.017418, 0.005877, 0.004750, 0.003589, 0.001511, 0.000828\}.$$

The total sum of the eigenvalues is

$$0.033973 = 0.017418 + 0.005877 + 0.004750 + 0.003589 + 0.001511 + 0.000828.$$

This sum equals the total volatility of all six excess returns as given by the sum of their variances

$$0.033973 = 0.001913 + 0.005358 + 0.000887 + 0.008771 + 0.011307 + 0.005737.$$

The proportionate contribution of the first factor to the total variance is $0.017418/0.03397 = 0.5127$. This suggests that a 1-factor CAPM explains 51.27% of the total variance of the six excess returns. To estimate the 1-factor CAPM, the intercepts (α_i) are estimated using the sample means. The slope parameters are estimated as

$$\widehat{\beta} = \sqrt{\widehat{\lambda}_1}\,\widehat{P}_1 = \sqrt{0.017418}\begin{bmatrix}
0.122268 \\
0.330706 \\
-0.056703 \\
0.535891 \\
0.720721 \\
0.256614
\end{bmatrix} = \begin{bmatrix}
1.6137 \times 10^{-2} \\
4.3646 \times 10^{-2} \\
-7.4835 \times 10^{-3} \\
7.0725 \times 10^{-2} \\
9.5119 \times 10^{-2} \\
3.3867 \times 10^{-2}
\end{bmatrix}.$$

These results show that gold moves in the opposite direction to the other assets, which is consistent with gold representing a hedge asset. Microsoft has the highest loading, equal to 9.5119×10^{-2}, showing that this asset responds the most to changes in the factor s_t compared to the other stocks. This result is consistent with Microsoft being an aggressive stock, at least in relation to the other stocks.

Simple comparison of the ordinary least squares estimates of the CAPM with the excess return on the market with an observable factor, as in Chapter 3, gives very different estimates of the beta-risk. Part of the reason for this is that the variance of s_t is by construction normalized to unity, whereas the variance of the excess return on the market

$r_{mt} - r_{ft}$ is not. To make the beta-risk estimates commensurate across the two estimated models, the estimate of s_t may be rescaled to achieve equivalence with the estimated variance of $r_{mt} - r_{ft}$, which in this case is $\widehat{\sigma}_m^2 = 0.042764^2$.

Defining σ_m as the standard deviation of the excess return on the market, then the standard 1-factor CAPM model is rewritten as

$$r_{it} - r_{ft} = \alpha_i + \beta_i \frac{\sigma_m}{\sigma_m} s_t + u_{it} = \alpha_i + \frac{\beta_{i1}}{\sigma_m}(\sigma_m s_t) + u_{it},$$

so that

$$E[(\sigma_m s_t)^2] = \sigma_m^2 E(s_t^2) = \sigma_m^2 \times 1 = \sigma_m^2.$$

Thus, the rescaled beta-risk estimates are obtained by dividing the loading vector β by the standard deviation of $r_{mt} - r_{ft}$ given by σ_m.

These rescaled beta estimates are

$$\widetilde{\beta} = \frac{\widehat{\beta}}{0.042764} = \begin{bmatrix} 1.6137 \times 10^{-2}/0.042764 \\ 4.3646 \times 10^{-2}/0.042764 \\ -7.4835 \times 10^{-3}/0.042764 \\ 7.0725 \times 10^{-2}/0.042764 \\ 9.5119 \times 10^{-2}/0.042764 \\ 3.3867 \times 10^{-2}/0.042764 \end{bmatrix} = \begin{bmatrix} 0.3773 \\ 1.0206 \\ -0.1750 \\ 1.6538 \\ 2.2243 \\ 0.7919 \end{bmatrix}.$$

The estimated $K = 1$ factor model is then

Exxon	:	$r_{1t} = 0.013836 + 0.3773\,\widehat{s}_t + \widehat{u}_{1t}$
GE	:	$r_{2t} = 0.019874 + 1.0206\,\widehat{s}_t + \widehat{u}_{2t}$
Gold	:	$r_{3t} = -0.003052 - 0.1750\,\widehat{s}_t + \widehat{u}_{3t}$
IBM	:	$r_{4t} = 0.008706 + 1.6538\,\widehat{s}_t + \widehat{u}_{4t}$
Microsoft	:	$r_{5t} = 0.017464 + 2.2243\,\widehat{s}_t + \widehat{u}_{5t}$
Walmart	:	$r_{6t} = 0.010084 + 0.7919\,\widehat{s}_t + \widehat{u}_{6t}.$

Figure 12.3 plots the excess market return and the rescaled latent factor $\widehat{s}_t$ for comparative purposes. The results show that there are some similarities in the estimated factor, $\widehat{s}_t$, and the market excess return, as well as some differences. The correlation between the two is 0.7614, showing that the first factor is highly correlated with the excess returns on the market.

12.4 DYNAMIC FACTOR MODELS: THE KALMAN FILTER

The discussion so far has concentrated on specifying and estimating factor models based on contemporaneous relationships among the observed variables. In principal components methodology, the aim is to explain the covariance or correlation matrix of the observed variables in terms of a reduced set of factor variates. Underlying this framework is the assumption that the unobserved factor is independently and identically distributed over time, an assumption that manifestly does not hold for much financial data.

An important feature of many financial time series is that they exhibit dynamic patterns of behavior that play a role in their relationship with other variables. It is therefore helpful to have a framework of analysis that accommodates this feature

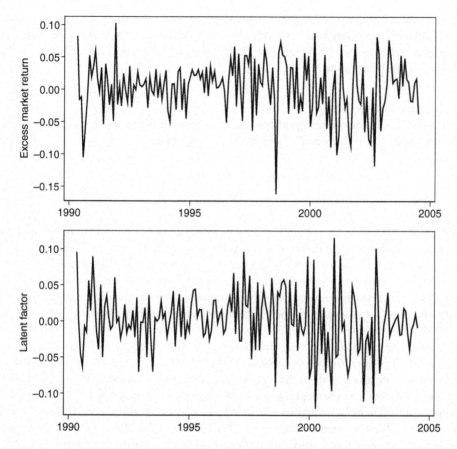

FIGURE 12.3 Time series plots of the excess return to the market and the scaled latent factor, $\widehat{s}_t$, based on the first principal component of the excess returns to the $N = 6$ US financial assets. Data are monthly for the period April 1990 to July 2004.

of financial data, allowing both contemporaneous and dynamic relationships to be captured by the factor variables.

The following table gives autocorrelations up to 6 lags on the 1-month, 1-year, and 5-year US Treasury yields plotted in Figure 12.1. The dynamics of the three series are similar, with the autocorrelations slowly decaying at an exponential rate. This time series behavior suggests that a single factor could potentially capture the serial correlations in all three yields.

Autocorrelation	Lag 1	Lag 2	Lag 3	Lag 4	Lag 5	Lag 6
1-month	0.977	0.948	0.921	0.887	0.852	0.819
1-year	0.980	0.950	0.917	0.883	0.849	0.815
5-year	0.936	0.855	0.786	0.727	0.670	0.630

If these time series dynamics of the Treasury yields are to be described in terms of a single factor, then it is necessary for the factor to have a dynamic structure capable of capturing the autocorrelation patterns in these yields. The Kalman filter provides a mechanism by which this can be achieved.

12.4.1 Univariate

To illustrate the Kalman filter algorithm, the following simple model is specified consisting of a single observable variable y_t and a single latent factor s_t

$$
\begin{aligned}
y_t &= \alpha + \beta s_t + u_t \quad &\text{[Measurement equation]} \\
s_t &= \phi s_{t-1} + v_t, \quad &\text{[State equation]}
\end{aligned}
\tag{12.15}
$$

where $u_t \sim N(0, \sigma^2)$ and $v_t \sim N(0, 1)$ are independent disturbances; and α, β, σ, and ϕ are unknown parameters. The variance of v_t is normalized here to be unity. This convention is consistent with the normalization adopted in the principal components approach. The representation of the model in equation (12.15) is known as a *state-space* system, which consists of a measurement equation (the equation of the observable variable y_t) and a state equation (the equation for the unobservable *state variable* or factor s_t).

The Kalman filter is an iterative algorithm that starts from an initial estimate of the factor, obtained from the state equation for the first observation, without using any information on the observed variable at time $t = 1$. This estimate of the factor is then used to compute an estimate of the observed variable at $t = 1$ based on the measurement equation. However, as the dependent variable is indeed observed at $t = 1$, an updated estimate of the latent factor is then obtained by using information on y_1. This sequential procedure is then applied to successive observations until observation T. In rolling through the sample, it is assumed that the parameters are known in equation (12.15), or at least represent some starting values that are given and used to initiate estimation. Details of estimation are discussed below.

In view of its sequential nature, the Kalman filter algorithm is couched in terms of conditional means and conditional variances. The following definitions are used

$$
y_{t|t-1} = E_{t-1}(y_t), \qquad s_{t|t-1} = E_{t-1}(s_t),
$$

to represent the conditional means at time t based on information at time $t - 1$, and

$$
V_{t|t-1} = E_{t-1}[(y_t - y_{t|t-1})^2], \qquad P_{t|t-1} = E_{t-1}[(s_t - s_{t|t-1})^2],
$$

to represent the corresponding conditional variances. Updates of the factor that also use observable information at time t, that is on y_t, are represented by the following corresponding conditional expectations

$$
s_{t|t} = E_t(s_t), \qquad P_{t|t} = E_{t-1}[(s_t - s_{t|t})^2],
$$

which are, respectively, the updated conditional mean and variance of the factor.

For the model given by equation (12.15), the Kalman filter equations are

Prediction: $s_{t|t-1} = \phi s_{t-1|t-1}$
$P_{t|t-1} = \phi^2 P_{t-1|t-1} + 1$

Observation: $y_{t|t-1} = \alpha + \beta s_{t|t-1}$
$V_{t|t-1} = \beta^2 P_{t|t-1} + \sigma^2$

Updating: $s_{t|t} = s_{t|t-1} + \dfrac{\beta P_{t|t-1}}{V_{t|t-1}} (y_t - y_{t|t-1})$

$P_{t|t} = P_{t|t-1} - \dfrac{\beta^2 P_{t|t-1}^2}{V_{t|t-1}}.$

At $t = 1$, starting values for $s_{1|0}$ and $P_{1|0}$ are commonly chosen as

$$s_{1|0} = 0 \qquad P_{1|0} = 1/(1 - \phi^2), \qquad\qquad (12.16)$$

although this is not always the case. The starting value for $s_{1|0}$ is its unconditional mean, and the starting value for $P_{1|0}$ is its unconditional variance (see Chapter 4).

It is instructive to rewrite the updating equation of the factor as

$$s_{t|t} - s_{t|t-1} = g_t(y_t - y_{t|t-1}),$$

where the parameter

$$g_t = \frac{\beta P_{t|t-1}}{V_{t|t-1}}$$

is known as the Kalman gain and represents the adjustment to the estimate of the factor once information on the observable variable at time t is used. The size of the adjustment equals the error in predicting the observable variable $(y_t - y_{t|t-1})$ from the estimate of the factor without y_t times the Kalman gain g_t.

Suppose that the first two observations on 5-year, zero-coupon Treasury bills, y_t, are given by $y_t = \{2, 5\}$, where the figures are percentage per annum yields. Assume for the moment that the parameters are known and given by $\alpha = 0.0$, $\beta = 0.5$, $\sigma = 0.1$, and $\phi = 0.8$. Letting the initial estimate of the factor be $s_{1|0} = 0.1$, the first step of the filter for $t = 1$ is

Prediction: $s_{1|0} = 0.1$

(initialization) $P_{1|0} = \dfrac{1}{1 - \phi^2} = \dfrac{1}{1 - 0.8^2} = 2.7778$

Observation: $y_{1|0} = \alpha + \beta s_{1|0} = 0.0 + 0.5 \times 0.1 = 0.05$
$V_{1|0} = \beta^2 P_{1|0} + \sigma^2 = 0.5^2 \times 2.7778 + 0.1^2 = 0.7045$

Updating: $s_{1|1} = s_{1|0} + \dfrac{\beta P_{1|0}}{V_{1|0}} (y_1 - y_{1|0}) = 0.1 + \dfrac{0.5 \times 2.7778}{0.7045} \times (2 - 0.05)$

$= 3.9444$

$P_{1|1} = P_{1|0} - \dfrac{\beta^2 P_{1|0}^2}{V_{1|0}} = 2.7778 - \dfrac{0.5^2 \times 2.7778^2}{0.7045} = 0.0396.$

Intuitively, the initial estimate of the factor of 0.1 results in an underestimate of the yield at $t = 1$, because $0.05 < 2$. By updating the estimate of the factor to 3.9444, a better estimate of the yield, y_t, at $t = 1$ is obtained. The second step at $t = 2$ follows the same process and gives

Prediction: $s_{2|1} = \phi s_{1|1} = 0.8 \times 3.9444 = 3.1555$

$P_{2|1} = \phi^2 P_{1|1} + 1 = 0.8^2 \times 0.0396 + 1 = 1.0253$

Observation: $y_{2|1} = \alpha + \beta s_{2|1} = 0.0 + 0.5 \times 3.1555 = 1.5778$

$V_{2|1} = \beta^2 P_{2|1} + \sigma^2 = 0.5^2 \times 1.0253 + 0.1^2 = 0.2663$

Updating: $s_{2|2} = s_{2|1} + \dfrac{\beta P_{2|1}}{V_{2|1}}(y_2 - y_{2|1}) = 3.1555 + \dfrac{0.5 \times 1.0253}{0.2663}$

$\times (5 - 1.5778)$

$= 9.7435$

$P_{2|2} = P_{2|1} - \dfrac{\beta^2 P_{2|1}^2}{V_{2|1}} = 1.0253 - \dfrac{0.5^2 \times 1.0253^2}{0.2663} = 0.03840.$

12.4.2 Multivariate

Consider a model where there are $N = 3$ variables and $K = 2$ factors

$$y_{1t} = \alpha_1 + \beta_{11} s_{1t} + \beta_{12} s_{2t} + u_{1t}, \quad u_{1t} \sim N(0, \sigma_1^2)$$
$$y_{2t} = \alpha_2 + \beta_{21} s_{1t} + \beta_{22} s_{2t} + u_{2t}, \quad u_{2t} \sim N(0, \sigma_2^2)$$
$$y_{3t} = \alpha_3 + \beta_{31} s_{1t} + \beta_{32} s_{2t} + u_{3t}, \quad u_{3t} \sim N(0, \sigma_3^2),$$

where the factors have AR(1) representations

$$s_{1t} = \phi_{11} s_{1t-1} + v_{1t}, \quad v_{1t} \sim N(0, 1)$$
$$s_{2t} = \phi_{22} s_{2t-1} + v_{2t}, \quad v_{2t} \sim N(0, 1).$$

This system is written in matrix notation as

$$\begin{bmatrix} y_{1t} \\ y_{2t} \\ y_{3t} \end{bmatrix} = \begin{bmatrix} \alpha_1 \\ \alpha_2 \\ \alpha_3 \end{bmatrix} + \begin{bmatrix} \beta_{11} & \beta_{12} \\ \beta_{21} & \beta_{22} \\ \beta_{31} & \beta_{32} \end{bmatrix} \begin{bmatrix} s_{1t} \\ s_{2t} \end{bmatrix} + \begin{bmatrix} u_{1t} \\ u_{2t} \\ u_{3t} \end{bmatrix}$$

$$\begin{bmatrix} s_{1t} \\ s_{2t} \end{bmatrix} = \begin{bmatrix} \phi_{11} & 0 \\ 0 & \phi_{22} \end{bmatrix} \begin{bmatrix} s_{1t-1} \\ s_{2t-1} \end{bmatrix} + \begin{bmatrix} v_{1t} \\ v_{2t} \end{bmatrix}.$$

For the general case of N variables $\{y_{1t}, y_{2t} \cdots, y_{Nt}\}$ and K factors $\{s_{1t}, s_{2t} \cdots, s_{Kt}\}$, the multivariate version of the state-space system is

$$y_t = A + B s_t + u_t, \quad u_t \sim N(0, R)$$
$$s_t = \Phi s_{t-1} + v_t, \quad v_t \sim N(0, I),$$

where $E(u_t u_t') = R$ and $E(v_t v_t') = I$ are, respectively, the covariance matrices of u_t and v_t. The dimensions of the parameter matrices are as follows: A is $(N \times 1)$, B is $(N \times K)$, Φ is $(K \times K)$, R is $(N \times N)$, and Q is $(K \times K)$.

The recursions of the multivariate Kalman filter are

Prediction:
$$s_{t|t-1} = \Phi s_{t-1|t-1}$$
$$P_{t|t-1} = \Phi P_{t-1|t-1}\Phi' + I$$

Observation:
$$y_{t|t-1} = A + Bs_{t|t-1}$$
$$V_{t|t-1} = BP_{t|t-1}B' + R$$

Updating:
$$s_{t|t} = s_{t|t-1} + P_{t|t-1}B'V_{t|t-1}^{-1}(y_t - y_{t|t-1})$$
$$P_{t|t} = P_{t|t-1} - P_{t|t-1}B'V_{t|t-1}^{-1}BP_{t|t-1}.$$

For further details, including extensions of the multivariate Kalman filter that allow for higher-order dynamics and exogenous or predetermined variables, see Harvey (1989) and Martin, Hurn, and Harris (2013).

12.4.3 Estimation and Factor Extraction

The discussion so far has concentrated on extracting the factor, s_t, assuming given values for the population parameters $\theta = \{A, B, \Phi, R\}$. In practical work these parameters must be estimated. If the factors are observed, then the parameters A and B are estimated by simply regressing y_t on a constant and s_t, while Φ is obtained by regressing s_t on s_{t-1}. But since the factor s_t is unobserved or latent, an alternative estimation strategy is needed.

A natural estimator of the parameters is the maximum likelihood estimator. To set up the likelihood, a recursive procedure is employed based on the sequence of conditional distributions given the previous sample history and the parameters. Thus, the conditional distribution of y_t given the history of observations to $t-1$ is

$$y_t \sim N(y_{t|t-1}, V_{t|t-1}),$$

in which $y_{t|t-1}$ and $V_{t|t-1}$ are obtained directly from the recursions of the Kalman filter and are therefore functions of all the parameters of the system. The corresponding conditional log-likelihood function for the tth observation using the form of the multivariate normal density is

$$\log L_t = -\frac{N}{2}\log(2\pi) - \frac{1}{2}\log|V_{t|t-1}| - \frac{1}{2}(y_t - y_{t|t-1})'V_{t|t-1}^{-1}(y_t - y_{t|t-1}).$$

For the entire sample of $t = 1, 2, \cdots, T$ observations on y_t, the normalized log-likelihood function is

$$\log L = \frac{1}{T}\sum_{t=1}^{T}\log L_t.$$

This log-likelihood function is constructed recursively. It is nonlinear in the parameters θ and an iterative algorithm is required to obtain the maximum likelihood estimates.

In many applications, an important objective is to extract estimates of the latent factors and interpret their time-series properties. The Kalman filter automatically provides estimates of these factors by means of the maximum likelihood estimates of the parameters of the state-space system together with an additional recursion that delivers smooth estimates of the unobserved state variables or latent factors. The approach is to make use of the property that the latent factors have a conditional normal distribution and the conditional mean of the distribution serves as a suitable estimate of the latent factor. Three possible choices, each depending on the form of the conditioning information set, are as follows

$$
\begin{array}{lll}
\text{One-step-ahead} & : & s_{t|t-1} = E_{t-1}(s_t) \\
\text{Filtered} & : & s_{t|t} = E_t(s_t) \\
\text{Smoothed} & : & s_{t|T} = E_T(s_t).
\end{array}
\tag{12.17}
$$

The one-step-ahead and filtered factor estimates are obtained directly from the recursions of the Kalman filter. The smoothed estimate takes account of all the data in the observed sample and is obtained by conditioning on all T observations. This full-set conditioning has the effect of generating smoother estimates of the factor than either the one-step or filtered estimates. This approach is also known as fixed-interval smoothing. The determining equations for the smoothed conditional mean and variance are given by the following expressions

$$
s_{t|T} = s_{t|t} + J_t(s_{t+1|T} - s_{t+1|t})
\tag{12.18}
$$

$$
P_{t|T} = P_{t|t} + J_t(P_{t+1|T} - P_{t+1|t})J_t',
\tag{12.19}
$$

where

$$
J_t = P_{t|t}\Phi'P_{t+1|t}^{-1}.
\tag{12.20}
$$

Constructing the smoothed estimates requires running the filter backward after the parameters have been estimated.

12.4.4 The Term Structure Revisited

Consider again the percentage annualized US Treasury yields for $N = 9$ maturities ranging from 1 month to 10 years for the period July 2001 to September 2010. A dynamic 1-factor model of the term structure is

$$
\begin{aligned}
r_{it} &= \alpha_i + \beta_i s_t + u_{it}, & u_{it} &\sim N(0, \sigma_i^2) \\
s_t &= \phi s_{t-1} + v_t, & v_t &\sim N(0, 1).
\end{aligned}
$$

This model contains 28 unknown parameters.

The maximum likelihood estimates of this dynamic 1-factor model are given in Table 12.1. The value of the log-likelihood function at the optimum is $\log L(\widehat{\theta}) = -115.559$. The estimates of the factor loadings $(\beta_1, \cdots, \beta_9)$ show that the latent factor has its greatest impact on the shorter maturities (less than 1 year), and this impact progressively diminishes in importance across the maturity spectrum. The estimates of the idiosyncratic parameters $(\sigma_1^2, \cdots, \sigma_9^2)$ are smallest for the 6-month yield, suggesting that this yield follows the factor s_t more closely than the other yields. The estimates of the intercept parameters $(\alpha_1, \cdots, \alpha_9)$ increase over the maturity spectrum, suggesting that on average the yield curve is upward sloping. The estimate of the parameter ϕ is 0.992, which is indicative that the latent factor is highly persistent.

Figure 12.4 gives the one-step-ahead estimates of the latent factor from the dynamic 1-factor model of the term structure of interest rates given in Table 12.1. These estimates are based on

$$
s_{t|t-1} = E_{t-1}(s_t),
$$

TABLE 12.1 Maximum likelihood estimates of a dynamic 1-factor model of the term structure of interest rates using monthly percentage annualized US Treasury yields for $N = 9$ maturities ranging from 1 month to 10 years for the period July 2001 to September 2010. Standard errors are in parentheses.

Yield	Intercept (α)	Loading (β)	Idiosyncratic (σ^2)
1-month	1.785 (1.393)	0.211 (0.015)	0.039 (0.006)
3-month	1.854 (1.416)	0.214 (0.015)	0.0134 (0.002)
6-month	1.999 (1.428)	0.216 (0.015)	0.003 (0.001)
1-year	2.149 (1.345)	0.204 (0.014)	0.012 (0.002)
2-year	2.477 (1.160)	0.176 (0.013)	0.089 (0.013)
3-year	2.783 (0.997)	0.151 (0.012)	0.149 (0.020)
5-year	3.340 (0.729)	0.110 (0.010)	0.209 (0.028)
7-year	3.739 (0.537)	0.081 (0.008)	0.230 (0.031)
10-year	4.089 (0.389)	0.058 (0.007)	0.203 (0.027)
		ϕ	
Factor		0.992 (0.008)	

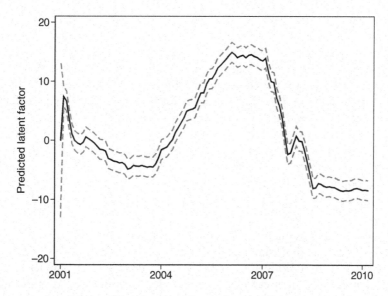

FIGURE 12.4 A plot of the one-step-ahead estimates of the latent factor in the term structure model together with 90% confidence bands. The data are monthly percentage annualized US Treasury yields for $N = 9$ maturities ranging from 1 month to 10 years for the period July 2001 to September 2010.

with the population parameters replaced by their maximum likelihood estimates. Also shown is the 90% confidence interval for the latent factor, which is obtained from the diagonal elements of the matrix $P_{t|t-1}$.

The confidence interval for the initial estimate of the factor is very wide. This result reflects the fact that the estimate of ϕ is close to 1, which, in turn, causes the initial estimate of the variance of the factor in equation (12.16) to be large. The confidence interval quickly narrows showing that the estimates at later points in time are more precise. The factor is relatively flat in the first part of the period, then rises reaching a peak around the end of 2006. As the loadings of the factor are larger on the shorter maturities than the longer maturities, this increase in the factor is associated with a narrowing of the spreads. From about mid-2007 the factor falls, resulting in a widening of spreads, and eventually stabilizes from 2009 onward.

12.5 A PARAMETRIC APPROACH TO FACTORS

An alternative approach to modeling the term structure was proposed by Diebold and Li (2006). This approach is intermediate between the use of observed factors and full estimation of latent factors. The model is given by

$$y_{it} = \beta_{i1} s_{1t} + \beta_{i2} s_{2t} + \beta_{i3} s_{3t} + u_{it}, \tag{12.21}$$

in which y_{it} is the yield on a bond with maturity τ_i, and u_{it} is a disturbance term. The factor loadings are based on the functional form suggested by Nelson and Siegel (1987),

$$\beta_{i1} = 1, \quad \beta_{i2} = \left(\frac{1 - e^{-\lambda \tau_i}}{\lambda \tau_i}\right), \quad \beta_{i3} = \left(\frac{1 - e^{-\lambda \tau_i}}{\lambda \tau_i} - e^{-\lambda \tau_i}\right).$$

In contrast to the other dynamic factor models of the term structure, all of the factor loadings in this formulation are functions of a single parameter, λ.

Estimation of the model proceeds in two steps. In the first step, Diebold and Li (2006) set $\lambda = 0.0609$, a value chosen to maximize the loading on the third factor at a maturity of 30 months. The resultant factor loadings are plotted against maturity in Figure 12.5. In the second step, a linear cross sectional regression is run in which the yields on the N maturities are regressed on the factor loadings β_{i1}, β_{i2}, and β_{i3}. This series of regressions then identifies the unobserved factors at each time point.

The data set comprises end-of-month price quotes (bid-ask average) for zero-coupon US Treasury bonds from January 1985 through December 2000 for monthly maturities:

$$\tau = \{1, 3, 6, 9, 12, 15, 18, 21, 24, 30, 36, 48, 60, 72, 84, 96, 108, 120\}.$$

These data are used to estimate $\widehat{s}_{1t}$, $\widehat{s}_{2t}$, and $\widehat{s}_{3t}$ using equation (12.21) and the resultant estimates for each t are plotted in Figure 12.6.

An important implication for applied work of the regression model in equation (12.21) is that the yield curve can be reconstructed for any time period according to

$$\widehat{y}_{it} = \beta_{i1} \widehat{s}_{1t} + \beta_{i2} \widehat{s}_{2t} + \beta_{i3} \widehat{s}_{3t}. \tag{12.22}$$

Figure 12.7 shows the estimated yield curves computed for the months of March, May, July, and August 1989, overlaid on a scatter plot of the observed yields for those months.

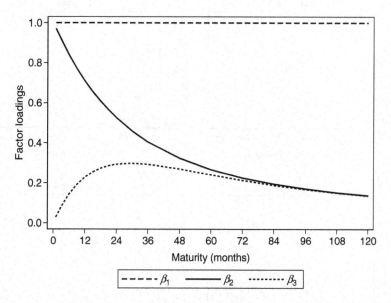

FIGURE 12.5 Factor loadings obtained from the Nelson–Siegel model of the yield curve with $\lambda = 0.0609$.

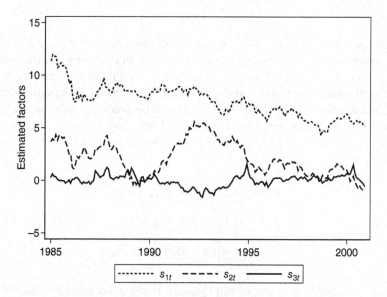

FIGURE 12.6 Time series plot of the estimated factors, s_{1t}, s_{2t}, and s_{3t}, using the factor regression model in equation (12.21). The data are US zero-coupon Treasury bond yields for 18 maturities from 1 month to 10 years for the period January 1985 to December 2000.

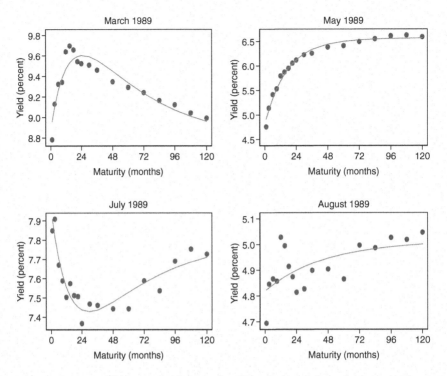

FIGURE 12.7 Forecast yield curves for the months of March, May, July, and August 1989, obtained by using the estimates $\widehat{s}_{1t}, \widehat{s}_{2t}$, and $\widehat{s}_{3t}$.

The results presented in Figure 12.7 suggest that the parametric factor loadings together with the estimated dynamic factors do a reasonable job in reconstructing the yield curve.

While the estimated yield curves in Figure 12.7 give a fairly accurate representation of the data, the real power of the approach is that if the time-series of estimated factors can be forecast successfully, then bond yields can be predicted more accurately than would be the case if the entire yield curve itself was being forecast. To generate the forecast, one approach is to fit AR(1) models to each of the estimated factors. These fitted regressions are

$$\widehat{s}_{1t} = \underset{(0.113)}{0.207} + \underset{(0.0147)}{0.968 \widehat{s}_{1\,t-1}} + \widehat{v}_{1t}$$

$$\widehat{s}_{2t} = \underset{(0.041)}{0.012} + \underset{(0.015)}{0.984 \widehat{s}_{2\,t-1}} + \widehat{v}_{2t}$$

$$\widehat{s}_{3t} = \underset{(0.018)}{-0.001} + \underset{(0.033)}{0.892 \widehat{s}_{3\,t-1}} + \widehat{v}_{3t}.$$

Using the techniques to forecast an AR(1) model that are discussed in Chapter 7, these models may be used to generate forecasts of the three factors, which in turn allow the entire yield curve to be forecast using equation (12.22). Instead of using univariate AR(1) models to forecast the factors, a multivariate model using a VAR could be used. The forecasting models could also be augmented by including macroeconomic explanatory variables, thereby linking forecasts of the yield curve directly to economic fundamentals and potentially improving longer-term forecasting performance.

12.6 STOCHASTIC VOLATILITY

A feature of modern financial econometrics is the attention paid to modeling the variance of financial asset returns or the square root of the variance, which is known as volatility. There is often much more structure and time-series interdependence to be explained in the variance of asset returns than in their levels. Chapters 13, 14, and 15 are devoted to methods of modeling time-varying variance.

One model not dealt with in those chapters is the so-called stochastic volatility model (Taylor, 1986) given by

$$r_t = \sqrt{h_t} z_t, \qquad\qquad z_t \sim N(0,1)$$
$$\log h_t = \alpha + \phi \log h_{t-1} + v_t, \qquad v_t \sim N(0,\sigma_v^2),$$

in which both z_t and v_t are random disturbance terms, and r_t represents centered returns. The model derives its name from the fact that the volatility of returns on the underlying security is itself treated as a stochastic process. In the model above, the presence of the disturbance term v_t in the second equation makes the variance, h_t, of r_t a time-dependent stochastic process—hence the t subscript on h_t and the volatility $\sqrt{h_t}$.

The reason for including a treatment of the stochastic volatility model in this chapter is that volatility is unobserved and can be expressed in terms of a latent factor model. Squaring both sides of the mean equation and taking logarithms in the model above gives

$$r_t^2 = h_t z_t^2$$
$$\log r_t^2 = \log h_t + \log z_t^2.$$

Defining $y_t = \log r_t^2$, $s_t = \log h_t$, and $u_t = \log z_t^2 + 1.27$, the measurement and state equations of the stochastic volatility model are

$$y_t = -1.27 + s_t + u_t, \qquad u_t \sim N(0, \pi^2/2)$$
$$s_t = \alpha + \phi s_{t-1} + v_t, \qquad v_t \sim N(0,\sigma_v^2),$$

in which u_t and v_t are disturbance terms. The value 1.27 in the equation for y_t follows from the property that $E[\log z_t^2] = -1.27$, so that $E(u_t) = 0$. It can also be shown that the variance of $\log z_t^2$ and hence u_t is $E(u_t^2) = \pi^2/2 = 4.9348$. A comparison of this model with equation (12.15) shows that all of the parameters in the measurement equation are identified and hence do not need to be estimated.

Consider the case where the asset is the £/\$ exchange rate. The centered daily returns on the £/\$ exchange rate, r_t, are shown in Figure 12.8 from 2 January 1979 to 13 February 2014. The estimated model is

$$y_t = -1.27 + \widehat{s}_t + \widehat{u}_t$$
$$\widehat{s}_t = -9.8257 + 0.2826 \widehat{s}_{t-1} + \widehat{v}_t,$$

with $\widehat{\sigma}_v = 4.4629$ and $\sigma_u = \widehat{\sigma}_u = \sqrt{4.9348}$.

An estimate of volatility is constructed from the definition of the factor s_t. If the object is to compute historical estimates of the volatility using all sample information,

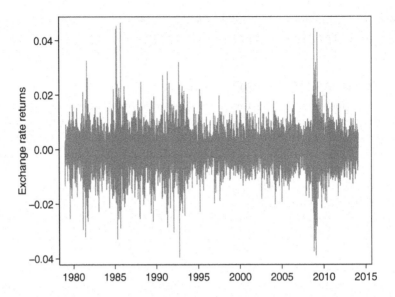

FIGURE 12.8 Plot of the centered daily returns on the £/$ exchange rate for the period 2 January 1979 to 13 February 2014.

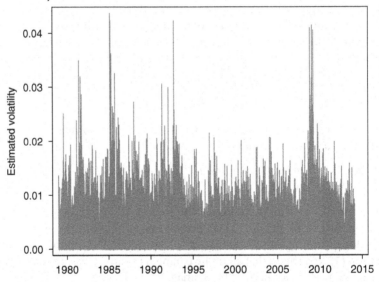

FIGURE 12.9 Plot of the volatility of the centered daily returns on the £/$ exchange rate for the period 2 January 1979 to 13 February 2014. The volatility is estimated using the smoothed latent factor.

then it is appropriate to use the smoothed estimator

$$\sqrt{\widehat{h_t}} = \exp\left(\frac{\widehat{s}_{t|T}}{2}\right),$$

which is plotted in Figure 12.9. The increases in volatility that occur during times of financial crises are evident in Figure 12.9, particularly during the oil glut crisis of the mid-1980s and the global financial crisis of 2008–2009. In these periods the estimates of volatility reach 0.04, which is well in excess of the mean of the volatility series 0.0038.

12.7 EXERCISES

The data required for the exercises are available for download as EViews workfiles (*.wf1), Stata datafiles (*.dta), comma delimited text files (*.csv), and as Excel spreadsheets (*.xlsx).

1. Multifactor Model of Interest Rates

> yields_us.*

The data are monthly observations on $N = 9$ US Treasury yields, expressed as annualized percentages, with maturities ranging from 1 month to 10 years, from July 2001 to September 2010.

(a) Plot the $N = 9$ yields and interpret their time series properties.

(b) Compute the (9×9) correlation matrix and discuss the contemporaneous relationships among the yields. Compute the eigenvalues of the correlation matrix and interpret the results.

(c) Estimate a $K = 3$ factor model and interpret the factor loadings.

(d) Plot the estimated factors, $\hat{s}_{1t}$, $\hat{s}_{2t}$, and $\hat{s}_{3t}$, and interpret their time series properties.

(e) How many factors would be included if the Bai and Ng method for choosing the optimal number of factors is used?

2. A Multifactor CAPM

> capm.*

The data are monthly yields on 5 US stocks and the commodity gold for the period April 1990 to July 2004. A principal component approach may be applied to estimating the multifactor CAPM given by

$$r_{it} - r_{ft} = \alpha_i + \sum_{j=1}^{K} \beta_{ij} s_{jt} + u_{it},$$

where s_{jt} are the unobserved latent factors.

(a) Compute the covariance matrix of the six returns and perform an eigen decomposition. Verify that the variances (diagonal terms) and the covariances (off-diagonal terms) can be recovered from the eigen decomposition.

(b) Compute the proportion of total volatility explained by the first three factors and interpret the results.

(c) Estimate the CAPM for $K = 1, 2$, and 3 factors.

(d) Use the Bai and Ng test to see whether or not a 3-factor model is preferred to the more traditional 1-factor model.

(e) Compare the estimates of the β-risk obtained for the $K = 3$ latent factor model with the β-risk obtained from a traditional multifactor CAPM model containing a market excess return and the Fama–French size and book-to-market factors.

3. A Dynamic Factor Model of Spreads

yields_us.*

The data are monthly observations on $N = 9$ US Treasury yields, expressed as annualized percentages, with maturities ranging from 1 month to 10 years, from July 2001 to September 2010.

(a) Estimate by maximum likelihood the following dynamic 1-factor model of the spread between the 1-year and 1-month yields

$$spread_t = \alpha + \beta s_t + u_t, \qquad u_t \sim N(0, \sigma^2)$$
$$s_t = \phi s_{t-1} + v_t, \qquad v_t \sim N(0, 1),$$

and interpret the parameter estimates. In particular, compare the estimate of ϕ with the first order sample correlation of the spread. Choose as starting values $\alpha = 0.1$, $\beta = 0.1$, $\sigma^2 = 0.1$, and $\phi = 0.9$.

(b) Repeat part (a) but replace the AR(1) model for s_t with the AR(2) specification

$$s_t = \phi_1 s_{t-1} + \phi_2 s_{t-2} + v_t.$$

Choose as starting values $\alpha = 0.1$, $\beta = 0.1$, $\sigma^2 = 0.1$, $\phi_1 = 0.2$, and $\phi_2 = 0.1$. Interpret the parameter estimates.

(c) Repeat parts (a) and (b) for the spread between the 6- and 1-month yields in the data file.

4. A Dynamic 1-Factor Model of the Term Structure

yields_us.*

The data are monthly observations on $N = 9$ US Treasury yields, expressed as annualized percentages, with maturities ranging from 1 month to 10 years, from July 2001 to September 2010.

(a) Estimate a dynamic 1-factor model of the $N = 9$ yields by maximum likelihood

$$r_{it} = \alpha_i + \beta_i s_t + u_{it}, \qquad u_{it} \sim N(0, \sigma_i^2)$$
$$s_t = \phi s_{t-1} + v_t, \qquad v_t \sim N(0, 1),$$

for $i = 1, 2, \cdots, 9$. Take the starting values to be those reported in Table 12.1.

(b) Re-estimate the model by imposing the restrictions

$$\beta_1 = \beta_2 = \beta_3 = \beta_4 = \beta_5 = \beta_6 = \beta_7 = \beta_8 = \beta_9 = \beta.$$

Interpret the parameter estimates. Test the validity of these restrictions.

(c) Based on your results in parts (a) and (b), extract and compare estimates of the unobserved factor s_t using the following methods:

   (i) the one-step-ahead prediction;
   (ii) the filtered estimate; and
   (iii) the smoothed estimate.

5. A Dynamic 2-Factor Model of the Term Structure

yields_us.*

The data are monthly observations on $N = 9$ US Treasury yields, expressed as annualized percentages, with maturities ranging from 1 month to 10 years, from July 2001 to September 2010.

(a) Estimate the following dynamic 2-factor model of the $N = 9$ yields by maximum likelihood

$$\begin{aligned}
r_{it} &= \alpha_i + \beta_{i1}s_{1t} + \beta_{i2}s_{2t} + u_{it}, & u_{it} &\sim N(0, \sigma_i^2) \\
s_{1t} &= \phi_1 s_{1t-1} + v_{1t}, & v_{1t} &\sim N(0, 1) \\
s_{2t} &= \phi_2 s_{2t-1} + v_{2t}, & v_{2t} &\sim N(0, 1),
\end{aligned}$$

for $i = 1, 2, \cdots, 9$. Interpret the estimated factors.

(b) Assuming the yields are ordered from shortest to longest maturities, re-estimate the model in part (a) by restricting the second factor to affect only the longer maturity yields (5-, 7-, and 10-year yields) by imposing the restrictions

$$\beta_{12} = \beta_{22} = \beta_{32} = \beta_{42} = \beta_{52} = \beta_{62} = 0.$$

Interpret the estimated factors.

(c) Estimate a dichotomous factor model by imposing the restrictions that s_{1t} just affects short maturities (less than 5 years) and s_{2t} just affects long maturities (greater than or equal to 5 years) by imposing the restrictions

$$\beta_{71} = \beta_{81} = \beta_{91} = 0.$$
$$\beta_{12} = \beta_{22} = \beta_{32} = \beta_{42} = \beta_{52} = \beta_{62} = 0.$$

Interpret the estimated factors.

6. Estimating Target Leverage

> leverage.*

The data are annual observations on three different measures of leverage, lv_{1t}, lv_{2t}, and lv_{3t}, for the US stock Air Products and Chemicals (APD) for the years 1971 to 2014. Assume that the firm's target leverage is an unobserved state variable, s_t, with AR(1) dynamics. This assumption gives rise to the following factor model:

$$lv_{it} = \alpha_i + \beta_i s_t + u_{it}, \qquad u_{it} \sim N(0, \sigma_i^2),$$
$$s_t = \phi_1 s_{t-1} + v_t, \qquad v_t \sim N(0, \sigma_v^2),$$

for $i = 1, 2, 3$.

(a) Discuss the possible strategies that can be used to identify the parameters of the system.
(b) Assume that $\sigma_v^2 = 1.0$. Estimate the model. Comment on your results focusing on the estimated persistence of the target leverage ratio, s_t, and which of the leverage measures, lv_{it}, most closely follows the target leverage.
(c) Now re-estimate the system omitting lv_{2t}. Compare and contrast your results with those obtained in part (b).

7. Parametric Model of the Yield Curve

> diebold.*

The data are the end-of-month price quotes (bid-ask average) for US Treasuries for the period January 1970 through December 2000, as used by Diebold and Li (2006).

(a) For monthly maturities defined by

$$\tau = \{1, 3, 6, 9, 12, 15, 18, 21, 24, 30, 36, 48, 60, 72, 84, 96, 108, 120\},$$

compute and plot the factor loadings given by

$$\beta_1 = 1, \quad \beta_2 = \left(\frac{1 - e^{-0.0609\tau_i}}{0.0609\tau_i} \right), \quad \beta_3 = \left(\frac{1 - e^{-0.0609\tau_i}}{0.0609\tau_i} - e^{-0.0609\tau_i} \right),$$

for $i = 1, 2, \cdots, 18$ monthly maturities.
(b) For each time period t, estimate the dynamic factors s_{1t}, s_{2t}, and s_{3t} in the cross sectional regression model

$$y_{it} = \beta_{i1} s_{1t} + \beta_{i2} s_{2t} + \beta_{i3} s_{3t} + u_{it},$$

in which u_{it} is a disturbance term.
(c) Using the estimated factors from part (b) and the parametric forms of the factor loadings, reconstruct the yield curve for the months of March, May, July, and August 1989. Plot these curves overlaid on scatter plots of the actual yield curves for these months.

(d) Using the estimated factors from part (b) and the parametric forms of the factor loadings, construct an estimate of the average yield curve. Plot this curve overlaid on a scatter plot of the actual average yield curve.

(e) Estimate AR(1) models for the fitted dynamic factors, $\widehat{s}_{1t}, \widehat{s}_{2t}$, and $\widehat{s}_{3t}$, and then redo parts (c) and (d) using one-step-ahead forecasts of the dynamic factors instead of the fitted values. Comment on your results.

(f) Redo part (e) using a VAR(1) model for the dynamic factors.

8. Stochastic Volatility Model of the Exchange Rate

> stochastic_volatility.*

The data are daily observations on the £/\$ exchange rate for the period 2 January 1979 to 13 February 2014. Consider the stochastic volatility model

$$
\begin{aligned}
y_t &= -1.27 + s_t + u_t, & u_t &\sim N(0, \pi^2/2) \\
s_t &= \alpha + \phi s_{t-1} + v_t, & v_t &\sim N(0, \sigma_v^2),
\end{aligned}
$$

where $y_t = \log r_t^2$, with r_t representing centered returns, and the factor is $s_t = \log h_t$, where $\sqrt{h_t}$ is the stochastic volatility of returns.

(a) Compute the ACF and the PACF of y_t and interpret its time series properties.

(b) Use the Kalman filter to estimate the parameters $\{\alpha, \phi, \sigma_v\}$ of the stochastic volatility model.

(c) Obtain the smoothed estimate of log variance and interpret the time-series properties of this series.

(d) Compute forecasts of y_t for the first 10 trading days after 13 February 2014.

9. Global and Regional Financial Integration

> integration.*

The data consist of daily stock prices in \$US of 10 Asian stocks (China, Hong Kong, Indonesia, Japan, Malaysia, Philippines, Singapore, South Korea, Taiwan, Thailand) as well as the US stock price, from 1 January 1997 to 27 May 2016, a sample size of $T = 5063$. Haldane and Hall (1991) identify changes in regional and global integration in financial markets over time by specifying the following time-varying parameter state-space model

$$
\begin{aligned}
\log P_{rt} - \log P_{it} &= \alpha_{it} + \beta_{it}(\log P_{rt} - \log P_{gt}) + u_{it}, & u_{it} &\sim N(0, \sigma_i^2) \\
\alpha_{it} &= \alpha_{it-1} + v_{1t}, & v_{1t} &\sim N(0, \sigma_{v1}^2) \\
\beta_{it} &= \beta_{it-1} + v_{2t}, & v_{2t} &\sim N(0, \sigma_{v2}^2),
\end{aligned}
$$

where P_{rt} is the regional stock price, P_{it} is the stock price of country i, P_{gt} is the global stock price, and u_{it}, v_{1t}, and v_{2t} are disturbance terms. Values of β_{it} near zero (one) suggest regional (global) integration because P_{it} is more influenced by P_{rt} (P_{gt}).

(a) Letting P_{rt} be the Japanese stock price, P_{gt} be the US stock price, and P_{it} be the Hong Kong stock price, estimate the Haldane and Hall model. Extract the smoothed estimates of the state variable β_{it} and interpret the changes in regional and global integration over time.

(b) Repeat part (a) where P_{it} is the stock price index for one of the following countries: Indonesia, Malaysia, Philippines, Singapore, South Korea, Taiwan, and Thailand.

(c) To understand the changing influence of China in the region, re-estimate the Haldane and Hall model where P_{rt} is the Chinese stock price index, P_{gt} is still the US stock price index, and P_{it} is the stock price from one of the following Asian countries: Hong Kong, Indonesia, Malaysia, Philippines, Singapore, South Korea, Taiwan, and Thailand. Extract the smoothed estimates of the state variable β_{it} for each of the Asian countries and discuss the influence of China in the Asian region.

Topics

CHAPTER 13

Univariate GARCH Models

When fund managers and individuals decide on financial investments, they consider potential returns on each investment, in relation to the risks that appear to be involved. Many of the goals of financial econometric work therefore involve modeling decisions in terms of the anticipated risk and the expected return of a particular investment. The empirical illustrations given in preceding chapters have often focused on specifying and estimating financial models of expected returns. These models typically seek to explain returns by characterizing the conditional mean of the return distribution. The set of conditioning variables usually involves lagged values of the dependent variable, various additional explanatory regressors, and sometimes combinations of these two. The conditional mean is obviously an important feature of the return distribution to study, estimate, and forecast, as it represents the payoff from investment. But other characteristics of the return distribution are important, especially the variance, which provides a rudimentary measure of the risk of investment.

From a financial perspective, modeling the variance of financial returns is potentially more interesting and relevant than the mean because it provides a crucial input into many aspects of financial decision-making. Examples include portfolio management, the construction of hedge ratios, the pricing of options, and the pricing of risk in general. Moreover, while mean returns may be challenging to explain empirically, the variance of returns is typically much easier to explain using historical data on past shocks and other observables that reflect changing risk conditions in financial markets. In implementing various strategies to explore market risk factors empirically, practitioners soon realized that an important characteristic of the return variance is that in most cases it is noticeably time-varying. In consequence, the same is true of the square root of the variance, which is commonly known as *volatility*.

The traditional approach to modeling time-varying variance is the generalized autoregressive conditional heteroskedasticity class of models (GARCH) due to Engle (1982) and Bollerslev (1986). This is a flexible class of volatility models that can capture a wide range of features that characterize time-varying risk. This class generalizes to multivariate settings in which time-varying models of both variances and covariances are dealt with. The multivariate model class is the subject matter of Chapter 14. An alternative, and more recent strategy for modeling volatility, known as realized volatility, is discussed in Chapter 15.

13.1 VOLATILITY CLUSTERING

To investigate the econometrics of modeling time-varying volatility in both a univariate and multivariate environment, the returns on six international stock markets are investigated. These are

SPX : Standard and Poors index from the United States;
DJX : Dow Jones index from the United States;
HSX : Hang Seng index from Hong Kong;
NKX : Nikkei index from Japan;
DAX : Deutscher Aktien index from Germany; and
UKX : FTSE index from the United Kingdom.

The data are daily log returns, r_t, from 5 January 1999 to 2 April 2014. This period covers a range of crises including the dot-com bubble in early 2000, the subprime crisis from mid 2007 to late 2008, the Great Recession from 2008 to 2010, and the European debt crisis from 2010.

One of the most documented features of financial asset returns is the tendency for large changes in asset prices to be followed by further large changes or reversals (producing market turmoil) or for small changes in prices to be followed by further small changes (leading to market tranquility). This phenomenon is known as volatility clustering, which highlights the property that the variation in financial returns is not constant over time but often appears to come in bursts of higher and lower variation. Figure 13.1 plots the annualized daily returns on the six international stock indices.

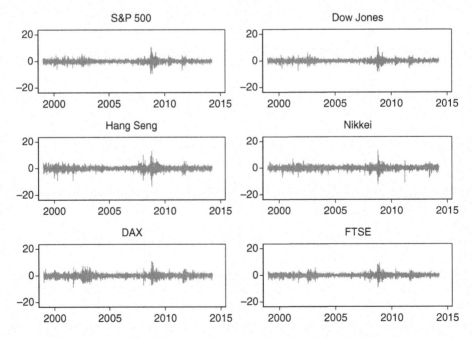

FIGURE 13.1 Annualized daily returns to six international stock market indices for the period 5 January 1999 to 2 April 2014.

The tendency for volatility to cluster is clearly evident in these plots, particularly the episode of high volatility during the crisis periods from July 2007 to the second half of 2008. There are also periods of relative tranquility when the magnitude of movements in the returns is relatively small.

A further implication of volatility clustering is that the unconditional distribution of returns on the asset is not a normal distribution. This result is highlighted in Figure 13.2, which plots the histogram of the daily returns on the DAX. The distribution of r_t is leptokurtic because it has a sharper peak and fatter tails (particularly in the left tail) than the best-fitting normal distribution, which is overlaid on the histogram of the returns.

To explore further the relationship between volatility clustering and leptokurtosis, consider a model of returns that is characterized by two regimes, namely, a tranquil regime in which the variance, $h_{tranquil}$, is low; and a turbulent regime in which the variance, $h_{turbulent}$, is high. It follows that $h_{tranquil} < h_{turbulent}$. In keeping with the volatility literature, the variance is represented by h, for heteroskedasticity, and not σ^2 as one might perhaps expect. This choice follows the original notation adopted by Engle (1982). Assuming that the means in the two regimes are the same,

$$\mu_{tranquil} = \mu_{turmoil} = \mu,$$

and that the returns in both these regimes are normally distributed, then

$$r_t \sim \begin{cases} N(\mu, h_{tranquil}) : \text{Tranquil regime} \\ N(\mu, h_{turbulent}) : \text{Turbulent regime} \end{cases}.$$

The tranquil regime is characterized by returns being close to their mean μ, whereas for the turbulent regime there are large positive and negative returns, which are relatively far from their mean of μ. Averaging the two distributions over the sample yields a

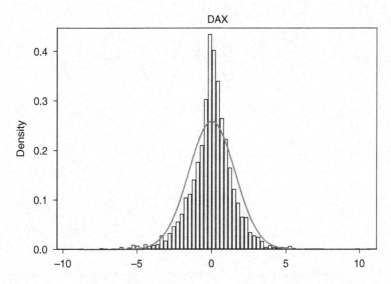

FIGURE 13.2 The distribution of the daily log returns on the DAX over the period 5 January 1999 to 2 April 2014. Superimposed on the histogram is a normal distribution with mean and variance equal to the sample mean and sample variance of the DAX returns.

leptokurtic distribution, with the sharp peak primarily corresponding to the returns during the tranquil periods. This distribution is computed as

$$f(r) = wN(\mu, h_{tranquil}) + (1 - w)N(\mu, h_{turbulent}),$$

in which the weight ω is the proportion of returns coming from each period.

A plot of the leptokurtic distribution is given in Figure 13.3 together with a plot of the standard normal distribution for comparative purposes. The weight used in generating the distribution is $w = 0.9$ so that 90% of returns come from the tranquil period. The parameters of the distributions in each of the regimes are $\mu = 0.02$, $h_{tranquil} = 0.5$ and $h_{turbulent} = 5.5$. The sharper peak is driven by the preponderance of returns in tranquil periods, while the fat tails largely correspond to the returns from the turbulent periods.

13.2 THE GARCH MODEL

One of the most widely used models of time variation in the variance of asset returns is the generalized autoregressive conditional heteroskedastic model, or simply GARCH (Engle, 1982; Bollerslev, 1986). This model is the analogue of the ARMA model of the conditional mean of asset returns (discussed in Chapter 4) but is now applied to explain the conditional variance. In contrast to the autocorrelations of asset returns, which from Chapters 2 and 4 are known to be weak, the autocorrelations of the variance of asset returns are strong and highly persistent. The GARCH model is a convenient vehicle for capturing this property. The model is used to characterize the volatility mechanism for returns in a broad range of asset markets and in these applications, it demonstrates strong empirical regularity in the sense that the estimated GARCH models are qualitatively very similar.

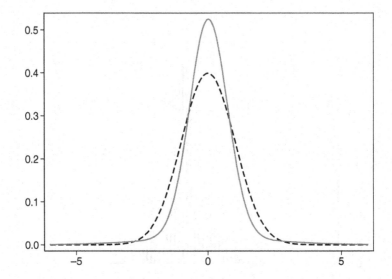

FIGURE 13.3 A simulated example of the distribution of returns constructed as a weighted sum of distributions from tranquil and turbulent regimes (solid line). A standard normal distribution (dashed line) is also plotted for comparative purposes.

13.2.1 Simple Models

To motivate the structure of the GARCH model, two earlier and simpler measures that can be used to capture time variation in the variance are first discussed. Once again, consistent with the convention in the volatility literature, the time-varying variance is represented by h_t and not σ_t^2.

(i) **Historical**

The simplest model of time-varying variance is based on the historically observed variance

$$h_t = \frac{1}{M} \sum_{j=1}^{M} r_{t-j}^2, \tag{13.1}$$

where r_t is the return on an asset, and M is the window over which the sample variance is computed. Technically speaking, for h_t to represent a true measure of sample variation, the sample mean $\bar{r}$ should be subtracted from r_t in the computation of equation (13.1). In practice, however, the sample mean for daily returns is numerically tiny and this centering calculation is often ignored. The advantage of the measure in equation (13.1) is that it is easy to compute, involving the choice of only one tuning parameter—the window length M. But the choice of M is important: If the window width is too long, then the computed estimate h_t reflects variation over a long period and fails to represent the time dynamics of variance at time t well enough; on the other hand, if the window width M is too short, the estimate will be very noisy. Typical values of M for daily returns that have been adopted in empirical work are $M = 22$ corresponding to a month, and $M = 252$ corresponding to a year.

(ii) **Exponentially Weighted Moving Average**

The exponentially weighted moving average model (EWMA) is another simple model of time-varying variance. This measure differs from the historical variance insofar as it allows for higher weights to be attached to more recent observations. The EWMA model of the variance is given by

$$
\begin{aligned}
h_t &= (1 - \lambda) \sum_{j=0}^{\infty} \lambda^j r_{t-j-1}^2 \\
&= (1 - \lambda) r_{t-1}^2 + (1 - \lambda) \left[\lambda r_{t-2}^2 + \lambda^2 r_{t-3}^2 + \cdots \right] \\
&= (1 - \lambda) r_{t-1}^2 + (1 - \lambda) \lambda \left[r_{t-2}^2 + \lambda r_{t-3}^2 + \cdots \right] \\
&= (1 - \lambda) r_{t-1}^2 + \lambda h_{t-1}.
\end{aligned}
\tag{13.2}
$$

The constant λ in equation (13.2) is known as the decay parameter. It governs how recent variances are weighted relative to more distant observations. The model depends crucially on this parameter, although no indication is given to explain how it should be estimated. In many cases a value is simply imposed a priori and then h_t can be computed recursively from the observations r_t^2 using equation (13.2). The value $\lambda = 0.94$, as suggested by the RiskMetrics Group, is a popular choice for updating daily volatility.

These two approaches deliver measures of variance at time t without the use of a specific econometric model and without econometric estimation. The conditional variation of returns at time t, $h\#$, is really an empirically unobserved latent time series variable that is associated with the return process. This variable may be constructively modeled, and the parameters on which it depends may be estimated directly from the observed returns data. Such a model accommodates the inherent randomness in the latent variable and provides a specific representation that may be used for purposes such as forecasting variance. The EWMA model is suggestive in this respect because it depends only on initial conditions and the unknown weighting parameter λ.

13.2.2 Specification

The GARCH model provides a flexible representation of the variance that addresses the shortcomings associated with the historical variance specification in equation (13.1) and the exponentially weighted moving average specification in equation (13.2). The GARCH(p,q) model is formulated using the following equations

$$
\begin{aligned}
r_t &= \mu_0 + u_t & \text{[Mean]} \\
h_t &= \alpha_0 + \sum_{i=1}^{q} \alpha_i u_{t-i}^2 + \sum_{i=1}^{p} \beta_i h_{t-i} & \text{[Variance]} \\
u_t &\sim N(0, h_t). & \text{[Distribution]}
\end{aligned}
\tag{13.3}
$$

The first component of the model is the mean (or conditional mean) specification, where the parameter μ_0 allows for returns to have a non-zero mean (or conditional mean). Given this simple specification for the mean, the disturbance term u_t effectively represents the re-centered returns

$$
r_t - \text{E}(r_t) = r_t - \text{E}_{t-1}(r_t) = r_t - \mu_0.
$$

The second component of the model is the conditional variance specification whereby

$$
h_t = \text{E}_{t-1}(u_t^2) = \text{E}_{t-1}\left(r_t - \text{E}_{t-1}(r_t)\right)^2,
$$

is a function of q lags of the squared disturbance term u_t^2 and p lags of the conditional variance h_t. The third component of the model is the choice of the distribution of the disturbance, which is specified to be normal with zero mean and variance h_t. Strictly speaking the distribution of u_t is conditionally normal. In most cases, conditioning is on the information set at time $t-1$. Throughout this chapter and also Chapters 14 and 15, the conditioning is suppressed for notational simplicity.

To understand the properties of the GARCH model in equation (13.3) consider an important special case given by the GARCH(1,1) model in which $q = p = 1$, resulting in the conditional variance specification

$$
h_t = \alpha_0 + \alpha_1 u_{t-1}^2 + \beta_1 h_{t-1}.
\tag{13.4}
$$

This model is now easily interpreted as a generalization of the EWMA model of equation (13.2) where instead of just one parameter (the delay parameter λ), there are now three unknown parameters: α_0, α_1, and β_1. The parameter β_1 determines how past shocks affect the conditional variance at time t. The initial impact of the previous shock on h_t is α_1. The effect of this shock feeds into the next period conditional variance through the lagged conditional variance, with the strength of the shock now equalling $\alpha_1\beta_1$. This process continues with the effects summarized as follows

$$\text{Period 1}: \alpha_1$$
$$\text{Period 2}: \alpha_1\beta_1$$
$$\vdots \qquad \vdots$$
$$\text{Period n}: \alpha_1\beta_1^{n-1}.$$

The larger is β_1, the longer is the memory of the shock. At the other extreme where $\beta_1 = 0$, the length of time a shock affects h_t is finite, with a memory of just one period. For this special case the model is known as the ARCH(1) model.

A simple extension to the GARCH model is to allow for the effects of additional explanatory variables, $x_{1t}, x_{2t} \cdots x_{Kt}$, on the conditional mean and variance. The GARCH model then becomes

$$r_t = \mu_0 + \sum_{k=1}^{K} \gamma_k x_{kt} + u_t \qquad \text{[Mean]}$$

$$h_t = \alpha_0 + \sum_{i=1}^{q} \alpha_i u_{t-i}^2 + \sum_{i=1}^{p} \beta_i h_{t-i} + \sum_{k=1}^{K} \psi_k x_{kt} \qquad \text{[Variance]}$$

$$u_t \sim N(0, h_t). \qquad \text{[Distribution]}$$

Examples of potential explanatory variables are lagged returns, trade volumes, and dummy variables to capture day-of-the-week effects and policy announcements.

A special case of the GARCH(1,1) model in equation (13.4) arises when $\alpha_1 + \beta_1 = 1$. In this case, there is persistent variance and the volatility series is nonstationary, a situation known as integrated GARCH or IGARCH, following the nomenclature of nonstationary models in Chapter 5. For this model, the variance is persistent in the sense that the conditional variance $E_{t-1}(u_{t+k}^2)$ taken k periods ahead depends on $h_t = E_{t-1}(u_t^2)$, so that current conditional variance information remains important in forecasts of variation indefinitely into the future. For instance, when $k = 1$

$$E_{t-1}(u_{t+1}^2) = E_{t-1}\left(\underset{t}{E} u_{t+1}^2\right)$$
$$= E_{t-1}\left(\alpha_0 + \alpha_1 u_t^2 + \beta_1 h_t\right)$$
$$= \alpha_0 + (\alpha_1 + \beta_1) h_t = \alpha_0 + h_t,$$

with a unit coefficient on h_t. In the case of an IGARCH(1,1) model, β_1 may be replaced by $1 - \alpha_1$.

13.2.3 Estimation

The parameters of the GARCH model and its extensions may be estimated by maximum likelihood using the methods discussed in Chapter 10.

Normal Distribution

The GARCH model in equation (13.3) specifies that the distribution of u_t is normal with zero mean and (conditional) variance h_t. From this specification, it may be deduced that the conditional distribution of r_t is

$$f(r_t|r_{t-1}, r_{t-2}, \cdots; \theta) = \frac{1}{\sqrt{2\pi h_t}} \exp\left(-\frac{(r_t - \mu_0)^2}{2h_t}\right).$$

where θ is a vector of the unknown parameters. Based on this distribution, the log likelihood function for an observation at time t is

$$\begin{aligned}
\log L_t(\theta) &= \log f(r_t|r_{t-1}, r_{t-2}, \cdots; \theta) \\
&= -\frac{1}{2}\log 2\pi - \frac{1}{2}\log h_t - \frac{1}{2}\frac{u_t^2}{h_t},
\end{aligned} \tag{13.5}$$

where

$$u_t = r_t - \mu_0$$

$$h_t = \alpha_0 + \sum_{i=1}^{q} \alpha_i u_{t-i}^2 + \sum_{i=1}^{p} \beta_i h_{t-i},$$

and $\theta = \{\mu_0, \alpha_1, \alpha_2, \cdots, \alpha_q, \beta_1, \beta_2, \cdots, \beta_p\}$.

To estimate the GARCH model using an iterative optimization algorithm, starting values are needed for the parameters together with some initial values for computing the conditional variance. In the case of the GARCH(1,1) model, the specification at observation $t = 1$ is

$$h_1 = \alpha_0 + \alpha_1 u_0^2 + \beta_1 h_0,$$

so that starting values for u_0 and h_0 are required in order to compute h_1. One possible choice of starting values is to set $u_0 = 0$ and to set h_0 equal to an estimate of the unconditional variance of r_t. Given these starting values for θ, the evaluation of the log likelihood function proceeds in the following manner.

(i) The disturbance term, u_t, is computed for all observations.
(ii) The conditional variance h_t is evaluated recursively using the values of u_t from the previous step.
(iii) The log likelihood function $\log L(\theta) = T^{-1} \sum_{t=1}^{T} \log L_t(\theta)$ is evaluated for the full sample of T observations.

An important aspect of the estimation is that the conditional variance, h_t, must always be positive at all observations. To restrict h_t to be positive, one strategy is to re-express the conditional variance in terms of positive components as

$$h_t = \alpha_0 + \sum_{i=1}^{q} \alpha_i^2 u_{t-i}^2 + \sum_{i=1}^{p} \beta_i^2 h_{t-i}.$$

Ensuring that the constraint $h_t > 0$ is satisfied is one of the major issues faced by the various specifications of multivariate GARCH models discussed in Chapter 14.

t Distribution

The GARCH model commonly assumes that the distribution of shocks is normal. It was earlier noted that the combination of conditional normality and GARCH variance yields an unconditional distribution of financial returns that is leptokurtotic. In practice, however, a GARCH model specified with normal disturbances is sometimes unable to capture all the leptokurtosis that is present in the observed data. To address this deficiency, a t distribution is commonly used to construct the log likelihood function for GARCH models.

Adopting the assumption that $u_t \sim St(0, h_t, v)$, where v is the degrees of freedom parameter, implies that the conditional distribution for the GARCH(1,1) model is now

$$f(r_t|r_{t-1}, r_{t-2}, \cdots; \theta) = \frac{\Gamma\left(\frac{v+1}{2}\right)}{\sqrt{\pi h_t (v-2)} \Gamma\left(\frac{v}{2}\right)} \left(1 + \frac{(r_t - \mu_0)^2}{h_t(v-2)}\right)^{-\left(\frac{v+1}{2}\right)},$$

where $\theta = \{\mu_0, \alpha_1, \alpha_2, \cdots, \alpha_q, \beta_1, \beta_2, \cdots, \beta_p, v\}$, and $v > 2$ is assumed. This expression for the density corresponds to the formulation in equation (10.9) used in Chapter 10, so that the variance of the conditional distribution is conveniently given directly by h_t. The log likelihood function for observation t is then

$$\log L_t(\theta) = -\frac{1}{2}\log(\pi(v-2)) - \frac{1}{2}\log h_t + \log\left(\Gamma\left(\frac{v+1}{2}\right)\right) - \log\left(\Gamma\left(\frac{v}{2}\right)\right)$$
$$- \left(\frac{v+1}{2}\right)\log\left(1 + \frac{(r_t - \mu_0)^2}{h_t(v-2)}\right),$$

with h_t representing the conditional variance from the GARCH(p,q) model. As before, an iterative optimization algorithm is needed to estimate the parameters of the model by maximum likelihood. The degrees of freedom parameter v is constrained to be positive and greater in value than 2 because if $v < 2$, the variance of the t distribution does not exist, in which case attempting to estimate the conditional variance is counterintuitive.

A GARCH(1,1) model is fitted to the six international stock market index returns for the period 5 January 1999 to 2 April 2014, with the results reported in Table 13.1. An interesting feature of the empirical results is the consistency of the parameter estimates across the different specifications. The estimates of β_1 are all in the vicinity of 0.9 and the estimates of α_1 all lie between 0.05 and 0.10. A feature of the results is that equity returns exhibit IGARCH characteristics since $\widehat{\alpha}_1 + \widehat{\beta}_1 \simeq 1$.

The degrees of freedom parameter for the t distribution indicates that the normal distribution may be a less appropriate choice in these examples and the assumption of normally distributed disturbances results in a misspecification of the log likelihood function. Provided that the conditional mean and variance specifications are not misspecified, estimates of the model's parameters are still consistent despite the fact that the shape of the distribution is incorrectly represented. But in this case standard errors need to be computed by means of quasi maximum likelihood standard errors, as discussed in Chapter 10, which use a combination of the Hessian and the outer product of the gradient of the log likelihood. In the context of GARCH models these standard errors are known as Bollerslev–Wooldridge standard errors (Bollerslev and Wooldridge, 1992).

TABLE 13.1 Parameter estimates of GARCH(1,1) models for the daily returns to six international stock market indices for log likelihood functions based on the normal and t distributions. The sample period is 5 January 1999 to 2 April 2014. Standard errors are in parentheses.

	SPX	DJX	HSX	NKX	DAX	UKX
	Normal Distribution					
μ_0	0.045	0.050	0.046	0.044	0.073	0.037
	(0.014)	(0.013)	(0.018)	(0.019)	(0.018)	(0.013)
α_0	0.014	0.013	0.012	0.041	0.024	0.014
	(0.002)	(0.002)	(0.003)	(0.007)	(0.004)	(0.003)
α_1	0.077	0.082	0.056	0.090	0.086	0.095
	(0.006)	(0.006)	(0.004)	(0.006)	(0.006)	(0.007)
β_1	0.913	0.907	0.939	0.893	0.903	0.896
	(0.006)	(0.007)	(0.005)	(0.007)	(0.007)	(0.007)
	t Distribution					
μ_0	0.059	0.057	0.051	0.053	0.085	0.047
	(0.013)	(0.013)	(0.017)	(0.019)	(0.017)	(0.013)
α_0	0.010	0.010	0.008	0.030	0.016	0.013
	(0.003)	(0.003)	(0.003)	(0.008)	(0.004)	(0.003)
α_1	0.079	0.082	0.050	0.074	0.084	0.095
	(0.009)	(0.009)	(0.006)	(0.008)	(0.009)	(0.010)
β_1	0.917	0.913	0.948	0.914	0.912	0.898
	(0.009)	(0.009)	(0.006)	(0.010)	(0.009)	(0.010)
ν	6.557	6.605	6.251	7.806	8.218	9.500
	(0.730)	(0.710)	(0.711)	(0.893)	(1.072)	(1.383)

13.3 ASYMMETRIC VOLATILITY EFFECTS

Consider the GARCH(1,1) model

$$r_t = \mu_0 + u_t$$
$$h_t = \alpha_0 + \alpha_1 u_{t-1}^2 + \beta_1 h_{t-1}.$$

In this model u_{t-1} measures shocks that embody the effects of news relevant to financial markets that arrived in period $t-1$. In no-news days, good and bad news balance and $u_{t-1} = 0$, whereas positive (negative) values of u_{t-1} represent good (bad) news. An important property of this GARCH(1,1) specification is that shocks of the same magnitude, positive or negative, result in the same increase in volatility h_t. That is, positive news with $u_{t-1} > 0$ has the same effect on the conditional variance as negative news $u_{t-1} < 0$ because it is only the absolute size of the news that matters since it is the squared function u_{t-1}^2 that enters the equation.

In the case of stock markets, an asymmetric response to news is supported by theory, in which case negative shocks $u_{t-1} < 0$ have a larger effect on the conditional variance. The heuristic explanation is that a negative shock raises the debt-equity ratio, thereby increasing leverage and consequently risk. It is this (aptly named) leverage effect that suggests bad news leads to a greater increase in conditional variance than good news.

There are two popular specifications in the GARCH class of model that relax the restriction of a symmetric response to the news.

(i) Threshold GARCH (TARCH)

The TARCH(1,1) specification (Glosten, Jagannathan, and Runkle, 1993; Zakoïan, 1994) of the conditional variance is

$$h_t = \alpha_0 + \alpha_1 u_{t-1}^2 + \beta_1 h_{t-1} + \lambda u_{t-1}^2 I_{t-1},$$

where I_{t-1} is an indicator variable defined as

$$I_{t-1} = \begin{cases} 1 : u_{t-1} \geq 0 \\ 0 : u_{t-1} < 0. \end{cases}$$

To make the asymmetry in the effect of news on the conditional variance explicit, this model can be written as

$$h_t = \begin{cases} \alpha_0 + (\alpha_1 + \lambda) u_{t-1}^2 + \beta_1 h_{t-1} : u_{t-1} \geq 0 \\ \alpha_0 + \alpha_1 u_{t-1}^2 + \beta_1 h_{t-1} \quad\quad : u_{t-1} < 0. \end{cases}$$

The leverage effect in equity markets would lead us to expect $\lambda < 0$, so that negative news, with $u_{t-1} < 0$, is associated with a higher effect on volatility than positive news of the same magnitude.

(ii) Exponential GARCH (EGARCH)

The EGARCH(1,1) specification (Nelson, 1991) of the conditional variance is

$$\log h_t = \alpha_0 + \alpha_1 \left| \frac{u_{t-1}}{\sqrt{h_{t-1}}} \right| + \lambda_1 \frac{u_{t-1}}{\sqrt{h_{t-1}}} + \beta_1 \log h_{t-1}.$$

An important advantage of the EGARCH specification is that the conditional variance is guaranteed to be positive at each point in time. This result follows from the fact that the variance is expressed in terms of $\log h_t$, so the actual variance is obtained by exponentiation. The parameter α_1 captures potential asymmetry in the effect of u_{t-1} on $\log h_t$. It is expected that $\alpha_1 < 0$, so negative news is associated with a higher effect than positive news of the same magnitude.

TARCH(1,1) models based on the normal distribution are fitted to daily returns from 5 January 1999 to 2 April 2014 for six international stock market indices. The results are reported in Table 13.2.

To illustrate the difference between the GARCH and TGARCH models, h_t is plotted against u_{t-1}. This plot is known as the news impact curve or NIC. The NICs for the Nikkei index are plotted in Figure 13.4. The major point to note is that the NIC of the simple GARCH model is symmetric. In the case of the TARCH model the NIC is asymmetric, with negative shocks having a larger impact on h_t than positive shocks. Inspection of the estimates of λ in Table 13.2 shows that the HSX, DAX, and FTSE indices generate similar news impact curves to the Nikkei. For the S&P 500 and Dow Jones indices, $\widehat{\alpha}_1 + \widehat{\lambda}_1 < 0$, so positive shocks actually reduce the conditional variance.

TABLE 13.2 Parameter estimates of TARCH(1,1) models based on the normal distribution for the daily returns on six international stock market indices. The sample period is 5 January 1999 to 2 April 2014. Standard errors are in parentheses.

	SPX	DJX	HSX	NKX	DAX	UKX
μ_0	0.003	0.013	0.024	0.015	0.026	−0.001
	(0.014)	(0.013)	(0.018)	(0.020)	(0.018)	(0.014)
α_0	0.014	0.013	0.016	0.053	0.029	0.017
	(0.001)	(0.001)	(0.003)	(0.008)	(0.003)	(0.002)
α_1	0.129	0.137	0.081	0.131	0.139	0.136
	(0.009)	(0.010)	(0.006)	(0.010)	(0.010)	(0.009)
β_1	0.938	0.926	0.939	0.889	0.911	0.920
	(0.005)	(0.006)	(0.005)	(0.008)	(0.007)	(0.007)
λ	−0.157	−0.149	−0.057	−0.090	−0.133	−0.143
	(0.010)	(0.010)	(0.006)	(0.008)	(0.009)	(0.010)

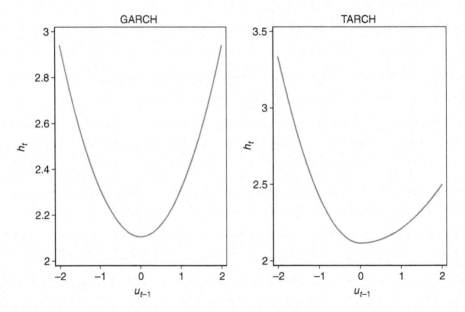

FIGURE 13.4 News Impact Curves for the GARCH(1,1) and TARCH(1,1) models estimated on daily returns on the Nikkei index from 5 January 1999 to 2 April 2014.

13.4 FORECASTING

To highlight the process of forecasting GARCH conditional variances, consider forecasting log returns over k periods where the conditional variance is a GARCH(1,1) model. The future k-period log return is

$$r_{T+1}(k) = r_{T+1} + r_{T+2} + \cdots + r_{T+k},$$

which has conditional variance

$$\text{var}(r_{T+1}(k)) = h_{T+1|T} + h_{T+2|T} + \cdots + h_{T+k|T}. \tag{13.6}$$

To generate the conditional variances in equation (13.6), consider the forecast of volatility at time $T+1$ by writing the GARCH(1,1) model at $T+1$,

$$h_{T+1} = \alpha_0 + \alpha_1 u_T^2 + \beta_1 h_T.$$

Taking conditional expectations based on information at time T, the one-step-ahead forecast is

$$h_{T+1|T} = E_T(h_{T+1}) = E_T(\alpha_0 + \alpha_1 u_T^2 + \beta_1 h_T)$$
$$= \alpha_0 + \alpha_1 u_T^2 + \beta_1 h_T,$$

since $E_T(u_T^2) = u_T^2$ and $E_T(h_T) = h_T$. Similarly, to forecast volatility at time $T+2$, the conditional variance is written at $T+2$ as

$$h_{T+2} = \alpha_0 + \alpha_1 u_{T+1}^2 + \beta_1 h_{T+1}.$$

Taking conditional expectations based on information at time T, the two-step-ahead forecast of h_{T+2} is

$$h_{T+2|T} = E_T(h_{T+2}) = E_T(\alpha_0 + \alpha_1 u_{T+1}^2 + \beta_1 h_{T+1})$$
$$= \alpha_0 + \alpha_1 E_T(u_{T+1}^2) + \beta_1 E_T(h_{T+1})$$
$$= \alpha_0 + \alpha_1 h_{T+1|T} + \beta_1 h_{T+1|T}$$
$$= \alpha_0 + (\alpha_1 + \beta_1) h_{T+1|T}, \tag{13.7}$$

since by definition $E_T(u_{T+1}^2) = h_{T+1|T}$ and $E_T(h_{T+1}) = h_{T+1|T}$. Extending this argument to $T+k$ gives

$$h_{T+k|T} = \alpha_0 + (\alpha_1 + \beta_1) h_{T+k-1|T}. \tag{13.8}$$

By recursive substitution for the term $h_{T+k-1|T}$ in equation (13.8) and using the results from equation (13.7), the conditional forecast of volatility for k periods ahead is found to be

$$h_{T+k|T} = \alpha_0 + (\alpha_1 + \beta_1)\alpha_0 + \cdots + (\alpha_1 + \beta_1)^{k-2}\alpha_0 + (\alpha_1 + \beta_1)^{k-1} h_{T+1|T}.$$

In summary, the forecasts for the GARCH(1,1) model are

$$h_{T+k|T} = \begin{cases} \alpha_0 + \alpha_1 u_T^2 + \beta_1 h_T & k = 1 \\ \alpha_0 + (\alpha_1 + \beta_1) h_{T+k-1|T} & k \geqslant 2. \end{cases}$$

Using these expressions in equation (13.6) generates the conditional variance of the k-period return

$$\text{var}(r_{T+1}(k)) = k\alpha_0 + \alpha_1 u_T^2 + ((\alpha_1 + \beta_1) + (\alpha_1 + \beta_1)^2 + \cdots + (\alpha_1 + \beta_1)^{k-1}) h_{T+1|T}.$$

In the special case of an IGARCH model where $\alpha_1 + \beta_1 = 1$, this expression simplifies to

$$\text{var}(r_{T+1}(k)) = k\alpha_0 + \alpha_1 u_T^2 + (k-1) h_{T+1|T}.$$

In practice, forecasts for the GARCH(1,1) model are computed by replacing the unknown parameters α_0, α_1, and β_1 and the unknown quantities u_T^2 and h_T by their respective sample estimates. The forecasts are computed recursively starting with

$$\widehat{h}_{T+1|T} = \widehat{\alpha}_0 + \widehat{\alpha}_1 \widehat{u}_T^2 + \widehat{\beta}_1 \widehat{h}_T.$$

Given this estimate, $\widehat{h}_{T+2|T}$ is computed from equation (13.7) as

$$\widehat{h}_{T+2|T} = \widehat{\alpha}_0 + (\widehat{\alpha}_1 + \widehat{\beta}_1)\widehat{h}_{T+1|T},$$

which, in turn, is used to compute $\widehat{h}_{T+3|T}$ and so on. To forecast higher order GARCH models the same recursive approach is adopted.

The forecast from a GARCH(1,1) model will converge relatively quickly to the long-term average volatility implied by the model, which is given by

$$h = \frac{\alpha_0}{1 - \alpha_1 - \beta_1}.$$

The unconditional variance h is defined so long as $\alpha_1 + \beta_1 < 1$. Figure 13.5 demonstrates this convergence for S&P 500 returns. A GARCH(1,1) model is fitted and then out-of-sample predictions are made for two different periods, the first starting on 1 January 2010 and the second on 1 July 2010. The forecasts in both cases converge to the long-term mean despite the fact the forecast starts below the long-term mean for the January forecast and above the long-term mean for the July forecast. The fact that the convergence occurs over a 12-month period indicates that the conditional volatility series is quite persistent. Notice that for the forecast starting in July 2010, the actual estimated conditional variance series drops off a lot more quickly than the forecast.

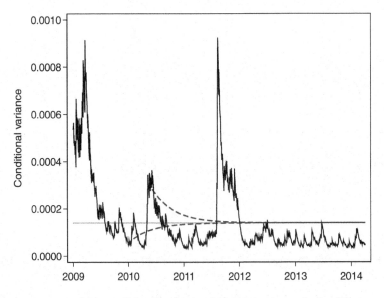

FIGURE 13.5 Forecasts of the conditional variance of S&P 500 returns obtained from a GARCH(1,1) model. Also shown is the estimated unconditional variance implied by the model. Both the forecasts beginning on 1 January 2010 and 1 July 2010 converge to the long-term mean.

One of the distinguishing features of the conditional variance literature has been the rapid proliferation in types of model available. Given this overwhelming choice, one of the more interesting results to emerge is that, despite its simplicity, when it comes to forecasting the conditional variance, the GARCH(1,1) model is difficult to beat (Hansen and Lunde, 2005).

The empirical efficacy of the GARCH(1,1) model for forecasting the conditional variance leads naturally to the question of assessing the accuracy of variance forecasts. In theory, determining the accuracy of the forecasts of the conditional variance can be accomplished using any of the statistical measures outlined in Chapter 7. In practice, however, this approach is not possible because the actual value of the conditional variance is never directly observed.

The standard method to assess volatility models, therefore, is to evaluate the forecast using a volatility proxy such as the squared return, r_t^2. Early attempts at forecast evaluation were based on Mincer–Zarnowitz regressions (Mincer and Zarnowitz, 1969) in which the realization of the variable of interest is regressed on the forecast using the model

$$r_t^2 = \delta_0 + \delta_1 \widehat{h}_t + e_t,$$

where e_t is a disturbance term. The null and alternative hypotheses are

$$H_0 : \delta_0 = 0 \text{ and } \delta_1 = 1$$
$$H_1 : \delta_0 \neq 0 \text{ or } \delta_1 \neq 1.$$

Under the null hypothesis $\widehat{h}_t$ is an unbiased estimator of r_t^2. The use of r_t^2 as a proxy is problematic, however, as returns that are large in absolute value may have a large impact on the estimation results. Two examples of alternative specifications that have been tried are

$$|r_t| = \delta_0 + \delta_1 \sqrt{\widehat{h}_t} + e_t$$
$$\log r_t^2 = \delta_0 + \delta_1 \log \widehat{h}_t + e_t,$$

which use transformations of the volatility proxy to reduce the impact of large returns.

Another approach is to use the measures of forecast performance outlined in Chapter 7 to assess volatility forecasts. This has been a particularly fertile area of research and has seen the development of new loss functions, such as the quasi-likelihood loss function, which is defined for observation t as

$$QLIKE = \log \widehat{h}_t + \frac{r_t^2}{\widehat{h}_t}.$$

The name QLIKE is derived from the similarity to the (negative) Gaussian log likelihood and its use as a quasi-likelihood in misspecified models. Specified in this way, the QLIKE function can become negative when dealing with very small returns because the term in $\log h_t$ will be negative and dominate the other term in the expression. To avoid this, an equivalent alternative specification (see Christoffersen, 2012), which is always positive, is given by

$$QLIKE = \frac{r_t^2}{\widehat{h}_t} - \log\left(\frac{r_t^2}{\widehat{h}_t}\right) - 1.$$

The QLIKE function has become very popular in evaluating variance forecasts. The major reason for this popularity is the fact that the QLIKE criterion is not symmetric. Figure 13.6 plots the MAE (see Chapter 7) and the QLIKE measures for forecasts ranging from 0.5 to 3.5 when the true value is 2. Unlike the MAE, the QLIKE penalizes underestimating volatility more heavily than overestimating it. This may be a desirable characteristic in a loss function if the risk manager is particularly conservative. Other loss functions based on economic notions of loss such as expected utility have also been proposed.

Table 13.3 provides a comparison of the forecasts generated by a GARCH(1,1) model fitted to S&P 500 returns against a forecast of the conditional variance using an exponentially weighted moving average of squared returns. The forecasts start at 1 July 2010 and are made for 500 days after this date. The EWMA forecast is computed using the weighting parameter 0.94 as suggested by RiskMetrics. The MAE, MAPE, and RMSE, as discussed in Chapter 7, are reported together with a simple t test of equal predictive accuracy. The QLIKE metric and associated t test are also reported. It is quite clear from these results that the GARCH(1,1) model dominates the EWMA in terms of forecasting accuracy. It is only in the MAPE case that the t test of equal predictive ability cannot be rejected at the 5% level; and in each case, the t statistic is negative indicating that the GARCH(1,1) loss function has a smaller value than the EWMA loss function.

13.5 THE RISK-RETURN TRADEOFF

The standard deviation is commonly used as a measure of risk in portfolio theory, as it captures the extent of the deviations of actual returns from their conditional mean. The larger the deviation the larger is the risk of the portfolio. To compensate an investor

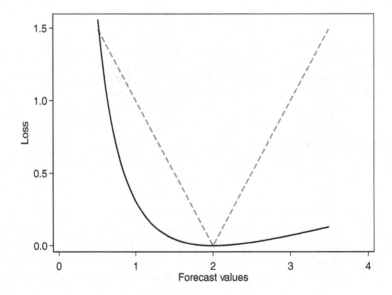

FIGURE 13.6 Simulated values of MAE (dashed line) and QLIKE (solid line) loss functions plotted for forecast values ranging from 0.5 to 3.5 when the hypothetical true value is 2.

TABLE 13.3 Forecast evaluations of the conditional variance of S&P 500 returns based on a GARCH(1,1) model and an EWMA model with weighting parameter 0.94. Forecasts begin on 1 July 2010 and are made for the subsequent 500 days. For each criterion, a simple t test of equal predictive accuracy and associated p value are reported.

Criterion	GARCH(1,1)	EWMA	t test	p value
MAE	0.0002	0.0003	−17.8953	0.0000
MAPE	1982.1100	2946.9700	−1.4640	0.1440
RMSE	0.0004	0.0004	−3.4602	0.0010
QLIKE	1.9864	2.0897	−1.9679	0.0490

for bearing more risk, an investor should receive a higher expected return, resulting in a positive relationship between the mean and the risk of the portfolio.

To model the trade-off between risk and return, the conditional mean of returns is specified to be a function of the conditional variance, h_t. The model, known as the GARCH-M model, is an extension of the CAPM with an allowance for time-varying risk to identify the risk and return preferences of investors. The augmented model is

$$r_{it} - r_{ft} = \mu_0 + \mu_1 h_t^\omega + \mu_2(r_{mt} - r_{ft}) + u_t$$
$$u_t \sim N(0, h_t) \tag{13.9}$$
$$h_t = \alpha_0 + \alpha_1 u_{t-1}^2 + \beta_1 h_{t-1},$$

with parameters $\theta = \{\mu_0, \mu_1, \mu_2, \alpha_0, \alpha_1, \beta_1\}$. The risk-return tradeoff is given by the term $\mu_1 h_t^\omega$. When $\omega = 0.5$ the risk-return tradeoff is specified in terms of the conditional standard deviation, $\sqrt{h_t}$, and when $\omega = 1.0$ the relationship is in terms of the conditional variance.

The GARCH-M version of the CAPM is estimated for 10 Fama–French industry portfolios using monthly data for the period January 1927 to December 2013. The critical parameters reflecting the risk preferences of investors are μ_1 and ω, and Table 13.4 summarizes the results relating to the trade-off parameter μ_1 for all 10 portfolios for $\omega = \{0.5, 1.0\}$. Inspection of the results for $\omega = 0.5$ shows that the Nondurables, Durables, and Retail portfolios exhibit the greatest trade-off, all with $\widehat{\mu}_1 \simeq 0.3$. The Utilities and Manufacturing portfolios have the smallest positive trade-offs, while the Energy and Health portfolios even exhibit a negative trade-off. The issue of a negative trade-off is investigated later by testing the strength of the risk-return relationships.

A test of a trade-off between risk and return is based on the hypotheses

$$H_0 : \mu_1 = 0 \quad \text{[No trade-off]}$$
$$H_1 : \mu_1 \neq 0. \quad \text{[Trade-off]}$$

The Wald test of these hypotheses is conveniently given by the t statistic. The p values of the models when $\omega = 0.5$ indicate that only the Durables portfolio has a statistically significant trade-off between risk and return at the conventional level of 5%. The results for the Nondurables and Retail portfolios are marginal, as is the result for the Health portfolio, which has the counterintuitive negative relationship. The situation is more promising for the ability of this model to capture the risk-return relationship when $\omega = 1.0$. The Nondurables, Durables, Retail, and Other portfolios all indicate a significant

TABLE 13.4 Estimates of the parameter μ_1 in the GARCH-M version of the CAPM in equation (13.9) with $\omega = \{0.5, 1.0\}$ for 10 Fama–French industry portfolios. The data are monthly excess returns for the period January 1927 to December 2013.

Portfolio	μ_1	t test	p value	AIC
$\omega = 0.5$				
Nondurables	0.286	1.859	0.063	4468.639
Durables	0.378	2.861	0.004	5718.193
Manufacturing	0.135	1.068	0.285	3925.937
Energy	−0.053	−0.430	0.667	5680.519
Technology	0.052	0.357	0.721	5188.485
Telecom	0.131	0.931	0.352	5156.026
Retail	0.301	1.886	0.059	4999.628
Health	−0.276	−1.881	0.060	5388.758
Utilities	0.011	0.120	0.904	5407.391
Other	0.115	1.170	0.242	4362.822
$\omega = 1.0$				
Nondurables	0.064	2.053	0.040	4467.797
Durables	0.039	2.403	0.016	5718.994
Manufacturing	0.044	1.299	0.194	3924.829
Energy	−0.010	−0.599	0.549	5680.353
Technology	0.001	0.062	0.950	5188.598
Telecom	0.016	0.741	0.459	5156.408
Retail	0.055	1.964	0.050	4998.995
Health	−0.029	−1.504	0.133	5390.037
Utilities	0.000	0.006	0.995	5407.404
Other	0.037	2.170	0.030	4360.769

risk-return tradeoff and the anomalous result for the Health portfolio is resolved because $\widehat{\mu}_1$ is not statistically significant.

Table 13.4 also reports the AIC which may be used to determine which choice of ω, 0.5 or 1.0, is consistent with the portfolio data. As discussed in Chapter 4, the AIC statistic is computed as

$$AIC = -2 \log L(\widehat{\theta}) + \frac{2K}{T},$$

where $K = 6$ is the number of estimated parameters in θ, which applies to both models. A comparison of the AICs for the two models associated with all 10 portfolios reveals an even split between the portfolios for which the statistic is minimized. The choice of $\omega = 0.5$ is appropriate for Nondurables, Technology, Telecommunications (Telecom in Table 13.4), Health, and Utilities; while the choice of $\omega = 1.0$ is best for Durables, Manufacturing, Energy, Retail, and Other.

13.6 HEATWAVES AND METEOR SHOWERS

An important application of GARCH models examines how volatility is transmitted through different regions of the world during the course of a global financial trading day (Ito, 1987; Ito and Roley, 1987; Engle, Ito, and Lin, 1990). The approach is to partition each 24-hour period (calendar day) into three major trading zones, namely, Japan (12am to 7am GMT), Europe (7am to 12:30pm GMT), and the United States (12:30pm to 9pm GMT), which is illustrated as follows:

$$
\begin{array}{ccc}
\text{Japan} & \text{Europe} & \text{U.S.} \\
\overbrace{\text{12am}\cdots\text{7am}} & \overbrace{\text{7am}\cdots\text{12:30pm}} & \overbrace{\text{12:30pm}\cdots\text{9pm}}
\end{array}
$$

$$
\underbrace{\qquad\qquad\qquad\qquad\qquad\qquad\qquad\qquad\qquad}_{\text{One Trading Day}}
$$

For other ways of defining a global trading day, see Dungey, Fakhrutdinova, and Goodhart (2009).

The calendar structure of the global trading day implies a particular form for the GARCH(1,1) framework used to model the conditional variance in each of the trading zones. Define r_{1t}, r_{2t}, and r_{3t} as the daily returns to the Japanese, the European, and the United States zones, respectively. The model is

$$
\begin{bmatrix} r_{1t} - \bar{r}_1 \\ r_{2t} - \bar{r}_2 \\ r_{3t} - \bar{r}_3 \end{bmatrix} = \begin{bmatrix} u_{1t} \\ u_{2t} \\ u_{3t} \end{bmatrix}, \quad \begin{bmatrix} u_{1t} \\ u_{2t} \\ u_{3t} \end{bmatrix} \sim N \left(\begin{bmatrix} 0 \\ 0 \\ 0 \end{bmatrix}, \begin{bmatrix} h_{1t} & 0 & 0 \\ 0 & h_{2t} & 0 \\ 0 & 0 & h_{3t} \end{bmatrix} \right)
$$

$$
\begin{bmatrix} h_{1t} \\ h_{2t} \\ h_{3t} \end{bmatrix} = \begin{bmatrix} \alpha_{10} \\ \alpha_{20} \\ \alpha_{30} \end{bmatrix} + \begin{bmatrix} 0 & 0 & 0 \\ \alpha_{21} & 0 & 0 \\ \alpha_{31} & \alpha_{32} & 0 \end{bmatrix} \begin{bmatrix} u_{1t}^2 \\ u_{2t}^2 \\ u_{3t}^2 \end{bmatrix} + \begin{bmatrix} \beta_{11} & 0 & 0 \\ 0 & \beta_{22} & 0 \\ 0 & 0 & \beta_{33} \end{bmatrix} \begin{bmatrix} h_{1t-1} \\ h_{2t-1} \\ h_{3t-1} \end{bmatrix}
$$

$$
+ \begin{bmatrix} \gamma_{11} & \gamma_{12} & \gamma_{13} \\ 0 & \gamma_{22} & \gamma_{23} \\ 0 & 0 & \gamma_{33} \end{bmatrix} \begin{bmatrix} u_{1t-1}^2 \\ u_{2t-1}^2 \\ u_{3t-1}^2 \end{bmatrix}. \tag{13.10}
$$

The structure of the global trading day is now apparent. Shocks at the start of the global trading day in Japan, u_{1t}^2, can potentially influence volatility on the same day in Europe and the United States via the coefficients α_{21} and α_{31}, respectively. In a similar way news from Europe, u_{2t}^2, can influence volatility in the United States on the same trading day, α_{32}, but not in Japan, as this market will already have closed. Events in the United States, however, will be transmitted to Japan and Europe only on the following day with parameters γ_{13} and γ_{23}, respectively. Similarly, a shock in Europe can only be transmitted to Japan on the following trading day with parameter γ_{12}. This implies that the γ_{ij} matrix on the lagged innovations is upper diagonal.

The aim is to examine international linkages in volatility between these regions and investigate in particular two patterns as possible descriptors of international volatility transmission.

(i) **Heatwave**
Volatility in any one region is primarily a function of the previous day's volatility in the same region ($\beta_{ii} \neq 0$).

(ii) **Meteor Shower**
Volatility in one region is driven primarily by volatility in the region immediately preceding it in terms of calendar time ($\alpha_{ij} \neq 0$).

To test this model, daily equity returns for the Nikkei, DAX, and the S&P 500 are used. The sample period is from 5 January 1999 to 2 April 2014. This example is illustrative only because there is some overlap between trading on the DAX and trading on the S&P 500. A technically correct implementation would be to use high-frequency data and compute returns in non-overlapping zones as

$$r_{it} = (\log P^c_{it} - \log P^o_{it})/\sqrt{nh_i}, \qquad i = 1, 2, 3,$$

in which P^c_{it} is a closing price of the relevant asset price in zone i on day t, and P^o_{it} is the opening price of the price in zone i on day t, and nh_i is the number of hours for which each non-overlapping zone i trades.[1]

Descriptive statistics for the log returns to the three indices representing the three major trading zones are presented in Table 13.5. While none of the returns series from the three zones exhibit large degrees of skewness, they all exhibit excess kurtosis. Formal testing using an LM test for ARCH (see Chapter 3) reveals that all the series have strong ARCH effects at the 5% level.

The system of equations in (13.10) can be estimated equation-by-equation using maximum likelihood. The estimation results, based on the log returns to the three representative equity price indices, are reported in Table 13.6, with the constant term in the variance equation suppressed.[2] There are two general conclusions that emerge from inspection of these results. First, all the lagged conditional variance terms, h_{it-1}, in the last row of Table 13.6 are statistically significant, a result that is consistent with the heatwave hypothesis being part of the explanation of the patterns in global volatility. Second, the meteor shower effect is also important: Japanese news affects Europe, and European news affects the United States on the same trading day. Note that in the case of Japan, the meteor shower effect shows up in the significance of the lagged influence of the US innovations, u^2_{3t-1}, on Japan. It is clear, therefore, that the pattern of volatility interaction in global foreign markets is a combination of both heatwaves and meteor showers. There

TABLE 13.5 Descriptive statistics for daily percentage log returns on the Nikkei, DAX, and the S&P 500 equity price indices. The sample period is 4 January 1999 to 2 April 2014.

Statistic	Nikkei	DAX	S&P 500
Mean	0.003	0.015	0.011
Std. dev.	1.512	1.542	1.273
Maximum	13.235	10.797	10.957
Minimum	−12.111	−8.875	−9.470
Skewness	−0.419	−0.019	−0.171
Kurtosis	9.628	7.413	10.893
ARCH	103.097	116.093	158.407
p value	(0.000)	(0.000)	(0.000)

---

[1] For an empirical application that looks at volatility transmission between time zones and across different financial markets, see Clements, Hurn, and Volkov (2015).

[2] These estimates are generated using Stata. The software treats additional terms in the conditional variance equation by entering them in exponentiated form.

TABLE 13.6 Coefficient estimates of the constituent equations of (13.10) for the Japanese, European, and US trading zones. The data are the percentage log returns on the Nikkei, DAX, and the S&P 500 equity price indices for the period 5 January 1999 to 2 April 2014. Coefficients with *p* values <0.05 are marked with an asterisk (*).

Variable	Nikkei	DAX	S&P 500
u_{1t}^2	–	0.0356*	−0.0320
u_{2t}^2	–	–	0.0646*
u_{3t}^2	–	–	–
u_{1t-1}^2	0.0850*	–	–
u_{2t-1}^2	−0.0258	0.0850*	–
u_{3t-1}^2	0.0764*	−0.0027	0.0814*
h_{it-1}	0.8832*	0.9024*	0.8992*

is no support for the conclusion that either one of these patterns dominates. This pattern of interaction suggests the transmission of news between different regions of the world on the same trading day is a potentially important explanation of volatility.

13.7 EXERCISES
The data required for the exercises are available for download as EViews workfiles (*.wf1), Stata datafiles (*.dta), comma delimited text files (*.csv), and as Excel spreadsheets (*.xlsx).

1. **Testing for Conditional Volatility in Hedge Fund Returns**

> hedgefunds.*

The data are daily percentage log returns, r_t, on 7 hedge fund indices (Convertible, Distressed, Equity, Event, Macro, Merger, and Neutral) and also the daily percentage returns to the S&P 500, Dow Jones, and NASDAQ stock market indices. The sample period is 1 April 2003 to 28 May 2010.

(a) A test of time-varying volatility is based on estimating the following ARCH equation by least squares

$$r_t^2 = \alpha_0 + \sum_{i=1}^{q} \alpha_i r_{t-i}^2 + v_t,$$

where v_t is a disturbance term. The test statistic is $ARCH = TR^2$, where R^2 is the coefficient of determination from the least squares regression. Under the null hypothesis of no ARCH the statistic is distributed asymptotically as χ^2 with q degrees of freedom. Perform a test of ARCH of orders $q = \{1, 2, 5, 10\}$ for each of the 7 hedge funds and compare the results of the tests.

(b) For each of the 7 hedge funds estimate the GARCH(1,1) model

$$r_t = \mu_0 + u_t$$
$$u_t \sim N(0, h_t)$$
$$h_t = \alpha_0 + \alpha_1 u_{t-1}^2 + \beta_1 h_{t-1}.$$

Comment on the results.

(c) A diagnostic test of the estimated model in part (b) is to redo the ARCH test in part (a), but with the returns, r_t, replaced by the standardized returns

$$z_t = \frac{r_t - \mu_0}{\sqrt{h_t}}.$$

If the null hypothesis of no ARCH in z_t cannot be rejected, then this result provides evidence that the conditional variance model is specified correctly. Apply the ARCH diagnostic test to the estimated models in part (b) and compare the results across the 7 hedge funds.

2. What Good is a Volatility Model?

> englepatton.*, englepatton_UPDATED.*

Engle and Patton (2001) use this question as the title of their paper. The data set is the original data used in the paper and consists of daily data for the period 23 August 1988 to 22 August 2000 on the Dow Jones and the US 3-month Treasury Bill rate.

(a) Plot the Dow Jones index and the percentage log returns and hence reproduce Figures 1 and 2 of the original paper and comment on any volatility clustering.

(b) Plot the correlogram of returns and squared returns for 20 lags and hence reproduce Figure 3 of the paper. Is there any significant dependence in squared returns?

(c) Compute the daily mean, variance, skewness, and kurtosis of the Dow Jones returns. Compute annualized volatility based on the assumption that there are 252 working days in a year. Comment on the results.

(d) Estimate a GARCH(1,1) for the Dow Jones returns and comment on the results. From the estimated conditional variance, compute and plot the annualized conditional volatility and hence reproduce Figure 4 of the paper.

(e) Estimate a TARCH model and compare and contrast the results with those reported in Table 4 of the paper. Are the results compatible with the conclusion that negative innovations have a greater impact on the conditional variance than positive innovations?

(f) Is the lagged level of the centered, 3-month US Treasury Bill important for modeling conditional volatility in a simple GARCH(1,1) framework?

(g) Use the updated data set that has observations on the Dow Jones and the US 3-month Treasury Bill rate from 23 August 1988 to 1 August 2017. Repeat parts (a)–(f) and compare and contrast your results with those obtained for the original data set.

3. GARCH Models of Global Equity Markets

> equities.*

The data file contains data from 29 July 2004 to 3 March 2009 on the Euro 50, FTSE 100, and S&P 500 equity price indices.

(a) Choose an equity market and plot the daily log return and the squared daily log return, and comment on the time series properties of these series.

(b) For the chosen equity market, estimate the GARCH(1,1) model

$$r_t = \mu_0 + u_t$$
$$h_t = \alpha_0 + \alpha_1 u_{t-1}^2 + \beta_1 h_{t-1}$$
$$u_t \sim N(0, h_t).$$

Comment on the parameter estimates of the model. Use the model to estimate the unconditional variance $h = \alpha_0/(1 - \alpha_1 - \beta_1)$, and compare this estimate with the variance of r_t.

(c) For the chosen equity market, estimate the GARCH-M model

$$r_t = \mu_0 + \mu_1 h_t + u_t$$
$$h_t = \alpha_0 + \alpha_1 u_{t-1}^2 + \beta_1 h_{t-1}$$
$$u_t \sim N(0, h_t),$$

where μ_1 represents the relative risk aversion parameter (Merton, 1973). Interpret the estimate of μ_1.

(d) The estimated models in parts (b) and (c) are based on the assumption that the GARCH conditional variance is specified correctly. Examine the appropriateness of this assumption by testing the standardized residuals for ARCH effects.

(e) Repeat parts (a) to (d) for a different equity market.

4. Time-varying Volatility in Asian Equity Markets

> hangseng.*, kospi.*, sse.*, szs,.* topix.*

The data files contain daily equity log returns on 5 Asian equity markets: the Hang Seng in Hong Kong, the KOSPI in Korea, the SSE and SZS in China, and the TOPIX in Japan. The Hang Seng and the two Chinese indices start 2 January 1996, the KOSPI starts 8 January and the Topix starts 4 January. All data end on 16 May 2017.

(a) Consider the autoregressive model

$$r_t = \mu_0 + \mu_1 r_{t-1} + u_t,$$

where r_t is the daily log return, and u_t is a disturbance term. Estimate this model for the Hang Seng and test for the presence of autocorrelation in equity returns by testing the restriction $\mu_1 = 0$.

(b) The model in part (a) assumes the disturbance u_t has a constant variance. Re-estimate this model for the Hang Seng index by assuming a TARCH$(1,1)$ conditional variance using the specification

$$r_t = \mu_0 + \mu_1 r_{t-1} + u_t$$
$$h_t = \alpha_0 + \alpha_1 u_{t-1}^2 + \beta_1 h_{t-1} + \lambda u_{t-1}^2 I_{t-1}$$
$$I_{t-1} = \begin{cases} 1 : u_{t-1} \geqslant 0 \\ 0 : u_{t-1} < 0 \end{cases}$$
$$u_t \sim N(0, h_t).$$

Retest for the presence of autocorrelation in equity returns by testing the restriction $\mu_1 = 0$ and compare the outcome of this test with the result obtained in part (a).

(c) Replace the normal distribution in part (b) by the t distribution and hence estimate the model

$$r_t = \mu_0 + \mu_1 r_{t-1} + u_t$$
$$h_t = \alpha_0 + \alpha_1 u_{t-1}^2 + \beta_1 h_{t-1} + \lambda u_{t-1}^2 I_{t-1}$$
$$I_{t-1} = \begin{cases} 1 : u_{t-1} \geqslant 0 \\ 0 : u_{t-1} < 0 \end{cases}$$
$$u_t \sim St(0, h_t, v),$$

where v is the degrees of freedom parameter. Redo the test for autocorrelation by testing the restriction $\mu_1 = 0$, and compare the outcome of the test with the results obtained in parts (a) and (b).

(d) Assess the estimated volatility model in part (c) by estimating the Mincer–Zarnowitz forecast regression equation

$$r_t^2 = \delta_0 + \delta_1 \widehat{h_t} + e_t,$$

where $\widehat{h_t}$ is the estimated conditional variance obtained in part (c), and e_t is a disturbance term. Test the joint restrictions $\delta_0 = 0$ and $\delta_1 = 1$ and interpret the outcome of the test.

(e) Repeat parts (a) to (d) for the other Asian stock market indices. Compare and contrast the results across the 5 indices.

5. **Value at Risk (VaR)**

techstocks.*

The data are daily equity prices from 13 March 1986 to 17 March 2017, on the S&P 500 index and 4 US technology stocks, namely, Apple, IBM, Intel, and Microsoft.

(a) For IBM estimate the constant mean model

$$r_t = \mu_0 + u_t$$
$$u_t \sim N(0, h),$$

where r_t is the daily percentage log return and u_t is a disturbance term. For a portfolio valued at \$1,000,000, compute the 1-day VaR with a maximum loss probability of 1% using

$$VaR = \mu_0 - 2.33\sqrt{h}.$$

Note that VaR is expressed in percentage terms as returns are defined in percentages.

(b) For IBM estimate the GARCH(1,1) model

$$r_t = \mu_0 + u_t$$
$$h_t = \alpha_0 + \alpha_1 u_{t-1}^2 + \beta_1 h_{t-1}$$
$$u_t \sim N(0, h_t).$$

Recompute the VaR in part (a) choosing the disturbance variance as follows

(i) The unconditional variance $\bar{h} = \alpha_0/(1 - \alpha_1 - \beta_1)$.
(ii) The conditional variance on 17 March 2017, $h_T = \alpha_0 + \alpha_1 u_{T-1}^2 + \beta_1 h_{T-1}$.
(iii) The 1-day ahead forecast of the conditional variance, $h_{T+1|T} = \alpha_0 + \alpha_1 u_T^2 + \beta_1 h_T$.

(c) Repeat parts (a) and (b) for the technology stocks Intel and Microsoft, as well as for the S&P 500.

(d) Repeat parts (a) and (b) for Apple, except define the mean equation as

$$r_t = \mu_0 + \mu_1 d_t + u_t,$$

where d_t is a dummy variable to capture the large fall in the price of Apple stock on 9 June 2014 resulting from a stock split

$$d_t = \begin{cases} 1 : 9 \text{ June } 2014 \\ 0 : \text{otherwise} \end{cases}.$$

6. **Heatwaves and Meteor Showers**

> stockindices.*

The data are daily equity prices from 4 January 1999 to 2 April 2014, on the Dow, DAX, FTSE, Hang Seng, Nikkei, and S&P 500 indices.

(a) Compute the percentage log returns on the DAX, Nikkei, and S&P 500 indices. Compute descriptive statistics for the three returns and discuss the results.

(b) Estimate the following GARCH(1,1) model for the centered returns on the Nikkei index

$$r_{1t} - \bar{r}_1 = u_{1t}$$
$$h_{11t} = \alpha_{10} + \alpha_{11} u_{1t-1}^2 + \beta_{11} h_{11t-1} + \alpha_{12} u_{2t-1}^2 + \alpha_{13} u_{3t-1}^2,$$

where $u_{2t-1}^2 = (r_{2t-1} - \bar{r}_2)^2$ and $u_{3t-1}^2 = (r_{3t-1} - \bar{r}_3)^2$ are, respectively, the lagged centered squared returns on the DAX and the S&P 500, which are treated as predetermined variables.

(c) Estimate the following GARCH(1,1) model for the centered returns on the DAX index

$$r_{2t} - \bar{r}_2 = u_{2t}$$
$$h_{22t} = \alpha_{20} + \alpha_1 u_{2t-1}^2 + \beta_{22} h_{22t-1} + \delta_{21} u_{1t}^2 + \alpha_{23} u_{3t-1}^2,$$

where $u_{1t}^2 = (r_{1t} - \bar{r}_1)^2$ is the squared centered returns on the Nikkei, and $u_{3t-1}^2 = (r_{3t-1} - \bar{r}_3)^2$ are the lagged centered squared returns on the S&P 500, which are treated as predetermined variables.

(d) Estimate the following GARCH(1,1) model for the centered returns on the S&P 500 index

$$r_{3t} - \bar{r}_3 = u_{3t}$$
$$h_{3t} = \alpha_{30} + \alpha_1 u_{3t-1}^2 + \beta_{33} h_{3t-1} + \delta_{31} u_{1t}^2 + \delta_{32} u_{2t}^2,$$

where $u_{1t}^2 = (r_{1t} - \bar{r}_1)^2$ and $u_{2t}^2 = (r_{1t} - \bar{r}_1)^2$ are, respectively, the lagged squared centered returns on the Nikkei and the DAX.

(e) Discuss the results in parts (b) to (d) in terms of heatwaves and meteor showers in volatility patterns between Japan, Europe, and the United States.

CHAPTER 14

Multivariate GARCH Models

I nvesting in financial securities is risky because of the inherent variability of future returns. Chapter 13 deals with modeling the time-varying variance of an individual asset, which directly impacts the risk of that asset. But understanding the co-movements of several financial returns and the extent of their individual risks is also of great practical importance, as investment decisions by firms and individuals rely on making assessments of the risks across different assets.

Asset pricing depends on the variances and covariances of the asset returns in a portfolio of financial assets. Risk management and asset allocation correspondingly requires updating optimal hedging positions in accordance with risk characteristics. These decisions in turn depend on variances and covariances of returns. In addition, forecasts of conditional covariance matrices of financial returns influence how large portfolios are managed in investment funds.[1] It follows, therefore, that specifying, estimating, and forecasting multivariate models of the conditional covariance matrix of a portfolio of assets are all matters of particular interest to the financial industry.

Let r_t denote a vector of N log returns, $r_t = \{r_{1t}, r_{2t}, \cdots, r_{Nt}\}$. The fundamental multivariate time-varying conditional covariance model addressed in this chapter is

$$r_t = E_{t-1}(r_t) + u_t$$
$$H_t = E_{t-1}(u_t u_t'),$$

where $u_t = \{u_{1t}, u_{2t}, \cdots, u_{Nt}\}'$ is a vector of disturbances, and H_t is the $(N \times N)$ conditional covariance matrix of u_t. The natural approach to modeling a time-varying conditional covariance matrix is to extend the univariate GARCH framework to a multivariate version in which both variances and covariances are allowed to be time-varying. In addition to multivariate GARCH (MGARCH) models, more recent developments focusing on the dynamics of the correlations among assets will be discussed.

---

[1] A 2012 survey of 139 North American investment managers representing $12 trillion worth of assets under management reported that the majority of managers use volatility and correlation forecasts to construct equity portfolios (Amenc et al., 2012).

14.1 MOTIVATION

Time-Varying β-risk

In Chapter 3 the β-risk of asset i is defined as

$$\begin{aligned}
\beta &= \frac{\text{cov}(r_{it} - r_{ft}, r_{mt} - r_{ft})}{\text{var}(r_{mt} - r_{ft})} \\
&= \frac{E[(r_{it} - r_{ft} - E[r_{it} - r_{ft}])(r_{mt} - r_{ft} - E[r_{mt} - r_{ft}])]}{E[(r_{mt} - r_{ft} - E[r_{mt} - r_{ft}])^2]},
\end{aligned} \tag{14.1}$$

where $r_{it} - r_{ft}$ is the excess return on the asset relative to the risk-free rate given by r_{ft}, and $r_{mt} - r_{ft}$ is the corresponding excess return on the market portfolio. The measure of β-risk by definition is constant, as it is based on the ratio of the unconditional covariance in the numerator between the excess returns on the asset and the market excess returns to the unconditional variance in the denominator of the market excess returns.

The restriction of constant β-risk may be unrealistic for practical work. Consequently, it is desirable to be able to relax this restriction and allow β-risk to be time-varying. This is formally achieved by replacing the unconditional expectations in equation (14.1) by the conditional expectations, resulting in the following specification of time-varying β-risk

$$\beta_t = \frac{E_{t-1}[(r_{it} - r_{ft} - E_{t-1}[r_{it} - r_{ft}])(r_{mt} - r_{ft} - E_{t-1}[r_{mt} - r_{ft}])]}{E_{t-1}[(r_{mt} - r_{ft} - E_{t-1}[r_{mt} - r_{ft}])^2]}, \tag{14.2}$$

where the numerator is the conditional covariance between the excess returns on the ith asset and the market based on information at time $t - 1$, and the denominator is the conditional variance of the market excess return. To operationalize the estimate of β_t in equation (14.2) it is necessary to specify models of the conditional variance and covariance. From Chapter 13 the GARCH model provides a suitable specification of the conditional variance of the excess returns on the market portfolio. But to specify a time-varying conditional covariance, it is necessary to formulate a bivariate volatility model in which conditional variances of the constituent assets and their conditional covariance are all modeled simultaneously.

Time-varying Portfolio Weights

Consider a portfolio containing $N = 2$ assets with log returns r_{1t} and r_{2t}. The optimal weights of the minimum variance portfolio from Chapter 3 are

$$w_1 = \frac{\text{var}(r_{2t}) - \text{cov}(r_{1t}, r_{2t})}{\text{var}(r_{1t}) + \text{var}(r_{2t}) - 2\,\text{cov}(r_{1t}, r_{2t})}, \quad w_2 = 1 - w_1, \tag{14.3}$$

where w_1 is the optimal weight allocated to asset 1 in the portfolio, and w_2 is the corresponding weight on asset 2. The weights w_1 and w_2 are assumed to be constant over time, as they are a function of the two unconditional variances and the unconditional covariance.

Restricting the portfolio weights to be constant suggests that there is no need to rebalance the portfolio to account for financial shocks. To relax this assumption and allow for time-varying portfolio weights, the unconditional expectations in equation (14.3) are replaced by conditional expectations. As with the time-varying model of β-risk, the conditional variances can be modeled using the GARCH specifications discussed in Chapter 13, whereas the conditional covariance is modeled by specifying a bivariate volatility model of the two log returns.

Value at Risk with Multiple Positions

Consider an equal weighted portfolio of $N = 2$ assets with respective returns r_{1t} and r_{2t}. The 1-day value at risk of the portfolio is

$$VaR = \sqrt{VaR_1^2 + VaR_2^2 + 2\rho VaR_1 VaR_2}, \qquad (14.4)$$

where VaR_i is the value at risk of asset i and

$$\rho = \frac{\text{cov}(r_{1t}, r_{2t})}{\sqrt{\text{var}(r_{1t}) \text{var}(r_{2t})}}$$

is the correlation between r_{1t} and r_{2t}. The maximum loss on the portfolio with a probability of 1% is

$$VaR_i = E(r_{it}) - 2.33\sqrt{\text{var}(r_{it})}, \quad i = 1, 2.$$

As the variances $\text{var}(r_{1t})$ and $\text{var}(r_{2t})$ and the correlation are all unconditional measures, the value at risk of the portfolio is restricted to be constant over time.

The restriction of a constant value at risk is likely to be invalid during periods of financial stress where the volatility of asset returns can be much higher than usual. To allow for a more accurate measure of the value at risk of the portfolio over time, and in particular during financial crises, the unconditional variances in equation (14.4) can be replaced by conditional variances using GARCH models. To allow for the correlation to be time-varying a bivariate volatility model is specified.

14.2 EARLY COVARIANCE ESTIMATORS

One approach to modeling multivariate volatility would be to construct multivariate versions of the historical variance and the exponentially weighted moving average estimate discussed in Chapter 13. If the asset log returns are collected into the vector $r_t = [r_{1t}\ r_{2t}\ r_{3t}\ \cdots\ r_{Nt}]'$, which for convenience is assumed to be re-centered by subtracting the respective sample means from the return vector, then the resulting measures are conditional sample covariance matrices.

Historical

The multivariate version of the historical estimate of the conditional covariance matrix of r_t is the sample moment matrix

$$H_t = \frac{1}{M} \sum_{j=1}^{M} r_{t-j} r_{t-j}'.$$

So the covariance matrix at time t is given as the sum of the outer products of the past log returns vector r_t calculated from the immediately preceding data point $t - 1$ going as far back as M. For daily data a typical choice of the window parameter M is 22, which corresponds to the number of trading days within a month, or 252, which is the number of trading days in a year. Setting $M = T$ results in a sample estimate of the unconditional covariance matrix, as it is based on the full observed sample. The forecast of volatility for k-periods ahead is simply given by the current value H_t irrespective of the value of the forecast horizon k.

Exponentially Weighted Moving Average

The multivariate version of the exponentially weighted moving average estimate of the conditional covariance matrix is

$$
\begin{aligned}
H_t &= (1-\lambda)\sum_{j=0}^{\infty}\lambda^j r_{t-j-1}r'_{t-j-1} \\
&= (1-\lambda)r_{t-1}r'_{t-1} + (1-\lambda)\left[\lambda r_{t-2}r'_{t-2} + \lambda^2 r_{t-3}r'_{t-3} + \cdots\right] \\
&= (1-\lambda)r_{t-1}r'_{t-1} + (1-\lambda)\lambda\left[r_{t-2}r'_{t-2} + \lambda r_{t-3}r'_{t-3} + \cdots\right] \\
&= (1-\lambda)r_{t-1}r'_{t-1} + \lambda H_{t-1},
\end{aligned}
$$

where λ represents the delay parameter. The delay parameter is similar to the parameter on the lagged conditional variance in the GARCH model discussed in Chapter 13, and thus controls the persistence in the system.

Constant Correlation Model

To capture time variation in the conditional covariance between two assets, the correlation

$$
\rho = \frac{\mathrm{cov}(r_{1t}, r_{2t})}{\sqrt{\mathrm{var}(r_{1t})}\sqrt{\mathrm{var}(r_{2t})}}, \tag{14.5}
$$

is arranged to give an expression for the covariance as

$$
\mathrm{cov}(r_{1t}, r_{2t}) = \rho\sqrt{\mathrm{var}(r_{1t})}\sqrt{\mathrm{var}(r_{2t})}. \tag{14.6}
$$

This expression shows that the covariance is the product of the constant correlation, ρ, and the two standard deviations, $\sqrt{\mathrm{var}(r_{1t})}$ and $\sqrt{\mathrm{var}(r_{2t})}$. This expression suggests that a time-varying covariance can be constructed by simply replacing the unconditional variances, $\mathrm{var}(r_{1t})$ and $\mathrm{var}(r_{2t})$, by their respective conditional variances based on univariate GARCH models and ρ is estimated using the sample correlation coefficient.

To illustrate the implementation of the constant correlation model, consider monthly log returns on Microsoft and the S&P 500 index for the period April 1990 to July 2004. Figure 14.1 gives the estimated GARCH(1,1) conditional variances for the two assets in the top panels. The estimate of the conditional covariance, given in the bottom panel, uses equation (14.6) with the correlation estimated to be $\widehat{\rho} = 0.5804$. Although this is a very simple approach, the major insight it provides has proved important in developing workable multivariate GARCH models. It is apparent that the conditional variances change over the sample, with Microsoft showing a marked increase in volatility at the time of the dot-com bubble in the early 2000s. Figure 14.1 also shows that the covariance and the variance of the market tend to decrease in step with each other in the first half of the sample, but appear to be out of alignment in the second half of the sample.

Using the conditional variance and covariance estimates reported in Figure 14.1, estimates of time-varying β-risk are plotted in Figure 14.2, together with the constant

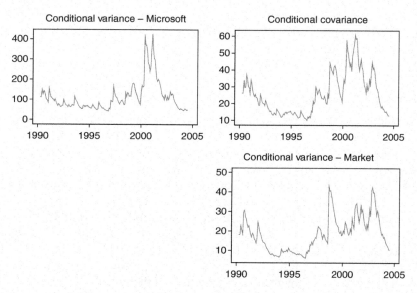

FIGURE 14.1 Conditional variances and covariance of Microsoft and the S&P 500 (market) index. The data are monthly from April 1990 to July 2004.

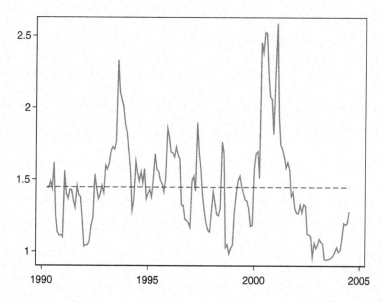

FIGURE 14.2 Estimated trajectory of time-varying β-risk for Microsoft based on the assumption of a constant correlation between Microsoft and the S&P 500 index. The constant β-risk estimated from a CAPM model of 1.447 is shown as the dashed line. The data are monthly from April 1990 to July 2004.

estimate of β-risk. There are some very large changes in the β-risk of Microsoft, ranging from around 0.2 at the end of 1995 to nearly 2.5 at the time of the dot-com bubble in early 2000. The sample average of the time-varying β-risk estimates is 1.196, which is a little lower than the estimated constant β-risk of 1.447.

14.3 THE BEKK MODEL

The conditional covariance estimators proposed thus far are based on the imposition of very strong restrictions on the parameters of the model. For the exponentially weighted moving average covariance estimator, there is a single parameter controlling the dynamics of all the conditional variances and covariances. Alternatively, for the conditional covariance estimator in equation (14.6), the correlation between the asset returns is restricted to be constant. To relax these restrictions when constructing conditional covariance estimators while still capturing the key features and flexibility of the univariate GARCH variance models discussed in Chapter 13, the multivariate GARCH model known as the BEKK model, due to Engle and Kroner (1995), is now presented.

Consider a set of N log returns $r_t = [r_{1t}\, r_{2t}\, r_{3t} \cdots r_{Nt}]'$. A time-varying estimate of the conditional covariance matrix requires construction of the matrix

$$H_t = \begin{bmatrix} h_{11t} & h_{12t} & \cdots & h_{1Nt} \\ h_{21t} & h_{22t} & \cdots & h_{2Nt} \\ \vdots & \vdots & \ddots & \vdots \\ h_{N1t} & h_{N2t} & \cdots & h_{NNt} \end{bmatrix}. \tag{14.7}$$

The conditional variances are located down the main diagonal, which are now defined as h_{iit}. The conditional covariances are located in the off-diagonal terms, which satisfy the symmetry restriction $h_{ijt} = h_{jit}$. In total there are $N(N+1)/2$ unique elements in H_t. In specifying a multivariate model of volatility an appropriate specification of H_t needs to preserve the property that it is positive definite. For a bivariate model with $N = 2$ in equation (14.7), the conditions for positive definiteness are

$$h_{11t} > 0$$
$$h_{11t}h_{22t} - h_{12t}^2 > 0.$$

The first requirement is that the conditional variance of r_{1t} is positive, a condition discussed already in Chapter 13 when specifying a GARCH model. The second condition is more involved. It requires the product interaction of the two conditional variances to exceed the square of the conditional covariance at each point in time t. A simple interpretation of this condition is

$$-1 < \frac{h_{12t}}{\sqrt{h_{11t}h_{22t}}} < 1,$$

giving the standard range condition on the correlation coefficient between r_{1t} and r_{2t}. Ensuring that this condition is satisfied at each t is not straightforward and becomes more difficult as the dimension N grows.

14.3.1 Specification

The first class of multivariate GARCH models satisfying the positive definiteness property while still being flexible enough to capture the dynamics of volatility and co-volatility over time is the BEKK model.[2] The BEKK model is a multidimensional analogue of the univariate GARCH model. Letting H_t be the conditional covariance matrix defined in equation (14.7) and u_t be the vector of disturbances, the BEKK specification for an MGARCH(1,1) model has the form

$$H_t = CC' + A u_{t-1} u'_{t-1} A' + B H_{t-1} B', \tag{14.8}$$

where C is an $(N \times N)$ lower triangular matrix of unknown parameters, and A and B are $(N \times N)$ matrices each containing N^2 unknown parameters associated with the lagged disturbances and the lagged conditional covariance matrix, respectively.

There are three different forms of the BEKK model, each of which is now presented for the bivariate case ($N = 2$).

(i) Asymmetric BEKK Model
    The parameter matrices are

$$C = \begin{bmatrix} c_{11} & 0 \\ c_{21} & c_{22} \end{bmatrix}, \quad A = \begin{bmatrix} a_{11} & a_{12} \\ a_{21} & a_{22} \end{bmatrix}, \quad B = \begin{bmatrix} b_{11} & b_{12} \\ b_{21} & b_{22} \end{bmatrix}.$$

This is the most general form of the BEKK model.

(ii) Symmetric BEKK Model
    The restrictions $a_{12} = a_{21}$ and $b_{12} = b_{21}$ are imposed so

$$C = \begin{bmatrix} c_{11} & 0 \\ c_{21} & c_{22} \end{bmatrix}, \quad A = \begin{bmatrix} a_{11} & a_{12} \\ a_{12} & a_{22} \end{bmatrix}, \quad B = \begin{bmatrix} b_{11} & b_{12} \\ b_{12} & b_{22} \end{bmatrix}.$$

(iii) Diagonal BEKK Model
    The restrictions $a_{12} = a_{21} = 0$ and $b_{12} = b_{21} = 0$ are imposed so

$$C = \begin{bmatrix} c_{11} & 0 \\ c_{21} & c_{22} \end{bmatrix}, \quad A = \begin{bmatrix} a_{11} & 0 \\ 0 & a_{22} \end{bmatrix}, \quad B = \begin{bmatrix} b_{11} & 0 \\ 0 & b_{22} \end{bmatrix}.$$

A special case of the BEKK model is where there is a single variable ($N = 1$), so the parameter matrices become scalars

$$C = [\, c_{11} \,], \quad A = [\, a_{11} \,], \quad B = [\, b_{11} \,].$$

The conditional covariance matrix now reduces to a scalar given by

$$H_t = h_{11t} = c_{11}^2 + a_{11}^2 u_{t-1}^2 + b_{11}^2 h_{11\,t-1},$$

which is the univariate GARCH(1,1) model discussed earlier but with the parameters now constrained to be positive. For the multivariate case with $N > 1$, equation (14.8) represents an application of the Cholesky decomposition (the matrix square root operator) discussed in Chapter 4.

---

[2] A multivariate GARCH model predating the BEKK model is the VECH model. This model is rarely used in practice because enforcing the positive definiteness condition on the conditional covariance matrix is difficult to achieve.

14.3.2 Estimation

Following the methods introduced in Chapter 10, for a sample of $t = 1, 2, \ldots, T$ observations, the log likelihood function of a multivariate GARCH model is given by

$$\log L = \frac{1}{T} \sum_{t=1}^{T} \log L_t = \frac{1}{T} \sum_{t=1}^{T} \log f(r_{1t}, r_{2t}, \cdots, r_{N,t}; \theta), \tag{14.9}$$

where $f(r_{1t}, r_{2t}, \cdots, r_{Nt}; \theta)$ is an N-dimensional conditional multivariate probability distribution, with the explicit conditioning suppressed for ease of notation, and θ is the vector of unknown parameters. To implement estimation by maximum likelihood methods, it is necessary to specify the functional form of the N-dimensional probability distribution. There are two popular choices in empirical applications.

1. **Multivariate normal distribution**

    The multivariate normal distribution is given by

    $$f(r_{1t}, r_{2t}, \cdots, r_{Nt}; \theta) = \left(\frac{1}{2\pi}\right)^{N/2} |H_t|^{-1/2} \exp\left(-0.5\, u_t' H_t^{-1} u_t\right),$$

    with the log likelihood function at time t taking the form

    $$\log L_t = \log f(r_{1t}, r_{2t}, \cdots, r_{Nt}; \theta)$$
    $$= -\frac{N}{2} \log(2\pi) - \frac{1}{2} \log|H_t| - \frac{1}{2} u_t' H_t^{-1} u_t. \tag{14.10}$$

2. **Standardized multivariate t distribution**

    The multivariate standardized t distribution is given by

    $$f(r_{1t}, r_{2t}, \cdots, r_{Nt}; \theta) = \frac{\Gamma\left(\frac{\nu+N}{2}\right)}{(\pi\,(\nu-2))^{N/2}\,\Gamma\left(\frac{\nu}{2}\right)}$$
    $$\times |H_t|^{-1/2} \left(1 + \frac{u_t' H_t^{-1} u_t}{\nu - 2}\right)^{-\left(\frac{\nu+N}{2}\right)},$$

    and the log likelihood function at time t takes the form

    $$\log L_t = \log f(r_{1t}, r_{2t}, \cdots, r_{Nt}; \theta)$$
    $$= \log \Gamma\left(\frac{\nu+N}{2}\right) - \frac{N}{2} \log(\pi\,(\nu-2)) - \log \Gamma\left(\frac{\nu}{2}\right)$$
    $$- \frac{1}{2} \log|H_t| - \left(\frac{\nu+N}{2}\right)\left(1 + \frac{u_t' H_t^{-1} u_t}{\nu - 2}\right). \tag{14.11}$$

    The parameter ν is the degrees of freedom parameter, and smaller values of ν represent heavier tails in the distribution. As $\nu \to \infty$, the multivariate standardized t distribution approaches the multivariate normal distribution.

In the log likelihood functions in equations (14.10) and (14.11), the disturbance vector is specified as

$$u_t = r_t - \mu,$$

in which r_t is an $(N \times 1)$ vector of log returns, μ is an $(N \times 1)$ vector of means, and H_t is the conditional covariance matrix. These log likelihood functions are maximized using an iterative optimization algorithm.

Consider estimating a bivariate diagonal BEKK model for the percentage excess returns to Microsoft, r_{1t}, and the S&P 500 index, r_{2t}, used in Section 14.1. The model is given by

$$r_{1t} = \mu_1 + u_{1t}$$

$$r_{2t} = \mu_2 + u_{2t},$$

with

$$u_t = \begin{bmatrix} u_{1t} \\ u_{2t} \end{bmatrix} \sim N(0, H_t)$$

$$H_t = \begin{bmatrix} h_{11t} & h_{12t} \\ h_{12t} & h_{22t} \end{bmatrix} = CC' + Au_{t-1}u'_{t-1}A' + BH_{t-1}B'$$

$$C = \begin{bmatrix} c_{11} & 0 \\ c_{21} & c_{22} \end{bmatrix}, \quad A = \begin{bmatrix} a_{11} & 0 \\ 0 & a_{22} \end{bmatrix}, \quad B = \begin{bmatrix} b_{11} & 0 \\ 0 & b_{22} \end{bmatrix}.$$

The maximum likelihood parameter estimates of the bivariate BEKK model using a log-likelihood function based on the normal distribution are

$$r_{1t} = 2.170 + \widehat{u}_{1t}$$

$$r_{2t} = 0.454 + \widehat{u}_{2t},$$

with estimated conditional covariance matrix, $\widehat{H}_t$, given by

$$\begin{bmatrix} \widehat{h}_{11t} & \widehat{h}_{12t} \\ \widehat{h}_{12t} & \widehat{h}_{22t} \end{bmatrix} = \begin{bmatrix} 9.784 & 0.000 \\ 1.279 & 0.795 \end{bmatrix} \begin{bmatrix} 9.784 & 1.279 \\ 0.000 & 0.795 \end{bmatrix}$$

$$+ \begin{bmatrix} 0.365 & 0.000 \\ 0.000 & 0.248 \end{bmatrix} \begin{bmatrix} \widehat{u}^2_{1t-1} & \widehat{u}_{1t-1}\widehat{u}_{2t-1} \\ \widehat{u}_{2t-1}\widehat{u}_{1t-1} & \widehat{u}^2_{2t-1} \end{bmatrix} \begin{bmatrix} 0.365 & 0.000 \\ 0.000 & 0.248 \end{bmatrix}$$

$$+ \begin{bmatrix} 0.875 & 0.000 \\ 0.000 & 0.941 \end{bmatrix} \begin{bmatrix} \widehat{h}_{11t-1} & \widehat{h}_{12t-1} \\ \widehat{h}_{12t-1} & \widehat{h}_{22t-1} \end{bmatrix} \begin{bmatrix} 0.875 & 0.000 \\ 0.000 & 0.941 \end{bmatrix}.$$

Figure 14.3 plots the time-varying conditional covariance between the excess returns on the market and Microsoft and the associated time-varying estimate of β-risk computed as $\widehat{h}_{12t}/\widehat{h}_{22t}$. These results should be compared with those in Figures 14.1 and 14.2, which were generated using the constant correlation assumption. The BEKK results produce a much steeper fall in the conditional covariance at the beginning of the sample than do the earlier constant correlation results. This major difference causes the time variation in β-risk to be quite different in the first half of the sample period. However, during the second half of the period, the impact of the dot-com bubble is manifest in the sharp increase in β-risk of Microsoft and this effect is common to both sets of results.

14.4 THE DCC MODEL

One of the drawbacks of the BEKK model is that it is difficult to apply to models containing multiple assets. In the case of a model with just $N = 3$ assets, the total number of unknown parameters of the asymmetric BEKK model in the matrices C, A, and B is $6 + 9 + 9 = 24$. The number of parameters rises quickly to $10 + 16 + 16 = 42$ for a

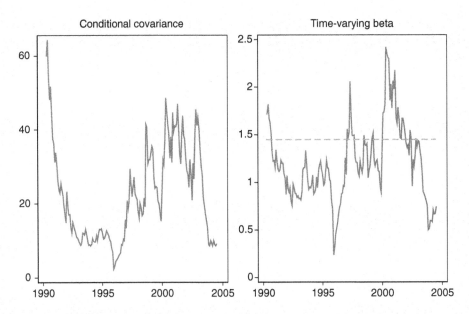

FIGURE 14.3 Trajectories of the time-varying covariance and associated time-varying beta estimated using a diagonal BEKK model for the percentage excess returns to Microsoft and the S&P 500 index. The data are monthly from April 1990 to July 2004.

model with $N = 4$ assets and to $15 + 25 + 25 = 65$ for $N = 5$ assets. This proliferation in parameters means that in practical work the BEKK model is effectively restricted to portfolios in which N is not too large, typically $N < 10$.

A solution to this parameter dimensionality problem was proposed by Engle (2002) using a different model specification known as the dynamic conditional correlation (DCC) model. This model is now one of the most widely adopted MGARCH specifications in empirical work.

14.4.1 Specification

The DCC model is based on specifying the conditional covariance matrix as

$$H_t = S_t R_t S_t, \tag{14.12}$$

where R_t is an $(N \times N)$ conditional correlation matrix, and S_t is a diagonal matrix containing the conditional standard deviations

$$S_t = \begin{bmatrix} \sqrt{h_{11t}} & & 0 \\ & \ddots & \\ 0 & & \sqrt{h_{NNt}} \end{bmatrix}. \tag{14.13}$$

This expression is the multivariate analogue of equation (14.6) in which the covariance between two assets is constructed from the product of the correlation and the two standard deviations. For the DCC model, the conditional variances are assumed to have univariate GARCH representations of the form

$$h_{iit} = \alpha_{i0} + \alpha_{i1}u^2_{it-1} + \beta_{i1}h_{iit-1}, \qquad i = 1, 2, \cdots N. \qquad (14.14)$$

The conditional correlation matrix R_t in equation (14.12) is defined as[3]

$$R_t = \text{diag}(Q_t)^{-1/2} Q_t \text{diag}(Q_t)^{-1/2}. \qquad (14.15)$$

The matrix Q_t represents a pseudo correlation matrix that has a GARCH(1,1) specification

$$Q_t = (1 - \alpha - \beta)Q + \alpha z_{t-1}z'_{t-1} + \beta Q_{t-1}, \qquad (14.16)$$

with unknown scalar parameters α and β, and $z_{it} = u_{it}/\sqrt{h_{it}}$ is a standardized disturbance. The definition of the intercept in the dynamics of Q_t as $(1 - \alpha - \beta)Q$ simplifies estimation because the intercept no longer has to be estimated separately. The matrix Q is the unconditional second moment matrix of standardized disturbances given by

$$Q = \frac{1}{T}\sum_{t=1}^{T} \begin{bmatrix} z^2_{1t} & z_{1t}z_{2t} & \cdots & z_{1t}z_{Nt} \\ z_{2t}z_{1t} & z^2_{2t} & \cdots & z_{2t}z_{Nt} \\ \vdots & \vdots & \ddots & \vdots \\ z_{Nt}z_{1t} & z_{Nt}z_{2t} & \cdots & z^2_{Nt} \end{bmatrix}. \qquad (14.17)$$

A special case of the DCC model is the constant correlation model (CCC) that arises when $\alpha = \beta = 0$, resulting in $Q_t = Q$ and $R_t = R$. In practice, the CCC model is estimated by specifying the covariance as

$$h_{ijt} = \rho_{ij}\sqrt{h_{iit}h_{jjt}}, \qquad (14.18)$$

where ρ_{ij} is the correlation coefficient and is treated as an additional parameter. There are no tests of constancy of correlations directly against the DCC model because the DCC model is only identified if correlations are changing (see Silvennoinen and Teräsvirta, 2009).

A variation of the DCC model that facilitates dealing with even larger portfolios of assets than the DCC model is the dynamic equicorrelation (DECO) model of Engle and Kelly (2009). The important limiting assumption required to achieve this greater flexibility is that the unconditional correlation matrix of financial returns has correlations that are equal across all N assets but not over time, as in the matrix

$$R_t = \begin{bmatrix} 1 & r_{12t} & \cdots & r_{1Nt} \\ r_{21t} & 1 & \cdots & \vdots \\ \vdots & \vdots & \ddots & r_{N-1Nt} \\ r_{N1t} & \cdots & r_{NN-1t} & 1 \end{bmatrix} = \begin{bmatrix} 1 & r_t & \cdots & r_t \\ r_t & 1 & \cdots & \vdots \\ \vdots & \vdots & \ddots & r_t \\ r_t & \cdots & r_t & 1 \end{bmatrix}.$$

By imposing this restriction on the correlation matrix the computation of the log-likelihood function is greatly simplified, making estimation of the unknown parameters feasible even for large numbers of assets.

---

[3] An alternative specification for the evolution of the correlation matrix, R_t, is provided by the varying correlation model (VCC) of Tse and Tsui (2002).

14.4.2 Estimation

The unknown parameters of the DCC multivariate GARCH model consist of the univariate GARCH parameters of the conditional variance equation (14.14) and the parameters α and β in equation (14.16). Estimation is based on maximum likelihood methods using the log likelihood in equation (14.9) but with the BEKK conditional covariance matrix in equation (14.8) replaced by the DCC conditional covariance matrix in equation (14.12).

To demonstrate the steps involved in computing the parameter estimates of the DCC model consider the case of $N = 2$ assets. Given starting values for the parameters $\theta = \{\alpha_{10}, \alpha_{11}, \beta_{11}, \alpha_{20}, \alpha_{21}, \beta_{21}, \alpha, \beta\}$, the steps required are as follows.

(i) Generate the conditional variances h_{11t} and h_{22t} from the univariate GARCH(1, 1) models

$$h_{11t} = \alpha_{10} + \alpha_{11} u_{1t-1}^2 + \beta_{11} h_{11t-1}$$
$$h_{22t} = \alpha_{20} + \alpha_{21} u_{2t-1}^2 + \beta_{21} h_{22t-1}.$$

(ii) Construct the standard deviation matrix

$$S_t = \begin{bmatrix} \sqrt{h_{11t}} & 0 \\ 0 & \sqrt{h_{22t}} \end{bmatrix}.$$

(iii) Compute the standardized residuals

$$\begin{bmatrix} z_{1t} \\ z_{2t} \end{bmatrix} = S_t^{-1} u_t = \begin{bmatrix} \dfrac{1}{\sqrt{h_{11t}}} & 0 \\ 0 & \dfrac{1}{\sqrt{h_{22t}}} \end{bmatrix} \begin{bmatrix} u_{1t} \\ u_{2t} \end{bmatrix} = \begin{bmatrix} \dfrac{u_{1t}}{\sqrt{h_{11t}}} \\ \dfrac{u_{2t}}{\sqrt{h_{22t}}} \end{bmatrix},$$

which are then used to compute the symmetric moment matrix

$$Q = \begin{bmatrix} q_{11} & q_{12} \\ q_{12} & q_{22} \end{bmatrix} = \frac{1}{T} \sum_{t=1}^{T} \begin{bmatrix} z_{1t}^2 & z_{1t} z_{2t} \\ z_{2t} z_{1t} & z_{2t}^2 \end{bmatrix}.$$

(iv) Construct the pseudo correlation matrix Q_t given by

$$Q_t = (1 - \alpha - \beta) \begin{bmatrix} q_{11} & q_{12} \\ q_{12} & q_{22} \end{bmatrix}$$
$$+ \alpha \begin{bmatrix} z_{1t-1}^2 & z_{1t-1} z_{2t-1} \\ z_{1t-1} z_{2t-1} & z_{2t-1}^2 \end{bmatrix} + \beta \begin{bmatrix} q_{11t-1} & q_{12t-1} \\ q_{12t-1} & q_{22t-1} \end{bmatrix}.$$

(v) Compute the correlation matrix

$$R_t = \begin{bmatrix} 1 & \dfrac{q_{12t}}{\sqrt{q_{11t} q_{22t}}} \\ \dfrac{q_{12t}}{\sqrt{q_{11t} q_{22t}}} & 1 \end{bmatrix} = \begin{bmatrix} 1 & \rho_{12t} \\ \rho_{12t} & 1 \end{bmatrix}.$$

(vi) The resultant DCC conditional covariance matrix is

$$
H_t = \begin{bmatrix} \sqrt{h_{11t}} & 0 \\ 0 & \sqrt{h_{22t}} \end{bmatrix} \begin{bmatrix} 1 & \rho_{12t} \\ \rho_{12t} & 1 \end{bmatrix} \begin{bmatrix} \sqrt{h_{11t}} & 0 \\ 0 & \sqrt{h_{22t}} \end{bmatrix}
$$

$$
= \begin{bmatrix} h_{11t} & \rho_{12t}\sqrt{h_{1t}h_{2t}} \\ \rho_{12t}\sqrt{h_{1t}h_{2t}} & h_{22t} \end{bmatrix}.
$$

Notice that the covariance (the off-diagonal terms of H_t are identical) is now time-varying as a result of the two GARCH model conditional variances h_{11t} and h_{22t} and the time-varying correlation $\rho_{12t} = q_{12t}/\sqrt{q_{11t}q_{22t}}$.

(vii) Use an iterative algorithm to estimate all of the parameters simultaneously by maximizing the log likelihood function in equation (14.9).

A simpler two stage procedure consists of estimating the univariate GARCH models one by one for each asset, thus providing estimates of the parameters $\theta_1 = \{\alpha_{10}, \alpha_{11}, \beta_{11}, \alpha_{20}, \alpha_{21}, \beta_{21}\}$. These parameter estimates are then used to construct the conditional covariance matrix and maximize the log likelihood function just with respect to the parameters $\theta_2 = \{\alpha, \beta\}$. The estimates $\widehat{\theta}_1$ are efficient, but those for $\widehat{\theta}_2$ are not because no account is taken of the fact that the univariate GARCH parameters are actually estimated. To generate correct standard errors for $\widehat{\theta}_2$, all that is required is to perform one iteration of the full log likelihood function and compute the standard errors from the corresponding covariance matrix of the resultant parameter estimates.

Maximum likelihood estimation of this class of model is illustrated using daily log returns on $N = 4$ US industry portfolios for the period 1 January 1990 to 31 December 2008. The industries considered are Consumer Goods (durables, nondurables, wholesale, retail, and services), Manufacturing (manufacturing, energy, and utilities), Technology (business equipment, telephone, and television transmission), and Health (healthcare, medical equipment, and drugs).

The log returns to the industry portfolios are plotted in Figure 14.4. It is immediately apparent that all the stocks experience a rise in volatility at the end of the sample period as the global financial crisis begins. There is also evidence that the dot-com bubble had a far greater influence on the volatility of the technology portfolio than on the other sector portfolios, an observation that confirms the potential advantages of estimating multivariate GARCH models to allow for volatility spillovers from one industry to another.

The DCC model and the CCC model are estimated using both the multivariate normal and multivariate standardized Student t distributions. The parameter estimates for the various models are reported in Table 14.1. For all four portfolios, the conditional variances have IGARCH features with $\alpha_{i1} + \beta_{i1} \approx 1$. This result indicates that the volatility of these portfolios is fairly persistent for both the CCC and DCC models. The adjustment parameters α and β on the DCC model are statistically significant and this suggests that there is prima facie evidence to support the claim that correlations are time-varying.

These results should, however, be regarded merely as preliminary evidence because testing the adequacy of the constant correlation assumption is a matter of ongoing research (Harvey and Thiele, 2016; Silvennoinen and Teräsvirta, 2016).

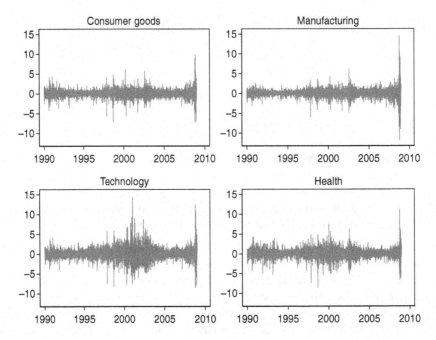

FIGURE 14.4   Daily log returns on 4 US industry portfolios from 1 January 1990 to 31 December 2008.

The symmetric correlation matrix for the CCC model, which contains the estimated values of the ρ_{ij} from equation (14.18) is given by

$$\widehat{R} = \begin{bmatrix} 1 & & & \\ \underset{(0.0006)}{0.7702} & 1 & & \\ \underset{(0.0006)}{0.7559} & \underset{(0.007)}{0.6913} & 1 & \\ \underset{(0.0007)}{0.7149} & \underset{(0.009)}{0.6224} & \underset{(0.0009)}{0.6160} & 1 \end{bmatrix}.$$

Since there are differences in the estimated correlations, these results provide only weak support for the DECO model.

14.5 OPTIMAL HEDGE RATIOS

Multivariate GARCH models can be used to estimate dynamic hedge ratios (Baillie and Myers, 1991). Consider an investor who sells futures contracts to hedge against movements in the spot price of an asset. The return on the hedged portfolio, r_{pt}, is

$$r_{pt} = r_{st} - \eta r_{ft},$$

where r_{st} is the return in the spot market, r_{ft} is the return on the futures contract, and η is the number of contracts the hedger sells for each unit of spot commodity, known as the hedge ratio. The expected return on the portfolio is

TABLE 14.1   Coefficient estimates for the DCC and CCC models using the multivariate normal and the multivariate standardized Student t distributions. The data are daily log returns of 4 industry portfolios using the following taxonomy: Consumer Goods = 1, Manufacturing = 2, Technology = 3, Health = 4. The sample period is 1 January 1990 to 31 December 2008. Standard errors are in parentheses.

Parameter	Normal Distribution		t Distribution	
	DCC	CCC	DCC	CCC
μ_{10}	0.052	0.054	0.053	0.049
	(0.011)	(0.010)	(0.010)	(0.010)
α_{10}	0.007	0.005	0.005	0.003
	(0.001)	(0.001)	(0.001)	(0.001)
α_{11}	0.058	0.041	0.049	0.033
	(0.004)	(0.004)	(0.004)	(0.003)
β_{11}	0.936	0.955	0.946	0.966
	(0.004)	(0.004)	(0.004)	(0.004)
μ_{20}	0.056	0.063	0.059	0.062
	(0.010)	(0.010)	(0.009)	(0.009)
α_{20}	0.004	0.003	0.003	0.002
	(0.001)	(0.001)	(0.001)	(0.001)
α_{21}	0.053	0.039	0.046	0.033
	(0.004)	(0.004)	(0.004)	(0.003)
β_{21}	0.943	0.959	0.951	0.968
	(0.004)	(0.004)	(0.004)	(0.003)
μ_{30}	0.057	0.063	0.064	0.063
	(0.013)	(0.014)	(0.013)	(0.013)
α_{30}	0.006	0.003	0.005	0.002
	(0.001)	(0.001)	(0.001)	(0.001)
α_{31}	0.050	0.043	0.044	0.037
	(0.004)	(0.004)	(0.004)	(0.003)
β_{31}	0.947	0.958	0.954	0.966
	(0.004)	(0.004)	(0.004)	(0.003)
μ_{40}	0.057	0.060	0.055	0.052
	(0.013)	(0.013)	(0.012)	(0.012)
α_{40}	0.009	0.005	0.006	0.003
	(0.002)	(0.002)	(0.002)	(0.001)
α_{41}	0.051	0.039	0.041	0.031
	(0.004)	(0.004)	(0.004)	(0.004)
β_{41}	0.943	0.958	0.954	0.969
	(0.005)	(0.005)	(0.005)	(0.004)
α	0.035		0.034	
	(0.002)		(0.002)	
β	0.952		0.952	
	(0.002)		(0.002)	
ν			9.089	6.605
			(0.499)	(0.298)

$$\mu_p = \mathrm{E}(r_{st} - \eta r_{ft}) = \mathrm{E}(r_{st}) - \eta \mathrm{E}(r_{ft}),$$

and the variance of the portfolio is

$$h_{pp} = \mathrm{E}[(r_{pt} - \mu_p)^2] = h_{ss} + \eta^2 h_{ff} - 2\eta h_{sf}. \qquad (14.19)$$

The optimal minimum variance portfolio is found by minimizing h_{pp} by choice of η. Differentiating the expression in equation (14.19) with respect to η gives

$$\frac{dh_{pp}}{d\eta} = 2\eta h_{ff} - 2h_{sf}.$$

Setting this derivative to zero and solving for η gives the optimal hedge ratio

$$\eta = \frac{h_{sf}}{h_{ff}}, \qquad (14.20)$$

which is the ratio of the covariance of the log returns on the spot and futures contracts to the variance of the return on futures. The objective of variance minimization assumes a high degree of risk aversion on the part of economic agents. However, Baillie and Myers (1989) show that if the expected log returns to holding futures are zero, the minimum variance hedging rule is also the expected utility-maximizing rule.

The expression for the optimal hedge ratio in equation (14.20) assumes that the covariance and the variance are constant. This, in turn, results in a hedge ratio that is also constant, implying that the hedger never rebalances the portfolio in response to shocks in the spot and futures markets. To relax the restriction of a constant hedge ratio, the covariance of the log returns on the spot and futures contracts and the variance of the return on the futures contract are specified as time-varying. The resultant dynamic hedge ratio is then

$$\eta_t = \frac{h_{sft}}{h_{fft}},$$

which is now the time-varying ratio of the conditional covariance of the log returns on the spot and futures contracts to the conditional variance of the return on futures. To model time variation in the conditional covariance and variance, a bivariate GARCH model is required.

Consider the problem of hedging the log returns to the four US industry portfolios using the daily log returns for the period 1 January 1990 to 31 December 2008 and the futures contract on the S&P 500 index for the same period. The constant hedge ratio for each of the industry portfolios is found by estimating the regression equation

$$r_{st} = \beta_0 + \beta_1 r_{ft} + u_t,$$

where r_{st} represents the log returns to the relevant industry portfolio, r_{ft} represents log returns to the 3-month S&P 500 futures contract, and u_t is a disturbance term. The constant hedge ratios are estimated to be 0.773, 0.787, 1.124, and 0.768, respectively, for the Consumer Goods, Manufacturing, Technology, and Health portfolios.

The dynamic hedge ratios are computed using bivariate DCC models specified for each industry portfolio relative to the S&P 500 futures contract. The model is estimated using the bivariate normal distribution. The parameter estimates for the bivariate models are not reported, but the dynamic hedge ratios for each industry portfolio are plotted in Figure 14.5.

For the consumer goods industry, the constant hedge ratio looks like a reasonable strategy and the value of the dynamic ratio seldom strays far from this constant value. The same conclusion cannot be drawn for the other three portfolios and particularly the manufacturing and technology industries. The dynamic hedge ratio for manufacturing is below the constant value for most of the early part of the sample and then switches to being above it after the dot-com bubble unwinds in the early 2000s. The effect of the dot-com bubble on high technology stocks is clear in Figure 14.5 and the advantage of using dynamic hedging is obvious. Finally, while the dynamic hedge ratio for the health portfolio fluctuates around the constant hedge ratio, the deviations during the early 1990s (above the constant ratio) and the dot-com bubble (below the line) suggest that dynamic hedging would provide a substantial reduction in risk exposure for this portfolio as well.

14.6 CAPITAL RATIOS AND FINANCIAL CRISES

The global financial crisis of 2008–2010 heightened awareness of the importance of systemic risk to financial policymaking. Brownlees and Engle (2016) introduce a method for determining the marginal expected shortfall (MES) of a financial institution, defined as the expected loss a financial firm would experience if the market declined substantially.

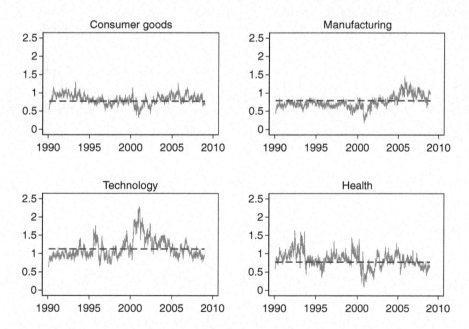

FIGURE 14.5 Dynamic hedge ratios (solid line) for 4 US industry portfolios hedged using the 3-month S&P 500 Index futures contract. The relevant time-varying variances and covariances are computed using a DCC model on daily data from 1 January 1990 to 31 December 2008. The optimal constant hedge ratio is shown by the dashed line.

In order to estimate the MES, a multivariate volatility model must be specified, estimated, and simulated to provide a view of the potential evolution of market and firm log returns.

The actual capital ratio (ACR) of a firm at time t is defined as

$$ACR_{it} = \frac{W_{it}}{W_{it} + D_{it}}, \tag{14.21}$$

where W_{it} is the firm's equity value, D_{it} is the book value of its debt, and $W_{it} + D_{it}$ represents the total value of the firm's assets. Table 14.2 gives the actual capital ratios of 18 financial institutions in the United States at the end of 2014, with the institutions sorted in terms of their equity values, W_{it}. The capital ratios range from a high of 42% (American Express) to a low of 8.9% (Citigroup). The important question is whether these capital ratios are sufficient for the firms to remain solvent during periods of financial distress in the future.

To determine whether the actual capital ratio is sufficient to withstand a large negative shock in the market, let the capital shortfall, CS_{it}, of a firm at time t be the negative of the difference between its equity value W_{it} and a proportion, κ, of its total assets $W_{it} + D_{it}$, measured as follows

$$CS_{it} = -(W_{it} - \kappa(W_{it} + D_{it})). \tag{14.22}$$

The firm is in financial distress if $W_{it} < k(W_{it} + D_{it})$, as the firm has a capital deficit and hence a (positive) capital shortfall. In this situation, the firm would need to raise additional financial capital. A systemic event occurs in the future at time $t + k$ when there is a large fall in the market (simple) return, R_{mt+k}, in excess of some threshold, c.

TABLE 14.2 Actual capital ratios of selected financial institutions on 31 December 2014. These ratios are defined as in equation (14.21).

Institution	Equity Value (E)	Actual Capital Ratios (ACR)
Wells Fargo	284385548	0.163666
JPMorgan Chase	233935868	0.092507
Bank of America	188139291	0.090744
Citigroup	163925596	0.089366
American Express	96266348	0.418410
Goldman Sachs Group	84421881	0.097466
Morgan Stanley	75947236	0.092937
Capital One Financial	45895407	0.151976
Bank of New York Mellon	45670055	0.116009
State Street	32773358	0.114548
SunTrust Banks	21849006	0.117233
Fifth Third Bank	16789143	0.123762
Northern Trust	15873037	0.134048
Regions Financial	14535576	0.124688
KeyCorp	12041918	0.131752
Huntington Bank	8568056	0.128700
Comerica	8416539	0.120482
Zions Bank	5785591	0.107296

The expected capital shortfall of a future systemic event given information at time t is

$$SRISK_{it} = E_t(CS_{it+k}|R_{mt+k} < c)$$
$$= kE_t(D_{it+k}|R_{mt+k} < c) - (1 - \kappa)E(W_{it+k}|R_{mt+k} < c). \quad (14.23)$$

Assuming that debt cannot be renegotiated, $E(D_{it+k}|R_{mt+k} < c) = D_{it}$, and using the result that the future equity value of the firm is $W_{it+k} = W_{it}(1 + R_{it+k})$, where R_{it+k} is the future return on the firm, the systemic risk of the firm is rewritten as

$$SRISK_{it} = \kappa D_{it} - (1 - \kappa)W_{it}(1 + MES_{it+k}), \quad (14.24)$$

where

$$MES_{it+k} = E_t(r_{it+k}|R_{mt+k} < c) \quad (14.25)$$

represents the marginal expected shortfall.

The safe capital ratio is defined as that ratio for which it is not necessary to raise any additional external capital during a crisis. By setting $SRISK_{it} = 0$ in equation (14.23) and rearranging the equation, the safe capital ratio for the firm at time t is a function of the MES and the prudential parameter κ, leading to the expresssion

$$SCR_{it} = \frac{\kappa}{1 - (1 - \kappa)MES_{it+k}}. \quad (14.26)$$

Consider estimating the $h = 1$ day marginal expected shortfall in equation (14.25) for Morgan Stanley, with $r_{it} = \log(1 + R_{it})$ and where the market excess return, r_{mt}, is given by the excess return on the S&P 500 index. The first step is to estimate the bivariate CCC model

$$r_{mt} = \mu_m + u_{mt}$$
$$r_{it} = \mu_i + u_{it},$$

where

$$u_t = \begin{bmatrix} u_{mt} \\ u_{it} \end{bmatrix} \sim N(0, H_t),$$

and the conditional variance matrix is

$$H_t = S_t R S_t = \begin{bmatrix} \sqrt{h_{mmt}} & 0 \\ 0 & \sqrt{h_{iit}} \end{bmatrix} \begin{bmatrix} 1 & \rho_{mi} \\ \rho_{mi} & 1 \end{bmatrix} \begin{bmatrix} \sqrt{h_{mmt}} & 0 \\ 0 & \sqrt{h_{iit}} \end{bmatrix},$$

in which ρ_{mi} is the constant correlation between market excess returns and Morgan Stanley excess returns. The conditional variances, h_{mmt} and h_{iit}, are generated from univariate GARCH(1,1) models using the specifications

$$h_{mmt} = \alpha_{m0} + \alpha_{m1}u_{mt-1}^2 + \beta_{m1}h_{mmt-1},$$
$$h_{iit} = \alpha_{i0} + \alpha_{i1}u_{1t-1}^2 + \beta_{i1}h_{iit-1}.$$

The parameter estimates of this bivariate CCC model using daily excess returns data for the period 14 December 2001 to 31 December 2014 are given in Table 14.3. The GARCH parameter estimates display typical empirical features of near integrated conditional volatility models, with estimates of the coefficients of the lagged squared residuals around 0.1 and estimates of the coefficients of the lagged conditional variances around 0.9, leading to an aggregate of the parameter estimates for each asset that is close to unity. The estimated correlation coefficient is $\hat{\rho}_{mi} = 0.7290$.

TABLE 14.3 Parameter estimates for a bivariate constant conditional correlation model for excess returns to Morgan Stanley and excess returns to the value weighted S&P 500 index using daily data from 14 December 2001 to 31 December 2014.

Parameter	Market		Morgan Stanley	
	Coefficient	Std. Err.	Coefficient	Std. Err.
μ_i	0.0694	0.0143	0.1012	0.0308
α_{i0}	0.0223	0.0034	0.0708	0.0134
α_1	0.0775	0.0074	0.0825	0.0084
β_1	0.8998	0.0091	0.9058	0.0091
ρ	0.7290	0.0082		

To compute the 1-day-ahead marginal expected shortfall at time $T + 1$, Brownlees and Engle (2016) suggest the following simple approximation

$$MES = -\rho_{mi}\sqrt{h_{iiT+1}}\,\frac{\phi(\tilde{c})}{\Phi(\tilde{c})},$$

in which $\tilde{c} = \log(1 + c)/\sqrt{h_{mmT+1}}$, and φ and Φ are, respectively, the standard normal density function and the cumulative standard normal density function. This formula can be extended to multiple days. A further extension is to use stochastic simulation of the estimated CCC model to compute a simulated MES.

14.7 EXERCISES

The data required for the exercises are available for download as `EViews` workfiles (*.wf1), `Stata` datafiles (*.dta), comma delimited text files (*.csv), and as `Excel` spreadsheets (*.xlsx).

1. **Time-Varying β-risk**

> capm.*

The data are monthly observations for the period April 1990 to July 2004 on the share prices of 5 US stocks, the price of gold, the S&P 500 stock market index, and the US Treasury bill (expressed as an annualized percentage), which represents the risk-free rate.

(a) Compute the daily percentage excess returns to Microsoft ($r_{it} - r_{ft}$) and the market portfolio ($r_{mt} - r_{ft}$). Estimate the β-risk of Microsoft using the CAPM

$$r_{it} - r_{ft} = \alpha + \beta(r_{mt} - r_{ft}) + u_t,$$

where u_t is a disturbance term. Interpret the estimate of β.

(b) Estimate GARCH(1,1) models for $r_{it} - r_{ft}$ and $r_{mt} - r_{ft}$ and use the following expression for the covariance

$$h_{imt} = \rho\sqrt{h_{1iit}}\sqrt{h_{mmt}},$$

to obtain an estimate of the conditional covariance between Microsoft and the market portfolio—where h_{iit} is the conditional variance of $r_{it} - r_{ft}$, h_{mmt} is the conditional variance of $r_{mt} - r_{ft}$, and ρ is the correlation parameter between $r_{it} - r_{ft}$ and $r_{mt} - r_{ft}$, which is estimated using the sample correlation coefficient. Use the conditional variance and covariance estimates to construct a time-varying estimate of β-risk. Comment on your results.

(c) Now consider the bivariate GARCH model

$$r_{it} - r_{ft} = \mu_i + u_{it}$$
$$r_{mt} - r_{ft} = \mu_m + u_{mt},$$

where the disturbance vector $u_t = (u_{it}, u_{mt})' \sim N(0, H_t)$. Estimate this model by maximum likelihood using a diagonal BEKK model and a CCC model for the conditional covariance matrix, H_t. Compute time-varying β-risk for each model and compare these estimates with the estimate obtained in part (a).

2. **Minimum Variance Portfolios with Time-Varying Weights**

> capm.*

The data are monthly observations for the period April 1990 to July 2004 on the share prices of 5 US stocks, the price of gold, the S&P 500 stock market index, and the US Treasury bill (expressed as an annualized percentage), which represents the risk-free rate.

(a) Let r_{1t} and r_{2t} represent, respectively, the percentage log returns on Microsoft and Walmart. Calculate the covariance matrix of r_{1t} and r_{2t} defined as

$$H = \begin{bmatrix} h_{11} & h_{12} \\ h_{12} & h_{22} \end{bmatrix}.$$

Use these estimates to construct a minimum variance portfolio of the stocks using as weights

$$w_1 = \frac{h_{22} - h_{12}}{h_{11} + h_{22} - 2h_{12}}, \quad w_2 = 1 - w_1.$$

Interpret the estimates of the portfolio weights w_1 and w_2.

(b) Estimate GARCH(1,1) models for r_{1t} and r_{2t}, and use the following expression for the covariance

$$h_{12t} = \rho \sqrt{h_{11t}} \sqrt{h_{22t}},$$

to obtain an estimate of the conditional covariance between Microsoft and Walmart—where h_{11t} and h_{22t} are, respectively, the conditional variances of r_{1t} and r_{2t}, and ρ is the correlation between r_{1t} and r_{2t}, which is estimated using the sample correlation.

(c) Using the estimates of h_{11t}, h_{22t}, and h_{12t} from part (b), compute time-varying minimum variance weights using the expressions

$$w_{1t} = \frac{h_{22t} - h_{12t}}{h_{11t} + h_{22t} - 2h_{12t}}, \quad w_{2t} = \frac{h_{11t} - h_{12t}}{h_{11t} + h_{22t} - 2h_{12t}}.$$

Plot the estimates of w_{1t} and w_{2t} and compare these estimates with the fixed portfolio weights computed in part (a).

(d) Repeat part (c) where the conditional covariance matrix is based on the diagonal BEKK specification

$$r_{1t} = \mu_1 + u_{1t}$$
$$r_{2t} = \mu_2 + u_{2t},$$

where

$$u_t = \begin{bmatrix} u_{1t} \\ u_{2t} \end{bmatrix} \sim N(0, H_t),$$

$$H_t = \begin{bmatrix} h_{11t} & h_{12t} \\ h_{12t} & h_{22t} \end{bmatrix} = CC' + Au_{t-1}u'_{t-1}A' + BH_{t-1}B',$$

$$C = \begin{bmatrix} c_{11} & 0 \\ c_{21} & c_{22} \end{bmatrix}, \quad A = \begin{bmatrix} a_{11} & 0 \\ 0 & a_{22} \end{bmatrix}, \quad B = \begin{bmatrix} b_{11} & 0 \\ 0 & b_{22} \end{bmatrix}.$$

Are the results significantly different to those obtained in (c)?

3. Hedge Funds

hedge funds.*

The data are daily percentage log returns from 1 April 2003 to 28 May 2010 on seven alternative hedge fund indices, namely, Convertible, Distressed, Equity, Event, Macro, Merger, and Neutral. Also included are the Dow, NASDAQ, and S&P 500 percentage log returns.

(a) Let r_{1t} and r_{2t} represent, respectively, the percentage log returns on convertible and distressed hedge funds. Calculate the covariance matrix of r_{1t} and r_{2t} defined as

$$H = \begin{bmatrix} h_{11} & h_{12} \\ h_{12} & h_{22} \end{bmatrix}.$$

Use these estimates to construct a minimum variance portfolio of the two hedge funds using as weights

$$w_1 = \frac{h_{22} - h_{12}}{h_{11} + h_{22} - 2h_{12}}, \quad w_2 = 1 - w_1.$$

Interpret the estimates of the portfolio weights w_1 and w_2.

(b) Consider constructing a minimum variance portfolio with time-varying weights by specifying the following bivariate GARCH model based on the diagonal BEKK specification

$$r_{1t} = \mu_1 + u_{1t}$$
$$r_{2t} = \mu_2 + u_{2t},$$

where $u_t = (u_{1t}, u_{2t})' \sim N(0, H_t)$, and the conditional covariance matrix H_t is specified as a diagonal BEKK model. Estimate the model and compute time-varying weights based on

$$w_{1t} = \frac{h_{22t} - h_{12t}}{h_{11t} + h_{22t} - 2h_{12t}}, \qquad w_{2t} = \frac{h_{11t} - h_{12t}}{h_{11t} + h_{22t} - 2h_{12t}}.$$

Plot the estimates of w_{1t} and w_{2t} and compare these estimates with the fixed portfolio weights computed in part (a).

(c) Consider the following time-varying parameter regression model

$$r_{2t} = \alpha + \beta_t (r_{2t} - r_{1t}) + e_t,$$

where e_t is a disturbance term, and β_t represents time-varying β-risk. Construct a minimum variance portfolio with time-varying weights by estimating the following bivariate model

$$r_{2t} = \mu_1 + u_{1t}$$
$$r_{2t} - r_{1t} = \mu_2 + u_{2t},$$

where $u_t = (u_{1t}, u_{2t})' \sim N(0, H_t)$, with H_t specified as a bivariate GARCH model based on the diagonal BEKK specification. Compare the estimated time-varying weights with the weights obtained in part (b).

(d) Repeat parts (a) to (c) for other pairs of hedge funds.

4. **Optimal Hedge Ratios for Industry Portfolios**

---
hedgeratio.*

The data are daily log returns on US industry portfolios for the period 1 January 1990 to 31 December 2008. The industries considered are Consumer Goods (Cnsmr), Manufacturing (Manuf), Technology (HiTec), and Health (Hlth). Also included is the return on the 3-month S&P 500 futures index.

(a) Plot the log returns to the four industry portfolios and comment on their time series properties.

(b) Estimate the linear regression

$$r_{st} = \alpha + \beta r_{ft} + u_t,$$

where r_{st} is the log return to an industry portfolio, r_{ft} is the log return to the 3-month S&P 500 futures index, and u_t is a disturbance term. Estimate the model for each of the four industry portfolios and interpret the estimates of β.

(c) Estimate a bivariate DCC model for the returns on the Consumer portfolio and the 3-month S&P 500 futures index. Use the results of the DCC model to provide an estimate of a dynamic hedge ratio for the Consumer portfolio. Compare the estimated time-varying hedge ratio with the constant hedge ratio estimate obtained in part (b).

(d) Repeat part (c) for the remaining three industry portfolios and comment on the results.

5. Hedge Funds and the GFC

> hedgefunds.*

The data are daily log returns to various hedge funds for the period 1 April 2003 to 28 May 2010 obtained from Hedge Fund Research, Inc. The hedge funds are Convertible, Distressed, Equity, Event, Macro, Merger, and Neutral.

(a) Estimate a bivariate DCC model for Merger hedge fund log returns and log returns to the S&P 500 index. Compute and plot an estimate of the time-varying correlation. Comment on your result.

(b) Repeat part (a) for the other six hedge funds. Discuss how successful the hedge funds were in minimizing exposure to systematic risk from the market during the subprime and global financial crises beginning in mid 2007.

(c) Now estimate a DCC model of the log returns on all seven hedge funds. Comment on whether or not a DECO model would be appropriate for this system.

6. Value at Risk with Multiple Positions

> techstocks.*

The data are daily equity prices from 13 March 1986 to 17 March 2017, on the S&P 500 index and four US technology stocks, namely, Apple, IBM, Intel, and Microsoft.

(a) Let r_{1t} be the percentage log-return on IBM and r_{2t} be the percentage log-return on Intel. Estimate the bivariate constant covariance model

$$r_{1t} = \mu_1 + u_{1t}$$
$$r_{2t} = \mu_2 + u_{2t},$$

where $u_t = (u_{1t}, u_{2t})' \sim N(0, H)$, and H is the covariance matrix

$$H = \begin{bmatrix} h_{11} & h_{12} \\ h_{12} & h_{22} \end{bmatrix}.$$

(b) The 1-day VaR with a maximum loss probability of 1% for each asset is

$$VaR_i = \mu_i - 2.33\sqrt{h_{ii}}, \quad i = 1, 2.$$

Compute the VaR for IBM and Intel and interpret the results.

(c) Now consider an equal-weighted portfolio containing IBM and Intel. The VaR on the portfolio is

$$VaR = \sqrt{VaR_1^2 + VaR_2^2 + 2\rho VaR_1 VaR_2},$$

where $\rho = h_{12}/\sqrt{h_{11}h_{22}}$ is the correlation between r_{1t} and r_{2t}. Use the estimates obtained in parts (a) and (b) to estimate the VaR on the portfolio.

(d) Now consider the bivariate conditional covariance model of r_{1t} and r_{2t} given
by

$$r_{it} = \mu_i + u_{it}, \quad i = 1, 2,$$

where $u_t = (u_{1t}, u_{2t})' \sim N(0, H_t)$, and H_t is the conditional covariance matrix

$$H_t = \begin{bmatrix} h_{11t} & h_{12t} \\ h_{12t} & h_{22t} \end{bmatrix},$$

based on the diagonal BEKK specification. Estimate this model and recompute
the VaR on the equal-weighted portfolio defined in part (c) based on the one-
day-ahead forecast of the conditional covariance matrix

$$H_{T+1|T} = CC' + A u_T u_T' A' + B H_T B',$$

where

$$C = \begin{bmatrix} c_{11} & 0 \\ c_{21} & c_{22} \end{bmatrix}, \quad A = \begin{bmatrix} a_{11} & 0 \\ 0 & a_{22} \end{bmatrix}, \quad B = \begin{bmatrix} b_{11} & 0 \\ 0 & b_{22} \end{bmatrix}.$$

(e) Repeat parts (a) to (d) for IBM and Microsoft.

(f) Repeat parts (a) to (d) for IBM and Apple, with the conditional mean specification for Apple adjusted to correct for the stock split on June 9, 2014.

CHAPTER 15

Realized Variance
and Covariance

The univariate and multivariate GARCH models of returns discussed in Chapters 13 and 14 provide a framework for modeling daily time-varying variances and covariances. These models are parametric. The main drivers that are used to explain the volatility of returns in these models are lagged shocks, which are determined as differences between observed and expected returns. The shocks are modeled to impact conditional variances and covariances by adopting specific functional form specifications. Common parametric functions include specifications in terms of squared shocks in the case of GARCH models and absolute values in the case of EGARCH models.

An alternative and more recent econometric approach to time-varying volatility estimation is nonparametric. The method starts from the premise that at each point in time asset price volatility is an unknown stochastic process. This process, which is known as the *quadratic variation* when it is accumulated over time, is unobserved; and it is a characteristic of the instantaneous price process, just as the variance of a random variable (the centered second moment) is an unobserved characteristic of that random variable. The variance of a random variable may be estimated with observed data and so too may the quadratic variation process of the price process. The essential difference is that the quadratic variation is a stochastic process, not a constant, and this process (like the price process itself) is subject to instantaneous random variation over time. The central idea in the estimation of this quadratic variation is to employ very high-frequency observations to ensure a nearly instantaneous focus in estimation.

This new methodology circumvents the need to adopt parametric functional forms by using within-day high-frequency data on financial asset returns to estimate the second-order moments for each day. Since the corresponding variances and covariances are based on observed, or realized, returns, they are referred to as *realized variances* and *realized covariances*, respectively. The sampling frequency of the returns data that is used to compute daily realized variance can potentially be hourly, half-hourly, 10-minute, 5-minute, or even transaction level (tick-by-tick) data. The precision of the variance estimates tends to increase as the sampling interval decreases as a result of the availability of more and more data infilling the gap between less frequently sampled data. Under certain conditions, the realized variance approaches its (random) population value, known as integrated variance or quadratic variation, as the interval between returns becomes infinitesimally small.

An important advantage of realized variance is that it provides a completely non-parametric measure of the true (random) variation of financial asset returns. Since this estimator does not require a parametric specification, it avoids potential misspecification bias from the use of an incorrect functional form. The realized variance measure has the added advantage that it admits a decomposition of variance into a continuous and a discontinuous component where the latter arises from possible instantaneous jumps that may occur in asset returns. Moreover, as realized variance is an observable nonparametric measure, it can be used to determine the accuracy of parametric variance forecasts based models such as GARCH specifications.

While it is the availability of high-frequency data that makes the computation of the realized variance feasible, there is a practical limit to the smallest sampling interval that may be available or may be appropriate to use in any given data set. At extremely high frequencies, microstructure properties in the trading process such as the bid-ask spread (see Chapter 16) and non-synchronous trading in financial assets become important in the measurement of realized variance. Such *microstructure noise* effects as they are called can potentially bias variance estimates, and various empirical devices have been devised to assist in identifying the presence of these effects in high-frequency data calculations. To inform on the potential presence of microstructure noise in computations, graphical plots known as *signature plots* may be used to measure the relationship and describe behavior between the realized variance and the sampling interval as that interval becomes small, thereby alerting investigators to potential problems in calculating realized variance. Moreover, when multiple asset returns are studied, trades are not necessarily synchronized in time across different assets. This lack of synchronicity inevitably affects the accuracy of estimates of realized covariance. The problem is known as the Epps effect and may be addressed by the construction of refresh prices.

15.1 HIGH-FREQUENCY DATA

Estimation of the daily realized variance of returns is based on the availability of high-frequency intraday data. An example of transactions data is given in Table 15.1, which provides a snapshot of a selection of the trades recorded on IBM on 3 January 2006, obtained from the TAQ (Ticks and Quotes) database. As the market opens at 09:30 and closes at 16:00, the total length of the trading day is 6.5 hours, or in terms of seconds, $6.5 \times 60 \times 60 = 23400$. The last entry of the first column shows that the number of recorded transactions is 6326, suggesting that there are $23400 - 6326 = 17074$ seconds (approximately two-thirds of the trading day) where no trades have taken place.

Table 15.1 gives the timestamp of each trade, the duration between trades (measured in seconds), the transaction price P_i (measured in US$), and the log price, $\log P_i = p_i$ (rounded to 4 decimal places). The first trade occurs 17 seconds after the market has opened. The next trade occurs a second later, with a duration time of 1 second between trades, while the third trade happens 27 seconds after the market opens, with a duration time between the second and third trades of 9 seconds. For the first two trades the price remains at $82.45, but it increases by 10 cents to $82.55 for the third trade. The last trade takes place 2 seconds before the market closes at 16:00, and the closing price is $82.06.

It is important to note that despite the increased use of fully automated or partly automated trading systems, data entry errors are still inevitable and are often encountered in high-frequency data sets. Consequently, substantial effort is required to ensure that the data are free from error and in this regard the data cleaning procedures recommended by Barndorff-Nielsen et al. (2009) provide a useful practical guide.

Table 15.1 shows that tick-by-tick data are not sampled at regular intervals, such as every 10 seconds, every 5 minutes, or even every hour. The log prices for the 6326 transactions in Table 15.1 are presented in panel (a) of Figure 15.1. The gaps present in the figure reflect the periods when no trade takes place. To produce data that are sampled at regular intervals, one recommended approach is to replace missing observations with the last recorded price (Hansen and Lunde, 2006). In panel (b) of Figure 15.1, 1-second data are presented for IBM based on this method. If the stock is highly liquid, the duration times between trades will be relatively short, resulting in only a small proportion of non-observed prices being replaced by previously recorded prices. Alternatively, if the market is thin and the stock trades infrequently, the proportion of non-trades being replaced by previous prices will be relatively high.

The log price for IBM on 3 January 2006 shows some variation over the course of the day. In the morning, there is a substantial downward movement followed by a recovery during the afternoon. It is this intraday variation in log prices that provides the basis for computing the realized variance of returns for the day. Let p_0 and p_1 represent, respectively, the opening and closing log price, and suppose that trades are recorded at 1-second intervals. If prices are sampled during a day at the rate of $1/M$ per second, in total there are $M + 1$ log prices consisting of the opening and closing prices as well as the $M - 1$ intraday log prices

TABLE 15.1 Tick-by-tick transaction prices and timestamps for trades of IBM on 3 January 2006. Log prices rounded to 4 decimal places.

Trade	Timestamp	Duration (seconds)	Price (US$)	Log Price
1	09:30:17	.	82.45	4.4122
2	09:30:18	1	82.45	4.4122
3	09:30:27	9	82.55	4.4134
⋮	⋮	⋮	⋮	⋮
12	09:30:57	4	82.42	4.4118
13	09:31:05	8	82.38	4.4113
14	09:31:06	1	82.38	4.4118
⋮	⋮	⋮	⋮	⋮
75	09:35:22	1	82.40	4.4116
76	09:35:44	22	82.36	4.4111
77	09:35:58	14	82.15	4.4085
⋮	⋮	⋮	⋮	⋮
6324	15:59:56	4	82.06	4.4075
6325	15:59:57	1	82.05	4.4073
6326	15:59:58	1	82.06	4.4075

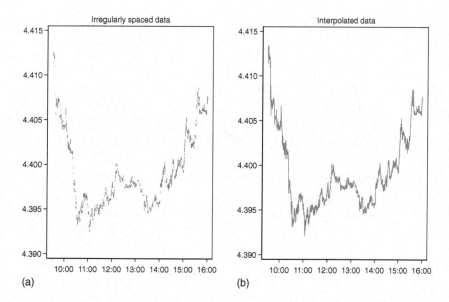

FIGURE 15.1 Time series plots of log prices for IBM on 3 January 2006. Panel (a) shows the 6326 irregularly spaced observations, while panel (b) shows the 23400 log prices based on interpolating the missing data using the previous log price.

$$\underbrace{p_0}_{\text{Opening log price}} \quad \underbrace{p_{1/M} \quad p_{2/M} \quad \cdots \quad p_{(M-1)/M}}_{\text{Intraday log prices}} \quad \underbrace{p_1}_{\text{Closing log price}}$$

In the case of a 6.5-hour trading day, the maximum number of prices that can be sampled is $M = 23400$. If instead prices are sampled every 5 seconds, then the number of prices sampled within a trading day reduces to $M = 23400/5 = 4680$. If sampling is every 1 minute, the number of prices sampled decreases further to $M = 23400/60 = 390$. The parameter M plays an important role in constructing the realized variance estimator of returns as well as in establishing the theoretical properties of this estimator.

15.2 REALIZED VARIANCE

To compute the realized variance for a trading day, consider the log returns based on a particular sampling frequency M

$$r_i = p_{i/M} - p_{(i-1)/M}, \qquad i = 1, 2, \cdots, M, \tag{15.1}$$

where p_i is the log price. For 1-second returns $M = 23400$, whereas for 1-minute returns $M = 390$. The sample variance of the M returns in equation (15.1) is defined in the usual way as

$$\text{var}(r_i) = \frac{1}{M} \sum_{i=1}^{M} (r_i - \bar{r})^2, \quad \bar{r} = \frac{1}{M} \sum_{i=1}^{M} r_i, \tag{15.2}$$

for a 1-second time interval when $M = 23400$, or for a 1-minute interval when $M = 390$. Table 15.2 provides a snapshot of the log prices at 1-minute intervals over the trading day, together with log returns for sampling frequencies of 5-minute ($M = 78$) and 10-minute ($M = 39$) intervals.

To convert the log-return variance in equation (15.2) from a within trading day frequency to a daily frequency, it is simply a matter of multiplying both sides of this equation by M. Moreover, as the within-day log returns correspond to very small changes in log prices, the average intraday return in equation (15.2) is approximately $\bar{r} = 0$. Performing these two steps on equation (15.2) results in the following expression for the realized variance of log returns on a particular trading day

TABLE 15.2   A snapshot of selected log returns on IBM for different sampling intervals computed using log prices recorded on 3 January 2006.

Time (seconds)	Minute closing log price (p_i)	Log return (r_i) 1-minute	5-minute	10-minute
09:30:00	4.4122	...	...	...
09:31:00	4.4118	−0.0004	...	...
09:32:00	4.4127	0.0008	...	...
09:33:00	4.4123	−0.0004	...	...
09:34:00	4.4121	−0.0002	...	...
09:35:00	4.4112	−0.0009	−0.0010	...
09:36:00	4.4085	−0.0027	...	...
09:37:00	4.4078	−0.0007	...	...
09:38:00	4.4062	−0.0016	...	...
09:39:00	4.4065	0.0002	...	...
09:40:00	4.4068	0.0004	−0.0044	−0.0054
09:41:00	4.4066	−0.0002	...	...
09:42:00	4.4068	0.0002	...	...
09:43:00	4.4072	0.0004	...	...
09:44:00	4.4073	0.0001	...	...
09:45:00	4.4070	−0.0004	0.0001	...
09:46:00	4.4067	−0.0002	...	...
09:47:00	4.4051	−0.0016	...	...
09:48:00	4.4051	0.0000	...	...
09:49:00	4.4055	0.0004	...	...
09:50:00	4.4054	−0.0001	−0.0016	−0.001464
09:51:00	4.4055	0.0001	...	...
09:52:00	4.4053	−0.0002	...	...
09:53:00	4.4049	−0.0004	...	...
09:54:00	4.4040	−0.0009	...	...
09:55:00	4.4043	0.0002	−0.0012	...
09:56:00	4.4049	0.0006	...	...
09:57:00	4.4039	−0.0010	...	...
09:58:00	4.4043	0.0004	...	...
09:59:00	4.4043	0.0000	...	...
10:00:00	4.4043	0.0000	0.0000	−0.0011
⋮	⋮	⋮	⋮	⋮
⋮	⋮	⋮	⋮	⋮
16:00:00	4.4075	−0.0001	0.0015	0.0007

$$RV(M) = \sum_{i=1}^{M} r_i^2,\tag{15.3}$$

which simply corresponds to summing the M squared log returns during the trading day.

Using the RV estimator in equation (15.3) and the log returns given in Table 15.2, the estimates of the realized variance for IBM on 3 January 2006 corresponding to three sampling frequencies are as follows.

1-minute RV

$$RV(M = 390) = \sum_{i=1}^{390} r_i^2 = (-0.0004)^2 + (0.0008)^2 + \cdots = 0.000118.$$

5-minute RV

$$RV(M = 78) = \sum_{i=1}^{78} r_i^2 = (-0.0010)^2 + (-0.0044)^2 + \cdots = 0.000163.$$

10-minute RV

$$RV(M = 39) = \sum_{i=1}^{39} r_i^2 = (-0.0054)^2 + (-0.0015)^2 + \cdots = 0.000155.$$

Figure 15.2 is known as the signature plot, and it graphs RV against sampling frequency, beginning with the highest sampling frequency of 1-second intervals and

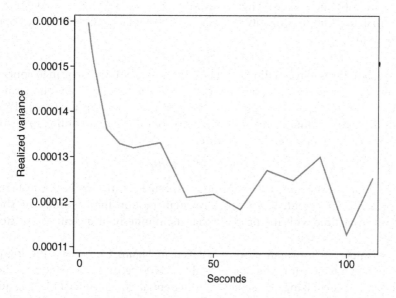

FIGURE 15.2 Signature plot of the estimated realized variance for IBM on 3 January 2006. Sampling intervals range from 1- to 110-second intervals.

ending with a sampling frequency of 110-second intervals. Inspection of the signature plot shows that the *RV* estimates are relatively high for smaller intervals and gradually decay as the sampling interval increases.

15.3 INTEGRATED VARIANCE

Although the finest sampling interval available for the IBM data is 1-second, in theory it is possible to abstract from this restriction and allow the interval to become infinitesimally small as $M \to \infty$. This situation is known as continuous sampling. As the realized variance estimator in equation (15.3) represents the sum of M log returns, as $M \to \infty$ this finite sum becomes a continuous one. The finite summation operator within the day in equation (15.3) is now replaced by an integral of the instantaneous variance of returns over that day, namely,

$$\text{plim} \sum_{i=1}^{M} r_i^2 = \int_{t-1}^{t} \sigma_s^2 ds, \tag{15.4}$$

whereas before, plim represents convergence in probability. In this instance the sample size approaches infinity by virtue of continuous sampling. The left-hand expression is the infinite sum of recorded squared log returns over the trading day, which is equivalent (in the limit) to the continuous sum over the trading day of the instantaneous variance σ_s^2 of returns. The integral on the right side of equation (15.4) is known as the *integrated variance (IV)*

$$IV = \int_{t-1}^{t} \sigma_s^2 ds, \tag{15.5}$$

which is a unit length partial segment of the quadratic variation process $\int_0^t \sigma_s^2 ds$.

The integrated variance is the random population analogue of the sample random quantity given by the realized variance estimator in equation (15.3). Equation (15.4) implies that the sample quantity (*RV*) is a consistent estimator of this population quantity so that

$$\text{plim } RV(M) = IV. \tag{15.6}$$

Since log returns r_i in equation (15.1) are computed as the change in log prices over a finite sampling interval, continuous log returns are computed over an infinitesimal time interval dt, and are denoted by dp_i, where the symbol d represents the (first) differential. This implies that continuous log returns dp_i evolve over time according to a stochastic differential equation of the following form

$$dp_t = \mu_t dt + \sigma_t dB_t, \tag{15.7}$$

where μ_t is the instantaneous conditional expected return, σ_t^2 is the instantaneous variance, and B_t represents a standard Brownian motion that captures the shocks to log returns over time with the property that its infinitesimal increment (or stochastic differential) is $dB_t \sim N(0, dt)$.

An example of Brownian motion is given in Figure 15.3 where the log price is simulated over a 6.5-hour trading day, equal to 23400 seconds. The simulated log price is achieved by discretizing the stochastic differential equation in (15.7) in terms of 1-second intervals of length $\Delta t = 1/23400$, with constant (as distinct from time-varying) parameters according to the stochastic difference equation

$$p_{i/M} = p_{(i-1)/M} + \mu \Delta t + \sigma \Delta B_{i/M}, \qquad i = 1, 2, \cdots, 23400, \qquad (15.8)$$

where $\Delta B_{i/M}$ is a normal random variable distributed as $N(0, \Delta t)$. The mean parameter is set at $\mu = 0.05/250 = 2 \times 10^{-4}$, which is a daily mean return assuming 250 trading days in the year, equivalent to an annual return of 5%. The integrated daily variance is set at $\sigma^2 = 0.04/250 = 1.6 \times 10^{-4}$, which corresponds to an annual volatility of $\sqrt{0.04} = 0.2$. Finally, the opening log price is chosen as $p_0 = 1$ so the actual price is $P_0 = \exp(1) = \$2.7183$, with the remaining 23400 observations at each second generated according to equation (15.8). The log price generally drifts upward over the full trading day as a result of the positive average daily return, with the closing price finishing somewhat above the opening price. During the course of the trading day the log price nonetheless experiences variations, resulting in high-frequency fluctuations in which direction is indeterminate over short periods coupled with longer periods of intermittent downward and upward movements.

As a rough test of the consistency property given in equation (15.6), the estimate of RV for a sampling interval of 1 second using the simulated data presented in Figure 15.3 is $RV = 0.000162$, which is very close to the population parameter value of $IV = 0.000160$. In fact, the consistency property of the estimate RV is robust to very general conditions arising from intraday volatility dynamics caused by complicated intraday trading patterns that are modeled by the time-varying instantaneous drift μ_t and instantaneous variance σ_t^2 in the more general stochastic differential equation given in (15.7).

The advantage of using intraday information to estimate the variance for the trading day is highlighted by a variance estimator that ignores all intraday information and just defines a single log return for the trading day equal to the range between the opening and closing prices

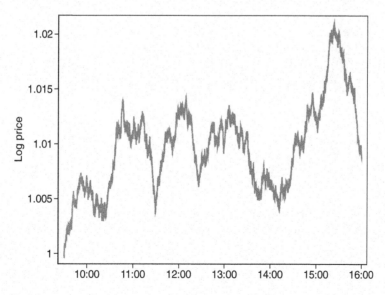

FIGURE 15.3 Simulated log prices from a continuous time model over a 6.5-hour trading day using the discretized stochastic differential equation in (15.8) with parameters $\mu = 0.05/250$, $\sigma^2 = 1.6 \times 10^{-4}$, and a 1-second step interval equal to $\Delta t = 1/23400$.

$$r_t = p_1 - p_0. \tag{15.9}$$

The estimator of *IV* in this case is simply the square of the range, r_t^2. In the case of the opening and closing log prices for IBM reported in Table 15.1, the range-based variance estimate for the trading day is

$$r_t^2 = (4.407451 - 4.412192)^2 = 0.0000225. \tag{15.10}$$

To understand the properties of the range-based variance estimator assume that log returns are normally distributed as $r_t \sim N(0, \sigma_t^2)$. From the relationship between the normal and chi-square distributions, the square of the standardized return, r_t/σ_t, is distributed as chi-square with one degree of freedom

$$\frac{r_t^2}{\sigma_t^2} \sim \chi_1^2.$$

Since $E_{t-1}(r_t^2) = \sigma_t^2$, the range-based variance estimator in equation (15.9) is an unbiased estimator of integrated volatility σ_t^2. However, unlike the realized variance estimator in equation (15.3), which from equation (15.5) is a consistent estimator of *IV*, the ranged-based variance estimator is not. This result follows from the property that the variance of a χ_1^2 random variable is a constant equal to 2, which does not decrease as the sample size increases simply because the sample size is fixed at 1 as a sample of a single observation. In fact, from the properties of the chi-square distribution as

$$\Pr(\chi_1^2 < 0.1) = 0.25,$$

the range-based variance estimator using r_t^2 is smaller than 10% of σ_t^2 with probability 25%.

The sample statistic $RV(M)$ has an asymptotic distribution that is mixed normal with mean *IV* and with (random) variance $(2/M)IQ$, where

$$IQ = \int_{t-1}^{t} \sigma_s^4 ds \tag{15.11}$$

is known as *integrated quarticity* (Barndorff-Nielsen and Shephard, 2002). Alternatively, the asymptotic distribution may be expressed in normalized form as

$$\sqrt{M}\frac{RV(M) - IV}{\sqrt{2IQ}} \xrightarrow{d} N(0, 1), \qquad \text{as } M \to \infty. \tag{15.12}$$

This expression has much in common with the variance estimator $\hat{\sigma}^2$ based on a random sample of size *T* of normally distributed variates with variance σ^2 for which

$$\sqrt{T}\frac{\hat{\sigma}^2 - \sigma^2}{\sqrt{2\sigma^4}} \xrightarrow{d} N(0, 1).$$

One apparent difference between these two results is that the asymptotic distribution of the latter is based on allowing the sample size (or time span) to increase ($T \to \infty$), whereas the former is based on allowing the number of intervals within a fixed time interval to increase without limit ($M \to \infty$) by a process of infill asymptotics.[1]

To use equation (15.12) to perform hypothesis tests on IV and compute confidence intervals for $RV(M)$, it is necessary to estimate IQ in equation (15.11), which is achieved by using the analogous realized quarticity statistic (Barndorff–Nielsen and Shephard, 2002).

$$RQ(M) = \frac{M}{3} \sum_{i=1}^{M} r_i^4. \tag{15.13}$$

Standard errors of $RV(M)$ are then computed as

$$se(RV) = \sqrt{\frac{2}{M} RQ(M)},$$

with p values based on the normal distribution. The corresponding self-normalized computable statistic in place of equation (15.12) is then given by

$$\sqrt{M} \frac{RV(M) - IV}{\sqrt{2RQ(M)}} \xrightarrow{d} N(0,1), \qquad \text{as } M \to \infty. \tag{15.14}$$

15.4 MICROSTRUCTURE NOISE

A feature of the RV estimates for IBM shown in the signature plot of Figure 15.1 is that as the sampling frequency increases from 10-second intervals to 1-second intervals, the RV estimates increase in magnitude from 0.000132 to 0.000169. Part of the reason for this behavior is the additional variability in log returns that occurs at very high frequencies due to microstructure noise arising from factors such as bid-ask bounce, the discreteness of price changes, and infrequent trading (see Chapter 16).

To explore the relationship between RV estimation and sampling frequency in the presence of microstructure effects, it is convenient to use a model in which these effects appear as additive noise. The following model of asset prices is commonly used and specifies that the observed log price, p_i, is determined by a market fundamental log price, f_i, with a random disturbance term, u_i, representing microstructure noise

$$p_i = f_i + u_i. \tag{15.15}$$

For simplicity, microstructure noise is often assumed to be distributed as $u_i \sim iid(0, \sigma_u^2)$ over time as well as being independent of the market fundamental log price f_i.

To show the effects of microstructure noise on the realized variance estimator, define the average realized variance as

$$\frac{RV(M)}{M} = \frac{1}{M} \sum_{i=1}^{M} r_i^2 = \frac{1}{M} \sum_{i=1}^{M} (p_{i/M} - p_{(i-1)/M})^2.$$

---

[1] Interestingly, the operation of the asymptotic theory leading to the two results is similar because of the independence of the Brownian motion infinitesimal increments dB_t in different intervals, even those that are immediately neighboring.

Substituting for price using equation (15.15) gives

$$\frac{RV(M)}{M} = \frac{1}{M} \sum_{i=1}^{M} (f_{i/M} - f_{(i-1)/M} + u_{i/M} - u_{(i-1)/M})^2. \tag{15.16}$$

Expanding this expression gives

$$\frac{RV(M)}{M} = \frac{1}{M} \sum_{i=1}^{M} (f_{i/M} - f_{(i-1)/M})^2 + \frac{1}{M} \sum_{i=1}^{M} (u_{i/M} - u_{(i-1)/M})^2$$

$$+ \frac{2}{M} \sum_{i=1}^{M} (f_{i/M} - f_{(i-1)/M})(u_{i/M} - u_{(i-1)/M}), \tag{15.17}$$

which decomposes the RV estimator in terms of the sample variance of the market fundamental price, the sample variance of the microstructure noise, and the cross-product term $(f_{i/M} - f_{(i-1)/M})(u_{i/M} - u_{(i-1)/M})$.

Allowing for infinite sampling by letting $M \to \infty$, the first term in equation (15.17) becomes

$$\text{plim} \frac{1}{M} \sum_{i=1}^{M} (f_{i/M} - f_{(i-1)/M})^2 = 0,$$

because

$$\text{plim} \sum_{i=1}^{M} (f_{i/M} - f_{(i-1)/M})^2 = IV,$$

by definition, which is a constant. The second term reduces to

$$\text{plim} \frac{1}{M} \sum_{i=1}^{M} (u_{i/M} - u_{(i-1)/M})^2 = 2\sigma_u^2,$$

a result that relies on

$$\text{plim} \frac{1}{M} \sum_{i=1}^{M} (u_{i/M})^2 = \text{plim} \frac{1}{M} \sum_{i=1}^{M} (u_{(i-1)/M})^2 = \sigma_u^2,$$

and the property that the u_i are mutually independent. The last term in equation (15.17) is zero because of the assumed independence between the noise u_i and the fundamental price f_i.

Based on these results, as $M \to \infty$ the average RV estimator in equation (15.17), in the presence of microstructure noise, converges to a constant given by twice the variance of the microstructure noise,

$$\text{plim} \frac{RV(M)}{M} = 2\sigma_u^2. \tag{15.18}$$

This expression implies that in the case of infinite sampling, RV is totally dominated by microstructure noise. This property explains why the signature plot in Figure 15.2 shows RV diverging to infinity as the sampling interval shrinks toward zero.

To circumvent the problems arising from the presence of microstructure noise, Andersen et al. (2001) proposed a conservative cut-off point suggested by the typical shape of a signature plot for computing RV by choosing 5-minute intervals to perform the computation. This choice of a 5-minute sampling interval rather than a smaller sampling interval helps control the impact of microstructure noise and has been affirmed in many later studies—see Liu, Patton, and Sheppard (2015) for further discussion. Once the sampling frequency has been established, the RV computation is repeated for every day in the sample in order to generate a daily time series of realized variance.

Instead of choosing a realized variance estimator based on a single sparse frequency such as the 5-minute interval for which the signature plot is stable, another approach proposed by Zhang, Mykland, and Aït-Sahalia (2005) is to use all of the information from K realized variance estimators constructed at sparse frequencies into a unique estimator. Letting $\{M_1, M_2, \cdots, M_k\}$ represent the sparse frequencies, the strategy is to compute the sample mean of these K realized variance estimators and (bias) adjust the mean by the realized variance estimator evaluated at a 1-second frequency, $M = 23400$, according to the following formula

$$RV_{ZMA} = \frac{1}{K} \sum_{k=1}^{K} RV_k(M_k) - \frac{\overline{M}}{M} RV(M), \tag{15.19}$$

where $\overline{M} = K^{-1} \sum_{k=1}^{K} M_k$ is the sample average of the sparse sampling frequencies. The choice of the number of realized variances K is estimated using the rule

$$K = \left(\frac{RQ}{12 \left(\widehat{\sigma}_u^2 \right)^2} \right)^{-1/3} M^{2/3}, \tag{15.20}$$

where $\widehat{\sigma}_u^2$ is an estimate of the microstructure noise variance given by

$$\widehat{\sigma}_u^2 = \frac{1}{2M} RV(M) = \frac{1}{2M} \sum_{i=1}^{M} r_i^2, $$

which uses the earlier result for the full data computation given in equation (15.18). Zhang et al. (2005) show that the estimator in equation (15.19) is consistent and asymptotically normal, although convergence occurs at the much slower rate of $M^{1/6}$ rather than the usual $M^{1/2}$ rate. An alternative approach to correcting the RV estimate for microstructure noise is given by Barndorff-Nielsen et al. (2008).

15.5 BIPOWER VARIATION AND JUMPS

The assumption that log prices adjust continuously over time according to the stochastic differential equation (15.7) is often violated in practice due to other factors affecting the price. These violations may be accommodated by formulating a more general model. One such model for the log price p_t of a financial asset combines a continuous sample path with a jump process by extending the stochastic differential equation (15.7) to the following augmented form

$$dp_t = \mu_t dt + \sigma_t dB_t + \kappa_t dN_t, \tag{15.21}$$

where $\kappa_t dN_t$ embodies the jump process. The model in equation (15.21) is called a *jump-diffusion* model. The jump component of the model comprises two components

(i) A binary integer process dN_t that records increments in an integer valued stochastic process N_t and identifies whether or not a jump occurs
(ii) A time-varying parameter process κ_t that controls the size and sign of the jump in log prices when the jump does occur.

If there are no jumps, $N_t = 0$ and the jump-diffusion model then reduces to the simpler model in equation (15.7). N_t is an integer-valued random variable and a common assumption is to let N_t be a Poisson process that counts the number of occurrences (here of jumps) that have occurred.[2] In this case, N_t has independent increments dN_t and is distributed as a Poisson random variable with parameter λ (commonly referred to as the *intensity parameter*) for which $E(N_t) = \lambda t$. For small values of λ the probability of a jump occurring is relatively small, resulting in sporadic large movements in log prices over time. For larger values of λ the probability of jumps increases, resulting in periods where there is a sequence of large movements in log prices as might occur during financial crises. For the extreme case of no jumps, $N_t = 0$, and the intensity parameter effectively is $\lambda = 0$.

Some of the properties of the jump diffusion model in equation (15.21) may be explored by simulating the following discretized jump diffusion model with constant parameters

$$p_{i/M} = p_{(i-1)/M} + \mu \Delta t + \sigma \Delta B_{i/M} + \kappa \Delta N_{i/M}, \qquad i = 1, 2, \cdots, 23400, \tag{15.22}$$

over a 6.5-hour trading day with a discretized time step of $\Delta t = 1/23400$, where the discretized jump process $\Delta N_{i/M}$ is defined as

$$\Delta N_{i/M} = \begin{cases} 1 : \text{With jump with probability } \lambda \Delta t \\ 0 : \text{No jump with probability } 1 - \lambda \Delta t \end{cases}. \tag{15.23}$$

The size of the jump in the log price is set at $\kappa = 0.02$, while the intensity parameter is chosen as $\lambda = 1.5$, resulting in a probability of $\lambda \Delta t = 1.5/23400 = 0.6410 \times 10^{-4}$ that a jump in the log price occurs during the trading day. The remaining parameters in equation (15.22) are chosen as before for the discretized stochastic differential equation in (15.8). The daily mean is $\mu = 0.05/250 = 2 \times 10^{-4}$, the daily integrated variance is $\sigma^2 = 0.04/250 = 1.6 \times 10^{-4}$, and the opening log price is $p_0 = 1$. The simulated log price during the trading day given in Figure 15.4 shows that the log price follows a continuous time path initially, with a single jump in the price in the middle of the trading day, followed by continuous movements in the price for the rest of the day.

Since the integrated variance σ_t^2 in equation (15.21) is by definition a continuous time process, it is important to extract the discontinuous time movements in log prices otherwise the usual *RV* estimates of *IV* will be biased and fail to reflect just the continuous movements alone. In the case where there is no microstructure noise, the relationship between *RV* and *IV* for continuous sampling ($M \to \infty$) is given by the following limit

---

[2] See Aït-Sahalia and Jacod (2012) for a discussion of other jump models.

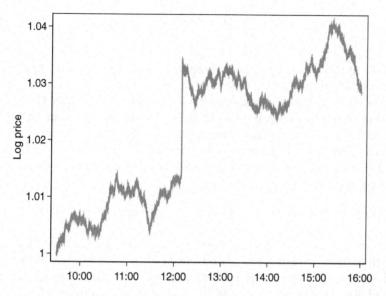

FIGURE 15.4 Simulated log prices over a 6.5-hour trading day using the discretized stochastic differential equation with Poisson jumps in equation (15.22). The parameters are $\mu = 0.05/250$, $\sigma^2 = 0.04250$, $\lambda = 1.5$, $\kappa = 0.02$, and a 1-second step interval equal to $\Delta t = 1/23400$.

$$\text{plim}RV(M) = IV + \sum_{t \in (0,1]} \kappa_t^2. \tag{15.24}$$

This expression reduces to equation (15.6) in the absence of jumps ($N_t = 0$), and then RV is a consistent estimate of IV. In general, the realized variance estimator is biased upward, as it is a function of the population variance (IV) plus the sum of all squared jump sizes (κ_t^2) that have occurred over the trading day.

To estimate IV in the presence of infrequent jumps, the realized variance estimator in equation (15.3) may be replaced by the realized bipower variance estimator (Barndorff-Nielsen and Shephard, 2004), which is given by the formula

$$BV(M) = \frac{\pi}{2} \sum_{i=2}^{M} |r_i| \times |r_{i-1}|. \tag{15.25}$$

A comparison of the realized variance and realized bipower variance estimators in equations (15.3) and (15.25), respectively, shows that the squared intraday log returns used to compute realized variance are replaced by the absolute values of the adjacent log returns, scaled by the constant $\pi/2$.

Barndorff-Nielsen and Shephard (2004) show that $BV(M)$ is a consistent estimator of integrated volatility so that

$$\text{plim } BV(M) = IV. \tag{15.26}$$

Combining the results in equations (15.24) and (15.26) suggests that the difference between the realized variance (RV) and realized bipower variance (BV) estimators provides an estimate of the total contribution of jumps to the total variation during the trading day

$$\text{plim}\left(RV\left(M\right) - BV\left(M\right)\right) = \sum_{t \in (0,1]} \kappa_t^2. \tag{15.27}$$

The statistic $RV(M) - BV(M)$ has an asymptotic distribution under the null hypothesis of no jumps, which can be used to test for the presence of jumps. A formal test of the presence of jumps is provided in Barndorff-Nielsen and Shephard (2004).

As a test of the consistency property of the bipower realized variance estimator given in equation (15.26) in the presence of jumps as well as the corresponding jump estimator given in equation (15.27), the RV and BV statistics are computed using the simulated 1-second data in Figure 15.4, which is based on a jump parameter of $\kappa = 0.02$. The alternative realized variance estimates are

$$RV(23400) = 5.63 \times 10^{-4}, \qquad BV(23400) = 1.67 \times 10^{-4}.$$

The robustness of the BV estimate in the presence of the jumps is demonstrated by the fact that the estimate is close to the true integrated variance value of $IV = 1.60 \times 10^{-4}$. By contrast, the realized variance estimator is influenced by the size of the jump, producing an upward biased estimate of 5.63×10^{-4}, which is more than twice as large as the true IV parameter value. Using equation (15.27) yields an estimate of the size of the jump of

$$RV(23400) - BV(23400) = 5.66 \times 10^{-4} - 1.65 \times 10^{-4} = 4.01 \times 10^{-4}.$$

As there is just one jump, this estimate agrees closely with the (squared) true jump parameter value of $\kappa^2 = 0.02^2 = 4.0 \times 10^{-4}$.

The realized bipower variance estimator is now applied to the IBM intraday data presented in Table 15.1, Figure 15.1, and the signature plot of Figure 15.2. The majority of recorded prices, precisely 98.8%, involve changes of at most 3 cents. The largest recorded change in price occurs shortly after the start of the trading day at 9:35:58, where there is a change in price of 21 cents. As this change in price is indeed very different to most of the other price changes, this suggests that it represents a discontinuous price jump during the trading day. To determine the relative importance of this change in price, and hence price jumps in general in the observed series, the realized bipower variance estimator in equation (15.25) is computed using a sampling frequency of 1 minute ($M = 390$), giving

$$
\begin{aligned}
BV(390) &= \frac{2}{\pi} \sum_{i=2}^{390} |r_i| \times |r_{i-1}| \\
&= \frac{2}{\pi} \left(|0.0008| \times |-0.0004| + |-0.0004| \times |0.0008| + \cdots\right) \\
&= 0.000103.
\end{aligned}
$$

The corresponding realized variance estimate for the same sampling frequency of 1 minute is $RV(390) = 0.000118$, which is slightly higher than the $BV(390)$ estimate. The difference in the two estimates yields an estimate of the contribution to total variation from the jump component of

$$RV(390) - BV(390) = 0.000118 - 0.000103 = 0.0000154.$$

The relative contributions to the total variation as estimated by RV are

$$\text{Continuous}: \quad 100 \times \frac{0.000103}{0.000118} = 87\%$$

$$\text{Jump} \quad : \quad 100 \times \frac{0.000015}{0.000118} = 13\%,$$

showing that the majority of the variation in IBM log prices during the trading day comes from continuous movements, with just 13% coming from discrete price jumps.

15.6 FORECASTING

The next step in the modeling process is to use the daily time series of realized variance to forecast future movements in volatility, a task that is central to pricing options and risk management. To generate out-of-sample variance forecasts, classical time series models can be used, including the class of ARMA models discussed in Chapter 4. A model that is found to be successful empirically is the heterogeneous autoregressive (HAR) realized variance model of Corsi (2009).

Let $RV_t^{(d)}$ represent the daily RV at day t. Now define the corresponding weekly and monthly respective estimates at each day according to

$$\begin{aligned}
\text{Weekly} \quad &: \quad RV_t^{(w)} = \frac{1}{5}(RV_t^{(d)} + RV_{t-1}^{(d)} + \cdots + RV_{t-4}^{(d)}) \\
\text{Monthly} &: \quad RV_t^{(m)} = \frac{1}{22}(RV_t^{(d)} + RV_{t-1}^{(d)} + \cdots + RV_{t-21}^{(d)}).
\end{aligned} \tag{15.28}$$

The HAR model is specified as the following autoregressive model

$$RV_t^{(d)} = \beta_0 + \beta_d RV_{t-1}^{(d)} + \beta_w RV_{t-1}^{(w)} + \beta_m RV_{t-1}^{(m)} + u_t, \tag{15.29}$$

where u_t is a disturbance term. This equation shows that the next-day variance is a function of three components that are designed to capture the role of heterogeneous traders: $RV_t^{(d)}$ reflects daily or higher trading frequency traders, $RV_t^{(w)}$ captures investors who typically rebalance their positions weekly, and $RV_t^{(m)}$ represents relatively long-term investors with investment horizons of 1 month or longer. An alternative formulation of the HAR model as adopted originally by Corsi (2009) is to re-express the variables in equation (15.29) in terms of realized volatilities (standard deviations) by taking the square root of the realized variances, $RV_t^{(d)}$, $RV_t^{(w)}$, and $RV_t^{(m)}$.

Substituting the weekly and monthly realized variance expressions into equation (15.29) shows that the HAR model represents a restricted AR(22) time series model in terms of the realized daily variance $RV_t^{(d)}$, with the total number of parameters restricted to just 4 parameters as given by $\{\beta_0, \beta_d, \beta_w, \beta_m\}$. A potential advantage of the HAR specification is that the model can yield relatively more precise estimates than an unrestricted AR(22) model, provided that the implied restrictions of the HAR model are indeed consistent with the data. As with autoregressive time series models, the parameters in equation (15.29) may be estimated by ordinary least squares.

To illustrate the estimation of the HAR model in equation (15.29), a daily realized variance time series for IBM from 4 January 2010 to 30 April 2013 is used. The daily log returns series and the constructed realized variance series are illustrated in Figure 15.5.

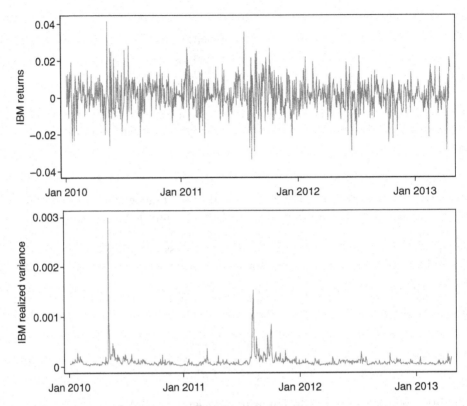

FIGURE 15.5 Plot of log returns and realized variance for IBM from 4 January 2010 to 30 April 2013.

Estimates of the parameters of the HAR model over the full sample period are presented in Table 15.3. To control for serial correlation in the error term, u_t, in equation (15.29), the standard errors are adjusted using the Newey–West estimator with the lag order chosen to be 6. Inspection of the results shows that the parameter estimates of β_d and β_m are statistically significant, suggesting the presence of multiple frequencies in determining the variance. By contrast, the parameter estimate associated with the weekly variance estimator is not statistically significant ($t = 1.11$).

To examine the forecasting properties of the HAR model for IBM, equation (15.29) is re-estimated using a moving window of 600 observations, which is used to generate

TABLE 15.3 Ordinary least squares estimates of the HAR model parameters for IBM from 4 January 2010 to 30 April 2013, with t statistics based on the Newey–West estimator with a lag order of 6.

Parameter	Variable	Estimate	t statistic
β_0	constant	0.00002	2.84
β_d	$RV_t^{(d)}$	0.44705	3.33
β_w	$RV_t^{(w)}$	0.07525	1.11
β_m	$RV_t^{(m)}$	0.23090	2.15

recursive 1-day-ahead forecasts of the realized variance. The total number of daily forecasts is 209, which are summarized using the MSE, MAE, and QLIKE statistics applied to the realized variance series (see Chapter 7 and Chapter 13 for discussions of the QLIKE statistic).

For comparison, the forecast properties of the AR(1), AR(3), and AR(22) time-series models are presented. The results of this forecasting experiment are given in Table 15.4, and these show that the AR(22) model performs the best, as it generates the smallest values of the forecast statistics. The HAR model is the next best performer followed by the AR(3) and the AR(1) models. The fact that the AR(22) model performs better than the HAR model in the case of the IBM data suggests that the restrictions imposed on the lag structure of the HAR model are not necessarily consistent with the data.

The forecast evaluations use realized variance RV when it is actually the integrated variance IV that is the ultimate objective in the forecasting experiment. This fact means that forecasts are presented in terms of a proxy for IV that is subject to measurement error, rather than IV itself. As RV is a consistent estimator of IV in the case of no jumps, the $RMSE$ statistic preserves the ranking of the models in terms of forecasting performance (Hansen and Lunde, 2005), as does the forecast statistic $QLIKE$ (Patton, 2011), whereas the forecast statistic MAE does not. To address the measurement error issue, Bollerslev, Patton, and Quaedvlieg (2016) extend the HAR forecasting model by allowing the autoregressive parameters $\{\beta_d, \beta_w, \beta_m\}$ in equation (15.28) to be time-varying. This extension is found to yield significant improvements in the accuracy of the forecasts.

15.7 THE REALIZED GARCH MODEL

Since realized variance RV is a consistent estimator of integrated variance IV, Hansen, Huang, and Shek (2012) propose a realized GARCH model by augmenting the GARCH specification discussed in Chapter 13 with the conditional variance h_t representing IV. Letting r_t represent daily log returns, the realized GARCH model has the following form,

$$
\begin{aligned}
r_t &= \mu_0 + u_t && \text{[Mean]} \\
h_t &= \alpha_0 + \alpha_1 RV_{t-1} + \beta_1 h_{t-1} && \text{[Variance]} \\
RV_t &= \delta_0 + \delta_1 h_t + v_t && \text{[RV]} \\
u_t &\sim N(0, h_t), \quad v_t \sim N(0, \sigma_v^2). && \text{[Disturbance Distributions]}
\end{aligned}
$$

TABLE 15.4 Comparison of the performance of the 1-day-ahead, out-of-sample forecasts for alternative models. The results are based on 209 recursive, one-day-ahead forecasts using a rolling window of 600 observations.

Forecast Statistic	Forecast Model			
	HAR	AR(1)	AR(3)	AR(22)
MSE($\times 10^{-9}$)	1.6333	1.7465	1.6954	1.5557
MAE($\times 10^{-5}$)	2.7680	2.9742	2.9029	2.6902
QLIKE	−8.6333	−8.6284	−8.6296	−8.6337

This specification is a bivariate model with dependent variables r_t and RV_t. There are two important features. First, the conditional variance involves replacing the usual lagged squared shock (u_{t-1}^2) in the standard GARCH model by RV_{t-1}. Second, the RV equation captures potential measurement error by using RV_t as a proxy for integrated volatility, defined here as h_t. For the special case of $\delta_0 = 0$ and $\delta_1 = 1$, RV_t represents an unbiased estimator of IV. This form of the model is easily extended to allow for additional lags, alternative functional forms, and asymmetries. Two extensions of the realized GARCH model are considered in the exercises.

Estimation of the realized GARCH model is relatively straightforward, as the likelihood function has a closed-form expression that can be decomposed into two components. By using the property that the joint probability equals the product of a marginal probability times a conditional probability, the joint density function of the two dependent variables r_t and RV_t at time t is expressed as

$$f(r_t, RV_t; \theta) = f(r_t; \theta_1) f(RV_t | r_t; \theta_1, \theta_2), \tag{15.30}$$

where $\theta = \{\theta_1, \theta_2\}$, with $\theta_1 = \{\mu_0, \alpha_0, \alpha_1, \beta_1\}$ and $\theta_2 = \{\delta_0, \delta_1, \sigma_v^2\}$. As in Chapters 13 and 14, conditioning on the lags $\{r_{t-1}, r_{t-2}, \cdots, RV_{t-1}, RV_{t-2}, \cdots\}$ is suppressed to simplify the presentation. For a sample of size T, the log likelihood function is

$$\log L(\theta) = \frac{1}{T} \sum_{t=1}^{T} \log f(r_t; \theta_1) + \frac{1}{T} \sum_{t=1}^{T} \log f(RV_t | r_t; \theta_1, \theta_2). \tag{15.31}$$

The log likelihood function of the realized GARCH model is

$$\log L(\theta) = -\frac{1}{2T} \sum_{t=1}^{T} \left(\log(2\pi) + \log(h_t) + \frac{r_t^2}{h_t} \right)$$

$$- \frac{1}{2T} \sum_{t=1}^{T} \left(\log(2\pi) + \log(\sigma_v^2) + \frac{(RV_t - \delta_0 - \delta_1 h_t)^2}{\sigma_v^2} \right)$$

$$= \log L_1(\theta_1) + \log L_2(\theta_1, \theta_2). \tag{15.32}$$

The term $\log L_1(\theta_1)$ represents the log likelihood function of the standard GARCH model discussed in Chapter 13, while $\log L_2(\theta_1, \theta_2)$ is the corresponding log likelihood function associated with RV_t.

The joint log likelihood function $\log L(\theta)$ in equation (15.32) is maximized with respect to θ using an iterative algorithm. An alternative 2-step estimation strategy that takes advantage of the decomposition of $\log L(\theta)$ in equation (15.32) is as follows. The first step involves maximizing $\log L_1(\theta_1)$ with respect to θ_1 and generating $\widehat{\theta}_1$ as well as the realized GARCH estimates $\widehat{h}_t$. The second step involves maximizing $\log L_2(\theta_1, \theta_2)$ with respect to θ_2, with $\theta_1 = \widehat{\theta}_1$ and h_t replaced by $\widehat{h}_t$ from the first step. Formally this step is implemented by simply regressing RV_t on $\widehat{h}_t$. Since $\widehat{h}_t$ is used in this step and not the true conditional variance h_t, the standard errors obtained from estimating this regression equation are incorrect, as they do not take into account the estimation error arising from the use of $\widehat{h}_t$. To generate correct standard errors, the log likelihood function in equation (15.32) is maximized in one iteration based on the estimates obtained from the 2-step estimation procedure.

The realized GARCH model is estimated using the daily open-to-close log returns (in percentage) on IBM from 4 January 2010 to 30 April 2013, which are plotted in Figure 15.5. For comparative purposes, the following GARCH(1,1) model is also estimated,

$$r_t = \mu_0 + u_t, \qquad u_t \sim N(0, h_t)$$
$$h_t = \alpha_0 + \alpha_1 u_{t-1}^2 + \beta_1 h_{t-1}.$$

The results from estimating the realized GARCH and standard GARCH models are reported in Table 15.5. Also reported are the full log likelihood value, $\log L(\widehat{\theta})$, and the partial log likelihood value, $\log L_1(\widehat{\theta}_1)$. The empirical results provide strong evidence in favor of the realized GARCH model over the standard GARCH model. First, the value of the partial log likelihood function of the realized GARCH model is -1.2060, which is greater than the associated value of the GARCH log likelihood function of -1.2467. Second, a comparison of the parameter estimates of α_1 for the two models shows that the estimate from the realized GARCH model is 0.5800, which is over five times larger than the estimate obtained from the standard GARCH model. Third, the parameter estimate of δ_1 in the realized variance equation is 0.8051, which is statistically significant, indicating that there is a strong relationship between integrated volatility h_t and realized variance RV_t.

15.8 REALIZED COVARIANCE

The analysis so far focusses on univariate models of realized variance. As with multivariate GARCH models, the analysis may be extended to N assets to allow for realized variances and covariances. This extension has the advantage of providing nonparametric time-varying estimates of correlations and β-risk, among other useful statistics.

In the case of 2 assets sampled at M intervals during a day, the realized covariance for a day is the product of the intraday log returns on the 2 assets summed over a day. Combining the realized covariance with the corresponding realized variances yields the (2×2) realized covariance matrix

TABLE 15.5 Maximum likelihood estimates of the realized GARCH and standard GARCH model parameters. Standard errors are computed using the OPG matrix.

Parameter	Realized GARCH		GARCH	
	Estimate	t statistic	Estimate	t statistic
μ_0	0.0134	0.5039	0.0159	0.5494
α_0	0.0620	1.6450	0.0564	3.0405
α_1	0.5800	8.8737	0.1151	5.1448
β_1	0.2193	10.5366	0.8150	20.4157
δ_0	0.3381	2.5830		
δ_1	0.8051	8.9092		
σ_v^2	1.5579	114.9562		
$\log L(\widehat{\theta})$	-2.8466			
$\log L_1(\widehat{\theta}_1)$	-1.2060		-1.2467	

$$RC(M) = \begin{pmatrix} \sum_{i=1}^{M} r_{1i}^2 & \sum_{i=1}^{M} r_{1i}r_{2i} \\ \sum_{i=1}^{M} r_{2i}r_{1i} & \sum_{i=1}^{M} r_{2i}^2 \end{pmatrix}, \tag{15.33}$$

where the realized variances are given on the diagonal, and the realized covariance is on the off diagonal. Extending this to N assets yields an $(N \times N)$ realized covariance matrix

$$RC(M) = \begin{pmatrix} \sum_{i=1}^{M} r_{1i}^2 & \sum_{i=1}^{M} r_{1i}r_{2i} & \cdots & \sum_{i=1}^{M} r_{1i}r_{Ni} \\ \sum_{i=1}^{M} r_{2i}r_{1i} & \sum_{i=1}^{M} r_{2i}^2 & \cdots & \sum_{i=1}^{M} r_{2i}r_{Ni} \\ \vdots & \vdots & \ddots & \vdots \\ \sum_{i=1}^{M} r_{Ni}r_{1i} & \sum_{i=1}^{M} r_{Ni}r_{2i} & \cdots & \sum_{i=1}^{M} r_{Ni}^2 \end{pmatrix}, \tag{15.34}$$

with the N realized variances down the diagonal and the $N(N-1)/2$ realized covariances in the off-diagonal cells. The realized covariance matrix in equation (15.33) or equation (15.34) is a consistent estimator of the integrated covariance (IC), which is written as

$$\text{plim}\, RC(M) \to IC. \tag{15.35}$$

This expression is the multivariate analogue of the consistency condition for the realized variance in equation (15.6). In the case of $N = 2$ assets, the integrated covariance matrix in equation (15.35) is defined as

$$IC = \begin{pmatrix} \int_{t-1}^{t} \sigma_{1s}^2 ds & \int_{t-1}^{t} \sigma_{1s}\sigma_{2s} ds \\ \int_{t-1}^{t} \sigma_{1s}\sigma_{2s} ds & \int_{t-1}^{t} \sigma_{2s}^2 ds \end{pmatrix}. \tag{15.36}$$

As with the construction of RV in the univariate case, the presence of microstructure noise can distort estimates based on realized covariances. As before, this distortion can be corrected by sampling more sparsely based on a signature plot analysis applied to the realized covariance. However, an additional issue arises in working with high-frequency multivariate data because financial assets are commonly traded at different timestamps. Epps (1979) showed that the effect of non-synchronous trading leads to a downward bias of the realized covariance estimator, commonly known as the Epps effect.

The Epps effect is demonstrated in Table 15.6 based on simulating the following discretized bivariate stochastic differential system

$$p_{i/M} = p_{(i-1)/M} + \mu \Delta t + \Omega^{1/2} \Delta B_{i/M}, \qquad i = 1, 2, \cdots, 23400, \tag{15.37}$$

where $p_{i/M}$ is a (2×1) vector of log prices with both of the initial log prices set at 1. In this system μ and Ω are, respectively, the daily vector of means and the integrated covariance matrix assuming 250 trading days in the year with parameter values

$$\mu = \begin{bmatrix} 0.05 \\ 0.05 \end{bmatrix} \frac{1}{250} = \begin{bmatrix} 2 \times 10^{-4} \\ 2 \times 10^{-4} \end{bmatrix},$$

$$\Omega = \begin{bmatrix} 0.04 & 0.03 \\ 0.03 & 0.05 \end{bmatrix} \frac{1}{250} = \begin{bmatrix} 1.6 \times 10^{-4} & 1.2 \times 10^{-4} \\ 1.2 \times 10^{-4} & 2.0 \times 10^{-4} \end{bmatrix},$$

and $\Delta B_{i/M}$ is a bivariate normal random variable distributed as $N(0, \Delta t)$. The square root of the covariance matrix $\Omega^{1/2}$ in equation (15.37) is given by the Cholesky decomposition of Ω. The simulation length is $\Delta t = 1/23400$, corresponding to 1-second tick intervals and a 6.5-hour trading day.

Table 15.6 gives the integrated and realized variances for the two assets, as well as the integrated and realized covariance. Non-synchronous trading is generated by randomly setting the two simulated log prices from equation (15.37) to zero and then filling in the pertinent log prices at these non-trade ticks by the previous log prices. The row corresponding to 100% is where all trades take place at each tick, with the result that the realized variances and the realized covariance show no evidence of bias. When the number of active trades is reduced to 75%, the realized variances still exhibit no bias, but the realized covariance is now biased downward by about 40%. The bias increases to over 70% when only 50% of potential trades take place, and to nearly 80% when only a quarter of all potential trades take place. In contrast, the realized variance estimates in the presence of non-synchronous trading still exhibit very little bias even in the most extreme case of 25% of ticks registering trades.

To correct for the Epps effect, Barndorff-Nielsen et al. (2011) propose a sampling scheme that generates synchronized prices across assets, known as the refresh time synchronization scheme. The first refresh time, $\tau(1)$, is that first time since the opening of the market when all assets have traded at least once. The refresh prices are then the current or the recent prices of the assets. The second refresh time, $\tau(2)$, is the next time all assets have been traded at least once since the first refresh time $\tau(1)$. Repeating this sequence yields in total M refresh times, $\tau(j), j = 1, 2, \cdots, M$, and corresponding M sets of synchronized refresh prices $p_{\tau(j)}$.

An example of non-synchronous trading is given in Table 15.7, which tabulates the transaction prices on three technology stocks (Dell, IBM, and Microsoft) during the first 20 seconds of trading on 4 January 2007. From the opening of the market at 09:30, Dell and Microsoft are traded at nearly every tick in the first 20 seconds, whereas IBM is traded more intermittently at practically half this rate.

TABLE 15.6 Demonstration of the Epps effect using a Monte Carlo simulation based on equation (15.37). The column headed Ticks gives the proportion of ticks at which all stocks are traded, so $\alpha\%$ means that there are only $\alpha\%$ ticks at which all stocks trade. All values are scaled by 10^4.

Ticks (%)	Asset 1		Asset 2		Assets 1 & 2	
	IV	RV	IV	RV	IC	RC
100	1.60	1.60	2.00	1.99	1.20	1.20
75	1.60	1.60	2.00	1.99	1.20	0.73
50	1.60	1.63	2.00	1.98	1.20	0.40
25	1.60	1.60	2.00	2.07	1.20	0.21

TABLE 15.7 Tick-by-tick transaction prices and refresh prices on Dell, IBM, and Microsoft, for the first 20 seconds of trading from the opening of the market at 09:30:00 on 4 January 2007. Missing values mean that a trade did not take place.

Time		Transaction Price			Refresh Price		
Real	Refresh	Dell	IBM	Microsoft	Dell	IBM	Microsoft
09:30:00		25.6207	.	29.6974			
09:30:01		25.6317	.	29.6955			
09:30:02		25.6500	.	29.6913			
09:30:03	$\tau(1)$	25.5407	97.2567	29.6806	25.5407	97.2600	29.6806
09:30:04		25.6600	.	29.6843			
09:30:05		25.6550	.	29.6813			
09:30:06		25.6720	.	29.6710			
09:30:07		25.6831	.	29.6707			
09:30:08	$\tau(2)$	25.5100	96.9850	29.6783	25.5100	96.9850	29.6783
09:30:09	$\tau(3)$	25.7000	96.9710	29.6887	25.7000	96.9710	29.6887
09:30:10	$\tau(4)$	25.7000	96.9680	29.6880	25.7000	96.9680	29.6880
09:30:11	$\tau(5)$	25.7000	97.0000	29.6959	25.7000	97.0000	29.6959
09:30:12	$\tau(6)$	25.5200	96.9625	29.7000	25.5200	96.9625	29.7000
09:30:13	$\tau(7)$	25.6886	97.1133	29.7000	25.6886	97.1133	29.7000
09:30:14	$\tau(8)$	25.7000	97.0950	29.6975	25.7000	97.0950	29.6975
09:30:15		25.6819	.	29.6903			
09:30:16		25.7000	.	29.6957			
09:30:17	$\tau(9)$	25.7000	97.2400	.	25.7000	97.2400	29.6957
09:30:18		.	.	29.6950			
09:30:19		.	.	29.6900			
09:30:20	$\tau(10)$	25.7067	97.2050	29.6964	25.7067	97.2050	29.6964

Inspection of Table 15.7 shows that the first refresh time occurs 3 seconds after trading begins at 09:30:03. In fact, at this point in time, there is perfect synchronization, as all three stocks trade at this point in time. The resulting refresh prices at $\tau(1)$ on Dell, IBM, and Microsoft are, respectively, 25.5407, 97.2600, and 29.6806. The second refresh time $\tau(2)$ occurs at 09:30:08. For the next 6 seconds (until 09:30:14) all the stocks are traded at each tick so that these times also represent refresh times, yielding a total of 8 refresh times out of a possible total of 14 since the start of trading. The next and 9th refresh time occurs at 09:30:17, as this is when IBM is the last of the three stocks to trade since the previous refresh time at $\tau(8)$. The refresh prices at $\tau(9)$ are 25.7000 for Dell, which traded at the same price that it traded at in the previous tick, 97.2400 for IBM, which is the price it traded at since the previous refresh price, and 29.6957, which is the price of Microsoft from the previous tick, as it did not trade at the current tick. In total, the procedure results in 6535 refresh prices for the three assets out of a maximum possible number of 23400 prices in the case of a 6.5-hour trading day.

Once the refresh times have been established, the intraday log returns are computed using the refresh prices. By construction, the log returns are not necessarily defined on the same time interval. Using these log returns to compute realized covariance in equation (15.34) yields a consistent estimator of the integrated covariance matrix IC, when $M \to \infty$, assuming that there are no distortions arising from the presence of microstructure noise. If this condition is not satisfied, then as with the computation of the realized variance, sampling from the refresh prices is chosen more sparsely when computing the realized variances and covariances using multivariate data.

The realized covariance matrix for Dell, IBM, and Microsoft, on 4 January 2007, using all $M = 6535$ refreshed log returns is

$$RC = \begin{pmatrix} 469.90 \times 10^{-5} & 1.12 \times 10^{-5} & 14.16 \times 10^{-5} \\ 1.12 \times 10^{-5} & 21.00 \times 10^{-5} & -2.90 \times 10^{-5} \\ 14.16 \times 10^{-5} & -2.90 \times 10^{-5} & 176.70 \times 10^{-5} \end{pmatrix}. \tag{15.38}$$

To identify the presence of any microstructure noise at relatively high frequencies, Figure 15.6 gives signature plots for the three variances down the main diagonal and the three covariances in the upper off-diagonal cells. In each figure, the x-axis represents the number of skipped refresh prices, starting at the highest frequency where all 6535 refresh prices are used, to the lowest frequency where every 363 ($\simeq 6535/18$) refresh prices are used.

Inspection of Figure 15.6 shows that as the number of refresh time prices increases, the three realized variances diverge and the three realized covariances become less stable. Figure 15.6 also shows that both the realized variances and the realized covariances stabilize if 54 or less refresh log returns are used. The three realized variances (after multiplying by 10^5) are 30.90, 6.65, and 13.20, while the three realized covariances (after

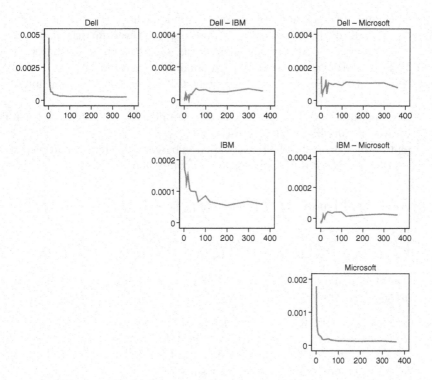

FIGURE 15.6 Realized variance and covariance signature plots for IBM, DELL, and Microsoft on 4 January 2007. The x-axis represents the number of skipped refresh prices.

multiplying by 10^5) are 4.90, 1.36, and 11.10. The full RC matrix based on 54 refresh log returns is

$$RC(54) = \begin{pmatrix} 30.9 \times 10^{-5} & 4.90 \times 10^{-5} & 1.36 \times 10^{-5} \\ 4.90 \times 10^{-5} & 6.65 \times 10^{-5} & 11.10 \times 10^{-5} \\ 1.36 \times 10^{-5} & 11.10 \times 10^{-5} & 13.20 \times 10^{-5} \end{pmatrix}. \tag{15.39}$$

The corresponding three realized correlation coefficients on 4 January 2007 are 0.34, 0.15, and 0.55.

15.9 EXERCISES

The data required for the exercises are available for download as EViews workfiles (*.wf1), Stata datafiles (*.dta), comma delimited text files (*.csv), and as Excel spreadsheets (*.xlsx).

1. **Signature Plot for IBM**

IBM3Jan2006.*

The data are tick-by-tick log prices for IBM on 3 January 2006. In total there are 6326 log prices in the trading day.

(a) Compute the squared daily close-to-open log return.
(b) Compute the RV based on log returns sampled at every ith tick for $i = 1, 2, ..., 30$ as opposed to equally spaced intervals. Compare these estimates with the squared daily close-to-open return obtained in part (a).
(c) Obtain the signature plot at every ith tick for $i = 1, 2, ..., 30$, and interpret its shape.
(d) Compute the RV based on log returns sampled at every 49th tick. What is the average sampling interval in this case?
(e) Compute the realized bipower variation based on log returns sampled at every 15th tick. What is the estimated jump component?

2. **A HAR Model of the USD/CHF Exchange Rate**

HARforecasting.*

The file contains daily realized variance data for IBM for the period 4 January 2010 to 30 April 2013.

(a) Estimate the HAR, AR(1), AR(3), and AR(22) models for the realized variance.
(b) Derive the set of restrictions that the HAR model imposes on the AR(22) parameters. Test these restrictions using the estimated HAR and unrestricted AR(22) models and interpret the results.

(c) Examine the one-step-ahead forecast performance of the HAR model relative to the AR(1), AR(3), and AR(22) models. When making predictions, re-estimate all candidate models based on a moving window of 600 observations. Calculate the MSE, MAE, and QLIKE for all the candidate models.

(d) Repeat step (c) for the two-step-ahead, out-of-the-sample prediction.

3. **Realized GARCH Models of the SPY Index**

realizedgarch4spy.*

The data are daily open-to-close log returns on the exchange-traded index fund, SPY, from 1 January 2002 to 31 December 2007 and the associated realized variance.

(a) Estimate a standard GARCH model

$$r_t = \mu_0 + u_t$$
$$h_t = \alpha_0 + \alpha_1 u_{t-1}^2 + \beta_1 h_{t-1}$$
$$u_t \sim N(0, h_t).$$

(b) Estimate the realized GARCH model

$$r_t = \mu_0 + u_t$$
$$h_t = \alpha_0 + \alpha_1 RV_{t-1} + \beta_1 h_{t-1}$$
$$RV_t = \delta_0 + \delta_1 h_t + v_t$$
$$u_t \sim N(0, h_t)$$
$$v_t \sim N(0, \sigma_v^2).$$

(c) Estimate the realized EGARCH model

$$r_t = \mu_0 + \sqrt{h_t} z_t$$
$$\log h_t = \alpha_0 + \alpha_1 \log RV_{t-1} + \beta_1 \log h_{t-1}$$
$$\log RV_t = \delta_0 + \delta_1 \log h_t + v_t$$
$$z_t \sim N(0, 1)$$
$$v_t \sim N(0, \sigma_v^2),$$

which differs from the standard realized GARCH specification because h_t and RV_t are expressed in natural logarithms.

(d) Estimate the following extension of the realized EGARCH model in part (c)

$$r_t = \mu_0 + \sqrt{h_t} z_t$$
$$\log h_t = \alpha_0 + \alpha_1 \log RV_{t-1} + \beta_1 \log h_{t-1}$$
$$\log RV_t = \delta_0 + \delta_1 \log h_t + \tau_0 z_t + \tau_1 (z_t^2 - 1) + v_t$$
$$z_t \sim N(0, 1)$$
$$v_t \sim N(0, \sigma_v^2),$$

where the expression $\tau_0 z_t + \tau_1 (z_t^2 - 1)$ in the RV equation allows for an asymmetric news impact curve between the variance and shocks to log returns, z_t, and τ_0 and τ_1 are parameters to be estimated.

(e) Compare and contrast the results in parts (a) to (d).

4. Realized GARCH Models of Global Equity Markets

> aord.*, dow.*, ftse.*

The data are daily log returns and realized variances on the Australian All Ordinaries Index, the Dow-Jones index, and the FTSE for the period 2 January 1996 to 16 May 2017. The realized variances are computed using the bipower variation estimator with 5-minute intraday data.

(a) For each equity market, plot the log returns and realized variance data and comment on their time series properties.

(b) For each equity market, estimate the GARCH model

$$r_t = \mu_0 + u_t$$
$$h_t = \alpha_0 + \alpha_1 u_{t-1}^2 + \beta_1 h_{t-1}$$
$$u_t|_{t-1} \sim N(0, h_t),$$

where r_t is the percentage daily log return.

(c) For each equity market, estimate the realized GARCH model

$$r_t = \mu_0 + u_t$$
$$h_t = \alpha_0 + \alpha_1 RV_{t-1} + \beta_1 h_{t-1}$$
$$RV_t = \delta_0 + \delta_1 h_t + v_t$$
$$u_t \sim N(0, h_t)$$
$$v_t \sim N(0, \sigma_v^2),$$

where r_t is the percentage daily log return on equities, and RV_t is the (squared) percentage realized variance.

(d) Compare the estimated models in parts (b) and (c).

5. Estimating Risk Aversion in Asian Equity Markets

> hangseng.*, kospi.*, sse.*, szs.*, topix.*

The data are daily log returns and realized variances on the Hang Seng index in Hong Kong, the KOSPI index in Korea, the SSE and SZS indices in China, and the TOPIX index in Japan. The Hang Seng and the two Chinese indices start on 2 January 1996, the KOSPI starts on 8 January and the TOPIX starts on 4 January. All the data series end on 16 May 2017. The realized variances are computed using the bipower variation estimator with 5-minute intraday data.

(a) For each equity market, plot the log returns and realized variance data and comment on their time series properties.

(b) For each equity market, estimate the following models where r_t is the percentage daily log return, and RV_t is the percentage realized variance.

(i) The GARCH-M model

$$r_t = \mu_0 + \mu_1 h_t + u_t$$
$$h_t = \alpha_0 + \alpha_1 u_{t-1}^2 + \beta_1 h_{t-1}$$
$$u_t \sim N(0, h_t).$$

(ii) The realized GARCH-M model

$$r_t = \mu_0 + \mu_1 h_t + u_t$$
$$h_t = \alpha_0 + \alpha_1 RV_{t-1} + \beta_1 h_{t-1}$$
$$RV_t = \delta_0 + \delta_1 h_t + v_t$$
$$u_t \sim N(0, h_t), \quad v_t \sim N(0, \sigma_v^2).$$

(iii) The combined realized GARCH-M model

$$r_t = \mu_0 + \mu_1 h_t + u_t$$
$$h_t = \alpha_0 + \alpha_1 RV_{t-1} + \alpha_2 u_{t-1}^2 + \beta_1 h_{t-1}$$
$$RV_t = \delta_0 + \delta_1 h_t + v_t$$
$$u_t \sim N(0, h_t), \quad v_t \sim N(0, \sigma_v^2).$$

(c) From the Merton (1973) inter-temporal CAPM, the relative risk aversion parameter is defined as

$$\gamma = \frac{\mu_1}{100},$$

where the parameter μ_1 is divided by 100 because r_t is expressed as a percentage, and hence h_t is expressed as a squared percentage. Compare the parameter estimates of γ based on the estimated models in part (b), and comment on the appropriateness of the alternative model specifications for estimating the relative risk aversion parameter.

6. **Realized Covariance Matrix for Dell, IBM, and Microsoft**

> ibmmsoftdell.*

Consider tick-by-tick transaction prices on Dell, IBM, and Microsoft traded on 4 January 2007, a total of 6535 refresh time prices.

(a) Compute the realized variances and covariances of the three technology stocks using all refresh time prices.

(b) Compute the realized variances and covariances of the three technology stocks at the refresh time prices using the skip intervals: 1, 2, 3, 6, 9, 11, 18, 22, 27, 33, 54, 66, 99, 121, 198, 297, 363.

(c) Obtain the signature plots for the three realized variances and the three realized covariances and interpret the patterns. Hence, estimate the realized covariance matrix of the three technology stocks.

(d) Use the results in part (c) to compute the realized correlations of the three stocks.

CHAPTER 16

Microstructure Models

Previous chapters have focused on specifying and estimating financial models when the available time series data are regularly spaced, such as daily, weekly, or monthly observations. Even with the higher frequency intraday data discussed in Chapter 15, irregularly spaced data is sometimes interpolated to yield regularly spaced data for analysis. Regularly spaced data are obviously convenient for econometric work, but this situation often does not match the way in which data are actually generated.

Most stock exchanges are now fully automated and operate limit order books that list the volumes of bids (offers to buy) and asks (offers to sell) with the associated bid and ask prices currently on offer. In addition to this order book information, actual trades and traded volumes are recorded. Consequently, there is now detailed high-frequency data at the level of individual trades measured in milliseconds, which is readily available to traders and automated (algorithmic) trading systems in real time. These large data sets can subsequently be used for financial econometric analysis. Although these data offer a rich environment for examining the behavior of financial markets, they create special challenges for modeling and estimation.

16.1 CHARACTERISTICS OF HIGH-FREQUENCY DATA

The major challenges posed by high-frequency data are related to a number of well-documented characteristics of these data.

(i) **Irregular observation times**: The data are recorded at the point in time when transactions occur and are therefore irregularly spaced. This characteristic poses an immediate complication for traditional econometric methods and models where observations are equispaced at some fixed interval.

(ii) **Temporal dependence**: Unlike lower frequency data, where the efficient markets hypothesis posits that financial returns will be uncorrelated, the mechanics, as well as the realities, of trading at frequent intervals most often induce strong temporal dependence in high-frequency returns.

(iii) **Leptokurtosis**: For all stocks, there are large numbers of time intervals during which prices do not change. So returns are zero, and flat price trading occurs. This feature contrasts with lower frequency returns data where there is almost always some movement in prices between observations. The result is that the empirical distribution of high-frequency returns has a large peak at zero. In consequence, leptokurtosis is even stronger in these data than in lower frequency observations.

(iv) **Discreteness**: Although the institutional feature of stock markets in which prices are quoted in discrete increments is now less prevalent than in the past, the empirical distribution of price changes is still often restricted to a finite number of discrete values. Discreteness in the return distribution gives rise to model classes where price changes are aggregated into broad categories. Econometric techniques for dealing with limited dependent variables then become relevant.

(v) **Diurnality**: High-frequency data exhibit strong intraday patterns. For most markets, volatility and the volume of trades are highest just after opening and just before closing, as investors open and close positions. The pattern of durations between trades mirrors the form of trade intensity, resulting in durations that have an inverted U-shape over the course of the trading day. Durations tend therefore to be highest around lunch time when trading is sluggish.

While there are some differences in institutional structure and regulation among major stock markets, there are also many common features. All centralized stock exchanges keep detailed records of transactions made on their exchanges. As a result, transactions-level data are now routinely available. Despite the ready availability of the data, entry errors are almost inevitable in high-frequency data, and a considerable amount of effort is often required to clean the data before analysis. For example, it is common for entry errors to occur when transaction prices are recorded outside the range of the bid-ask spread. This aspect of applied modeling and implementation will not be explored here. As noted in Chapter 15, readers are referred to Barndorff-Nielsen et al. (2009), who provide useful practical guidance on data cleaning.

16.2 LIMIT ORDER BOOK

Table 16.1 provides an example of the kind of high-frequency data sets that are now widely used in financial econometrics. The data represent a snapshot of the top of the order book for the first 20 trades on the Australian resources stock BHP Billiton at the opening of trading on 1 September 2011. The transactions data are recorded at the millisecond level, with the 20 trades all occurring within 9 seconds of the opening of the Australian market at 10:10.[1]

The Australian Stock Exchange operates a fully automated, limited order book in which liquidity is provided in the form of *limit orders*, which are orders not necessarily for immediate execution but are rather offers to buy or sell a certain number of shares at a particular price. These orders are placed in the order book and ranked by price and time. The columns in Table 16.1 called *bid volume* (Bid Vol) and *ask volume* (Ask Vol) are

---

[1] The Australian stock market opens at 10am Sydney time, but it is not until 10:10 that all stocks are trading. Consequently, the effective starting time of the market is often taken to be 10:10 in empirical work.

therefore numbers of shares available in terms of these limit orders at the current best bid and ask prices. This limited information, which does not show the depth of the order book in terms of levels of prices and the volumes at each level below the current best bid and ask prices, is known as the top of the book. Transactions take place in response to *market orders*, which are orders for immediate execution; a buy order is executed at the ask price and a sell order is executed at the bid price. Generally speaking, these prices will not coincide; and the ask price will be above the bid price, and the difference is known as the bid-ask spread. Traditionally, the bid-ask spread was regarded as compensation for market makers who provided liquidity in the market for a particular stock by standing ready to buy or sell any quantity of the stock required for a transaction to take place.

The first entry in Table 16.1 indicates a market order for 1521 BHP shares that is buyer initiated, indicated by +1 in the Buy/Sell column. The transaction occurs at the ask price of 39.83, with the ask volume being reduced from 3317 to 1796, a difference of 1521. There is no change in either the best bid or ask price as a result of the transaction. The second market order is also a buy order, this time for 61 BHP shares. Notice that now the ask volume increases rather than decreases. This indicates that the order book was replenished by more limit orders on the ask side. The third market order is a seller initiated order, indicated by −1 in the Buy/Sell column, for 1256 BHP shares. Interestingly, the bid volume decreases by more than this number of shares, and this is accompanied by a fall in the available ask volume as well. These movements are due to cancellations of limit orders on both the bid and ask side of the limit order book.

Another transaction of interest is the fifth entry, which is a sell order for 357 shares. This order exhausts the bid volume in the order book at the current bid price of $39.82,

TABLE 16.1 A snapshot of transactions-level data at the millisecond level for the Australian resources stock BHP Biliton, at the opening of trading on 1 September 2011. The first 20 transactions are shown.

Date	Time	Volume	Buy/Sell	Bid	Bid Vol	Ask	Ask Vol	Spread
09/01/2011	10:10:00.033	1521	1	39.82	4311	39.83	3317	0.01
09/01/2011	10:10:00.185	61	1	39.82	4311	39.83	1796	0.01
09/01/2011	10:10:01.584	1256	−1	39.82	2204	39.83	2631	0.01
09/01/2011	10:10:02.830	482	−1	39.82	839	39.83	896	0.01
09/01/2011	10:10:03.103	357	−1	39.82	357	39.83	896	0.01
09/01/2011	10:10:03.508	757	−1	39.81	1622	39.82	1236	0.01
09/01/2011	10:10:03.585	500	1	39.81	865	39.82	1236	0.01
09/01/2011	10:10:03.930	765	−1	39.81	765	39.82	736	0.01
09/01/2011	10:10:03.954	500	1	39.80	2354	39.81	500	0.01
09/01/2011	10:10:04.238	500	−1	39.81	500	39.82	736	0.01
09/01/2011	10:10:04.239	236	1	39.80	2336	39.81	236	0.01
09/01/2011	10:10:04.835	3	−1	39.82	3	39.84	5369	0.02
09/01/2011	10:10:05.674	336	−1	39.81	2342	39.84	5369	0.03
09/01/2011	10:10:07.388	1875	−1	39.81	2342	39.84	5369	0.03
09/01/2011	10:10:08.248	2221	−1	39.80	2221	39.83	1546	0.03
09/01/2011	10:10:08.268	71	−1	39.79	1528	39.80	2779	0.01
09/01/2011	10:10:08.272	5	−1	39.79	1457	39.80	2779	0.01
09/01/2011	10:10:09.119	14	−1	39.79	1052	39.80	3805	0.01
09/01/2011	10:10:09.320	1344	1	39.79	1038	39.80	3805	0.01
09/01/2011	10:10:09.537	332	−1	39.79	1038	39.80	2461	0.01

and as a consequence, the next quoted best bid price is $39.81. This entry illustrates that price changes occur when the volume in the order book at the current price is exhausted, either by market orders or a combination of market orders and cancelled limit orders, and is not replenished by the arrival of additional liquidity in the form of new limit orders. The ability to buy or sell significant amounts of a stock quickly and with little price impact is an important feature of an asset known as the *liquidity* of the asset. In the open order book, the liquidity of the stock can be gauged directly in terms of the volumes of the stock available at the best bid and ask prices. The liquidity of the stock is also evident in the market depth or the stack. The market depth refers to the number of price levels containing bids of offers at a particular time, and it is therefore possible to gauge liquidity by the bid orders on one side of the book of various sizes and prices and the offer orders at various sizes and prices on the other side.

16.3 BID-ASK BOUNCE

One of the most fundamental propositions in finance is the efficient markets hypothesis, which posits that asset returns are uncorrelated (see Chapter 2). However, this proposition does not necessarily hold when returns are computed using high-frequency data. Figure 16.1 contains the autocorrelation function for the 5-minute returns on the Australian stock BHP Billiton over the period 4 January 2011 to 28 December 2012. The autocorrelation function demonstrates that there is significant dependence in the returns. The autocorrelations up to lag 5 are all negative, and the 95% confidence interval is $\pm 1.96/\sqrt{33761} = \pm 0.0107$, implying that autocorrelations for lags 1 to 3 are all statistically significant.

One explanation for the occurrence of autocorrelation in high-frequency returns data is that recorded transactions occur at either the bid price or the ask price, and switching

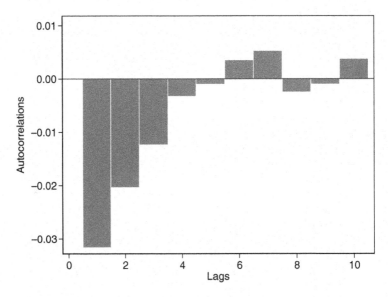

FIGURE 16.1 Autocorrelation function of price changes for the Australian resource stock BHP Billiton sampled at a fixed 5-minute frequency from 4 January 2011 to 28 December 2012.

between the bid and ask prices induces the dependence in returns. This dependence still occurs even if the true price[2] of the asset does not exhibit autocorrelation. To formalize this dependence structure, consider the following model, due to Roll (1984), where the observed log price p_t is specified as a function of the true market log price f and the spread between the bid log price p^b and the ask log price p^a according to

$$p_t = f + \frac{p^a - p^b}{2} I_t = f + \frac{s}{2} I_t, \tag{16.1}$$

where

$$s = p^a - p^b.$$

The variable I_t is a binary random indicator that causes the price to increase if there is a buyer and to decrease if there is a seller

$$I_t = \begin{cases} +1 : \text{with probability } 0.5 \text{ (buyer)} \\ -1 : \text{with probability } 0.5 \text{ (seller).} \end{cases} \tag{16.2}$$

Even though the true market log price (f), as well as the bid (p^b) and ask (p^a) log prices are assumed to be constant in equation (16.1), p_t nonetheless still changes over time as a result of the switching variable I_t in equation (16.2). Despite the simplicity of the model's specification, a number of insightful results can be drawn. The first result is that the expected log price equals the true market log price

$$E(p_t) = E\left(f + \frac{s}{2} I_t\right) = f + \frac{s}{2} E(I_t) = f,$$

as $E(I_t) = (1) \times 0.5 + (-1) \times 0.5 = 0.0$. Even though the true price is unobservable, the actual log price equals f on average.

The second result of the model in equation (16.1) is that returns are dependent over time. To demonstrate this result, equation (16.1) is re-expressed in terms of log returns Δp_t, using the first difference operator, Δ, as

$$\Delta p_t = \Delta f + \frac{s}{2} \Delta I_t. \tag{16.3}$$

The first-order autocovariance of returns is

$$\text{cov}(\Delta p_t, \Delta p_{t-1}) = \text{cov}\left(\frac{s}{2} \Delta I_t, \frac{s}{2} \Delta I_{t-1}\right) = \frac{s^2}{4} \text{cov}(\Delta I_t, \Delta I_{t-1}) = -\frac{s^2}{4}, \tag{16.4}$$

as $\text{cov}(\Delta I_t, \Delta I_{t-1}) = -1$. Since the bid-ask spread is positive $(s > 0)$, this implies that the first-order autocovariance is negative, a result that is consistent with the negative autocorrelation identified in Figure 16.1. In fact, this equation can be rearranged to generate an expression for the spread s as a function of the autocovariance

$$s = 2\sqrt{-\text{cov}(\Delta p_t, \Delta p_{t-1})}.$$

---

[2] The true price of a financial asset may be understood as the underlying efficient price of the asset that would apply if the market were fully efficient, with no institutional frictions such as those induced by the bid-ask spread, and where full information would be available to traders on both sides of the market.

Using the 5-minute BHP log returns data, the first-order autocovariance is estimated as -0.0000423, resulting in an estimate of the spread of

$$\hat{s} = 2\sqrt{0.0000423} = 0.01300.$$

Computing the sample mean of the observed spreads gives a value of 0.01244, which is very close to the estimated value of s.

The third property of Roll's model is that autocovariances greater than 1 lag are zero

$$\text{cov}(\Delta p_t, \Delta p_{t-k}) = 0, \quad k > 1.$$

This result, combined with the first-order covariance expression in equation (16.1), suggests that returns based on transactions data follow a first-order moving average process, as discussed in Chapter 4. Of course, the estimated autocorrelation function presented in Figure 16.1 suggests that returns exhibit a more complex structure than that predicted by the MA(1) structure of this model, on which readers are referred to Russell and Engle (2007).

16.4 INFORMATION CONTENT OF TRADES

To identify the information content of trades, Hasbrouck (1991) specifies a dynamic demand and supply model using transactions data. Let ΔP_t represent the change in price between two trades and vol_t the size of the trade order given by

$$vol_t = \begin{cases} + : & \text{buyer} \\ - : & \text{seller,} \end{cases}$$

also known as the signed volume. The model is specified as

$$\Delta P_t = \phi_1 + \sum_{i=1}^{L} \phi_{11i} \Delta P_{t-i} + \sum_{i=0}^{L} \phi_{12i} vol_{t-i} + u_{1t}$$

$$vol_t = \phi_2 + \sum_{i=1}^{L} \phi_{21i} \Delta P_{t-i} + \sum_{i=1}^{L} \phi_{22i} vol_{t-i} + u_{2t},$$

(16.5)

where u_{1t} and u_{2t} are disturbances representing unanticipated movements in prices and volumes, respectively. Note that although the index t is a maintained usage, it is understood here that the events are being modeled in transactions time rather than clock time.

A special feature of the model is the inclusion of contemporaneous volumes, vol_t, as an explanatory variable in the price equation in order to capture privately available information of a trade. The parameter on this variable is expected to be positive $\phi_{120} > 0$, as buyer initiated transactions ($vol_t > 0$) should lead to higher prices and seller initiated transactions ($vol_t < 0$) should result in lower prices.

The models in equation (16.5) represent a recursive system in which each of the equations can be estimated one at a time by ordinary least squares. Data on the transactions of BHP shares given in Table 16.1 are used to estimate equation (16.5), with the price computed as the average of the bid and ask prices

$$P_t = \frac{P_t^b + P_t^a}{2}.$$

The results are given in Table 16.2 where the lag structure is set at $L = 6$ lags. The parameter estimate of ϕ_{120} is positive and statistically significant.

To reveal the information content of trades on prices, Figure 16.2 contains the impulse responses of an unanticipated one-unit increase in volumes on the price P_t, which is obtained by cumulating the impulse responses of ΔP_t. The impulse responses are computed by noting that the recursive model in equation (16.5) is equivalent to a vector autoregression transformed by a Cholesky decomposition to identify the structural shocks u_{1t} and u_{2t} as discussed in Chapter 4. The impulse response function converges after about 6 transactions, suggesting that it takes approximately 6 transactions for private information to become public information.

TABLE 16.2 Estimating equation (16.5) in transactions time for quote revisions, ΔP_t, and signed volume, vol_t. The data are tick data for BHP Billiton transactions data for the month of September 2011 recorded at the millisecond level. Standard errors are in parentheses.

Variable	ΔP_t	vol_t
ΔP_{t-1}	−0.2407	−0.4303
	(0.0023)	(0.0097)
ΔP_{t-2}	−0.1025	−0.2171
	(0.0024)	(0.0100)
ΔP_{t-3}	−0.0479	−0.1059
	(0.0024)	(0.0100)
ΔP_{t-4}	−0.0197	−0.0695
	(0.0024)	(0.0100)
ΔP_{t-5}	−0.0101	−0.0292
	(0.0024)	(0.0100)
ΔP_{t-6}	−0.0064	0.0007
	(0.0023)	(0.0097)
vol_t	0.0924	—
	(0.0006)	
vol_{t-1}	0.0325	0.0921
	(0.0006)	(0.0025)
vol_{t-2}	0.0147	0.0537
	(0.0006)	(0.0025)
vol_{t-3}	0.0096	0.0341
	(0.0006)	(0.0025)
vol_{t-4}	0.0059	0.0285
	(0.0006)	(0.0025)
vol_{t-5}	0.0038	0.0156
	(0.0006)	(0.0025)
vol_{t-6}	0.0020	0.0133
	(0.0006)	(0.0025)
constant	−0.0000	0.0000
	(0.0000)	(0.0001)

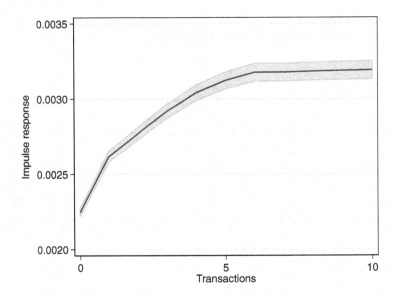

FIGURE 16.2 The cumulative impulse response function for price changes and signed volume. Impulse responses are based on a Cholesky decomposition that allows signed volume to influence price changes contemporaneously. The data are the transactions data for BHP Billiton recorded at the millisecond level for the month of September 2011.

The bivariate structural VAR model in equation (16.5) has been extended to allow for the market impact of limit order placements and short-term liquidity dynamics in the limit order book (Eisler, Bouchard, and Kockelkoren, 2012; Hautsch and Huang, 2012; Lo and Hall, 2015). These models study the impact of limit order arrivals and cancellations on price and how liquidity is replenished following specific liquidity shocks.

16.5 MODELING PRICE MOVEMENTS IN TRADES

An important property of transaction prices is that they are quoted in discrete units, with the effect that price changes are represented by a finite number of discrete values; see, for example, Hausman, Lo, and MacKinlay (1992). A related issue is that for many transactions, there is no associated movement in price. This phenomenon is highlighted in Figure 16.3, which gives histograms of changes in bid prices and ask prices for the BHP transactions data in Table 16.1. The number of transactions where there are no changes in price dominate the number of transactions that have either positive or negative price movements.

Movements in prices that are defined qualitatively are commonly known as limited dependent variables, as the information of changes in prices is limited to just the direction of the movement. Models containing qualitative dependent variables can be estimated using maximum likelihood methods, although an iterative algorithm is needed, as it is necessary to introduce a nonlinear structure on the model to preserve the qualitative characteristics of the dependent variable.

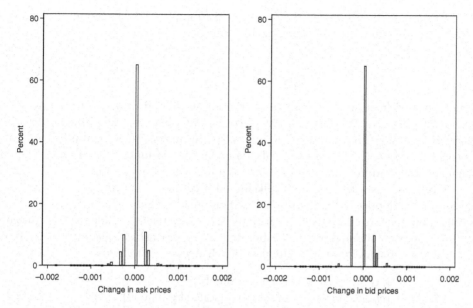

FIGURE 16.3 Histograms of changes in the bid and ask prices of BHP Billiton using transactions data recorded at the millisecond level for the month of September 2011.

16.5.1 Binary Dependent Variable

Suppose that the direction of the price movement for a trade at time t is classified as

$$y_t = \begin{cases} 0 : \Delta P_t \leq 0 & \text{[Price falls or does not change]} \\ 1 : \Delta P_t > 0. & \text{[Price rises]} \end{cases} \tag{16.6}$$

The variable y_t is a binary variable, as it takes on two values, with 1 signifying a price increase and 0 signifying a fall or no change in price.

To preserve the binary features of the dependent variable y_t, assume that the probability of a price rise is determined by the normal cumulative distribution function

$$\Pr(y_t = 1) = \Phi_t = \int_{-\infty}^{\alpha + \beta x_t} \phi(s) \, ds, \tag{16.7}$$

where x_t is an explanatory variable that determines price movements, and α and β are unknown parameters. By definition, the probability of a price not increasing is

$$\Pr(y_t = 0) = 1 - \Phi_t = 1 - \int_{-\infty}^{\alpha + \beta x_t} \phi(s) \, ds = \int_{-\infty}^{-(\alpha + \beta x_t)} \phi(s) \, ds,$$

because of the symmetry property of the normal distribution. The probability distribution function has the effect of imposing a nonlinear relationship linking the qualitative dependent variable y_t and the explanatory variable x_t. The choice of a normal cumulative distribution function for Φ_t yields what is known as a *probit model*. Other choices may be used, including the choice of a logistic distribution function, which leads to a *logit model*.

To estimate the parameters $\theta = \{\alpha, \beta\}$ in equation (16.7) by maximum likelihood, the log likelihood function for T transactions is

$$\log L(\theta) = \frac{1}{T} \sum_{t=1}^{T} (y_t \log \Phi_t + (1 - y_t) \log(1 - \Phi_t)), \qquad (16.8)$$

where Φ_t is defined in equation (16.7). The log likelihood contains two terms. The first term is the part of the log likelihood corresponding to occasions when prices are increasing ($y_t = 1$), and the second term corresponds to occasions when prices are not increasing ($y_t = 0$). Given that the log likelihood function is nonlinear in the parameters, an iterative algorithm is used to estimate θ, as discussed in Chapter 10.

Table 16.3 gives the maximum likelihood estimates obtained by estimating the probit model of price changes for BHP based on the log likelihood in equation (16.8), with robust standard errors given in parentheses. The dependent variable y_t is constructed from changes in the average of the bid and ask prices using equation (16.6). The explanatory variables in x_t used to model price changes are as follows

$$
\begin{aligned}
y_{t-1} \quad &= \text{lagged dependent variable} \\
vol_{t-1} \quad &= \text{volume of the trade (scaled by 100000)} \\
trade_{t-1} \quad &= \text{indicator} = 1/0 \text{ if trade is buyer/seller initiated} \\
dur_t \quad &= \text{duration from last trade (in seconds)} \\
spread_{t-1} \quad &= \text{spread between the bid and ask prices.}
\end{aligned}
$$

Also given in Table 16.3 are the results obtained by ignoring the qualitative nature of the dependent variable and simply regressing y_t on a constant and the set of explanatory variables. This model is known as the linear probability model and is presented as a basis of comparison.

TABLE 16.3   Parameter estimates for the linear probability, probit, and ordered probit models of changes in the mid-price of BHP Billiton. The data are recorded at the millisecond level for the month of September 2011. Robust standard errors are reported in parentheses.

Variable	Linear Probability	Probit	Ordered Probit
y_{t-1}	0.0056	−0.0097	−0.1111
	(0.0019)	(0.0106)	(0.0074)
vol_{t-1}	1.3652	5.1278	0.4566
	(0.0560)	(0.2718)	(0.1354)
$trade_{t-1}$	0.1764	0.8583	0.8199
	(0.0008)	(0.0050)	(0.0036)
dur_t	0.0005	0.0030	−0.0040
	(0.0002)	(0.0008)	(0.0006)
$spread_{t-1}$	6.7685	32.9487	−1.5818
	(0.2041)	(0.7842)	(0.7326)
constant	0.1012	−1.6394	
		(0.0026)	(0.0107)
c_0	—	—	−1.1289
			(0.0094)
c_1	—	—	1.0950
			(0.0094)

The probit and linear probability models yield the same qualitative results for signs on all the slope coefficients but one. The exception is the lagged dependent variable y_{t-1}, whose coefficient estimate is negative and statistically insignificant for the probit model and positive and significant for the linear probability model. The coefficient on the indicator variable, $trade_{t-1}$, is positive in both models, indicating that buy-initiated trades tend to drive positive price changes. This result is consistent with those obtained in Section 16.4. The other coefficient estimates from the probit and linear probability models all have positive signs, implying that increases in volumes, spread, and duration lead to price increases.

The marginal effects of a change in an explanatory variable on the probability of a price increase can be determined in the probit model by differentiating Φ_t in equation (16.7) with respect to x_t as follows

$$\frac{\partial \Pr(y_t = 1)}{\partial x_t} = \frac{\partial \Phi}{\partial x_t} = \phi(\alpha + \beta x_t)\beta, \tag{16.9}$$

where $\phi(\cdot)$ is the probability density function of the standard normal distribution. Since $\phi(\cdot)$ depends on the values of x_t, the marginal effects are computed for alternative values of the data.[3] In the linear probability model, because the relationship between y_t and x_t is linear, the marginal effect is simply given by the parameter β.

The estimates of the marginal effects, evaluated at the maximum likelihood estimates in Table 16.3, are reported in Table 16.4. As expected in view of the linearization involved in the delta method, there is a good agreement between the estimates of the marginal effects reported in Table 16.3 and the coefficient estimates of the linear probability model. The two exceptions are the coefficients of y_{t-1} and $spread_{t-1}$. In the case of the former, the estimated coefficient in the probit model is not statistically significant and neither is the marginal effect. In the case of the spread, however, the coefficient appears to be well resolved, and the discrepancy between the linear model and the marginal effect derived from the probit model is unexpected.

TABLE 16.4   Estimates of the marginal effects of the probit model of changes in the price of BHP Billiton. The data are recorded at the millisecond level for the month of September 2011. Standard errors are computed using the delta method.

Variable	Marginal Effect	Standard Error	t statistic	p value
y_{t-1}	−0.0021	0.0023	−0.9200	0.3600
vol_{t-1}	1.1205	0.0588	19.0700	0.0000
$trade_{t-1}$	0.1875	0.0009	203.7800	0.0000
dur_t	0.0007	0.0002	3.7000	0.0000
$spread_{t-1}$	0.3469	0.1608	2.1600	0.0310

[3] Standard errors of the marginal effects are computed using the delta method. For a description of how the delta method is implemented, see Martin, Hurn, and Harris (2013), pp. 101–104.

16.5.2 Ordered Dependent Variable

In the case of the binary variable defined in equation (16.6), trades corresponding to constant prices and price falls are classified together. A more general approach is to separate these two situations and adopt a three-regime classification as

$$
y_k = \begin{cases} 1 : \Delta p_t < 0 & \text{[Price falls]} \\ 2 : \Delta p_t = 0 & \text{[No change]} \\ 3 : \Delta p_t > 0. & \text{[Price rises].} \end{cases} \tag{16.10}
$$

The probabilities associated with each of the three outcomes are

$$
\begin{aligned}
\Phi_{1t} &= \Pr(y_t = 1) = \Phi(c_0 - \beta x_t) \\
\Phi_{2t} &= \Pr(y_t = 2) = \Phi(c_1 - \beta x_t) - \Phi(c_0 - \beta x_t) \\
\Phi_{3t} &= \Pr(y_t = 3) = 1 - \Phi(c_1 - \beta x_t),
\end{aligned}
$$

where the Φ_{jt} $j = 1, 2, 3$ are cumulative normal distribution functions that satisfy the property

$$
\Phi_{1t} + \Phi_{2t} + \Phi_{3t} = 1.
$$

As before, x_t is an explanatory variable with slope parameter β. The parameters c_0 and c_1 represent intercept parameters for the first two regimes, commonly known as the cut-off points, which satisfy the restriction $c_0 < c_1$ to ensure that the probabilities of each outcome are positive. Since the probabilities are based on the cumulative normal distribution, the model is referred to as an ordered probit model.

To estimate the parameters $\theta = \{c_0, c_1, \beta\}$ by maximum likelihood, the log likelihood for T transactions is specified as

$$
\log L(\theta) = \frac{1}{T} \sum_{t=1}^{T} (I_{1t} \log \Phi_{1t} + I_{2t} \log \Phi_{2t} + I_{3t} \log \Phi_{3t}),
$$

where $I_{jt} = 1$ if $y_{jt} = j$ for $j = 1, 2, 3$. As with the probit model, the log likelihood is a nonlinear function of θ that is estimated using a nonlinear algorithm.

The results of computing the maximum likelihood parameter estimates using the transactions data on BHP are given in Table 16.3. The probit and ordered probit parameter estimates have the same signs for y_{t-1}, vol_{t-1}, and $trade_{t-1}$ but the opposite signs for dur_t and $spread_{t-1}$.

The marginal effects of change in x_t on the probabilities of each regime are as follows:

(i) Regime 1 ($\Delta p_t < 0$):

$$
\frac{\partial \Pr(y_t = 1)}{\partial x_t} = -\beta \underbrace{\phi(c_0 - \beta x_t)}_{>0}.
$$

If $\beta > 0$, the probability of a fall in price decreases if x_t increases.

(ii) Regime 2 ($\Delta p_t = 0$):

$$
\frac{\partial \Pr(y_t = 2)}{\partial x_t} = [\phi(c_1 - \beta x_t) - \phi(c_0 - \beta x_t)] \beta.
$$

The sign of the marginal effect is ambiguous because it depends on relative sizes of the two densities.

(iii) Regime 3 ($\Delta p_t > 0$):

$$\frac{\partial \Pr(y_t = 3)}{\partial x_t} = \beta \underbrace{\phi \left(c_1 - \beta x_t \right)}_{>0}.$$

The change in the probability for this case has the same sign as β.

As with marginal effects of the probit model, standard errors of the ordered probit marginal effects are computed using the delta method.

The marginal effects of the ordered probit model are reported in Table 16.5 for the three regimes in equation (16.10). The mean-reverting tendency of the change in prices is now readily apparent by inspecting the marginal effects of y_{t-1}. For the $\Delta p_t < 0$ regime, the marginal effect is positive, suggesting a reversal in price, while mean reversal in the opposite direction occurs for the $\Delta p_t > 0$ regime, as there the marginal effect is negative. An increase in volumes, (vol), lowers (raises) the probability of a price fall (increase). The influence of a buyer-initiated trade ($trade = 1$) to raise prices has its strongest effect in the $\Delta p_t > 0$ regime. The effect of the spread ($spread$) is interesting. If the price change is expected to be negative, then increasing the spread increases the probability of a fall in price. If the price change is expected to be positive, however, increasing the spread reduces the probability of prices increasing.

TABLE 16.5   Estimates of the marginal effects of the ordered probit model of changes in the price of BHP Billiton for the month of September 2011. Standard errors are computed using the delta method.

Variable	Regime	Marginal Effect	Standard Error	t statistic	p value
y_{t-1}	$\Delta p_t < 0$	0.0244	0.0016	15.08	0.000
	$\Delta p_t = 0$	0.0006	0.0001	7.01	0.000
	$\Delta p_t > 0$	−0.0249	0.0017	−15.08	0.000
vol_{t-1}	$\Delta p_t < 0$	−0.1002	0.0297	−3.37	0.001
	$\Delta p_t = 0$	−0.0023	0.0007	−3.07	0.002
	$\Delta p_t > 0$	0.1024	0.0304	3.37	0.001
$trade_{t-1}$	$\Delta p_t < 0$	−0.1798	0.0007	−267.20	0.000
	$\Delta p_t = 0$	−0.0041	0.0005	−7.85	0.000
	$\Delta p_t > 0$	0.1839	0.0007	253.54	0.000
dur_t	$\Delta p_t < 0$	0.0009	0.0001	6.20	0.000
	$\Delta p_t = 0$	0.0000	0.0000	5.01	0.000
	$\Delta p_t > 0$	−0.0009	0.0001	−6.20	0.000
$spread_{t-1}$	$\Delta p_t < 0$	0.3469	0.1608	2.16	0.031
	$\Delta p_t = 0$	0.0079	0.0035	2.23	0.026
	$\Delta p_t > 0$	−0.3548	0.1642	−2.16	0.031

16.6 MODELING DURATIONS

In Chapter 10, it was argued that the distribution of durations between trades, d_t, may be approximated by an exponential distribution

$$f(d_t | d_{t-1}, d_{t-2}, \cdots ; \theta) = \frac{1}{\mu_t} \exp\left(-\frac{d_t}{\mu_t}\right), \qquad \mu_t > 0, \tag{16.11}$$

where μ_t is the conditional mean of the exponential distribution. Figure 16.4 is a histogram of the durations for BHP Billiton data for the month of September 2011. The durations d_t are computed in milliseconds but then rounded up to the nearest second. The mean duration is 3.181 seconds, and the standard deviation is 4.722 seconds. The 99th percentile is 24 seconds, and the four largest durations between trades are 85, 90, 91, and 98 seconds, respectively. The histogram of the durations shows that the assumption of an exponential distribution for the durations is not an unrealistic one.

An important method used in empirical finance to explain the duration between trades, $d\#$, is the autoregressive conditional duration (ACD) framework due to Engle and Russell (1998). In addition to assuming that d_t is distributed exponentially as in equation (16.11), the conditional mean of durations is specified as

$$\mu_t = \alpha_0 + \sum_{j=1}^{q} \alpha_j d_{t-j} + \sum_{j=1}^{p} \beta_j \mu_{t-j}. \tag{16.12}$$

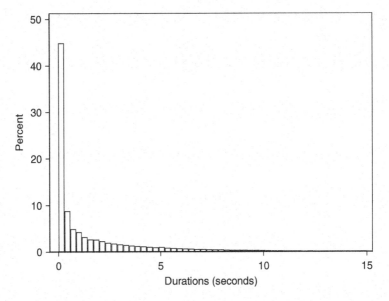

FIGURE 16.4 Histogram of the durations between trades for the Australian resource stock BHP Billiton for the month of September 2011. Overall, there are 185517 durations included, once overnight and opening transactions have been deleted.

To ensure that the conditional mean is stationary, the condition

$$\sum_{j=1}^{q}\alpha_j + \sum_{j=1}^{p}\beta_j < 1,$$

is needed; and to ensure that $\mu_t > 0$, it is usual to require that $\alpha_0 > 0$, $\alpha_j > 0$, and $\beta_j > 0$ for all j.

The log likelihood function at observation t for the ACD model with $p = q = 1$ is

$$\log L_t = -\log \mu_t - \frac{d_t}{\mu_t},$$
$$\mu_t = \alpha_0 + \alpha_1 d_{t-1} + \beta_1 \mu_{t-1},$$
(16.13)

which is maximized with respect to the parameters $\theta = \{\alpha_0, \alpha_1, \beta_1\}$ using an iterative algorithm.

The exponential ACD model is very similar to the univariate GARCH model for the conditional variance of returns introduced in Chapter 13. It turns out that the ACD model can be estimated as if it were a GARCH model by specifying the dependent variable in terms of $\sqrt{d_t}$ and by not having a constant term in the mean equation. The model is

$$\sqrt{d_t} = v_t, \qquad v_t \sim N(0, h_t),$$
$$h_t = \alpha_0 + \alpha_1 v_{t-1}^2 + \beta_1 h_{t-1}.$$
(16.14)

The specification in equation (16.14) is equivalent to that in equation (16.13), with h_t playing the role of μ_t. Where the two approaches differ is in the construction of the log likelihood function. The specification in equation (16.14) requires that the log likelihood function be based on the assumption that v_t is normally distributed. The true distribution of v_t is not known, so the parameter estimates obtained by this process are quasi maximum likelihood estimates. Interestingly, the parameter estimates returned by these two procedures are identical. As with all quasi maximum likelihood estimators (see Chapter 10), however, robust standard errors should be used if the GARCH approach is chosen.

The assumption that the durations are exponentially distributed as in equation (16.11) may be too restrictive, and the more flexible Weibull distribution may be a more appropriate choice. The standardized Weibull distribution for durations is

$$f(d_t | d_{t-1}, d_{t-2}, \cdots; \theta) = \lambda \left[\Gamma\left(1 + \frac{1}{\lambda}\right) \right] \frac{d_t^{\lambda - 1}}{\mu_t^{\lambda}} \exp\left[-\left(\frac{d_t \Gamma\left(1 + \frac{1}{\lambda}\right)}{\mu_t} \right)^{\lambda} \right],$$

in which $\Gamma(\cdot)$ is the gamma function, and λ is an unknown parameter. Using the result that $\Gamma(2) = 1$, it follows that the restriction $\lambda = 1$ reduces the Weibull distribution to the exponential distribution. The log likelihood function for observation t is

$$\log L_t = \log \lambda + \lambda \log \Gamma\left(1 + \frac{1}{\lambda}\right) + (\lambda - 1)\log d_t - \lambda \log \mu_t - \left(\frac{d_t \Gamma\left(1 + \frac{1}{\lambda}\right)}{\mu_t}\right)^{\lambda},$$

which is maximized with respect to the parameters $\theta = \{\lambda, \alpha_0, \alpha_1, \beta_1\}$ using an iterative algorithm. Maximum likelihood estimates of the exponential ACD model (based on both the normal and exponential log likelihood functions) and Weibull ACD model are reported in Table 16.6.

The results in Table 16.6 confirm that the parameter estimates obtained from the normal and exponential likelihoods are identical. Note, however, that the standard errors are not the same. The expected conditional duration based on the estimated normal log likelihood is

$$\widehat{\mu} = \frac{0.0111}{1 - 0.0333 - 0.996281} = 2.846,$$

which is consistent with the actual unconditional average duration of 2.490. It is clear that the durations are very persistent as

$$0.0333 + 0.9628 = 0.9961.$$

A final comment on the results in Table 16.6 concerns the choice of distribution for the durations. It appears that the Weibull distribution is the more appropriate choice for modeling BHP durations because the point estimate of the parameter λ is significantly different from 1. A t test of this hypothesis yields a p value of 0.000. This fact may help to explain why the robust standard errors reported for the normal likelihood are closer to those obtained by the outer product of gradients formula for the Weibull model.

A final issue concerns the diurnal patterns in the durations. Most high-frequency data exhibit daily patterns, and this is no different for durations. A simple way to take account of the daily variation in the durations is to express each duration as a fraction of the expected duration for that particular time of day. This expected duration can easily

TABLE 16.6   Maximum likelihood estimates of the ACD model based on the normal, exponential, and Weibull log likelihood functions. The data are durations between trades on the stock BHP Billiton for the month of September 2011. The data are recorded at the millisecond level, but the durations are rounded to seconds. Standard errors are based on the outer product of gradients matrix except for the normal log likelihood function where quasi maximum likelihood standard errors are reported.

Parameter	Normal	Exponential	Weibull
α_0	0.0111	0.0111	0.0261
	(0.0014)	(0.0002)	(0.0017)
α_1	0.0333	0.0333	0.0523
	(0.0021)	(0.0002)	(0.0015)
β_1	0.9628	0.9628	0.9441
	(0.0025)	(0.0003)	(0.0016)
λ	—	—	0.4598
			(0.0011)

be obtained from the fitted values of a regression of durations on a set of hourly dummy variables. Figure 16.5 shows a plot of the coefficients of the hourly dummy variables for the BHP data. The diurnal pattern is clearly evident, with longer durations during the middle part of the day when volatility and volume are lower.

16.7 MODELING VOLATILITY IN TRANSACTIONS TIME

An important characteristic of transactions data is its irregular time interval spacing, which results in returns between transactions being computed at different frequencies. To correct for differences in frequencies when applying a GARCH model, as discussed in Chapter 13, to transactions data, to model time-varying volatility per unit of time, Engle (2000) suggests standardizing returns by the duration between trades.

Defining r_t as the return between transaction t and $t - 1$, and d_t as the corresponding duration, the dependent variable is

$$y_t = \frac{r_t}{\sqrt{d_t}}. \tag{16.15}$$

A GARCH(1,1) applied to transactions data for y_t is specified as

$$y_t = \mu_0 + u_t, \qquad u_t \sim N(0, h_t),$$
$$h_t = \alpha_0 + \alpha_1 u_{t-1}^2 + \beta_1 h_{t-1}. \tag{16.16}$$

The unknown parameters $\theta = \{\mu_0, \alpha_0, \alpha_1, \beta_1\}$ are estimated by maximum likelihood using an iterative algorithm based on the procedures discussed in Chapter 13. In

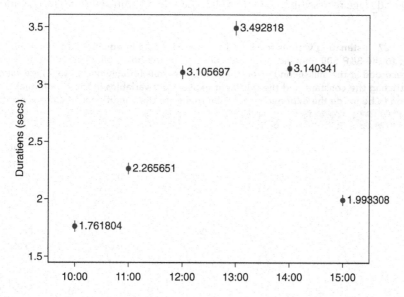

FIGURE 16.5 Estimated coefficients of a regression of BHP durations on a set of hourly dummy variables. The numbers shown are the point estimates on the hourly dummy variables. The data are millisecond observations for September 2011, with durations rounded to seconds.

estimating the GARCH model, the dependent variable y_t in equation (16.15) is centered, thereby reducing the unknown parameters to $\theta = \{\alpha_0, \alpha_1, \beta_1\}$.

The column headed (1) in Table 16.7 provides the results from estimating the GARCH model using transactions data on the S&P 500 E-mini Index futures contract, which trades on the Chicago Mercantile Exchange. The price of each trade is recorded with a timestamp in milliseconds, which covers a 2-hour period from 08:30 to 10:30 Chicago time (or 14:30 to 16:25 GMT) on 3 January 2012. The data are sourced from the Thomson Reuters Tick History database. A striking feature of the parameter estimates of the conditional variance of standardized returns is that the parameter estimate of α_1 tends to be larger, and the parameter estimate of β_1 tends to be smaller than the corresponding estimates obtained in Chapter 13 using regularly spaced daily data. Moreover, the implied persistence of this model is

$$\widehat{\alpha}_1 + \widehat{\beta}_1 = 0.2036 + 0.5666 = 0.7702,$$

which is well below the value often found in lower frequency data. This empirical result is indicative of a general consensus that the persistence of volatility is generally lower in intraday data.

The GARCH model in equation (16.16) is now extended in one of two ways. The first is to allow for dynamics in the conditional mean specification. This is motivated by the property discussed in Section 16.3 that returns calculated for transactions data are autocorrelated. Following Engle (2000), an ARMA(1,1) model is specified. In estimating this form of the GARCH model, the approach is to filter the standardized returns in equation (16.15) by first regressing y_t on a constant and y_{t-1}, and then regressing y_t on a constant, y_{t-1}, and the lagged residuals from the first-stage regression. The residuals from this second-stage regression are then used as the filtered adjusted standardized returns.

TABLE 16.7   Estimating various forms of the GARCH model in equation (16.18). The data are returns to the S&P 500 mini index futures contract for the hours 08:30 to 10:30 on 3 January 2012 recorded at the millisecond level. The GARCH models for columns (2) to (4) are estimated by restricting the constant and the pertinent explanatory variables in the conditional variance equation to be inside the exponential function to ensure the conditional variance is positive.

Parameter	(1)	(2)	(3)	(4)
α_0	0.0000	−15.9753	−16.1646	−15.5020
	(0.0000)	(0.0311)	(0.0342)	(0.0400)
α_1	0.2036	0.1483	0.0866	0.0447
	(0.0565)	(0.0197)	(0.0168)	(0.0034)
β_1	0.5666	0.0114	−0.0283	0.1052
	(0.1085)	(0.0107)	(0.0109)	(0.0063)
γ_1		0.0029	0.0026	0.0013
		(0.0001)	(0.0001)	(0.0001)
γ_2			0.0428	0.0504
			(0.0053)	(0.0045)
γ_3				−1.5868
				(0.0575)

The second extension of the GARCH model in equation (16.16) is to allow for additional explanatory variables to explain the conditional variance. Engle (2000) suggests a number of potential specifications of increasing complexity, which are nested within the following general form

$$h_t = \alpha_0 + \alpha_1 u_{t-1}^2 + \beta_1 h_{t-1} + \gamma_1 d_t^{-1} + \gamma_2 \mu_t^{-1} + \gamma_3 \frac{d_t}{\mu_t}, \qquad (16.17)$$

in which d_t is the current duration, and μ_t is the expected current duration defined in equation (16.12). On the basis that long durations between trades indicate little news and low volatility, the parameter on d_t^{-1} is expected to be $\gamma_1 > 0$. A similar argument applies to expected durations μ_t. The term d_t/μ_t is interpreted as representing surprises in durations, but there are no a priori expectations as to the sign of γ_3.

Estimation of the model in equation (16.16), with h_t replaced by the extended GARCH specification in equation (16.17) combined with an allowance for dynamics in the conditional mean proceeds as follows. First, filter the standardized returns y_t using the two-stage regression procedure discussed previously to purge any dynamics in the conditional mean. Second, estimate an ACD model of durations in order to generate an estimate of the expected duration for the current trade, $\widehat{\mu}_t$. Finally, estimate the GARCH model with μ_t in equation (16.17) replaced by $\widehat{\mu}_t$. To ensure positivity of the conditional variance h_t, the GARCH specification is transformed by expressing h_t as

$$h_t = \exp\left(\alpha_0 + \gamma_1 d_t^{-1} + \gamma_2 \mu_t^{-1} + \gamma_3 d_t/\mu_t\right) + \alpha_1 u_{t-1}^2 + \beta_1 h_{t-1}. \qquad (16.18)$$

The results of estimating alternative GARCH models of increasing complexity based on equation (16.18) are given in columns (2) to (4) of Table 16.7. The parameter estimate of γ_1 is positive and statistically significant, showing that longer durations between trades correspond to low news and hence low volatility, thereby providing support for the no news, low-volatility hypothesis. A similar result also holds for the effect of conditional durations on volatility, as γ_2 is also positive and statistically significant. The sign of the coefficient γ_3 on duration surprises is negative, indicating that a shorter than expected duration (or greater incoming news) drives up volatility.

16.8 EXERCISES

The data required for the exercises are available for download as EViews workfiles (*.wf1), Stata datafiles (*.dta), comma delimited text files (*.csv), and as Excel spreadsheets (*.xlsx).

1. Bid-Ask Bounce

bhp5minreturns.*

The data are the 5-minute price changes recorded for the Australian resource stock BHP Billiton over the period 4 January 2011 to 28 December 2012. Overnight price changes have been omitted.

(a) Compute summary statistics for the price change data and comment on the results.

(b) Plot a histogram of the price changes overlaid with a normal distribution. Is there any evidence of leptokurtosis?

(c) Plot the autocorrelation function for price changes for lags 1 to 10. Discuss the pattern of the autocorrelations.

(d) Simulate $T = 10000$ observations of the following MA(3) model

$$y_t = u_t - 0.03u_{t-1} - 0.02u_{t-2} - 0.01u_{t-3}, \qquad u_t \sim N(0, 0025),$$

using starting values of 0 where necessary. Compute the autocorrelation function of y_t for lags 1 to 10 and compare the result with the plot obtained in (c).

(e) Compute Roll's (1984) theoretical approximation to the average bid-ask spread and compare this approximation to the actual average bid-ask spread.

(f) Suppose that the price is now given by

$$p_t = f_t + \frac{s}{2} I_t,$$

where s is the spread, and the fundamental price f_t is

$$f_t = f_{t-1} + u_t, \qquad u_t \sim N(0, \sigma^2).$$

Derive expressions for $E[(\Delta p_t)^2]$ and $E(\Delta p_t \Delta p_{t-1})$.

2. Information Content of Trades

bhpfull.*

The data are transactions data at the millisecond level for the Australian resource stock BHP Billiton for the month of September 2011.

(a) Estimate the equation

$$\Delta P_t = \phi_1 + \sum_{i=1}^{6} \phi_{11i} \Delta P_{t-i} + \sum_{i=0}^{6} \phi_{12i} vol_{t-i} + u_t,$$

in which vol_t is a measure of signed volume and

$$\Delta P_t = P_t - P_{t-1} \qquad P_t = \frac{P_t^a + P_t^b}{2}.$$

Comment on the results.

(b) Estimate a bivariate VAR(6) for ΔP_t and vol_t. Perform a Cholesky decomposition on the estimated covariance matrix of the VAR residuals and derive an estimate of the contemporaneous effect of vol_t on ΔP_t. Verify that this estimate is identical to that obtained in part (a).

(c) Compute the impulse response function and cumulative impulse response function for an orthogonal, 1 standard deviation shock to vol_t. Comment on the results.

(d) Test for the pattern of Granger causality between vol_t and ΔP_t by testing the following null hypotheses

$$H_0 : vol_t \nrightarrow \Delta P_t, \qquad H_0 : \Delta P_t \nrightarrow vol_t.$$

(e) The analysis so far has simply assumed that 6 lags be included in the VAR. Check this assumption using information criteria.

(f) Hasbrouck (1991) extends the bivariate VAR model to three variables by allowing for a nonlinear effect from trade volumes. Let $z_t = vol_t^2$; then the extended VAR model becomes

$$\Delta P_t = \phi_1 + \sum_{i=1}^{L} \phi_{11i} \Delta P_{t-i} + \sum_{i=0}^{L} \phi_{12i} vol_{t-i} + \sum_{i=0}^{L} \phi_{13i} z_{t-i} + u_{1t}$$

$$vol_t = \phi_2 + \sum_{i=1}^{L} \phi_{21i} \Delta P_{t-i} + \sum_{i=1}^{Lq} \phi_{22i} vol_{t-i} + \sum_{i=1}^{L} \phi_{23i} z_{t-i} + u_{2t}$$

$$z_t = \phi_3 + \sum_{i=1}^{L} \phi_{31i} \Delta P_{t-i} + \sum_{i=1}^{L} \phi_{32i} vol_{t-i} + \sum_{i=1}^{L} \phi_{33i} z_{t-i} + u_{3t}.$$

Estimate this model and compare the results obtained in the bivariate case.

3. **Modeling Price Movements of Trades**

> bhpdurations.*

The data consist of trades on BHP shares for the month of September 2011.

(a) Compute the histogram for the change in the bid price and interpret the result. Repeat the question for the ask price.

(b) Construct the qualitative variable of price movements

$$y_t = \begin{cases} 0 : \Delta P_t \le 0 & \text{[Price falls or does not change]} \\ 1 : \Delta P_t > 0. & \text{[Price rises]} \end{cases}$$

Estimate a probit model by maximum likelihood with y_t as the dependent variable and with the following explanatory variables

y_{t-1} = lagged dependent variable
vol_{t-1} = volume of the trade (scaled by 100000)
$trade_{t-1}$ = indicator = 1/0 if trade is buyer/seller initiated
dur_t = duration from last trade (in seconds)
$spread_{t-1}$ = spread between the bid and ask prices.

Use as starting estimates the parameter estimates of the linear probability model. Interpret the parameter estimates by computing the marginal effects.

(c) Construct the qualitative variable of price movements

$$y_t = \begin{cases} 1 : \Delta p_t < 0 & \text{[Price falls]} \\ 2 : \Delta p_t = 0 & \text{[No change]} \\ 3 : \Delta p_t > 0. & \text{[Price rises]} \end{cases}$$

Estimate an ordered probit model by maximum likelihood with y_t as the dependent variable and with the same set of explanatory variables as defined in part (b). Interpret the parameter estimates by computing the marginal effects.

4. Household Finance

$$\boxed{\text{empirical\_finance.*}}$$

The file contains panel data on the risk behavior of households across four waves: 2002, 2006, 2010, and 2014. The data are based on the HILDA panel survey conducted in Australia.

Consider the following model of risk preferences

$$y_i = \beta_0 + \sum_{j=1}^{10} \beta_j x_{ji} + u_i,$$

where y_i is the dependent variable that determines risk behavior, x_{ji}, are the control variables, and u_i is a disturbance term with zero mean and constant variance.

(a) Letting the dependent variable y_i be the ordered variable measuring risk preferences according to

$$y_i = \begin{cases} 0 : \text{None} \\ 1 : \text{Average} \\ 2 : \text{Above-Average} \\ 3 : \text{Substantial,} \end{cases}$$

estimate the ordered probit model by maximum likelihood and discuss the factors determining household risk preferences.

(b) Repeat part (a) except use the binary preference variable

$$y_i = \begin{cases} 0 : \text{None} \\ 1 : \text{Some risk.} \end{cases}$$

Hence, estimate the probit model by maximum likelihood and discuss the factors determining household risk preferences.

(c) Now consider using data on actual risk behavior by letting the dependent variable be the binary stock holding decision variable

$$y_i = \begin{cases} 0 : \text{Do not hold stocks} \\ 1 : \text{Hold stocks.} \end{cases}$$

Estimate the probit model of stock holding by maximum likelihood and discuss the factors determining household stock holding. Are these factors consistent with the factors identified in parts (a) and (b)?

(d) Data on the risky price ratio consists of households who own risky assets ($y_i > 0$) and households who do not ($y_i = 0$). This is a two-regime model known as the tobit model. Define the indicator variable

$$I_i = \begin{cases} 1 : \text{Household owns risky assets} \\ 0 : \text{Household does not own risky assets.} \end{cases}$$

The log likelihood for N households is

$$\log L(\theta) = \frac{1}{N}\sum_{i=1}^{N}(-I_i\log\sigma + I_i\log(\phi_i) + (1-I_i)\log(1-\Phi_i)),$$

where I_i is an indicator function and ϕ_i and Φ_i are, respectively, the normal density and cumulative normal distribution function

$$\phi_i = \frac{1}{\sqrt{2\pi}}\exp\left(-\frac{(y_i-\alpha-\beta x_i)^2}{2\sigma^2}\right), \quad \Phi_i = \int_{-\infty}^{\alpha+\beta x_i}\phi(s)\,ds.$$

Using the same set of explanatory variables contained in the probit and ordered probit models, estimate the tobit model and interpret the parameter estimates.

(e) Repeat parts (a) to (d) but allow for changes in risk over time using fixed effects. Do the results change?

5. **An ACD Model of Index Futures**

usdurations. *

The data consist of transactions on the S&P 500 E-mini Index futures contract from 08:30 to 10:30 Chicago time (or 14:30 to 16:25 GMT) on 3 January 2012, corresponding to a sample size of $T = 30686$ recorded trades. The price of each trade is recorded with a timestamp in milliseconds.

(a) Defining d_t as the duration between transaction t and $t-1$, estimate the empirical distribution and interpret its shape.
(b) Assuming that durations are exponentially distributed with density

$$f(d_t;\mu) = \frac{1}{\mu}\exp\left(-\frac{d_t}{\mu}\right), \quad \mu > 0,$$

compute the maximum likelihood estimator of the unknown parameter μ.
(c) Estimate the Engle–Russell ACD model by maximum likelihood assuming that durations are exponentially distributed

$$f(d_t|d_{t-1},d_{t-2},\cdots;\theta) = \frac{1}{\mu_t}\exp\left(-\frac{d_t}{\mu_t}\right), \quad \mu_t > 0,$$

$$\mu_t = \alpha_0 + \alpha_1 d_{t-1} + \beta_1\mu_{t-1}.$$

Use the estimated model to compute the long-run estimate of durations, and compare this estimate with the estimate of μ obtained in part (b).
(d) Re-estimate the ACD model in part (c) where durations are now assumed to be distributed according to the standardized Weibull distribution

$$f(d_t|d_{t-1},d_{t-2},\cdots;\theta) = \lambda\left[\Gamma\left(1+\frac{1}{\lambda}\right)\right]\frac{d_t^{\lambda-1}}{\mu_t}\exp\left[-\left(\frac{\Gamma\left(1+\frac{1}{\lambda}\right)}{\mu_t}\right)^\lambda\right],$$

in which $\Gamma(\cdot)$ is the gamma function. Perform a test of the hypothesis $\lambda = 1$, and interpret the result.

6. An ACD Model of BHP Trades

bhpdurations.*

The data consist of trades on BHP shares for the month of September 2011. The durations between trades are expressed in seconds.

(a) Estimate the exponential ACD model basing the log likelihood function on the normal distribution. The model is given by

$$\sqrt{d_t} = v_t, \qquad v_t \sim N(0, h_t),$$
$$h_t = \alpha_0 + \alpha_1 v_{t-1}^2 + \beta_1 h_{t-1}.$$

Interpret the results.

(b) Compute the expected unconditional mean duration from the model and, compare this value with the unconditional sample mean of the duration variable.

(c) Generate dummy variables for each of the 6 trading hours of the day. Regress the duration variable against the hourly dummies and comment on your results.

(d) Remove the diurnal pattern from the duration variable using this regression approach and re-estimate the model in part (a) on this purged variable. Compare your results with those in (a).

(e) Now estimate the model on the raw duration variable but include the dummy variables in the conditional duration equation in exponential form. Compare your results with those obtained in (a) and (d).

7. GARCH Model in Transaction Time

usdurations.*

The data consist of transactions on the S&P 500 E-mini Index futures contract from 08:30 to 10:30 Chicago time (or 14:30 to 16:25 GMT) on 3 January 2012. The price of each trade is recorded with a timestamp in milliseconds.

(a) Let r_t represent the return between transaction t and $t-1$, and d_t be the corresponding duration. Construct and plot the variable

$$y_t = \frac{r_t}{\sqrt{d_t}},$$

and interpret its time-series properties.

(b) Estimate a GARCH(1,1) for y_t given by

$$y_t = \mu_0 + u_t, \qquad u_t \sim N(0, h_t),$$
$$h_t = \alpha_0 + \alpha_1 u_{t-1}^2 + \beta_1 h_{t-1}.$$

Interpret the parameter estimates $\theta = \{\alpha_0, \alpha_1, \beta_1\}$.

(c) Compute the standardized residuals

$$z_t = \frac{\widehat{u}_t}{\sqrt{\widehat{h}_t}},$$

and plot the empirical distribution of z_t using a histogram. Comment on the shape of the histogram and discuss the implications for modeling transaction returns.

(d) Re-estimate the model in part (b), but allow the dynamics of the conditional mean to follow an ARMA(1,1) model.

(e) Redo part (b) where the conditional variance equation is augmented to include the variables d_t^{-1}, μ_t^{-1}, and d_t/μ_t, where μ_t is the conditional mean of durations obtained from an ACD model.

CHAPTER 17

Options

A financial option is the right to buy (known as a *call option*) or sell (known as a *put option*) an asset in the future at a particular price known as the exercise or *strike price* (see Chapter 1). The option may be exercised at the specified strike price either on or prior to a specified date that is part of the option contract. If the option expiration date passes and the option has not been exercised, then the buyer of the option loses the cash outlay (the so-called premium) to the seller. If an asset's current price is above (below) the strike price by the amount of the premium, the holder of a call (put) option can earn a positive payoff by exercising the option immediately or by selling the option on the secondary market.

Options fall into the class of financial securities that are known as derivatives, which, as the name implies, derive their value from some underlying base security or financial asset such as a stock or currency. As with all financial assets, one of the most fundamental concerns is pricing. Because options derive their value from the value of other more primitive assets, the mechanism of valuation is inevitably more complex because consideration must be given to the value of the base asset and the risk associated with holding that asset over time.[1]

In the formal option pricing models presented in this chapter, the key determinants of the price of an option are the type of option, the exercise price, the maturity of the contract, the discount rate, and the model underlying how the asset price, on which the option is written, evolves over time from time t to when the contract expires in the future. Of critical importance is the variance of the returns on the underlying asset, σ^2, which must be estimated in order to price an option. Several methods may be used to generate estimates of σ^2, but even in the simplest of all option pricing models, the relationship between the price of the option and σ^2 is nonlinear. Estimating the parameters of option

---

[1] The first steps in developing a theory for derivative and option valuation were made by Robert Merton, Fischer Black, and Myron Scholes. Their work led to the formulation of a model and pricing formula, known as *Black–Scholes*, that takes into account the mean value and volatility of the fundamental asset. The key research was published by Black and Scholes (1973) in a pioneering paper. Merton and Scholes were awarded the 1996 Nobel Prize in Economics for their work on pricing options. Fischer Black died in 1995 and was not included in the Nobel Prize because the awards are not made posthumously.

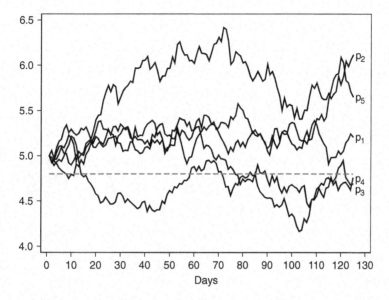

FIGURE 17.1   Five potential sample paths for the underlying asset price, p_t, over a 6-month (125 day) time horizon, $h = 0.5$, with initial price $p_0 = 5$. The horizontal dashed line is the strike price $k = 4.8$.

pricing models therefore requires an iterative approach using the methods discussed in Chapter 10 to obtain the maximum likelihood estimate.

Extending the specification of the asset pricing model to allow for additional complexities raises the level of difficulty in modeling and estimation. Relevant features to take into account in the asset pricing model are among those considered earlier, such as more complex dynamics, time-varying volatility, volatility smiles and smirks, heteroskedastic pricing errors, and nonnormal asset return distributions. All these features of the data increase the complexity of the relationship between the option price and the unknown parameters of the asset pricing model. These complexities correspondingly raise the computational burden of computing parameter estimates.

17.1 OPTION PRICING BASICS

Consider an investor at time t who wants to have the option to purchase an asset in the equity market h periods in the future at time $t + h$ and at a price equal to k. This type of contract is known as a call option. How much should the investor be prepared to pay for the option contract now? To work out the price of this contract, it is necessary to understand the mechanism by which the equity price p_t evolves.

Figure 17.1 gives 5 potential sample paths that the price of the equity can follow over a 6-month time horizon assuming 250 trading days in a year, $h = 0.5$, all beginning at $p_0 = 5$, the spot price at the time when the option contract is written, and with a strike price of $k = 4.8$. The time paths of the asset price p_t are based on simulating the log-price based on the AR(1) model

$$\log p_{t+\Delta t} - \log p_t = \left(r - \frac{1}{2}\sigma^2\right)\Delta t + \sqrt{\sigma^2 \Delta t}\, z_{t+h}, \qquad z_{t+h} \sim N(0,1), \qquad (17.1)$$

in which the (annualized) interest rate is $r = 0.05$, the (annualized) volatility is set at $\sigma = 0.2$, and $\Delta t = 1/250$ represents daily movements.

For three of the sample paths for the price in Figure 17.1, namely, cases 1, 2, and 5, the call contract is *in-the-money* at $t + h$ because

$$p_{1,125} = 5.2104 > 4.8, \qquad p_{2,125} = 6.1121 > 4.8, \qquad p_{5,125} = 5.6535 > 4.8.$$

This suggests that in 6 months time the investor could exercise the option contract in any of these three cases and make a positive payoff by purchasing the equity at time $t + h$ for the price k and immediately selling the equity on the future spot market at the corresponding price p_{t+h}. The payoffs for these three cases are

$$PAYOFF_1 = 5.2104 - 4.80 = 0.4104$$
$$PAYOFF_2 = 6.1121 - 4.80 = 1.3121$$
$$PAYOFF_5 = 5.6535 - 4.80 = 0.8535.$$

For cases 3 and 4 the contract is *out-of-the-money* at $t + h$

$$p_{3,125} = 4.69 < 4.8, \qquad p_{4,125} = 4.75 < 4.8.$$

The option would therefore not be exercised in these cases resulting in payoffs of

$$PAYOFF_3 = PAYOFF_4 = 0.$$

Intuitively, a fair price for this call option contract at the time it matures is the average of the payoffs of the five potential time paths given in Figure 17.1

$$\begin{aligned} PAYOFF &= \frac{1}{5}\sum_{i=1}^{5} PAYOFF_i \\ &= \frac{0.4104 + 1.3121 + 0.00 + 0.00 + 0.8535}{5} \\ &= 0.5152. \end{aligned}$$

Since the contract is written at t, and not at $t + h$, the average payoff at $t + h$ is discounted back to t at the risk-free annualized rate of interest r according to the formula

$$c_t = \exp(-rh)\frac{1}{5}\sum_{i=1}^{5} PAYOFF_i.$$

The factor $\exp(-rh)$ in this expression discounts the future average payoff back 6 months. So, for example, if $r = 0.05$ the price of the 6-month call option ($h = 0.5$) is

$$c_t = \exp(-rh)\frac{1}{5}\sum_{i=1}^{5} PAYOFF_i = \exp(-0.05 \times 0.5) \times 0.5152 = 0.5025.$$

It follows that \$0.5025 is the price the investor should pay for the option contract based on these 5 potential time paths.

Allowing for N time paths the option price is

$$c_t = \exp(-rh)\frac{1}{N}\sum_{i=1}^{N} PAYOFF_i. \tag{17.2}$$

The effect of increasing the number of simulation paths N from $N = 5$ to $N = 200$ on the price of the option is summarized in Table 17.1. As the number of time paths approaches infinity, $N \to \infty$, then the sample average approaches its conditional expectation (by the ergodic theorem or the law of large numbers) in which case the option price in equation (17.2) is given by

$$c_t = \exp(-rh)\,\mathrm{E}_t(PAYOFF) = \exp(-rh)\,\mathrm{E}_t(p_{t+h} - k). \tag{17.3}$$

The expression for a call option in equation (17.3) suggests that there are three important ingredients involved in pricing options.

(i) *Forecasting*

Options are concerned with purchasing an asset in the future, say at time $t + h$, where h represents the maturity of the contract. This forward looking behavior means that it is necessary to consider the (conditional) forecast distribution of the price of this asset, $f(p_{t+h}|p_t)$, where conditioning represents information available at time t when the decision is being made. For simplicity, the conditioning may be assumed to be solely a function of the current price of the asset p_t.

(ii) *Conditional Mean*

The price of the asset that an investor is prepared to pay in the future is equal to the conditional mean of the price distribution in the future, which is given by the formula

$$\mu_{t+h|t} = \int_0^\infty p_{t+h} f(p_{t+h}|p_t)\,dp_{t+h}. \tag{17.4}$$

(iii) *Truncation*

Only positive payoffs in the future are valued—that is, ones for which $p_{t+h} - k > 0$. The relevant conditional mean of an option is therefore a truncated conditional mean, which when discounted by the risk-free annualized rate of interest r gives the price of the call option as

$$c_t = \exp(-rh)\int_k^\infty (p_{t+h} - k)f(p_{t+h}|p_t)\,dp_{t+h}. \tag{17.5}$$

TABLE 17.1   Monte Carlo prices based on alternative numbers of simulation paths, N, of a call option exercised at maturity. Simulations are based on equation (17.2). The option contract is for a strike price of \$4.8 that matures in 6 months ($h=0.5$). The spot price is $p_0=5$, the annualized risk-free rate of interest is $r=0.05$, and the annualized volatility is set at $\sigma=0.2$.

N	Option Price
5	0.5025
10	0.3822
50	0.4248
100	0.4757
200	0.4639

17.2 THE BLACK–SCHOLES OPTION PRICE MODEL

In the first formal option pricing model, known as the Black–Scholes model (Black and Scholes, 1973), it is assumed that the natural logarithm of the asset price evolves according to an AR(1) process of the form

$$\log p_{t+h} - \log p_t = (r - \frac{1}{2}\sigma^2)h + \sqrt{\sigma^2 h}\, z_{t+h}, \qquad z_{t+h} \sim N(0,1). \qquad (17.6)$$

European Call Option

Based on the process in equation (17.6) Black and Scholes (1973) provide an analytical solution for the call option price defined in equation (17.5). This particular option is known as a European call option because the contract can only be exercised at the time of maturity. For a forecast horizon of h the conditional forecast distribution, $f(p_{t+h}|p_t)$, in equation (17.5) is lognormal

$$f(p_{t+h}|p_t) = \frac{1}{p_{t+h}\sqrt{2\pi\sigma^2 h}} \exp\left[-\frac{(\log p_{t+h} - \mu_t)^2}{2\sigma^2 h}\right], \qquad (17.7)$$

in which $\mu_t = \log p_t + (r - \sigma^2/2)h$.

Figure 17.2 illustrates the properties of the forecast distribution, $f(p_{t+h}|p_t)$, for selected time horizons of 1 month ($h = 1/12$), 3 months ($h = 3/12$), and 6 months ($h = 6/12$), with an initial price $p_0 = 5$, a risk-free annualized rate of interest of $r = 0.05$, and an annualized volatility of $\sigma = 0.2$. The 1-month forecast distribution is the most compact distribution, with dispersion increasing for longer time horizons.

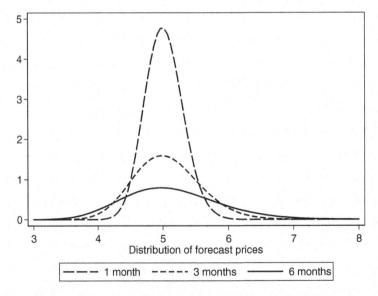

FIGURE 17.2 Forecast distributions of the asset price for selected time horizons of 1 month ($h = 1/12$), 3 months ($h = 3/12$), and 6 months ($h = 6/12$). The distributions are simulated from the lognormal distribution in equation (17.7) with initial price $p_0 = 5$, risk-free annualized rate of interest $r = 0.05$, and volatility $\sigma = 0.2$.

The solution of the Black–Scholes price for a European call option is obtained by substituting equation (17.7) into equation (17.5) and rearranging the expression to give

$$c_t = \exp(-rh) \int_k^{\infty} (p_{t+h} - k) \frac{1}{p_{t+h}\sqrt{2\pi\sigma^2 h}} \exp\left[-\frac{(\log p_{t+h} - \mu_t)^2}{2\sigma^2 h}\right] dp_{t+h}$$

$$= \exp(-rh) I_1 - \exp(-rh) I_2, \tag{17.8}$$

where I_1 and I_2 are integral expressions.

Using the lognormal distribution in equation (17.7) the first integral is

$$I_1 = \int_k^{\infty} p_{t+h} f\left(p_{t+h} | p_t\right) dp_{t+h}$$

$$= \exp\left[\log p_t + \left(r - \frac{1}{2}\sigma^2\right)h + \frac{\sigma^2 h}{2}\right] \times \Phi\left(\frac{\log\left(p_t/k\right) + \left(r + \frac{1}{2}\sigma^2\right)h}{\sigma\sqrt{h}}\right)$$

$$= p_t \exp\left[\left(r - \frac{1}{2}\sigma^2\right)h + \frac{\sigma^2 h}{2}\right] \times \Phi\left(\frac{\log\left(p_t/k\right) + \left(r + \frac{1}{2}\sigma^2\right)h}{\sigma\sqrt{h}}\right)$$

$$= p_t e^{rh} \Phi(d_t),$$

where $\Phi(\cdot)$ represents the cumulative distribution function of the normal distribution, and $d_t = \left(\log\left(p_t/k\right) + \left(r + \frac{1}{2}\sigma^2\right)h\right)\Big/\sqrt{\sigma^2 h}$.

The second integral is

$$I_2 = \int_k^{\infty} f\left(p_{t+h} | p_t\right) dp_{t+h} = \int_k^{\infty} \frac{1}{p_{t+h}\sqrt{2\pi\sigma^2 h}} \exp\left[-\frac{(\log p_{t+h} - \mu_t)^2}{2\sigma^2 h}\right] dp_{t+h},$$

where $\mu_t = \log p_t + (r - \sigma^2/2)h$. Using $z = (\log p_{t+h} - \mu_t)/\sigma\sqrt{h}$ as a change of variable, this integral becomes

$$I_2 = \int_k^{\infty} \frac{1}{p_{t+h}\sqrt{2\pi\sigma^2 h}} \exp\left[-\frac{(p_{t+h} - \mu_t)^2}{2\sigma^2 h}\right] dp_{t+h} = \int_{-\infty}^{\frac{\mu_t - \log k}{\sigma\sqrt{h}}} \frac{1}{\sqrt{2\pi}} \exp\left[-\frac{z^2}{2}\right] dz,$$

which simplifies as

$$I_2 = \Phi\left(\frac{\mu_t - \log k}{\sigma\sqrt{h}}\right) = \Phi(d_t - \sigma\sqrt{h}).$$

Substituting the expressions for I_1 and I_2 in equation (17.8) and simplifying gives the Black–Scholes price of a European call option contract as

$$c_t = p_t \Phi(d_t) - ke^{-rh}\Phi(d_t - \sigma\sqrt{h}),$$

$$d_t = \frac{\log\left(p_t/k\right) + \left(r + \frac{1}{2}\sigma^2\right)h}{\sigma\sqrt{h}}. \tag{17.9}$$

The term $\Phi(d_t - \sigma\sqrt{h})$ represents the probability the option is exercised in a risk neutral world. So $k\Phi(d_t - \sigma\sqrt{h})$ is the strike price times the probability that the strike price is paid. The term $p_t\,\Phi(d_t)$ is the discounted expected value that the price at maturity is p_{t+h} provided that $p_{t+h} > k$.

In the extreme case where the distribution of p_t is not truncated so that $k = 0$ and $p_t - k = p_t$, then $d_t \to \infty$ and it follows that

$$\lim_{k \to 0} \Phi(d_t) \to 1.$$

The result is that the price of the call option is in fact the current price of the asset, $c_t = p_t$. Viewed from another perspective, if $k = 0$ the conditional mean of the price at $t + h$ for a lognormal random variable is simply $p_t \exp(rh)$, which reduces to p_t when discounted back to the present, t, using $\exp(-rh)$ as the discount factor.

Applying the expression in equation (17.9) to compute the option price based on the option contract inputs given in Table 17.1 yields a value for d_t of

$$\begin{aligned}
d_t &= \frac{\log(p_t/k) + (r + \tfrac{1}{2}\sigma^2)h}{\sigma\sqrt{h}} \\
&= \frac{\log(5.00/4.80) + (0.05 + 0.5 \times 0.2^2) \times 0.5}{0.2 \times \sqrt{0.5}} = 0.5361.
\end{aligned}$$

Since

$$\Phi(d_t) = \Phi(0.5361) = 0.7041,$$

$$\Phi(d_t - \sigma\sqrt{h}) = \Phi(0.5361 - 0.2\sqrt{0.5}) = \Phi(0.3947) = 0.6535,$$

the Black–Scholes price of a European call option is

$$\begin{aligned}
c_t &= p_t\Phi(d_t) - ke^{-rh}\Phi(d_t - \sigma\sqrt{h}) \\
&= 5.00 \times 0.7041 - 4.80 \times \exp(-0.05 \times 0.5) \times 0.6535 = 0.4611.
\end{aligned}$$

Comparing this price and the simulated option prices reported in Table 17.1 shows that as the number of sample paths increases to $N = 200$, the eventual numerical price of 0.4639 for $N = 200$ is very close to the analytical price of 0.4611, with an error of less than 1%.

European Put Option

A European put option provides the right to sell an asset at the strike price of k when the contract matures at $t + h$, so the discounted payoff is

$$put_t = e^{-rh}E_t\left[\max\left(k - p_{t+h}, 0\right)\right]. \tag{17.10}$$

As p_t follows a lognormal distribution and evolves according to equation (17.6), the Black–Scholes expression for a European put option is

$$\begin{aligned}
put_t &= ke^{-r_t h}\Phi(-d_t + \sigma\sqrt{h}) - p_t\Phi(-d_t), \\
d_t &= \frac{\log\left(p_t/k\right) + \left(r + \tfrac{1}{2}\sigma^2\right)h}{\sigma\sqrt{h}},
\end{aligned} \tag{17.11}$$

whereas before $\Phi(z)$ is the standard normal cumulative distribution.

Equity Option

If a stock earns dividends (equal to a continuous dividend stream at the rate q per annum), the asset price equation in equation (17.6) is re-expressed as

$$\log p_{t+h} - \log p_t = (r - q - \frac{1}{2}\sigma^2)h + \sqrt{\sigma^2 h} z_{t+h}, \qquad z_{t+h} \sim N(0,1). \tag{17.12}$$

The Black–Scholes price for a European call option paying a continuous dividend yield is

$$c_t = p_t e^{-qh} \Phi(d_t) - ke^{-rh} \Phi(d_t - \sigma\sqrt{h}), \tag{17.13}$$

where now

$$d_t = \frac{\log(p_t/k) + (r - q + \frac{1}{2}\sigma^2)h}{\sigma\sqrt{h}}. \tag{17.14}$$

Currency Option

To price currency options let p_t represent the exchange rate between two currencies, which is assumed to evolve according to

$$\log p_{t+h} - \log p_t = (r - i - \frac{1}{2}\sigma^2)h + \sqrt{\sigma^2 h} z_{t+h}, \qquad z_{t+h} \sim N(0,1), \tag{17.15}$$

where r is the domestic interest rate and i is the foreign interest rate. Equation (17.15) represents uncovered interest rate parity as the expected depreciation of the exchange rate, $E_t[\log p_{t+h} - \log p_t]$, is proportional to the interest rate differential between the two countries, $r - i$. The Black–Scholes price for a European currency call option is

$$c_t = p_t e^{-ih} \Phi(d_t) - ke^{-rh} \Phi(d_t - \sigma\sqrt{h}),$$
$$d_t = \frac{\log(p_t/k) + (r - i + \frac{1}{2}\sigma^2)h}{\sigma\sqrt{h}}. \tag{17.16}$$

17.3 A FIRST LOOK AT OPTIONS DATA

The data consist of $N = 27695$ contracts on European call options written on the S&P 500 index on 4 April 1995, between 09:00 and 15:00. All duplicate observations are removed and all the option prices satisfy the no arbitrage lower bound condition

$$LB = \max\left(p_t e^{-qh} - ke^{-rh}, 0\right).$$

Summary statistics for the data are reported in Table 17.2. The call option prices (c_t) are computed as the average of the bid-ask prices, which range from a minimum of $1.0350 to a maximum of $156.2500, with an average price of $60.3602 and a standard deviation of $30.9778. There are 30 different strike prices, k, and 3 different maturities, h, resulting in a total of $30 \times 3 = 90$ unique contracts for the day. The strike price ranges from $350 to $550. The lowest four strike prices are $350, $375, $400, and $410; these then increase in steps of $5 to $535 for the second highest strike price, and $550 for the highest strike price.

The three different maturities correspond to options expiring in May, June, and September, with the respective number of days until maturity being 45, 73, and 167 days,

TABLE 17.2 Summary statistics for the $N = 27695$ European call options written on the S&P 500 index on 4 April 1995. Maturity, h, is expressed as a proportion of days per annum, the stock price, p_t, is adjusted for dividends, and the interest rate, r, is the 3-month US Treasury bill rate on the day equal to 0.059.

Statistic	Option Price (c_t)	Strike Price (k)	Maturity (h)	Stock Price (p_t)
Minimum	$1.0350	$350.0000	0.123288	$496.4390
Maximum	$156.2500	$550.0000	0.457534	$502.9450
Mean	$60.36025	$449.2538	0.270635	$499.8471
St. Dev.	$30.97777	$33.8460	0.141486	$1.9290

or expressed as a proportion of the number of days within a year, the maturities are $45/365 = 0.123288$, $73/365 = 0.2$, and $167/365 = 0.457534$, respectively. The stock price, p_t, is the synchronously recorded price of the index at the time the quote is recorded. As dividends are paid on the S&P 500 index, the stock price is adjusted for dividends by multiplying the index by e^{-qh} where q is computed as the average annual rate of dividends paid on the index over 1995. Inspection of Table 17.2 shows that the dividend adjusted stock price varies over the day, with an average price of $499.8471 and ranging from a minimum of $496.4390 to a maximum of $502.9450. Finally, the interest rate, $r = 0.0591$, is the annualized 3-month Treasury bill rate on 4 April 1995, which is assumed to be constant over the trading day.

17.4 ESTIMATING THE BLACK–SCHOLES MODEL

An important feature of the Black–Scholes option price model is that the only unknown parameter is the standard deviation (σ) of the returns on the stock for which the option contract is written. All the remaining components used to price an option based on the Black–Scholes model are specified by the contract. There are two broad methods for estimating σ. The first is based on the prevailing prices in the stock market and the second is based on prices in the options market.

17.4.1 Historical Approach

The standard deviation (σ) in the Black–Scholes expression for the price of a European call option in equation (17.9) corresponds to the standard deviation of returns on the stock for which the option is written. Hence, a natural estimator of σ is simply the standard deviation of the observed stock returns. As σ needs to be expressed in annual terms, the estimate typically needs to be scaled. This approach is commonly referred to as the historical method.

Suppose that stock prices (p_t) are measured daily. The steps to compute σ are as follows. First, compute daily returns from the stock prices as

$$y_t = \log(p_t) - \log(p_{t-1}). \tag{17.17}$$

For a sample of T daily observations on returns, now compute an estimate of the variance of the daily stock log returns in equation (17.17) as

$$\hat{\sigma}_y^2 = \frac{1}{T-1} \sum_{t=1}^{T} (y_t - \bar{y})^2, \tag{17.18}$$

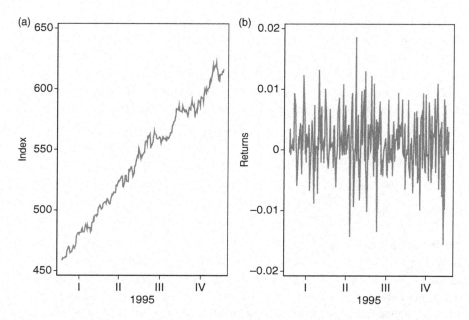

FIGURE 17.3 Daily data on the S&P 500 index and associated log returns for 2 January to 31 December 1995.

where $\bar{y}$ is the sample mean of y_t. An estimate of the annualized variance is then

$$\hat{\sigma}^2 = 250\hat{\sigma}_y^2,$$

where 250 is chosen to represent the number of trading days that exist within a calendar year. Finally, an estimate of the annualized volatility parameter is

$$\hat{\sigma} = \sqrt{250}\hat{\sigma}_y. \tag{17.19}$$

Alternatively, if stock returns are monthly, then the estimate of the annualized volatility is $\hat{\sigma} = \sqrt{12}\hat{\sigma}_y$.

To illustrate estimating the volatility of stock prices historically, consider panel (a) of Figure 17.3, which plots the daily S&P 500 index for the period 2 January to 31 December 1995. Panel (b) of Figure 17.3 contains the corresponding daily log returns $y_t = \log p_t - \log p_{t-1}$.

The mean of the daily log returns is $\bar{y} = 0.001133$, while the estimate of the returns variance is

$$\hat{\sigma}_y^2 = \frac{1}{T-1} \sum_{t=1}^{T} (y_t - \bar{y})^2 = \frac{0.006067}{259 - 1} = 2.3516 \times 10^{-5},$$

and the standard deviation is

$$\hat{\sigma}_y = \sqrt{2.3516 \times 10^{-5}} = 4.8493 \times 10^{-3}.$$

The annualized estimate of the volatility in stock returns is

$$\hat{\sigma} = \sqrt{250 \times \hat{\sigma}_y^2} = \sqrt{250 \times 2.3516 \times 10^{-5}} = 7.67 \times 10^{-2}, \tag{17.20}$$

or 7.67% per annum. Expressing the annualized value in terms of calendar days, the estimate increases to

$$\sqrt{365 \times 2.3516 \times 10^{-5}} = 9.26 \times 10^{-2}, \tag{17.21}$$

or 9.26% per annum. As an alternative historical estimate of the volatility, instead of using the full year of daily returns, if just the returns in May are used

$$\hat{\sigma}_y = 0.006572,$$

yielding an annualized estimate of volatility of

$$\hat{\sigma} = \sqrt{365} \times \hat{\sigma}_y = \sqrt{365} \times 0.006572 = 12.56 \times 10^{-2}, \tag{17.22}$$

or 12.56% per annum.

17.4.2 Implied Approach

Given $i = 1, 2, \cdots, N$ observations on the observed market prices of option contracts c_i and the corresponding timestamped price p_i of the underlying asset the option is written on, it is possible to back out an estimate of the volatility, σ. This is commonly referred to as the implied estimate of volatility, as the estimate represents the implied value of volatility that must have been used to price the option in the first place.

To formalize the empirical model to estimate σ, consider the equation

$$c_i = c_i^{BS}(\sigma) + u_i, \tag{17.23}$$

where c_i represents the observed price of the ith option, and $c_i^{BS}(\sigma)$ is the Black-Scholes price of the ith option contract given the volatility parameter σ. In the case of a European call option, the Black–Scholes price for the ith option contract is

$$c_i^{BS} = p_i \Phi(d_i) - k_i e^{-r_i h_i} \Phi(d_i - \sigma\sqrt{h_i}), \tag{17.24}$$

where d_i is defined as

$$d_i = \frac{\log(p_i/k_i) + (r_i + \frac{1}{2}\sigma^2)h_i}{\sigma\sqrt{h_i}}. \tag{17.25}$$

The disturbance term

$$u_i = c_i - c_i^{BS}(\sigma), \tag{17.26}$$

represents the pricing error, as it measures the difference between the observed price in the market for a call option and the price that would be predicted by the Black–Scholes model if volatility equaled σ. The pricing error represents a random variable that is assumed to be independent across contracts and distributed as a normal random variable, with zero mean and constant variance ω^2 so that

$$u_i \sim N(0, \omega^2). \tag{17.27}$$

To estimate $\theta = \{\sigma^2, \omega^2\}$ in the model in equations (17.23) and (17.27) by maximum likelihood, the logarithm of the likelihood is given by

$$\log L = -\frac{1}{2}\log(2\pi\omega^2) - \frac{1}{2}\frac{1}{N}\sum_{i=1}^{N}\frac{(c_i - c_i^{BS}(\sigma))^2}{\omega^2}, \tag{17.28}$$

where N is the number of option contracts in the sample. Since the systematic component $c_i^{BS}(\sigma)$ in equation (17.24) is a nonlinear function of σ, an iterative algorithm is needed to estimate θ.

Using log returns on the S&P 500 option contracts written on 4 April 1995, the maximum likelihood estimate of σ^2 is

$$\hat{\sigma}^2 = 0.0170, \tag{17.29}$$

with standard error $se(\hat{\sigma}^2) = 2.98 \times 10^{-5}$. The (implied) volatility estimate is then

$$\hat{\sigma} = \sqrt{0.0170} = 13.05 \times 10^{-2},$$

or 13.05%, which is comparable to the estimate of 12.56% based on the historical approach given in equation (17.22) using May returns in 1995. The parameter estimate of the pricing error variance is

$$\hat{\omega}^2 = 0.9249, \tag{17.30}$$

which has standard error $se(\hat{\omega}^2) = 0.7975 \times 10^{-2}$.

17.4.3 The Greeks

After estimation of the Black–Scholes model, various sensitivity parameters can be constructed that are useful in hedging portfolios and risk management. These quantities measure the sensitivity of the value of the portfolio to a change in an underlying parameter. They are denoted by Greek letters[2] and are collectively known as *The Greeks*. In the case of the Black–Scholes model, the most commonly used Greeks on a call option with price c, for a non-dividend-paying stock are as follows.

(i) **Delta**

The Delta (denoted Δ) parameter of an option measures the rate of change of the option price with respect to a change in the underlying price of the asset

$$\Delta = \frac{\partial c}{\partial p} = \Phi(d), \tag{17.31}$$

where $d = (\log(p/k) + (r + \sigma^2/2)/h)/(\sigma\sqrt{h})$. By definition, Δ lies between 0 and 1 and represents the implied probability that the option will expire in-the-money. An estimate of this probability can be obtained by replacing σ in the formula for Δ by either the historical or the implied estimator, $\hat{\sigma}$.

(ii) **Gamma**

The Gamma (denoted by Γ) parameter of an option measures the rate of change in the option's Δ with respect to a change in the underlying price of the asset. Given the definition of Δ, the Gamma is the second derivative of the option price with respect to the underlying price of the asset, namely,

$$\Gamma = \frac{\partial^2 c}{\partial p^2} = \frac{\phi(d)}{p\sigma\sqrt{h}}. \tag{17.32}$$

---

[2] The convention of using Greek letters probably developed out of the traditional use of α and β in asset pricing.

For relatively small values of Γ, Δ adjusts slowly to changes in p, whereas for relatively large values of Γ the Δ is highly sensitive to changes in p.

(iii) **Theta**

The Theta (denoted by Θ) parameter of an option measures the rate of change in the option value with respect to a decrease in the time to maturity

$$\Theta = -\frac{\partial c}{\partial h} = -\frac{p\phi(d)\sigma}{2\sqrt{h}} - rke^{-rh}\Phi(d - \sigma\sqrt{h}). \tag{17.33}$$

In general, $\Theta < 0$ with the negative value reflecting the fact that an option loses its value as it approaches maturity. Since h is measured in years, it is usual to divide Θ by 365 so that the quoted figure indicates the amount (per underlying share) that the option loses in one day.

(iv) **Vega**

The Vega quantity measures sensitivity to volatility—the change in the option value with respect to a change in volatility. This quantity is denoted by the Greek letter v, but the term Vega is not the name of any Greek letter

$$v = \frac{\partial c}{\partial \sigma} = p\sqrt{h}\phi(d). \tag{17.34}$$

Inspection of this expression shows that $v > 0$, so an increase in volatility increases the price of the option.

Table 17.3 gives estimates of the Greeks (Delta, Gamma, Theta, and Vega) for the first and last 10 contracts in the data set as well as for 10 intermediate contracts out of the total 27695 European call options written on the S&P 500 index on 4 April 1995. The first 10 contracts are out-of-the-money, as $p < k$; the 10 intermediate contracts are (near) at-the-money, as $p \simeq k$; and the last 10 contracts are in-the-money, as $p > k$. Volatility is based on the implied estimate of $\hat{\sigma} = 0.1305$.

The Delta in equation (17.31) of the first 10 contracts implies relatively low estimated probabilities, between 0.21 and 0.37, of finishing in-the-money. For the at-the-money contracts, the probability is estimated to be slightly above 0.5. For the last set of contracts, all of the Deltas are 1.0, suggesting that these contracts are a sure bet to mature in-the-money. The Gamma of the at-the-money contracts is higher than it is for the out-of-the-money and in-the-money contracts, a result that follows immediately from equation (17.32). In other words, at-the-money options are relatively more susceptible to movements in p than the other types of options.

For all the option contracts, the Theta in equation (17.33) is negative, demonstrating that the value of each contract diminishes as it approaches maturity. A comparison of the at-the-money option contracts 1002 and 1003 shows that the fall in the value of the option is higher for the May contract than for the June contract, as the former is closer to maturity. The daily loss of the May option is $44.9241/365 = \$0.1231$, compared to a loss of $34.8983/365 = 0.0956$ for the June option. Finally, the Vega in equation (17.34) is $v = 0$ for the in-the-money options, showing that volatility has no discernible impact on these options. This is not the case for the out-of-the-money and at-the-money options, where an increase in volatility raises the value of the option.

TABLE 17.3 The Greeks for 10 out-of-the-money, 10 at-the-money, and 10 in-the-money European call option contracts written on the S&P 500 index on 4 April 1995.

Contract	Strike	Maturity	Stock Price	Delta	Gamma	Theta	Vega
1	550	0.458	496.874	0.212	0.007	−19.796	97.327
2	535	0.458	496.726	0.312	0.008	−25.605	118.847
3	535	0.458	497.091	0.315	0.008	−25.773	119.417
4	535	0.458	497.101	0.315	0.008	−25.778	119.432
5	535	0.458	498.277	0.325	0.008	−26.315	121.226
6	530	0.458	496.983	0.353	0.009	−27.571	124.850
7	530	0.458	497.022	0.353	0.009	−27.588	124.902
8	530	0.458	497.052	0.353	0.009	−27.601	124.942
9	530	0.458	498.504	0.366	0.009	−28.231	126.808
10	530	0.458	498.504	0.366	0.0085	−28.231	126.808
⋮				⋮			⋮
1001	500	0.458	496.587	0.6075	0.0088	−34.897	129.106
1002	500	0.458	496.597	0.6076	0.0088	−34.898	129.100
1003	500	0.200	499.934	0.5908	0.0133	−44.924	86.877
1004	500	0.200	499.944	0.5909	0.0133	−44.926	86.872
1005	500	0.200	499.944	0.5909	0.0133	−44.926	86.872
1006	500	0.458	496.617	0.6078	0.0088	−34.902	129.089
1007	500	0.458	496.617	0.6078	0.0088	−34.902	129.089
1008	500	0.200	499.953	0.5910	0.0133	−44.929	86.867
1009	500	0.200	499.963	0.5911	0.0133	−44.931	86.862
1010	500	0.200	499.963	0.5911	0.0133	−44.931	86.862
⋮				⋮			⋮
27686	350	0.200	501.734	1.000	0.000	−20.442	0.000
27687	350	0.200	501.814	1.000	0.000	−20.442	0.000
27688	350	0.200	501.814	1.000	0.000	−20.442	0.000
27689	350	0.200	501.834	1.000	0.000	−20.442	0.000
27690	350	0.200	501.854	1.000	0.000	−20.442	0.000
27691	350	0.200	501.854	1.000	0.000	−20.442	0.000
27692	350	0.200	501.864	1.000	0.000	−20.442	0.000
27693	350	0.200	501.873	1.000	0.000	−20.442	0.000
27694	350	0.200	501.883	1.000	0.000	−20.442	0.000
27695	350	0.200	501.883	1.000	0.000	−20.442	0.000

17.5 TESTING THE BLACK–SCHOLES MODEL

The Black–Scholes model imposes very strong restrictions on the underlying process, which can be tested using various inferential methods. Let the Black–Scholes model be rewritten as

$$c_i = p_i \Phi(d_i) - k_i e^{-r h_i} \Phi(d_i - \sigma \sqrt{h_i}) + u_i, \tag{17.35}$$

where

$$d_i = \frac{\log(p_i/k_i) + (r + \frac{1}{2}\sigma^2)h_i}{\sigma \sqrt{h_i}},$$

and u_i is the pricing error with the property

$$u_i \sim N(0, \omega^2).$$

Three tests of the model are now investigated.

17.5.1 Bias

The model in equation (17.35) does not contain an intercept, suggesting that the conditional mean of the call option price equals the Black–Scholes price

$$E(c_i | p_i) = p_i \Phi(d) - ke^{-rh} \Phi(d - \sigma \sqrt{h}),$$

as $E(u_i) = 0$. This result is interpreted as the call option price being unbiased. To allow for the possibility that the observed option prices are biased, the empirical model in equation (17.35) is extended to include an intercept

$$c_i = \beta_0 + p_i \Phi(d) - ke^{-rh} \Phi(d - \sigma \sqrt{h}) + u_i, \tag{17.36}$$

where β_0 is the unknown intercept. A test of the unbiasedness property is that the intercept is zero and is based on the hypothesis $H_0 : \beta_0 = 0$. This restriction can be tested using a standard t test. Performing the test based on estimating equation (17.36) by maximum likelihood yields

$$t = \frac{0.8105}{0.0091} = 88.81,$$

a result that indicates a strong rejection of unbiasedness.

17.5.2 Heteroskedasticity

An important assumption of the regression model in equation (17.5) is that the variance of the disturbance term, ω^2, is constant across all contract types. To relax the assumption of homoskedasticity, dummy variables defined for strikes and/or maturities can be used to allow the disturbance variance to change over the sample. For example, dummy variables on the three types of maturities (h_i) in the stock option data set would be defined as

$$D_{MAY,i} = \begin{cases} 1 : h_i = 0.123288 \\ 0 : \text{otherwise} \end{cases}$$

$$D_{JUNE,i} = \begin{cases} 1 : h_i = 0.200000 \\ 0 : \text{otherwise} \end{cases} \tag{17.37}$$

$$D_{SEPT,i} = \begin{cases} 1 : h_i = 0.457534 \\ 0 : \text{otherwise} \end{cases}$$

corresponding, respectively, to May, June, and September option contracts.

Only two of the three dummy variables need to be included in the equation to be estimated if the model already contains an intercept term. The resulting model specifies the variance as

$$\omega_i^2 = \exp\left(\alpha_0 + \alpha_1 D_{MAY,i} + \alpha_2 D_{JUNE,i}\right),$$

where only 2 of the 3 dummy variables are needed because the variance equation includes an intercept. A joint test of the restrictions

$$H_0 : \alpha_1 = \alpha_2 = 0,$$

is a test of homoskedasticity. The Wald test of the restrictions yields the test statistic $\chi_2^2 = 23668.42$, with a p value of 0.0000. This outcome shows significant evidence of heteroskedasticity in the call prices.

17.5.3 Volatility Smiles and Smirks

In estimating option price models, the data consist of option contracts corresponding to various strike prices and various maturities. In fact, the present data consist of 90 different types of call option contracts used in the combined data set, as there are 30 different strike prices and 3 types of maturities. An important feature of the estimated model is that there is just a single estimate of the volatility parameter σ, regardless of the type of option contract. This is a restriction of the model that can be tested by re-estimating the model for alternative strike prices and alternative maturities.

A natural way to determine the validity of the assumption that volatility is invariant to strike prices is to group the data corresponding to each strike price and re-estimate the Black–Scholes model for each group. If the Black–Scholes model is consistent with the data, then the estimates of volatility associated with each group should not be statistically different. Volatility estimates that are different across groups may be interpreted as evidence against the Black–Scholes model. In practical work, this outcome is commonly present when implied volatility is plotted against the strike price. Two types of relationships between volatility and the strike price usually emerge in such plots, depending on the type of option contract.

  (i) Volatility Smile: There is a U-shape relationship between volatility and the strike price, centered around the at-the-money options.
  (ii) Volatility Smirk or Skew: There is an inverse relationship between volatility and the strike price, with volatility being relatively high for in-the-money options and low for out-of-the-money options.

Volatility smiles are commonly found for currency options, whereas downward sloping implied volatility (known as volatility skew or smirk) tends to be found for stock options, as the following example demonstrates. Such deviations from the constant volatility framework of the Black–Scholes model became common in American markets following the 1987 stock market crash, which increased awareness of extreme outcomes and the possible presence of heavy tailed distributions rather than a normal distribution in determining stock market outcomes.

Figure 17.4 gives the results from estimating the option price model separately for the 29 strike prices ranging from 350 to 535 (the strike price of 550 is excluded because there is only one observation) for the European call options written on the S&P 500 index on 4 April 1995. There is an inverse relationship between the (implied) volatility and the strike price, with volatility falling from 0.35 for the smallest strike price to around 0.1 for the highest strike price, hence demonstrating the so-called volatility smirk. This result is in stark contrast to the assumption of the Black–Scholes model in which the volatility is assumed to be constant across strike prices. The results illustrated in Figure 17.4 suggest that the Black–Scholes model is misspecified. A likelihood ratio test of a volatility smirk is investigated in the exercises.

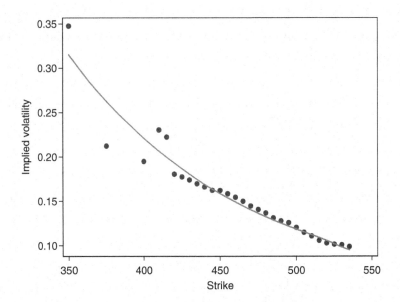

FIGURE 17.4 The volatility skew or smirk of call options written on the S&P 500 index on 4 April 1995. The implied volatility is obtained by fitting the Black–Scholes option price to European call option prices for each strike price separately.

17.6 OPTION PRICING AND GARCH VOLATILITY

An alternative approach is to estimate the constant mean model with a GARCH conditional variance

$$\log p_t - \log p_{t-1} = \mu + u_t$$
$$\sigma_{yt}^2 = \alpha_0 + \alpha_1 u_{t-1}^2 + \beta_1 \sigma_{yt-1}^2$$
$$u_t \sim N(0, \sigma_{yt}^2),$$

where μ is the mean return and σ_{yt}^2 is the GARCH conditional variance. The variance is now time-varying, with the memory controlled by the parameters α_1 and β_1.

The log likelihood function is

$$\log L = -\frac{1}{2}\log(2\pi) - \frac{1}{2}\frac{1}{T}\sum_{t=1}^{T}\sigma_{yt}^2 - \frac{1}{2}\frac{1}{T}\sum_{t=1}^{T}\frac{\left(\log p_t - \log p_{t-1} - \mu\right)^2}{\sigma_{yt}^2}$$

$$= -\frac{1}{2}\log(2\pi) - \frac{1}{2}\frac{1}{T}\sum_{t=1}^{T}\left(\alpha_0 + \alpha_1 u_{t-1}^2 + \beta_1 \sigma_{yt-1}^2\right)$$

$$- \frac{1}{2}\frac{1}{T}\sum_{t=1}^{T}\frac{\left(\log p_t - \log p_{t-1} - \mu\right)^2}{\alpha_0 + \alpha_1 u_{t-1}^2 + \beta_1 \sigma_{yt-1}^2},$$

where the unknown parameters are $\theta = \{\mu, \alpha_0, \alpha_1, \beta_1\}$. Maximizing the log likelihood function requires an iterative solution, as the log likelihood is a nonlinear function of the parameters.

Using the log returns on the S&P 500 index for the period 2 January to 31 December 1997, the maximum likelihood estimates of this model are

$$\widehat{\mu} = 0.001144, \quad \widehat{\alpha}_0 = 1.29 \times 10^{-6}, \quad \widehat{\alpha}_1 = 0.0128, \quad \widehat{\beta}_1 = 0.9357.$$

An estimate of the long-run variance from the GARCH estimates is

$$\widehat{\sigma}_y^2 = \frac{\widehat{\alpha}_0}{1 - \widehat{\alpha}_1 - \widehat{\beta}_1} = \frac{1.29 \times 10^{-6}}{1 - 0.0128 - 0.9357} = 2.5049 \times 10^{-5}.$$

The annualized volatility based on the long-run GARCH estimate is

$$\widehat{\sigma} = \sqrt{250} \times 2.5049 \times 10^{-5} = 3.9606 \times 10^{-4}.$$

This GARCH estimate of volatility is smaller than the estimate based on the historical approach. Figure 17.5 highlights the reason for the difference: The conditional variance is very low in the first part of the period but eventually climbs to about 0.005, an estimate that is consistent with the constant variance model.

17.7 THE MELICK–THOMAS OPTION PRICE MODEL

An important feature of the Black–Scholes model is that the price of the underlying asset is taken to be lognormally distributed. This assumption is equivalent to assuming that the returns on the underlying asset are normally distributed. There is strong empirical evidence to reject this assumption, which suggests that the Black–Scholes model may deliver incorrect option prices or poor approximations to them in cases where log

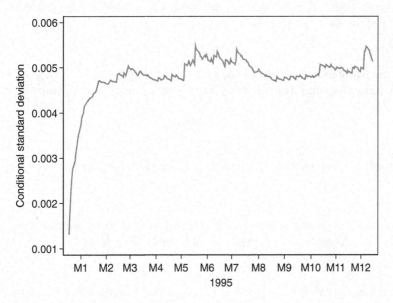

FIGURE 17.5 Plot of the estimated conditional volatility of log returns on the S&P 500 index obtained by estimating a GARCH(1,1) model using daily data for the period 2 January 1995 to 31 January 1995.

normality fails. An implication of this failure is that portfolios containing options may not be hedged appropriately under Black–Scholes pricing methods.

To relax the lognormality assumption, Melick and Thomas (1997) assume that the distribution of the asset price is a mixture of lognormals, resulting in the empirical option pricing model in equation (17.23) being re-specified as

$$c_i = \alpha c_{1i}^{BS}(\sigma_1) + (1 - \alpha) c_{2i}^{BS}(\sigma_2) + u_i, \tag{17.38}$$

where $c_{ji}^{BS}(\sigma_j)$, $j = 1, 2$ is the Black–Scholes price corresponding to the jth regime given by

$$c_{ji}^{BS} = p_i \Phi(d_{ji}) - k_i e^{-rh_i} \Phi(d_{ji} - \sigma_j \sqrt{h_i}), \tag{17.39}$$

with constant volatility, σ_j, $j = 1, 2$ and

$$d_{ji} = \frac{\log(p_i/k_i) + (r + \frac{1}{2}\sigma_j^2)h_i}{\sigma_j \sqrt{h_i}}. \tag{17.40}$$

The parameter $0 \leq \alpha \leq 1$ is the mixing parameter that weights the two subordinate lognormal distributions.

The unknown parameters in $\theta = \{\sigma_1^2, \sigma_2^2, \alpha, \omega^2\}$ are estimated by maximum likelihood methods. Assuming as before that the pricing errors u_i are normally distributed according to equation (17.27), the log likelihood function in equation (17.28) is

$$\log L = -\frac{1}{2}\log(2\pi\omega^2) - \frac{1}{2}\frac{1}{N}\sum_{i=1}^{N}\frac{(c_i - \alpha c_{1i}^{BS}(\sigma_1) - (1 - \alpha)c_{2i}^{BS}(\sigma_2))^2}{\omega^2}, \tag{17.41}$$

which is maximized with respect to θ using an iterative algorithm.

Using the S&P 500 index option contracts on 4 April 1995, the maximum likelihood estimates of the two variances are

$$\hat{\sigma}_1^2 = 0.0009, \quad \hat{\sigma}_2^2 = 0.0426, \tag{17.42}$$

with respective standard errors of $se(\hat{\sigma}_1^2) = 1.7 \times 10^{-5}$ and $se(\hat{\sigma}_2^2) = 16.6 \times 10^{-5}$, implying that the two lognormal distributions have very different shapes. The mixing parameter estimate is

$$\hat{\alpha} = 0.5516, \tag{17.43}$$

with standard error $se(\hat{\alpha}) = 0.0016$, suggesting that these two distributions have roughly equal weights. However, a test of equal weights based on the t statistic

$$t = \frac{0.5516 - 0.5}{0.0016} = 32.907, \tag{17.44}$$

results in a rejection of the null hypothesis that $\alpha = 0.5$ at conventional significance levels. Finally, the estimate of the variance of the pricing error is

$$\hat{\omega}^2 = 0.1407, \tag{17.45}$$

with standard error $se(\hat{\omega}^2) = 0.0008$. As this estimate is smaller than the estimate given in equation (17.30) for the lognormal model, the result indicates that the lognormal mixture model provides a significant improvement in the pricing of options over the Black–Scholes model.

17.8 NONLINEAR OPTION PRICING

The Black–Scholes option price in equation (17.35) shows that there is a nonlinear relationship between the option price, c_i^{BS}, and the remaining arguments, p_i, k_i, h, r_i, and σ. For more general option price models, it is not always possible to derive an analytic expression for the price of the option. One way to proceed is to use a semi-nonparametric approach such as artificial neural networks (ANN) to model the nonlinear dependence. These methods provide a flexible way to approximate nonlinear processes and are now often implemented with machine learning algorithms that assist in identifying a suitable framework for practical use. (For an introduction, see Martin, Hurn, and Harris, 2013).

A simple example of an ANN model of option prices is

$$c_i = \alpha_0 + \alpha_1 \left(p_i - k_i \right) + \alpha_2 h_i + \alpha_3 L_i + u_i, \tag{17.46}$$

where

$$L_i = \frac{1}{1 + \exp\left[-(\gamma_0 + \gamma_1 \left(p_i - k_i \right) + \gamma_2 h_i) \right]},$$

and $u_i \sim N(0, \omega^2)$ is a disturbance term. The logistic function, L_i, represents the artificial neural network and is commonly referred to as a squasher because it dampens the impact of large movements in asset prices p_i. The logistic function is perhaps the most commonly used squasher, although other alternatives such as the cumulative normal distribution and the hyperbolic tangent are also used. To estimate all the unknown parameters of the model contained in the vector $\theta = \{\alpha_0, \alpha_1, \alpha_2, \alpha_3, \gamma_0, \gamma_1, \gamma_2, \omega^2\}$, an iterative algorithm must be used to maximize the log likelihood function based on the assumption that the disturbances are normally distributed.

Having estimated the ANN, it is possible to compute various hedge parameters to be used in a risk management strategy. For example, the Delta is estimated as

$$\widehat{\Delta} = \frac{\partial \widehat{c}_i}{\partial p_i} = \widehat{\alpha}_1 + \widehat{\alpha}_3 \widehat{\gamma}_1 \widehat{l}_i,$$

where

$$\widehat{l}_i = \frac{\exp\left[-\left(\widehat{\gamma}_0 + \widehat{\gamma}_1 \left(p_i - k_i \right) + \widehat{\gamma}_2 h_i \right) \right]}{\left(1 + \exp\left[-\left(\widehat{\gamma}_0 + \widehat{\gamma}_1 \left(p_i - k_i \right) + \widehat{\gamma}_2 h_i \right) \right] \right)^2}$$

is the logistic density function. Differentiating $\widehat{\Delta}$ by p_i produces an estimate of the Gamma. An estimate of the Theta is given by

$$\widehat{\Theta} = \frac{\partial \widehat{c}_i}{\partial h_i} = \widehat{\alpha}_2 + \widehat{\alpha}_3 \widehat{\gamma}_2 \widehat{l}_i.$$

17.9 USING OPTIONS TO ESTIMATE GARCH MODELS

Estimates of volatility discussed previously are based either on historical methods (using returns) or on implicit methods (using option prices). A more general strategy is to combine both methods and use data on asset returns and options prices in order to improve precision in the estimation of the GARCH parameters. There are two ways to do this: the direct approach in which data on observed option prices are used, and the indirect approach in which the VIX index is used. The direct approach is computationally demanding because analytical solutions for option prices based on GARCH conditional variances are not available. In this case, numerical solutions are needed to compute option prices, which makes estimation by maximum likelihood highly involved.

An innovative approach, proposed by Kanniainen, Lin, and Yang (2014), circumvents the computational demands of the direct approach. To understand this indirect approach to computing the parameters of GARCH models using both returns and options data based on the VIX, consider the GARCH-M conditional variance model introduced in Chapter 13

$$r_t - r_{ft} = \mu_0 + \mu_1 \sigma_{yt} + u_t$$
$$u_t \sim N(0, \sigma_{yt}^2) \tag{17.47}$$
$$\sigma_{yt}^2 = \alpha_0 + \alpha_1 u_{t-1}^2 + \beta_1 \sigma_{yt-1}^2, \tag{17.48}$$

where $r - r_{ft}$ is the excess log return, expressed as a percentage. The parameter μ_1 represents the market price of risk. Defining the standardized random variable $z_t = u_t / \sigma_{yt}$, this model is conveniently rewritten as

$$r_t - r_{ft} = \mu_0 + \mu_1 \sigma_{yt} + \sigma_{yt} z_t$$
$$\sigma_{yt}^2 = \alpha_0 + \alpha_1 \sigma_{yt-1}^2 z_{t-1}^2 + \beta_1 \sigma_{yt-1}^2. \tag{17.49}$$

The use of the VIX is motivated by the property that it approximates the 1-month variance swap rate on the S&P 500 index, thereby providing a measure of the risk-neutral expectation of integrated variance over a month (Bollerslev, Gibson, and Zhou, 2011). Formally, the relationship between the VIX and the conditional variance σ_{yt}^2 is expressed as

$$\frac{1}{252} VIX_t^2 = \frac{1}{M} E_t \sum_{j=1}^{M} \sigma_{yt+j}^2 + v_t, \tag{17.50}$$

where v_t is a disturbance term capturing the approximation error between the observed variance using the squared VIX and the expected variance based on the average of the future expected conditional variances over the month. The scaling of the squared VIX by $1/252$ converts the VIX from an annualized measure of volatility based on calendar days to a daily variance measure in order to make it commensurate with the daily conditional variance σ_{yt}^2. As returns, and hence the conditional variance σ_{yt}^2, are computed using trading days, M is set at $M = 22$ to represent the number of trading days in a month. The conditional expectations operator E_t is defined with respect to the risk-neutral distribution, as this is the measure that is used to price options.

To operationalize the use of equation (17.50) to estimate the GARCH parameters, it is necessary to re-express the conditional variance σ_{yt}^2 in equation (17.49) in terms of the risk-neutral probabilities. This is achieved by assuming that the risk-neutral probabilities z_t^* are related to z_t in equation (17.49) by the expression

$$z_t^* = z_t + \mu_1, \tag{17.51}$$

where μ_1 is the risk parameter defined in equation (17.49). Substituting equation (17.51) for z_t in equation (17.49) yields the risk-neutral expression of the conditional variance

$$r_t - r_{ft} = \mu_0 + \sigma_{yt}^2 z_t^*$$

$$\sigma_{yt}^2 = \alpha_0 + \alpha_1 \sigma_{yt-1}^2 \left(z_t^* - \mu_1\right)^2 + \beta_1 \sigma_{yt-1}^2. \tag{17.52}$$

Now using this expression in equation (17.50) gives the following linear relationship

$$\frac{1}{252} VIX_t^2 = \delta_0 + \delta_1 \sigma_{yt+1}^2 + v_t, \tag{17.53}$$

where $v_t \sim N(0, \sigma_v^2)$ is a disturbance term. The parameters δ_0 and δ_1 are given by

$$\delta_0 = \frac{\alpha_0}{1 - \alpha_1 - \beta_1} \left(1 - \frac{\left(1 - \psi^M\right)}{(1 - \psi) \times M}\right), \quad \delta_1 = \frac{\left(1 - \psi^M\right)}{(1 - \psi) \times M}, \tag{17.54}$$

with

$$\psi = \alpha_1 + \beta_1 + \alpha_1 \mu_1^2.$$

These expressions are obtained by replacing the $E_t \sigma_{yt+k}^2$ terms in equation (17.50) using the conditional GARCH forecast expressions given in Chapter 13—see Kanniainen et al. (2014) for further details. Since $\sigma_y^2 = \alpha_0/(1 - \alpha_1 - \beta_1)$ is the unconditional variance, the term $\delta_0 + \delta_1 \sigma_{yt+1}^2$ represents a weighted average of σ_y^2 and σ_{yt+1}^2 with weighting parameter $(1 - \psi^M)/((1 - \psi)M)$.

To estimate the GARCH parameters by maximum likelihood, the log likelihood function contains two components. The first is associated with the returns model in equation (17.49), which is discussed in Chapter 13. The second is associated with the VIX equation (17.53) that has the effect of imposing a number of cross-equation restrictions on the parameters of the two models, as δ_0 and δ_1 are functions of the parameters in the returns model. Assuming normal disturbances for z_t in equation (17.49) and v_t in equation (17.53), the joint log likelihood

$$\log L = \log L_1(r_t; \theta) + \log L_2(VIX_t; \theta), \tag{17.55}$$

is maximized with respect to the unknown parameters $\theta = \{\mu_0, \mu_1, \alpha_0, \alpha_1, \beta_1\}$ using an iterative algorithm.

Using daily percentage excess returns on the S&P 500 index from 2 January 2004 to 9 August 2017, with the risk-free rate chosen as the 1-month US Treasury bond yield, the GARCH model in equation (17.48) is estimated by maximum likelihood methods, with the results presented in Table 17.4.

TABLE 17.4 Estimated GARCH(1,1) models based on the one-equation model using returns and the combined model using both returns and the VIX. Standard errors are in parentheses.

Model	Parameter						log L
	μ_0	μ_1	α_0	α_1	β_1	σ_v	
GARCH	−0.049	0.131	0.019	0.099	0.880		−1.280
	(0.000)	(0.017)	(0.002)	(0.007)	(0.008)		
GARCH + VIX	−0.050	0.132	0.015	0.101	0.882	0.104	−48.722
	(0.000)	(0.005)	(0.000)	(0.000)	(0.000)	(0.000)	

As a preliminary step in estimating the joint log likelihood in equation (17.55), equation (17.53) is estimated by least squares, where σ_{yt+1}^2 is replaced by the estimated conditional variance $\hat{\sigma}_{yt+1}^2$ from the estimated returns model. The estimated equation for the VIX is

$$\frac{1}{252} VIX_t^2 = 0.638 + 0.840\hat{\sigma}_{yt+1}^2 + \hat{v}_t. \tag{17.56}$$

If the cross-equation restrictions in equation (17.54) are to be satisfied, the implied estimates of δ_0 and δ_1 should be similar in magnitude to the estimates in equation (17.56). Substituting the estimates of the returns model reported in Table 17.4 into the expression for ψ gives

$$\hat{\psi} = 0.100657 + 0.881816 + 0.100657 \times 0.131961^2 = 0.984226.$$

The implied estimates of δ_0 and δ_1 are, respectively,

$$\hat{\delta}_0 = \frac{0.015141}{1 - 0.100657 - 0.881816}\left(1 - \frac{\left(1 - 0.984226^{22}\right)}{(1 - 0.984226) \times 22}\right) = 0.129$$

$$\hat{\delta}_1 = \frac{\left(1 - 0.984226^{22}\right)}{(1 - 0.984226) \times 22} = 0.851.$$

The implied estimate of δ_1 matches the least squares estimate of 0.840 in equation (17.56). In the case of the estimate of δ_0, there is less of an agreement, with the implied estimate of 0.129 being less than the least squares estimate of 0.638 reported in equation (17.56). The maximum likelihood estimates from maximizing the joint log likelihood in equation (17.55) are given in Table 17.4. A comparison of the two sets of estimates shows that they are qualitatively very similar.

17.10 EXERCISES

The data required for the exercises are available for download as EViews workfiles (*.wf1), Stata datafiles (*.dta), comma delimited text files (*.csv), and as Excel spreadsheets (*.xlsx).

1. Historical Volatility

sp500_1995.*

The data are daily observations on the S&P 500 index from 2 January to 31 December 1995.

(a) Compute daily log returns, r_t, and plot them. Comment on the time series properties of the log returns.

(b) Compute the daily mean and variance of r_t.

(c) Compute an annualized estimate of the volatility, σ, of stock returns assuming that there are 250 trading days in the year.

(d) Consider the constant mean model

$$\log p_t - \log p_{t-1} = \mu + u_t$$
$$u_t \sim N(0, \sigma_y^2),$$

where γ is the mean return, and σ_y is the daily historical volatility.

(i) Derive the log likelihood function for this model.

(ii) Estimate the parameters in $\theta = \{\mu, \sigma_y^2\}$ by maximum likelihood. Use these estimates to compute the annualized volatility, σ, and compare this estimate to that obtained in part (c).

(e) Repeat part (d) replacing the assumption of constant variance with the GARCH model of the conditional variance

$$\log p_t - \log p_{t-1} = \mu + u_t$$
$$\sigma_{yt}^2 = \alpha_0 + \alpha_1 u_{t-1}^2 + \beta_1 \sigma_{yt-1}^2$$
$$u_t \sim N(0, \sigma_{yt}^2),$$

where μ is the mean return, and σ_{yt}^2 is the conditional variance.

2. **Estimating Volatility Using Option Prices**

---
stock_option.*

The data file contains European call options data written on the S&P 500 index on 4 April 1995. The total number of contracts is 27695. The data include the prices of call options, c, the strike price of the contract, k, maturity of the contract, h, the stock price at the time of the contract, p, and the interest rate, r.

(a) Consider the Black–Scholes model

$$c_i = p_i \Phi(d_i) - k_i e^{-rh_i} \Phi(d_i - \sigma \sqrt{h_i}) + u_i$$
$$u_i \sim N(0, \omega^2),$$

where the unknown parameters are $\theta = \{\sigma^2, \omega^2\}$ and

$$d_i = \frac{\log(p_i/k_i) + (r + \frac{1}{2}\sigma^2)h_i}{\sigma \sqrt{h_i}}.$$

Compute the maximum likelihood estimate of θ. Interpret the implied volatility parameter estimate and compare it with the historical volatility estimate based on stock prices.

(b) An extension of the Black–Scholes model is

$$c_i = \beta_0 + p_i \Phi(d_i) - k_i e^{-rh_i} \Phi(d_i - \sigma \sqrt{h_i}) + u_i$$
$$u_i \sim N(0, \omega^2),$$

where d_i is defined in part (a), and the unknown parameters are $\theta = \{\sigma^2, \omega^2, \beta_0\}$. Perform a test for bias by using an LR test of the hypothesis $\beta_0 = 0$. Interpret the result of the test.

(c) To determine if the bias identified in part (b) depends on the maturity of the contract, estimate the model

$$c_i = \beta_0 + \beta_1 D_{MAY,i} + \beta_2 D_{JUNE,i} + p_i \Phi(d_i) - k_i e^{-rh_i} \Phi(d_i - \sigma \sqrt{h_i}) + u_i$$
$$u_i \sim N(0, \omega^2),$$

where d_i is defined in part (a),

$$D_{MAY,i} = \begin{cases} 1 : \text{May} \\ 0 : \text{otherwise} \end{cases}$$
$$D_{JUNE,i} = \begin{cases} 1 : \text{June} \\ 0 : \text{otherwise,} \end{cases}$$

and the unknown parameters are $\theta = \{\sigma^2, \omega^2, \beta_0, \beta_1, \beta_2\}$. Perform a likelihood ratio test of the hypothesis $\beta_1 = \beta_2 = 0$. Interpret the result of the test.

(d) Estimate the model

$$c_i = \beta_0 + p_i \Phi(d_i) - k_i e^{-rh_i} \Phi(d_i - \sigma\sqrt{h_i}) + u_i$$
$$u_i \sim N(0, \omega_i^2),$$

where d_i is defined in part (a), the disturbance variance is specified as

$$\omega_i^2 = \exp\left(\gamma_0 + \gamma_1 DUM_{MAY,i} + \gamma_2 DUM_{JUNE,i}\right),$$

with $DUM_{MAY,i}$ and $DUM_{JUNE,i}$ defined in part (c), and the unknown parameters are $\theta = \{\sigma^2, \omega^2, \gamma_0, \gamma_1, \gamma_2\}$. Perform a likelihood ratio test of the hypothesis $\gamma_1 = \gamma_2 = 0$. Interpret the result of the test.

(e) Consider the following generalization of the Black–Scholes model where volatility is a function of moneyness

$$c_i = p_i \Phi(d_i) - k_i e^{-rh_i} \Phi(d_i - \sigma_i\sqrt{h_i}) + u_i$$
$$u_i \sim N(0, \omega^2),$$

in which

$$d_i = \frac{\log(p_i/k_i) + (r + \frac{1}{2}\sigma_i^2)h_i}{\sigma_i\sqrt{h_i}}$$
$$\sigma_i^2 = \exp\left(\alpha_0 + \alpha_1 DUM\_AT_i + \alpha_2 DUM\_IN_i\right).$$

The relevant dummy variables are defined as

$$DUM\_AT_i = \begin{cases} 1 : 0.97 < \dfrac{p_i}{k_i} < 1.03 \\ 0 : \text{otherwise} \end{cases}$$
$$DUM\_IN_i = \begin{cases} 1 : 1.03 < \dfrac{p_i}{k_i} \\ 0 : \text{otherwise,} \end{cases}$$

representing, respectively, at-the-money and in-the-money options.

(i) Estimate the parameters $\theta = \{\alpha_0, \alpha_1, \alpha_2, \omega^2\}$. Interpret the results.

(ii) Perform a likelihood ratio test of constant volatility.

3. Volatility Smirk in Stock Options

stock_option.*

Consider the European call options data written on the S&P 500 index on 4 April 1995.

(a) For each strike price, $k_i, i = 1, 2, \cdots, 29$ (which excludes $k = 550$), estimate the implied volatility σ of the Black–Scholes model. Plot the volatility estimates against the strike prices and show that there is a volatility smirk.

(b) Perform a likelihood ratio test of the assumption of constant volatility (Black–Scholes) against the alternative of a smirk.

(c) Repeat part (b), but allow for the pricing model to include a constant bias.

4. Term Structure of the Volatility Smirk

stock_option.*

Consider the European call options data written on the S&P 500 index on 4 April 1995.

(a) Estimate the implied volatility, σ, of the Black–Scholes model for May option contracts, ($h = 0.123288$). In computing the volatility, it may be necessary to restrict the range of the strike prices as for some deep in-the-money and deep out-of-the-money contracts, there may be no observations available corresponding to just May contracts.

(b) Repeat part (a) for June option contracts, ($h = 0.2$), and September option contracts, ($h = 0.457534$).

(c) Plot the three volatility estimates obtained in (a) and (b) and discuss the results.

5. Estimating the Implied Volatility of S&P 500 Stock Options

sp500.*

The data file contains 675 option contracts written on the S&P 500 index on 28 and 29 December 1995.

(a) Compute an estimate of the average volatility, σ, using the model

$$c_i = p_i \Phi(d_i) - k_i e^{-rh_i} \Phi(d_i - \sigma \sqrt{h_i}) + u_i$$
$$u_i \sim N(0, \omega^2),$$

where the unknown parameters are $\theta = \{\sigma^2, \omega^2\}$ and

$$d_i = \frac{\log(p_i/k_i) + (r + \frac{1}{2}\sigma^2)h_i}{\sigma \sqrt{h_i}}.$$

Note that k_i is the exercise price, which equals p_i for at-the-money options, $h_i = 0.25$ is the option's maturity expressed as a proportion of a year, and $\Phi(z)$ is the standard normal cumulative distribution.

(b) Suggest an alternative estimate of σ using the spot data series and compare this estimate with the one obtained from part (a).

6. **Melick–Thomas Option Price Model**

> stock_option.*

The data file contains European call options data written on the S&P 500 index on 4 April 1995. The total number of contracts is 27695. The data include the prices of call options, c, the strike price of the contract, k, maturity of the contract, h, the stock price at the time of the contract, p, and the interest rate, r.

Consider the Melick–Thomas option price model

$$c_i = \alpha c_{1i}^{BS}(\sigma_1) + (1 - \alpha) c_{2i}^{BS}(\sigma_2) + u_i,$$

$$c_{ji}^{BS} = p_i \Phi(d_{ji}) - k_i e^{-rh_i} \Phi(d_{ji} - \sigma_j \sqrt{h_i})$$

$$d_{ji} = \frac{\log(p_i/k_i) + (r + \frac{1}{2}\sigma_j^2)h_i}{\sigma_j \sqrt{h_i}},$$

in which $0 \le \alpha \le 1$ is the mixing parameter that weights the two subordinate lognormal distributions.

(a) Estimate the parameters $\theta = \{\sigma_1^2, \sigma_2^2, \alpha, \omega^2\}$ by maximum likelihood and interpret the results.

(b) Re-estimate the model, but allow for a constant bias term in the mean.

7. **Artificial Neural Networks (ANN)**

> ann.*

The data are 93 stock call option prices based on Black–Scholes at a point in time for a range of exercise prices (31 in total) and maturities (3 in total). The underlying asset price is $p = \$65$, the expected annual return is $r = 0.1$, and annual volatility is $\sigma = 0.2$.

(a) Estimate the following regression equation by ordinary least squares

$$c_i = \beta_0 + \beta_1 (p_i - k_i) + \beta_2 h_i + u_i,$$

where u_i is a disturbance term, and $i = 1, 2, ..., 93$. Compare the actual and fitted option prices and discuss the suitability of this equation for modeling call option prices.

(b) Estimate by maximum likelihood the ANN model

$$c_i = \alpha_0 + \alpha_1 (p_i - k_i) + \alpha_2 h_i + \alpha_3 L_i + u_i,$$

where

$$L_i = \frac{1}{1 + \exp\left[-\left(\gamma_0 + \gamma_1 (p_i - k_i) + \gamma_2 h_i\right)\right]},$$

and $u_i \sim N(0, \omega^2)$ is a disturbance term. Compare the actual and fitted option prices, and discuss the suitability, both statistical and theoretical, of this equation for modeling call option prices.

(c) For both the linear model estimated in part (a) and the ANN model estimated in part (b), compute the Delta hedge for an exercise price $k = \$65$ (at-the-money option) and maturity $h = 0.25$, and compare these estimates with the Black–Scholes delta hedge

$$\frac{\partial c}{\partial p} = \Delta = \Phi(d),$$

with

$$d = \frac{\log(p/k) + \left(r + \frac{1}{2}\sigma^2\right)h}{\sigma\sqrt{h}}.$$

(d) For both the linear model estimated in part (a) and the ANN model estimated in part (b), compute the Delta hedge for an exercise price $k = \$70$ (out-of-the-money option) and maturity $h = 0.25$, and compare these estimates with the Black–Scholes delta hedge.

(e) For both the linear model estimated in part (a) and the ANN model estimated in part (b), compute the Delta hedge for an exercise price $k = \$60$ (in-the-money option) and maturity $h = 0.25$, and compare these estimates with the Black–Scholes Delta hedge.

(f) For both the linear model estimated in part (a) and the ANN model estimated in part (b), compute an estimate for the call option price for a two-year option, that is $h = 2$, with an exercise price of $k = \$70$, and compare these estimates with the Black–Scholes price.

8. Using Option Prices to Estimate GARCH Models

> garch_vix. *

The data are daily observations for the period 1 April 2004 to 9 August 2017, on the S&P 500 index, the VIX, and the 1-month US Treasury bill yield (expressed as an annualized percentage).

(a) Compute the daily percentage excess log returns on the S&P 500 index using the 1-month Treasury Bill rate as the risk-free rate. Plot the squared excess returns, and compare this series with the series $VIX_t^2 / 252$.

(b) Estimate the GARCH-M model for returns

$$r_t = \mu_0 + \mu_1 \sigma_{yt} + u_t$$
$$\sigma_{yt}^2 = \alpha_0 + \alpha_1 u_{t-1}^2 + \beta_1 \sigma_{yt-1}^2$$
$$u_t \sim N(0, \sigma_y^2),$$

where r_t is the daily percentage excess return on the S&P 500 index, u_t is a disturbance term, and μ_1 is the market price of risk. Estimate the model and interpret the estimates. Let the log likelihood value be denoted as $\log L_1$.

(c) Estimate the following regression equation by least squares

$$\frac{1}{252} VIX_t^2 = \delta_0 + \delta_1 \sigma_{yt+1}^2 + v_t,$$

where $v_t \sim N(0, \sigma_v^2)$ is a disturbance term, and δ_0 and δ_1 are unknown parameters. Let the log likelihood value be denoted as $\log L_2$.

(d) Use the estimates of the GARCH-M model in part (b) to construct estimates of δ_0 and δ_1 based on the expressions

$$\delta_0 = \frac{\alpha_0}{1 - \alpha_1 - \beta_1} \left(1 - \frac{\left(1 - \psi^k\right)}{(1 - \psi) k} \right), \quad \delta_1 = \frac{\left(1 - \psi^k\right)}{(1 - \psi) k},$$

with $\psi = \alpha_1 + \beta_1 + \alpha_1 \mu_1^2$ and $k = 22$. Compare these estimates with the estimates obtained in part (c).

(e) Now re-estimate the GARCH-M model in part (b) by combining this equation with the VIX equation in part (c) subject to the restrictions in part (d). Compare the parameter estimates with the estimates based just on returns.

(f) Test the restrictions in part (d) by performing a likelihood ratio test comparing the constrained log likelihood function from part (e) and the unconstrained log likelihood function given by $\log L_1 + \log L_2$, which are obtained, respectively, from the estimated models in parts (b) and (c). Interpret the results of the test.

CHAPTER 18

Extreme Values and Copulas

The assumption of normality is widely adopted in finance. This usage stems partly from mathematical convenience and partly from a concern to represent behavior during normal market periods in which there are no extremes. In the case of risk management, for instance, the value at risk (VaR) of a portfolio based on the assumption of normality (see Chapter 7) may be regarded as evaluating the risk of a loss in portfolio value during normal times of trading.

Risk managers are often much more interested in potential losses in portfolio value that can occur in more extreme situations such as the Black Monday episode on 19 October 1987 or the more recent financial crisis of 2008–2010. During these episodes, markets experienced extreme falls in the value of equities that exceeded five times the empirical standard deviation and were therefore inconsistent with a generating mechanism for equity returns based on a normal distribution. Such considerations lead to the use of extreme value distributions.

One aspect of the analysis of extreme value distributions in finance concerns the tail behavior of univariate distributions of asset returns. Extending this analysis to modeling the joint distribution of asset returns enables a shift in focus to joint tail behavior in asset return distributions and the dependence of returns during extreme periods. Once again, both left and right tails of the distribution are important. Understanding the joint behavior of extreme returns is particularly important for risk management when computing the VaR of a portfolio containing multiple assets. It is also an important component of models of systemic risk (see Chapter 14) and contagion (Bae, Karolyi, and Stultz, 2003).

Moving from univariate to multivariate analyses of extreme behavior is complicated because analytical solutions based on multivariate extreme value distributions may not always be convenient or even available. An alternative approach, which is now common in the literature and in financial industry practice, is to use *copulas* to assist in developing analytic solutions. This approach is adopted in this chapter. The copula method simplifies analysis by writing the joint density function in decomposed form in terms of its individual marginal distributions (which may be expressed in terms of univariate extreme value distributions) and a function that combines the marginals to produce a joint distribution in which there is dependence among the random variables.[1]

18.1 MOTIVATION

Figure 18.1 contains daily percentage log returns of the S&P 500, from 4 January 1960 to 17 March 2017. There exist large negative spikes as well as large positive spikes, with the largest occurring on Black Monday, where the index fell by 22.90%. Descriptive statistics given in Table 18.1 show that for a mean daily return of 0.0247% with an (empirical) standard deviation of 0.9865%, a fall of −22.90% represents more than 22 standard deviations from its mean. Given that a normal distribution is characterized by having 99.73% of its distribution within ±3 standard deviations of the mean, the fall in the S&P 500 on Black Monday clearly constitutes an extreme event.

It is not surprising that risk managers have particular interest in extreme components of the distribution such as the minimum and the maximum statistics. As functions of a sequence of realizations, these statistics are themselves random variables. Their probability distributions are derived using extreme value theory. The distribution of the minimum statistic provides information on the left tail of the distribution and represents a measure of the potential losses faced by investors who hold a long position in a portfolio. The distribution of the maximum statistic provides information on the right

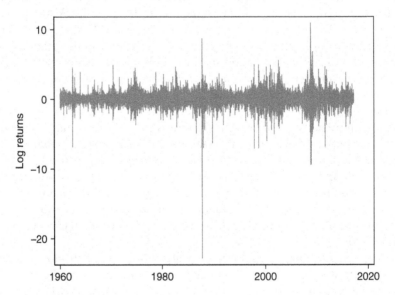

FIGURE 18.1   Daily percentage log returns on the S&P 500 index, from 4 January 1960 to 17 March 2017.

---

[1] The first copula used in finance was the Gaussian copula, originally proposed by Li (1999, 2000). It has the dubious alleged distinction of being partly responsible for the Wall Street collapse in 2008 because of its failure to capture the potential impact of extreme events that can arise with heavy tailed distributions (MacKenzie and Spears, 2014).

TABLE 18.1 Descriptive statistics on the daily percentage log returns of the S&P 500 from 4 January 1960 to 20 March 2017.

Statistic	Value
Mean	0.0247
Median	0.0131
Standard Deviation	0.9865
Maximum	10.9572
Minimum	−22.8997
Skewness	−1.0285
Kurtosis	31.3226
Jarque–Bera	501480.0000
p value	0.0000

tail of the distribution and represents a measure of the potential losses faced by an investor who has a short position in a portfolio.

Studying the form of the tails of a distribution is important in determining the existence of moments such as the mean and the variance, as well as higher order moments including skewness and kurtosis. The heavier (or fatter) the tails of a distribution are, the fewer the number of moments that exist. In the extreme case, where no integer order moments of a distribution exist, the distribution does not even possess a finite mean.[2] Calculations that lead to financial inputs based on sample moments do not have population analogues in such cases. An important example of a distribution whose moments do not exist is the Cauchy distribution (see Chapter 10), which is a special case of the t distribution in which the degrees of freedom parameter is $\nu = 1$. For this distribution the sample mean can be calculated, but this quantity has no population analogue and does not satisfy a law of large numbers. Instead, in such cases, it is useful to deal with the sample quantiles such as the median and interquartile range rather than the sample mean and sample standard deviation.

18.2 EVIDENCE OF HEAVY TAILS

18.2.1 Order Statistics

The descriptive statistics on the percentage log returns of the S&P 500 from 4 January 1960 to 17 March 2017 given in Table 18.1 show that the biggest daily fall (the minimum $r_{(1)}$) is −22.90%, corresponding to Black Monday; and the biggest daily rise (the maximum $r_{(T)}$) is 10.96%, following the $700 billion bailout plan of the US government enacted on 3 October 2008. A more extensive list of extreme movements is given in Table 18.2, which contains the biggest daily changes in the S&P 500 in excess of ±6%, ordered from the largest negative to the largest positive returns. These movements represent approximately more than 6 empirical standard deviations from the average daily return. Inspection of Table 18.2 shows that there are more extreme falls (16) than there are extreme rises (8). Interestingly, while the period of the global financial crisis in

---

[2] Fractional moments of order less than unity may still exist even when the mean is not finite.

TABLE 18.2 Extreme movements in the daily percentage log returns of the S&P 500 from 4 January 1960 to 17 March 2017. Dates reflect daily movements in excess of ±6%.

Negative Returns			Positive Returns		
Order Stat.	Date	Return (%)	Order Stat.	Date	Return (%)
$r_{(1)}$	10/19/1987	−22.90	$r_{(T-7)}$	11/21/2008	6.13
$r_{(2)}$	10/15/2008	−9.47	$r_{(T-6)}$	03/10/2009	6.17
$r_{(3)}$	12/01/2008	−9.35	$r_{(T-5)}$	24/11/2008	6.27
$r_{(4)}$	09/29/2008	−9.20	$r_{(T-4)}$	13/11/2008	6.69
$r_{(5)}$	10/26/1987	−8.64	$r_{(T-3)}$	03/23/2009	6.84
$r_{(6)}$	10/09/2008	−7.92	$r_{(T-2)}$	10/21/1987	8.71
$r_{(7)}$	10/27/1997	−7.11	$r_{(T-1)}$	10/28/2008	10.25
$r_{(8)}$	08/31/1998	−7.04	$r_{(T)}$	10/13/2008	10.96
$r_{(9)}$	01/08/1988	−7.01			
$r_{(10)}$	11/20/2008	−6.95			
$r_{(11)}$	05/28/1962	−6.91			
$r_{(12)}$	08/08/2011	−6.90			
$r_{(13)}$	10/13/1989	−6.32			
$r_{(14)}$	11/19/2008	−6.31			
$r_{(15)}$	10/22/2008	−6.29			
$r_{(16)}$	04/14/2000	−6.00			

2008 does not yield a single negative movement that comes close to the magnitude of the fall experienced on Black Monday in 1987, this period is nonetheless characterized by more extreme movements than any other financial crisis between 1960 and 2017.

The big movements in the returns on the S&P 500 listed in Table 18.2 represent the order statistics, with the ordering running from the lowest (largest negative) to the highest (largest positive). Let

$$r_1, r_2, \cdots, r_T, \tag{18.1}$$

represent the log returns of a time series for a sample size of length T. The order statistics from ordering the returns from the lowest return to the highest return are denoted as

$$r_{(1)}, r_{(2)}, \cdots, r_{(T)}, \tag{18.2}$$

where $r_{(i)}$ represents the ith order statistic. The first order statistic $r_{(1)}$ represents the minimum return, while the last order statistic $r_{(T)}$ represents the maximum return.

For the returns on the S&P 500, the first order statistic is $r_{(1)} = -22.90\%$, corresponding to 19 October 1987 and the largest order statistic is $r_{(T)} = 10.96\%$, which occurred on 13 October 2008. The second order statistic is $r_{(2)} = -9.47\%$, on 15 October 2008, which occurs two days after the largest order statistic $r_{(T)}$ and potentially represents a market correction to the big movement in the US equity market on 13 October.

Each order statistic in equation (18.2) has a distribution, as does the joint distribution of the full set of T order statistics. The goal of this chapter is to construct useful models of extreme events. The focus is therefore on the distributions of the first and largest order statistics and explaining their characteristics. In principle, this is achieved by constructing empirical probability distributions of the first and last order statistics and using these distributions for inference. But from a sampling perspective, there is just a single realization of the minimum value and a single realization of the maximum value in one sample of data, which does not provide sufficient information to construct the relevant empirical distributions. To circumvent this problem, the strategy is to generate non-overlapping subsamples of T observations. It is common to choose subsamples based on a month, or a quarter, or even a year. For the S&P 500, data adopting a monthly interval results in 687 subsamples.

The empirical distribution of the first order statistics for each of the 687 samples is presented in the left-hand panel of Figure 18.2. The empirical distribution is negatively skewed, with the most extreme observation in the left tail corresponding to the drop in the stock market on Black Monday, when the market fell 22.90%. This distribution is unimodel with a peak occurring at negative returns between −1% and −2%. The corresponding empirical distribution of the largest order statistic is given in the right-hand panel of Figure 18.2 by extracting the maximum return from each of the 687 monthly subsamples. The shape of this distribution tends to be a mirror image of the empirical distribution of the minimum, being positively skewed and with the peak occurring at a positive return between 1% and 1.5%.

18.2.2 Standardized t Distribution
The approach proposed in Chapter 10 to capture the effects of extreme values in the returns distribution is to replace the normal distribution by a distribution exhibiting heavy tails such as the (standardized) t distribution. The resulting model may then be estimated by maximum likelihood. For example, consider the model

$$r_t = \mu + \sigma z_t, \qquad z_t \sim St(0, 1, v), \tag{18.3}$$

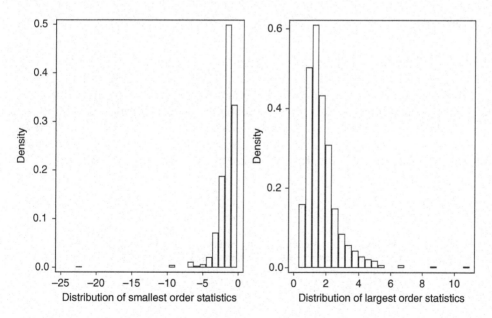

FIGURE 18.2 Empirical distributions of the minimum and maximum order statistics based on 687 monthly subsamples of the daily percentage log returns of the S&P 500 for the period 4 January 1960 to 20 March 2017.

where $St(0, 1, \nu)$ represents the standardized t distribution

$$f(z_t; \nu) = \frac{\Gamma((\nu + 1)/2)}{\Gamma(\nu/2)\sqrt{(\nu - 2)\pi}}\left(1 + \frac{z_t^2}{\nu - 2}\right)^{-(\nu+1)/2},\tag{18.4}$$

which has zero mean, unit variance, and degrees of freedom parameter $\nu > 2$. Apart from providing additional flexibility for modeling extreme returns, the t distribution also provides evidence about the existence of the population moments. In the extreme case where the degrees of freedom parameter approaches infinity ($\nu \to \infty$), the t distribution approaches the normal distribution, which has the property that all moments exist. As ν decreases in magnitude so do the number of moments that exist. In the case of the standardized t distribution in equation (18.4), it is assumed that $\nu > 2$ so that the mean and variance exist, which is useful in empirical work.

Using the estimation methods established in Chapter 10, the unknown parameters $\theta = \{\mu, \sigma, \nu\}$ of the returns model in equations (18.3) and (18.4) are estimated by maximum likelihood methods using an iterative algorithm. Using the percentage log returns on the S&P 500 given in Figure 18.1, the maximum likelihood estimates are given in Table 18.3 with standard errors based on the outer product of the gradients. The daily mean and standard deviation are estimated to be 0.04% and 1.08%, respectively. An estimate of tail heaviness in the returns distribution is given by the degrees of freedom parameter (ν), which is estimated to be 2.87. Since this estimate is greater than 2 but less than 3, the first two moments of the S&P 500 returns distribution exist; but none of the higher order moments are finite, including skewness and kurtosis. This empirical result provides support for the previous observation concerning the common presence of outliers in return distributions, which make these distributions incompatible with a normal distribution.

18.3 EXTREME VALUE THEORY

By construction, the standardized t distribution defined in equation (18.4) is a symmetric distribution with equal mass in the negative and positive tails of the distribution. The symmetric shape characteristic of this distribution may be too restrictive, especially for return distributions that exhibit skewness. Such characteristics are indeed the case for S&P 500 returns, as highlighted in Table 18.2. Not only are some of the actual returns found to be extreme in magnitude, as evidenced in the large negative return occurring on Black Monday, but the extreme returns in the negative tail are larger in magnitude and

TABLE 18.3 Maximum likelihood estimates of the returns model with t distribution disturbances as in equations (18.3) and (18.4). The data are the percentage log returns on the S&P 500 from 4 October 1960 to 17 April 2017. Standard errors are based on the outer product of the gradients formula.

Parameter	Estimate	Standard Error
μ	0.0397	0.0061
σ	1.0757	0.0307
ν	2.8715	0.0861
$\log L$	−1.2668	

greater in number than those in the right tail. These features clearly indicate a skewed distribution.

Moreover, from a risk management point of view there may only be interest in one of the tails of the distribution. This would be the case if the risk manager is long in a portfolio (owning stock and having the right to sell, or holding an option and having the right to exercise or sell it before expiration) so the focus of attention will be on the left tail. Alternatively, if the risk manager is short in a portfolio (having borrowed to sell shares with a need to repay with interest later or having sold an option giving the holder the right to exercise the option later) then the positive tail would be the focus.

An alternative approach to using the t distribution to model extreme returns, which by construction uses all of the returns to model the full distribution, is to focus solely on the extreme parts of the distribution as given by the lowest, $r_{(1)}$, and the highest, $r_{(T)}$, order statistics as discussed in Section 18.2.1. This is the approach of extreme value theory. Because the main focus of this approach is on the extreme returns, it has the potential to provide a more accurate estimate of the tails of the distribution. This has the added advantage for risk managers that downside and upside risks can be priced separately.

18.3.1 Distribution Types

The standardized random variable corresponding to the minimum return $r_{(1)}$ is defined as the ratio

$$z = \frac{r_{(1)} - \mu}{\sigma}, \tag{18.5}$$

where μ (location) and σ (scale) are parameters that are to be determined from the data. There are three important extreme value probability distributions commonly used in practice, namely,

$$
\begin{aligned}
\text{Fréchet } (k < 0): \quad & f(z) = (1+kz)^{1/k-1}\exp[-(1+kz)^{1/k}], & z < -1/k \\
\text{Gumbel } (k = 0): \quad & f(z) = \exp[z - \exp(z)], & -\infty < z < \infty \\
\text{Weibull } (k > 0): \quad & f(z) = (1+kz)^{1/k-1}\exp[-(1+kz)^{1/k}], & z > -1/k.
\end{aligned} \tag{18.6}
$$

The extreme value distributions in equation (18.6) are derived based on the assumption that returns are independently and identically distributed, although these expressions still hold even when returns display some form of dependence. The unknown parameter k represents the shape parameter that governs the tail behavior of the extreme value densities. The shape parameter k is often represented by the parameter

$$\alpha = -1/k, \tag{18.7}$$

which is commonly known as the tail index of the distribution. This parameter is helpful and can be used in practice to identify the existence of moments: Smaller values of α correspond to the existence of a smaller number of moments. For $0 < \alpha \le 1$, no moments exist. For $1 < \alpha \le 2$, the mean exists but not the variance. For $2 < \alpha \le 3$, the mean and the variance exist, but higher order moments such as skewness and kurtosis do not. For $3 < \alpha \le 4$, the first three moments now exist from the mean, variance, and skewness, but not kurtosis. Finally, for $4 < \alpha \le 5$, all of the first four moments exist.

To understand the properties of the extreme value distributions in equation (18.6), Figure 18.3 provides a plot of the three densities and for comparison a plot of the standardized normal density. Both the Fréchet ($k < 0$) and Gumbel ($k = 0$) extreme value densities are negatively skewed, with the Fréchet exhibiting a longer negative tail. This shows that as k becomes more negative the density has more of its probability mass in the left tail. In comparison, the Weibull ($k > 0$) extreme value density is positively skewed, which, from inspection of Figure 18.3, appears more compact than even the normal density.

18.3.2 Estimation

The extreme value distributions in equation (18.6) together with the definition of the standardized random variable in equation (18.5) are based on the unknown parameters $\theta = \{\mu, \sigma, k\}$. Two estimators are presented. The first is based on the Hill estimator, which provides an estimate of the shape parameter k. The second is based on the maximum likelihood principle, which provides estimates of all three unknown parameters.

Hill Estimator

The Hill estimator provides a nonparametric method for computing the shape parameter k that uses the order statistics. In the case of the left tail of the distribution, this estimator is defined as

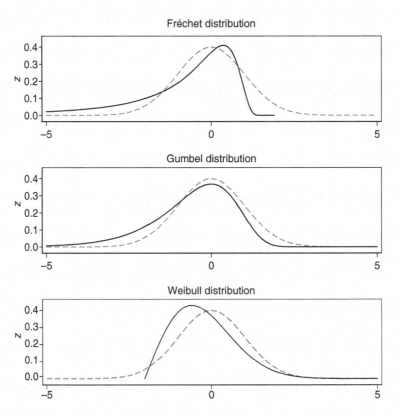

FIGURE 18.3 Plots of the extreme value probability density functions (solid lines) of the first order statistic in equation (18.6). The standard normal density function (dashed lines) is plotted for comparison.

$$\widehat{k}_q = -\frac{1}{q}\sum_{i=1}^{q}\left(\log(-r_{(i)}) - \log(-r_{(q+1)})\right)$$

$$= \log(-r_{(q+1)}) - \frac{1}{q}\sum_{i=1}^{q}\log(-r_{(i)}), \tag{18.8}$$

which is the difference between the logarithm of the negative $q+1$ order statistic compared to the average of the logarithm of the negative lower q order statistics. The parameter q is chosen as a positive integer that stabilizes the estimate of k. As the Hill estimator in equation (18.8) contains terms such as $\log(-r_{(i)})$, it is only applicable to those returns that are negative. The asymptotic distribution of this estimator as $q \to \infty$ is

$$\sqrt{q}(\widehat{k}_q - k) \xrightarrow{d} N(0, k^2). \tag{18.9}$$

In practice, the asymptotic variance, k^2, is replaced by a consistent estimator, $\widehat{k}_q^2$, in order to conduct inference and construct confidence intervals.

To demonstrate the implementation of the Hill estimator, consider the daily percentage returns presented in Figure 18.1 for the period 4 January 1960 to 17 March 2017. Sorting the data to compute the order statistics and extracting just the negative values reduces the available number of observations to 6757 to estimate the parameter k. The order statistics are

$r_{(1)}$	$r_{(2)}$	$\cdots$	$r_{(100)}$	$r_{(101)}$	$\cdots$	$\cdots$	$r_{(6757)}$
-22.89972	-9.46951		-3.00239	-3.0022			-0.00076.

The calculations for computing k based on $q = 100$ are

$$\widehat{k}_{100} = \log(-r_{(101)}) - \frac{1}{100}\sum_{i=1}^{100}\log(-r_{(i)})$$

$$= \log(3.00226) - \frac{\log(22.89972) + \log(9.46951) + \cdots + \log(3.00239)}{100}$$

$$= -0.33567.$$

The full set of k estimates are reported in Figure 18.4 for $q = \{1, 2, \cdots, 500\}$. Inspection of this figure shows that the estimates of k based on values of $q < 100$ are still relatively noisy but stabilize for $q \geq 100$.

A test of the Gumbel distribution ($k = 0$) based on $q = 500$ and using the asymptotic distribution in equation (18.9) with the asymptotic variance of k^2 replaced by the consistent estimator $\widehat{k}_q^2$ yields a statistic evaluated under the null hypothesis of

$$\frac{\sqrt{q}(\widehat{k}_q - k)}{\widehat{k}_q} = \frac{\sqrt{500}(-0.352284 - 0)}{0.352284} = -22.361,$$

which is distributed asymptotically as $N(0, 1)$. The p value is 0.000, showing a strong rejection of the Gumbel distribution in favor of the Fréchet distribution.

Maximum Likelihood Estimator

The maximum likelihood estimator of the unknown parameters in $\theta = \{\mu, \sigma, k\}$ is based on the extreme value distribution of the first order statistic $r_{(1)}$. To generate a sample of

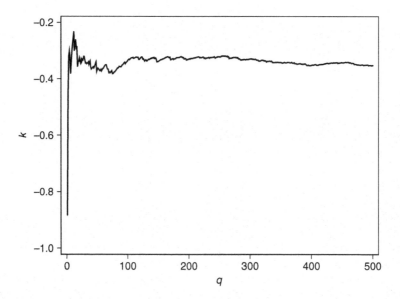

FIGURE 18.4 Application of the Hill estimator in equation (18.8) to determine the shape parameter k using the daily stock returns from Figure 18.1.

first order statistics, the 1-month subsamples of $r_{(1)}$ given in Figure 18.3 are used. From equations (18.5) and (18.6), the extreme value distribution for $r_{(1)}$ is as follows

$$f(r_{(1)}) = \begin{cases} \dfrac{1}{\sigma}(1+kz)^{1/k-1}\exp\left[-(1+kz)^{1/k}\right], & k \neq 0 \\ \dfrac{1}{\sigma}\exp[z-\exp(z)], & k = 0. \end{cases} \qquad \textbf{(18.10)}$$

The log likelihood function at observation (month) t is

$$\log f(r_{(1)}) = \begin{cases} -\log\sigma + \left(\dfrac{1}{k}-1\right)\log(1+kz) - (1+kz)^{1/k}, & k \neq 0 \\ -\log\sigma + z - \exp(z), & k = 0, \end{cases}$$

and the maximum likelihood estimator θ is obtained by maximizing the log likelihood function

$$\log L = \frac{1}{N}\sum_{t=1}^{N}\log f(r_{(1)}). \qquad \textbf{(18.11)}$$

As equation (18.11) is a nonlinear function of the unknown parameters, an iterative algorithm is used to compute the maximum likelihood estimates.

   The results of maximizing equation (18.11) for the monthly observations on the first order statistic for the S&P 500 data are given in Table 18.4. The estimate of k is $\widehat{k} = -0.2142$, which suggests that the Fréchet distribution is the appropriate extreme value distribution for modeling the distribution of the first order statistic. This estimate is

TABLE 18.4 Maximum likelihood estimates of the extreme value distribution in (18.10) for the first order statistic $r_{(1)}$, based on the $N=687$ monthly sub-samples of the first order statistics presented in Figure 18.2. Standard errors are based on the outer product of the gradients.

Parameter	Estimate	Standard Error
μ	−1.1503	0.0269
σ	0.6195	0.0219
k	−0.2142	0.0262
$\log L$	−1.2197	

similar in magnitude to the Hill estimate given in Figure 18.4. Performing a Wald test of the null hypothesis that the extreme value distribution is the Gumbel distribution $(k = 0)$ yields a t statistic of

$$t = \frac{-0.2142 - 0.0}{0.0262} = -8.18.$$

The value of this statistic is highly significant, resulting in a strong rejection of the null hypothesis in favor of the Fréchet extreme value distribution.

18.3.3 Implications for Univariate VaR Calculations
Extreme value theory is now used to compute the VaR of a portfolio with probability $p = 0.01$. Assuming a long position is taken, it is the left tail of the distribution that is appropriate, resulting in a VaR of

$$\text{VaR} = \begin{cases} \mu - \dfrac{\sigma}{k}\left(1 - \left(-n\log\left(1-p\right)\right)^{k}\right), & k \neq 0 \\ \mu + \sigma \log\left(-n\log\left(1-p\right)\right), & k = 0, \end{cases} \tag{18.12}$$

where n is the average number of days in the subsamples used to estimate the parameters by maximum likelihood methods.

Upon replacing the unknown parameters in equation (18.12) by their maximum likelihood estimates in Table 18.4 and noting that the maximum likelihood estimates are based on 1-month subsamples (with $n \approx 21$), the VaR for the 1% quantile is

$$\text{VaR} = \widehat{\mu} - \frac{\widehat{\sigma}}{\widehat{k}}\left(1 - \left(-n\log(1-p)\right)^{\widehat{k}}\right)$$

$$= -1.1503 - \frac{0.6195}{-0.2142}\left(1 - \left(-21 \times \log\left(1 - 0.01\right)\right)^{-0.2142}\right)$$

$$= -2.2939.$$

The pertinent lower percentage return corresponding to the 1% tail is −2.2939%, or −0.022939. For a long position of a portfolio valued at $1,000,000$, the 1-day VaR with 1% risk is

$$1000000 \times (-0.022936) = -22939,$$

Thus, the 1-day VaR(1) $= \$22,939$, which corresponds to a fall in the value of the $\$1,000,000$ portfolio of $\$22,939$ with 1% probability.

18.4 MODELING DEPENDENCE USING COPULAS

The focus of extreme value theory is on modeling the tails of univariate distributions so as to capture nonnormal extreme movements in asset returns. Now the analysis is extended to modeling joint events using multivariate distributions of asset returns. Modeling joint events is especially important in asset management, as the calculation of the VaR of a portfolio with multiple positions requires computing how each of the assets making up the portfolio interact with each other. During periods of financial stress, this requires modeling the probability that the returns on multiple assets simultaneously occur in the tails. The conditional probability that one financial return occurs in the tail of the distribution, given that another financial return is also in the tail, is known as the tail dependence of a multivariate distribution.

As a general rule, constructing models of multivariate asset returns is more complicated than specifying univariate models due to mathematical complexities arising from higher dimensions and the need to specify the dependence structure linking asset returns. When the focus is on extreme events and their potential interaction, it is particularly helpful to continue to utilize the form of the univariate distributions of the component variables where tail behavior is clearly evident. A convenient analytic approach that enables this to be accomplished is the use of copulas.

The copula method relies on a fundamental decomposition that writes a multivariate distribution in terms of a function of its individual marginal distributions. The linkage function that achieves this decomposition is known as the copula. In the analysis of a portfolio of asset returns, this decomposition means that the joint probability distribution is written explicitly in terms of the univariate distributions of each asset return separately with a copula linkage function that characterizes interactions between the marginals and thereby enables the univariate distributions to interact with each other to allow asset returns to be dependent. When it is expressed in this form, the joint distribution is sometimes known as a copula distribution. The analysis that follows focuses on bivariate models for simplicity. But all the key ideas and methods extend to the multivariate case. For a general review of copulas and applications in economics and finance, see Trivedi and Zimmer (2005), Patton (2012), and Fan and Patton (2014).

To motivate the use of copulas in modeling the dependence between asset returns, Figure 18.5 provides a scatter plot of the daily percentage log-returns on the S&P 100 and the S&P 600 from 17 August 1995 to 20 May 2011. The S&P 100 index contains the largest US firms, and the S&P 600 index covers the small-cap range of stocks. Inspection of the scatter plot suggests the two returns are strongly positively related, which is confirmed by the correlation coefficient that equals 0.8368. The scatter plot also shows strong dependence between the two returns in the tails of the distribution, where large negative (positive) returns in one index are matched by large negative (positive) returns in the other index.

Let the asset returns of the S&P 100 and the S&P 600 be represented, respectively, by r_1 and r_2, with joint probability distribution function $F(r_1, r_2)$, and marginal probability distribution functions $F_1(r_1)$ and $F_2(r_2)$. Two examples of joint distribution functions are the multivariate normal and multivariate t distributions discussed in Chapter 14. A copula representation of a joint probability distribution function is based on the mathematical result that any joint distribution such as $F(r_1, r_2)$ can be expressed in terms of its marginal distributions $F_1(r_1)$ and $F_2(r_2)$ and a copula function C as

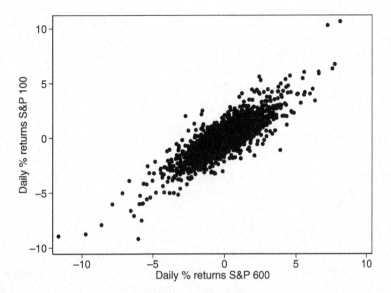

FIGURE 18.5 Scatter plot of the daily percentage log returns of the S&P 100 and the S&P 600 indices for the period from 17 August 1995 to 20 May 2011.

$$F(r_1, r_2) = C(F_1(r_1), F_2(r_2)). \tag{18.13}$$

This result is known as Sklar's theorem and is named after the American mathematician Abe Sklar who discovered it. A corresponding result applies to the joint probability density function and the marginal density functions when these exist.

In practical applications, it is particularly useful to characterize the copula $C(\cdot, \cdot)$ using a linkage function that depends explicitly on a parameter that measures the extent of the interaction or dependence between the component distributions. In such cases, the joint distribution is written as

$$F(r_1, r_2) = C(F_1(r_1), F_2(r_2); \delta), \tag{18.14}$$

where $C(\cdot, \cdot; \delta)$ represents a parametric copula function that determines the strength of the dependency between the two asset returns, which is controlled by the unknown parameter δ. A positive (negative) value of δ shows positive (negative) dependence. The importance of this specification is that it shows that $F(r_1, r_2)$ can be conveniently decomposed into two parts.

(i) **The marginal components** that capture the univariate behaviors of the individual asset returns given by $F_1(r_1)$ and $F_2(r_2)$.
(ii) **The dependence component** that captures the jointly interactive behavior of the asset returns embodied in the copula function $C(\cdot, \cdot; \delta)$.

This analytic separation of the marginal and dependence components of the joint distribution makes joint modeling much easier. Estimation can be broken down into two steps: In the first stage, univariate models for each asset return are specified and estimated separately; and in the second stage, the univariate models are combined using a particular copula specification for $C(\cdot; \delta)$, with δ estimated by maximum likelihood methods.

This separation of the joint distribution into univariate and multivariate components is very similar to the modeling strategy of the CCC and DCC multivariate GARCH models discussed in Chapter 14 and explored later in Section 18.7.

An alternative way of presenting the copula specification of the joint probability distribution function in equation (18.14) is to define the marginal probability distribution functions as

$$u_1 = F_1(r_1) = \int_{-\infty}^{r_1} f_1(s)ds, \quad u_2 = F_2(r_2) = \int_{-\infty}^{r_2} f_2(s)ds, \tag{18.15}$$

where u_i represents the probability that returns are less than r_i. By construction, u_i is defined over the unit interval $[0, 1]$. Substituting these expressions into the copula in equation (18.14) gives

$$F(r_1, r_2) = C(u_1, u_2; \delta). \tag{18.16}$$

This expression shows that the bivariate copula function $C(u_1, u_2; \delta)$ can be viewed as a mapping from the unit square $[0, 1]^2$, which captures all possible combinations of u_1 and u_2, to the unit interval $[0, 1]$ and which represents the probability range of the joint probability distribution function $F(r_1, r_2)$.

In view of the probability integral transforms in equation (18.15) applied to each component, the random vector $(u_1, u_2) = (F_1(r_1), F_2(r_2))$ has uniformly distributed marginals. The copula C of u_1, u_2; is therefore defined as the joint cumulative distribution function of (u_1, u_2). In consequence, the copula function contains all of the information concerning the dependence structure between the components (r_1, r_2), whereas the marginal cumulative distribution functions $F_i(r_i)$ contain all information on the marginal distributions.

18.5 PROPERTIES OF COPULAS

There exist many families of alternative types of copulas. A primary distinguishing feature of the copulas used in financial applications is the dependence structure of the tails of the joint distribution of asset returns. Five commonly used copula specifications are discussed in the following sections. Their properties are highlighted by presenting in Figure 18.6 scatter plots of 10000 pairs of simulated asset returns, using the different copulas summarized in Table 18.5. The steps for simulating each copula specification are given in Appendix E.

Gaussian Copula
The Gaussian copula is perhaps the most famous copula, and it has been widely used in empirical finance. This copula is expressed in terms of Gaussian/normal distribution functions as

$$C(u_1, u_2; \delta) = F_{12}(F^{-1}(u_1), F^{-1}(u_2); \delta), \quad -1 < \delta < 1, \tag{18.17}$$

where $F_{12}(r_1, r_2; \delta)$ is the cumulative distribution of a bivariate normal variable given by

$$F_{12}(r_1, r_2; \delta) = \int_{-\infty}^{r_1} \int_{-\infty}^{r_2} \frac{1}{2\pi\sqrt{1 - \delta^2}} \exp\left[-\frac{w_1^2 - 2\delta w_1 w_2 + w_2^2}{2(1 - \delta^2)}\right] dw_1 dw_2, \tag{18.18}$$

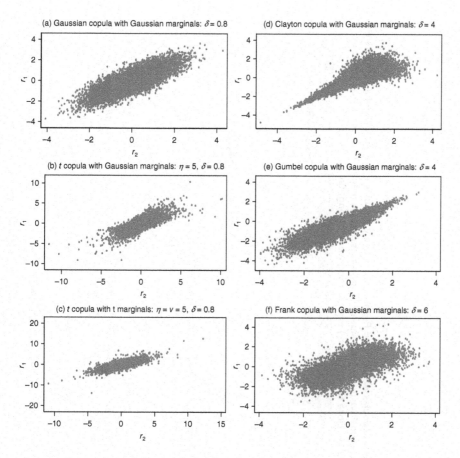

FIGURE 18.6 Scatter plots of simulated data from bivariate Gaussian, t; Clayton, Gumbel, and Frank copulas, all with Gaussian marginals; and from t copula with t marginals. The sample size is 10000.

which has zero means, unit variances, and dependence parameter δ. The function $u_i = F(r_i)$ is the univariate cumulative distribution of a standard normal distribution, which is a probability integral transform that maps the return r_i to the uniform random variable u_i.

The inverse of this mapping from u_i to r_i is given by the inverse cumulative distribution $F^{-1}(u_i)$. The inverse cumulative distribution function is commonly known as the quantile function. For the Gaussian copula the dependence parameter δ is equivalent to the correlation parameter, which lies in the range $-1 < \delta < 1$, with positive (negative) values representing positive (negative) dependence between returns. For the special case of independent returns the correlation parameter is $\delta = 0$, with the Gaussian copula reducing to what is known as the product copula $C(u_1, u_2) = u_1 u_2$. A common way of expressing the Gaussian copula in equation (18.17) is

$$C(u_1, u_2; \delta) = \Phi_{12}(\Phi^{-1}(u_1), \Phi^{-1}(u_2); \delta),$$

where the notation Φ is used to denote the cumulative distribution function of the standard normal distribution.

TABLE 18.5 Summary of the properties of alternative bivariate copulas where F and F_{12} are, respectively, the univariate and bivariate cumulative distribution functions. The dependence parameter is δ, where a positive (negative) value of δ represents positive (negative) dependence. The lower and upper tail measures are τ_L and τ_U, respectively, with values close to zero (unity) representing weak (strong) tail behavior.

Type	Copula Specification, $C(u_1, u_2; \delta)$	Dependence	Tail Properties Left	Tail Properties Right
Gaussian	$F_{12}(F^{-1}(u_1), F^{-1}(u_2); \delta)$	$-1 < \delta < 1$	Weak ($\tau_L = 0$)	Weak ($\tau_U = 0$)
t	$F_{12}(F^{-1}(u_1, \nu_1), F^{-1}(u_2, \nu_2); \delta, \eta)$	$-1 < \delta < 1$	Strong ($\tau_L = 2F(x; 1+\eta)$) with $x = -(1+\eta)^{1/2}(1-\delta)^{1/2}(1+\delta)^{-1/2}$	Strong ($\tau_U = 2F(x; 1+\eta)$)
Clayton	$(u_1^{-\delta} + u_2^{-\delta} - 1)^{-1/\delta}$	$0 < \delta < \infty$	Strong ($\tau_L = 2^{-1/\delta}$)	Weak ($\tau_U = 0$)
Gumbel	$\exp\left(-\left((-\log u_1)^\delta + (-\log u_2)^\delta\right)^{1/\delta}\right)$	$1 \le \delta < \infty$	Weak ($\tau_L = 0$)	Strong ($\tau_U = 2 - 2^{1/\delta}$)
Frank	$-\dfrac{1}{\delta}\log\left(1 + \dfrac{(e^{-\delta u_1} - 1)(e^{-\delta u_2} - 1)}{e^{-\delta} - 1}\right)$	$-\infty < \delta < \infty$	Weak ($\tau_L = 0$)	Weak ($\tau_U = 0$)

Panel (a) of Figure 18.6 provides a scatter plot of the simulated returns from the Gaussian copula with $\delta = 0.8$ and $N(0, 1)$ marginals for u_1 and u_2. The scatter has an elliptical shape with a positive slope as $\delta > 0$. Inspection of the tails of the scatter plot shows that the Gaussian copula generates moderate tail behavior. The marginals of the copula in this case are specified to be normal distributions, so $u_i = F(r_i)$. The Gaussian copula in equation (18.17) therefore reduces to the bivariate normal distribution function as

$$
\begin{aligned}
C(u_1, u_2; \delta) &= F_{12}(F^{-1}(u_1), F^{-1}(u_2); \delta) \\
&= F_{12}(F^{-1}(F(r_1)), F^{-1}(F(r_2)); \delta) \\
&= F_{12}(r_1, r_2; \delta),
\end{aligned}
$$

where the last step is based on the property $F^{-1}(F(r_i)) = r_i$. This result would not follow, however, if the marginals were specified to be nonnormal distributions. In fact, the marginals do not even have to be of the same type. One marginal could be a t distribution and the other could be a gamma distribution.

t Copula

A popular alternative to the Gaussian copula is the t copula in view of the ability of the t distribution to capture the heavy tailed distributions that are commonly observed in asset returns. The t copula is obtained by replacing the normal cumulative distribution functions in equation (18.17) by the corresponding t distribution functions so that

$$
C(u_1, u_2; \delta, v_1, v_2, \eta) = F_{12}(F^{-1}(u_1; v_1), F^{-1}(u_2; v_2); \delta, \eta), \tag{18.19}
$$

where $F_{12}(r_1, r_2; \delta, \eta)$ is the cumulative distribution function of a bivariate t distribution given by

$$
F_{12}(r_1, r_2; \delta, \eta) = \int_{-\infty}^{r_1} \int_{-\infty}^{r_2} \frac{1}{2\pi\sqrt{1-\delta^2}} \left(1 + \frac{w_1^2 - 2\delta w_1 w_2 + w_2^2}{\eta(1-\delta^2)} \right)^{-\frac{\eta+2}{2}} dw_1 dw_2,
$$

in which $\eta > 1$ represents the degrees of freedom parameter that controls the thickness of the tails of the joint distribution. Dependence is controlled by the parameter δ, which allows for positive and negative dependence, and independence if $\delta = 0$. The marginal function $F^{-1}(u_i; v_i)$, $i = 1, 2$ represents the quantile function of a univariate t random variable with degrees of freedom $v_i > 1$. For the special case where $\eta \to \infty$ the t copula in equation (18.19) approaches the Gaussian copula in equation (18.17).

Scatter plots of simulated returns from the t copula, with dependence parameter $\delta = 0.8$ and degrees of freedom parameter $\eta = 5$, are given in panel (b) of Figure 18.6 for normal marginals and in panel (c) of Figure 18.6 for t marginals with $v_1 = v_2 = 5$ degrees of freedom. In this case, since the marginals have the same degrees of freedom parameter as the t copula, simulating this copula is equivalent to simulating the returns from a bivariate t distribution. Comparison of the Gaussian copula in panel (a) of Figure 18.6 and the t in panel (b) of Figure 18.6 shows that the latter exhibits greater tail behavior than the former. By specifying t marginals for u_1 and u_2 as well, panel (c) of Figure 18.6 reveals even greater dependence in the tails of the joint distribution. Given the strong tail behavior observed in Figure 18.5 for the S&P 100 and the S&P 600 indices, a t copula, with or without normal marginals, is potentially a far more appropriate specification than the Gaussian copula for modeling the joint distribution of the two indices.

Clayton Copula

The Clayton copula is another copula that has proved useful in empirical finance. Unlike the t distribution, which can generate strong tail behavior in both the left and right tails, the Clayton copula only allows for lower tail dependence. For this reason, the Clayton copula is especially important in modeling the joint behavior of asset returns during periods of financial crisis when multiple assets jointly experience large negative returns. The Clayton copula has the following form

$$C(u_1, u_2; \delta) = (u_1^{-\delta} + u_2^{-\delta} - 1)^{-1/\delta}, \qquad 0 < \delta < \infty, \tag{18.20}$$

where δ controls the degree of dependence between the two asset returns. As δ is restricted to be positive it can only generate positive dependence. Independence occurs as $\delta \to 0$, in which case $C(u_1, u_2; \delta) \to u_1 u_2$, the product copula.

Panel (d) of Figure 18.6 provides a scatter plot of the simulated returns from the Clayton copula with normal marginals for u_1 and u_2 and dependence parameter $\delta = 4$. The positive dependence of the simulated asset returns is highlighted by the positively sloped scatter. The asymmetric tail behavior of the Clayton copula is evident in the tight scatter of simulated negative returns in comparison with the wide scatter in the right tail.

Gumbel Copula

The Gumbel copula effectively represents the mirror of the Clayton copula, as it only allows for positive dependence in the tails. This would suggest that the Gumbel copula is potentially relevant in modeling asset returns during bull markets when assets are characterized by large positive returns. The Gumbel copula is defined as

$$C(u_1, u_2; \delta) = \exp\left(-\left((-\log u_1)^\delta + (-\log u_2)^\delta\right)^{1/\delta}\right), \qquad 1 \le \delta < \infty, \tag{18.21}$$

where δ is the dependence parameter, with $\delta = 1$ representing independence as the Gumbel copula reduces to the product copula in this case.

The properties of the Gumbel copula are illustrated in panel (e) of Figure 18.6, which provides a scatter plot of the simulated returns from the Gumbel copula, with $\delta = 4$ and normal marginals for u_1 and u_2. The positive dependence between the simulated returns is revealed by the positively sloped scatter, while the strong positive tail behavior of the Gumbel copula is highlighted by the tight scatter that exists for the positive simulated returns and much wider scatter that appears for the negative returns.

Frank Copula

The final copula considered here is the Frank copula, which is given by

$$C(u_1, u_2; \delta) = -\frac{1}{\delta} \log\left(1 + \frac{\left(e^{-\delta u_1} - 1\right)\left(e^{-\delta u_2} - 1\right)}{e^{-\delta} - 1}\right), \qquad -\infty < \delta < \infty, \tag{18.22}$$

where δ controls the degree of dependence. Setting $\delta = 0$ corresponds to independence, whereas $\delta > 0$ ($\delta < 0$) corresponds to positive (negative) dependence.

Simulated returns from the Frank copula are given in panel (f) of Figure 18.6, with dependence parameter $\delta = 6$ and normal marginals. The positively sloped scatter highlights the positive association of the simulated returns. This copula generates symmetric tails, as do the Gaussian and t copulas, but a comparison of the scatter plots demonstrates that the Frank copula tails are even weaker than the tails of the Gaussian copula. This property suggests that the Frank copula is better suited to modeling the main body of the distribution of asset returns rather than the tails of the distribution.

The properties of the copulas presented by the scatter plots of simulated asset returns in Figure 18.6 demonstrate the tail properties of the various copulas. A more formal expression of tail behavior is obtained by determining the probability that the return on an asset is in the tails of the distribution given that the return on another asset is in the tails. In the case of the lower tail of the distribution, since large negative returns in r_i correspond to small values of u_i, the following conditional probability is suggested

$$\Pr[u_1 \leq q | u_2 \leq q] = \frac{\Pr[u_1 \leq q, u_1 \leq q]}{\Pr[u_2 \leq q]}, \tag{18.23}$$

in which q represents a value close to zero for the left tail, and the right side of the equation follows from the definition of a conditional probability. Since by definition $u_i = F(r_i)$, this expression is rewritten as

$$\begin{aligned}
\Pr[u_1 \leq q | u_2 \leq q] &= \frac{\Pr[F_1(r_1) \leq q, F_2(r_2) \leq q]}{\Pr[F_2(r_2) \leq q]} \\
&= \frac{\Pr\left[r_1 \leq F_1^{-1}(q), r_2 \leq F_2^{-1}(q)\right]}{\Pr\left[r_2 \leq F_2^{-1}(q)\right]} \\
&= \frac{F_{12}(F_1^{-1}(q), F_2^{-1}(q))}{F_2\left(F_2^{-1}(q)\right)} \\
&= \frac{C(q, q; \delta)}{q},
\end{aligned}$$

where the last step in the numerator is based on the definition of a copula. Evaluating this expression for small values of q and taking the limit as $q \to 0$ gives the following measure of lower tail dependence,

$$\tau_L = \lim_{q \to 0} \frac{C(q, q; \delta)}{q}. \tag{18.24}$$

By definition $0 \leq \tau_L \leq 1$, with small (large) values of τ_L representing weak (strong) lower tail dependence. The lower tail measures for the various copulas are summarized in Table 18.5. The weak lower tail dependence of the Gaussian, Gumbel, and Frank copulas identified by the scatter plots in Figure 18.6 is confirmed by a lower tail dependence parameter of $\tau_L = 0$ for these copulas. For the t and Clayton copulas, τ_L approaches unity for increasing values of the dependence parameter δ.

Similarly, a measure of dependence in the upper tail is obtained by defining the conditional probability when the u_i are close to unity as this corresponds to large positive returns. Explicitly, in place of equation (18.23)

$$\Pr[u_1 > q | u_2 > q] = \frac{\Pr[u_1 > q, u_1 > q]}{\Pr[u_2 > q]}. \tag{18.25}$$

Using the definition of a copula and evaluating this expression for values of q approaching 1.0 gives the following measure of upper tail dependence in the limit

$$\tau_U = \lim_{q \to 1} \frac{1 - 2q + C(q, q; \delta)}{1 - q}. \tag{18.26}$$

By definition $0 \le \tau_U \le 1$, with small (large) values of τ_U representing weak (strong) upper tail dependence. The upper tail measures for the various copulas are given in Table 18.5. The measure is zero for the Gaussian, Clayton, and Frank copulas and approaches unity for the t and Gumbel copulas for increasing values of the dependence parameter δ.

18.6 ESTIMATING COPULA MODELS

Let r_{1t} and r_{2t} be daily log returns at time t, which are assumed to be

$$r_{1t} = \mu_1 + \sigma_1 z_{1t}$$
$$r_{2t} = \mu_2 + \sigma_2 z_{2t} \tag{18.27}$$
$$F(r_{1t}, r_{2t}) = C(F_1(r_{1t}), F_2(r_{2t}); \delta),$$

where μ_i and σ_i are, respectively, the mean and standard deviation of r_{it}; and the joint distribution function of r_{1t} and r_{2t} is specified via the copula $C(\cdot)$ with dependence parameter δ, from equation (18.14). The unknown parameters are $\theta = \{\mu_1, \sigma_1, \mu_2, \sigma_2, \delta\}$ plus any additional parameters in the copula specification and its marginals, such as the degrees of freedom parameters in the case of the t distribution and marginals.

To estimate θ by maximum likelihood it is necessary to derive the joint density function $f(r_{1t}, r_{2t}; \theta)$. Applying the chain rule of differentiation (see Appendix A) to the joint distribution function $F(r_{1t}, r_{2t})$ gives

$$\begin{aligned}
f(r_{1t}, r_{2t}; \theta) &= \frac{\partial^2}{\partial r_{1t} \partial r_{2t}} F(r_{1t}, r_{2t}) \\
&= \frac{\partial^2}{\partial r_{1t} \partial r_{2t}} C(F_1(r_{1t}), F_2(r_{2t}); \delta) \\
&= \frac{\partial^2 C(F_1, F_2; \delta)}{\partial F_1 \partial F_2} \frac{\partial F_1(r_{1t})}{\partial r_{1t}} \frac{\partial F_2(r_{2t})}{\partial r_{2t}} \\
&= C_{12}(F_1(r_{1t}), F_2(r_{2t}); \delta) f_1(r_{1t}; \mu_1, \sigma_1) f_2(r_{2t}; \mu_2, \sigma_2), \tag{18.28}
\end{aligned}$$

where

$$C_{12}(F_1(r_{1t}), F_2(r_{2t}); \delta) = \frac{\partial^2 C(F_1, F_2; \delta)}{\partial F_1 \partial F_2}$$
$$f_i(r_{it}; \mu_i, \sigma_i) = \frac{\partial F_i(r_{it})}{\partial r_{it}}, \quad i = 1, 2.$$

For $t = 1, 2, \cdots, T$ observations the log likelihood function is

$$\log L = \frac{1}{T} \sum_{t=1}^{T} \log f(r_{1t}, r_{2t}; \theta)$$

$$= \log L_c(\theta) + \log L_1(\mu_1, \sigma_1) + \log L_2(\mu_2, \sigma_2), \qquad (18.29)$$

where

$$\log L_c(\theta) = \frac{1}{T} \sum_{t=1}^{T} \log C_{12}(F_1(r_{1t}; \mu_1, \sigma_1), F_2(r_{2t}; \mu_2, \sigma_2); \delta)$$

$$\log L_i(\mu_i, \sigma_i) = \frac{1}{T} \sum_{t=1}^{T} \log f_i(r_{it}; \mu_i, \sigma_i), \quad i = 1, 2.$$

To maximize the log likelihood function with respect to the full set of unknown parameters, θ, an iterative algorithm is generally needed.

Given the recursive structure of the log likelihood function in equation (18.29), it is possible to estimate the parameters in two stages. Let $\theta = \{\theta_1, \theta_2\}$, where $\theta_1 = \{\mu_1, \sigma_1, \mu_2, \sigma_2\}$ are the parameters of the marginals, and $\theta_2 = \{\delta\}$ is the dependence parameter of the copula. In the first stage, θ_1 is estimated by maximizing the log likelihoods $\log L_1(\mu_1, \sigma_1)$ and $\log L_2(\mu_2, \sigma_2)$ separately with respect to their own parameters. Given $\widehat{\theta}_1 = \{\widehat{\mu}_1, \widehat{\sigma}_1^2, \widehat{\mu}_2, \widehat{\sigma}_2^2\}$, in the second stage the copula parameter θ_2 is chosen to maximize $\log L_c(\theta_2)$, with θ_1 replaced by $\widehat{\theta}_1$. The two-stage parameter estimates $\widehat{\theta}_1$ and $\widehat{\theta}_2$ are both consistent. But only the standard errors of $\widehat{\theta}_1$ are correct as usually calculated. The standard errors of $\widehat{\theta}_2$ are conditional on the first stage and therefore fail to take into account that $\widehat{\theta}_1$ is estimated and random. One way to circumvent this problem is to use the two-step estimates as starting values in a further joint optimization of the likelihood with respect to $\theta = \{\theta_1, \theta_2\}$ based on the full log likelihood function.

Copula models for the percentage daily log returns on the S&P 100, r_{1t}, and the S&P 600, r_{2t}, presented in Figure 18.5 for the period 17 August 1995 to 30 May 2011, are now specified and estimated. Four models are considered, consisting of a Gaussian copula with normal marginals (Model 1), a Gaussian copula with t marginals (Model 2), a t copula with t marginals (Model 3), and a Clayton copula with t marginals (Model 4). The log likelihood functions at time t for each copula model are as follows.

Model 1: Gaussian copula with normal marginals

$$\log L_t = -\log(2\pi) - \frac{1}{2} \log \left(\sigma_1^2 \sigma_2^2 \left(1 - \delta^2 \right) \right) - \frac{z_{1t}^2 + z_{2t}^2 - 2\delta z_{1t} z_{2t}}{2 \left(1 - \delta^2 \right)},$$

with parameters $\theta = \{\mu_1, \sigma_1, \mu_2, \sigma_2, \delta\}$, and where $z_{it} = (r_{it} - \mu_i)/\sigma_i$.

Model 2: Gaussian copula with t marginals

$$\log L_t = -\frac{1}{2} \log \left(1 - \delta^2 \right) - \frac{q_{1t}^2 + q_{2t}^2 - 2\delta q_{1t} q_{2t}}{2 \left(1 - \delta^2 \right)} + \frac{1}{2} (q_{1t}^2 + q_{2t}^2)$$

$$+ \log \left(\frac{1}{\sigma_1} f(z_{1t}; v) \right) + \log \left(\frac{1}{\sigma_2} f(z_{2t}; v) \right),$$

with parameters $\theta = \{\mu_1, \sigma_1, \mu_2, \sigma_2, \delta, \nu\}$, and where for $i = 1, 2$, $q_{it} = \Phi^{-1}(F(z_{it}; \nu))$, $z_{it} = (r_{it} - \mu_i)/\sigma_i$, $f(z_{it}; \nu)$, and $F(z_{it}; \nu)$ are the probability density function and the cumulative distribution function of the t distribution with ν degrees of freedom,[3] respectively, and $\Phi^{-1}(\cdot)$ is the quantile function of the standard normal distribution.

Model 3: t copula with t marginals

$$\log L_t = -\log(2\pi) - \frac{1}{2}\log(1 - \delta^2) - \frac{\eta + 2}{2}\log\left(1 + \frac{q_{1t}^2 + q_{2t}^2 - 2\delta q_{1t}q_{2t}}{\eta(1 - \delta^2)}\right)$$

$$- \log f(q_{1t}; \eta) - \log f(q_{2t}; \eta) + \log\left(\frac{1}{\sigma_1}f(z_{1t}; \nu)\right) + \log\left(\frac{1}{\sigma_2}f(z_{2t}; \nu)\right),$$

with parameters $\theta = \{\mu_1, \sigma_1, \mu_2, \sigma_2, \delta, \eta, \nu\}$, and where for $i = 1, 2$, $q_{it} = F^{-1}(F(z_{it}; \nu); \eta)$, $z_{it} = (r_{it} - \mu_i)/\sigma_i$.[4]

Model 4: Clayton copula with t marginals

$$\log L_t = \log(1 + \delta) - (1 + \delta)(\log u_{1t} + \log u_{2t}) - (2 + 1/\delta)\log(u_{1t}^{-\delta} + u_{2t}^{-\delta} - 1)$$

$$+ \log\left(\frac{1}{\sigma_1}f(z_{1t}; \nu)\right) + \log\left(\frac{1}{\sigma_2}f(z_{2t}; \nu)\right),$$

with parameters $\theta = \{\mu_1, \sigma_1, \mu_2, \sigma_2, \delta, \nu\}$, and where $z_{it} = (r_{it} - \mu_i)/\sigma_i$ and $u_{it} = F(z_{it}, \nu)$.

The maximum likelihood parameter estimates of the four copula models are presented in Table 18.6. A number of conclusions can be drawn from the results presented there. First, there is strong evidence of positive dependence between r_{1t} and r_{2t}, as the estimates of δ are positive and significant for all models. Second, when t marginals are used the degrees of freedom parameter estimates range between 2.6 (Model 4) and 4.3 (Model 2), thereby providing evidence that asset returns exhibit heavy tails. Third, Models 3 and 4 provide evidence of tail dependence among r_{1t} and r_{2t}, whereas Models 1 and 2 assume no tail dependence, as they are based on a Gaussian copula. For Model 3, the lower and upper tail dependence estimates are

$$\widehat{\tau}_L = \widehat{\tau}_U = 2F\left(-(\widehat{\eta} + 1)^{1/2}(1 - \widehat{\delta})^{1/2}(1 + \widehat{\delta})^{-1/2}; 1 + \widehat{\eta}\right) = 0.4835.$$

For Model 4, the lower tail estimate is

$$\widehat{\tau}_L = 2^{-1/\widehat{\delta}} = 0.7280,$$

whereas the upper tail dependence estimate is $\widehat{\tau}_U = 0$, which immediately follows from the properties of the Clayton copula. Evidence of tail behavior is supported by the value of the log likelihood for the t copula, which is larger in magnitude than the two Gaussian copula log likelihood values. Moreover, the log likelihood of the t copula dominates the

---

[3] Hence, the variance of z_{it} is $\nu/(\nu - 2)$, and the variance of r_{it} is $\sigma_i^2 \nu/(\nu - 2)$.

[4] When $\eta \neq \nu$, $F^{-1}(F(z_{it}; \nu); \eta) \neq z_{it}$, as $F^{-1}(\cdot; \eta)$ is the quantile function of the t distribution with η degrees of freedom, while $F(\cdot; \nu_i)$ is the cumulative distribution function of the t distribution with ν degrees of freedom.

TABLE 18.6 Maximum likelihood estimates of the Gaussian copula with normal marginals (Model 1) and t marginals (Model 2), the t copula with t marginals (Model 3), and the Clayton copula with t marginals (Model 4). The data are daily percentage returns on the S&P 100 and S&P 600 indices for the period 17 August 1995 to 30 May 2011.

Parameter	Model 1	Model 2	Model 3	Model 4
μ_1	0.0202	0.0404	0.0468	0.1648
	(0.0208)	(0.0163)	(0.0164)	(0.0153)
σ_1	1.6809	0.8181	0.7411	0.6586
	(0.0183)	(0.0256)	(0.0253)	(0.0213)
μ_2	0.0335	0.0570	0.0670	0.1945
	(0.0228)	(0.0184)	(0.0185)	(0.0171)
σ_2	2.0343	1.0665	0.9764	0.8579
	(0.0263)	(0.0324)	(0.0325)	(0.0272)
δ	0.8368	0.8175	0.8151	2.1837
	(0.0032)	(0.0042)	(0.0064)	(0.0532)
ν	–	4.1756	3.6433	2.6498
		(0.2122)	(0.1900)	(0.1007)
η	–	–	4.5330	–
			(0.4373)	
$\log L$	−2.8504	−2.7194	−2.6895	−2.7889

Clayton log likelihood, which is a reflection of the restriction imposed by the Clayton copula of no upper tail dependence, a result that is rejected from inspection of the upper tail of the scatter plot of the returns in Figure 18.5.

18.7 MGARCH MODEL USING COPULAS

The multivariate GARCH (MGARCH) class of models discussed in Chapter 14 provides a flexible framework to estimate models that allow for both time-varying variances and covariances. An underlying theme in the development of MGARCH models is the ability to specify flexible models without resorting to a proliferation of parameters that can make estimation by maximum likelihood infeasible. The CCC model is a framework in which univariate GARCH models are estimated for each series and are then used to generate time-varying conditional variances and covariances, assuming that the correlations associated with the covariances are constant. This two-stage process is comparable to specifying and estimating a copula model to generate a multivariate GARCH model from a sequence of univariate GARCH models.

To highlight the features of a copula MGARCH model, consider the constant mean model in equation (18.27) but allow the conditional variances, h_{it}, to be time-varying. In the case of N assets, the marginal models are specified as

$$r_{it} = \mu_i + u_{it}, \qquad u_{it} \sim N(0, h_{it}), \qquad i = 1, 2, \cdots, N$$
$$u_{it} = \sqrt{h_{it}}\, z_{it} \tag{18.30}$$
$$h_{it} = \alpha_{i0} + \alpha_{i1} u_{it-1}^2 + \beta_{i1} h_{it-1}.$$

To allow for dependence among asset returns and hence the standardized variables z_{it}, a Gaussian copula with Gaussian marginals is specified with a constant symmetric dependence correlation matrix

$$\delta = \begin{pmatrix} 1 & \delta_{12} & \cdots & \delta_{1N} \\ \delta_{21} & 1 & \cdots & \delta_{2N} \\ \vdots & \vdots & \ddots & \vdots \\ \delta_{N1} & \delta_{N2} & \cdots & 1 \end{pmatrix}. \tag{18.31}$$

Estimation of the parameters of the copula MGARCH model proceeds in two stages. First, the univariate GARCH models in equation (18.30) are estimated separately for each asset using the maximum likelihood methods discussed in Chapter 13. The next stage is to standardize the time series using the parameter estimates obtained in the first stage, and estimate the correlation matrix of the standardized time series

$$z_{1t} = \frac{r_{1t} - \mu_1}{\sqrt{h_{1t}}}, \quad z_{2t} = \frac{r_{2t} - \mu_2}{\sqrt{h_{2t}}}, \cdots, z_{Nt} = \frac{r_{Nt} - \mu_N}{\sqrt{h_{Nt}}}, \tag{18.32}$$

with the unknown parameters replaced by their maximum likelihood estimates from the first stage.

As an empirical illustration the copula MGARCH model is estimated for $N = 4$ assets consisting of the percentage log returns on three technology stocks—IBM (r_{1t}), INTEL (r_{2t}), Microsoft (r_{3t})—and the market factor as given by the S&P 500 (r_{4t}). The returns are daily with the sample starting on 13 March 1986 and ending on 17 March 2017. The results from estimating the 4 GARCH models in equation (18.30) are given in Table 18.7.

For each of the $N = 4$ estimated GARCH models presented in Table 18.7, the standardized residuals in equation (18.32) are computed. The estimated correlation matrix in equation (18.31) is

$$\widehat{\delta} = \begin{pmatrix} 1.0000 & 0.3342 & 0.2514 & 0.5432 \\ 0.3342 & 1.0000 & 0.2589 & 0.4560 \\ 0.2514 & 0.2589 & 1.0000 & 0.3728 \\ 0.5432 & 0.4560 & 0.3728 & 1.0000 \end{pmatrix}. \tag{18.33}$$

The strongest observed dependence is between IBM and the S&P 500 with correlation $\widehat{\delta}_{14} = 0.5432$. Microsoft and IBM have the smallest level of dependence with correlation $\widehat{\delta}_{31} = 0.2514$.

For comparative purposes, an MGARCH CCC model as described in Chapter 14 is estimated. The resultant matrix of estimated constant correlation parameters, $\widehat{\rho}_{ij}$, obtained from the model is

TABLE 18.7 Maximum likelihood parameter estimates of the univariate GARCH models in equation (18.30), which represent the marginals for the copula MGARCH model. The sample period is 13 March 1986 to 17 March 2017.

Parameter	IBM (r_{1t})		INTEL (r_{2t})		Microsoft (r_{3t})		S&P 500 (r_{4t})	
	Est.	S.E.	Est.	S.E.	Est.	S.E.	Est.	S.E.
μ	0.0061	0.0100	−0.0394	0.0234	0.0053	0.0301	0.0562	0.0092
α_0	0.2329	0.0099	0.0095	0.0014	2.3778	0.1178	0.0171	0.0013
α_1	0.4801	0.0044	0.0549	0.0020	0.1040	0.0041	0.0918	0.0022
β_1	0.6249	0.0050	0.9628	0.0011	0.6734	0.0154	0.8952	0.0033

$$\widehat{\rho} = \begin{pmatrix} 1.0000 & 0.3342 & 0.2514 & 0.5432 \\ 0.3218 & 1.0000 & 0.2589 & 0.4560 \\ 0.2638 & 0.2993 & 1.0000 & 0.3728 \\ 0.5204 & 0.4802 & 0.4338 & 1.0000 \end{pmatrix}.$$

The estimated correlation matrix is almost identical to $\widehat{\delta}$ in equation (18.33), indicating the copula model does a good job of capturing the correlation between the assets.

18.8 EXERCISES

The data required for the exercises are available for download as EViews workfiles (*.wf1), Stata datafiles (*.dta), comma delimited text files (*.csv), and as Excel spreadsheets (*.xlsx).

1. **Statistical Properties of S&P 500 Equity Returns**

> spx.*

The data file contains daily equity prices on the S&P 500 from 1 January 1960 to 17 March 2017.

(a) Compute and plot the daily percentage log returns for the S&P 500, and interpret their time series properties.

(b) Compute descriptive statistics (mean, standard deviation, minimum, maximum), of the S&P 500 returns. Identify the dates of the minimum and the maximum, and determine how many standard deviations these values are from the mean return.

(c) Consider the following model of returns r_t, given by

$$r_t = \mu + \sigma z_t, \qquad z_t \sim St(0, 1, \nu),$$

where $St(0, 1, \nu)$ represents the standardized t distribution whose probability density function is

$$f(z_t; \nu) = \frac{\Gamma((\nu+1)/2)}{\Gamma(\nu/2)\sqrt{(\nu-2)\pi}} \left(1 + \frac{z_t^2}{\nu-2}\right)^{-(\nu+1)/2},$$

with zero mean, unit variance, and degrees of freedom parameter ν. Estimate the degrees of freedom parameter ν and interpret the value of this estimate in terms of the tail shape of the distribution and the number of finite moments of r_t.

2. **Empirical Distribution of Order Statistics**

> spxorderstats.*

The data file contains the monthly observations on the first and last order statistics from monthly subsamples of percentage daily returns on the S&P 500 from 4 January 1960 to 17 March 2017.

(a) Compute and interpret the descriptive statistics (mean, standard deviation, skewness, kurtosis) on the monthly series of the first order statistic. Plot the empirical distribution (histogram) of the first order statistic and interpret its shape.

(b) Repeat part (a) for the monthly series on the largest order statistic.

(c) Consider estimating k for the left tail of the distribution. Using just the negative order statistics, compute the Hill estimator in equation (18.8) of the index parameter k for $q = \{100, 250, 500\}$. Interpret the results.

(d) Consider estimating k for the right tail of the distribution. Using just the positive order statistics, compute the Hill estimator

$$\widehat{k}_q = \frac{1}{q} \sum_{i=1}^{q} \left(\log(r_{(i)}) - \log(r_{(q+1)}) \right),$$

of the parameter k for $q = \{100, 250, 500\}$. Interpret the results.

3. Simulating the Fréchet Distribution

This exercise demonstrates how to simulate data from a Fréchet distribution with cumulative distribution function given by

$$F(x) = e^{-x^{-\alpha}},$$

where α is the tail index.

(a) Draw 1000 uniform independent random numbers $u_1, u_2, \cdots, u_{1000}$.

(b) Choosing an index parameter $\alpha = 5$, generate draws from the Fréchet distribution using the expression (known as the inverse transform method)

$$x_i = \left(-\log u_i \right)^{-1/\alpha}.$$

Plot the simulated data and interpret its behavior.

(c) Repeat part (b) for $\alpha = \{2.5, 2.0, 1.5, 1.0, 0.5\}$.

(i) For each value of α, graph the empirical distribution and interpret its shape.

(ii) For each value of α identify the existence of the mean and the variance of x.

4. Maximum Likelihood Estimation of Extreme Value Distributions

> spxorderstats.*

The data file contains monthly observations on the first and last order statistics from monthly subsamples of percentage daily returns on the S&P 500 from 4 January 1960 to 17 March 2017.

(a) Consider the extreme value distribution of the first order statistic. Defining

$$z = \frac{r_{(1)} - \mu}{\sigma},$$

it follows that

$$f(r_{(1)}) = \begin{cases} \dfrac{1}{\sigma}(1+kz)^{1/k-1}\exp\left[-(1+kz)^{1/k}\right] & k \neq 0 \\[2ex] \dfrac{1}{\sigma}\exp\left[z-\exp(z)\right] & k = 0, \end{cases}$$

where $\theta = \{\mu, \sigma, k\}$ are unknown parameters. Construct the log likelihood function and compute the maximum likelihood estimates using the 1-month subsamples of the first (minimum) order statistic.

(b) Assuming a long position in a portfolio of $1,000,000, compute the 1-day VaR for $p = 5\%$ risk.

(c) Repeat part (b) for a 5-day horizon by using the result

$$\mathrm{VaR}(h) = h^{-k}\mathrm{VaR}(1),$$

where the horizon is set at $h = 5$.

(d) Repeat parts (b) and (c) but assume a short position in a portfolio of $1,000,000 based on

$$\mathrm{VaR} = \begin{cases} \mu + \dfrac{\sigma}{k}\left(1-(-n\log(1-p))^k\right) & k \neq 0 \\[2ex] \mu + \sigma\log(-n\log(1-p)) & k = 0. \end{cases}$$

(e) Define

$$z = \frac{r_{(T)} - \mu}{\sigma},$$

so that the extreme value distribution of the last order statistic is

$$f(r_{(T)}) = \begin{cases} \dfrac{1}{\sigma}(1+kz)^{1/k-1}\exp\left[-(1+kz)^{1/k}\right] & k \neq 0 \\[2ex] \dfrac{1}{\sigma}\exp\left[z-\exp(z)\right] & k = 0, \end{cases}$$

where $\theta = \{\mu, \sigma, k\}$ are unknown parameters. Construct the log likelihood function and compute the maximum likelihood estimates using the 1-month subsamples of the last (maximum) order statistic.

5. **Allowing for Time Dependence in Extreme Value Distributions**

---
spx.*

The data file contains the monthly observations on the first and last order statistics from monthly subsamples of percentage daily returns on the S&P 500 from 4 January 1960 to 17 March 2017.

(a) To allow for dependent returns in extreme value theory arising from time-varying volatility, estimate the following GARCH(1,1) model of asset returns

$$r_t = \mu + u_t$$
$$h_t = \alpha_0 + \alpha_1 u_{t-1}^2 + \beta_1 h_{t-1}$$
$$u_t \sim N(0, h_t).$$

(b) Using the results in part (a) construct the standardized residual

$$z_t = \frac{r_t - \mu}{h_t},$$

and estimate the shape parameter k using the Hill estimator and interpret the result.

6. **Estimating Copulas for NASDAQ and DJIA indices**

> sp100sp600djianasdaq.*

The data file contains daily equity log returns on the NASDAQ and the DJIA from 17 August 1995 to 20 May 2011, as well as the S&P 100 and the S&P 600.

(a) Let r_{1t} and r_{2t} be, respectively, the percentage log returns on the NASDAQ and the DJIA. Compute a scatter plot of the two series and discuss the dependence structure between the two asset returns.

(b) Consider a bivariate model for r_{1t} and r_{2t} given by the marginal models

$$r_{1t} = \mu_1 + \sigma_1 z_{1t}, \qquad\qquad z_{1t} \sim N(0, 1)$$
$$r_{2t} = \mu_2 + \sigma_2 z_{2t}, \qquad\qquad z_{2t} \sim N(0, 1),$$

in which the dependence structure between z_{1t} and z_{2t} is determined by the Gaussian copula with parameter δ. Estimate $\theta = \{\mu_1, \sigma_1, \mu_2, \sigma_2, \delta\}$ by maximum likelihood and interpret the estimate of δ.

(c) Repeat part (b), but replace the normal marginals by t marginals as follows

$$r_{1t} = \mu_1 + \sigma_1 z_{1t}, \qquad\qquad z_{1t} \sim St(v)$$
$$r_{2t} = \mu_2 + \sigma_2 z_{2t}, \qquad\qquad z_{2t} \sim St(v).$$

Estimate $\theta = \{\mu_1, \sigma_1, \mu_2, \sigma_2, \delta, v\}$ by maximum likelihood. Also estimate the lower and the upper tail dependence.

(d) Repeat part (c) where the Gaussian copula is replaced by the t copula with η degrees of freedom. Use maximum likelihood to estimate $\theta = \{\mu_1, \sigma_1, \mu_2, \sigma_2, \delta, v, \eta\}$. Estimate the lower and the upper tail dependence.

(e) Repeat part (d) where the t copula is replaced by the Clayton copula. Estimate $\theta = \{\mu_1, \sigma_1, \mu_2, \sigma_2, v, \delta\}$. Estimate the lower tail dependence and the upper tail dependence.

7. **An MGARCH Copula Model of Asset Returns**

> copula.*

The data file contains daily equity prices on the S&P 500 from 13 March 1986 to 17 March 2017, as well as four technology stocks, namely, Apple, IBM, Intel, and Microsoft.

(a) Consider the following $N = 4$ asset model consisting of the percentage log returns on three technology stocks, IBM (r_{1t}), INTEL (r_{2t}), Microsoft (r_{3t}), and the market factor as given by the S&P 500 (r_{4t})

$$r_{it} = \mu_i + u_{it}, \qquad u_{it} \sim N(0, h_{it}), \qquad i = 1, 2, 3, 4$$

$$u_{it} = \sqrt{h_{it}} z_{it}$$

$$h_{it} = \alpha_{i0} + \alpha_{i1} u_{it-1}^2 + \beta_{i1} h_{it-1}.$$

Compute the maximum likelihood estimates of the model for each asset over the sample period 13 March 1986 to 17 March 2017.

(b) Use the estimates in part (a) to compute the standardized residuals $z_{it}, i = 1, 2, 3, 4$ to estimate the dependence parameters of the Gaussian copula

$$\delta = \begin{pmatrix} 1 & \delta_{12} & \delta_{13} & \delta_{14} \\ \delta_{21} & 1 & \delta_{23} & \delta_{24} \\ \delta_{31} & \delta_{32} & 1 & \delta_{34} \\ \delta_{41} & \delta_{42} & \delta_{43} & 1 \end{pmatrix}.$$

(c) Compare the estimates of the dependence matrix δ in part (b) with the correlation matrix obtained by estimating a full MGARCH CCC model.

(d) Repeat parts (a) to (c) for an expanded $N = 5$ asset model that includes Apple (r_{5t}). Choose the returns equation for Apple as

$$r_{5t} = \mu_5 + \beta d_t + u_{5t}, \qquad u_{5t} \sim N(0, h_{5t})$$

$$u_{5t} = \sqrt{h_{5t}} z_{5t}$$

$$h_{5t} = \alpha_{50} + \alpha_{51} u_{5t-1}^2 + \beta_{51} h_{5t-1},$$

where d_t is a dummy variable to correct for the stock split on 9 June 2014.

CHAPTER 19

Concluding Remarks

The methods and the theories that this book explores belong to the rapidly growing edifice of financial econometrics. Exploration of its expanding structure of models, methods, and findings reveals an architecture that brings together ideas from financial theory, regulation, and the financial industry, with the practical characteristics of financial data and an econometric toolkit designed to address them. The treatment in this book has emphasized these linkages. But it only just opens the door. The arena beyond is vast, like the financial universe to which it relates. There is much more for the student and interested reader to discover, from the deeper underpinnings of mathematical finance and its probabilistic foundations to the exciting passage through which these ideas are translated into the empirical models that are used in financial econometrics.

Readers can be inspired by the short history and flourishing literature of this subject, which began with simple models to explain asset prices and their volatility, moved on to tackle complex phenomena such as the pricing of financial derivatives, and proceeded through a rich avenue of applications to study recent problems associated with financial crises and stock market crashes. As the financial universe grows, new challenges emerge for which models need to be created and econometric methodologies developed. Some of these challenges are posed by phenomena such as ultra-high frequency trading and the multidimensional nature of financial market microstructure; others arise from the requirements of high dimensional financial portfolio analysis, the nature of algorithmic trading, and its wider impact on financial markets and financial stability. The more that is learned about this rapidly evolving world of finance and its manifold links with economic activity, the more there is yet to discover.

In a subject that has over a short span of time given rise to its own professional society, a dedicated journal, and to Nobel Prize awards in Economics, there is evidently great scope for the young scholar. The skill of the financial econometrician draws on an accumulating body of knowledge in financial theory, an appreciation of the diverse nature of financial data, the capacity to develop econometric tools fashioned to address the express purpose at hand, and the practical ability to implement these tools.

This book has sought to provide a basic training in selected aspects of this skill set. Much has been covered but many gaps remain. The lessons learned may assist in a career in the financial industry, open up the prospect of further study, or lead to applied policy research in government agencies or commentary in financial journalism or consulting. Much can now be achieved with standard econometric software and the econometric methods covered in this book's introductory treatment. May these tools prove to be a useful companion to readers wherever their professional endeavors take them.

Mathematical Preliminaries

A.1 SUMMATION NOTATION

Consider a set of T observations on the variable y given by $\{y_1, y_2, \cdots, y_T\}$. Notation to sum all of these items is given by

$$\sum_{t=1}^{T} y_t = y_1 + y_2 + \cdots + y_T.$$

The limits on the summation sign determine where to start and end summing. For example

$$\sum_{t=3}^{T-1} y_t = y_3 + y_4 + \cdots + y_{T-1}.$$

Some or all of the limits (and subscripts on the variables) may be dropped, in which case the following expressions are equivalent

$$\sum_{t=1}^{T} y_t = \sum_{t} y_t = \sum y_t = \sum y.$$

Let two series be given by $\{y_1, y_2, \cdots, y_T\}$ and $\{x_1, x_2, \cdots, x_T\}$. Some basic rules of summation notation are the following.

1. Addition

$$\sum_{t=1}^{T} (y_t + x_t) = \sum_{t=1}^{T} y_t + \sum_{t=1}^{T} x_t.$$

2. Subtraction

$$\sum_{t=1}^{T} (y_t - x_t) = \sum_{t=1}^{T} y_t - \sum_{t=1}^{T} x_t.$$

3. Scalar product

$$\sum_{t=1}^{T} k y_t = k \sum_{t=1}^{T} y_t,$$

where k is a constant.

4. Scalar addition

$$\sum_{t=1}^{T} k = Tk,$$

where k is a constant.

Consider, for example, the problem of demonstrating that

$$\sum_{t=1}^{T} (y_t - \bar{y}) = 0,$$

where

$$\bar{y} = \frac{1}{T} \sum_{t=1}^{T} y_t$$

is the sample mean. Using the subtraction rule gives

$$\sum_{t=1}^{T} (y_t - \bar{y}) = \sum_{t=1}^{T} y_t - \sum_{t=1}^{T} \bar{y}.$$

From the scalar addition rule with $k = \bar{y}$, the second term is $\sum_{t=1}^{T} \bar{y} = T\bar{y}$, in which case

$$\sum_{t=1}^{T} (y_t - \bar{y}) = \sum_{t=1}^{T} y_t - T\bar{y}.$$

From the definition of the sample mean, $T\bar{y} = \sum_{t=1}^{T} y_t$, so that

$$\sum_{t=1}^{T} (y_t - \bar{y}) = \sum_{t=1}^{T} y_t - \sum_{t=1}^{T} y_t = 0.$$

Similarly, it can be shown that

$$\sum_{t=1}^{T} (y_t - \bar{y})^2 = \sum_{t=1}^{T} y_t^2 - T\bar{y}^2,$$

where $\bar{y}$ is the sample mean defined earlier.

Expand the quadratic expression inside the summation sign as

$$\sum_{t=1}^{T} (y_t - \bar{y})^2 = \sum_{t=1}^{T} (y_t^2 + \bar{y}^2 - 2y_t\bar{y}).$$

Use the summation and subtraction rules to generate

$$\sum_{t=1}^{T} (y_t - \bar{y})^2 = \sum_{t=1}^{T} y_t^2 + \sum_{t=1}^{T} \bar{y}^2 - 2\sum_{t=1}^{T} y_t\bar{y}.$$

From the scalar addition rule, with $k = \bar{y}^2$, the second term is $\sum_{t=1}^{T} \bar{y}^2 = T\bar{y}^2$, in which case

$$\sum_{t=1}^{T} (y_t - \bar{y})^2 = \sum_{t=1}^{T} y_t^2 + T\bar{y}^2 - 2\sum_{t=1}^{T} y_t\bar{y}.$$

From the scalar product rule, the third term is $2\sum_{t=1}^{T} y_t\bar{y} = 2\bar{y}\sum_{t=1}^{T} y_t$, in which case

$$\sum_{t=1}^{T} (y_t - \bar{y})^2 = \sum_{t=1}^{T} y_t^2 + T\bar{y}^2 - 2\bar{y}\sum_{t=1}^{T} y_t.$$

From the definition of the sample mean, $T\bar{y} = \sum_{t=1}^{T} y_t$, so the last term becomes $2\bar{y}\sum_{t=1}^{T} y_t = 2\bar{y} \times T\bar{y}$. Using this expression in the previous expression gives

$$\sum_{t=1}^{T} (y_t - \bar{y}) = \sum_{t=1}^{T} y_t^2 + T\bar{y}^2 - 2\bar{y} \times T\bar{y} = \sum_{t=1}^{T} y_t^2 + T\bar{y}^2 - 2T\bar{y}^2 = \sum_{t=1}^{T} y_t^2 - T\bar{y}^2.$$

As a final example, consider the function

$$f(y_t) = \theta \exp(-\theta y_t),$$

where θ is a constant. Find

$$\sum_{t=1}^{T} \log f(y_t).$$

Substituting in the expression for $f(y_t)$ gives

$$\sum_{t=1}^{T} \log f(y_t) = \sum_{t=1}^{T} \log (\theta \exp(-\theta y_t)).$$

Using the following rules of logarithms

$$\log(ab) = \log a + \log b,$$
$$\log(\exp a) = a,$$

it follows that

$$\sum_{t=1}^{T} \log f(y_t) = \sum_{t=1}^{T} (\log \theta - \theta y_t).$$

Using the subtraction rule

$$\sum_{t=1}^{T} \log f(y_t) = \sum_{t=1}^{T} \log \theta - \sum_{t=1}^{T} \theta y_t.$$

From the scalar addition rule, the first term becomes $\sum_{t=1}^{T} \log \theta = T \log \theta$ so that

$$\sum_{t=1}^{T} \log f(y_t) = T \log \theta - \sum_{t=1}^{T} \theta y_t.$$

From the scalar product rule $\sum_{t=1}^{T} \theta y_t = \theta \sum_{t=1}^{T} y_t$, the final expression becomes

$$\sum_{t=1}^{T} \log f\left(y_t\right) = T \log \theta - \theta \sum_{t=1}^{T} y_t.$$

This expression is used to derive the maximum likelihood estimator of the parameter, θ, for an exponential distribution.

A.2 EXPECTATIONS OPERATOR

Let y be a random variable that takes the discrete values $y_1, y_2, \cdots, y_T$ with associated probabilities $p\left(y_1\right), p\left(y_2\right), \cdots, p\left(y_T\right)$. The expectations operator is defined as

$$\mathrm{E}[y] = \sum_{t=1}^{T} y_t p\left(y_t\right),$$

or more generally

$$\mathrm{E}\left[g\left(y\right)\right] = \sum_{t=1}^{T} g\left(y_t\right) p\left(y_t\right).$$

Note that the expectations are defined with respect to a discrete random variable. For a continuous random variable, the summation operator is replaced by an integral. Some important examples of the expectations operator are

Mean : $\mu_y = \mathrm{E}[y],$

Variance : $\mathrm{var}\left(y\right) = \sigma_y^2 = \mathrm{E}\left[\left(y - \mu_y\right)^2\right],$

Skewness : $sk = \dfrac{\mathrm{E}\left[\left(y - \mu_y\right)^3\right]}{\sigma_y^3},$

Kurtosis : $kt = \dfrac{\mathrm{E}\left[\left(y - \mu_y\right)^4\right]}{\sigma_y^4},$

Covariance : $\mathrm{cov}\left(y, x\right) = \sigma_{yx} = \mathrm{E}\left[\left(y - \mu_y\right)\left(x - \mu_x\right)\right],$

Correlation : $\mathrm{cor}\left(y, x\right) = \rho_{yx} = \dfrac{\mathrm{cov}\left(y, x\right)}{\sqrt{\mathrm{var}\left(y\right)\mathrm{var}\left(x\right)}} = \dfrac{\sigma_{yx}}{\sigma_y \sigma_x}.$

Some basic rules are as follows.

1. Addition

$$\mathrm{E}(y + x) = \mathrm{E}(y) + \mathrm{E}(x),$$

where y and x are random variables.

2. Subtraction

$$\mathrm{E}(y - x) = \mathrm{E}(y) - \mathrm{E}(x),$$

where y and x are random variables.

3. Expectation of a constant

$$E(k) = k,$$

where k is a constant.

4. Scalar product

$$E(ky) = kE(y),$$

where y is a random variable, and k is a constant.

5. Variance of a linear function of a single random variable y

$$\text{var}\,(a + by) = b^2\,\text{var}\,(y),$$

where y and x are random variables, and a and b are constants.

6. Variance of a linear function of two random variables y and x (with correlation)

$$\text{var}\,(ay + bx) = a^2\,\text{var}\,(y) + b^2\,\text{var}\,(x) + 2ab\,\text{cov}\,(y,x)$$
$$= a^2\sigma_y^2 + b^2\sigma_x^2 + 2ab\sigma_{yx},$$

or

$$\text{var}\,(ay + bx) = a^2\sigma_y^2 + b^2\sigma_x^2 + 2ab\sigma_y\sigma_x\rho_{yx},$$

where y and x are random variables, and a and b are constants.

7. Variance of a linear function of two random variables y and x (without correlation)

$$\text{var}\,(ay + bx) = a^2\,\text{var}\,(y) + b^2\,\text{var}\,(x)$$
$$= a^2\sigma_y^2 + b^2\sigma_x^2,$$

where y and x are random variables, and a and b are constants.

A.3 DIFFERENTIATION

The first derivative of the function $y = f(x)$ is written as dy/dx or sometimes as $f'(x)$. The second derivative is given by

$$\frac{d^2y}{dx^2} = \frac{d}{dx}\left(\frac{dy}{dx}\right),$$

which is the derivative of the first derivative, or more compactly $f''(x)$. Higher order derivatives can also be computed.

There are a number of important rules of differentiation.

1. Power function

$$y = x^n \quad \text{then} \quad \frac{dy}{dx} = nx^{n-1}.$$

Problems of the form

$$y = \frac{1}{x^n},$$

may be handled by rewriting the expression as

$$y = x^{-n},$$

and using the rule for power functions, in which case

$$y = x^{-n} \quad \text{then} \quad \frac{dy}{dx} = -nx^{-n-1} = -\frac{n}{x^{n+1}}.$$

2. Product Rule

$$y = g(x)f(x) \quad \text{then} \quad \frac{dy}{dx} = \frac{df}{dx}g(x) + \frac{dg}{dx}f(x).$$

3. Chain Rule

$$y = u(f(x)) \quad \text{then} \quad \frac{dy}{dx} = \frac{du}{df}\frac{df}{dx}.$$

4. Quotient Rule

$$y = \frac{g(x)}{f(x)} \quad \text{then} \quad \frac{dy}{dx} = \frac{\frac{dg}{dx}f(x) - \frac{df}{dx}g(x)}{f(x)^2}.$$

This rule is based on applying the product and chain rules and using the derivative of a power function. To see this, write y as a product

$$y = \frac{g(x)}{f(x)} = f(x)^{-1}g(x).$$

Using the product rule where $f(x)$ is replaced by $f(x)^{-1}$, together with the chain rule where $u[f(x)] = f(x)^{-1}$, gives

$$\frac{dy}{dx} = -f(x)^{-2}\frac{df}{dx}g(x) + f(x)^{-1}\frac{dg}{dx} = \frac{\frac{dg}{dx}f(x) - \frac{df}{dx}g(x)}{f(x)^2}.$$

5. Exponential function

$$y = \exp(f(x)) \quad \text{then} \quad \frac{dy}{dx} = \exp(f(x))\frac{df}{dx}.$$

6. Logarithmic function (natural)

$$y = \log f(x) \quad \text{then} \quad \frac{dy}{dx} = \frac{1}{f(x)}\frac{df}{dx}.$$

7. Logarithmic differentiation

$$y = a^x \quad \text{then} \quad \frac{dy}{dx} = a^x \log a.$$

To prove this result, write

$$y = a^x = e^{\log a^x} = e^{x \log a}.$$

Using the rule of differentiating an exponential function, it follows that

$$\frac{dy}{dx} = e^{x \log a} \log a = a^x \log a.$$

A.4 TAYLOR SERIES EXPANSIONS

A Taylor series is a representation of a function that is evaluated at a particular point in terms of the value of the function and its derivatives at another neighboring point. This series takes the form of a polynomial function, which is extremely convenient in both analytic and practical work. The existence of a Taylor series representation depends on the existence of the derivatives of the function in this neighborhood. The Taylor series may be a finite sum with a remainder term or an infinite series (a convergent sum of an infinite number of terms), depending on the properties of the function and the function's derivatives.

A.4.1 Single Variable Case

Consider the function $f(x)$, where x is a scalar. An approximation of this function around the point a is given by selecting a number of terms of the following so-called Taylor series expansion

$$f(x) = f(a) + \frac{1}{1!} \frac{df}{dx}\bigg|_{x=a} (x-a) + \frac{1}{2!} \frac{d^2f}{dx^2}\bigg|_{x=a} (x-a)^2$$

$$+ \frac{1}{3!} \frac{d^3f}{dx^3}\bigg|_{x=a} (x-a)^3 + \cdots,$$

where

$$\frac{d^nf}{dx^n}\bigg|_{x=a} = f^{(n)}(a)$$

is the nth derivative evaluated at a. This is potentially an infinite expansion if the derivatives all exist; but in practice the series is usually truncated to produce an approximation. Note that this truncated expansion delivers a polynomial approximation to the function.

A second-order Taylor series expansion, for example, is (note the use of the approximation symbol $\simeq$ in this representation)

$$f(x) \simeq f(a) + \frac{1}{1!} \frac{df}{dx}\bigg|_{x=a} (x-a) + \frac{1}{2!} \frac{d^2f}{dx^2}\bigg|_{x=a} (x-a)^2.$$

Under certain very rigorous conditions, a function may be represented exactly in terms of a convergent infinite power series by its Taylor series in an interval around $x = a$ as

$$f(x) = \sum_{k=0}^{\infty} \frac{f^{(k)}(a)}{k!} (x-a)^k.$$

Even when this is possible, the interval in which the series converges will usually be finite, giving an explicit radius of convergence of the power series. Such series have a long history in mathematics, but their first general treatment and means of construction were provided by the English mathematician Brook Taylor in 1715, after whom the series expansion is named.

The function $f(x)$ may be represented in terms of a finite number of the Taylor series terms complemented with a remainder. Many different forms exist. But the most common are of the following type

$$f(x) = \sum_{k=0}^{K} \frac{f^{(k)}(a)}{k!} (x-a)^k + R_{K+1}(x),$$

where $R_{K+1}(x)$ is the remainder term given by

$$R_{K+1}(x) = \frac{f^{(K+1)}(\xi_a)}{(K+1)!} (x-a)^{K+1},$$

and ξ_a is a real number between x and a. This form of the remainder term is known as the Lagrange form, after the eighteenth century Italian-French mathematician Joseph-Louis Lagrange, whose work in analysis is best known in economics and finance because of his development of the now-ubiquitous technique of Lagrange multipliers. The explicit form of the Taylor series remainder $R_{K+1}(x)$ involves the use of a mean-value theorem, which leads to the evaluation of the derivative $f^{(K+1)}(\xi_a)$ at the intermediate point ξ_a.

Consider a first-order Taylor series expansion of the function $f(x) = \exp(-x^2)$ around $a = 1$. The derivative (using the Chain rule) is

$$\frac{df}{dx} = -2x\exp(-x^2).$$

Evaluating all terms at $a = 1$ gives

$$f(1) = \exp(-1^2) = 0.368,$$
$$\left.\frac{df}{dx}\right|_{x=1} = -2 \times 1 \times \exp(-1^2) = -0.736.$$

Substituting into the first-order Taylor series expansion gives

$$f(x) \simeq f(1) + \frac{1}{1!}\left.\frac{df}{dx}\right|_{x=0}(x-1)$$
$$\simeq 0.368 + 1 \times (-0.736) \times (x-1)$$
$$\simeq 1.104 - 0.736x.$$

To check the quality of the approximation, consider the value at $x = 1.1$

$$f(1) \simeq 1.104 - 0.736 \times 1.1 = 0.294.$$

Comparing to the exact value $\exp(-1.1^2) = 0.298$, the first-order Taylor series expansion provides an approximation that is correct to the second decimal place.

Consider a second-order Taylor series expansion of the exponential function $f(x) = \exp(x)$ around $a = 0$. The derivatives are

$$\frac{df}{dx} = \exp(x), \qquad \frac{d^2f}{dx^2} = \exp(x).$$

Evaluating all terms at $a = 0$, gives

$$f(0) = \exp(0) = 1$$
$$\left.\frac{df}{dx}\right|_{x=0} = \exp(0) = 1$$
$$\left.\frac{d^2f}{dx^2}\right|_{x=0} = \exp(0) = 1.$$

Substituting into the second-order Taylor series expansion gives

$$f(x) \simeq f(0) + \frac{1}{1!} \frac{df}{dx}\bigg|_{x=0} (x-0) + \frac{1}{2!} \frac{d^2f}{dx^2}\bigg|_{x=0} (x-0)^2$$

$$\simeq 1 + 1 \times (x-0) + \frac{1}{2} \times (x-0)^2$$

$$\simeq 1 + x + \frac{x^2}{2}.$$

To check the quality of the approximation, consider the value at $x = 1$,

$$f(1) \simeq 1 + 1 + \frac{1^2}{2} = 2.5.$$

Comparing to the exact value $\exp(1) = 2.7183$, the second-order Taylor series expansion provides a reasonable approximation. Extending the approximation to the third order gives

$$f(x) \simeq 1 + x + \frac{x^2}{2} + \frac{x^3}{6}.$$

The value of the approximation at $x = 1$ is

$$f(x) \simeq 1 + 1 + \frac{1^2}{2} + \frac{1^3}{6} = 2.6667,$$

which is now accurate to the first decimal point.

Consider a third-order Taylor series expansion of the natural logarithmic function $f(x) = \log x$ around $a = 1$. The derivatives are

$$\frac{df}{dx} = \frac{1}{x}, \qquad \frac{d^2f}{dx^2} = -\frac{1}{x^2}, \qquad \frac{d^3f}{dx^3} = \frac{2}{x^3}.$$

Evaluating all the terms at $a = 1$ gives

$$f(1) = \log(1) = 0$$

$$\frac{df}{dx}\bigg|_{x=1} = \frac{1}{1} = 1$$

$$\frac{d^2f}{dx^2}\bigg|_{x=1} = -\frac{1}{1^2} = -1$$

$$\frac{d^3f}{dx^3}\bigg|_{x=1} = \frac{2}{1^3} = 2.$$

Substituting into the third-order Taylor series expansion gives

$$f(x) \simeq f(1) + \frac{1}{1!} \frac{df}{dx}\bigg|_{x=1} (x-1) + \frac{1}{2!} \frac{d^2f}{dx^2}\bigg|_{x=1} (x-1)^2 + \frac{1}{3!} \frac{d^3f}{dx^3}\bigg|_{x=1} (x-1)^3$$

$$\simeq 0 + 1 \times (x-1) + \frac{1}{2} \times (-1) \times (x-1)^2 + \frac{1}{6} \times 2 \times (x-1)^3$$

$$\simeq (x-1) - \frac{1}{2} \times (x-1)^2 + \frac{1}{3} \times (x-1)^3.$$

To check the quality of the approximation, consider the value at $x = 2$,

$$f(2) \simeq (2-1) - \frac{1}{2} \times (2-1)^2 + \frac{1}{3} \times (2-1)^3 = 0.833.$$

Comparing this approximation to the exact value $\log(2) = 0.693$, the third-order Taylor series expansion provides only a very rough approximation and is not accurate even to the first decimal place. More terms in the Taylor series are needed to deliver a more accurate approximation in this case. For instance, the fifth-order Taylor series is

$$f(2) \simeq (2-1) - \frac{1}{2} \times (2-1)^2 + \frac{1}{3} \times (2-1)^3 - \frac{1}{4} \times (2-1)^4 + \frac{1}{5} \times (2-1)^5 = 0.783,$$

which is closer to the true value but still not a good approximation. The reason is that the Taylor series for $\log x$ converges absolutely[1] only in a small neighborhood of $x=1$ (in fact, the neighborhood $0 < x < 2$). For $x = 2$, the series does converge but only conditionally[2] in view of the alternating signs in the terms in the series, that is,

$$f(2) = \sum_{k=1}^{\infty} \frac{(-1)^{k-1}}{k}.$$

If we evaluate the third-order Taylor series at $a = 1.5$, which is much closer to unity, then

$$f(1.5) \simeq (1.5 - 1) - \frac{1}{2} \times (1.5 - 1)^2 + \frac{1}{3} \times (1.5 - 1)^3 = 0.416,$$

compared with the exact value $\log(1.5) = 0.405$, and so the approximation is now correct to the first decimal place.

A.4.2 Multiple Variable Case

The Taylor series expansion can be applied to functions containing several variables. For simplicity, consider the bivariate function $f(x, y)$, where x and y are the arguments. An approximation of this function around the points a and b, corresponding to x and y, respectively, is given by the Taylor series expansion

$$f(x, y) = f(a, b)$$
$$+ \frac{1}{1!} \left(\frac{\partial f}{\partial x} \Big|_{x=a, y=b} (x-a) + \frac{\partial f}{\partial y} \Big|_{x=a, y=b} (y-b) \right)$$
$$+ \frac{1}{2!} \left(\frac{\partial^2 f}{\partial x^2} \Big|_{x=a, y=b} (x-a)^2 + \frac{\partial^2 f}{\partial y^2} \Big|_{x=a, y=b} (y-b)^2 \right.$$
$$\left. + 2 \times \frac{\partial^2 f}{\partial x \partial y} \Big|_{x=a, y=b} (x-a)(y-b) \right)$$
$$+ \text{ higher order terms.}$$

Consider a second-order Taylor series expansion of the function $f(x, y) = x^3 y + x^2 y + 1$, around $a = 0$ and $b = 1$. The derivatives are

$$\frac{\partial f}{\partial x} = 3x^2 y + 2xy, \qquad \frac{\partial f}{\partial y} = x^3 + x^2,$$
$$\frac{\partial^2 f}{\partial x^2} = 6xy + 2y, \qquad \frac{\partial^2 f}{\partial y^2} = 0, \qquad \frac{\partial^2 f}{\partial x \partial y} = 3x^2 + 2x.$$

---

[1] A series $\sum_{k=1}^{\infty} a_k$ converges absolutely if $\sum_{k=1}^{\infty} |a_k| < \infty$.

[2] The series $\sum_{k=1}^{\infty} \frac{(-1)^{k-1}}{k}$ does not converge absolutely because $\sum_{k=1}^{\infty} |\frac{(-1)^{k-1}}{k}| = \sum_{k=1}^{\infty} \frac{1}{k} = \infty$.

Evaluating all terms at $a = 0$ and $b = 1$ gives

$$f(0,1) = 0^3 \times 1 + 0^2 \times 1 + 1 = 1$$

$$\left. \frac{\partial f}{\partial x} \right|_{x=0, y=1} = 3 \times 0^2 \times 1 + 2 \times 0 \times 1 = 0$$

$$\left. \frac{\partial f}{\partial y} \right|_{x=0, y=1} = 0^3 + 0^2 = 0$$

$$\left. \frac{\partial^2 f}{\partial x^2} \right|_{x=0, y=1} = 6 \times 0 \times 1 + 2 \times 1 = 2$$

$$\left. \frac{\partial^2 f}{\partial y^2} \right|_{x=0, y=1} = 0$$

$$\left. \frac{\partial^2 f}{\partial x \partial y} \right|_{x=0, y=1} = 3 \times 0^2 + 2 \times 0 = 0.$$

Substituting these values into the Taylor series expansion gives

$$f(x,y) = x^3 y + x^2 y + 1$$
$$\simeq 1 + \frac{1}{1!} \left(0 \times (x - 0) + 0 \times (y - 1) \right)$$
$$+ \frac{1}{2!} \left(2 \times (x - 0)^2 + 0 \times (y - 1)^2 + 2 \times 0 \times (x - 0)(y - 1) \right)$$
$$\simeq 1 + x^2,$$

as a second-order approximation of the function $x^3 y + x^2 y + 1$ about its value at $(x, y) = (0, 1)$.

A.5 MATRIX ALGEBRA

Matrices provide a convenient and compact way of collating information on systems of equations. To motivate the use of matrices, the following example shows the steps involved to solve a system of equations using standard operations.

Consider the following system of equations

$$4y_1 + 2y_2 = 5, \tag{A.1}$$
$$y_1 + 3y_2 = 10. \tag{A.2}$$

To obtain the solution of this system, reduce the system to a single equation by subtracting four times the second equation (A.2) from the first equation (A.1), to eliminate y_1, giving

$$2y_2 - 12y_2 = 5 - 40$$
$$-10y_2 = -35.$$

Rearranging this equation gives the solution for y_2

$$y_2 = 3.5.$$

Using the solution of y_2 in equation (A.2) and rearranging gives the solution of y_1 as well,

$$y_1 = 10 - 3 \times y_2 = 10 - 3 \times 3.5 = -0.5.$$

A.5.1 Definitions

An $(M \times N)$ matrix is an array of numbers ordered into M rows and N columns

$$A = \begin{pmatrix} a_{11} & a_{12} & \cdots & a_{1N} \\ a_{21} & a_{22} & \cdots & a_{2N} \\ \vdots & \vdots & \ddots & \vdots \\ a_{M1} & a_{M2} & \cdots & a_{MN} \end{pmatrix}.$$

The numbers of rows and columns of the matrix are also referred to as the dimensions of the matrix.

1. Column vector: If there is just one column ($N = 1$) then A is called a column vector,

$$A = \begin{pmatrix} a_{11} \\ a_{21} \\ \vdots \\ a_{M1} \end{pmatrix}.$$

2. Row vector: If there is just one row ($M = 1$) then A is called a row vector,

$$A = \begin{pmatrix} a_{11} & a_{12} & \cdots & a_{1N} \end{pmatrix}.$$

3. Scalar: If there is just one column ($N = 1$) and one row ($M = 1$) then A is called a scalar,

$$A = \begin{pmatrix} a_{11} \end{pmatrix}.$$

A.5.2 Summation of Matrices

Two $(M \times N)$ matrices are added element by element

$$\begin{pmatrix} a_{11} & a_{12} & \cdots & a_{1N} \\ a_{21} & a_{22} & \cdots & a_{2N} \\ \vdots & \vdots & \ddots & \vdots \\ a_{M1} & a_{M2} & \cdots & a_{MN} \end{pmatrix} + \begin{pmatrix} b_{11} & b_{12} & \cdots & b_{1N} \\ b_{21} & b_{22} & \cdots & b_{2N} \\ \vdots & \vdots & \ddots & \vdots \\ b_{M1} & b_{M2} & \cdots & b_{MN} \end{pmatrix}$$

$$= \begin{pmatrix} a_{11} + b_{11} & a_{12} + b_{12} & \cdots & a_{1N} + b_{1N} \\ a_{21} + b_{21} & a_{22} + b_{22} & \cdots & a_{2N} + b_{2N} \\ \vdots & \vdots & \ddots & \vdots \\ a_{M1} + b_{M1} & a_{M2} + b_{M2} & \cdots & a_{MN} + b_{MN} \end{pmatrix},$$

or more compactly

$$A + B = \begin{pmatrix} a_{ij} + b_{ij} \end{pmatrix}.$$

Consider the two matrices

$$A = \begin{pmatrix} 1 & 5 \\ 2 & 3 \\ 3 & 6 \end{pmatrix}, \quad B = \begin{pmatrix} 2 & 6 \\ 5 & 2 \\ 1 & 5 \end{pmatrix}.$$

Then

$$A + B = \begin{pmatrix} 1 & 5 \\ 2 & 3 \\ 3 & 6 \end{pmatrix} + \begin{pmatrix} 2 & 6 \\ 5 & 2 \\ 1 & 5 \end{pmatrix} = \begin{pmatrix} 3 & 11 \\ 7 & 5 \\ 4 & 11 \end{pmatrix}.$$

Note that to be able to add two matrices together, they must have the same dimensions.

A.5.3 Multiplication of Matrices

The product of an $(M \times N)$ matrix A and an $(N \times Q)$ matrix B is

$$\underset{(M \times N)}{A} \times \underset{(N \times Q)}{B} = \underset{(M \times Q)}{C},$$

where C is $(M \times Q)$. The elements of C are computed as

$$c_{ij} = \sum_{k=1}^{N} a_{ik} b_{kj}.$$

That is, the element c_{ij} is obtained by multiplying the ith row by the jth column. Note that matrix multiplication requires that the matrices involved are *conformable* in the sense that the column dimension of the first matrix in the product, A, must be the same as the row dimension of the second matrix in the product, B, for the product to be computed. In this case, the requirement is satisfied as the column dimension of A is N, which equals the row dimension of B.

Consider the two matrices

$$A = \begin{pmatrix} 1 & 5 \\ 2 & 3 \\ 3 & 6 \end{pmatrix}, \quad B = \begin{pmatrix} 2 & 5 & 1 & 4 \\ 6 & 2 & 5 & 3 \end{pmatrix},$$

with $M = 3$, $N = 2$, and $Q = 4$. Then

$$A \times B = \begin{pmatrix} 1 & 5 \\ 2 & 3 \\ 3 & 6 \end{pmatrix} \times \begin{pmatrix} 2 & 5 & 1 & 4 \\ 6 & 2 & 5 & 3 \end{pmatrix} = \begin{pmatrix} 32 & 15 & 26 & 19 \\ 22 & 16 & 17 & 17 \\ 42 & 27 & 33 & 30 \end{pmatrix},$$

which is a (3×4) matrix. Thus

Row 1 by Column 1 : $1 \times 2 + 5 \times 6 = 32$
Row 1 by Column 2 : $1 \times 5 + 5 \times 2 = 15$

Row 3 by Column 4 : $3 \times 4 + 6 \times 3 = 30$.

If α is a scalar, and A is an $(M \times N)$ matrix, then

$$\alpha \times A = C,$$

where C is $(M \times N)$ with elements computed as

$$c_{ij} = \alpha a_{ij}.$$

Consider the scalar $\alpha = 5$ and matrix A

$$A = \begin{pmatrix} 1 & 5 \\ 2 & 3 \\ 3 & 6 \end{pmatrix},$$

then

$$\alpha \times A = 5 \times \begin{pmatrix} 1 & 5 \\ 2 & 3 \\ 3 & 6 \end{pmatrix} = \begin{pmatrix} 5 & 25 \\ 10 & 15 \\ 15 & 30 \end{pmatrix}.$$

A.5.4 Identity Matrix

The identity matrix is an $(N \times N)$ matrix with unity along the main diagonal and zeros elsewhere, given by

$$I = \begin{pmatrix} 1 & 0 & \cdots & 0 \\ 0 & 1 & \cdots & 0 \\ \vdots & \vdots & \ddots & \vdots \\ 0 & 0 & \cdots & 1 \end{pmatrix} = diag(1, 1, \cdots, 1).$$

An important property of the identity matrix is

$$I \times A = A \times I = A,$$

where A is $(N \times N)$.

A.6 TRANSPOSITION OF A MATRIX

The transpose of an $(M \times N)$ matrix

$$A = (a_{ij}),$$

is the $(N \times M)$ matrix

$$A' = (a_{ji}).$$

That is, the transpose of a matrix rearranges the elements in a matrix so that the columns become the rows and the rows become the columns.

Consider the (3×2) matrix

$$A = \begin{pmatrix} 1 & 5 \\ 2 & 3 \\ 3 & 6 \end{pmatrix}.$$

The transpose is

$$A' = \begin{pmatrix} 1 & 2 & 3 \\ 5 & 3 & 6 \end{pmatrix},$$

which is a (2×3) matrix.

Let A be $(M \times N)$ and B be $(N \times K)$ in which case AB is an $(M \times K)$ matrix. An important result of the transpose operation is that

$$(AB)' = B'A',$$

which is a $(K \times M)$ matrix.

A.7 SYMMETRIC MATRIX

The $(N \times N)$ matrix A is symmetric if

$$(a_{ij}) = (a_{ji}),$$

or in terms of the transpose

$$A = A'.$$

Consider the (3×3) matrix

$$A = \begin{pmatrix} 1 & 5 & 2 \\ 5 & 3 & 6 \\ 2 & 6 & 8 \end{pmatrix}.$$

This matrix is symmetric because

$$a_{12} = a_{21} = 5, \qquad a_{31} = a_{13} = 2, \qquad a_{23} = a_{32} = 6.$$

A.7.1 Determinant of a Matrix

The determinant of a matrix A, denoted $|A|$, is a scalar. If A is a (2×2) matrix

$$A = \begin{pmatrix} a_{11} & a_{12} \\ a_{21} & a_{22} \end{pmatrix},$$

the determinant is

$$|A| = a_{11}a_{22} - a_{12}a_{21}.$$

Consider the (2×2) matrix

$$A = \begin{pmatrix} 1 & 5 \\ 2 & 3 \end{pmatrix}.$$

The determinant is

$$|A| = a_{11}a_{22} - a_{12}a_{21} = 1 \times 3 - 5 \times 2 = -7.$$

Determinants can be defined for general $(N \times N)$ matrices, although the analytic expressions quickly become complicated and involve many summations of products of the elements of the matrix. In practical work, determinants are usually computed numerically by computer algorithms.

A.7.2 Inverse of a Matrix

If it exists, the inverse of a square matrix A, denoted A^{-1}, has the property that

$$AA^{-1} = I,$$

where I is the identity matrix. The inverse of the (2×2) matrix A

$$A = \begin{pmatrix} a_{11} & a_{12} \\ a_{21} & a_{22} \end{pmatrix},$$

is

$$A^{-1} = \frac{1}{a_{11}a_{22} - a_{12}a_{21}} \begin{pmatrix} a_{22} & -a_{12} \\ -a_{21} & a_{11} \end{pmatrix}.$$

Note that the term

$$a_{11}a_{22} - a_{12}a_{21} = |A|,$$

is the determinant of A.

A scalar example is

$$A = (2), \quad A^{-1} = (0.5).$$

A (2×2) example is

$$A = \begin{pmatrix} 4 & 2 \\ 1 & 3 \end{pmatrix}, \quad A^{-1} = \frac{1}{4 \times 3 - 2 \times 1} \begin{pmatrix} 3 & -2 \\ -1 & 4 \end{pmatrix} = \begin{pmatrix} 0.3 & -0.2 \\ -0.1 & 0.4 \end{pmatrix}.$$

Consider the following (2×2) diagonal matrix

$$A = \begin{pmatrix} 4 & 0 \\ 0 & 3 \end{pmatrix}, \quad A^{-1} = \frac{1}{4 \times 3 - 0 \times 0} \begin{pmatrix} 3 & -0 \\ -0 & 4 \end{pmatrix} = \begin{pmatrix} 1/4 & 0 \\ 0 & 1/3 \end{pmatrix}.$$

In general,

$$A = \begin{pmatrix} a_{11} & 0 \\ 0 & a_{22} \end{pmatrix}, \quad A^{-1} = \begin{pmatrix} 1/a_{11} & 0 \\ 0 & 1/a_{22} \end{pmatrix},$$

in which case the inverse is simply obtained by inverting the diagonal elements.

Consider the linear set of equations

$$Ay = B.$$

Then the solution is given by pre-multiplying both sides by A^{-1}

$$A^{-1}Ay = A^{-1}B.$$

Since $A^{-1}A = I$, then

$$y = A^{-1}B.$$

Returning to the original example where $N = 2$, the system of equations is

$$4y_1 + 2y_2 = 5$$
$$y_1 + 3y_2 = 10.$$

The matrix representation of this system is

$$\begin{pmatrix} 4 & 2 \\ 1 & 3 \end{pmatrix} \begin{pmatrix} y_1 \\ y_2 \end{pmatrix} = \begin{pmatrix} 5 \\ 10 \end{pmatrix},$$

which has solution

$$\begin{pmatrix} y_1 \\ y_2 \end{pmatrix} = \begin{pmatrix} 4 & 2 \\ 1 & 3 \end{pmatrix}^{-1} \begin{pmatrix} 5 \\ 10 \end{pmatrix} = \begin{pmatrix} 0.3 & -0.2 \\ -0.1 & 0.4 \end{pmatrix} \begin{pmatrix} 5 \\ 10 \end{pmatrix} = \begin{pmatrix} -0.5 \\ 3.5 \end{pmatrix},$$

so that as before, $y_1 = -0.5$ and $y_2 = 3.5$.

A.7.3 Definiteness of a Matrix

Consider the $(N \times N)$ matrix A and the $(N \times 1)$ vector y, which is any non-zero vector. Definiteness of a matrix refers to the sign of the scalar

$$y'Ay,$$

which is known as a quadratic form in the vector y with matrix A. There are four relevant cases concerning definiteness of a matrix.

(i)	Positive definite	:	$y'Ay > 0$
(ii)	Positive semi-definite	:	$y'Ay \geqslant 0$
(iii)	Negative definite	:	$y'Ay < 0$
(iv)	Negative semi-definite	:	$y'Ay \leq 0$

A convenient way to determine the definiteness of a matrix is based on the use of determinants. The idea is illustrated in the following simple cases.

1. Scalar case: Let A be a scalar

$$A = (a_{11}).$$

Then

(i)	Positive definite	:	$a_{11} > 0$
(ii)	Positive semi-definite	:	$a_{11} \geq 0$
(iii)	Negative definite	:	$a_{11} < 0$
(iv)	Negative semi-definite	:	$a_{11} \leq 0$

2. Bivariate case: Let A be a (2×2) matrix

$$A = \begin{pmatrix} a_{11} & a_{12} \\ a_{21} & a_{22} \end{pmatrix}.$$

Then the conditions for definiteness are

(i)	Positive definite	:	$a_{11} > 0, a_{11}a_{22} - a_{12}a_{21} > 0$
(ii)	Positive semi-definite	:	$a_{11} \geq 0, a_{11}a_{22} - a_{12}a_{21} \geq 0$
(iii)	Negative definite	:	$a_{11} < 0, a_{11}a_{22} - a_{12}a_{21} > 0$
(iv)	Negative semi-definite	:	$a_{11} \leq 0, a_{11}a_{22} - a_{12}a_{21} \geq 0$

If the scalar matrix A is

$$A = (\ 2 \ ),$$

then

$$a_{11} = 2 > 0,$$

so that A is a positive definite matrix.

If the scalar matrix A is

$$A = (\ -2 \ ),$$

then

$$a_{11} = -2 < 0,$$

so that A is a negative definite matrix.

Consider the (2×2) matrix A

$$A = \begin{pmatrix} 4 & 2 \\ 1 & 3 \end{pmatrix}.$$

Since

$$a_{11} = 4 > 0, \quad a_{11}a_{22} - a_{12}a_{21} = 4 \times 3 - 2 \times 1 = 10 > 0,$$

A is a positive definite matrix.

Consider the (2×2) matrix A

$$A = \begin{pmatrix} -4 & 1 \\ 2 & -3 \end{pmatrix}.$$

Since

$$a_{11} = -4 < 0, \quad a_{11}a_{22} - a_{12}a_{21} = (-4) \times (-3) - 1 \times 2 = 10 > 0,$$

A is a negative definite matrix.

Positive and negative definiteness can also be defined for matrices of dimension $N > 2$.

A.7.4 Differentiation and Matrices

Consider the scalar function $f(y)$ that is a function of the $(N \times 1)$ vector

$$y = \begin{pmatrix} y_1 \\ y_2 \\ \vdots \\ y_N \end{pmatrix}.$$

Two examples of a scalar function involve the sum and product of the elements of y

$$f(y) = \sum_{i=1}^{N} y_i \quad \text{and} \quad f(y) = y_1 y_2 \cdots y_N.$$

The scalar function can be differentiated with respect to each element of y

$$\frac{\partial f}{\partial y_1}, \frac{\partial f}{\partial y_2}, \dots, \frac{\partial f}{\partial y_N}.$$

All of these derivatives can be conveniently summarized as a vector. Since y is an $(N \times 1)$ column vector, then the vector of derivatives, the gradient vector, is also an $(N \times 1)$ column vector given by

$$G = \frac{\partial f}{\partial y} = \begin{pmatrix} \dfrac{\partial f}{\partial y_1} \\ \dfrac{\partial f}{\partial y_2} \\ \vdots \\ \dfrac{\partial f}{\partial y_N} \end{pmatrix}.$$

Alternatively, if the transpose of y is a $(1 \times N)$ row vector, then the vector of derivatives with respect to y' is also a $(1 \times N)$ row vector given by

$$\frac{\partial f}{\partial y'} = \begin{pmatrix} \dfrac{\partial f}{\partial y_1} & \dfrac{\partial f}{\partial y_2} & \cdots & \dfrac{\partial f}{\partial y_N} \end{pmatrix}.$$

The key idea to note here is that when differentiating a function f with respect to a vector y, the dimension of the function of derivatives expands according to the dimension of y.

Now consider the set of second derivatives of the scalar f with respect to all of the elements in y

Derivative of $\dfrac{\partial f}{\partial y_1}$ wrt y_1 to y_N : $\quad \dfrac{\partial^2 f}{\partial y_1^2} \quad \dfrac{\partial^2 f}{\partial y_1 \partial y_2} \quad \dfrac{\partial^2 f}{\partial y_1 \partial y_3} \quad \cdots \quad \dfrac{\partial^2 f}{\partial y_1 \partial y_N}$

Derivative of $\dfrac{\partial f}{\partial y_2}$ wrt y_1 to y_N : $\quad \dfrac{\partial^2 f}{\partial y_2 \partial y_1} \quad \dfrac{\partial^2 f}{\partial y_2^2} \quad \dfrac{\partial^2 f}{\partial y_2 \partial y_3} \quad \cdots \quad \dfrac{\partial^2 f}{\partial y_2 \partial y_N}$

$$\vdots \qquad\qquad \vdots \qquad \vdots \qquad \vdots \qquad \ddots \qquad \vdots$$

Derivative of $\dfrac{\partial f}{\partial y_N}$ wrt y_1 to y_N : $\quad \dfrac{\partial^2 f}{\partial y_N \partial y_1} \quad \dfrac{\partial^2 f}{\partial y_N \partial y_2} \quad \dfrac{\partial^2 f}{\partial y_N \partial y_3} \quad \cdots \quad \dfrac{\partial^2 f}{\partial y_N^2}.$

These derivatives are conveniently summarized by the Hessian matrix

$$H = \frac{\partial^2 f}{\partial y \partial y'} = \begin{pmatrix} \dfrac{\partial^2 f}{\partial y_1^2} & \dfrac{\partial^2 f}{\partial y_1 \partial y_2} & \dfrac{\partial^2 f}{\partial y_1 \partial y_3} & \cdots & \dfrac{\partial^2 f}{\partial y_1 \partial y_N} \\[2mm] \dfrac{\partial^2 f}{\partial y_2 \partial y_1} & \dfrac{\partial^2 f}{\partial y_2^2} & \dfrac{\partial^2 f}{\partial y_2 \partial y_3} & \cdots & \dfrac{\partial^2 f}{\partial y_2 \partial y_N} \\[2mm] \vdots & \vdots & \vdots & \ddots & \vdots \\[2mm] \dfrac{\partial^2 f}{\partial y_N \partial y_1} & \dfrac{\partial^2 f}{\partial y_N \partial y_2} & \dfrac{\partial^2 f}{\partial y_N \partial y_3} & \cdots & \dfrac{\partial^2 f}{\partial y_N^2} \end{pmatrix}.$$

The first column contains the derivatives of the $(N \times 1)$ gradient vector with respect to y_1 (the first element of y'). The second column contains the derivatives of the $(N \times 1)$ gradient vector with respect to y_2 (the second element of y'), etc.

Consider differentiating the scalar

$$f = A'y,$$

where A and y are $(N \times 1)$ column vectors

$$A = \begin{pmatrix} a_1 \\ a_2 \\ \vdots \\ a_N \end{pmatrix}, \qquad y = \begin{pmatrix} y_1 \\ y_2 \\ \vdots \\ y_N \end{pmatrix}.$$

Then

$$\frac{\partial f}{\partial y} = \frac{\partial A'y}{\partial y} = A.$$

Notice that the result is A, not its transpose A'. As already mentioned, the dimension of the derivative must be the same as the dimension of y, which implies that the result must be an $(N \times 1)$ vector. This can only occur for A because A' is $(1 \times N)$.

Note that

$$f = A'y = \sum_{i=1}^{N} a_i y_i.$$

The derivatives are given by the ($N \times 1$) column vector

$$\frac{\partial f}{\partial y} = \begin{pmatrix} \dfrac{\partial f}{\partial y_1} \\[2mm] \dfrac{\partial f}{\partial y_2} \\[1mm] \vdots \\[1mm] \dfrac{\partial f}{\partial y_N} \end{pmatrix} = \begin{pmatrix} a_1 \\ a_2 \\ \vdots \\ a_N \end{pmatrix}.$$

This suggests that

$$\frac{\partial f}{\partial y} = \frac{\partial A'y}{\partial y} = A.$$

Consider differentiating the scalar

$$f = y'Ay,$$

where A is an ($N \times N$) symmetric matrix, and y is an ($N \times 1$) column vector

$$A = \begin{bmatrix} a_{11} & a_{12} & \cdots & a_{1N} \\ a_{21} & a_{22} & \cdots & a_{2N} \\ \vdots & \vdots & \ddots & \vdots \\ a_{N1} & a_{N2} & \cdots & a_{NN} \end{bmatrix}, \qquad y = \begin{bmatrix} y_1 \\ y_2 \\ \vdots \\ y_N \end{bmatrix}.$$

Then

$$\frac{\partial f}{\partial y} = \frac{\partial y'Ay}{\partial y} = 2Ay,$$

which is ($N \times 1$). Again notice that this result is consistent with the general result that the derivative must have the same dimension as y.

The proof is given for the $N = 2$ case. First note that

$$f = y'Ay = \sum_{i=1}^{N} \sum_{j=1}^{N} y_i y_j a_{ij}.$$

For example, if

$$A = \begin{pmatrix} 6 & 2 \\ 2 & 3 \end{pmatrix} \qquad y = \begin{pmatrix} y_1 \\ y_2 \end{pmatrix},$$

then

$$y'Ay = 6y_1^2 + 3y_2^2 + 4y_1 y_2.$$

Computing the derivatives gives

$$\frac{\partial y'Ay}{\partial y_1} = 12y_1 + 4y_2, \qquad \frac{\partial y'Ay}{\partial y_2} = 4y_1 + 6y_2.$$

In matrix notation, the result is

$$\frac{\partial y'Ay}{\partial y} = \begin{pmatrix} 12 & 4 \\ 4 & 6 \end{pmatrix} \begin{pmatrix} y_1 \\ y_2 \end{pmatrix}$$

$$= 2Ay.$$

Consider the second derivatives of the scalar

$$f = y'Ay,$$

where A is an $(N \times N)$ symmetric matrix and y is an $(N \times 1)$ column vector

$$A = \begin{pmatrix} a_{11} & a_{12} & \cdots & a_{1N} \\ a_{21} & a_{22} & \cdots & a_{2N} \\ \vdots & \vdots & \ddots & \vdots \\ a_{N1} & a_{N2} & \cdots & a_{NN} \end{pmatrix}, \qquad y = \begin{pmatrix} y_1 \\ y_2 \\ \vdots \\ y_N \end{pmatrix}.$$

Then

$$\frac{\partial^2 f}{\partial y \partial y'} = \frac{\partial y'Ay}{\partial y \partial y'} = 2A,$$

which is $(N \times N)$.

From the results of the first derivative

$$\frac{\partial f}{\partial y} = \frac{\partial y'Ay}{\partial y} = 2Ay.$$

Now differentiate again with respect to the $(1 \times N)$ row vector y', giving

$$\frac{\partial^2 f}{\partial y \partial y'} = \frac{\partial y'Ay}{\partial y \partial y'} = \frac{2Ay}{\partial y \partial y'} = 2A.$$

A.7.5 Expectations and Matrices

The expectations operator $E(\cdot)$ may be applied to matrices element by element.

1. Let y be a scalar random variable. Then

$$E(y) = \mu,$$

where μ represents the mean of y.

2. Let y be an $(N \times 1)$ vector of random variables

$$y = \begin{pmatrix} y_1 \\ y_2 \\ \vdots \\ y_N \end{pmatrix}.$$

Taking expectations gives

$$E(y) = \begin{pmatrix} E(y_1) \\ E(y_2) \\ \vdots \\ E(y_N) \end{pmatrix} = \begin{pmatrix} \mu_1 \\ \mu_2 \\ \vdots \\ \mu_N \end{pmatrix},$$

where μ_i represents the mean of y_i.

3. Let y be an $(M \times N)$ matrix of random variables

$$y = \begin{pmatrix} y_{11} & y_{12} & y_{13} & \cdots & y_{1N} \\ y_{21} & y_{22} & y_{23} & \cdots & y_{2N} \\ \vdots & \vdots & \vdots & \ddots & \vdots \\ y_{M1} & y_{M2} & y_{M3} & \cdots & y_{MN} \end{pmatrix}.$$

Taking expectations gives

$$E(y) = \begin{pmatrix} E(y_{11}) & E(y_{12}) & E(y_{13}) & \cdots & E(y_{1N}) \\ E(y_{21}) & E(y_{22}) & E(y_{23}) & \cdots & E(y_{2N}) \\ \vdots & \vdots & \vdots & \ddots & \vdots \\ E(y_{M1}) & E(y_{M2}) & E(y_{M3}) & \cdots & E(y_{MN}) \end{pmatrix}.$$

4. Let y be an $(N \times 1)$ vector of random variables

$$y = \begin{pmatrix} y_1 \\ y_2 \\ \vdots \\ y_N \end{pmatrix},$$

which are assumed to have zero means. Then

$$E(yy') = E\left[\begin{pmatrix} y_1 \\ y_2 \\ \vdots \\ y_N \end{pmatrix} \begin{pmatrix} y_1 & y_2 & \cdots & y_N \end{pmatrix} \right]$$

$$= E\left[\begin{pmatrix} y_1^2 & y_1 y_2 & y_1 y_3 & \cdots & y_1 y_N \\ y_2 y_1 & y_2^2 & y_2 y_3 & \cdots & y_2 y_N \\ \vdots & \vdots & \vdots & \ddots & \vdots \\ y_N y_1 & y_N y_2 & y_N y_3 & \cdots & y_N^2 \end{pmatrix} \right]$$

$$= \begin{pmatrix} E(y_1^2) & E(y_1 y_2) & E(y_1 y_3) & \cdots & E(y_1 y_N) \\ E(y_2 y_1) & E(y_2^2) & E(y_2 y_3) & \cdots & E(y_2 y_N) \\ \vdots & \vdots & \vdots & \ddots & \vdots \\ E(y_N y_1) & E(y_N y_2) & E(y_N y_3) & \cdots & E(y_N^2) \end{pmatrix}$$

$$= \begin{pmatrix} \sigma_1^2 & \sigma_{12} & \sigma_{13} & \cdots & \sigma_{1N} \\ \sigma_{21} & \sigma_2^2 & \sigma_{23} & \cdots & \sigma_{2N} \\ \vdots & \vdots & \vdots & \ddots & \vdots \\ \sigma_{N1} & \sigma_{N2} & \sigma_{N3} & \cdots & \sigma_N^2 \end{pmatrix},$$

where σ_i^2 is the variance of y_i, and σ_{ij} is the covariance of y_i and y_j.

Properties of Estimators

This appendix is concerned with the properties of estimators. These properties fall into two categories—finite sample properties and asymptotic properties. The former are typically difficult to establish except for simple cases. In consequence, attention is most often given to asymptotic properties. These characterize large sample behavior by means of the limit properties of the estimator as the sample size tends to infinity. For the sake of simplicity, the discussion here focuses exclusively on the case of the sample mean. To emphasize that the sample mean is a function of the sample size, it is now written with a T subscript.

$$\widehat{\mu}_T = \frac{1}{T} \sum_{t=1}^{T} x_t,$$

which is used to estimate the population mean, μ, given a sample of T observations $\{x_1, x_2, \cdots, x_T\}$ that are drawn from a population with mean μ.

B.1 FINITE SAMPLE PROPERTIES

B.1.1 Unbiasedness

An unbiased estimator is one whose mathematical expectation is equal to the true value of the population parameter, or

$$\mathrm{E}(\widehat{\mu}_T) = \mu.$$

The (frequentist) interpretation of the mathematical expectation is that in repeated sampling of the population, the sample mean estimator $\widehat{\mu}_T$ will on average yield the true population value. If the sampling distribution of the estimator is symmetric, the property of unbiasedness means that the distribution of $\widehat{\mu}_T$ is centered on the true population value μ. If $\mathrm{E}(\widehat{\mu}_T) \neq \mu$, then the estimator is said to be biased. If there is bias, then $\mathrm{E}(\widehat{\mu}_T)$ provides information about the location of the finite sample distribution of $\widehat{\mu}_T$, giving the mean of that sampling distribution.

The expected value of the sample mean, $\widehat{\mu}_T$, is

$$\mathrm{E}(\widehat{\mu}_T) = \mathrm{E}\left(\frac{1}{T}\sum_{t=1}^{T} x_t\right) = \frac{1}{T}\sum_{t=1}^{T} \mathrm{E}(x_t) = \frac{1}{T}T\mu = \mu,$$

so that the sample mean is an unbiased estimator of the population mean in random sampling where $E(x_t) = \mu$. Notice that unbiasedness does not depend on the sample size and is an exact finite sample property.

B.1.2 Efficiency

While unbiasedness concerns the location of a sampling distribution in relation to the true value of a parameter, efficiency refers to the dispersion of the sampling distribution of $\widehat{\mu}_T$ about the true value. This dispersion is often measured by the variance of the sampling distribution. An estimator is said to be *efficient* when it is both unbiased and has minimum variance in the class of all other unbiased estimators. One way to show that an estimator is efficient is to demonstrate that its variance attains the so-called Cramér–Rao lower bound. The Cramér–Rao inequality establishes a lower bound for the covariance matrix of any unbiased estimator (see, for example, Martin, Hurn, and Harris, (2013)). Finite sample efficient estimators are always minimum variance, unbiased estimators. Although the Cramér–Rao inequality is a powerful general result, its use requires that the distribution of the underlying population be known because it is derived using likelihood theory (see Chapter 10). Moreover, in view of the stringency of the criteria involved, finite sample efficient estimators are uncommon in practical work.

A property that is less strict than efficiency and much easier to establish is the minimum variance estimator for the class of linear unbiased estimators. An estimator that satisfies this condition is known as the best linear unbiased estimator (BLUE). It is possible to demonstrate that $\widehat{\mu}_T$ is the BLUE of μ. A linear estimator has the form

$$\widehat{\theta}_T = \sum_{t=1}^{T} \omega_t x_t, \tag{B.1}$$

in which ω_t are weights to be determined, and the data, x_t, are independently and identically distributed. Under random sampling, this estimator has expected value and variance given by

$$E(\widehat{\theta}_T) = \sum_{t=1}^{T} \omega_t E(x_t) = E(x_t) \sum_{t=1}^{T} \omega_t$$

$$\text{var}(\widehat{\theta}_T) = \sum_{t=1}^{T} \omega_t^2 \text{var}(x_t) = \text{var}(x_t) \sum_{t=1}^{T} \omega_t^2,$$

respectively. Since $\text{var}(x_t)$ is a constant, the best (minimum variance) linear unbiased estimator then solves

$$\min_{\omega_t} \sum_{t=1}^{T} \omega_t^2 \quad \text{subject to} \sum_{t=1}^{T} \omega_t = 1.$$

Recognize that

$$\sum_{t=1}^{T} \omega_t = 1 \Rightarrow \omega_1 = \left(1 - \sum_{t=2}^{T} \omega_t\right),$$

so that

$$\min \mathcal{L}(\omega_2, \cdots, \omega_T) = \left(1 - \sum_{t=2}^{T} \omega_t\right)^2 + \sum_{t=2}^{T} \omega_t^2.$$

The first-order conditions for a minimum require that for any j

$$\frac{\partial \mathcal{L}}{\partial \omega_j} = -2\left(1 - \sum_{t=2}^{T} \omega_t\right) + 2\omega_j = -2\omega_1 + 2\omega_j = 0.$$

It therefore follows that $\omega_1 = \omega_j \ \forall j$ and this requires that $\omega_t = 1/T$. From equation (B.1) it follows that

$$\widehat{\theta}_T = \widehat{\mu}_T = \frac{1}{T}\sum_{t=1}^{T} x_t.$$

In other words, the BLUE of the population mean is the sample mean under random sampling.

B.2 ASYMPTOTIC PROPERTIES

The limiting properties of an estimator or test statistic as the sample size increases indefinitely are known as large sample or asymptotic properties. In view of their complexity, most procedures that are now in use in financial econometrics are justified in terms of their asymptotic properties. Simulation studies are then used to explore their finite sample behavior and to determine whether reliance may be placed on asymptotic properties and the conditions under which this is so. When asymptotic properties are shown in finite sample simulations to be unreliable, for instance in distortions of the size of statistical tests, modifications to testing procedures have been developed to improve their finite sample performance. These modifications include resampling, subsampling, and bootstrap methods which are discussed in more advanced textbooks.

B.2.1 Consistency

Consistency is the large sample property of an estimator $\widehat{\mu}_T$ that characterizes how the distance between $\widehat{\mu}_T$ and the true value μ diminishes in a probabilistic sense to zero as the sample size T increases to infinity. A consistent estimator is one where information continues to accumulate fast enough about the true value as the sample size grows to ensure that eventually the estimator converges to the true value. It is important to understand that even though $\widehat{\mu}_T$ approaches μ, the approach is probabilistic, not deterministic, because $\widehat{\mu}_T$ forms a sequence of random variables and not a deterministic sequence. This idea is expressed formally as

$$\text{plim}\,\widehat{\mu}_T = \mu,$$

where "plim" denotes convergence in probability. The property of consistency is satisfied when the estimator $\widehat{\mu}_T$ is asymptotically unbiased and its variance or another measure of dispersion converges to zero as T increases. However, these conditions are much stronger than is required. It is often possible to demonstrate that an estimator is consistent even in cases where the finite sample mean and variance of the estimator are not finite. Consistency is often regarded as a minimum requirement for a useful estimator in the sense that if the population remains stable, an infinite amount of random sample information should be sufficient to learn about the characteristics of that population.

It has already been established that $\widehat{\mu}_T$ is an unbiased estimator of μ and it is therefore also asymptotically unbiased. The variance of $\widehat{\mu}_T$ is

$$\text{var}(\widehat{\mu}_T) = \text{var}\left(\frac{1}{T}\sum_{t=1}^{T} x_t\right) = \frac{1}{T^2}\sum_{t=1}^{T} \text{var}(x_t) = \frac{1}{T^2}T\sigma^2 = \frac{\sigma^2}{T},$$

which becomes smaller as T becomes larger. It follows therefore that $\widehat{\mu}_T$ is a consistent estimator of μ and satifies

$$\text{plim}\,\widehat{\mu}_T = \mu,$$

or

$$\frac{1}{T}\sum_{t=1}^{T} x_t = \widehat{\mu}_T \xrightarrow{p} \mu.$$

The second statement, which emphasizes that a sample moment converges in probability to its population counterpart, is an example of an important class of results in statistics called laws of large numbers (see Martin et al., 2013).

The consistency of the sample mean as an estimator of the population mean is demonstrated in Figure B.1. In the left panel, for sample sizes less than $T < 50$, $\widehat{\mu}_T$ is rather erratic. For samples greater than $T > 100$, $\widehat{\mu}_T$ becomes closer and closer to μ as T increases. Notice that even though $\widehat{\mu}_T$ approaches μ, it never quite equals μ because $\widehat{\mu}_T$ is a random

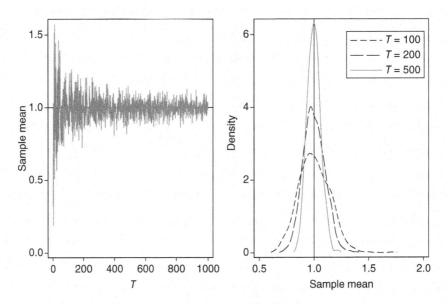

FIGURE B.1 Visualizing the consistency of the sample mean as an estimator of the population mean when the population is the chi-squared distribution with one degree of freedom, that is, $\mu = 1$. In the left panel the sample mean is used to estimate the population mean for samples of increasing size, T. In the right panel, the sampling distributions of the sample mean are computed for samples of size 100, 200, and 500 using 10000 draws to construct the distribution in each case.

variable and not a deterministic sequence. The right panel shows the distributions of the estimator $\widehat{\mu}_T$ for three sample sizes (100, 200, 500). For sample size 500, the distribution is apparently much tighter around unity than that of the distributions based on samples of size 100 and 200.

B.2.2 Asymptotic Normality

The behavior of the sampling distribution of an estimator as the sample size becomes infinitely large is complicated by the fact that for consistent estimators, the variance of the distribution tends to become infinitely small as $T \to \infty$. Consequently, it is usual to work with scaled versions of the distributions of the form $\sqrt{T}(\widehat{\mu}_T - \mu)$ in which the distribution is centered about the population value of the parameter (in this case, the mean μ) and scaled (usually by the square root of the sample size) to ensure that its variance is constant as T grows. Central limit theorems[1] are invoked to establish the conditions under which the distribution of a suitably standardized and centered estimator converges to a normal distribution.

The Lindberg–Lévy central limit theorem states that the distribution of the centered and scaled sample mean $\widehat{\mu}_T$ of independently and identically distributed drawings of a random variable with finite mean μ and finite variance σ^2 converges to a normal distribution with mean 0 and variance σ^2 as the sample size increases. Formally, the theorem states that

$$\sqrt{T}(\widehat{\mu}_T - \mu) \xrightarrow{d} N(0, \sigma^2),$$

where the notation $\xrightarrow{d}$ is read as "converges in distribution to," and the asymptotic variance of the sample mean is in fact σ^2. Alternatively, the implied asymptotic distribution of $\widehat{\mu}_T$ may be written in the form

$$\widehat{\mu}_T \overset{a}{\sim} N\left(\mu, \frac{\sigma^2}{T}\right),$$

where $\overset{a}{\sim}$ is taken to mean "is asymptotically distributed as." Note that there is no requirement that the population is a normal distribution for the appropriately scaled sampling distribution of the sample mean to converge to a normal distribution. Although the Lindberg–Lévy version of the central limit theorem does require a random sample that comprises independent and identically distributed drawings, there are many other central limit theorems that considerably relax this assumption and allow for weakly dependent and heterogeneously distributed observations.

Figure B.2 illustrates the asymptotic normality of the sampling distribution of the sample mean. In this instance, the *iid* drawings are taken from a population that is a χ^2_1 distribution in which $\mu = 1$ and $\sigma^2 = 2$. By the Lindberg–Lévy central limit theorem

$$\sqrt{T}(\widehat{\mu}_T - 1) \xrightarrow{d} N(0, 2).$$

The distributions of the sample mean for sample sizes of 100 and 500 are shown together with the relevant (asymptotic) normal distribution.

---

[1] The term *central limit theorem* was introduced by the Hungarian mathematician George Pólya in 1920 to characterize the property that a limit distribution of a standardized sum of random variables is normal under certain conditions.

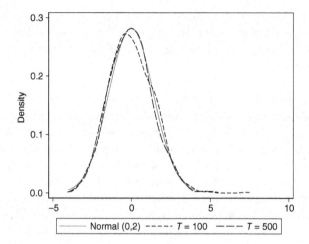

FIGURE B.2 The appropriately centered and scaled distribution of the sample mean approaches the normal distribution as the sample size grows. The sample mean is asymptotically normally distributed.

Linear Regression Model in Matrix Notation

Define the following column vectors

$$y = \begin{pmatrix} y_1 \\ y_2 \\ \vdots \\ y_T \end{pmatrix}, \quad \beta = \begin{pmatrix} \beta_0 \\ \beta_1 \\ \vdots \\ \beta_k \end{pmatrix}, \quad u = \begin{pmatrix} u_1 \\ u_2 \\ \vdots \\ u_T \end{pmatrix}, \quad \widehat{\beta} = \begin{pmatrix} \widehat{\beta}_0 \\ \widehat{\beta}_1 \\ \vdots \\ \widehat{\beta}_k \end{pmatrix}, \quad \widehat{u} = \begin{pmatrix} \widehat{u}_1 \\ \widehat{u}_2 \\ \vdots \\ \widehat{u}_T \end{pmatrix},$$

and the matrix

$$X = \begin{pmatrix} 1 & x_{11} & \cdots & x_{1K} \\ 1 & x_{21} & \cdots & x_{2K} \\ \vdots & \vdots & \cdots & \vdots \\ 1 & x_{T1} & \cdots & x_{TK} \end{pmatrix}.$$

The population multiple regression model is written in observation form as

$$y = X\beta + u,$$

and the ordinary least squares estimator of β is given by

$$\widehat{\beta} = \left(X'X\right)^{-1} X'y.$$

The only requirement here is that the matrix inverse $\left(X'X\right)^{-1}$ exists. For this requirement to be met, the matrix X is required to be of full rank, that is, no column of X is a linear combination of the remaining columns. It can be further shown that

$$\mathrm{E}(\widehat{\beta}) = \beta,$$
$$\mathrm{var}(\widehat{\beta}) = \sigma_u^2 \left(X'X\right)^{-1},$$

where $\sigma_u^2 = \mathrm{var}(u_t)$. The asymptotic distribution of the ordinary least squares estimator is

$$\widehat{\beta} \overset{a}{\sim} N(\beta, \sigma_u^2 (X'X)^{-1}),$$

or, equivalently, in centered form

$$\sqrt{T}(\widehat{\beta} - \beta) \overset{a}{\sim} N(0, \sigma_u^2 (X'X/T)^{-1}).$$

As with the bivariate regression model discussed in Section 3.1, the disturbance variance σ^2 is replaced by the least squares estimator $\widehat{\sigma}^2$, which is written in matrix notation as

$$\widehat{\sigma}_u^2 = \frac{\widehat{u}'\widehat{u}}{T},$$

where

$$\widehat{u} = y - X\widehat{\beta}$$

is the vector of least squares residuals. Alternatively, the denominator in the variance estimator $\widehat{\sigma}^2$ may be replaced by $T - K - 1$, where $K + 1$ is the number of columns in the matrix X, which delivers an unbiased estimator of σ^2.

The least squares formulas for the multiple regression model are demonstrated using the same data as used in Chapter 3. The estimates for the Nondurables portfolio reported in Table 3.1 are now computed using the matrix formulation. The y and X matrices, respectively, are

$$y = \begin{pmatrix} -0.92 \\ 3.16 \\ 2.46 \\ 3.12 \\ 7.88 \\ -2.03 \\ \vdots \\ 2.95 \\ -4.00 \\ 1.94 \\ 4.75 \\ 1.29 \\ 2.65 \end{pmatrix}, \quad X = \begin{pmatrix} 1 & -0.11 \\ 1 & 4.11 \\ 1 & -0.15 \\ 1 & 0.52 \\ 1 & 5.40 \\ 1 & -2.04 \\ \vdots & \vdots \\ 1 & 5.65 \\ 1 & -2.69 \\ 1 & 3.76 \\ 1 & 4.17 \\ 1 & 3.12 \\ 1 & 2.81 \end{pmatrix}.$$

The following moment matrices are needed

$$X'X = \begin{pmatrix} 1044.0000 & 673.3100 \\ 673.3100 & 31147.2117 \end{pmatrix}, \quad X'y = \begin{pmatrix} 724.7300 \\ 23740.9082 \end{pmatrix}.$$

The least squares estimates are then deduced as follows

$$\begin{aligned} \widehat{\beta} &= (X'X)^{-1}X'y \\ &= \begin{pmatrix} 1044.0000 & 673.3100 \\ 673.3100 & 31147.2117 \end{pmatrix}^{-1} \begin{pmatrix} 724.7300 \\ 23740.9082 \end{pmatrix} \\ &= \begin{pmatrix} 0.000971 & -0.000021 \\ -0.000021 & 0.000033 \end{pmatrix} \begin{pmatrix} 724.7300 \\ 23740.9082 \end{pmatrix} \\ &= \begin{pmatrix} 0.2055 \\ 0.7578 \end{pmatrix}, \end{aligned}$$

and the residual variance is

$$\widehat{\sigma}_u^2 = \frac{\widehat{u}'\widehat{u}}{T-2} = \frac{5026.2404}{1044-2} = 4.8236.$$

These estimates agree with the estimates reported in Section 3.1 for the bivariate model using summation notation.

Finally, the asymptotic covariance matrix of the least squares estimator $\widehat{\beta}$, with σ_u^2 replaced by $\widehat{\sigma}_u^2$, is

$$\mathrm{var}(\widehat{\beta}) = \widehat{\sigma}^2 \left(X'X\right)^{-1}$$

$$= 4.823 \times \begin{pmatrix} 0.000971 & -0.000021 \\ -0.000021 & 0.000033 \end{pmatrix}$$

$$= \begin{pmatrix} 0.004686 & -0.000101 \\ -0.000101 & 0.000157 \end{pmatrix}.$$

Extracting the diagonal elements of this matrix and computing the square roots of these terms produces the standard errors of the least squares estimators

$$se(\widehat{\alpha}) = \sqrt{0.0047} = 0.0684, \qquad se(\widehat{\beta}) = \sqrt{0.0002} = 0.0125.$$

Numerical Optimization

There are many important estimation techniques in econometrics for which a closed-form solution of the estimator does not exist. Applications in financial econometrics frequently lead to such problems. Two cases of particular importance are found in Chapters 9 and 10, which deal with GMM and maximum likelihood estimation, where extremum estimation procedures are employed. For notational simplicity and without loss of generality, the discussion here will focus on maximum likelihood estimation. The maximum likelihood estimator of θ is given by

$$\widehat{\theta} = \arg\max_{\theta} \log L(\theta).$$

By convention, optimization algorithms are usually presented in terms of function minimization. To accommodate maximum likelihood within this framework, the maximization problem is re-expressed as a minimization function where the parameters, θ, are obtained by minimizing the *negative* of the log-likelihood function with respect to θ,

$$\widehat{\theta} = \arg\min_{\theta} \left(-\log L(\theta)\right).$$

In both these cases, the solution for θ is found using a numerical algorithm.

Optimization algorithms routinely require computation of the first-order derivatives, $G(\theta)$, and second-order derivatives, $H(\theta)$, of the target function $L(\theta)$. These are, respectively,

$$
G(\theta) = \begin{bmatrix} \dfrac{\partial \log L(\theta)}{\partial \theta_1} \\[2mm] \dfrac{\partial \log L(\theta)}{\partial \theta_2} \\[2mm] \vdots \\[2mm] \dfrac{\partial \log L(\theta)}{\partial \theta_K} \end{bmatrix}, \quad
H(\theta) = \begin{bmatrix} \dfrac{\partial^2 \log L(\theta)}{\partial \theta_1 \partial \theta_1} & \dfrac{\partial^2 \log L(\theta)}{\partial \theta_1 \partial \theta_2} & \cdots & \dfrac{\partial^2 \log L(\theta)}{\partial \theta_1 \partial \theta_K} \\[2mm] \dfrac{\partial^2 \log L(\theta)}{\partial \theta_2 \partial \theta_1} & \dfrac{\partial^2 \log L(\theta)}{\partial \theta_2 \partial \theta_2} & \cdots & \dfrac{\partial^2 \log L(\theta)}{\partial \theta_2 \partial \theta_K} \\[2mm] \vdots & \vdots & \vdots & \vdots \\[2mm] \dfrac{\partial^2 \log L(\theta)}{\partial \theta_K \partial \theta_1} & \dfrac{\partial^2 \log L(\theta)}{\partial \theta_K \partial \theta_2} & \cdots & \dfrac{\partial^2 \log L(\theta)}{\partial \theta_K \partial \theta_K} \end{bmatrix}.
$$

Most software packages automatically compute accurate numerical approximations to $G(\theta)$ and $H(\theta)$.

Numerical algorithms begin by taking starting values for the unknown parameter θ and then iterating until a convergence criterion is satisfied. Given some initial guess or estimate $\widehat{\theta}_k$, which is assumed to be near the optimal value θ at which a minimum is attained, the first-order Taylor series expansion of $G(\widehat{\theta})$ about $\widehat{\theta}_k$ gives the approximation

$$G(\widehat{\theta}) \simeq G(\widehat{\theta}_k) + H(\widehat{\theta}_k)(\widehat{\theta} - \widehat{\theta}_k). \tag{D.1}$$

The minimum of the objective function occurs where $G(\widehat{\theta}) = 0$, so setting the expression in equation (D.1) equal to zero, solving for $\widehat{\theta}$, gives

$$\widehat{\theta} = \widehat{\theta}_k - H(\widehat{\theta}_k)^{-1}G(\widehat{\theta}_k).$$

This result suggests an iterative scheme of the form

$$\widehat{\theta}_{k+1} = \widehat{\theta}_k - H(\widehat{\theta}_k)^{-1}G(\widehat{\theta}_k), \tag{D.2}$$

which is indeed the basis of the three most common iterative algorithms, described below, that are used by software packages including Stata or EViews. The second term on the right side of (D.2) provides a correction step to $\widehat{\theta}_k$ leading to the updated estimate $\widehat{\theta}_{k+1}$.

1. Newton–Raphson

The Newton–Raphson update is

$$\widehat{\theta}_{k+1} = \widehat{\theta}_k - \alpha_k H(\widehat{\theta}_k)^{-1}G(\widehat{\theta}_k),$$

where α_k is a parameter that controls the step size and is chosen to ensure that the function value is reduced at each iteration. The algorithm converges quickly in the vicinity of the optimum, but it can be troublesome when $H(\widehat{\theta}_k)$ cannot be computed with sufficient accuracy or when there are multiple optima.

2. BHHH

The Berndt, Hall, Hall, and Hausman (BHHH) algorithm approximates $H(\widehat{\theta})$ by using the outer product of the gradient vector, $J(\widehat{\theta})$, defined in Chapter 10 as

$$J(\widehat{\theta}_k) = \frac{1}{T}\sum_{t=1}^{T} \frac{\partial \log L_t}{\partial \theta} \frac{\partial \log L_t}{\partial \theta'}.$$

The BHHH update is

$$\widehat{\theta}_{k+1} = \widehat{\theta}_k + \alpha_k J(\widehat{\theta}_k)^{-1}G(\widehat{\theta}_k).$$

This algorithm is usually more stable than Newton–Raphson but does not converge as quickly.

3. BFGS

The Broyden, Fletcher, Goldfarb, and Shanno (BFGS) algorithm builds up an approximation to $H(\widehat{\theta})$ in successive iterations starting from an initial estimate, which is usually the identity matrix. The general form for the updating sequence is

$$\widehat{\theta}_{k+1} = \widehat{\theta}_k - \alpha_k A(\widehat{\theta}_k)^{-1}G(\widehat{\theta}_k),$$
$$A_k = A_{k-1} + U_k,$$

where A_k is the estimate of $H(\widehat{\theta})$ at the kth iteration, and U_k is an update matrix. The details of the update are not important except for the fact that it is designed to ensure that $A(\widehat{\theta}_k)$ is well behaved and converges to an accurate estimate of $H(\widehat{\theta})$ as the number of iterations increases.

In theory, there is little basis for choosing among these algorithms. In practice, there are three broad guidelines worth noting.

(i) There is a consensus that the BFGS algorithm is the best practical choice for most applications.

(ii) Newton–Raphson is particularly efficient if the starting values are known to be in the vicinity of the optimum. This is often the case in simulation studies where the true parameters of the data generating process are known.

(iii) The BHHH algorithm is particularly well suited for estimating autoregressive conditional volatility models (Chapters 13 and 14) and autoregressive conditional duration models (Chapter 16).

Simulating Copulas

This appendix shows how to simulate pairs of dependent random variables from copulas. In all cases considered here, the marginals are assumed to be $N(0,1)$, although other marginal distributions could be adopted. In the case of the Gaussian copula with normal marginals, this is equivalent to simulating directly from a bivariate normal distribution.

Bivariate Gaussian Copula

Step 1: Draw two independent $N(0,1)$ random numbers, z_1 and z_2.

Step 2: Generate r_1 and r_2 from the Gaussian copula as

$$r_1 = z_1$$
$$r_2 = z_1\delta + z_2\sqrt{1-\delta^2},$$

for a given dependence parameter δ.

Bivariate Student t Copula

Step 1: Draw random variables from the Gaussian copula as

$$x_1 = z_1$$
$$x_2 = z_1\delta + z_2\sqrt{1-\delta^2},$$

where z_1 and z_2 are independent normals.

Step 2: Draw a χ^2_η random variable, s, where η is the degrees of freedom parameter, and generate the Student t random variables

$$v_1 = \frac{x_1}{\sqrt{s/\eta}}, \qquad v_2 = \frac{x_2}{\sqrt{s/\eta}}.$$

The vector (v_1, v_2) has a bivariate t distribution with η degrees of freedom and correlation parameter δ.

Step 3: Set

$$u_1 = F(v_1; \eta), \qquad u_2 = F(v_2; \eta),$$

where $F(\cdot; \eta)$ is the cumulative distribution function of the univariate Student t distribution with η degrees of freedom. The variates u_1, u_2 are now uniformly distributed on $[0, 1]^2$

Step 4: Transform the uniform random variables, u_1 and u_2, from the Student t copula using the normal quantile function Φ^{-1}

$$r_1 = \Phi^{-1}(u_1), \qquad r_2 = \Phi^{-1}(u_2),$$

where Φ is the cumulative normal distribution function.

Bivariate Clayton Copula

Step 1: Generate two independent uniform random numbers on the unit interval, v_1 and v_2.

Step 2: Generate two random variables, u_1 and u_2, as

$$u_1 = v_1$$
$$u_2 = \left(v_1^{-\delta} \left(v_2^{-\delta/(\delta+1)} - 1 \right) + 1 \right)^{-1/\delta},$$

for a given dependence parameter δ.

Step 3: Transform the uniform random numbers, u_1 and u_2, from the Clayton copula using the normal quantile function

$$r_1 = \Phi^{-1}(u_1), \qquad r_2 = \Phi^{-1}(u_2).$$

Bivariate Gumbel Copula

The steps to simulate a Gumbel copula with dependence parameter δ are more involved than they are for the other copulas. For more details, see Trivedi and Zimmer (2005).

Step 1: Draw a random variable w from $U(0, \pi)$.

Step 2: Draw a random variable x from the exponential distribution with mean of 1.

Step 3: Generate the random variable

$$k = \frac{\sin((1-\alpha)w)(\sin(\alpha w))^{\alpha/(1-\alpha)}}{(\sin(w))^{1/(1-\alpha)}},$$

where $\alpha = 1/\delta$ is the inverse of the dependence parameter.

Step 4: Generate the random variable

$$y = \left(\frac{k}{x} \right)^{(1-\alpha)/\alpha}.$$

Step 5: Generate two independent uniform random variables v_1 and v_2.

Step 6: Generate two random variables u_1 and u_2, as

$$u_1 = \exp\left(-\left(-\frac{\log v_1}{y} \right)^{1/\delta} \right), \qquad u_2 = \exp\left(-\left(-\frac{\log v_2}{y} \right)^{1/\delta} \right).$$

Step 7: Transform u_1 and u_2, from the Gumbel copula using the normal quantile function as

$$r_1 = \Phi^{-1}(u_1), \qquad r_2 = \Phi^{-1}(u_2).$$

Bivariate Frank Copula

Step 1: Generate two independent uniform random numbers on the unit interval, v_1 and v_2.

Step 2: Generate two random variables u_1 and u_2 as

$$u_1 = v_1$$

$$u_2 = -\frac{1}{\delta} \log \left(1 + \frac{v_2 \left(1 - e^{-\delta}\right)}{v_2 \left(e^{-\delta v_1} - 1\right) - e^{-\delta v_1}} \right),$$

for a given dependence parameter δ.

Step 3: Transform u_1 and u_2 from the Frank copula using the normal quantile function

$$r_1 = \Phi^{-1}(u_1), \qquad r_2 = \Phi^{-1}(u_2).$$

BIBLIOGRAPHY

Adams, R., Almeida, H., and Ferreira, D. 2009. Understanding the relationship between founder-CEOs and firm performance. *Journal of Empirical Finance*, **16**, 136–150.

Aït-Sahalia, Y. 1996. Testing continuous-time models of the spot interest rate. *Review of Financial Studies*, **9**, 385–426.

Aït-Sahalia, Y., and Jacod, J. 2012. Analyzing the spectrum of asset returns: Jump and volatility components in high frequency data. *Journal of Economic Literature*, **50**, 1007–1050.

Akaike, H. 1974. A new look at the statistical model identification. *I.E.E.E. Transactions on Automatic Control*, **19**, 716–723.

Akaike, H. 1976. Canonical correlation analysis of time series and the use of an information criterion. In: Mehra, R., and Lainotis, D. G. (eds.), *System Identification: Advances and Case Studies*, 52–107. New York: Academic Press.

Aldrich, J. 1997. RA Fisher and the making of maximum likelihood 1912–1922. *Statistical Science*, **12**, 162–176.

Amenc, N., Goltz, F., Tang, L., and Vaidyanathan, V. 2012. *EDHEC-Risk North American Index Survey 2011*. Tech. rept. EDHEC-Risk Institute Publication.

Andersen, T. G., Bollerslev, T., Diebold, F. X., and Labys, P. 2001. The distribution of exchange rate volatility. *Journal of the American Statistical Association*, **96**, 42–55.

Anderson, R. C., and Reeb, D. M. 2003. Founding-family ownership and firm performance: Evidence from the S&P 500. *Journal of Finance*, **58**, 1301–1327.

Anderson, T. W., and Hsiao, C. 1981. Estimation of dynamic models with error components. *Journal of the American Statistical Association*, **76**, 598–606.

Andrews, D. W. K. 2001. Testing when a parameter is on the boundary of the maintained hypothesis. *Econometrica*, **69**, 683–734.

Andrews, D. W. K., and Stock, J. H. 2005. *Inference with weak instruments*. Working Paper. National Bureau of Economic Research, Cambridge, Mass.

Arellano, M., and Bond, S. 1991. Some tests of specification for panel data: Monte Carlo evidence and an application to employment equations. *Review of Economic Studies*, **58**, 277–297.

Arellano, M., and Bover, O. 1995. Another look at the instrumental variable estimation of error-components models. *Journal of Econometrics*, **68**, 29–51.

Bae, K. H., Karolyi, G. A., and Stultz, R. M. 2003. A new approach to measuring financial contagion. *Review of Financial Studies*, **16**, 717–763.

Bai, J., and Ng, S. 2002. Determining the number of factors in approximate factor models. *Econometrica*, **70**, 191–221.

Baillie, R. T., and Myers, R. J. 1989. *Modeling commodity price distributions and estimating the optimal futures hedge*. Working Paper. Columbia University.

Baillie, R. T., and Myers, R. J. 1991. Bivariate GARCH esimation of the optimal commodity futures hedge. *Journal of Applied Econometrics*, **6**, 109–124.

Bali, T. G., and Peng, L. 2006. Is there a risk–return trade-off? Evidence from high-frequency data. *Journal of Applied Econometrics*, **21**, 1169–1198.

Baltagi, B. H., and Kao, C. 2000. Nonstationary panels, cointegration in panels and dynamic panels: A survey, 7–52. In: Baltagi, B. H. (ed), *Nonstationary Panels, Panel Cointegration and Dynamic Panels*. Amsterdam: Elsevier.

Banerjee, A., Dolado, J. J., Galbraith, J. W., and Hendry, D. F. 1993. *Co-integration, Error Correction, and the Econometric Analysis of Non-Stationarity*. Advanced Texts in Econometrics. Oxford: Oxford University Press.

Barndorff-Nielsen, O. E., and Shephard, N. 2002. Econometric analysis of realized volatility and its use in estimating stochastic volatility models. *Journal of Royal Statistical Society, Series B*, **64**, 253–280.

Barndorff-Nielsen, O. E., and Shephard, N. 2004. Power and bipower variation with stochastic volatility and jumps. *Journal of Financial Econometrics*, **2**, 1–37.

Barndorff-Nielsen, O. E., Hansen, P. R., Lunde, A., and Shephard, N. 2008. Designing realized kernels to measure the ex post variation of equity prices in the presence of noise. *Econometrica*, **76**, 1481–1536.

Barndorff-Nielsen, O. E., Hansen, P. R., Lunde, A., and Shephard, N. 2009. Realized kernels in practice: Trades and quotes. *Econometrics Journal*, **12**, C1–C32.

Barndorff-Nielsen, O. E., Hansen, P. R., Lunde, A., and Shephard, N. 2011. Multivariate realised kernels: Consistent positive and semi-definite estimators of the covariance of equity prices with noise and non-synchronous trading. *Journal of Econometrics*, **162**, 149–169.

Bartlett, M. S. 1950. Periodogram analysis and continuous spectra. *Biometrika*, **37**, 1–16.

Bates, J., and Granger, C. W. J. 1969. The combination of forecasts. *Operations Research Quarterly*, **20**, 451–468.

Becker, R., Clements, A. E., Doolan, M. B., and Hurn, A. S. 2015. Selecting volatility forecasting models for portfolio allocation purposes. *International Journal of Forecasting*, **31**, 849–861.

Bekaert, G., and Hoerova, M. 2016. What do asset prices have to say about risk appetite and uncertainty? *Journal of Banking and Finance*, 67, 103–118.

Bekaert, G., Hoyem, K., Hu, W-Y., and Ravina, E. 2017. Who is internationally diversified? Evidence from 401(k) plans of 296 firms. *Journal of Financial Economics*, 124, 86–112.

Bergstrom, A. R. 1967. *The Construction and Use of Economic Models*. London: English Universities Press.

Black, F., and Scholes, M. 1973. The pricing of options and corporate liabilities. *Journal of Political Economy*, **81**, 637–654.

Blundell, R., and Bond, S. 1998. Initial conditions and moment restrictions in dynamic panel data models. *Journal of Econometrics*, **87**, 115–143.

Bollerslev, T. 1986. Generalized autogressive conditional heteroskedasticity. *Journal of Econometrics*, **31**, 307–327.

Bollerslev, T., and Wooldridge, J. M. 1992. Quasi-maximum likelihood estimation and inference in dynamic models with time-varying covariances. *Econometric Reviews*, **11**, 143–172.

Bollerslev, T., Gibson, M., and Zhou, H. 2011. Dynamic estimation of volatility risk premia and investor risk aversion from option-implied and realized volatilities. *Journal of Econometrics*, **160**, 235–245.

Bollerslev, T., Patton, A. J., and Quaedvlieg, R. 2016. Exploiting the errors: A simple approach to improved volatility forecasting. *Journal of Econometrics*, **192**, 1–18.

Bonhomme, S., and Manresa, E. 2015. Grouped patterns of heterogeneity in panel data. *Econometrica*, **83**, 1147–1184.

Bound, J., Jaeger, D., and Baker, R. 1995. Problems with instrumental variable estimation when the correlation between the instruments and the endogenous explanatory variables is weak. *Journal of the American Statistical Association*, **90**, 443–450.

Brennan, M. J., and Schwartz, E. S. 1980. Analyzing convertible bonds. *Journal of Financial and Quantitative Analysis*, **15**, 907–929.

Brockwell, P. J., and Davis, R. A. 1991. *Time Series: Theory and Methods*. 2nd ed. New York: Springer Verlag.

Brownlees, C., and Engle, R. F. 2016. SRISK: A conditional capital shortfall measure of systemic risk. *Review of Financial Studies*, **30**, 48–79.

Buckland, S. T., Burnham, K. P., and Augustin, N. H. 1997. Model selection: An integral part of inference. *Biometrics*, **53**, 603–618.

Burnham, K. P., and Anderson, D. R. 2002. *Model selection and multimodel inference: A practical information theoretic approach*. 2nd ed. New York: Springer.

Campbell, J. Y., and Shiller, R. J. 1987. Cointegration and tests of present value models. *Journal of Political Economy*, **95**, 1062–1088.

Campbell, J. Y., and Shiller, R. J. 1991. Yield spreads and interest rate movements: A bird's eye view. *Review of Economic Studies*, **58**, 495–514.

Campbell, J. Y., and Yogo, M. 2006. Efficient tests of stock return predictability. *Journal of Financial Economics*, **81**, 27–60.

Campbell, J. Y., Lo, A. W., and MacKinlay, A. C. 1997. *The Econometrics of Financial Markets*. Princeton, New Jersey: Princeton University Press.

Carhart, M. M. 1997. On persistence in mutual fund performance. *Journal of Finance*, **52**, 57–82.

Chan, K. C., Karolyi, G. A., Longstaff, F. A., and Sanders, A. B. 1992. An empirical comparison of alternative models of the short term interest rate. *Journal of Finance*, **52**, 1209–1227.

Chao, J. C., and Phillips, P. C. B. 1999. Model selection in partially nonstationary vector autoregressive processes with reduced rank structure. *Journal of Econometrics*, **91**, 227–271.

Cheng, X., and Phillips, P. C. B. 2009. Semiparametric cointegrating rank selection. *The Econometrics Journal*, **12**, S83–S104.

Cheng, X., and Phillips, P. C. B. 2012. Cointegrating rank selection in models with time-varying variance. *Journal of Econometrics*, **169**, 155–165.

Chernozhukov, V., and Hansen, C. 2008. The reduced form: A simple approach to inference with weak instruments. *Economics Letters*, **100**, 68–71.

Choi, I. 2001. Unit root tests for panel data. *Journal of International Money and Finance*, **20**, 249–272.

Christoffersen, P. F. 2012. *Elements of Financial Risk Management*. Oxford: Academic Press.

Clemen, R. T. 1989. Combining forecasts: A review and annotated bibliography. *International Journal of Forecasting*, **5**, 559–581.

Clements, A. E., Hurn, A. S., and Volkov, V. V. 2015. Volatility patterns in global financial markets. *Journal of Empirical Finance*, **32**, 3–18.

Cochrane, J. H. 2008. The dog that did not bark: A defense of return predictability. *Review of Financial Studies*, **21**, 1533–1575.

Corbae, D., Lim, K.-G., and Ouliaris, S. 1992. On cointegration and tests of forward market unbiasedness. *Review of Economics and Statistics*, **74**, 728–732.

Corsi, F. 2009. A simple approximate long-memory model of realized volatility. *Journal of Financial Econometrics*, **7**, 174–196.

Cox, J. C., Ingersoll, J. E., and Ross, S. A. 1985. A theory of the term structure of interest rates. *Econometrica*, **53**, 385–407.

Cramér, H. 1946. *Mathematical Methods of Statistics*. Princeton University Press.

Davidson, R., and MacKinnon, J. G. 1989. Testing for consistency using artificial regressions. *Econometric Theory*, **5**, 363–384.

Davidson, R., and MacKinnon, J. G. 1993. *Estimation and Inference in Econometrics*. Oxford: Oxford University Press.

Diba, B. T., and Grossman, H. I. 1988. Explosive rational bubbles in stock prices? *American Economic Review*, **78**, 520–530.

Dickey, D. A., and Fuller, W. A. 1979. Distributions of the estimators for autoregressive time series with a unit root. *Journal of the American Statistical Association*, **74**, 427–431.

Dickey, D. A., and Fuller, W. A. 1981. Likelihood ratio statistics for autogressive time series with a unit root. *Econometrica*, **49**, 1057–1072.

Diebold, F. X., and Li, C. 2006. Forecasting the term structure of government bond yields. *Journal of Econometrics*, **130**, 337–364.

Diebold, F. X., and Mariano, R. S. 1995. Comparing predictive accuracy. *Journal of Business and Economic Statistics*, **13**, 253–263.

Diebold, F. X., and Yilmaz, K. 2009. Measuring financial asset return and volatility spillovers, with application to global equity. *Economic Journal*, **119**, 158–171.

Diebold, F. X., Gunther, T. A., and Tsay, R. S. 1998. Evaluating density forecasts with applications to financial risk managment. *International Economic Review*, **39**, 863–883.

Dungey, M., and Jacobs, J. P. A. M., and Lestano, L. 2015. The internationalization of financial crises: Banking and currency crises 1883–2008. *North American Journal of Banking and Finance*, **32**, 29–47.

Dungey, M., Fakhrutdinova, L., and Goodhart, C. A. E. 2009. After-hours trading in equity futures markets. *Journal of Futures Markets*, **29**, 114–136.

Durbin, J. 1959. Efficient estimation of parameters in moving-average models. *Biometrika*, **46**, 306–316.

Durbin, J. 1988. Maximum likelihood estimation of the parameters of a system of simultaneous regression equations. *Econometric Theory*, **4**, 159–170.

Eisler, Z., Bouchard, J.-P., and Kockelkoren, J. 2012. The price impact of order book events: Market orders, limit orders and cancellations. *Quantitative Finance*, **12**, 1395–1419.

Elliott, G. 2011. *Averaging and the optimal combination of forecasts.* Unpublished manuscript, UCSD.

Elliott, G., and Timmerman, A. 2008. Economic forecasting. *Journal of Economic Literature*, **46**, 3–56.

Elliott, G., and Timmerman, A. 2016. *Economic Forecasting.* Princeton, New Jersey: Princeton University Press.

Elliott, G., Rothenberg, T. J., and Stock, J. H. 1996. Efficient tests for an autoregressive unit root. *Econometrica*, **64**, 813–836.

Engle, R. F. 1982. Autoregressive conditional heteroskedasticity with estimates of the variance of United Kingdom inflation. *Econometrica*, **50**, 987–1008.

Engle, R. F. 2000. The econometrics of ultra-high-frequency data. *Econometrica*, **68**, 1–22.

Engle, R. F. 2002. Dynamic conditional correlation. A simple class of multivariate generalized autoregressive conditional heteroskedasticity models. *Journal of Business and Economic Statistics*, **20**, 339–350.

Engle, R. F., and Colacito, R. 2006. Testing and valuing dynamic correlations for asset allocation. *Journal of Business and Economic Statistics*, **24**, 238–253.

Engle, R. F., and Granger, C. W. J. 1987. Cointegration and error correction: Representation, estimation and testing. *Econometrica*, **55**, 251–276.

Engle, R. F., and Kelly, B. 2009. *Dynamic equicorrelation.* Unpublished manuscript.

Engle, R. F., and Patton, A. J. 2001. What good is a volatility model? *Quantitative Finance*, **1**, 237–245.

Engle, R. F., and Russell, J. R. 1998. Autoregressive conditional duration: A new model for irregularly spaced transaction data. *Econometrica*, **66**, 1127–1162.

Engle, R. F., Ito, T., and Lin, W.-L. 1990. Meteor showers or heat waves? Heteroskedastic intra-daily volatility in the foreign exchange market. *Econometrica*, **58**, 525–542.

Epps, T. W. 1979. Comovements in stock prices in the very short run. *Journal of the American Statistical Association*, **74**, 291–298.

Evans, G. W. 1991. Pitfalls in testing for explosive bubbles in asset prices. *American Economic Review*, **81**, 922–930.

Fama, E. F. 1965. The behavior of stock market prices. *Journal of Business*, **38**, 34–105.

Fama, E. F., and French, K. R. 1988. Permanent and transitory components of stock prices. *Journal of Political Economy*, **96**, 246–273.

Fama, E. F., and French, K. R. 1993. Common risk factors in the returns on stocks and bonds. *Journal of Financial Economics*, **33**, 3–56.

Fama, E. F., and MacBeth, J. D. 1973. Return, risk and equilibrium: Empirical tests. *Journal of Political Economy*, **81**, 607–636.

Fan, Y., and Patton, A. J. 2014. Copulas in econometrics. *Annual Review of Economics*, **6**, 179–200.

Ferson, W. E., and Harvey, C. R. 1992. Seasonality and consumption-based asset pricing. *Journal of Finance*, **47**, 511–552.

Fisher, R. A. 1932. *Statistical Methods for Research Workers*. Edinburgh: Oliver and Boyd.

Flannery, M. J., and Hankins, K. W. 2013. Estimating dynamic panel models in corporate finance. *Journal of Corporate Finance*, **19**, 1–19.

Fleming, J., Kirby, C., and Ostdiek, B. 2001. The economic value of volatility timing. *Journal of Finance*, **56**, 329–352.

Fleming, J., Kirby, C., and Ostdiek, B. 2003. The economic value of volatility timing using realized volatility. *Journal of Financial Economics*, **67**, 473–509.

Garratt, A., Koop, G., and Vahey, S. P. 2008. Forecasting substantial data revisions in the presence of model uncertainty. *Economic Journal*, **18**, 1128–1144.

Ghosh, A., and Bera, A. K. 2005. *Smooth test for density forecast evaluation*. Unpublished manuscript.

Ghysels, E., Santa-Clara, P., and Valkanov, R. 2005. There is a risk-return trade-off after all. *Journal of Financial Economics*, **76**, 509–548.

Gibbons, M., Ross, S. A., and Shanken, J. 1989. A test of the efficiency of a given portfolio. *Econometrica*, **57**, 1121–1152.

Glosten, L. R., Jagannathan, R., and Runkle, D. E. 1993. On the relation between the expected value and the volatility of the nominal excess return on stocks. *Journal of Finance*, **48**, 1779–1801.

Gordon, M. J. 1959. Dividends, earnings and stock prices. *Review of Economics and Statistics*, **41**, 99–105.

Goyal, A., and Welch, I. 2003. Predicting the equity premium with dividend ratios. *Management Science*, **49**, 639–654.

Goyal, A., and Welch, I. 2008. A comprehensive look at the empirical performance of equity premium prediction. *Review of Financial Studies*, **21**, 1455–1508.

Granger, C. W. J. 1969. Investigating causal relations by econometric models and cross-spectral methods. *Econometrica*, **37**, 424–438.

Granger, C. W. J., and Newbold, P. 1974. Spurious regressions in econometrics. *Journal of Econometrics*, **2**, 111–120.

Granger, C. W. J., and Ramanathan, R. 1984. Improved methods for combining forecasts. *Journal of Forecasting*, **3**, 197–204.

Haldane, A. G., and Hall, S. G. 1991. Sterling's relationship with the Dollar and the Deutschemark: 1976–89. *Economic Journal*, **101**, 436–443.

Hall, A. R. 2005. *Generalized Method of Moments*. Oxford: Oxford University Press.

Hamilton, J. D. 1994. *Time Series Analysis*. Princeton, New Jersey: Princeton University Press.

Hannan, E. J. 1980. The estimation of the order of an ARMA process. *Annals of Statistics*, **8**, 1071–1081.

Hannan, E. J., and Quinn, B. G. 1979. The determination of the order of an autoregression. *Journal of the Royal Statistical Society (Series B)*, **41**, 190–195.

Hansen, L. P. 1982. Large sample properties of generalized method of moments estimators. *Econometrica*, **50**, 1029–1054.

Hansen, L. P., and Singleton, K. J. 1982. Generalized instrumental variables estimation of nonlinear rational expectations models. *Econometrica*, **50**, 1269–1286.

Hansen, L. P., Heaton, J., and Yaron, A. 1996. Finite-sample properties of some alternative GMM estimators. *Journal of Business and Economic Statistics*, **14**, 262–280.

Hansen, P. R., and Lunde, A. 2005. A forecast comparison of volatility models: Does anything beat a GARCH(1,1)? *Journal of Applied Econometrics*, **20**, 873–889.

Hansen, P. R., and Lunde, A. 2006. Realized volatility and market microstructure noise. *Journal of Business and Economic Statistics*, **24**, 127–161.

Hansen, P. R., Huang, Z., and Shek, H. H. 2012. Realized GARCH: A joint model for returns and realized measures of volatility. *Journal of Applied Econometrics*, **27**, 877–906.

Harvey, A. C. 1989. *Forecasting, Structural Time Series Models and the Kalman Filter*. Cambridge: Cambridge University Press.

Harvey, A. C., and Thiele, S. 2016. Testing against changing correlation. *Journal of Empirical Finance*, **38**, 575–589.

Hasbrouck, J. 1991. Measuring the information content of stock prices. *Journal of Finance*, **46**, 179–207.

Hausman, J. A. 1978. Specification tests in econometrics. *Econometrica*, **46**, 1251–1271.

Hausman, J. A., Lo, A. W., and MacKinlay, A. C. 1992. An ordered probit analysis of transactions stock prices. *Journal of Financial Economics*, **31**, 319–379.

Hautsch, N., and Huang, R. 2012. The market impact of a limit order. *Journal of Economic Dynamics and Control*, **36**, 501–522.

Hendry, D. F., and Clements, M. 2004. Pooling of forecasts. *Econometrics Journal*, **7**, 1–31.

Hwang, J., and Sun, Y. 2018. Simple, robust, and accurate F and t tests in cointegrated systems. *Econometric Theory*, **34**, 949–984.

Im, K. S., Pesaran, M. H., and Shin, Y. 2003. Testing for unit roots in heterogeneous panels. *Journal of Econometrics*, **115**, 53–74.

Ito, T. 1987. The intra-daily exchange rate dynamics and monetary policy after the G5 agreement. *Journal of Japanese and International Economies*, **1**, 275–298.

Ito, T., and Roley, V. V. 1987. News from the U. S. and Japan: Which moves the Yen/Dollar exchange rate? *Journal of Monetary Economics*, **19**, 255–278.

Jarque, C. M., and Bera, A. K. 1987. A test for normality of observations and regression residuals. *International Statistical Review*, **55**, 163–172.

Jensen, M. C. 1968. The performance of mutual funds in the period 1945–1964. *Journal of Finance*, **23**, 389–416.

Johansen, S. 1988. Statistical analysis of cointegration vectors. *Journal of Economic Dynamics and Control*, **12**, 231–254.

Johansen, S. 1991. Estimation and hypothesis testing of cointegration vectors in Gaussian vector autoregressive models. *Econometrica*, **59**, 1551–1580.

Johansen, S. 1995. *Likelihood-based Inference in Cointegrated Vector Autoregressive Models*. Oxford: Oxford University Press.

Judson, R. A., and Owen, A. L. 1996. Estimating dynamic panel data models: A practical guide for macroeconomists. *Working Paper, Federal Reserve Board of Governors*.

Kanniainen, J., Lin, B., and Yang, H. 2014. Estimating and using GARCH models with VIX data for option valuation. *Journal of Banking and Finance*, **43**, 200–211.

Kao, C., Chiang, M. H., and Chen, B. 1999. International R&D spillovers: An application of estimation and inference in panel cointegration. *Oxford Bulletin of Economics and Statistics*, **61**, 693–711.

Kapetanios, G., Labhard, V., and Price, S. 2008. Forecasting using Bayesian and information-theoretic model averaging: An application to UK inflation. *Journal of Business and Economic Statistics*, **26**, 33–41.

Kasparis, I., Andreou, E., and Phillips, P. C. B. 2015. Nonparametric predictive regression. *Journal of Econometrics*, **185**, 468–494.

Kim, M. J., Nelson, C. R., and Startz, B. 1991. Mean reversion in stock prices? A reappraisal of the empirical evidence. *Review of Economic Studies*, **58**, 515–528.

Kiviet, J. 1995. On bias, inconsistency and efficiency of various estimators in dynamic panel data models. *Journal of Econometrics*, **68**, 53–78.

Kleibergen, Frank. 2002. Pivotal statistics for testing structural parameters in instrumental variables regression. *Econometrica*, **70**, 1781–1803.

Kostakis, A., Magdalinos, T., and Stamatogiannis, M. P. 2014. Robust econometric inference for stock return predictability. *The Review of Financial Studies*, **28**, 1506–1553.

Kwiatkowski, D. P., Phillips, P. C. B., Schmidt, P., and Shin, Y. 1992. Testing the null hypothesis of stationarity against the alternative of a unit root: How sure are we that economic series have a unit root? *Journal of Econometrics*, **54**, 159–178.

Levin, A., Lin, C. F., and Chu, C.-J. 2002. Unit root tests in panel data: Asymptotic and finite-sample properties. *Journal of Econometrics*, **108**, 1–24.

Li, D. X. 1999. The valuation of basket credit derivatives. *CreditMetrics Monitor*, April, 34–50.

Li, D. X. 2000. On default correlation: A copula function approach. *Journal of Fixed Income*, **9**, 43–54.

Liu, L., Patton, A. J., and Sheppard, K. 2015. Does anything beat 5-minute RV? A comparison of realized measures across multiple asset classes. *Journal of Econometrics*, **187**, 293–311.

Lo, D. K., and Hall, A. D. 2015. Resiliency of the limit order book. *Journal of Economic Dynamics and Control*, **61**, 222–244.

Lütkepohl, H. 2005. *New Introduction to Multiple Time Series Analysis*. New York: Springer.

MacKenzie, D., and Spears, T. 2014. The formula that killed Wall Street? The Gaussian copula and modeling practices in investment banking. *Social Studies of Science*, **44**, 393–417.

MacKinnon, J. G. 1991. Critical values for cointegration tests. In: Engle, R. F., and Granger, C. W. J. (eds.), *Long-Run Economic Relationships: Readings in Cointegration*, 266–276. New York: Oxford University Press.

MacKinnon, J. G. 1994. Approximate asymptotic distribution functions for unit-root and cointegration tests. *Journal of Business and Economic Statistics*, **12**, 167–176.

Maddala, G. S., and Wu, S. 1999. A comparative study of unit root tests with panel data and a new simple test. *Oxford Bulletin of Economics and Statistics*, **61**, 631–652.

Malmendier, U., and Nagel, S. 2011. Depression babies: Do macroeconomic experiences affect risk taking? *Quarterly Journal of Economics*, **126**, 373–416.

Mann, H. B., and Wald, A. 1943. On the statistical treatment of linear stochastic difference equations. *Econometrica*, **11**, 173–220.

Martin, V. L., Hurn, A. S., and Harris, D. 2013. *Econometric Modeling with Time Series: Specification, Estimation and Testing*. New York: Cambridge University Press.

Melick, W. R., and Thomas, C. P. 1997. Recovering an asset's implied PDF from option prices: An application to crude oil during the Gulf crisis. *Journal of Financial and Quantitative Analysis*, **32**, 91–115.

Merton, R. C. 1973. An intertemporal capital asset pricing model. *Econometrica*, **41**, 867–887.

Merton, R. C. 1980. On estimating the expected return on the market: An exploratory investigation. *Journal of Financial Economics*, **8**, 323–361.

Millar, R. B. 2011. *Maximum Likelihood Estimation and Inference: With Examples in R, SAS and ADMB.* Chichester: John Wiley and Sons, Inc.

Mincer, J., and Zarnowitz, V. 1969. The Evaluation of Economic Forecasts. In: Zarnowitz, V. (ed.), *Economic Forecasts and Expectations*, 3–46. New York: National Bureau of Economic Research.

Nelson, C. R., and Siegel, A. F. 1987. Parsimonious modeling of yield curves. *Journal of Business*, **60**, 473–489.

Nelson, D. B. 1991. Conditional heteroskedasticity in asset returns: A new approach. *Econometrica*, **59**, 347–370.

Newey, W. K., and West, K. D. 1987. A simple, positive semi-definite, heteroscedasticity and autocorrelation consistent covariance matrix. *Econometrica*, **55**, 703–708.

Ng, S., and Perron, P. 2001. Lag length selection and the construction of unit root tests with good size and power. *Econometrica*, **69**, 1519–1554.

Nickell, S. 1981. Biases in dynamic models with fixed effects. *Econometrica*, **49**, 1417–1426.

Patton, A. J. 2011. Data-based rankings of realised volatility estimators. *Journal of Econometrics*, **161**, 284–303.

Patton, A. J. 2012. A review of copula models for economic time series. *Journal of Multivariate Analysis*, **110**, 4–18.

Patton, A. J., and Sheppard, K. 2009. Evaluating volatility forecasts. In: Andersen, T. G., Davis, R. A., Kreiss, J. P., and T., Mikosch (eds.), *Handbook of Financial Time Series*, 801–838. Berlin: Springer-Verlag.

Pérignon, C., and Smith, D. R. 2010. The level and quality of value-at-risk disclosure by commerical banks. *Journal of Banking and Finance*, **34**, 362–377.

Phillips, P. C. B. 1980. The exact distribution of instrumental variable estimators in an equation containing n + 1 endogenous variables. *Econometrica*, **48**, 861–878.

Phillips, P. C. B. 1986. Understanding spurious regressions in econometrics. *Journal of Econometrics*, **33**, 311–340.

Phillips, P. C. B. 1987. Time series regression with a unit root. *Econometrica*, **55**, 277–301.

Phillips, P. C. B. 1989. Partially identified econometric models. *Econometric Theory*, **5**, 181–240.

Phillips, P. C. B. 1994. Some exact distribution theory for maximum likelihood estimators of cointegrating coefficients in error correction models. *Econometrica*, **62**, 73–93.

Phillips, P. C. B. 1995. Fully modified least squares and vector autoregression. *Econometrica*, **63**, 1023–1078.

Phillips, P. C. B. 1996. Econometric model determination. *Econometrica*, **64**, 763–812.

Phillips, P. C. B. 1998. New tools for understanding spurious regressions. *Econometrica*, **66**, 1299–1325.

Phillips, P. C. B. 2002. New unit root asymptotics in the presence of deterministic trends. *Journal of Econometrics*, **111**, 323–353.

Phillips, P. C. B. 2006. A remark on bimodality and weak instrumentation in structural equation estimation. *Econometric Theory*, **22**, 947–960.

Phillips, P. C. B. 2014a. On confidence intervals for autoregressive roots and predictive regression. *Econometrica*, **82**, 1177–1195.

Phillips, P. C. B. 2014b. Optimal estimation of cointegrated systems with irrelevant instruments. *Journal of Econometrics*, **178**, 210–224.

Phillips, P. C. B., and Bykhovskaya, A. 2020. Point optimal testing with roots that are functionally local to unity. *Journal of Econometrics*, **Forthcoming.**

Phillips, P. C. B., and Gao, W. Y. 2017. Structural inference from reduced forms with many instruments. *Journal of Econometrics*, **199**, 96–116.

Phillips, P. C. B., and Hansen, B. E. 1990. Statistical inference in instrumental variables regressions with I(1) errors. *Review of Economic Studies*, **57**, 99–125.

Phillips, P. C. B., and Lee, C. C. 1995. Efficiency gains from quasi-differencing under nonstationarity. In: *Athens Conference on Applied Probability and Time Series Analysis*. Lecture Notes in Statistics, vol. 115, 300–314. New York: Springer.

Phillips, P. C. B., and Lee, J. H. 2013. Predictive regression under various degrees of persistence and robust long-horizon regression. *Journal of Econometrics*, **177**, 250–264.

Phillips, P. C. B., and Loretan, M. 1991. Estimating long-run equilibria. *Review of Economic Studies*, **58**, 407–436.

Phillips, P. C. B., and Moon, H. R. 1999. Linear regression limit theory for nonstationary panel data. *Econometrica*, **67**, 1057–1111.

Phillips, P. C. B., and Ouliaris, S. 1990. Asymptotic properties of residual based tests for cointegration. *Econometrica*, **58**, 165–193.

Phillips, P. C. B., and Perron, P. 1988. Testing for a unit root in time series regression. *Biometrika*, **75**, 335–346.

Phillips, P. C. B., and Yu, J. 2011. Dating the timeline of financial bubbles during the subprime crisis. *Quantitative Economics*, **2**, 455–491.

Phillips, P. C. B., Shi, S., and Yu, J. 2015a. Testing for multiple bubbles: Historical episodes of exuberance and collapse in the S&P 500. *International Economic Review*, **56**, 1043–1078.

Phillips, P. C. B., Shi, S., and Yu, J. 2015b. Testing for multiple bubbles: Limit theory of real time detectors. *International Economic Review*, **56**, 1079–1134.

Phillips, P. C. B., Wu, Y., and Yu, J. 2011. Explosive behaviour in the 1990s NASDAQ: When did exuberance escalate asset values? *International Economic Review*, **52**, 201–226.

Poterba, J. M., and Summers, L. H. 1988. Mean reversion in stock prices: Evidence and Implications. *Journal of Financial Economics*, **22**, 27–59.

Pratt, J. W. 1976. F. Y. Edgeworth and R. A. Fisher on the efficiency of maximum likelihood estimation. *The Annals of Statistics*, **4**, 501–514.

Rajan, R. G., and Zingales, L. 1995. What do we know about capital structure? Some evidence from international data. *Journal of Finance*, **50**, 1421–1460.

Reinhart, C. M., and Rogoff, K. S. 2009. *This Time is Different: Eight Centuries of Financial Folly.* Princeton, New Jersey: Princeton University Press.

Roll, R. 1984. A simple implicit measure of the effective bid-ask spread in an efficient market. *Journal of Finance*, **39**, 1127–1139.

Russell, J. R., and Engle, R. F. 2007. Analysis of high-frequency data. In: Aït-Sahalia, Y., and Hansen, L. P. (eds.), *Handbook of Financial Econometrics*, 383–426. Elsevier.

Said, S. E., and Dickey, D. A. 1984. Testing for unit roots in autoregressive-moving average models of unknown order. *Biometrika*, **71**, 599–607.

Saikkonen, P. 1991. Asymptotically efficient estimation of cointegration regressions. *Econometric Theory*, **7**, 1–21.

Samuelson, P. 1965. Proof that anticipated prices fluctuate randomly. *Industrial Management Review*, **6**, 41–49.

Sargan, J. D. 1958. The estimation of economic relationships using instrumental variables. *Econometrica*, **26**, 393–415.

Sargan, J. D. 1959. The estimation of relationships with autocorrelated residuals by the use of instrumental variables. *Journal of the Royal Statistical Society, Series B*, **21**, 91–105.

Schwarz, G. 1978. Estimating the dimension of a model. *Annals of Statistics*, **6**, 461–464.

Sharpe, W. F. 1966. Mutual fund performance. *Journal of Business*, **39**, 199–138.

Shiller, R. J. 1981. Do stock prices move too much to be justified by subsequent changes in dividends? American Economic Review, 71, 421–436.

Shiller, R. J. 1984. Stock prices and social dynamics. Brookings Papers on Economic Activity, 98, 457–510.

Silvennoinen, A., and Teräsvirta, T. 2009. Multivariate GARCH models. In: Andersen, T. G., Davis, R. A., Kreiss, J.-P., and Mikosch, T. (eds.), *Handbook of Financial Time Series*, 201–229. Berlin, Heidelberg: Springer.

Silvennoinen, A., and Teräsvirta, T. 2016. Testing constancy of unconditional variance in volatility models by misspecification and specification tests. *Studies in Nonlinear Dynamics and Econometrics*, **20**, 347–364.

Sims, C. A. 1980. Macroeconomics and reality. *Econometrica*, **48**, 1–48.

Smith, J., and Wallis, K. F. 2009. A simple explanation of the forecast combination puzzle. *Oxford Bulletin of Economics and Statistics*, **71**, 302–355.

Solnik, B., and Roulet, J. 2000. Dispersion as cross-sectional correlation. *Financial Analysts Journal*, **56**, 54–61.

Staiger, D., and Stock, J. H. 1997. Instrumental variables with weak instruments. *Econometrica*, **65**, 557–586.

Stambaugh, R. F. 1999. Predictive regressions. *Journal of Financial Economics*, **54**, 375–421.

Stigler, S. M. 1978. Francis Ysidro Edgeworth, Statistician. *Journal of the Royal Statistical Society. Series A (General)*, **141**, 287–322.

Stock, J. H., and Watson, M. W. 1993. A simple estimator of cointegration vectors in higher order integrated systems. *Econometrica*, **61**, 783–820.

Stock, J. H., and Watson, M. W. 2001. A comparison of linear and nonlinear univariate models for forecasting macroeconomic time series. In: Engle, R. F., and White, H. (eds.), *Cointegration, Causality, and Forecasting: Festschrift in Honor of Clive W. J. Granger*, 1–44. Oxford: Oxford University Press.

Stock, J. H., and Yogo, M. 2005. Testing for weak instruments in linear IV regression. In: Stock, J. H., and Andrews, D. W. K. (eds.), *Identification and Inference for Econometric Models: A Festschrift in Honor of Thomas Rothenberg*, 80–108. Cambridge: Cambridge University Press.

Stock, J. H., Wright, J. H., and Yogo, M. 2002. A survey of weak instruments and weak identification in generalized method of moments. *Journal of Business and Economic Statistics*, **20**, 518–529.

Su, L., Shi, Z., and Phillips, P. C. B. 2016. Identifying latent structures in panel data. *Econometrica*, **84**, 2215–2264.

Taylor, S. J. 1986. *Modeling Financial Time Series*. Chichester: John Wiley and Sons, Inc.

Timmerman, A. 2006. Forecast Combinations. In: Elliott, G., Granger, C. W. J., and Timmerman, A. (eds.), *Handbook of Economic Forecasting*, vol. 1, 135–196. Amsterdam: North Holland.

Toda, H. Y., and Yamamoto, T. 1995. Statistical inference in vector autoregressions with possibly integrated processes. *Journal of Econometrics*, **66**, 225–250.

Treynor, J. L. 1966. How to rate management investment funds. *Harvard Business Review*, **43**, 63–75.

Trivedi, P. K., and Zimmer, D. M. 2005. Copula modelling: An introduction for practitioners. *Foundations and Trends in Econometrics*, **1**, 1–111.

Tse, Y. K., and Tsui, A. K. C. 2002. A multivariate generalized autoregressive conditional heteroscedasticity model with time-varying correlations. *Journal of Business and Economic Statistics*, **20**, 351–362.

van der Vaart, A. W. 2000. *Asymptotic Statistics*. Vol. 3. Cambridge: Cambridge University Press.

van der Vaart, A. W., and Wellner, J. A. 1996. *Weak Convergence and Empirical Processes*. New York: Springer.

Vasicek, O. 1977. An equilibrium characterization of the term structure. *Journal of Financial Economics*, **5**, 177–188.

White, H. 1980. A heteroskedasticity-consistent covariance matrix estimator and a direct test for heteroskedasticity. *Econometrica*, **48**, 817–838.

Winkler, R. L., and Clemen, R. T. 1992. Sensitivity of weights in combined forecasts. *Operations Research*, **40**, 609–614.

Zakoïan, J. M. 1994. Threshold heteroskedastic models. *Journal of Economic Dynamics and Control*, **18**, 931–944.

Zhang, L., Mykland, P. A., and Aït-Sahalia, Y. 2005. A tale of two time scales: Determining integrated volatility with noisy high-frequency data. *Journal of the American Statistical Association*, **100**, 1394–1411.

AUTHOR INDEX

SUBJECT INDEX